501
MUST-SEE MOVIES

Bounty Books

Publisher: Polly Manguel

Project Editor: Emma Beare

Designer: Ron Callow/Design 23

Production Manager: Neil Randles

Photographs Courtesy of the Kobal Collection

First published in Great Britain in 2004 by Bounty Books
a division of Octopus Publishing Group Limited
2-4 Heron Quays, London E14 4JP
An Hachette Livre UK Company

Reprinted 2005 (three times), 2006 (twice), 2007 (twice)

Copyright © 2004 Octopus Publishing Group Limited

A CIP catalogue record is available from the British Library

ISBN: 978-0-753710-67-8

Printed and bound in China

Contents

Introduction

501 Must-see Movies – 'Define 'must see'!' I hear you exclaim through gritted teeth. Cinephiles are notoriously opinionated – passionate about auteur, actors, directors, cinematographers, or cameramen. They know their genres; they know their plots, sub-plots, sub-texts, homage and allusions, the context and the history, the perfectionist care that has gone into each angle and frame. They know too who was in the frame to star, who backed out, who failed to show, which directors gave the studio bosses grey hair prematurely, as their schedules and budgets sky rocketed into the stratosphere and which low-budget gems have made cinema history. They have plotted the career paths and listed the achievements of the most influential players. They can define and defend German Expressionism, French New Wave, Italian Modernism, Post Modernism and Film Noir and predict next year's box office blockbusters and 'sleepers' from the 'best-boy' credits. Are you that cinephile?

If so, there is no doubt that you will take issue with some of the 501 movies described in these pages. Of necessity the selection is subjective to some degree. However, before you slam this (beautifully illustrated) book down in disgust because your favourite isn't included, or raise your blood pressure as you disagree with the opinions of our six expert contributors, consider. For every expert there is a novice, someone who has not seen every movie on the planet but who would like to make an informed choice at their local video store or art-house cinema; someone who is starting a film club or aspires to be a director or cinematographer. That someone will be fascinated by the wealth of background detail, the pithy plot outlines, the Academy Awards for which each movie

was nominated and which of those it actually won –
who will learn the career development of directors,
actors, screenplay writers and then sit down and enjoy,
maybe for the first time, one of the extraordinary,
ground-breaking, beautiful, avant-garde, memorable,
startling, shocking or amusing films described here.
Don't you envy those movie virgins? Then, of course,
there are the many of us who just enjoy the
entertainment and magic of a movie masterpiece, in
the quiet and dark of our local cinema, or who long for
just such a reference work as this to check our failing
memories against the facts.

So how did we define 'must see'? Well first we
made selections from the genres Action/Adventure &
Epic, Comedy, Drama, Horror, Musical, Mystery &
Thriller, Romance, Science Fiction & Fantasy, War and
Western, then consulted the many lists of 'favourite' or
'best' movies that have been compiled. Our expert
critics had their own views of course. Then we looked
at the body of work each director, actor, cameraman
and crew contributed to the decade or decades
featured in the chronology of this book. We looked at
films which complemented or contrasted with one
another within their genre or which reflected the era
in which they were made.

Here you will find astonishing achievements in
special effects before and after CGI, brave
cinematographical experiments, courageous social
commentary, staggering performances, debuts and
swan-songs. With this book at your elbow you can start
and stop angry debates, be stimulated, informed and
amused and all before the lights go down and the
credits roll. But then, please watch the films described
here and form your own opinions. Enjoy!

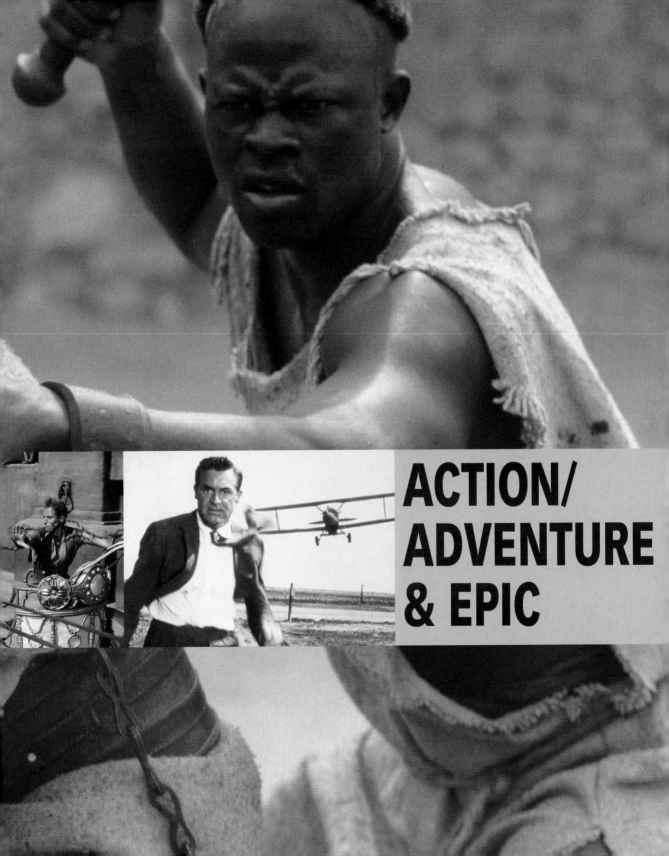

ACTION/ ADVENTURE & EPIC

The Four Horsemen of the Apocalypse

Born to a half-French, half-German family, Julio (Valentino), the son of an Argentinian cattle baron, is forced to reconsider his decadent and uncommitted way of life with the advent of World War I.

A continent-spanning epic that drew huge audiences, *The Four Horsemen of the Apocalypse* tapped the popular anti-war and anti-German sentiment of the time (it was banned in Germany) and established Rudolph Valentino as silent cinema's seminal 'Latin Lover'. With its reconstructed locations, which ranged from high-society Paris to the South American pampas, its scenes of World War I battlefields and the invasion of a French village by German soldiers, the film was conceived and marketed as an out-and-out spectacular to compete with the major works made a few years earlier by the pioneer filmmaker, D.W.Griffith.

When it was screened in major cities the film played with the full paraphernalia of large orchestras and backstage sound effects for the battle scenes. And with the death of Valentino in 1926, the film was revived. In 1992, the film was re-released in a restored version by Kevin Brownlow with an orchestral accompaniment by Carl Davis.

USA, 1921
DIRECTOR:
Rex Ingram
CAST INCLUDES:
Rudolph Valentino, Pomeroy Cannon,
Bridgetta Clark
SCREENPLAY:
June Mathis from the novel by
Vicente Blasco Ibanez
CINEMATOGRAPHY:
John F.Seitz
**PRODUCER/
PRODUCTION COMPANIES:**
Rex Ingram
Metro Pictures Corporation

The Iron Horse

After Davy Brandon's (O'Brien) father is killed by an Indian tribe led by a white man, Brandon strives to realize his father's ambition of building an American transcontinental railway.

Brandon is also wooing his childhood sweetheart, Miriam (Bellamy), but discovers that she is already married. Her husband, Peter Jesson (Chadwick), is the man who killed his father.

Dubbed an 'historical super-western', *The Iron Horse* certainly had all the trappings of an epic production: a fair-sized habitation had to be built in Arizona, where most of the film was shot, to house the cast and crew numbering some 6,000 people. It was to the young John Ford that supervision of this vast project was

entrusted. Not yet thirty years old in 1924, Ford had been churning out one-and two-reelers since 1917 and *The Iron Horse* was his first production on such a scale.

The themes that would dominate Ford's work – the 'settling' of the West, the ambiguous incursion of 'civilization' into its 'wilderness' – are all present and correct in this early, silent example of his work in the Western genre. Along with the building of the transcontinental railway the film also features other key generic sequences: a cattle drive, an Indian attack and a bar-room brawl, as well as the appearance of legendary and historical figures such as Abraham Lincoln, Wild Bill Hickok and Buffalo Bill.

USA, 1924
DIRECTOR:
John Ford
CAST INCLUDES:
George O'Brien, Madge Bellamy,
Charles Deward Bull, Cyril Chadwick
SCREENPLAY:
Charles Kenyon, John Russell (story),
Charles Kenyon
CINEMATOGRAPHY:
George Schneiderman
PRODUCER/
PRODUCTION COMPANIES:
John Ford/Fox Film Corporation

Napoléon

FRANCE, 1927
DIRECTOR:
Abel Glance
CAST INCLUDES:
Albert Dieudonné, Vladimir
Roudenko, Edmond Van Daële,
Alexandre Koubitzky
SCREENPLAY:
Abel Glance
CINEMATOGRAPHY:
Léonce-Henri Burel, Jules Kruger,
Joseph-Louis Mundwiller, Torpkoff
PRODUCER/
PRODUCTION COMPANIES:
Films Abel Gance/
Société générale des films.

Beginning in his schooldays, the film charts the life of Napoleon, from his flight from Corsica, through the French Revolution (where a real storm is intercut with a political storm) and the Terror, culminating in his invasion of Italy in 1797.

Abel Gance's bio-pic of Napoleon is one of silent cinema's monumental achievements. But this six-hour account of the Emperor's life, from schoolboy to victorious general, was intended by Gance as merely the first of a five-part account. The requisite list of statistics can be trotted out regarding the film's epic ambition: three year's worth of research and writing, thousands of extras, a dozen or so cameramen employed, not to mention the millions of francs spent in production. But these statistics pale in the face of the sheer range of techniques Gance used to tell his story, especially in the innovative use of camera movement to render a storm-tossed ship, a galloping horse, even a snowball in flight.

Perhaps the most celebrated of all Gance's technical coups is the final twenty-minute triptych sequence, which alternates wide-screen panoramic shots with multiple-image montages projected simultaneously on three screens, a process named 'Polyvision'. Gance's Napoléon endures not only for the epic scale of the story and its treatment, but also and equally as an outstanding example of cinema in its early years being explored for its experimental possibilities as a still new visual medium.

Cleopatra

48 BC. Cleopatra, Queen of Egypt (Colbert), is facing a palace revolt and welcomes the arrival of Julius Caesar (William) as a way of securing her power under Roman rule. When Caesar, whom she has led astray, is killed Cleopatra transfers her attentions to Marc Antony (Wilcoxon) whom she attempts to seduce and manipulate.

The characteristic opulence of De Mille's take on the story of the legendary Egyptian asp-clasper is well encapsulated by its poster tag-line: 'A love affair that shook the world set in a spectacle of thrilling magnificence'. For which, read 'campy', 'grandiose' and 'ludicrous historically'. All the key qualities, in short, that one expects of one of classical Hollywood's masters of spectacle. The sets, designed by Hans Dreier, are strikingly opulent, especially those constructed for the barge scene in which Cleopatra seduces Marc Antony. The blatant sensuality of Colbert's portrayal of the Egyptian queen, as well as the revealing costumes, demonstrate how DeMille profited from a certain latitude in Hollywood's pre-censorship, pre-Hays' Code period.

USA, 1934
DIRECTOR:
Cecil B. DeMille
CAST INCLUDES:
Claudette Colbert, Warren William,
Henry Wilcoxon, Joseph Schildkraut,
Ian Keith
SCREENPLAY:
Bartlett Cormack, Waldemar Young,
Vincent Lawrence
CINEMATOGRAPHY:
Victor Milner
**PRODUCERS/PRODUCTION
COMPANIES:**
Cecil B. DeMille/Paramount Pictures
**ACADEMY AWARD
NOMINATIONS (1935)**
Best Assistant Director: Cullen Tate
Best Film Editing: Anne Bauchens
Best Sound Recording:
Franklin Hansen
Best Picture
ACADEMY AWARDS
Best Cinematography: Victor Milner

The Adventures of Robin Hood

USA, 1938
DIRECTOR:
Michael Curtiz & William Keighley
CAST INCLUDES:
Errol Flynn, Olivia De Havilland,
Basil Rathbone, Claude Rains,
Patric Knowles
SCREENPLAY:
Norman Reilly Raine, Seton I Miller
CINEMATOGRAPHY:
Tony Gaudio, Sol Polito
PRODUCER/
PRODUCTION COMPANIES:
Hal B Wallis, Henry Blanke/
First National Pictures Inc.,
Warner Bros.
ACADEMY AWARD
NOMINATIONS (1939)
Outstanding Production:
Warner Brothers-First National
ACADEMY AWARDS
Best Art Direction: Carl Jules Weyl,
Best Film Editing: Ralph Dawson
Best Music, Original Score:
Erich Wolfgang Korngold

Sir Robin of Locksley (Flynn) falls foul of the Norman authorities and turns outlaw when Prince John (Rains) usurps his brother's succession to the throne. Fleeing to Sherwood Forest, Sir Robin becomes Robin Hood, gathering around him a band of Merry Men. Robin woos and wins Lady Marian (de Havilland) who feeds him news of John's plots. When Marian is captured, Robin and his men storm Nottingham Castle to rescue her.

The film that set the all-action standard by which other screen swashbucklers would be judged, Curtiz's take on the Sherwood Forest saga of 'robbing from the rich to give to the poor' is distinguished by Flynn's thrusting charisma as the film's lead (having pipped James Cagney, who was the director's original first choice, to the role).

Flynn plays Sir Robin of Locksley the renegade aristo who, with his merry band of forest-dwelling marauders, confronts the

corrupt ruling class of the day. Graced with a brilliantly choreographed, climactic swordfight between Flynn and Basil Rathbone as the villainous Sir Guy of Gisbourne, during which the action cuts between the men and their shadows, *The Adventures of Robin Hood* is graced with an Oscar-winning score by Erich Korngold and still-sparkling Technicolor cinematography (an innovation in the 1930s) which was digitally enhanced for Warner's 2003 re-release of the film.

Alexander Nevsky

In the 13th century, Russia is invaded by Teutonic knights. A Russian prince, Alexander Nevsky (Cherkasov), calls the people to arms to drive back the invaders.

Alexander Nevsky heralded Eisenstein's return to filmmaking after ten years of politically-induced inactivity. The film's source lay in the Soviet regime's growing perception of the threat of Nazi Germany and Eisenstein was called upon to make a historical epic based on events in the thirteenth century, when Russians led by Prince Alexander Nevsky repelled an invasion by German knights.

Alexander Nevsky was Eisenstein's first sound film and the director's collaboration with the Soviet composer Sergei Prokofiev was unusual in its scope. Prokofiev composed his score based on the director's sketches and shot plans and Eisenstein cut the final footage to match movement and sound. One of the most outstanding examples of Eisenstein's visual creativity is the famous 'Battle on the Ice' scene, with its extremely stylized shots. Filmed in high summer, the scene was thoroughly fabricated; lens filters were used to alter the light of the summer skies and ice and snow were made from melted glass, chalk and salt. The most widely known of Soviet films of the 1930s, *Alexander Nevsky* restored Eisenstein's reputation.

USSR, 1938
DIRECTOR:
Sergei Eisenstein, Dmitri Vasilyev
CAST INCLUDES:
Nikolai Cherkasov,
Nikolai Okhlopkov,
Andrei Abrikosov, Dmitri Orlov
SCREENPLAY:
Sergei M Eisenstein,
Pyotr Pavlenko
CINEMATOGRAPHY:
Eduard Tisse
**PRODUCER/
PRODUCTION COMPANIES:**
Mosfilm

USA, 1939
DIRECTOR:
Victor Fleming
CAST INCLUDES:
Clark Gable, Vivien Leigh,
Olivia de Havilland, Hattie McDaniel,
Thomas Mitchell, Leslie Howard,
George Reeves
SCREENPLAY:
Sidney Howard from the novel
by Margaret Mitchell
CINEMATOGRAPHY:
Ernest Haller
PRODUCER/
PRODUCTION COMPANIES:
David O. Selznick/
Selznick International Pictures
ACADEMY AWARD
NOMINATIONS (1940)
Best Actor in a Leading Role:
Clark Gable
Best Actress in a Supporting Role:
Olivia de Havilland
Best Music, Original Score:
Max Steiner; Best Sound Recording:
Samuel Goldwyn Studio Sound
Department, Thomas T. Moulton
Best Special Effects: John R.
Cosgrove, Fred Albin, Arthur Johns
ACADEMY AWARDS
Best Actress in a Leading Role:
Vivien Leigh
Best Actress in a Supporting Role:
Hattie McDaniel
Best Art Direction: Lyle Wheeler
Best Cinematography:
Ernest Haller, Ray Rennahan
Best Director:
Victor Fleming
Best Film Editing: Hal C. Kern,
James E. Newcom
Outstanding Production:
Selznick International Pictures
Best Writing, Screenplay:
Sidney Howard, Technical
Achievement Award

Gone with the Wind

Adapted from Margaret Mitchell's best-selling novel of the American South during the years of the Civil War and Reconstruction, *Gone with the Wind* was a monumental piece of Hollywood filmmaking in every conceivable respect. Costing $4.25 million (roughly equivalent to $50 million today) and lasting over three and a half hours, the film won ten Oscars, a record that stood until 1959 when *Ben-Hur* won eleven.

Director Victor Fleming – who was brought in after three weeks by producer David O. Selznick to replace the original director, George Cukor – presided over a number of technical innovations and cinematic firsts on the film. These included staging, for the burning of Atlanta, what was then the largest fire scene ever shot; the use of matte paintings to complete partially constructed sets (only the second use of this technique with Technicolor film); establishing the unknown actress Vivien Leigh who had been cast as Scarlett O'Hara through a talent search (Katherine Hepburn and Paulette Goddard had both been considered for the role) and securing the first Academy Award for a black person (Hattie McDaniel, winning Best Supporting Actress for her role as 'Mammy'). *Gone with the Wind* can be properly considered as the prototype of the Hollywood 'blockbuster'.

The Sea Hawk

Geoffrey Thorpe (Flynn), a buccaneer, is hired by Queen Elizabeth I (Robson) to harass the Spanish Armada which is waiting to attack England. Thorpe surprises them with attacks on their galleons.

For *The Sea Hawk*, Warners reunited the team that had made *The Adventures of Robin Hood* (1938) a successful production: director Michael Curtiz, composer Erich Wolfgang Korngold and actors Errol Flynn, Claude Rains and Alan Hale. Flynn is energetically charming as the roguish Thorpe, secret lover of the Queen and a privateer against Spain and Claude Rains is the villainous Spanish envoy, Don José. Shot in black and white rather than Technicolor, this high-seas swashbuckler was in part intended to be a morale-boosting exercise that would encourage the British in their fight against Germany.

USA, 1940
DIRECTOR:
Michael Curtiz
CAST INCLUDES:
Errol Flynn, Brenda Marshall,
Claude Rains, Alan Hale,
Flora Robson
SCREENPLAY:
Howard Koch, Seton I. Miller
CINEMATOGRAPHY:
Sol Polito
**PRODUCER/
PRODUCTION COMPANIES:**
Henry Blanke, Hal B. Wallis/
Warner Bros.
**ACADEMY AWARD
NOMINATIONS (1941)**
Best Art Direction:
Anton Grot
Best Music, Scoring:
Erich Wolfgang Korngold
Best Sound Recording: Warner Bros.
Studio Sound Department,
Nathan Levinson
Best Special Effects (Photographic
Effects): Byron Haskin; Sound Effects
by Nathan Levinson.

The Treasure of the Sierra Madre

USA, 1948
DIRECTOR:
John Huston
CAST INCLUDES:
Humphrey Bogart, Walter Huston,
Tim Holt, Bruce Bennett
SCREENPLAY:
John Huston from the novel
by B. Traven
CINEMATOGRAPHY:
Ted D. McCord
PRODUCER/
PRODUCTION COMPANIES:
Henry Blanke, Jack L. Warner/
Warner Bros.
ACADEMY AWARD
NOMINATIONS (1949)
Best Motion Picture: Warner Bros.
Best Writing, Screenplay:
John Huston
ACADEMY AWARDS
Best Actor in a Supporting Role:
Walter Huston
Best Director:
John Huston

Having been swindled by a crooked contractor, Dobbs (Bogart) and Curtin (Holt), a couple of adventurers, meet up with Howard (Huston), an old prospector, who tells them the hills are full of gold. The trio set off to hunt for the bounty but greed gradually gets the better of them.

In this 'quest for gold' picture, John Huston cast Humphrey Bogart in one of the most noxious roles of the actor's career. As Fred C. Dobbs, Bogart is the epitome of paranoid venality who, despite having his life saved twice by his fellow treasure-hunters, spirals into greed-induced madness. Having developed a taste and facility for location shooting while making propaganda films during World War II, Huston convinced Warners to let him shoot for ten weeks in Mexico and the film's portrait of the slow-burn dissolution of the trio of adventurers gains much from the sun-bleached mountainside settings.

This is an adventure film in which the quest is not an end in itself but the alibi for a fatalistic character study in which the moral differences between an older, wiser man (Huston, the director's father, who won an Oscar for his performance) and the mistrustful, middle-aged Dobbs become starkly apparent, and between which Curtin, the younger man, must choose. Jack Warner, the film's producer, is reputed to have seen *The Treasure of the Sierra Madre* and said 'It's one of the best films made since movies started talking'.

The African Queen

At the beginning of World War I, Charlie Allnut (Bogart) ferries supplies in his old steamer *The African Queen* to villages in East Africa. When the Reverend Samuel Sayer (Morley) dies, Charlie agrees to take Sayer's sister, Rose (Hepburn) back to civilization at the same time as confronting German forces.

Opposites attract when starched-skirt British missionary Rose Sayer and coarse, gin-guzzling Canadian river-trader Charlie Allnut are thrown together on Bogey's boat while evading the Germans. Under the influence of Hepburn's moral rectitude, Bogart moves from cynical individualism to a sense of committed action, attacking a German gunboat. And love, of course, blossoms between the unlikely pair.

Huston insisted that the film be shot on location (a style of shooting that was by no means as common then as now) on the Ruiki river in the then Belgian Congo, maintaining that this was the only way to invest authenticity and believability into the couple's tribulations and growing romance.

Adapted from a C.S.Forester novel by Huston and critic James Agee, *The African Queen* is an unashamed yarn combining implausible romance and high adventure which is greatly enlivened by the smart interplay of two Hollywood greats at the top of their respective games.

USA, 1951
DIRECTOR:
John Huston
CAST INCLUDES:
Humphrey Bogart, Katharine Hepburn, Robert Morley, Peter Bull
SCREENPLAY:
James Agee and John Huston from the novel by C.S. Forester
CINEMATOGRAPHY:
Jack Cardiff
**PRODUCER/
PRODUCTION COMPANIES:**
Sam Spiegel, John Woolf/
Horizon Pictures, Romulus Films
**ACADEMY AWARD
NOMINATIONS (1952)**
Best Actress in a Leading Role:
Katherine Hepburn
Best Director: John Huston
Best Writing, Screenplay:
James Agee
ACADEMY AWARDS
Best Actor in a Leading Role:
Humphrey Bogart

The Wages of Fear
Le Salaire de la peur

In the South American jungle, an American oil company pays four men to deliver supplies of highly sensitive nitroglycerene to a remote oil field. A hostile rivalry develops between the two sets of drivers: the slightest jolt to either of their trucks will result in death.

The *Wages of Fear* is a 'road movie' with only one possible destination: Hell. Henri-Georges Clouzot's bleakly pessimistic, black-and-white thriller was a huge international success on its release, thanks to the unerring skill with which the director builds the tension to breaking point. The film's four main characters together represent a vision of the 'international adventurer' not as charming, risk-taking rogue but as corrupt and cynical mercenary.

The first half of the film is devoted to establishing the squalid and oppressive conditions in which this group of junk-town dogs find themselves, holed up in a poor part of Venezuela. A fire in an oil well gives them the chance to break out of their dead-end lives when an American petrochemical company hires them for the nearly suicidal job of transporting the explosives to the well. On the pitted and perilous roads, the two trucks they drive are virtual time-bombs primed to detonate at any moment, and their unbearably tense journey occupies the latter half of the film. *The Wages of Fear* is an adventure-thriller with strong philosophical and political overtones: a vision of capitalist degradation finding its irredeemably corrupt personification in the four drivers. In 1977, William Friedkin delivered an inferior remake called *Sorcerer*.

FRANCE/ITALY, 1953
DIRECTOR:
Henri-Georges Clouzot
CAST INCLUDES:
Yves Montand, Charles Vanel, Peter van Eyck, Antonio Centa, Darling Légitimus
SCREENPLAY:
Henri-Georges Clouzot, Jérôme Géronimi from the novel by Georges Arnaud
CINEMATOGRAPHY:
Armand Thirard
PRODUCER/ PRODUCTION COMPANIES:
Raymond Borderie, Henri-Georges Clouzot/CICC, Filmsonor S.A., Fono Roma, Vera Films
CANNES FILM FESTIVAL (1953)
Grand Prize: Henri-Georges Clouzot Special Mention: Charles Vanel for his acting performance

The Seven Samurai
Shichinin no samurai

A veteran samurai (Shimura) answers a village's request for protection from marauding bandits. He assembles a team of six other samurai and they teach the townspeople how to defend themselves. When forty bandits attack the village a fight to the death ensues.

Although set in 16th century Japan *The Seven Samurai*, as Kurosawa readily acknowledged, was heavily indebted to Hollywood westerns and particularly to John Ford. From its opening shot of galloping horsemen silhouetted against the horizon to its story of an elite team of warriors being assembled to protect a threatened village, the film was innovative with its influences – it would eventually be re-made by John Sturges as *The Magnificent Seven*.

The film takes time, a leisurely 207 minutes, establishing the individual characters of the team of samurai and detailing their ambiguous relations with the villagers they are hired to protect. It builds steadily to the magnificent climactic rain-drenched battle scene, which is rendered as an orgy of chaotic, kinetic action, all slashing limbs and splashing mud. Kurosawa's genius for pictorial composition and choreographed movement made *The Seven Samurai* a perfect example of epic, bravura filmmaking.

JAPAN, 1954
DIRECTOR:
Akira Kurosawa
CAST INCLUDES:
Takashi Shimura, Toshirô Mifune,
Yoshio Inaba, Seiji Miyaguchi,
Minoru Chiaki
SCREENPLAY:
Akira Kurosawa, Shinobu Hashimoto,
Hideo Oguni
CINEMATOGRAPHY:
Asakazu Nakai
**PRODUCER/
PRODUCTION COMPANIES:**
Sojiro Motoki/
Toho Company Ltd.
**ACADEMY AWARD
NOMINATIONS (1957)**
Best Art Direction-Set Decoration:
So Matsuyama
Best Costume Design,
Black-and-White: Kôhei Ezaki

The Ten Commandments

USA, 1956
DIRECTOR:
Cecil B. DeMille
CAST INCLUDES:
Charlton Heston, Yul Brynner,
Anne Baxter, Edward G. Robinson,
Yvonne De Carlo
SCREENPLAY:
J.H. Ingraham (novel), A.E. Southon
(novel), Dorothy Clarke Wilson
(novel), Æneas MacKenzie, Jesse
Lasky Jr., Jack Gariss,
Fredric M. Frank (screenplay)
CINEMATOGRAPHY:
Loyal Griggs
PRODUCER/
PRODUCTION COMPANIES:
Cecil B. DeMille/
Motion Picture Associates, Inc.,
Paramount.
ACADEMY AWARD
NOMINATIONS (1957)
Best Art Direction: Hal Pereira,
Walter H. Tyler, Albert Nozaki
Best Set Decoration: Samuel M.
Comer, Ray Moyer
Best Cinematography: Loyal Griggs
Best Costume Design: Edith Head,
Ralph Jester, John Jensen, Dorothy
Jeakins, Arnold Friberg
Best Film Editing: Anne Bauchens
Best Motion Picture: Cecil B. DeMille
Best Sound Recording: Paramount
Studio Sound Department,
Loren L. Ryder
ACADEMY AWARDS
Best Effects, Special Effects:
John P. Fulton

Moses (Heston) leads the slaves from the tyranny of the Egyptian pharaoh (Brynner) and into the desert where he receives the Word of God. Moses attracts the attentions of Queen Nefertiti (Baxter) until he rebels and is sent into exile.

De Mille had already made an earlier version of *The Ten Commandments* in 1923, before this epic 1956 reprise of the biblical story. Shot in widescreen Technicolor and lasting nearly four hours, *The Ten Commandments* set the standard by which many epics, biblical or otherwise, would be measured. DeMille pulled out all the stops in terms of special effects: the images of Moses turning his staff into a snake and the Nile into blood were unprecedented visual innovations at the time and the parting of the Red Sea remains one of Hollywood's most treasured 'miracles' of special effects.

22

War and Peace

Focused around Napoleon's 1812 invasion of Russia, the film follows the lives of three aristocratic Russians, Natasha (Hepburn), Pierre (Fonda) and Bolkonsky (Ferrer), over the course of fifteen years.

Another epic Dino D. Laurentiis/Carlo Ponti co-production, this $6 million costume-drama adaptation of Leo Tolstoy's equally epic novel *War and Peace* was Paramount's second big production of 1956, the other being DeMille's *The Ten Commandments*. Moving from lavish ballroom scenes to huge battle reconstructions, Vidor pulled out all the stops in the film's three hours, making the most of Jack Cardiff's sumptuous colour cinematography and the VistaVision widescreen format to create some opulent compositions of movement and colour.

ITALY/USA, 1956
DIRECTOR:
King Vidor
CAST INCLUDES:
Audrey Hepburn, Henry Fonda,
Mel Ferrer, Vittorio Gassman,
Herbert Lom
SCREENPLAY:
Bridget Boland, Mario Camerini,
Robert Westerby from the novel
by Leo Tolstoy
CINEMATOGRAPHY:
Jack Cardiff
PRODUCER/
PRODUCTION COMPANIES:
Dino de Laurentiis/
Ponti-De-Laurentiis Productions,
Paramount.
ACADEMY AWARD
NOMINATIONS (1957)
Best Cinematography: Jack Cardiff
Best Costume Design:
Marie De Matteis
Best Director: King Vidor

The Vikings

USA, 1958
DIRECTOR:
Richard Fleischer
CAST INCLUDES:
Kirk Douglas, Tony Curtis,
Ernest Borgnine, Janet Leigh,
James Donald
SCREENPLAY:
Dale Wasserman from the novel by
Edison Marshall
CINEMATOGRAPHY:
Jack Cardiff
PRODUCER/
PRODUCTION COMPANIES:
Jerry Bresler/Brynaprod S.A.

Einar (Douglas) and Erik (Curtis) are two Viking half-brothers; one is a great warrior, the other an ex-slave but neither knows the identity of the other. When the throne of Northumbria becomes free, the brothers compete for it.

'Mightiest of Men, Mightiest of Spectacles, Mightiest of Motion Pictures!' boasted the poster for Richard Fleicher's *The Vikings* in which Kirk Douglas and Tony Curtis' competitive on-screen chemistry was first enjoyed before being further exploited, two years later, in *Spartacus*. Shot on location in Norway, preparations for the film included a year's pre-production and historical research to lend authenticity to its reconstructed longships and epic battle scenes. Its box-office success can be seen to have paved the way for future Viking epics, including *The Long Ships* (1963), which was directed by the cinematographer on *The Vikings*, Jack Cardiff.

North by Northwest

An advertising executive, Roger O. Thornhill (Grant), is mistaken for a government agent by a gang of spies and is pursued across the US, while being helped by the beautiful Eve Kendall (Saint).

One of Hitchcock's best-loved classics, *North by Northwest* is a mistaken-identity caper movie in which the master of suspense puts the ever-suave Cary Grant through his paces (it would be the fourth and final collaboration between the actor and director) as a man on the run in a mystifying game of cat-and-mouse. Or perhaps that should be crop-duster and quarry. The film features two of cinema's most famous set-pieces: the chase scene in which Grant is terrorized by a biplane that harries him across empty fields; and the equally famous, but less mysteriously unsettling, climactic scene in which Grant and Saint are chased across the monumental presidential sculptures of Mount Rushmore. In between the pursuit sequences the two leads engage in frisky thrust-and-parry dialogue, as though they'd somehow wandered out of a romantic comedy into a big-budget thriller and can't quite get their bearings. For all its set-piece action, *North by Northwest* is Hitchcock in light, likeable mode. The fearsome and intimate malevolence of *Psycho* was only a year away.

USA, 1959
DIRECTOR:
Alfred Hitchcock
CAST INCLUDES:
Cary Grant, Eva Marie Saint, James Mason, Jessie Royce Landis
SCREENPLAY:
Ernest Lehman
CINEMATOGRAPHY:
Robert Burks
PRODUCER/
PRODUCTION COMPANIES:
Herbert Coleman, Alfred Hitchcock/ Metro-Goldwyn-Mayer (MGM)
ACADEMY AWARD
NOMINATIONS (1960)
Best Art Direction:
William A. Horning, Robert Boyle, Merrill Pye
Best Set Decoration:
Henry Grace, Frank McKelvy
Best Film Editing: George Tomasini
Best Writing, Story and Screenplay written directly for the screen:
Ernest Lehman

Ben-Hur

USA, 1959
DIRECTOR:
William Wyler
CAST INCLUDES:
Charlton Heston, Jack Hawkins,
Haya Harareet, Stephen Boyd,
Hugh Griffith
SCREENPLAY:
Karl Turnberg from the novel
by Lew Wallace
CINEMATOGRAPHY:
Robert L Surtees
PRODUCER/
PRODUCTION COMPANIES:
Sam Zimbalist, William Wyler
Metro-Goldwyn-Mayer (MGM)
ACADEMY AWARD
NOMINATIONS (1960)
Best Writing Screenplay Based on
Material from Another Medium:
Karl Turnberg
ACADEMY AWARDS
Best Actor in a Leading Role:
Charlton Heston
Best Actor in a Supporting Role:
Hugh Griffith
Best Art Direction-Set Decoration:
William A. Horning, Edward Carfagno,
Hugh Hunt
Best Cinematography:
Robert L. Surtees
Best Costume Design:
Elizabeth Haffenden
Best Director: William Wyler
Best Film Editing: Ralph E. Winters,
John D. Dunning
Best Music: Miklos Rozsa
Best Motion Picture: Sam Zimbalist
Best Sound: MGM Studio Sound
Department-Franklin E. Milton
Best Effects-Special Effects:
A. Arnold Gillespie (visual)
Robert MacDonald (visual)
Milo B. Lory (audible)

Jerusalem at the beginning of the 1st century. Judah Ben-Hur (Heston) is a rich Jewish prince and merchant who welcomes his old friend Messala (Boyd) when he arrives as commanding officer of the Roman legions. But tensions develop between them and Messala contrives to have Judah framed and condemned to life as a galley slave and to send his mother and sister to prison. Judah swears to seek his revenge.

Still legendary, this vast biblical epic remains the grandest of the widescreen Hollywood blockbusters of the 1950s. Subtitled: 'A Tale of the Christ', and opening with an overture playing against a shot of Michelangelo's Sistine Chapel, the grandiose nature of the film's ambitions are asserted right from the start. An adaptation of a 1926 film of the same name, Wyler's 1959 version was the most expensive film ever made at the time, costing $15 million and almost bankrupting a financially unstable MGM, and involving six years of pre-production and six months of location shooting in Italy.

The film's scenes of chariot-racing remain one of the iconic moments of all-out Hollywood spectacle, taking up twenty minutes of the film's nearly four hours and they took three months of filming on what was then the largest single set ever constructed. Charlton Heston, who, three years earlier, had played Moses in DeMille's *The Ten Commandments*, took on the role of Judah Ben-Hur, the wronged and rebellious Jewish prince after other major stars, including Rock Hudson, Burt Lancaster and Marlon Brando, had turned it down. It made him a matinée idol. The gargantuan nature of the production carries all the way to the Academy Awards, where *Ben-Hur* shares the record for most awards (eleven) with *Titanic*.

Spartacus

Spartacus (Douglas) was born and raised a slave. After being trained as a gladiator, he turns on his masters and leads the other slaves in rebellion. Under Spartacus, the rebels travel to southern Italy, where they intend to cross the sea to return to their homes. Two Roman statesmen, the republican Gracchus (Laughton) and the militarist Crassus (Olivier), attempt to manipulate the rebels for their own political benefit.

In the 1960s, *Spartacus* was seen as being the first 'intellectual epic' since the days of silent cinema, in which the ideas were as central as the action sequences. And *Spartacus* indeed combines both the cerebral and the spectacular in its concentration on the political machinations taking place around the slave rebellion. With its stellar international cast, an intelligent screenplay (by then-blacklisted writer, Dalton Trumbo), the film was produced by its lead actor Kirk Douglas and is reputed to have definitively put its director, Stanley Kubrick, off working on a big-budget Hollywood picture ever again without complete independence. Today, elements of the film inevitably appear dated but it remains a rousing, immensely confident piece of epic filmmaking and was re-released in a restored version in 1991.

USA, 1960
DIRECTOR:
Stanley Kubrick
CAST INCLUDES:
Tony Curtis, Kirk Douglas,
Laurence Olivier, Jean Simmons,
Charles Laughton
SCREENPLAY:
Dalton Trumbo from the novel
by Howard Fast
CINEMATOGRAPHER:
Russell Metty
**PRODUCER/
PRODUCTION COMPANIES:**
Kirk Douglas, James C. Katz
(1991 restoration)/
Bryna Productions, Inc.,
Universal-International
**ACADEMY AWARD
NOMINATIONS (1961)**
Best Film Editing: Robert Lawrence
Best Music,Score: Alex North
ACADEMY AWARDS
Best Actor in a Supporting Role:
Peter Ustinov
Best Art Direction:
Alexander Golitzen, Eric Orbom
Best Set Decoration:
Russell A. Gausman, Julia Heron,
Best Cinematography: Russell Metty
Best Costume Design: Valles,
Bill Thomas

Lawrence of Arabia

GB, 1962
DIRECTOR:
David Lean
CAST INCLUDES:
Peter O'Toole, Alec Guinness,
Anthony Quinn, Jack Hawkins,
Omar Sharif, Arthur Kennedy
SCREENPLAY:
T.E.Lawrence (writings), Robert Bolt,
Michael Wilson (sc.)
CINEMATOGRAPHY:
Freddie Young
PRODUCER/
PRODUCTION COMPANIES:
Sam Spiegel, Robert A. Harris (for
1989 reconstruction & restoration)/
Horizon Pictures
ACADEMY AWARD
NOMINATIONS (1963)
Best Actor in a Leading Role:
Peter O'Toole
Best Supporting Actor: Omar Sharif
Best Writing, Screenplay Based on
Material from Another Medium:
Robert Bolt, Michael Wilson
ACADEMY AWARDS
Best Art Direction: John Box,
John Stoll, Dario Simoni
Best Cinematography: Fred A. Young
Best Director: David Lean
Best Film Editing: Anne Coates
Best Music, Score: Maurice Jarre
Best Picture: Sam Speigel
Best Sound: Shepperton Studio
Sound Department, John Cox

During World War I, young lieutenant T.E.Lawrence is seconded to act as an observer with Prince Feisal, the leader of an Arab tribal army. Lawrence decides to stay and help the Prince and to keep him on the side of the Allies against the Turks.

'Four hours long, with no stars, and no women, and no love story, and not much action either': Omar Sharif's description of David Lean's epic would hardly make a ringing poster endorsement, yet the film was a great success, not least at the 1963 Academy Awards where it took seven Oscars. The film's subject is the First World War exploits of T.E Lawrence, who played a crucial role in enlisting Arab tribes to fight alongside the British against Turkey. Lawrence was a complicated historical figure, a social and sexual non-conformist whose own legendary self-image he was happy to help construct, and the film doesn't entirely skirt these issues.

Lawrence of Arabia is, more than anything else, one of the great desert movies. Shot in 70mm (rather than on 35mm and then blown up), there are moments when it's evident that what Lean wants to do most is film the heat-haze and distance and to convey the desert mystery of shimmering vastness between sand and sky. In other words, it's one of those films that you simply cannot see on television. A restored version, with an extra 35 minutes added, was released in 1989.

Zulu

On January 22 1879, the British Army suffers one of its worst defeats when Zulu forces massacres 1,500 of its troops. After the battle, a Zulu force of over 4,000 advances on a small British outpost at Rorke's Drift guarded by 139 Welsh infantrymen. The film focuses on the ensuing 12-hour battle.

Telling the story of a small detachment of British troops holding out against overwhelming numbers in a last-ditch battle, *Zulu* is notable for featuring Michael Caine in his first major screen role. Making his name in an uncharacteristic role, Caine plays Lt. Gonville Bromhead, a young aristocrat with no combat experience. With some memorable set pieces in a burning hospital and on the perimeter walls of the soldiers' isolated outpost, *Zulu* is a 'Boy's Own' tale of military honour and derring-do. The troops' expectation of an inevitable Zulu attack leads to a steady ratcheting-up of tension over the film's first hour, enlivened by the interplay of the characters.

Actor Stanley Baker also produced the film, working with director Cy Endfield – their collaborations also included *Hell Drivers* (1957) and *Sands of the Kalahari* (1965). The budget of $2m was relatively small and the production had to deal with location-based adversity (the film was shot in Natal, South Africa): the first eleven days of the shoot were lost to bad weather which, nevertheless, allowed for intense rehearsals so that when shooting started the pace was so rapid that the production caught up with the original schedule. Only 500 Zulus were available to work on the film, with 4,000 required for the battle scenes, so artificial figures were created: watch carefully as they gather on the hilltops and look out for the legless, pre-digital Zulus.

GB, 1964
DIRECTOR:
Cy Endfield;
CAST INCLUDES:
Michael Caine, Stanley Baker, Jack Hawkins, Ulla Jacobsson, James Booth
CINEMATOGRAPHY:
Stephen Dade
SCREENPLAY:
Cy Endfield from the article by John Prebble
PRODUCER/ PRODUCTION COMPANIES:
Stanley Baker, Cy Endfield/ Diamond Films.

GB, 1965
DIRECTOR:
David Lean
SCREENPLAY:
Robert Bolt from the novel
by Boris Pasternak
CAST INCLUDES:
Omar Sharif, Julie Christie,
Rod Steiger, Alec Guiness,
Tom Courtney, Ralph Richardson
CINEMATOGRAPHY:
Freddie Young, Nicolas Roeg
**PRODUCER/
PRODUCTION COMPANIES:**
David Lean, Carlo Ponti/
Metro-Goldwyn-Mayer (MGM),
SoStar S.A.
**ACADEMY AWARD
NOMINATIONS (1966)**
Best Actor in a Supporting Role:
Tom Courtenay
Best Director: David Lean
Best Film Editing: Norman Savage
Best Picture: Carlo Ponti
Best Sound: Metro-Goldwyn-Mayer
British Studio Sound Department,
A. W. Watkins, and Metro-Goldwyn-
Mayer Studio Sound Department,
Franklin E. Milton
ACADEMY AWARDS
Best Art Direction: John Box,
Terry Marsh, Dario Simoni;
Best Cinematography: Freddie Young
Best Costume Design: Phyllis Dalton
Best Music, Score: Maurice Jarre
Best Writing, Screenplay Based on
Material From Another Medium:
Robert Bolt

Dr Zhivago

Told in flashback, the film follows the life of surgeon-poet Yuri Zhivago (Sharif) through the days of the Russian Revolution, World War I, the Russian Civil War and the years of Stalin's Terror. How can Zhivago's love for Lara (Christie) survive such upheavals?

Adapted from Boris Pasternak's novel, Lean's epic is a 3-hour long panorama of fifty years' worth of Russian history told through the lens of the love affair between Zhivago, a humanist, artist and medic, and Lara, the young woman who becomes his muse. Robert Bolt's heavily abridged adaptation of Pasternak's novel retained its central theme of the individual's place in history but Lean was criticized for using the epochal upheavals of war and revolution as the backdrop to a love story, creating a 'picture postcard' view of history.

Lean recreated revolution-era Russia on sets built in Spain and Canada, shooting most of the scenes during winter and the director's much-vaunted attention to detail and stunning period set-pieces made the film a huge success. It was re-released in a restored version for its 30th anniversary in 1995.

The Charge of the Light Brigade

The film chronicles the events that led to the British involvement in the Crimean War, notably the Seige of Sebastopol and the Battle of Balaclava.

Richardson's account of the ill-fated British military campaign against Russian forces in the Crimean War is a very sixties exercise in colliding genre elements: scrupulous period production values meeting epic-scale battle reconstructions and anti-Establishment satire.

The film's tone, a drawn-out retrospective raspberry blown at the complacency of the 19th century officer class and the romantic myth of military glory, make it something of a companion to another contemporary anti-war film, Robert Altman's *M*A*S*H* (1970). Richardson's film's passionate provocation draws much of its venom from Charles Wood's barbed, witty screenplay, while Richard William's animated sequences add distancing interludes and a veritable parade of top brass thesps – Gielgud, Howard, Redgrave, Andrews – fruitily incarnate the major historical players.

The first two-thirds of the film set the scene on the home-front where gung-ho militarism and jingoistic press coverage stokes up the coming slaughter on the Crimean fields portrayed with sweeping panache in the final third of the film.

GB, 1968
DIRECTOR:
Tony Richardson
CAST INCLUDES:
Trevor Howard, Vanessa Redgrave,
John Gielgud, Harry Andrews,
Jill Bennett, David Hemmings
CINEMATOGRAPHY:
David Watkin
SCREENPLAY:
Charles Wood
PRODUCER/
PRODUCTION COMPANIES:
Neil Hartley/Woodfall Films

The Lion in Winter

GB, 1968
DIRECTOR:
Anthony Harvey
CAST INCLUDES:
Katharine Hepburn, Peter O'Toole,
Nigel Terry, Anthony Hopkins
SCREENPLAY:
James Goldman from his play
CINEMATOGRAPHY:
Douglas Slocombe
**PRODUCER/
PRODUCTION COMPANIES:**
Martin Poll/Haworth Productions, Ltd.
Avco Embassy.
**ACADEMY AWARD
NOMINATIONS (1969)**
Best Actor in a Leading Role:
Peter O'Toole
Best Costume Design: Margaret Furse
Best Director: Anthony Harvey
Best Picture: Martin Poll
ACADEMY AWARDS
Best Actress in a Leading Role:
Katharine Hepburn
Best Music,Original Score for a Motion
Picture Not a Musical:
John Barry
Best Writing, Screenplay Based on
Material From Another Medium:
James Goldman.

1183. Court intrigues develop around which of Henry II's (O'Toole) four sons will succeed him. Henry favours his youngest son (Terry), while his wife, Eleanor of Aquitaine (Hepburn), has other plans for the oldest (Hopkins), Richard the Lionhearted.

The action in *The Lion in Winter* is less violent than verbal, a matter more of royal skullduggery than set-piece swordfights. The battlefield here is the English court of King Henry II at Christmas where, in the company of his sons and wife, Eleanor of Aquitaine (who lives imprisoned in a French tower), the fifty year-old King is deciding on his successor. Adapted from James Goldman's play, the film's emphasis is on the intrigues, schemes and power-plays between the royal family and, in keeping with his theatrical source, director Harvey opted to cast leading stage performers for the supporting roles; the film saw the screen debuts of Anthony Hopkins, Nigel Terry and Timothy Dalton as the child king of France. Restricting the action largely to the castle confines, this is a waspish depiction of dynastic struggles where the themes of love, honour and loyalty are explored through poisonous repartee and cunning stratagems.

Waterloo

ITALY/RUSSIA, 1970
DIRECTOR:
Sergei Bondarchuk
CAST INCLUDES:
Rod Steiger, Christopher Plummer,
Virginia McKenna, Jack Hawkins,
Orson Welles
SCREENPLAY:
Sergei Bondarchuk,
Vittorio Bonicelli, H.A.L. Craig
CINEMATOGRAPHY:
Armando Nannuzzi
**PRODUCERS/
PRODUCTION COMPANIES:**
Thomas Carlisle, Dino De Laurentiis/
Dino de Laurentiis Cinematografica,
Mosfilm

Napoleon (Steiger) escapes from imprisonment on Elba causing the French Army to defect from the King back to him. The Duke of Wellington (Plummer) faces Napoleon with a ragtag army of Britons, Belgians, Prussians and mercenaries. The two meet at Waterloo where the fate of Europe will be decided.

Waterloo was one of the many elephantine international co-productions that the Italian producer Dino De Laurentiis specialized in making throughout the 1960s and 1970s and was a commercial disaster on its release. Director Sergei Bondarchuk, having already cut his teeth on the mammoth Soviet film version of *War and Peace* (1956) which was reputed to have cost around $100 million, worked with an international cast of big name actors and called on cohorts of the Red Army for kinetic recreations of the battle scenes.

Lasting for four hours in its Russian version, the Americans slashed two hours off the film's running time making an already sprawling story almost incomprehensible in places. Bondarchuk filmed on location in the Ukraine and Italy, with interiors being shot at Cinecittá Studios in Rome, and the film's historical accuracy was ensured by technical advisor Willoughby Gray who drew on the extensive notes of his great grandfather, who had fought on the British side at Waterloo. The battle scenes are fast-paced orgies of zooming, tracking airborne camera movement that effectively capture the vast scale of this epic historical conflict.

Aguirre: The Wrath of God
Aguirre, der Zorn Gottes

In 16th century South America, a group of Spanish conquistadors descend the Amazon River in search of El Dorado, the legendary 'City of Gold'. As the expedition party falls foul of the local Indians and suffers disease and hunger it slowly falls apart. The megalomaniac second-in-command Don Lope de Aguirre (Kinski) seizes control.

Described as 'one of the great river films', Herzog's Amazonian epic charts the descent into disillusionment, despair and self-destruction of the group seeking the ever-elusive city and the riches it promises.

This is cinema of primal savagery, as much in its aesthetic minimalism of handheld cameras aboard lurching rafts, as for its portrayal of civilization succumbing to murderous atavism, at the centre of which is the explosive, gargoyle-like presence of Klaus Kinski as the messianic adventurer, Don Lope de Aguirre.

Herzog's insistent concentration on the power of place - the river, its swamps and forests – and the emphasis on filth, disease and brutality produce an environment of unforgiving cruelty in which he grounds the film's allegory of the human capacity for self-delusion.

GERMANY/PERU/MEXICO, 1972
DIRECTOR:
Werner Herzog
CAST INCLUDES:
Klaus Kinski, Alejandro Repulles, Cecilia Rivera, Helena Rojo, Dan Ades, Peter Berling
SCREENPLAY:
Werner Herzog
CINEMATOGRAPHY:
Thomas Mauch
**PRODUCER/
PRODUCTION COMPANIES:**
Werner Herzog/Hessischer Rundfunk, Werner Herzog Filmproduktion [de]

The Poseidon Adventure

USA, 1972
DIRECTOR:
Ronald Neame
CAST INCLUDES:
Gene Hackman, Ernest Borgnine,
Red Buttons, Roddy McDowall,
Shelley Winters, Stella Stevens
CINEMATOGRAPHY:
Harold E. Stine
SCREENPLAY:
Wendell Mayes, Stirling Silliphant
from the novel by Paul Gallico
PRODUCER/
PRODUCTION COMPANIES:
Irwin Allen/Irwin Allen Production
20th Century-Fox, Kent Productions
ACADEMY AWARD
NOMINATIONS (1973)
Best Actress in a Supporting Role:
Shelley Winters
Best Art Direction: William Creber
Best Set Decoration: Raphael Bretton
Best Cinematography:
Harold E. Stine
Best Costume Design:
Paul Zastupnevich
Best Film Editing: Harold F. Kress
Best Music, Original Dramatic Score:
John Williams
Best Sound: Theodore Soderberg,
Herman Lewis
Special Achievement Award (Visual
Effects): L. B. Abbott,
A. D. Flowers
ACADEMY AWARDS
Best Music, Original Song: Al Kasha,
Joel Hirschhorn

New Year's Eve, a luxury cruise liner, the S.S. *Poseidon*, is on its final voyage before being dismantled. An undersea earthquake unleashes a flood of tidal waves which capsize the ship, turning it upside down. A small crew of survivors trapped onboard must fight their way to safety.

Along with *The Towering Inferno* (1974), *The Poseidon Adventure* is one of the best of Hollywood's crop of 1970s disaster movies. Which is not to say that it hasn't acquired a certain camp patina over time, thanks largely to the now-dated special effects and the countless *Airplane* send-ups of the genre. (Guess who plays the Poseidon's Cap'n? None other than Leslie Nielsen.) Despite this, the race-against-time narrative in which characters develop under extreme duress makes for a satisfying depiction of ship-bound peril.

The motley bunch of survivors includes Gene Hackman as a tough-minded, liberal preacher, Ernest Borgnine as a blowhard cop constantly competing with Hackman for leadership of the group, the cop's ex-prostitute wife (Stevens) and an assortment of differently-aged others whose chief function is to gain our sympathy only to perish tragically. It seems strange to say it but, today, there's something almost comforting about the vision of disaster that the movie delivers.

Enter the Dragon

A martial arts expert (Lee) is hired by an intelligence agency to uncover the criminal activities of Mr. Han (Shih) who sponsors a martial arts' competition set on an island near Hong Kong. Lee infiltrates the competition and teams up with two other agents to avenge his sister's death and to destroy Han's drugs and prostitution ring.

Enter the Dragon is a lurid seventies spectacle which succeeded in adapting elements of the hugely popular Bond films – Lee's infiltration of an island fortress, the manic super-villain Mr. Han – to the grind-house genres of exploitation and Kung-Fu movies, bringing Hong Kong action cinema to an international audience.

With several tournament fight-scenes, a cat burglar sequence and a climactic showdown set in a hall of mirrors between Lee and Mr. Han, this was the work that made Lee a legend, largely because it was his last completed film. Lee died, aged 32, before the film was released, but *Enter the Dragon* remains a highly influential cult precursor of the recent renaissance of martial arts' films.

USA, 1973
DIRECTOR:
Robert Clouse
CAST INCLUDES:
Bruce Lee, John Saxton, Kien Shih,
Jim Kelly
SCREENPLAY:
Michael Allin
CINEMATOGRAPHY:
Gilbert Hubbs
PRODUCER/
PRODUCTION COMPANIES:
Bruce Lee, Paul Heller,
Fred Weintraub/
Concorde Productions Inc.,
Sequoia Productions,
Warner Bros.

USA, 1973
DIRECTOR:
Franklin J. Schaffner
CAST INCLUDES:
Steve McQueen, Dustin Hoffman,
Victor Jory, Don Gordon,
Anthony Zerbe
CINEMATOGRAPHY:
Fred J. Koenekamp
SCREENPLAY:
Dalton Trumbo, Lorenzo Semple Jr.
from the novel by Henri Charrière
PRODUCER/
PRODUCTION COMPANIES:
Robert Dorfmann,
Franklin J. Schaffner/
Allied Artists Pictures Corporation,
Corona-General, Solar Productions
ACADEMY AWARDS (1973)
Best Music, Original Dramatic Score:
Jerry Goldsmith

Papillon

1931: Henri 'Papillon' Charrière is a petty criminal wrongly convicted of murder and sentenced to life imprisonment in a penal colony in French Guyana, South America. Dega (Hoffman) is also a resident of the colony. Papillon makes repeated attempts to escape but is always recaptured and thrown into solitary confinement.

Based on the 'true story' of Henri Charrière, whose nickname 'Papillon' (French for 'butterfly') was the title of his bestselling account of escape from a penal colony, Schaffner's film version cast Steve McQueen as the dogged escapee. The film strives for grimy authenticity in its depiction of the penal colony as a brutal hellhole. With each escape attempt, Papillon is set on an endurance course of blood, sweat and leprosy which the spectator goes through with him. The film marked the end of a run of highly successful films for McQueen, including *The Great Escape*, *Bullitt* and *The Getaway* in which he established his screen persona as a rugged, impassive survivor.

USA, 1974
DIRECTOR:
Irwin Allen, John Guillermin
CAST INCLUDES:
Steve McQueen, Paul Newman,
William Holden, Fred Astaire,
Faye Dunaway
CINEMATOGRAPHY:
Fred Koenekamp, Joseph Biroc
SCREENPLAY:
Stirling Silliphant from the novels *The Tower* by Richard Martin Stern and *The Glass Inferno* by Thomas N. Scortia & Frank M. Robinson
PRODUCER/
PRODUCTION COMPANIES:
Irwin Allen, Sidney Marshall/
Irwin Allen Production,
20th Century-Fox, Warner Bros.
ACADEMY AWARD
NOMINATIONS (1975)
Best Actor in a Supporting Role:
Fred Astaire
Best Art Direction: William Creber,
Ward Preston
Best Set Decoration: Raphael Bretton
Best Picture: Irwin Allen
Best Sound: Theodore Soderberg,
Herman Lewis.
ACADEMY AWARDS
Best Cinematography:
Fred Koenekamp, Joseph Biroc
Best Film Editing: Harold F. Kress,
Carl Kress
Best Music, Original Song:
Al Kasha and Joel Hirschhorn

The Towering Inferno

During a celebratory party, a newly-built skyscraper bursts into flames. A courageous fire captain (McQueen) on the outside and the desperate architect (Newman) trapped inside struggle to save the guests.

Directed by Irwin Allen, who produced *The Poseidon Adventure*, *The Towering Inferno* replaces the former film's stricken ship with a 130-storey skyscraper wreathed in flames and fills the structure with a similarly ill-assorted group of would-be survivors. *Earthquake*, yet another

example of the popular big-budget disaster movie, was released in the same year but *Inferno* came top at the US box office helped, no doubt, by the twinning of star leads Steve McQueen and Paul Newman. Running at over two and a half hours long, the film drains every last bit of tension from the initial premise and makes great play with its ever more spectacular effects and stunts.

The Man Who Would Be King

The Man Who Would Be King sees director John Huston in epic adventure mode. Sean Connery and Michael Caine as Danny Dravout and Peachy Carneham, play a pair of soldiers of fortune who tire of their blackmailing and gun-smuggling antics in colonial India and set their sights on a greater prize: their own kingdom in the mountains of Afghanistan. This is a 'Boy's Own' action-adventure tale, set in exotic locations. It has, however, a self-conscious literary twist to it; while it was derived from Rudyard Kipling, Huston shows the storyteller transcribing the yarn but it is being related to him by an aged Peachy. And while ostensibly a broad parody of the imperialist 'great game' as played by a couple of dirty rotten scoundrels in uniform, a few of the film's gags may have something of a rancidly jingoistic tang for today's more sensitive PC palettes. As Peachy says of Danny, 'He's not a god, but an Englishman. The next best thing!'

USA/GB, 1975
DIRECTOR:
John Huston
CAST INCLUDES:
Michael Caine, Sean Connery, Christopher Plummer, Saeed Jaffrey, Shakira Caine
SCREENPLAY:
Gladys Hill, John Huston from the story by Rudyard Kipling
CINEMATOGRAPHY:
Oswald Morris
**PRODUCER/
PRODUCTION COMPANIES:**
John Foreman/
Allied Artists-Columbia Pictures Production, Devon Film
**ACADEMY AWARD
NOMINATIONS (1976)**
Best Art Direction-Set Decoration: Alexander Trauner, Tony Inglis Peter James
Best Costume Design: Edith Head
Best Film Editing: Russell Lloyd
Best Writing, Screenplay Adapted From Other Material: John Huston, Gladys Hill

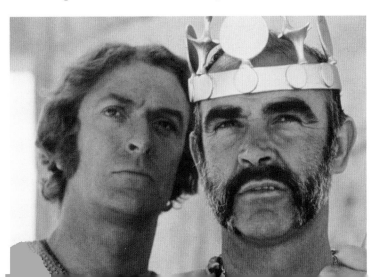

Raiders of the Lost Ark

A highly entertaining romp of an action film that throws in everything from giant spiders to Nazi villains, biblical and Egyptian mythology, thrills, spills and special effects, *Raiders of the Lost Ark* marked the first collaboration between Spielberg and George Lucas, the two most commercially successful American filmmakers. *Raiders* was the first of Spielberg's all-action Indiana Jones films, followed by *Indiana Jones and the Temple of Doom* (1984) and *Indiana Jones and the Last Crusade* (1989). While *Raiders* was acknowledged by the director to be a tribute to the action serials of his youth, it's a truly post-modern cornucopia of cinematic styles and genres, drawing on westerns, horror films, war and Bond movies. Spielberg also described his vision of Harrison Ford's character as a combination of Errol Flynn in *The Adventures of Don Juan* and Humphrey Bogart in *The Treasure of the Sierra Madre*; an American critic summed up his appeal nicely when he described Indiana Jones as being as 'indestructible as a cartoon coyote'.

USA, 1981
DIRECTOR:
Steven Spielberg;
CAST INCLUDES:
Harrison Ford, Karen Allen,
Paul Freeman, Ronald Lacey,
Denholm Elliott
SCREENPLAY:
George Lucas & Philip Kaufman
(story), Lawrence Kasdan
CINEMATOGRAPHY:
Douglas Slocombe
**PRODUCER/
PRODUCTION COMPANIES:**
Frank Marshall/
Lucasfilm, Ltd., Paramount
**ACADEMY AWARD
NOMINATIONS (1982)**
Best Cinematography:
Douglas Slocombe
Best Director: Steven Spielberg
Best Music, Original Score:
John Williams
Best Picture: Frank Marshall
Special Achievement Award
(Sound Effects Editing):
Ben Burtt, Richard L. Anderson
ACADEMY AWARDS
Best Art Direction-Set Decoration:
Norman Reynolds, Leslie Dilley,
Michael Ford
Best Film Editing: Michael Kahn
Best Sound: Bill Varney,
Steve Maslow, Gregg Landaker,
Roy Charman
Best Visual Effects: Richard Edlund,
Kit West, Bruce Nicholson,
Joe Johnston
Special Achievement Award
(Sound Effects Editing):
Ben Burtt, Richard L. Anderson

Fitzcarraldo

GERMANY/PERU, 1982
DIRECTOR:
Werner Herzog
CAST INCLUDES:
Klaus Kinski, Claudia Cardinale,
José Lewgoy, Miguel Angel Fuentes,
Paul Hittscher
SCREENPLAY:
Werner Herzog
CINEMATOGRAPHY:
Thomas Mauch
**PRODUCER/
PRODUCTION COMPANIES:**
Werner Herzog, Willi Segler,
Lucki Stipetic/Filmverlag der Autoren,
Pro-ject Filmproduktion, Werner
Herzog Filmproduktion, Wildlife Films
(Peru), ZDF

An obsessive Irish opera enthusiast (Kinski) plans to build an opera house in the Peruvian jungle. First, he has to make his fortune and decides on a rubber plantation on an inhospitable stretch of the river. Fitzgerald recruits local Indians to haul his riverboat over the mountain that stands between him and the realization of his dreams.

With its central image of a ship being hauled over a mountain, Herzog's epic account of Irish adventurer Brian Sweeney Fitzgerald's visionary attempt to build an opera house in the depths of the Amazonian jungle is a film about the costs of obsession. Fitzgerald is dismissed as 'conquistador of the useless' after his plans to build a trans-Andean railroad and to sell ice in the area have both foundered. But his

monomaniac dedication to realizing his vision finds unlikely allies including the seemingly hostile native Indians, who name him 'Fitzcarraldo'.

Made before the days when such epic quests could be safely mocked up with the aid of digital effects, Herzog took his crew down the Amazon and it's hard not to see the character of Fitzcarraldo, the risk-taking visionary, as the director's alter-ego. Given the extraordinarily chaotic nature of the film's production (detailed in Les Blank's aptly titled documentary *Burden of Dreams* (1982)), which involved the loss of the two previously-cast leads (Jason Robards and Mick Jagger) with Herzog having to start over again after a year's worth of filming, plus injuries and deaths among the crew, not to mention Kinski's legendary volatility, it's clear that there were equal degrees of obsession at work on either side of the camera.

Gandhi

The story of the life of Mohandas K. 'Mahatma' Gandhi, from his days as a struggling anti-racist lawyer in apartheid-era South Africa to becoming Indian leader. Returning to India, Gandhi sees the British treating Indians as second-class citizens. He inspires his countrymen to rise against the British through non-violent means.

Attenborough's account of the life and tumultuous times of Mahatma Gandhi is truly epic in both scope and scale. Covering five decades worth of Indian history, the film follows the blueprint of David Lean's *Lawrence of Arabia*: beginning with the death of the protagonist, following with his funeral and flashing back to his life's achievements. Attenborough's commitment to the project was itself epic, the director had begun researching the project twenty years earlier and had been planning it for the best part of four decades.

Before CGI allowed filmmakers to create digital crowd scenes, *Gandhi* set the record for the sheer number of extras: a quarter of a million extras were employed for a single scene. Kingsley's extraordinary chameleon-like performance won him an Academy Award; one of the nine that the film earned.

USA/GB/INDIA, 1982
DIRECTOR:
Richard Attenborough
CAST INCLUDES:
Ben Kingsley, Candice Bergen, Roshan Seth, Edward Fox, John Gielgud
SCREENPLAY:
John Briley
CINEMATOGRAPHY:
Ronnie Taylor, Billy Williams
PRODUCER/
PRODUCTION COMPANIES:
Richard Attenborough, Rani Dubé, Carolina Bank/Goldcrest Film International, Indo-British, International Film Investors, National Film Development Corporation of India (NFDC)
ACADEMY AWARD
NOMINATIONS (1983)
Best Makeup: Tom Smith
Best Music, Original Score: Ravi Shankar, George Fenton
Best Sound: Gerry Humphreys, Robin O'Donoghue, Jonathan Bates, Simon Kaye
ACADEMY AWARDS
Best Actor in a Leading Role: Ben Kingsley
Best Art Direction-Set Decoration: Stuart Craig, Bob Laing, Michael Seirton
Best Cinematography: Billy Williams, Ronnie Taylor;
Best Costume Design: John Mollo, Bhanu Athaiya
Best Director: Richard Attenbrough
Best Film Editing: John Bloom
Best Picture: Richard Attenborough
Best Writing, Screenplay Written Directly for the Screen: John Briley

The Right Stuff

USA, 1983
DIRECTOR:
Philip Kaufman
CAST INCLUDES:
Sam Shepard, Scott Glenn, Ed Harris,
Dennis Quaid, Fred Ward
SCREENPLAY:
Philip Kaufman from the book
by Tom Wolfe
CINEMATOGRAPHY:
Caleb Deschanel
PRODUCER/
PRODUCTION COMPANIES:
Irwin Winkler, Robert Chartoff/
Robert Chartoff-Irwin Winkler
Production, The Ladd Company
through Warner Bros.
ACADEMY AWARD
NOMINATIONS (1984)
Best Actor in a Supporting Role:
Sam Shepard
Best Art Direction: Geoffrey Kirkland,
Richard J. Lawrence, W. Stewart
Campbell, Peter Romero
Best Set Decoration: Pat Pending,
George R. Nelson
Best Cinematography:
Caleb Deschanel
Best Picture:
Irwin Winkler and Robert Chartoff
Best Sound Effects Editing:
Jay Boekelheide
ACADEMY AWARDS
Best Film Editing: Glenn Farr,
Lisa Fruchtman, Stephen A. Rotter,
Douglas Stewart, Tom Rolf
Best Music, Original Score: Bill Conti
Best Sound: Mark Berger, Tom Scott,
Randy Thom, David MacMillan

During the early days of the American space programme, seven test pilots are selected to become astronauts in Project Mercury. They must undergo gruelling training if the Americans are going to win the race against the Soviets and be the first to send a manned mission into space.

The Right Stuff is based on Tom Wolfe's 1979 best-seller about the early days of the US space programme, when test pilots were pushing planes towards MACH speeds that would pull them beyond the earth, and when debates were still active over whether space-flights should go unmanned or carry 'Spam in a can', as ace test pilot Chuck Yeager described manned missions.

A study of daredevil heroism derived from the real-life exploits of Yeager (Shepard), John Glen (Ed Harris) and the first astronauts, Philip Kaufman's gripping epic features striking special effects and stunning aerial cinematography but doesn't stint at examining the political and media machinations at work in the American desire to send the first man into space. On its release, the film didn't fare well at the box office, probably being slightly ahead of its time in its ironical perspective on the American idea of heroism.

Greystoke: The Legend of Tarzan, Lord of the Apes

1886: Africa. A shipwreck strands the Greystokes, a British couple of noble lineage, in the wilds where the woman gives birth to a boy. After the death of his parents, the child is raised by apes. Twenty years later, the young man, now known as Tarzan (Lambert), rescues a wounded Belgian explorer, Phillippe D'Arnot (Holm), and nurses him back to health. D'Arnot determines to take Tarzan back to civilization and restore him to his rightful place on the Greystoke estate.

The intriguing premise of Greystoke might be stated thus: 'You may take the Lord out of the Jungle, but can you take the Jungle out of the Lord?' Hugh Hudson re-interprets Edgar Rice Burrough's character Tarzan as a 'noble savage' caught in the face-off between nature and nurture, between the 'civilization' of Edwardian aristocracy and his own 'primitivism'. It's a revisionist reading of the Tarzan story, then, in which the 'natural' superiority of the upper classes comes in for a drubbing, but one that doesn't stint on jungle-bound spectacle, especially in the attention the film pays to describing the ape community in which the young man is raised.

Christopher Lambert excels as the feral interloper, awkwardly coming to terms with a new society that contains its own fair share of barbarism, while romancing the genteel Jane, played by then-newcomer Andie McDowell. It's a fitting coincidence, in a film which pays such attention to the acquisition of language (Tarzan goes from mastering the nuances of grunts and screeches to lapsing into French and learning Latin), that McDowell's lines should have been dubbed by Glenn Close who would later voice Kala, Tarzan's ape mother, for the Disney *Tarzan*. Something of an anguished, intimate epic.

USA, 1984
DIRECTOR:
Hugh Hudson
CAST INCLUDES:
Ralph Richardson, Ian Holm,
Christopher Lambert,
Andie MacDowell
SCREENPLAY:
Robert Towne (as P.H.Vazak),
Michael Austin from the novel by
Edgar Rice Burroughs
CINEMATOGRAPHY:
John Alcott
PRODUCER/
PRODUCTION COMPANIES:
Stanley S. Canter, Hugh Hudson/
Edgar Rice Burroughs Inc., WEA
Records, Warner Bros.
ACADEMY AWARD
NOMINATIONS (1985)
Best Actor in a Supporting Role:
Ralph Richardson
Best Makeup: Rick Baker,
Paul Engelen
Best Writing, Screenplay Based on
Material from Another Medium:
P.H. Vazak, Michael Austin.

A Passage to India

UK/USA,1984
DIRECTOR:
David Lean
CAST INCLUDES:
Judy Davis, Victor Banerjee,
Peggy Ashcroft, James Fox,
Alec Guinness
SCREENPLAY:
David Lean from the novel
by E.M. Forster
CINEMATOGRAPHY:
Ernest Day
PRODUCER/
PRODUCTION COMPANIES:
John Brabourne, Richard B. Goodwin/
EMI Films Ltd, Home Box Office
(HBO), Thorn EMI Screen
Entertainment
ACADEMY AWARD
NOMINATIONS (1985)
Best Actress in a Leading Role:
Judy Davis
Best Art Direction-Set Decoration:
John Box, Hugh Scaife
Best Cinematography: Ernest Day
Best Costume Design:
Judy Moorcroft
Best Director: David Lean
Best Film Editing: David Lean
Best Picture: John Brabourne and
Richard Goodwin
Best Sound: Graham V. Hartstone,
Nicolas Le Messurier, Michael A.
Carter, John Mitchell
Best Writing, Screenplay Based on
Material from Another Medium:
David Lean
ACADEMY AWARDS
Best Actress in a Supporting Role:
Peggy Ashcroft
Best Music, Original Score:
Maurice Jarre

India, the 1920s: tensions develop between Indians and colonial Britons when a young English woman, Adela Quested (Davis), who has travelled to India to visit her fiancé accuses the young Muslim Doctor Aziz H. Ahmed (Banerjee) of rape.

It had been fourteen years since his last feature film, *Ryan's Daughter*, when David Lean returned to filmmaking with his 1984 adaptation of E.M. Forster's celebrated novel, *A Passage to India*. It explores the barely suppressed resentment and racism existing between the British Raj and its Indians and its poisonous effects when Adela presses the charge and the doctor goes on trial. Lean treats the subject matter on a characteristically grand scale and this historical costume drama was one of the key films of the 'heritage cinema' genre that was so popular in 1980s British filmmaking.

Ran

Lord Hidetora (Nakadai) is an aging Japanese warlord who intends to divide his kingdom between his three sons. The elder two are satisfied while the youngest believes his father has gone mad and predicts conflict between his older brothers.

Made when Kurosawa was 75, *Ran* (meaning 'chaos') was the venerable director's version of Shakespeare's *King Lear*, a project that took ten years to reach the screen and, at $12 million, was the most expensive film ever made in Japan. The film is less a straightforward stage-to-screen adaptation (Lear's daughters are gender-swapped to sons) than an examination of greed, betrayal and disloyalty to the codes of personal honour placed within a dynastic power struggle that finds bloody expression on the battlefield. Kurosawa had amply demonstrated his mastery of staging epic action scenes in films, such as *The Seven Samurai* (1954), *Yojimbo* (1961) and *Kagemusha* (1980) and *Ran* was proof that his ability to orchestrate epic slices of movement and colour remained that of a cinematic virtuoso. In 1985, French director Chris Marker produced an informative making-of documentary.

JAPAN/FRANCE, 1985
DIRECTOR:
Akira Kurosawa
CAST INCLUDES:
Tatsuya Nakadai, Akira Terao,
Jinpachi Nezu, Daisuke Ryu,
Mieko Harada
SCREENPLAY:
Masato Ide, Akira Kurosawa,
Hideo Oguni based on *King Lear*
by William Shakespeare
CINEMATOGRAPHER:
Takao Saito, Masaharu Ueda,
Asakazu Nakai
**PRODUCER/
PRODUCTION COMPANIES:**
Serge Silberman, Masato Hara/
Greenwich Film, Nippon Herald Films,
Herald Ace Production,
Orion Classics
**ACADEMY AWARD
NOMINATIONS (1986)**
Best Art Direction: Yoshiro Muraki,
Shinobu Muraki
Best Cinematography: Takao Saito,
Masaharu Ueda, Asakazu Nakai
Best Director: Akira Kurosawa
ACADEMY AWARDS
Best Costume Design: Emi Wada

The Mission

Father Gabriel (Irons), a Spanish Jesuit, travels to the South American wilderness to build a mission in order to convert native Indians. Mendoza (De Niro), a slave hunter, is converted and joins Irons in his mission. When Spain sells the colony to Portugal, both must defend the mission against the Portugese aggressors.

Director Roland Joffé and producer David Puttnam followed the international success of *The Killing Fields* with this epic story of the confrontation between missionaries and colonizers in the jungles of South America. While undeniably spectacular and featuring committed performances by Robert De Niro and Jeremy Irons. *The Mission* was not as well received as the production team's previous film. It is, in part, an epistolary epic, employing the device of letters to explain what happened to the mission founded by Father Gabriel and which Mendoza, who killed his brother, has joined. The missionaries crave a society in which Christian natives will live peacefully with Spanish and Portuguese alike. But the colonial governors would rather enslave the Indians and order the destruction of the mission. Gabriel and Mendoza disagree on how to respond: one believing in the power of prayer and passive resistance, the other in armed rebellion.

UK/USA 1986
DIRECTOR:
Roland Joffé
CAST INCLUDES:
Robert De Niro, Jeremy Irons,
Cherie Lunghi, Ray McAnally,
Aidan Quinn
CINEMATOGRAPHY:
Chris Menges
SCREENPLAY:
Robert Bolt
PRODUCER/
PRODUCTION COMPANIES:
Fernando Ghia, David Puttnam,
Iain Smith/Enigma Productions,
Goldcrest Films Ltd., Kingsmere
Productions Ltd., Warner Bros.
ACADEMY AWARD
NOMINATIONS (1987)
Best Art Direction-Set Decoration:
Stuart Craig, Jack Stephens
Best Costume Design: Enrico Sabbatini
Best Director: Roland Joffé
Best Film Editing: Jim Clark
Best Music, Original Score:
Ennio Morricone
Best Picture: Fernando Ghia,
David Puttnam
ACADEMY AWARDS
Best Cinematography: Chris Menges

Top Gun

Lt. Pete 'Maverick' Mitchell (Cruise), a fighter pilot, is sent to the Top Gun Naval Flying School where he strives to be the best pilot and is attracted to Charlotte Blackwood (McGillis), a civilian tutor.

Although, in essence, a barely disguised recruitment film for the US Air Force, *Top Gun* features some breathtaking aerial sequences in which Cruise and colleagues engage in all manner of dog-fighting daredevilry. As the ultra-competitive, yet conflicted 'Maverick', Cruise has a rival in another 'top gun' airman known as 'Iceman' (Kilmer), an air-ace Dad whose mysterious death still troubles him and a love-interest in the shape of earth-bound instructor 'Charlie' (McGillis). It's clearly not the emotional and psychological aspects of the story that interest director Tony Scott but the gung-ho airborne action, which is riveting.

USA, 1986
DIRECTOR:
Tony Scott
CAST INCLUDES:
Tom Cruise, Kelly McGillis, Val Kilmer, Anthony Edwards, Tom Skerritt
SCREENPLAY:
Jim Cash, Jack Epps Jr. from an article by Ehud Yonay
CINEMATOGRAPHY:
Jeffrey L. Kimball
**PRODUCER/
PRODUCTION COMPANIES:**
Don Simpson, Jerry Bruckheimer/ Don Simpson/Jerry Bruckheimer Production, Paramount
**ACADEMY AWARD
NOMINATIONS (1987)**
Best Film Editing: Billy Weber, Chris Lebenzon
Best Sound: Donald O. Mitchell, Kevin O'Connell, Rick Kline, William B. Kaplan
Best Sound Effects Editing: Cecelia Hall, George Watters
ACADEMY AWARDS
Best Music, Original Song: Giorgio Moroder, Tom Whitlock

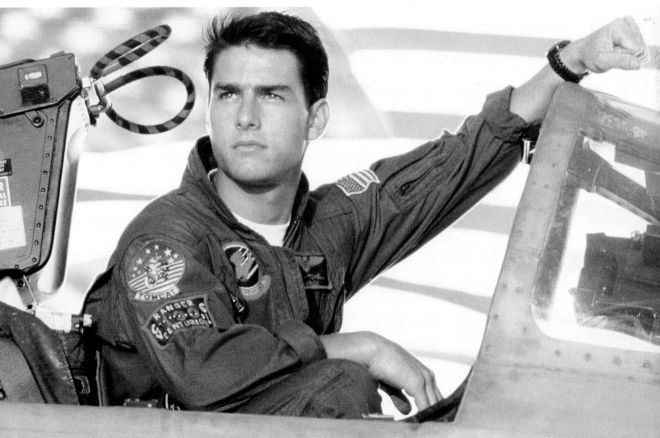

The Last Emperor

FRANCE, ITALY, GB, 1987
DIRECTOR:
Bernardo Bertolucci
CAST INCLUDES:
John Lone, Joan Chen, Peter O'Toole,
Tao Wu
SCREENPLAY:
Henry Pu-yi, Mark Peploe, Bernardo
Bertolucci from the book
by Henry Pu-yi
CINEMATOGRAPHY:
Vittorio Storaro
PRODUCER/
PRODUCTION COMPANIES:
Jeremy Thomas/
AAA Productions, Recorded Picture
Company, Screenframe Ltd.,
Soprofilms, TAO Film, Yanco Films Ltd.
ACADEMY AWARDS (1988)
Best Art Direction:
Ferdinando Scarfiotti, Bruno Cesari,
Osvaldo Desideri
Best Cinematography: Vittorio Storaro
Best Costume Design: James Acheson
Best Director: Bernardo Bertolucci
Best Film Editing: Gabriella Cristiani
Best Music, Original Score:
Ryuichi Sakamoto, David Byrne,
Cong Su
Best Picture: Jeremy Thomas
Best Sound: Bill Rowe, Ivan Sharrock
Best Writing, Screenplay Based on
Material from Another Medium:
Mark Peploe, Bernardo Bertolucci

At the age of three, Pu Yi is named Emperor of China. The film follows his life through his brief reign, his abdication and decline into a dissolute lifestyle to his final days as a humble gardener in the Peking Botanical Gardens.

The Last Emperor was the film with which Bernardo Bertolucci went beyond his self-proclaimed status as one of the 'sons' of Jean-Luc Godard and a leading light of 1960s and 1970s European art cinema, reaching out to the widest possible international audience. While *The Last Emperor* retains certain conventions of the 'historical epic', especially in the way that the life of a single individual – in this case, Pu Yi, the child Emperor – is used as a prism through which to address a nation's history, Bertolucci's approach is that of a director who has fully absorbed the refinements of cinematic modernism. Pu-Yi is a paradoxically passive character to be at the heart of such an epic; sealed within an opulent, hermetic court and occupying a position that represents only ceremonial significance, he is dubbed 'the Emperor of Nothing' whose story is told in an intricately interwoven tapestry of flash-forward and flash-back.

As well as using authentic costumes and thousands of extras, Bertolucci shot entirely on location in the People's Republic of

China and was given permission to film inside the Forbidden City, the vast imperial complex of 250 acres and 9,999 rooms. With this combination of real locations and his strange, dreamlike use of space and colour, Bertolucci fashioned an epic spectacle that managed to be both sumptuously grand and psychologically intimate. His triumph would pay off in terms of public, critical and Academy Award acclaim and lead to him making two subsequent 'intimate epics': *The Sheltering Sky* (1990) and *Little Buddha* (1994).

Die Hard

USA, 1988
DIRECTOR:
John McTiernan
CAST INCLUDES:
Bruce Willis, Allan Rickman,
Bonnie Bedelia, Reginald Veljohsnon
SCREENPLAY:
Jeb Stuart, Steven E de Souza from
the novel by Roderick Thorp
CINEMATOGRAPHY:
Jan de Bont
PRODUCER/
PRODUCTION COMPANIES:
Joel Silver, Lawrence Gordon/
20th-Century Fox, Gordon Company,
Silver Pictures
ACADEMY AWARD
NOMINATIONS (1989)
Best Effects-Sound Editing:
Stephen H. Flick, Richard Shorr
Best Effects-Visual: Richard Edlund,
Al DiSarro, Brent Boates,
Thaine Morris
Best Film Editing: Frank J. Urioste,
John F. Link
Best Sound: Don Bassman,
Kevin F. Cleary, Richard Overton,
Al Overton

During a Christmas trip to Los Angeles, New York cop John McClane (Willis) is trapped in a skyscraper when a group of terrorists occupy the building. His wife (Bedelia) is among the group captured by the charismatic terrorist leader (Rickman). McClane is all that stands between the hostages and their captors.

In the language of the 'high-concept' pitch beloved of 80s Hollywood *Die Hard*, with its combination of gung-ho action and skyscraper-set peril, could be described as 'Rambo meets The Towering Inferno'. This was the first of three films – *Die Hard II* (1990) and *Die Hard: With a Vengeance* (1995) would follow – in which Willis established himself as one of Hollywood's principal vest-wearing, gun-toting action men, having previously been best known for playing a smirking private-eye in the US television series *Moonlighting*. But alongside the cat-and-mouse interplay between Willis' resourceful, wise-cracking cop and Rickman's suave and ruthless terrorist, it's the building that's the star. The lift shafts, heating ducts and sheer glass façades of the Nakatomi Corporation's high-rise HQ become the setting for a catalogue of violent confrontations, high-adrenalin stunts and huge explosions.

Speed

Jack Traven (Reeves), a young cop, must save the passengers of a bus that has a bomb set to explode if the bus goes below 50 MPH.

Speed is one of those films that does exactly what it says in the title; it tears along with the machine-tooled precision of a big-budget action film intent on dispensing wall-to-wall thrills, stunts and special effects. An inventive thriller that starts with hostages trapped in an elevator and continues with two chases, one on a bus, another on a subway train, *Speed* pits a resourceful bomb-disposal expert (Reeves) against a maniac ex-cop with a grudge (Hopper) who is orchestrating the mayhem. Featuring Sandra Bullock as the woman who must keep her foot to the pedal on the bomb-primed bus, the film also revealed Keanu Reeves to be a compelling action-hero – next stop: *The Matrix*. Director Jan de Bont, who had worked as a cinematographer on action movies such as *Total Recall* and *Die Hard* delivers a compelling white-knuckle ride all the way to the subway station.

USA, 1994
DIRECTOR:
Jan de Bont
CAST INCLUDES:
Keanu Reeves, Dennis Hopper,
Sandra Bullock,
Joe Morton, Jeff Daniels
CINEMATOGRAPHY:
Andrzej Bartkowiak
SCREENPLAY:
Graham Yost
**PRODUCER/
PRODUCTION COMPANIES:**
Mark Gordon/
20th Century Fox.
**ACADEMY AWARD
NOMINATIONS (1995)**
Best Film Editing: John Wright
Best Sound Effects Editing:
Stephen Hunter Flick
ACADEMY AWARDS
Best Sound: Gregg Landaker,
Steve Maslow, Bob Beemer,
David R. B. MacMillan

True Lies

USA, 1994
DIRECTOR:
James Cameron
CAST INCLUDES:
Arnold Schwarzenegger,
Jamie Lee Curtis, Tom Arnold,
Art Malik, Bill Paxton, Tia Carrere
SCREENPLAY:
James Cameron,
Claude Zidi, Simon Michael,
Didier Kaminka
CINEMATOGRAPHY:
Russell Carpenter
**PRODUCERS/
PRODUCTION COMPANIES:**
James Cameron, Stephanie
Austin/Lightstorm Entertainment Inc.,
20th-Century Fox
**ACADEMY AWARD
NOMINATIONS (1995)**
Best Visual Effects: John Bruno,
Thomas L. Fisher, Jacques Stroweis,
Patrick McClung

Harry Tasker (Schwarzenegger) works for a top-secret organization, Omega Sector and is investigating a group of Arab terrorists involved in smuggling nuclear weapons. His wife Helen (Curtis), who believes Harry to be a computer salesman, feels neglected by her husband and begins a flirtation with a man who pretends to be a spy (Paxton). Harry spies on his wife and when they are both kidnapped by the terrorists, Harry is forced to reveal his true identity to Helen. They manage to escape, only to learn that the terrorists have kidnapped their teenage daughter and are threatening to explode a nuclear warhead in Miami.

True Lies has Schwarzenegger playing a semi-parodic, self-reflexive version of his well-established action-hero role (though not as self-reflexive as 1993's *The Last Action Hero*); his Harry Tasker is a secret undercover operative who's also a husband and father and must keep his job secret from his wife. This allows director James Cameron to attempt an unlikely fusion of two seemingly incompatible genres – the action-adventure film and the screwball comedy – which doesn't quite come off. Whether it was conceived to broaden the actor's range and humanize his *'Terminator'* persona (basically, he's James Bond as family-man here), the film's concentration on the husband and wife relationship lacks the conviction of the action sequences which, as one would expect from Cameron, come thick, fast and increasingly spectacular.

Braveheart

13th century Scotland. A Scottish rebel, William Wallace (Gibson), leads an uprising against the cruel English reign of Edward the Longshanks (McGoohan) who plans to take the Scottish crown for himself. His father died trying to bring freedom to the Scots when he was a young boy, so Wallace, with the support of Robert the Bruce (MacFadyen), takes on the invader.

Hardly the last word in historical accuracy, Gibson's directorial debut, an account of thirteenth century Scots taking on their evil British oppressors, is a wattle-and-daub epic of muddy, bloody battles. Gibson plays freedom fighter William Wallace as an ultra-macho mythical warrior, a resourceful military strategist and a martyr-in-the-making (dying on the rack, his last word is 'Freedom!'), while also enjoying dalliances with a French princess (Marceau) and an old flame (McCormack).

Budgeted at around $53 million and given an R rating for its scenes of 'brutal medieval warfare', *Braveheart* bagged six Academy Awards including Best Director. While the battle scenes are something to behold, the real interest lies in the way Gibson ups the ante in Hollywood cinema's enduring fascination with the spectacle of broken, bloodied male bodies where narcissism and masochism combine to create the image of warrior-star. The next stop for Gibson would be obvious, *The Passion of the Christ*, the ultimate in celluloid bloodletting.

USA, 1995
DIRECTOR:
Mel Gibson
CAST INCLUDES:
Mel Gibson, Sophie Marceau, Brian Cox, Patrick McGoohan, Catherine McCormack, Angus MacFadyen
CINEMATOGRAPHY:
John Toll
SCREENPLAY:
Randall Wallace
PRODUCER/
PRODUCTION COMPANIES:
Bruce Davey, Alan Ladd Jr., Mel Gibson/20th-Century Fox, BH Finance CV, Icon Entertainment International/Paramount Pictures, The Ladd Company
ACADEMY AWARD
NOMINATIONS (1996)
Best Costume Design: Charles Knode
Best Film Editing: Steven Rosenblum
Best Music, Original Dramatic Score: James Horner
Best Sound: Andy Nelson, Scott Millan, Anna Behlmer, Brian Simmons
Best Writing, Screenplay Written Directly for the Screen: Randall Wallace
ACADEMY AWARDS
Best Cinematography: John Toll
Best Director: Mel Gibson
Best Makeup: Peter Frampton, Paul Pattison, Lois Burwell
Best Picture: Mel Gibson, Alan Ladd, Jr. and Bruce Davey
Best Sound Effects Editing: Lon Bender, Per Hallberg

Crouching Tiger, Hidden Dragon
Wo Hu Cang Long

HONG KONG/USA, 2000
DIRECTOR:
Ang Lee
SCREENPLAY:
Hui-Ling Wang, James Schamus, Kua Jung Tsai (Sc.) from the novel by Du Lu Wang
CAST INCLUDES:
Yun Fat Chow, Michelle Yeoh, Pei-Pei Chang, Ziyi Zhang
CINEMATOGRAPHY:
Peter Pau
PRODUCER/
PRODUCTION COMPANIES:
Ang Lee, Bill Kong, Hsu Li Kong/ Asia Union Film & Entertainment Ltd., China Film Company Production Corporation, Columbia Pictures Film Production Asia, EDKO Film Ltd, Good Machine, Sony Pictures Classics, United China Vision, Zoom Hunt International Productions Company Ltd.
ACADEMY AWARD
NOMINATIONS (2001)
Best Costume Design: Tim Yip
Best Director: Ang Lee
Best Film Editing: Tim Squyres
Best Music, Original Song: 'A Love Before Time.' Music by Jorge Calandrelli and Tan Dun, Lyric by James Schamus
Best Picture: Bill Kong, Hsu Li Kong and Ang Lee
Best Writing, Screenplay Based on Material Previously Produced or Published: Wang Hui Ling, James Schamus and Tsai Kuo Jung
ACADEMY AWARDS
Best Foreign Language Film: (Taiwan)
Best Cinematography: Peter Pau
Best Music, Original Score: Tan Dun
Best Art Direction-Set Decoration: Tim Yip

Li Mu Bai (Fat) is a warrior whose sword, the magic Green Destiny, is stolen. Li must recover it while also avenging the death of his father at the hands of the evil Jade Fox (Chang). He is joined in his quest by Yu Shu Lien (Yeoh), the unacknowledged love of his life.

'*Sense and Sensibility*' with swordfights' was how screenwriter and stalwart Ang Lee-collaborator James Schamus described the Hong Kong-born director's foray into martial arts action cinema. Lee's reputation as a master of finessed psychological dramas (*Eat, Drink, Man, Woman, The Ice Storm*) and period costume dramas (*Sense and Sensibility*) did not appear to make him the obvious contender to deliver a kung-fu epic, least of all one in Mandarin Chinese which was to make it to the multiplexes and multi-Oscar acclaim.

Set in the mythical Chinese past, *Crouching Tiger* is a film about honour, betrayal and supernaturally gifted warriors who are able to effortlessly defy gravity. The fight sequences are breathtaking, with the actors scaling walls, leaping from roof to roof and, in one memorable scene, literally fighting it out in the treetops courtesy of Yuen Wo-Ping's 'wire-fu' choreography (which also featured in *The Matrix*). The action adds to the film's richly romantic epic sweep, further enhanced by the commanding presences of Fat and Yeoh and a swooning score performed by cellist Yo Yo Ma.

Gladiator

AD 180. General Maximus Decimus Meridius (Crowe) is named 'Keeper of Rome' by the dying Emperor Marcus Aurelius (Harris) after successfully vanquishing the Barbarian hordes. But the Emperor's son, Commodus (Phoenix) has other ideas. Following a foiled execution, Maximus flees to his Spanish home to discover his wife and son have been murdered. Enslaved and trained as a gladiator, Maximus is one of a troupe of warriors called to Rome for the gladiatorial games where he is soon involved in plots to overthrow the emperor.

With a mammoth $100 million budget and a four-month shoot in four countries, director Ridley Scott aimed, with *Gladiator*, to revive the genre of the 'ancient epic'; a genre which had not proved to be much of a crowd-puller since the international vogue in the 1960s for 'swords and sandals' spectaculars such as *Spartacus* (1960) and *The Fall and the Rise of the Roman Empire* (1964). Today, the thousands of extras mandatory in such epic undertakings may be multiplied thanks to CGI, and *Gladiator* is one of the prime examples of the new cinematic fashion for 'pixellated antiquity'. As well as using CGI to recreate the Colosseum in Rome – where the authentically bone-crunching, blood-soaked gladiatorial combat is staged as recreations of famous battles – there was another, unexpected use found for Scott's special effects team: the death, during filming, of Oliver Reed (playing the gladiator trainer, Proximo) called for a stealthy dose of digital reanimation.

USA/GB, 2000
DIRECTOR:
Ridley Scott
SCREENPLAY:
David Franzoni (story),
David Franzoni, John Logan,
William Nicholson (screenplay)
CAST INCLUDES:
Russell Crowe, Joaquin Phoenix,
Connie Nielsen, Oliver Reed,
Richard Harris
CINEMATOGRAPHY:
John Mathieson
**PRODUCER/
PRODUCTION COMPANIES:**
David Franzoni, Branko Lustig,
Douglas Wick/DreamWorks SKG,
Scott Free Productions,
Universal Pictures
**ACADEMY AWARD
NOMINATIONS (2001)**
Best Art Direction: Arthur Max,
Crispian Sallis
Best Cinematography:
John Mathieson
Best Film Editing Pietro Scalia
Best Writing, Screenplay Written
Directly for the Screen:
David Franzoni. John Logan,
William Nicholson, David Franzoni
Best Sound: Scott Millan,
Bob Beemer, Ken Weston
ACADEMY AWARDS
Best Actor in a Leading Role:
Russell Crowe
Best Costume Design: Janty Yates
Best Director: Ridley Scott
Best Visual Effects: John Nelson,
Neil Corbould, Tim Burke,
Rob Harvey
Best Picture: Douglas Wick, David
Franzoni, Branko Lustig
Best Sound: Scott Millan, Bob
Beemer, Ken Weston

The Lord of the Rings: The Fellowship of the Ring

NEW ZEALAND/USA 2001
DIRECTOR:
Peter Jackson
CAST INCLUDES:
Elijah Wood, Orlando Bloom,
Ian McKellen, Liv Tyler,
Christopher Lee, Cate Blanchett,
Sala Baker
CINEMATOGRAPHY:
Andrew Lesnie
SCREENPLAY:
Fran Walsh, Philippa Boyens,
Peter Jackson from the novel
by J.R.R. Tolkien
PRODUCER/
PRODUCTION COMPANIES:
Peter Jackson, Fran Walsh,
Barrie M. Osborne/New Line Cinema,
Wingnut Films Production
ACADEMY AWARD
NOMINATIONS (2002)
Best Actor in a Supporting Role:
Ian McKellen
Best Art Direction: Grant Major,
Dan Hennah
Best Costume Design: Ngila Dickson,
Richard Taylor
Best Director: Peter Jackson
Best Film Editing: John Gilbert
Best Music, Original Song: Enya,
Nicky Ryan, Roma Ryan
Best Picture: Peter Jackson,
Fran Walsh and Barrie M. Osborne
Best Sound: Christopher Boyes,
Michael Semanick, Gethin Creagh,
Hammond Peek
Best Writing, Screenplay Based on
Material Previously Produced or
Published: Fran Walsh,
Philippa Boyens, Peter Jackson
ACADEMY AWARDS
Best Cinematography:
Andrew Lesnie
Best Makeup: Peter Owen,
Richard Taylor
Best Music, Original Score:
Howard Shore
Best Visual Effects:
Jim Rygiel, Randall William Cook,
Richard Taylor, Mark Stetson

An ancient ring thought lost for centuries has been found, given to a Hobbit named Frodo (Wood). When Gandalf (McKellen) discovers that this is the One Ring of the Dark Lord Sauron (Baker), Frodo must make an epic quest to the Cracks of Doom to destroy it.

Director Peter Jackson's screen adaptation of J.R.R. Tolkien's mammoth Middle Earth trilogy is an epic feat in itself: three films – *The Lord of the Rings: The Fellowship of the Ring* (2001), *The Two Towers* (2002) and *The Return of the King* (2003) – filmed over an 18-month production period between 1999 and 2001 at a cost of $300 million. Jackson's combination of the landscape of his native New Zealand, where the films were shot, and extensive use of CGI have served to make his 'Ring Cycle' the standard not only for fantasy cinema but for modern epic cinema in general. But while the films have proved immensely popular, retaining the mystery, mood and imaginative scope of the source material, *The Lord of the Rings: The Fellowship of the Ring* is sombre, violent and almost morbidly death-obsessed. Taken all together, Jackson's epic vision of Tolkien's Middle Earth is a landscape of final battles, mythical monsters and age-old quests that is rendered throughout with spectacular panache.

Master and Commander: The Far Side of the World

During the Napoleonic Wars, HMS *Surprise*, a British frigate, and a larger French warship, the *Acheron*, hunt one another off the South American coast.

Peter Weir's film brings to the screen characters from Patrick O'Brien's highly regarded series of seafaring novels and centres on the relationship between naval officer Capt. Jack Aubrey, whose crew call him 'Lucky Jack', and the ship's surgeon Stephen Maturin, a pair of firm friends and conversational sparring partners. Opening with a prolonged, bravura battle scene set in the foggy South Atlantic, the film takes time to establish the characters of the crew, their everyday on-board relations and their reactions to the fierce weather and violent skirmishes with the French battleship that stalks them. The film's core lies in the relationship between Capt. Aubrey and Maturin – who find frequent respite from the violence of their lives by playing string duets together – the one is a military traditionalist, the other tending to a more rationalist, scientific world-view.

USA, 2003
DIRECTOR:
Peter Weir
CAST INCLUDES:
Russell Crowe, Paul Bettany,
James D'Arcy, Edward Woodall,
Chris Larkin
SCREENPLAY:
Peter Weir, John Collee from the
novels by Patrick O'Brian
CINEMATOGRAPHY:
Russell Boyd; Producer:
Samuel Goldwyn Jr., Peter Weir,
Duncan Henderson
PRODUCER/
PRODUCTION COMPANIES:
Peter Weir, Alan B. Curtiss, Samuel
Goldwyn Jr., Duncan Henderson/
20th-Century Fox, Universal Pictures,
Miramax Films Production
ACADEMY AWARD
NOMINATIONS (2004)
Best Art Direction: William Sandell
Best Set Decoration: Robert Gould
Best Costume Design: Wendy Stites
Best Director: Peter Weir
Best Film Editing: Lee Smith
Best Makeup: Edouard Henriques,
Yolanda Toussieng
Best Picture: Samuel Goldwyn Jr.,
Peter Weir, Duncan Henderson
Best Sound Mixing: Paul Massey,
D.M. Hemphill and Arthur Rochester
Best Visual Effects: Dan Sudick,
Stefen Fangmeier, Nathan
McGuinness, Robert Stromberg
ACADEMY AWARDS
Best Cinematography: Russell Boyd
Best Sound Editing: Richard King

Pirates of the Caribbean: The Curse of the Black Pearl

USA 2003
DIRECTOR:
Gore Verbinski
CAST INCLUDES:
Johnny Depp, Geoffrey Rush,
Orlando Bloom,
Keira Knightley, Jack Davenport
CINEMATOGRAPHY:
Dariusz Wolski; Screenplay: Ted Elliott
(screenplay & story), Terry Rossio,
(screenplay & story), Stuart Beattie
(story), Jay Wolpert (story)
**PRODUCER/
PRODUCTION COMPANIES:**
Jerry Bruckheimer/
Walt Disney Pictures Production,
Buena Vista
**ACADEMY AWARD
NOMINATIONS (2004)**
Best Actor in a Leading Role:
Johnny Depp
Best Makeup: Ve Neill, Martin Samuel
Best Sound Editing: Christopher
Boyes, George Watters
Best Sound Mixing: Christopher
Boyes, David Parker, David Campbell
and Lee Orloff
Best Visual Effects: John Knoll,
Hal Hickel, Charles Gibson,
Terry Frazee

Jack Sparrow (Depp) is an inept pirate who rescues Elizabeth Swann (Knightley) who is then kidnapped by Barbossa (Rush), captain of the pirate ship the *Black Pearl*. Barbossa and crew are cursed to sail the seas as the living dead unless they make a sacrifice to restore them to life. Jack and Will Turner (Bloom), a heroic blacksmith, set off to rescue Elizabeth.

Pirates of the Caribbean is a special-effects swashbuckler for kids, an action-adventure film as theme-park ride. Literally so: at a budget of $100 million, Disney adapted for the screen one of its most popular theme park attractions. Unabashedly scary fun, in which Johnny Depp's roguishly incompetent brigand and Orlando Bloom's capable blacksmith take on sword-wielding hordes of undead pirates; the film runs through all the possible variations of high-seas skulduggery in a non-stop carnival of chases and fight scenes. As Elizabeth, Keira Knightley is no tremulous damsel, battling with the best of them in this tongue-in-cheek romp.

Troy

1193 B.C., Paris (Bloom), a prince of Troy woos Helen (Kruger), Queen of Sparta, from her husband, Menelaus (Gleeson), setting the kingdoms of Mycenae and Greece at war with Troy. The Greeks sail to Troy and lay siege. Achilles (Pitt), the greatest hero among the Greeks meets Hector (Bana), the eldest son of Priam, King of Troy in the ensuing battles.

It's not often that one finds a Hollywood movie that has Homer given a writing credit but Wolfgang Petersen's *Troy* confirmed that, after *Gladiator*, Hollywood trusted the newly revitalized 'ancient epic' genre to pull in the crowds: the 'swords and sandals' spectaculars of yore were reborn as 'toga and pixels' mega-bucks productions. But among all the mythical action, there's a curious absence at the heart of *Troy*. For while Achilles et al. were the original warrior super-heroes, they were the playthings of capricious gods and monsters, alive to a world of myth and legend in which they fully believed. Yet Petersen, for all the miraculous CGI effects at his disposal, modestly balked at the prospect of bringing the Greek gods to the big screen, suspicious that modern audiences would find them laughably unbelievable. A strange but telling failure of nerve which leaves spectacular options open for other, more ambitious directors.

USA, 2004
DIRECTOR:
Wolfgang Petersen
CAST INCLUDES:
Brad Pitt, Orlando Bloom, Eric Bana, Diane Kruger, Brendan Gleeson
SCREENPLAY:
David Benioff from the poem by Homer
CINEMATOGRAPHY:
Roger Pratt
PRODUCER/ PRODUCTION COMPANIES:
Wolfgang Petersen, Diana Rathbun, Colin Wilson/Plan B Productions Inc., Radiant Productions, Warner Bros.

COMEDY

Safety Last

USA, 1923
DIRECTOR:
Fred C. Newmeyer, Sam Taylor
CAST INCLUDES:
Harold Lloyd, Mildred David,
Bill Strothers, Noah Young
SCREENPLAY:
Story by Jean C. Havez,
Hal Roach, Sam Taylor; titles by
HM Walken, Tim Whelan
CINEMATOGRAPHY:
Walter Lundin
**PRODUCERS/
PRODUCTION COMPANIES:**
Hal Roach/Hal Roach Studios Inc.,
Pathé

The Boy wants to better himself in order to marry the Girl, so he leaves his home town for the big city and becomes a salesman in a large department store. He shares an apartment with the Pal who is a 'human fly' – an expert in scaling high buildings. The Boy gets into all kinds of trouble at work, but hides this from the Girl who believes he's already been promoted. She follows him to the city where the Boy manages to fool her by 'borrowing' the general manager's office. The Boy then persuades his bosses to pay him a large sum for arranging a publicity stunt whereby the Pal will climb up the building – attracting huge crowds. However, when the Pal is chased off by a policeman, the Boy has to do the climb himself. After defeating a host of life-threatening hazards, he reaches the top to find the Girl waiting for him.

Safety Last was the best-known of Lloyd's feature films. The story line is merely the route to the great final climb, one of the classic sequences of silent cinema, and Lloyd never revealed how he did it. Various stunt men were, indeed, employed, but close and medium shots without back projection show that he climbed to a goodly height himself, negotiating such obstacles as pigeons, nervous spectators, a dog, a net, a malicious plank of wood, a photographer's flash and a collapsing clock. Each of these obstacles is a comic scene in itself, and the whole sequence takes up a good third of the film.

The General

When the American Civil War breaks out, Johnnie Gray (Keaton) tries to enlist with the Confederates; however, the army feel he's of more use in his job as the engineer on 'his' locomotive 'The General'. His girlfriend Annabelle (Mack) leaves him, believing he's too much of a coward to fight. A year later, Annabelle is kidnapped when Union renegades hijack 'The General'. Johnnie sets off after train and girl, rescues them both and returns to the South with valuable battle information and a Union General whom he finds hiding in the cab of his train. He is rewarded with a commission and the now adoring attention of Annabelle.

For many, this is Keaton's masterpiece, if not one of the greatest action-comedy movies of all time although, at the time, critical and audience response was lukewarm. The story was based on a true tale, *The Great Locomotive Chase*. However, that memoir had been told from the viewpoint of the Northern raiders, and Keaton realized that he could only make a sympathetic hero out of a Southern man. In any event, the original story had ended with the Northern hijackers being caught, and several of them being executed.

The General is a visual treasure trove. Apart from the glorious location shooting and the great attention to historical detail, Keaton did all his own very risky train stunts. He even managed to arrange for a real train to crash off a burning bridge into a deep ravine. The engine is still believed to be down there, somewhere.

USA, 1926
DIRECTORS:
Clyde Bruckman, Buster Keaton
CAST INCLUDES:
Buster Keaton, Marion Mack,
Charles Henry Smith, Richard Allen,
Glen Cavender, Joe Keaton
SCREENPLAY:
Al Boasberg, Charles Smith,
Buster Keaton, Clyde Bruckman,
Paul Gerard Smith (uncredited),
adapted from the memoir *The Great
Locomotive Chase* by William
Pittenger (uncredited)
CINEMATOGRAPHY:
Bert Haines, Dev Jennings
**PRODUCERS/
PRODUCTION COMPANIES:**
Buster Keaton,
Jospeh M. Schenk/Buster Keaton
Productions Inc./United Artists

Show People

Would-be starlet Peggy Pepper (Davies) arrives at MGM, hoping to become a great actress. Instead she becomes a hit as the *ingénue* in slapstick comedies starring Bully Boone (Haines). As she watches the preview of her first movie, she swears that one day she'll reduce the audience to tears, not laughter. When she does become a dramatic actress, she and Billy drift apart. Soon she is preparing to marry her smarmy leading man, but Billy manages to spoil her luxury wedding. Then, one day, Billy and Peggy meet up again – on the set of a WWII picture directed by King Vidor.

King Vidor persuaded millionaire William Randolph Hearst to allow his lovely mistress, Davies, to star in this (silent) movie, roughly based on the career of Gloria Swanson. Hearst preferred her in costume dramas, but the rest of Hollywood knew her to be a fine comedienne and she wickedly 'sent up' the silent star to the delight of subsequent audiences. Indeed, many believe this to be Davies' best film. *Show People* is full of in-jokes about show people. At an all-star luncheon, the 'real' stars include Mae Murray, Renée Adorée, John Gilbert and Douglas Fairbanks. For Billy and Peggy's final reunion, Vidor restages part of his *The Big Parade* (1925) as the set on which they meet.

USA, 1928
DIRECTOR:
King Vidor
CAST INCLUDES:
Marion Davies, William Haines,
Dell Henderson, Paul Ralli,
Tenen Holtz, Harry Gribbon,
Sidney Bracey, Polly Moran,
Albert Conti
SCREENPLAY:
Story by Laurence Stallings,
Wanda Tuchock; titles by
Agnes Christine Johnston,
Ralph Spence.
CINEMATOGRAPHY:
John Arnold
**PRODUCERS/
PRODUCTION COMPANIES:**
Irving Thalberg
(uncredited)/Cosmopolitan Pictures,
Metro-Goldwyn-Mayer (MGM)

Duck Soup

USA, 1933
DIRECTOR:
Leo McCarey
CAST INCLUDES:
Groucho Marx, Harpo Marx,
Chico Marx, Zeppo Marx,
Margaret Dumont. Louis Calhern
SCREENPLAY:
Bert Kalmar, Harry Ruby, with
additional dialogue by
Arthur Sheekman and Nat Perrin
CINEMATOGRAPHY:
Henry Sharp
**PRODUCERS/PRODUCTION
COMPANIES:**
Herman J. Mankiewicz/ (uncredited)/
Paramount Pictures

Mrs Teasdale (Dumont), a wealthy citizen of Freedonia, offers to donate $20 million to save that little country from bankruptcy, but only if her candidate, Rufus T. Firefly (Groucho) is installed as the new president. Firefly, an unsympathetic and undiplomatic character, decides that he wishes to be married to Mrs Teasdale's money. However Ambassador Trentino (Calhern) of Sylvania (the little country next door) also intends to wed Mrs Teasdale, both for her money and as the first step in his plot to take over Freedonia. Confusion on all sides is worsened by two under-skilled spies, Pinky (Harpo) and Chicolini (Chico), who are most probably working for Sylvania.

Duck Soup was the last of the Marx Brothers' five-picture deal with Paramount and, sadly, it flopped at the box-office.

However, although the mass public didn't warm to their fire-cracker humour until their next film, *A Night at the Opera* (1934), Marx buffs count it as one of their best. Director Leo McCarey already had a fine comedy record. It was he who suggested the famous mirror routine in which Groucho is pretty sure that the moustachioed face looking back at him is not his reflection, but can't quite catch 'it' out. *Duck Soup*'s script, dialogue, jokes and one-liners were all also superb. Furthermore, this was a Marx Brothers film with a message. It has many harsh things to say about war, government and dictators, but as this was done Marx-style, with buffoonery and sarcasm, many just found it disrespectful (including Mussolini, who banned it).

It's a Gift

USA, 1934
DIRECTOR:
Norman Z. McLeod
CAST INCLUDES:
W.C. Fields, Kathleen Howard,
Jean Rouverol, Julian Madison,
Tommy Bupp, Baby LeRoy,
Tammany Young
SCREENPLAY:
Jack Cunningham from the play *The Comic Supplement* by
J.P. McEvoy and an original story by
W.C. Fields (as Charles Bogle), plus
contributions from Claude Binyon,
Lou Breslow, Howard J. Green,
Harry Ruskin, John Sinclair,
Johnny Sinclair, Paul Girard Smith,
Eddie Welch, Garnett Weston
(all uncredited)
CINEMATOGRAPHY:
Henry Sharp
**PRODUCERS/
PRODUCTION COMPANIES:**
William LeBaron/Paramount Pictures

After leaving Mrs Bisonette (Howard) to her endless grievances, Harold Bisonette (Fields) goes to his store to find that his inept assistant, Everett (Young), has agreed to mind Baby Dunk (LeRoy), and now the store is covered in molasses while an angry customer yells for kumquats and a blind one destroys half his merchandize while looking for a stick of chewing gum. Suddenly, however, he comes into enough money to purchase, by mail-order, his dream of a ranch in an orange grove. He sets off for California, only to discover that he's bought one dead tree and a tumbledown shack. Things take an upswing, however, when his family leave him and a rich man appears who wants to buy his land.

It's a Gift is Fields at his most side-splitting. This is Fields in henpecked mode. Henpecked Fields merely mutters, and tries to accomplish simple acts in the face of a tempest of opposition. The classic set-pieces include his attempt to get a quiet wife-free night's sleep on the porch, hindered by everyman and his milk bottles, coconuts, garbage cans, and babies. As so often, Fields' character is alone with only his bumbling ineptness to protect him from an appalling family and a cruel world. Yet, we do not pity him. We can only admire a man with such strong inner resolve ('I never drink anything stronger than gin before breakfast') and such an astute judgement of character ('Anyone who hates dogs and children can't be all bad').

Modern Times

The Little Tramp (Chaplin) is a factory worker whose conveyor-belt job is to tighten the nuts on pieces of machinery. He is used as a guinea pig in tests on 'the Billows Feeding Machine', a practical device which automatically feeds your men while at work, 'Don't stop for lunch; be ahead of your competitor'. After a hilarious 'disagreement' with this machine, he cracks under the strain, goes berserk and is sent to a lunatic asylum. On his release, he is arrested and jailed for supposedly being a Communist. Once outside jail again, he finds life so tough that he tries hard to get re-arrested, but to no avail. He links up with an orphaned waif (Goddard) who is on the run, and the two are last seen walking hand-in-hand down a country road.

Chaplin's rearguard action against sound continued in *Modern Times*. Even though the film is billed as his first sound film, in fact the spoken word only comes through machines such as the prison warden's radio or the sinister voice of 'the Mechanical Salesman' over the phonograph. Charlie does sing a song, but in gibberish – albeit explained by his hand gestures. He also wrote a complete script and even filmed some of it before deciding that silence (with music) is best. It was this attack on the grinding life of the worker that enabled the House of Un-American Activities to pronounce Chaplin a Communist and force him to leave the country. In 1999, however, *Modern Times* came fourth on a list of forty-five films that the Vatican regarded as suitable for viewing by the faithful.

USA, 1936
DIRECTOR:
Charles Chaplin
CAST INCLUDES:
Charlie Chaplin, Paulette Goddard,
Henry Bergman, Tiny Sandford,
Chester Conklin
SCREENPLAY:
Charles Chaplin
CINEMATOGRAPHY:
Rollie Tothero
**PRODUCERS/
PRODUCTION COMPANIES:**
Charles Chaplin/Charlie Chaplin
Productions, United Artists

COMEDY

Nothing Sacred

USA, 1937
DIRECTOR:
William A. Wellman
CAST INCLUDES:
Carole Lombard, Fredric March,
Charles Winninger, Walter
Connolly, Sig Ruman
SCREENPLAY:
Ben Hecht, Ring Lardner Jr.
(uncredited), Budd Schulberg
(uncredited) from the story by
James H. Street
CINEMATOGRAPHY:
W. Howard Greene
**PRODUCERS/
PRODUCTION COMPANIES:**
David O. Selznick/Selznick
International Pictures

Reporter Wally Cook (March) is in the black books of editor Oliver Stone (Connolly), over a hoax that backfired, and is relegated to obituaries. He hears of Hazel Flagg (Lombard), a typist in Vermont who has contracted radium poisoning and only has a few months to live. Sensing a front-page sob story, he finds Hazel and persuades her that, if he takes her to New York, its sympathetic citizens will give her a wonderful time. Indeed, the Mayor of New York hands her the key to the city. However, it now transpires that Hazel isn't sick; she, too was hoaxing and the two hoaxers now fall in love. When doctors confirm that Hazel is in perfect health, the couple slip away but, to avoid scandal, they announce Hazel's death in the papers first.

This kind of black comedy was new in 1937, and some critics were troubled by their amusement at such a nasty little story about such bad behaviour. However, they concluded that comedy was perhaps better concerned with hypocrisy and humbug than with silly social intrigues and marital squabbles. *Nothing Sacred* is a superb amalgamation of talent. Val Lewton, then in Selznick's story department, found the original tale and sent it to Ben Hecht in New York. Hecht and his co-writers turned it into a slick smart satire with simmering dialogue. William Wellman brought the passion and technical mastery he'd hitherto invested in action and adventure films; and Selznick was, as ever, an involved and creative producer. Frederick March was excellent – and Carole Lombard was perfect.

Way Out West

Stanley (Laurel) and Ollie (Hardy) travel to Brushwood Gulch to fulfil their promise of delivering a dead prospector's gold-mine deeds to his daughter Mary (Lawrence). The saloon-owner Mickey Finn (Finlayson) is Mary's guardian, but he wants the deeds for himself. He tells his wife Lola Marcel (Lynn) to pretend to be Mary, and Stan and Ollie give the deeds to her. Lola then gets Mary to sign the lease over to her as guardian. Then Stan and Ollie discover the real Mary, and the battle is on to get the deeds back for her.

Way Out West contains some of the most delightful pieces of Stan & Ollie business. At one point, they do an exquisite soft-shoe shuffle. Another finds them singing a still-sought-after version of 'Trail of the Lonesome Pine'. Their attempt to rescue Mary from her wicked guardians involves a rope, a pulley, and Ollie as a counterbalance being pulled up by Stan who lets go for a moment so that he can 'spit on me hands'. There's the grand tickling scene, and the one where Stan lights a lamp with his flaming thumb, plus when he gets a lift on a stagecoach by showing a leg. They have as many ideas in a scene as most directors can produce for a whole film, and at least as many laughs.

USA, 1937
DIRECTOR:
James W. Horne
CAST INCLUDES:
Stan Laurel, Oliver Hardy,
Sharon Lynn, James Finlayson,
Rosina Lawrence, Stanley Fields
SCREENPLAY:
Charles Rogers, Felix Adler,
James Parrott, James W. Horne
(uncredited), Arthur V. Jones
(uncredited) from a story by
Jack Jevne, Charles Rogers
CINEMATOGRAPHY:
Art Lloyd, Walter Lundin
PRODUCERS/
PRODUCTION COMPANIES:
Stan Laurel, Hal Roach//Hal Roach
Studios Inc., Metro-Goldwyn-Mayer
(MGM), Stan Laurel Productions
ACADEMY AWARD
NOMINATIONS (1938)
Best Music, Score: Marvin Hatley

Bluebeard's Eighth Wife

USA, 1938
DIRECTOR:
Ernst Lubitsch
CAST INCLUDES:
Claudette Colbert, Gary Cooper,
Edward Everett Horton, David Niven,
Elizabeth Patterson, Herman Bing,
SCREENPLAY:
Billy Wilder, Charles Bracket,
Charlton Andrews (play translation)
from the play *La huitième femme de
Barbe-Bleu* by Alfred Savoir
CINEMATOGRAPHY:
Leo Tover
**PRODUCERS/
PRODUCTION COMPANIES:**
Ernst Lubitsch/Paramount Pictures

Michael Brandon (Cooper) is a very wealthy American playboy who likes getting married, but isn't so good at staying married. Shortly after parting from wife Number Seven, he meets the lovely Nicole de Loiselle (Colbert) in a department store – and proposes. However, at their engagement party, Nicole learns of the previous seven wives and only agrees to marry Michael if he promises her a huge settlement – she needs the money for her destitute father (Edward Everett Horton) – should he divorce her. However, after she has driven him to the brink of divorce (and into a lunatic asylum in the process), she realizes she wants him after all. . .

The director Ernst Lubitsch was known as the Paramount stylist. He could make the frothiest – or even, as here, the most malicious – little story into the most sophisticated or screwball of comedies. In those early days of Studio dominance, Lubitsch remained a law unto himself: he chose his stories, scriptwriters and stars – and determined the final edit of his films. However, Paramount had nothing to fear for the public loved Lubitsch movies: they were light and sparkling and dealt with subjects dear to the American heart – money and sex. For *Bluebeard*, he chose the cool, laconic Gary Cooper as his hero and as the backdrop for Claudette Colbert's Nicole. Colbert, one of Hollywood's most versatile and gifted actresses, had been born in Paris and had Parisian chic in every elegant sway of her slender hips. However, Colbert was, first and foremost, a comedienne and, in *Bluebeard* – with the guidance of the 'Lubitsch touch' – her seemingly effortless talent for comedy blossomed to the full.

Bringing Up Baby

Dr David Huxley (Grant), a stuffy young palaeontologist due to be married in two days, and only one bone short of a priceless dinosaur skeleton, hopes that, during a game of golf, he can persuade a potential donor to give him the money he needs to acquire the final bone. There he meets Susan Vance (Hepburn), a scatty young socialite with a hyperactive dog called George, who steals first his golf ball and then his car. On reaching her home, they are greeted by Baby, a young leopard that Susan's brother in Brazil has posted to her for safekeeping.

Smitten Susan's subsequent chaotic actions revolve around her efforts to keep David with her and away from his fiancée – efforts which include stealing his clothes, dressing him in a frilly négligé and ordering him to keep Baby calm by serenading it with 'I Can't Give You Anything But Love'. In the end, everyone lives happily ever after – except the dinosaur, which didn't make it.

For many, *Bringing Up Baby* is the definitive screwball comedy. Hawks certainly included all the ingredients: *double entendres*, rapid-fire delivery of witty dialogue, slap-stick, and supposedly intelligent people performing mad-cap capers.

Although much revered today, on its release *Bringing Up Baby* was both a commercial and a critical flop. Howard Hawks brought the film in way over budget, and viewers and reviewers were labelling Hepburn 'box-office poison' – however good a comedienne she showed herself to be. Hepburn and Hawks both parted company with RKO, but each went on to greater things while, in the course of time, *Bringing Up Baby*, too, gained the recognition it had always deserved.

USA, 1938
DIRECTOR:
Howard Hawks
CAST INCLUDES:
Cary Grant, Katharine Hepburn,
Charles Ruggles, May Robson
SCREENPLAY:
Dudley Nichols and Hagar Wilde from
a story by Hagar Wilde
CINEMATOGRAPHY:
Russell Metty
PRODUCERS/
PRODUCTION COMPANIES:
Howard Hawks/RKO Radio
Pictures Inc.

Midnight

USA, 1939
DIRECTOR:
Mitchell Leisen
CAST INCLUDES:
Claudette Colbert, Don Ameche,
John Barrymore, Francis Lederer,
Mary Astor, Elaine Barrie,
Hedda Hopper, Rex O'Malley,
Monty Woolley, Armand Kaliz
SCREENPLAY:
Charles Brackett and Billy Wilder
from a story by
Edwin Justus Mayer and
Franz Schulz
CINEMATOGRAPHY:
Charles Lang
**PRODUCERS/
PRODUCTION COMPANIES:**
Arthur Hornblower Jr./Paramount
Pictures

Eve Peabody (Colbert) – American, penniless and living in Paris – is hired by Georges (Barrymore), a jealous husband, to use her charms to distract Jacques (Lederer), a gigolo who is having a 'dalliance' with Georges' wife Helene (Astor). Although Eve has a boyfriend, Tibor (Ameche), she agrees to the plan because Tibor is naught but a handsome taxi driver. To show Helene that Jacques is only after her money, Georges elevates Eve to the status of a Baroness. Anxious to win her lover back, and suspecting that Eve's title is phoney, Helene gets ready to expose her at a grand ball. However, at the moment of climax, Tibor appears, announcing himself as Baron Czerny and Eve's husband. After a few more twists and turns, everyone does live happily ever after.

Midnight is often overlooked because the pages on the films of 1939 are already full to overflowing. However, it is a super-classy, smart-ass comedy of elegant adultery, with superbly witty characterization and dialogue by Wilder and Bracket. It is Paramount at its best. Moreover, all the cast were individually on top form and were working together with a scintillating rapport. Noone would have guessed that Barrymore was reading his lines from cue cards or that beneath Mary Astor's furs and black ensembles nestled an imminent arrival – baby Anthony. The cast's comic timing was impeccable, the clothes were beautiful and Paramount gave their ace Art Director, Hans Dreier, a free hand in designing Paris.

His Girl Friday

Ace reporter Hildy Johnson (Russell) goes to the quick-witted, self-serving managing editor Walter Burns (Grant) – who is also her boss and ex-husband – to tell him that she's leaving the paper and is about to marry Bruce Baldwin (Bellamy) an insurance salesman. Burns realizes he wants Hildy back both as wife and crack reporter. He uses every trick in the book to discredit Baldwin, and tempts Hildy with a front-page story about Earl Williams (Qualen), a possibly innocent man who has been convicted of murder. Williams escapes from prison and, with the police on his tail, heads for the newspaper where the staff hide him in a roll-top desk. In the thick of the excitement, Hildy becomes aware that she doesn't want to leave her job and that the man she really loves is Burns.

In Hecht and MacArthur's original play, *The Front Page*, the male Hildy (Hildebrandt) has decided to quit working for Burns' trashy tabloid. Ten years later, while casting for the role of Burns, Howard Hawkes, had his secretary read Hildy's lines and liked the new slant a female lead gave to the story. With Ben Hecht's permission, Hildebrandt became Hildegaard and scriptwriter Lederer wrote in a romantic sub-plot that heightened the editor-reporter relationship. Another of the film's key elements was the pace of everything. The movie made use of overlapping dialogue, simultaneous conversations, rapid-fire delivery, sarcastic insults and plot twists – all the necessary ingredients of a screwball masterpiece but at twice the usual speed and volume. So, take a very deep breath before you start watching *His Girl Friday*; you won't get the chance of another one until the end.

USA, 1940
DIRECTOR:
Howard Hawks
CAST INCLUDES:
Cary Grant. Rosalind Russell, Ralph Bellamy, Gene Lockhart, Porter Hall, John Qualen
SCREENPLAY:
Charles Lederer from the play *The Front Page* by Ben Hecht and Charles MacArthur
CINEMATOGRAPHY:
Joseph Walker
PRODUCERS/ PRODUCTION COMPANIES:
Howard Hawks/Columbia Pictures Corporation

Sullivan's Travels

USA, 1941
DIRECTOR:
Preston Sturges
CAST INCLUDES:
Joel McCrea, Veronica Lake,
Robert Warwick,
William Demarest,
Franklin Pangborn, Porter Hall,
Byron Foulger, Margaret Hayes,
Robert Greig, Eric Blore
SCREENPLAY:
Preston Sturges
CINEMATOGRAPHY:
John (F.) Seitz
PRODUCERS/
PRODUCTION COMPANIES:
Preston Sturges
(uncredited)/Paramount

John L. Sullivan (McCrea) is a Hollywood director who wishes to stop making 'fluffy' comedies and direct a significant film about human suffering. When it is pointed out to him that he knows nothing of suffering, given his background and upbringing, he dresses as a hobo with only ten cents in his pocket, and sets off to find out. To begin with, the quest is very difficult because his privileged world – in the shape of studio publicists – won't leave him alone. He meets up with a young woman (Lake), disillusioned with Hollywood, who decides to join him. Eventually, the pair do meet with and share the suffering of the homeless and the hopeless, and the inescapability of poverty. He witnesses chain-gang convicts laughing at a Mickey Mouse cartoon and finally realizes the true value of laughter – that it can be, if only for a moment, a lifeline of escape and a ray of hope.

Preston Sturges had been writing sought-after scripts for nearly a decade but, come the forties, he thought it time to direct them himself. *Sullivan's Travels* was his third, and already he was beginning to frighten the studio. Here was a film by a comedy director about a comedy director and a beautiful woman wandering around in filthy clothes looking for poverty. Eventually, Paramount side-stepped the problem by coming up

with the tagline: 'Veronica Lake's on the take'. To lovers of comedy, this movie offers a banquet of brilliant dialogue and one-liners, and McCrea and Lake's onscreen relationship quite simply 'rocks'. For many, this is Sturges' best.

To Be or Not to Be

Joseph Tura (Benny) and his wife Maria (Lombard) lead a troupe of actors in Poland before and during the Nazi occupation. Maria is having a liaison with bomber pilot Lt Sobinski (Stack). Every night, Sobinski waits in the audience until Tura begins 'To Be or Not to Be . . .' and then leaves the auditorium for Maria's dressing room, knowing that her husband is safely stuck on the stage for some time. Sobinski, who is part of a Polish squadron based in England, suspects Professor Siletsky (Ridges) of being a Nazi spy. Siletsky is indeed a double agent. He has been collecting names of members of the Warsaw underground to give to the Nazis and the Tura troupe is recruited to intercept these incriminating lists.

Lubitsch doesn't have much scope for subtlety when working with Jack Benny. When the troupe begins their very risky job of impersonating the Nazis who have been chosen to receive the lists of underground names, Tura delightedly opts to mis-represent 'Concentration Camp Ernie' (Erhardt). Lombard's job, meanwhile, is to encourage the advances of the traitor Siletsky to which end she finishes her kisses with the whispered words 'Heil Hitler'. However, Lubitsch leaves us in no doubt that the end justifies the means. The whole cast meld their different strands of this classic comedy into a seamless whole. Bad taste maestro Mel Brooks directed the excellent 1983 remake.

USA, 1942
DIRECTOR:
Ernst Lubitsch
CAST INCLUDES:
Carole Lombard, Jack Benny,
Robert Stack, Felix Bressart,
Lionel Atwill, Stanley Ridges,
Sig Ruman, Tom Dugan
SCREENPLAY:
Edwin Justus Mayer from a story by
Ernst Lubitsch (uncredited), Melchior
Lengyel
CINEMATOGRAPHY:
Rudolph Maté
PRODUCERS/
PRODUCTION COMPANIES:
Ernst Lubitsch/Romaine Film
Corporation
ACADEMY AWARD
NOMINATIONS (1943)
Best Music, Scoring of a Dramatic or
Comedy Picture:
Werner R. Heymann

Road to Morocco

USA, 1942
DIRECTOR:
David Butler
CAST INCLUDES:
Bing Crosby, Bob Hope,
Dorothy Lamour, Anthony Quinn,
Dona Drake, Yvonne De Carlo
SCREENPLAY:
Frank Butler and Don Hartman
CINEMATOGRAPHY:
William C. Mellor
PRODUCERS/
PRODUCTION COMPANIES:
Paul Jones/Paramount Pictures
ACADEMY AWARD
NOMINATIONS (1943)
Best Sound, Recording:
Loren L. Ryder (Paramount SSD)
Best Writing, Original Screenplay:
Frank Butler, Don Hartman

Jeff (Crosby) and Turkey (Hope) find themselves raft-wrecked on an Arabian shore. They hitch a camel ride to an exotic city where Jeff sells Turkey as a slave, but is annoyed to discover that Turkey's new owner is the beautiful Princess Shalmar (Lamour) of Karameesh who wishes to marry him. Jeff resolves to rescue Turkey who isn't at all grateful until he learns that Mullay Kassim (Quinn), a menacing Arabian Sheik, wishes to marry the Princess, and will kill anyone who gets in his way . . .

Two years earlier, Paramount had popped Bing Crosby, Bob Hope and Dorothy Lamour into *Road to Singapore*, a one-off musical of which no one had any particular expectations. However, the chemistry of the three stars, and the idiotic hilarity of the Hope-Crosby ad libs made the movie a 'smasheroo', and Paramount hastened to repeat the formula. From Singapore the trio travelled to Zanzibar and then on to Morocco. At the start of *Road to Morocco*, the boys are marooned on a Mediterranean beach; at the end, they 'raft' back into New York harbour. In the middle, *Morocco* spoofed all the 'political incorrectness' that Arab peoples regularly suffered in movies – albeit from no elevated motive. The script was excellent, and Crosby gained a hit from crooning 'Moonlight Becomes You' to Lamour.

Kind Hearts and Coronets

Louis Manzzini's mother was the youngest daughter of Ethelred d'Ascoyne, Duke of Chalfont – until she ran off with a penniless opera singer and her family disowned her. Louis (Price) grows up having to work in a draper's shop. After his mother's death, an embittered Louis determines to avenge them both and reclaim the Chalfont title, to which end he murders his way though the d'Ascoyne family – and rounds things off by marrying Edith (Hobson), the widow of one of his murdered cousins. Shortly afterwards, he is wrongly charged with the death of the husband of his mistress, Sibella (Greenwood), and put in jail. Sibella has him acquitted on the understanding that he will dispose of Edith and marry her, and all seems well, until he remembers the very detailed memoirs that he had started to write while in his prison cell . . .

Kind Hearts and Coronets is Robert Hamer's masterful matching of the elegance of both word and image. The original novel's author, Roy Horniman, had been an admirer of Oscar Wilde, and Hamer made sure that the element of Wildean wit was retained in the script. Many scenes are explained by Louis's voice-over as he reveals, in flash-back, the contents of his memoirs. At all times both narrative and dialogue are counter-pointed by exquisite visual touches. For instance, after Louis decides to blow up his photographer cousin, and is taking tea with Edith (the soon-to-be widow), a plume of dark smoke appears outside the window, a silent testimony to another hindrance eliminated.

However, the element of the film most readily remembered is the extraordinary acting feat of (Sir) Alec Guinness who plays all eight of the remaining d'Ascoynes (other than Louis): a general, a cleric, an admiral, a banker, an amateur photographer, the present Duke, young Henry – and Lady Agatha, his suffragette aunt. He does this so skilfully that one merely observes with interest the many, very different members of the d'Ascoyne family, and not his sublime talent.

GB, 1949
DIRECTOR:
Robert Hamer
CAST INCLUDES:
Alec Guinness, Dennis Price,
Valerie Hobson, Joan Greenwood
SCREENPLAY:
Robert Hamer and John Dighton,
based on the novel *Israel Rank* by
Roy Horniman
CINEMATOGRAPHY:
Douglas Slocombe
**PRODUCERS/
PRODUCTION COMPANIES:**
Michael Balcon/Ealing Studios

Born Yesterday

USA, 1950
DIRECTOR:
George Cukor
CAST INCLUDES:
Judy Holliday, William Holden,
Broderick Crawford,
Howard St John
SCREENPLAY:
Albert Mannheimer, based on the
play by Garson Kanin
CINEMATOGRAPHY:
Joseph Walker
PRODUCERS/
PRODUCTION COMPANIES:
S. Sylvan Simon/Columbia
ACADEMY AWARD
NOMINATIONS (1951)
Best Director: George Cukor
Best Picture: S. Sylvan Simon
Best Writing, Screenplay:
Albert Mannheimer
Best Costume Design,
Black-and-White:
Jean Louis
ACADEMY AWARDS
Best Actress in a Leading Role:
Judy Holliday

Harry Brock (Crawford), a self-made junk-metal tycoon, arrives in Washington to establish an illegal business cartel – with the assistance of grateful Washington politicians whose ambitions he will finance. However, he wants his mistress, Billie (Holliday) – an ex-chorus-line 'dumb broad' who regularly beats him at gin rummy – to grace his arm on social occasions. To this end, he hires journalist Paul Verrall (Holden) to put some ideas into her head and to get her to talk 'nice'. Two ideas quickly take root: that she likes Verrall and wants his undivided attention, and that she doesn't like her sugar-daddy's business dealings and no longer wishes to put her signature to them. The not-so-dumb Billie learns fast, and soon both men have a great deal more to handle than they ever expected.

Judy Holliday had already made Garson Kanin's play, *Born Yesterday*, a stage hit by the time Columbia boss Harry Cohn bought it (for the then record sum of one million dollars). However, Holliday had not, at that time, done much on screen, and Cohn resisted all of Kanin's entreaties to give her the part. Instead, he spent two years screen-testing actresses – from other studios as well as Columbia – to no avail. Eventually, the frustrated Kanin concocted an elaborate plot. He and his wife Ruth Gordon had written the screenplay for the new Katharine Hepburn-Spencer Tracy vehicle, *Adam's Rib* (1949), over at MGM. The story was set around the trial of Doris Attinger, a woman on trial for shooting her blatantly philandering husband. Holliday was cast as Attinger, and both stars and writers gave her every chance to shine. When her performance won her a Best Actress Golden Globe, Harry Cohn could object no longer to giving her the role of Billie.

Born Yesterday is more than a screwball comedy. Kanin enriches the script with an acute awareness of the political and social post-war situation in America. However, Holliday's Billie is the classic screen example of tough cookie gets an education, makes good – and gets the guy.

Les Vaçances de M. Hulot
Mr. Hulot's Holiday

The accident-prone Monsieur Hulot (Tati) is on his way to a vacation in a normally quiet seaside town in Brittany, spluttering and backfiring in his Archaic Amilcar. Decked out in his holiday gear – hat, trousers pulled up too high, stripey socks and smoking his pipe – Hulot sets out, with his bouncing stride, to become a friendly vacationer with the others in the hotel and at the beach. He is polite, considerate, and well meaning. However, wherever he goes and whatever he does, chaos follows.

Tati doesn't need a plot for his films; neither does he focus on himself as the central character. His films are, however, structured and pre-planned in minute detail. He fills his scenes with people and objects and leaves the viewer to decide where to look. Sometimes he is at the centre, as (in *Monsieur Hulot's Holiday*) when his tiny kayak folds up around him, panicking the vacationers who take him for a shark. At other times he is irrelevant, as when a station full of people, unable to understand the announcements, are left careering from one platform to another. Tati is able to be both satirical and kind, both awkward and graceful. He is the gentle genius of comedy who produced a handful of masterpieces – and this is one.

FRANCE, 1953
DIRECTOR:
Jacques Tati
CAST INCLUDES:
Jacques Tati, Nathalie Pascaud,
Michèle Rolla, Valentine Camax,
Louis Perrault, André Dubois
SCREENPLAY:
Jacques Tati, Henri Marquet,
Pierre Aubert (uncredited),
Jacques Lagrange (uncredited), from
a story by Jacques Tati and
Henri Marquet, with dialogue by
Jacques Tati and Henri Marquet
CINEMATOGRAPHY:
Jacques Mercanton, Jean Mousselle
PRODUCERS/
PRODUCTION COMPANIES:
Fred Orain and Jacques Tati
(uncredited)/Cady Films,
Specta Films [FR]
ACADEMY AWARD
NOMINATIONS (1956)
Best Writing, Story and Screenplay:
Jacques Tati, Henri Marquet

USA, 1959
DIRECTOR:
Billy Wilder
CAST INCLUDES:
Marilyn Monroe, Tony Curtis,
Jack Lemmon, George Raft,
Pat O'Brien, Joe E. Brown
SCREENPLAY:
Billy Wilder and I.A.L. Diamond, from
the story by Robert Thoeren,
Michael Logan
CINEMATOGRAPHY:
Charles Lang Jr.
PRODUCERS/
PRODUCTION COMPANIES:
Billy Wilder/Ashton Productions,
The Mirisch Corporation
ACADEMY AWARD
NOMINATIONS (1960)
Best Actor in a Leading Role:
Jack Lemmon
Best Art Direction-Set
Decoration, (B/W):
Ted Haworth, Edward G. Boyle
Best Cinematography, (B/W):
Charles Lang:
Best Director: Billy Wilder
Best Writing, Screenplay Based on
Material from Another Medium:
Billy Wilder, I.A.L. Diamond
ACADEMY AWARDS
Best Costume Design,
Black-and-White: Orry-Kelly

Some Like It Hot

Chicago, 1929. Joe (Curtis) and Jerry (Lemmon), two unemployed musicians (sax and bass), have just landed a speakeasy job when a police raid means the boys must scram to avoid arrest. Minutes later they witness the St Valentine's Day Massacre – and are themselves seen by the mobsters. To get out of town, they dress up and join – as Josephine and Daphne - an all-women's orchestra on it's way to Florida. Joe falls for the band's singer, Sugar Kane (Monroe), and invents another persona – Junior, a young millionaire – in order to win her. An elderly millionaire Osgood Fielding III (Brown) falls in love with Daphne. The mobsters turn up again, and have to be eluded. After that, Joe and Osgood propose – and Sugar and Daphne accept.

Nothing in *Some Like It Hot* – an all-time favourite film – fails. Despite all the reported problems of working with a 'dazed and confused' Marilyn, the outcome is superb. Wilder even manages to get Shakespearean, playing Sugar and Junior as high comedy, and Daphne and Osgood as the clowns. The best drag movie till *Tootsie* (1982) – and maybe then some.

Move Over, Darling

USA, 1963
DIRECTOR:
Michael Gordon
CAST INCLUDES:
Doris Day, James Garner,
Polly Bergen, Thelma Ritter,
Fred Clark, Chuck Connors
SCREENPLAY:
Hal Kanter and Jack Sher from the
1940 story *My Favourite Wife*, and
the 1940 screenplay *My Favourite
Wife*, both by Bella Spewack,
Sam Spewack; also story *Move Over
Darling* by Leo McCarey
CINEMATOGRAPHY:
Daniel L. Fapp
**PRODUCERS/
PRODUCTION COMPANIES:**
Martin Melcher, Aaron
Rosenberg/Arcola Pictures (as
Melcher-Arcola Productions)

Ellen, aka Eve (Day), missing and legally dead for five years, returns to her husband, Nick (Garner) just after Nick has got remarried – to the sexy Bianca (Bergen). Ellen had survived a plane crash over the Pacific Ocean and had been on a desert island, with no phone or sun cream, albeit with fellow survivor Stephen, aka Adam (Conners) until rescued by a US submarine. Ellen realizes that she must take things slowly – even her children don't recognize her – but her mother-in-law (Ritter) doesn't and takes out a bigamy order against her son. A sojourn in jail gives Nick time to sort out which wife he really wants to keep.

This giddy tale, first filmed as *My Favourite Wife* (1940), was being remade as *Something's Got To Give*, with Marilyn Monnroe – but Marilyn died. Doris Day and James Garner then stepped in, and the confluence of their comedic talents created this bright, funny, sixties marital comedy. Life on set was often hard for Day. On this occasion she was working with a cracked rib, after an over-enthusiastic move by Garner, and was later car-washed, although the producers did, thoughtfully, leave this scene till the last day in case the car-wash detergents gave them any problems with her skin.

The Pink Panther

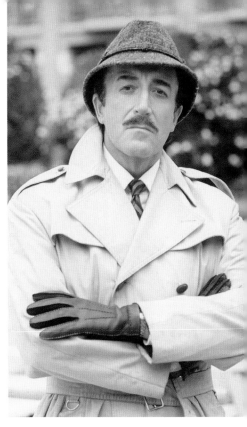

The Pink Panther, the largest diamond in the world, belongs to Dala, an Indian Princess, who takes it with her on holiday to an exclusive Swiss ski resort. It is no co-incidence that at the resort is also Sir Charles Lytton, an infamous jewel thief known as 'The Phantom'. Hot on the heels of The Phantom is the French detective, Inspector Clouseau. Unfortunately, Clouseau doesn't know whose heels he's looking for, nor that his beautiful wife Simone (Capucine) is The Phantom's lover and accomplice . . .

Peter Sellers deserves the credit for the success of *The Pink Panther*, and its sequels. Inspector Clouseau is his inspiration. He created an astoundingly inept character: bumbling, fumbling, maladroit, clueless, clumsy, ineffectual and very bad at French. Fortunately, Clouseau was also loveable, and his international fan base blossomed. The suave, elegant David Niven, as the gentleman jewel thief, was a further piece of admirable casting. The animated Pink Panther of the credit sequence, accessorized by Henry Mancini's 'Pink Panther' theme, also went on to become its own series.

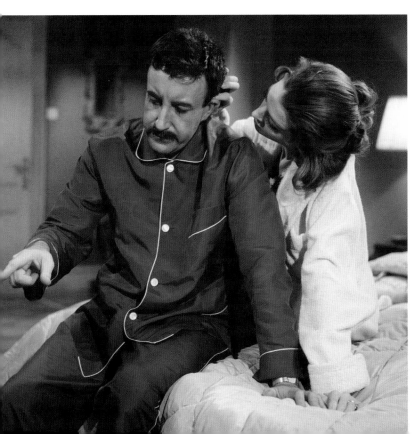

GB/USA, 1963
DIRECTOR:
Blake Edwards
CAST INCLUDES:
David Niven, Peter Sellers,
Robert Wagner, Capucine,
Brenda De Banzie, Colin Gordon,
John LeMesurier, James Lanphier,
Claudia Cardinale
SCREENPLAY:
Maurice Richlin, Blake Edwards
CINEMATOGRAPHY:
Philip (H.) Lathrop
**PRODUCERS/
PRODUCTION COMPANIES:**
Martin Jurow/The Mirisch
Corporation [US]
**ACADEMY AWARD
NOMINATIONS (1965)**
Best Music, Score – Substantially
Original: Henry Mancini

The Fortune Cookie

USA, 1966
UK TITLE:
Meet Whiplash Willie
DIRECTOR:
Billy Wilder
CAST INCLUDES:
Jack Lemmon, Walter Matthau,
Ron Rich, Judi West
SCREENPLAY:
I.A.L. Diamond, Billy Wilder
CINEMATOGRAPHY:
Joseph LaShelle
**PRODUCERS/PRODUCTION
COMPANIES:**
Billy Wilder/Phalanx-Jaelem,
The Mirisch Corporation
**ACADEMY AWARD
NOMINATIONS (1967)**
Best Art Direction, Set
Decoration (B/W):
Robert Luthardt, Edward G. Boyle
Best Cinematography (B/W):
Joseph LaShelle
Best Writing, Story and Screenplay
Written Directly for the Screen:
Billy Wilder, I.A.L. Diamond
ACADEMY AWARDS
Best Actor in a Supporting Role:
Walter Matthau

While filming a US football game, TV cameraman Harry Hinkle (Lemmon) suffers a minor concussion when accidentally knocked over by Luther 'Boom Boom' Jackson (Rich) of the Cleveland Browns. Hinkle's brother-in-law, 'Whiplash Willie' Gingrich (Matthau), a shyster lawyer, convinces him to pretend his legs have been paralyzed and sue the National Football League. Hinkle would have refused, but he thinks his 'injury' and claim may be a way of getting back at his ex-wife Sandy (West). The insurance company suspects a phoney claim and starts its investigations. Meantime, Boom Boom is devastated by the damage he has done, and sets out to take care of Harry and get him better.

Jack Lemmon and Billy Wilder had already forged a very successful working relationship through *The Apartment* (1960) and *Irma La Douce* (1963), but *The Fortune Cookie* was the first outing of the incomparable Lemmon-Matthau comedy pairing. Lemmon had been offered both Frank Sinatra and Jackie Gleason as co-stars, but he insisted on Matthau. This gem of a partnership nearly didn't happen, however: a few weeks after shooting commenced, Matthau had a heart attack – but recovered and was able to continue. Wilder's thought-provoking script is extremely cynical, and it set up the ferocious love-hate banter that was to be the Lemmon-Matthau trademark for a further nine films together.

The Producers

Accountant Leo Bloom (Wilder) tells down-on-his-luck producer Max Bialystock (Mostel), who has to charm wealthy widows to raise money for his plays, that he could make far more money from an outright flop. None of his 'angels' would expect anything back from a flop. Their formula for failure is a musical called *Springtime for Hitler*. It boasts a dance line of jackbooted chorus girls and such catchy lyrics as 'Don't be stupid, be a smarty! Come and join the Nazi Party'. The reactions on the audience's faces during the first act register complete horror. However, by the end of the evening, the house is in raptures and the critics have rushed off to write eulogies for the morning papers. Bialystock is ruined – his flop is a hit!

Mel Brooks is unquestionably the monarch of the worst possible taste, but the nerve of a man who could manifest such an idea, in any shape or form, is awesome. Furthermore, *The Producers* was released in 1968 when, all over Europe and America, people were marching against oppression and aggression. However, the movie is achingly funny: the dialogue and the sight gags are – painful. There is not a gram of subtlety anywhere; everywhere is ear-splitting frenzy. On-stage is marginally calmer than off. Mostel's Bialystock, with a fringe of hair swept over from neck to neck, is forcefully desperate; Wilder's Bloom is timidly hysterical. Brooks said of his movie that it 'rose below vulgarity'.

USA, 1968
AKA SPRINGTIME FOR HITLER
USA, 1967
DIRECTOR:
Mel Brooks
CAST INCLUDES:
Zero Mostel, Gene Wilder, Kenneth Mars, Estelle Winwood, Renée Taylor, Christopher Hewett, Lee Meredith
SCREENPLAY:
Mel Brooks
CINEMATOGRAPHY:
Joseph (F.) Coffey
**PRODUCERS/
PRODUCTION COMPANIES:**
Sidney Glazier/Crossbow Productions, Metro-Goldwyn-Mayer (MGM), Springtime Productions
**ACADEMY AWARD
NOMINATIONS (1969)**
Best Actor in a Supporting Role: Gene Wilder
ACADEMY AWARDS
Best Writing, Story and Screenplay – Written Directly for the Screen: Mel Brooks

USA, 1968
DIRECTOR:
Gene Saks
CAST INCLUDES:
Jack Lemmon, Walter Matthau,
John Fiedler, Herb (Herbert)
Edelman, (as Herbert Edelman),
David Sheiner, Larry Haines,
Monica Evans, Carole Shelley
SCREENPLAY:
Neil Simon (also play)
CINEMATOGRAPHY:
Robert B. Hauser
**PRODUCERS/
PRODUCTION COMPANIES:**
Howard W. Koch/Paramount Pictures
**ACADEMY AWARD
NOMINATIONS (1969)**
Best Film Editing: Frank Bracht
Best Writing, Screenplay Based on
Material from Another Medium:
Neil Simon

The Odd Couple

Felix (Lemmon) has broken up with his wife and she's thrown him out. He paces the streets of New York trying to commit suicide, but doesn't succeed. He goes round to the flat of his poker mate, Oscar (Matthau), a writer, who offers to let Felix share his apartment. Unfortunately, Felix is neurotically house proud, while Oscar (already divorced) is a normally contented slob who is being tidied towards a murderous breakdown. Oscar sets up a double date for them both (Felix: 'Funny, I haven't thought of a woman in weeks.' Oscar: 'I fail to see the humour.'), but even that fails as the girls merely end-up weeping in sympathy with a sobbing Felix. Finally, Oscar throws Felix out (Felix: 'In other words, you're throwing me out.' Oscar: 'Not in other words. Those are the perfect words.'), but the neatnik comes up with a surprising solution to his housing problems.

Neil Simon's play (based, he says, on the experiences of his brother Danny when he got divorced) was a 'Smash!' on Broadway and in cities all over the USA prior to being filmed. However, for the movie version, Lemmon and Matthau did encapsulate so perfectly Simon's unforgettable characters in their polarized roles, and radiated such a powerful love-hate magnetism, that a piece of movie-comedy magic was born.

Harold and Maude

Harold Chasen (Cort), nearly twenty years old, walks slowly and dramatically down the staircase of his manorial home, lights some candles and then hangs himself. His mother (Pickles) is mildly irritated; she's seen it all before. Shortly afterwards, while attending someone else's funeral (noone he knows) Harold realizes someone is trying to attract his attention, and thus he meets nearly-eighty-year-old Maude; she likes strangers' funerals too. Maude, a bundle of energy, takes Harold, a bundle of gloom, back to her railway-car home. She teaches him to dance, sing, rescue sad trees and 'borrow' cars and motorbikes. She teaches him kindly ways of living for today, and zany ways of having fun. She includes him in her life and her lunatic adventures until he is ready to open up to love.

USA, 1971
DIRECTOR:
Hal Ashby
CAST INCLUDES:
Ruth Gordon, Bud Cort,
Vivian Pickles, Cyril Cusack,
Charles Tyner, Ellen Greer
SCREENPLAY:
Colin Higgins
CINEMATOGRAPHY:
John Alonzo
PRODUCERS/PRODUCTION COMPANIES:
Colin Higgins, Charles B.
Mulvehill/Paramount Pictures

A young man deeply damaged by his refrigerated, upper-class upbringing; an elderly lady dancing and twirling to Cat Stevens; is it all too dated? In 2003, the American magazine *Entertainment Weekly* did a poll of the Top 50 Cult Movies, and Harold and Maude is there at # 4, behind *This Is Spinal Tap* (1984), *The Rocky Horror Picture Show* (1975) and *Freaks* (1932), so perhaps not. Hal Ashby came to directing with a broad hands-on experience of the film industry. Here, he shows his gift for blending edgy partners – the blackly comical and the nearly whimsical. Ruth Gordon, however, never lets Maude sink into whimsy: she's too spunky and matter-of-fact, and her one-liners are too funny. Harold's 'one-liners' are visual – the series of priceless fake suicides that he stages in an effort to have a conversation with his mother.

What's Up, Doc?

In a hotel in San Francisco sit four identical tartan overnight bags. One contains rare rocks that are on their way to a conference of musicologists. One is full of valuable jewellery, one has top-secret government documents and one has a change of clothes. Shy, bespectacled, musicology Professor Howard Bannister (O'Neal) is there with the rocks – and his fiancée, Eunice (Kahn), hoping to get a research grant from rich Mr Larabee (Pendleton). A thief is there to steal the jewellery, and a spy is there to filch the documents. Judy (Streisand) is there to cadge a free meal and stays on to further her growing interest in Howard and to become a liability to anyone whose path crosses hers. All resolves itself after a rip-roaring chase through the streets of San Francisco.

What's Up, Doc? was number 3 at the box-office for 1972, so audiences clearly delighted in Bogdanovich's happy homage to the screwball comedies of the thirties (particularly Bringing Up Baby); certainly, Streisand's Judy is every bit as unrestful as Katharine Hepburn's Susan. Madeline Kahn had been a regular on the US 'Comedy Tonight' series, but this was her first feature film and it clearly showed her gifts as an 'oddball' comedienne. The film also showed, many murmured, how funny Streisand could be – before she lost her sense of humour. Furthermore, the side-splitting court-room scene is there because Bogdanovich plucked Liam Dun from his casting director's chair, and set him down on the throne of Judge Maxwell.

USA, 1972
DIRECTOR:
Peter Bogdanovich
CAST INCLUDES:
Barbra Streisand, Ryan O'Neal,
Madeline Kahn, Kenneth Mars,
Austin Pendleton, Michael Murphy,
Philip (Phil) Roth, Randy Quaid
SCREENPLAY:
Buck Henry, David Newman,
Robert Benton from a story by Peter
Bogdanovich
CINEMATOGRAPHY:
László Kovács
(Director of Photography)
**PRODUCERS/
PRODUCTION COMPANIES:**
Peter Bogdanovitch/Saticoy
Productions

Everything You Always Wanted to Know About Sex*
*But were afraid to ask

USA, 1972
DIRECTOR:
Woody Allen
CAST INCLUDES:
Woody Allen, John Carradine,
Lou Jacobi, Louise Lasser,
Anthony Quayle, Tony Randall,
Lynn Redgraves, Burt Reynolds,
Gene Wilder
SCREENPLAY:
Woody Allen from the book by
David Reuben
CINEMATOGRAPHY:
David M. Walsh
**PRODUCERS/
PRODUCTION COMPANIES:**
Charles H. Joffe, Jack Rollins
(uncredited)/Rollins-Joffe Productions

Seven significant questions about sex are answered in the film's seven episodes. 1. Do Aphrodisiacs Work? A court fool (Allen), who has fallen in love with the Queen (Redgrave), obtains a love potion. It works, but it doesn't help to open her chastity belt. 2. What is Sodomy? A shepherd complains to a doctor (Wilder) that his sheep, Daisy, no longer loves him. The doctor offers to treat Daisy, but he too falls deeply in love with her and embarks on an affair which lands him on Skid Row. 3. Do Some Women Have Trouble Reaching Orgasm? Gina (Lasser) finds that sexy husband Fabrizio (Allen) does nothing for her in the bedroom, but that sex in public places can turn her on. 4. Are Transvestites Homosexuals? Sam, nearly caught trying on his mother-in-law's clothes, escapes to the street where his handbag is snatched. The police arrive to help. 5. What Are Sex Perverts? On the TV game-show 'What's My Perversion', celebrities try to guess a guest's special preferences. 6. Are the Findings of Doctors and Clinics Who Do Sexual Research and Experiments Accurate? When Victor Shakapopolis (Allen) meets up with a fellow sexologist, the eccentric and unorthodox Dr Bernardo (Carradine), Bernardo's latest experiment, a giant breast, breaks free and rampages across the countryside. 7. What Happens During Ejaculation? A man is out on a date when his body's control centre finds his erection is losing steam. Sperm #1 (Allen) becomes very anxious about where it is – or isn't – going to end up.

It's clear that all director/scriptwriter Woody Allen needed from David Reuben's book was the title and the chapter headings. The rest of the genius is Allen's own. Noone who has seen the film will forget the tears in the eyes of Gene Wilder as he gazes at Daisy, nor the neurotic nihilism of Woody Allen's Sperm # 1 as it observes it's dwindling chances of being able to make the leap.

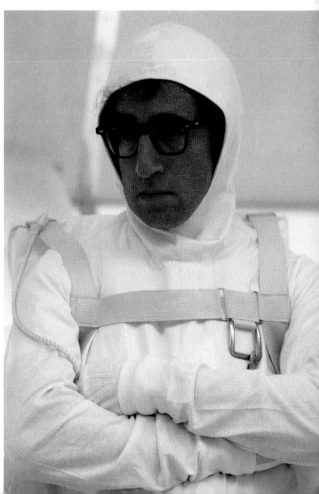

Blazing Saddles

USA, 1974
DIRECTOR:
Mel Brooks
CAST INCLUDES:
Cleavon Little,
Gene Wilder, Slim Pickens,
Harvey Korman, Madeline Kahn,
Mel Brooks, Burton Gilliam,
Dom DeLuise
SCREENPLAY:
Mel Brooks, Norman Steinberg,
Andrew Bergman, Richard Pryor,
Alan Uger, from a story by
Andrew Bergman
CINEMATOGRAPHY:
Joseph Biroc
PRODUCERS/
PRODUCTION COMPANIES:
Michael Hertzberg/Crossbow
Productions for Warner Bros.
ACADEMY AWARD
NOMINATIONS (1975)
Best Actress in a Supporting Role:
Madeline Kahn
Best Film Editing:
John C. Howard, Danford B. Greene
Best Music, Original Song:
John Morris (music), Mel Brooks
(lyrics) for the song 'Blazing Saddles'

Rescued from a railroad-gang, Black Bart (Little) is appointed by a corrupt speculator and a crooked Governor (both played by Brooks) to be the sheriff of Rock Ridge. Their hope is that the townsfolk will become so hostile and demoralized that it will be easy to overcome their resistance to selling up and leaving, so that a profitable railroad can be built through their land. Black Bart finds an unexpected ally in the drunken – but one-time gunslinger legend – Waco Kid (Wilder), and the two come up with a plan to fool the would-be land-stealers and their henchmen by creating a replica cardboard town. After many wild adventures, they ride off into the sunset – in a limousine.

Alongside the sexual revolution and flower power of the sixties and seventies, strode the fast-growing power of the black civil-rights movement in America. Hollywood rushed to create new black super-hero roles, and 'Blaxploitation' movies were born in which the super-stud black hero – Shaft, Superfly – always comes out on top – but is also suitably street-wise and controversial.

For *Blazing Saddles*, Mel Brooks – prince of atrocious taste –

chose a breathtakingly incorrect formula: he would show up Hollywood's new black moral consciousness for what it was while simultaneously spoofing the Western. Black Bart, therefore, quickly reveals that he is as incompetent as a sheriff as at everything else, while the thing that 'real' cowboys do best is fart.

Gloriously over-the-top moments include the great bean-fart campfire, honky-tonk singer Lili Von Shtupp's (Kahn) rendition of a Destry-type Dietrich torch-song, complete with the (Mae) Western aside: 'Is that a ten-gallon hat or are you just enjoying the show?', and Count Basie and his jazz band playing the film's score in the middle of a desert.

The release of *Blazing Saddles* was greeted with a lot of critical farts that had petered out by the time (1983) the movie became the world's biggest box-office Western.

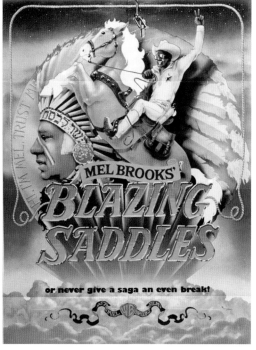

Monty Python and the Holy Grail

GB, 1975
DIRECTORS:
Terry Gilliam and Terry Jones
CAST INCLUDES:
Graham Chapman, John Cleese,
Eric Idle, Terry Gilliam, Terry
Jones, Michael Palin,
Connie Booth, Carol Cleveland
SCREENPLAY:
Graham Chapman, John Cleese,
Eric Idle, Terry Gilliam, Terry Jones,
Michael Palin
CINEMATOGRAPHY:
Terry Bedford (uncredited)
**PRODUCERS/
PRODUCTION COMPANIES:**
Mark Forstater, John Goldstone,
Michael White/Michael White
Productions, National Film Trustee
Company, Python (Monty)
Pictures Limited

A horseless King Arthur jogs across the countryside followed by a servant banging coconut shells together. The knight may be Sir Galahad the Pure, Sir Lancelot the Brave, Sir Bedevere the Quiet, Sir Robin the Not-Quite-So-Brave-as-Sir Lancelot or Sir Not-Appearing-In-This-Film.

The *Monty Python* team wanted their version of the King Arthur legend to be 'a film completely different from some of the other films which aren't quite the same as this one is'. They elected to achieve this by means of satire, whimsy and aggressive eccentricity, and by complementing their random gag-making with the visually imaginative creation of a mock-medieval landscape, with every intention of deliberately courting controversy. Their success is summed up by all the critics who said of the film: 'Makes *Ben-Hur* look like an Epic.'

Animal House

USA, 1978
DIRECTOR:
John Landis
CAST INCLUDES:
John Belushi, Tim Matheson,
John Vernon, Verna Bloom,
Tom Hulce, Cesare Danova,
Peter Riegert, Mary Louise Weller,
Kevin Bacon, Donald Sutherland
SCREENPLAY:
Harold Ramis, Douglas Kenney,
Chris Miller
CINEMATOGRAPHY:
Charles Correll
**PRODUCERS/
PRODUCTION COMPANIES:**
Ivan Reitman,
Matty Simmons/Universal Pictures

Faber College, 1962. Some years ago, John 'Bluto' Blutarsky (Belushi) and Eric 'Otter' Statton (Matheson) were refused admittance to Omega, the WASP college, and consigned to Delta, the crap college where the only thing the students do best is behave atrociously. Bluto and Otter are now at the forefront of Delta's toga parties, drunken binges, pot-smoking orgies and food fights. The college principal despises them and, following the fraternity's abysmal exam results, the whole of Delta is expelled. The Delta dorks decide that the best way to declare war on the college is to wreck the annual homecoming parade . . .

National Lampoon's Animal House (the film's original release title) was based on the American college-humour magazine, *National Lampoon*. Script-writer Chris Miller also drew on his own college experiences in the Alpha Delta Phi fraternity at Dartmouth, while Harold Ramis added his reminiscences of high jinks at Washington University in St Louis. Time was tight: the University of Oregon rationed the crew to one month for the entire shoot. However, this enforced schedule was no problem for director John Landis who had completed production on

Schlock! (1973) in thirteen days and *Kentucky Fried Movie* (1977) in twenty three days.

'Frantic', 'gross' and 'crude' are words frequently and lovingly applied to *Animal House*. The relentless pace of John Belushi's Bluto was the work of a consummate (and fondly remembered) professional. *Animal House* became one of the top-earners in Universal's history and spawned many imitations, but it remained, for a considerable time, the most successful comedy movie ever produced.

Airplane!

The experiences of Ted Striker (Hays) as a fighter pilot have left him with a deeply entrenched phobia of flying. However, when his air-hostess girlfriend, Elaine (Hagerty), dumps him, he realizes he must follow her on her next flight if he is to win her back. Fortunately, he doesn't eat the poisonous fish that the airline serves for dinner but, as most of the crew (and the passengers) do, it falls to Ted to land the plane. With help from Emily and an unflappable doctor (Nielsen), and in spite of help from a high-as-a-kite ground-controller (Bridges) and an inflatable automatic pilot, Ted manages to land the plane safely.

Disaster movies had been one of the most successful Hollywood genres of the seventies, with such successes as *The Towering Inferno, Avalanche* and *Earthquake* – and the whole series of *Airport* movies. By the end of the decade, these catastrophe films were running thin on ideas, and the relentless parodying provided by *Airplane!* not only tolled their death-knell but gave rise to a new style of knock-about spoof movie. *Airplane!*'s plot was based on Arthur Hailey's screenplay for the fifties B-movie *Zero Hour.* The AZZ team – Abrahams, Zucher and Zucher – held on to the B-movie tension (with the help of such B-movie stars as Bridges, Stack and Nielsen) – and added a laugh a second. They'd been practising the laughs in *The Kentucky Fried Movie* (1977), and the hilarity now came tumbling out of the bucket. 'Parody may be the lowest form of humour', observed *Variety* on *Airplane!*'s release, 'but few comedies in ages have rocked the laugh-metre this hard.'

USA, 1980
DIRECTOR:
Jim Abrahams, David Zucker, Jerry Zucker
CAST INCLUDES:
Robert Hays, Julie Hagerty, Lloyd Bridges, Leslie Nielsen, Robert Stack, Peter Graves, Lorna Patterson
SCREENPLAY:
Jim Abrahams, David Zucker and Jerry Zucker, based on the teleplay *Flight Into Danger* by Arthur Hailey (uncredited) and the screenplay *Zero Hour* by Arthur Hailey, Hall Bartlett and John C. Champion (all uncredited)
CINEMATOGRAPHY:
Joseph Biroc
PRODUCERS/ PRODUCTION COMPANIES:
Howard W. Koch, Jon Davison/Paramount Pictures

Tootsie

USA, 1982
DIRECTOR:
Sydney Pollack
CAST INCLUDES:
Dustin Hoffman, Jessica Lange,
Teri Garr, Dabney Coleman,
Charles Durning, Bill Murray,
Sydney Pollack, George Gaynes,
Geena Davis
SCREENPLAY:
Larry Gelbart, Murray Schisgal,
Barry Levinson (uncredited)
Elaine May (uncredited) from a story
by Don McGuire, Larry Gelbart
CINEMATOGRAPHY:
Owen Roizman
PRODUCERS/
PRODUCTION COMPANIES:
Sydney Pollack,
Dick Richards, Ronald L. Schwary
(uncredited)/Columbia Pictures
Corporation, Delphi, Mirage,
Punch Productions Inc.
ACADEMY AWARD
NOMINATIONS (1983)
Best Actor in a Leading Role:
Dustin Hoffman
Best Actress in a Supporting Role:
Teri Garr
Best Cinematography:
Owen Roizman
Best Director: Sydney Pollack
Best Film Editing: Fredric Steinkamp,
William Steinkamp
Best Music, Original Song: Dave
Grusin (music), Alan Bergman (lyrics),
Marilyn Bergman (lyrics) for the song
'It Might Be You'
Best Picture: Sydney Pollack,
Dick Richards
Best Sound: Arthur Piantadosi,
Les Fresholtz, Rick Alexander (as
Dick Alexander), Les Lazarowitz
Best Writing, Screenplay Written
Directly for the Screen:
Larry Gelbart, Murray Schisgal,
Don McGuire
ACADEMY AWARDS
Best Actress in a Supporting Role:
Jessica Lange

Actor Michael Dorsey (Hoffman) is a deeply motivated young actor who has been branded 'unemployable': he says 'perfectionist', they say 'difficult'. Feeling that he knows exactly why girlfriend Sandy (Garr) didn't get chosen for a daytime hospital soap, he dresses as a women, auditions as Dorothy Michaels – and lands the role of Emily. Now he has to keep up his female guise – not easy as he's fallen for his co-star, Julie (Lange), and Julie's father (Durning) has fallen for Dorothy. Eventually, he can stand it no more, and 'outs' himself during an episode of the soap.

Tootsie's film crew realized that, if they had bad news for Hoffman, they should keep it until he was playing Dorothy, because he was 'much nicer as a woman'. *Toostie* is one of the top-grossing comedies of all time, and comes second on the American Film Institute's recent list of funniest-ever US movies – after that other great drag movie, *Some Like It Hot* (1959).

Trading Places

Louis Winthorpe III (Aykroyd) is a rich young broker who works at the commodities firm of Duke and Duke. Billy Ray Valentine (Murphy) is a con-man who 'works' outside Duke and Duke. Randolph (Bellamy) and Mortimer (Ameche) are the two elderly Duke brothers. They like a bet and decide to gamble on 'nurture versus nature'. They set Louis up with a drugs charge and a spell in jail, and give his job and his house to Billy Ray. Louis does badly; deprived of his props he turns (ineptly) to crime. Billy does well: he's good at the job and takes care of the house. However, he realizes all will be over when the old guys settle their bet. He and Louis get together to turn the tables on the Dukes.

John Landis was riding high after *(National Lampoon's) Animal House* (1978) and *The Blues Brothers* (1980). For *Trading Places*, he took a very archetypal theme – rich guy becomes poor guy, and poor guy becomes rich guy – and added a well-chosen cast, a fine script with excellent comic dialogue, and his own funny and delicate touches. There are also, underpinning it all, some need-to-look-at questions about – not nature and nurture – but money.

USA, 1983
DIRECTOR:
John Landis
CAST INCLUDES:
Dan Aykroyd, Eddie Murphy, Ralph Bellamy, Don Ameche, Denholm Elliott, Jamie Lee Curtis, Kristin Holby, Paul Gleason, Alfred Drake, Bo Diddley, Frank Oz, James Belushi
SCREENPLAY:
Timothy Harris, Herschel Weingrod
CINEMATOGRAPHY:
Robert Paynter
PRODUCERS/ PRODUCTION COMPANIES:
Aaron Russo/Cinema Group Ventures, Paramount Pictures
ACADEMY AWARD NOMINATIONS (1984)
Best Music, Original Song Score and Its Adaptation or Best Adaptation Score: Elmer Bernstein

All of Me

USA, 1984
DIRECTOR:
Carl Reiner
CAST INCLUDES:
Steve Martin, Lily Tomlin,
Victoria Tennant, Madolyn Smith,
Richard Libertini
SCREENPLAY:
Phil Alden Roninson from the novel
Me Too by Edwin Davis III
CINEMATOGRAPHY:
Richard H. Kline
**PRODUCERS/
PRODUCTION COMPANIES:**
Stephen J. Friedman/Kings Road
Productions, Old Time, Universal
Pictures

When the eccentric and wealthy Edwina Cutwater (Tomlin) learns that she is dying, she arranges for her soul to be transferred, by self-styled guru Prahka Lasa (Libertini), into the body of the young and lovely Terry (Tennant), for a sizeable sum. Roger Cobb (Martin) is the lawyer hired merely to sort out the final legalities but, on Edwina's death, her soul is somehow transferred to him and duly takes over the right side of his body – leaving him with what's left.

When *The Jerk* – directed by Carl Reiner and starring Steve Martin in his first comedy – appeared in 1979, it was a hit. However, the reviews were so bad that Martin decided to follow it with the very 'unusual' musical drama, *Pennies From Heaven* (1981). This was a flop, and his next three movies fared little better. Then Carl Reiner phoned him with a script 'about a girl who gets into a guy's body'. Martin took some persuading to go with a story even odder than *Pennies*, but finally agreed. *All of Me* was released in 1984. The public loved it, and Steve Martin was duly elevated to major comic star – a star that is still shining brightly. Lily Tomlin, too, received many plaudits for her Edwina. Even Victoria Tennant – the former soap-kitten – was able to cast a new persona as a downright evil minx.

This is Spinal Tap

USA, 1984
DIRECTOR:
Rob Reiner
CAST INCLUDES:
Rob Reiner, R.J. Parnell, David Kaff,
Tony Hendra, Michael McKean,
Christopher Guest, Harry Shearer,
Fran Drescher
SCREENPLAY:
Christopher Guest, Michael McKean,
Harry Shearer,
Rob Reiner
CINEMATOGRAPHY:
Peter Smokler
**PRODUCERS/
PRODUCTION COMPANIES:**
Karen Murphy/Spinal Tap Prod.

The next project from film director Marty DiBergi (Reiner), is a documentary about Spinal Tap, a British heavy-metal band which has the enviable reputation of being 'one of England's loudest'. The band is on the US leg of their come-back tour which is scheduled to coincide with their new album, 'Sniff the Glove'. However, the tour is plagued with problems. The album hasn't arrived, there are hotel mix-ups, their Stonehenge stage set appears in miniature form, some of the venues are appalling and all of the audiences are dwindling. Through it all, DiBergi observes, films and interviews to make a worthy filmed tribute to his favourite band.

This is perhaps the spoof to end all spoofs. The inescapable factor that leads *This is Spinal Tap* fans to a weak-kneed worship of a film about a bunch of dim-witted musicians playing unbelievably bad songs with excruciatingly bad lyrics is that – they could be real. Reiner's acute ear for the vernacular of 1980s rock bands and the tedious, reverential films made about them is faultless. Only the truly terrible songs remind us that this is parody par excellence.

The Breakfast Club

Five high-school students, who would not normally seek out each other's company, have to spend a Saturday together – in detention. Brian the geek (Hall), Alison the basket-case (Sheedy), Andy the jock (Estevez), John Bender the jerk (Nelson) and Claire the prom queen (Ringwald). They start off at each other's throats but loosen up during a pot-smoking session, and begin to see that they have far more in common than the stereotypes that separate them.

Director Hughes recognized the plight of 1980s teenagers and saw beyond the definitions inflicted on them by parents and teachers. His empathy with the wounds that hormones and changing family values could cause was a theme he returned to again and again.

The film's title came from a phrase used at a school he knew: people who had been on detention were designated members of the Breakfast Club. Hughes shot the film in sequence in several schools in Northbook, Illinois – one of which he had attended himself. Cast and crew were expected to eat lunch in the cafeteria of whichever school was the current location.

Hughes wrote the script for the film in only a few days, but then got the young cast to rehearse it several times as a play before shooting began, allowing the story to develop during that process. *The Breakfast Club* was the teenage-angst, Brat Pack movie that cast the mould for those that followed.

USA, 1985
DIRECTOR:
John Hughes
CAST INCLUDES:
Emilio Estevez,
Anthony Michael Hall,
Judd Nelson, Molly Ringwald,
Paul Gleason, Ally Sheedy
SCREENPLAY:
John Hughes
CINEMATOGRAPHY:
Thomas Del Ruth
PRODUCERS/
PRODUCTION COMPANIES:
John Hughes, Ned Tanen/A&M Films,
Universal Pictures

Ferris Bueller's Day Off

It's a beautiful day in Chicago, and Ferris Bueller (Broderick) has decided that school is not the place for him today and so, after persuading his parents that he's at death's door, he calls in sick. He next persuades his best buddy, Cameron (Ruck), to 'borrow' his father's irreplaceable 1961 red Ferrari, and they then swing by school to kidnap Ferris's girlfriend, Sloane (Sara). The trio now set off on a joy-ride around Chicago which includes joining a street parade, whereupon Ferris commandeers a microphone and treats Chicago to his (brass-band-backed) rendition of 'Twist and Shout'. Meantime, the school principal (Jones) is after him, as is Ferris's jealous kid sister Jeannie (Grey); both are fed up with the way Ferris is 'always getting away with things'. The day off also gives Ferris the chance to do something important: to give his depressed friend Cameron some time and encouragement.

Ferris Bueller's Day Off is one of the funniest and most delightful of John Hughes' 'Brat Pack' comedies. It is also the only one that doesn't feature Anthony Michael Hall and Molly Ringwald. Hall had been offered the part of Cameron, but turned it down lest he be typecast. (Cameron was, in fact, played by a 30-year-old Alan Ruck.) The film does, however, have Brat-Packer Charlie Sheen in a side-splitting cameo role as a drugged-to-the-eyeballs boy that spiteful sister Jeannie encounters at a police station. To get the necessary spaced-out effect, full method acting would have been a step too far, but Sheen did keep himself awake for 48 hours before the scene was shot.

USA, 1986
DIRECTOR:
John Hughes
CAST INCLUDES:
Matthew Broderick, Alan Ruck,
Mia Sara, Jeffrey Jones,
Jennifer Grey, Cindy Pickett,
Charlie Sheen
SCREENPLAY:
John Hughes
CINEMATOGRAPHY:
Tak Fujimoto
**PRODUCERS/
PRODUCTION COMPANIES:**
John Hughes, Tom
Jacobson/Paramount Pictures

A Fish Called Wanda

Wanda (Curtis), a normal diamond-loving woman, Otto (Kline) her jewel-thief boyfriend (ex-CIA and a psychopath), the robbery's mastermind, George (Georgeson), and a verbally challenged animal-lover K-K-K-Ken (Palin) pull off a successful jewellery heist. Wanda then decides she wants all the diamonds for herself and tips the cops off about George – only to find she doesn't know where George has stashed the loot. She sets out to seduce George's tight-assed lawyer, Archie Leach, in whom George may have confided. A complex double-crossing caper ensues during which Archie falls in love, Otto becomes dangerously jealous, George stays safely out of the way and K-K-K-Ken's heart is broken when Otto eats his tropical fish – one of which is called Wanda.

Embroiled in *A Fish Called Wanda* – 'A tale of murder, lust, greed, revenge and seafood' – are two Hollywood stars (Curtis and Kline), two members of the British *Monty Python* team (Cleese and Palin) and Charles Crichton, a director of such notably English Ealing comedies as *The Lavender Hill Mob* (1951). Somehow, this odd mix complemented each other beautifully. Cleese requested Crichton to write the film as an old-fashioned romantic comedy, and that worked, too. The movie was the sleeper of the summer if 1988. In fact, it went into a deep sleep: it opened in the USA on 15 July and didn't hit the number 1 spot until 16 September – a record for sleepiness which may well still hold today. (PS: Cleese called his character Archie Leach because the real Archie Leach – i.e. Cary Grant – and he both came from the English town of Weston- super-Mare.)

USA/GB, 1988
DIRECTOR:
Charles Crichton, John Cleese
(uncredited)
CAST INCLUDES:
John Cleese, Jamie Lee Curtis,
Kevin Kline, Michael Palin,
Maria Aitken, Tom Georgeson,
Patricia Hayes, Geoffrey Palmer
SCREENPLAY:
John Cleese from the story by
John Cleese and Charles Crichton
CINEMATOGRAPHY:
Alan Hume
**PRODUCERS/
PRODUCTION COMPANIES:**
Michael Shamberg/MGM, Prominent
Features, Star Partners Limited
Partnership
**ACADEMY AWARD
NOMINATIONS (1989)**
Best Director:
Charles Crichton
Best Writing, Original Screenplay:
John Cleese, Charles Crichton
ACADEMY AWARDS
Best Actor in a Supporting Role:
Kevin Kline

The Naked Gun: From the Files of Police Squad

USA, 1988
DIRECTOR:
David Zucker
CAST INCLUDES:
Leslie Nielsen, Priscilla Presley,
Ricardo Montalban,
George Kennedy, O.J. Simpson,
Susan Beaubian, Nancy Marchand,
Jeannette Charles
SCREENPLAY:
Jim Abrahams, David Zucker,
Pat Proft Jerry Zucker after the
television series *Police Squad* by
Jim Abrahams, David Zucker,
Jerry Zucker
CINEMATOGRAPHY:
Robert (M.) Stevens
**PRODUCERS/
PRODUCTION COMPANIES:**
Robert K. Weiss/Paramount Pictures

Fresh from tackling terrorism in Beirut, Lt Frank Drebin (Nielsen) is immediately detailed to investigate the near-fatal shooting of a fellow officer, Detective Nordberg (Simpson). Drebin starts the job where Nordberg left off, at a company owned by the much-respected Victor Ludwig (Montalban) whose assistant, Jane (Presley), Drebin falls for. Thanks to years of experience and granite-jawed determination (and Jane), Drebin uncovers a dastardly plot, by Ludwig, to assassinate Queen Elizabeth II when she attends a baseball game while on her state visit to the USA.

Acclaimed, when it first appeared, as the best movie ever made with the words 'Naked', 'Gun' and 'The' in the title; although, after the initial acclaim, a few sad people challenged the word 'The'. From the creators of *Airplane!* (1980) and the brief but unforgettable (now that it's a cult) TV spoof series *Police Squad* next came this spoof police movie. Jokes, visual gags and achingly funny moments are so rained upon the viewer that laugh he/she must. The Zuchers, Abrahams and Proft have also taken the trouble to create endearing and well-rounded characters so that, despite the mayhem, the viewer still cares about what's happening to them. John Houseman, as an unflappable driving instructor, is irrepressibly funny in this, his last movie. *The Naked Gun 2 1/2: The Smell of Fear* (1991), and *Naked Gun 33 1/3: The Final Insult* (1994) followed.

Big

Young Josh (Moscow), at 12, is just starting on the stage of being an awkward in-between. One minute it's Little League baseball: the next, it's standing beside a blonde princess at a carnival fairground and being told you're too short to go on the ride. In that moment of mortification, young Josh encounters a fortune-telling machine, and wishes that he'll become big. The next morning finds him with a 30-year-old body and a face he doesn't recognize. He runs away to New York with best-mate Billy (Rushton) and gets a job in a toy factory. So in tune is he with the company's product that he is soon moving up the career ladder. Despite, however, the attentions of the attractive Susan (Perkins), Josh has begun to realize that all he wants to do is find the magic machine, and get back to normal.

Tom Hanks always played his 12-year-old Josh as a 12-year-old, and won a Best-Actor Golden Globe and an Oscar nomination for his success. He was helped in this by Penny Marshall who had young Moscow play each of big Josh's scenes first, so that Hanks could absorb the reactions and body-language of a real 12-year-old.

The director, Penny Marshall, provides the perfect pace for this film about a boy who just wants to be tall enough to be popular – but gets a whole lot more than he bargained for. The scriptwriters contributed the delightful story and dialogue that aptly illustrated the boy-in-man's-body problems: On the occasion when he's told about a woman co-worker who '. . . will wrap her legs around you till you beg for mercy', he innocently responds with 'Well, I'll be sure to stay away from her, then'.

USA, 1988
DIRECTOR:
Penny Marshall
CAST INCLUDES:
Tom Hanks, Elizabeth Perkins,
Robert Loggia, John Heard,
Jared Rushton, David Moscow,
Jon Lovitz, Mercedes Ruehl
SCREENPLAY:
Gary Ross, Anne Spielberg
CINEMATOGRAPHY:
Barry Sonnenfeld
PRODUCERS/
PRODUCTION COMPANIES:
James L. Brooks,
Robert Greenhut/20th Century Fox,
Gracie Films
ACADEMY AWARD
NOMINATIONS (1989)
Best Actor in a Leading Role:
Tom Hanks
Best Writing, Original Screenplay:
Gary Ross, Anne Spielberg

Home Alone

USA, 1990
DIRECTOR:
Chris Columbus
CAST INCLUDES:
Macaulay Culkin, Joe Pesci,
Daniel Stern, John Heard,
Catherine O'Hara
SCREENPLAY:
John Hughes
CINEMATOGRAPHY:
Julio Macat
**PRODUCERS/
PRODUCTION COMPANIES:**
John Hughes/20th Century Fox
**ACADEMY AWARD
NOMINATIONS (1991)**
Best Music, Original Score:
John Williams
Best Music, Original Song:
John Williams (music),
Leslie Bricusse (lyrics) For the song
'Somewhere in My Memory'

The McCallister clan have gathered in Peter and Kate's Chicago home prior to flying off to spend Christmas in Paris. In the chaos of leaving, they overlook 8-year-old Kevin (Culkin). Once in the air, his absence is noticed but snowstorms prevent his distraught mother (O'Hara) from getting back to him. Kevin can't believe his luck. He watches forbidden videos, eats his favourite junk food, rifles through his brother's things and sleeps in his parents' bed. He does get scared, and when two burglars, Harry and Marv (Pesci and Stern) decide to break into the house he gets really scared. However, courage and resourcefulness come to the fore as he devises elaborate and painful booby traps to deter them. However, by the time his family do get home, he's very pleased to see them.

Macaulay Culkin had already appeared in a couple of films, but his extraordinarily self-possessed and all-encompassing performance in *Home Alone* launched him to child superstardom. He earned $100,000 for the film; by the time he made *Home Alone 2* (1992) he was commanding $5 million. John Hughes, who'd already snared the teenage market (e.g. *The Breakfast Club*, 1985), both wrote and produced this massive Christmas hit. It did what it set out to with maximum hilarity, and Culkin was the cutest kid on the block for a long time. Indeed, *Home Alone*, at that time, earned an entry in the *Guinness Book of World Records* as the Highest Comedy Box-Office-Grosser with international earnings of $533 million.

Groundhog Day

Phil Conners (Murray), is a nasty, cynical, people-hating TV weather-man. This year, as every year, on 2 February, he makes a much-resented trip to Punxsutawney, the 'Groundhog Capital', to broadcast the big news from Groundhog Day: if Punxsutawney Phil (the Groundhog) appears, then spring has come; if he doesn't it's six more months of winter. However, on awaking the next morning, it's Groundhog Day again . . . and on the next day, and the next. For a while, he enjoys taking advantage of his *déjà-vu* knowledge – especially of how to impress his long-suffering producer, Rita (MacDowell). Next, frustration leads him to various forms of suicide, but he still wakes up the next day. Finally, however, though time and space remain stuck, he realizes that things within him are changing. He starts on the long job – for which he needs many Groundhog Days – of becoming a loveable human being.

There haven't been many movies that play with concurrent time. There are a few of the order of *It's a Wonderful Life* (1946) where how things might have been are examined as a way of re-evaluating how things are. In *Groundhog Day*, the method is not once-around shock tactics; its message is 'You stay here and keep doing it till you get it right'. The fact that such a potentially grim situation (Phil Connors goes through 2 February 34 times) is hilarious owes it's weak-at-the-knees thanks to Rubin and Ramis' script and to the deep well of comedy talent that is Bill Murray.

USA, 1993
DIRECTOR:
Harold Ramis
CAST INCLUDES:
Bill Murray, Andie MacDowell, Chris Elliott, Stephen Tobolowsky, Brian Doyle-Murray, Maria Geraghty
SCREENPLAY:
Danny Rubin, Harold Ramis from a story by Danny Rubin
CINEMATOGRAPHY:
John Baily
PRODUCERS/PRODUCTION COMPANIES:
Trevor Albert, Harold Ramis/Columbia Pictures Corporation

USA, 1997
DIRECTOR:
George Armitage
CAST INCLUDES:
John Cusak, Minnie Driver, Alan
Arkin, Dan Aykroyd, Joan Cusak
SCREENPLAY:
Tom Jankiewicz, D.V. DeVincentis,
Steve Pink, John Cusack from a story
by Tom Jankiewicz
CINEMATOGRAPHY:
Jamie Anderson
**PRODUCERS/
PRODUCTION COMPANIES:**
Susan Arnold, Roger Birnbaum,
Donna Arkoff Roth/Caravan Pictures,
Hollywood Pictures, New Crime
Productions

Grosse Pointe Blank

Martin Q. Blank (Cusak) is a hitherto successful hit man who has just hit burnout. After a bungled job, he gets the chance to redeem himself through a contract in Detroit. His old High School is in the Detroit suburb of Grosse Pointe and, co-incidentally, it's holding his 10-year reunion. Once in Grosse Pointe, he searches out Debi (Driver), the girlfriend he stood up at the school prom. He discovers that various people are out to kill him, including fellow hit man, Mr Groces (Aykroyd) whose Assassin's Union he has refused to join. His improving relationship with Debi goes sour when he has to kill a would-be assassin at the reunion dance and when he learns the name on his current hit contract.

This is dead-pan comedy of a high order. The perennially boyish-looking Cusak does a fine job of persuading us that he is a professional assassin. He placed *Blank* very much in the mould of 'Zen and the Art of Assassination'; all the nitty-gritty bits of the job are meticulously planned and carried out; the corpse is simply the outcome of a job well done. Like many perfectionist professionals, he hasn't a clue how to conduct a relationship – but he discovers he wants to learn. Furthermore, his moral code has been to kill only bad people, but once his emotions have started to surface, it's much harder to make that distinction. Grosse Pointe Blank is a family affair: apart from John and sister Joan, brother Bill and sister Ann are in there, too.

Austin Powers: International Man of Mystery

It's swinging 1967. The vicious, though childish, Dr Evil (Myers), who has failed to kill his arch-enemy, British Secret Agent Austin Powers (Myers) – he of the Union-Jack underpants, albeit dentally challenged – resolves to escape by means of his cryogenic freezing capsule, and come back later. Powers bravely offers to be frozen too, ready to destroy Dr Evil when he returns. It's now 1997. Dr Evil thaws out, steals a nuclear weapon and holds the world to ransom. Austin Powers, however, is ready for him – debonair, defiant and defrosted – together with his new assistant, Vanessa Kensington (Hurley), whose job is to re-acclimatize Powers to the no-fun nineties. Dr Evil discovers that the nineties are more about dysfunctional family therapy than world domination and escapes again in his cryogenic capsule.

For Austin 'Groovy, baby!' Powers, secret-agenting is his vocation. He would, indeed, like to do much more of it, if only there was more time between shags. Nevertheless, whenever possible, he offers his country the highest standards: 'Personally, before I'm on the job, I like to give my undercarriage a bit of a 'how's your father'.' On being thawed out, he immediately rushes to see 'if all my bits and pieces are still working'. Austin 'Shall we shag now, or shall we shag later?' Powers is not just a homage to 007 and a sixties send-up, it's full of little-boy, lavatory humour that has even been known to make girls laugh – on a good-hair day. In addition, Myers' Austin 'It's my bag, baby!' Powers provides all the joys of appalling velvet fashion statements, matted hairy chests and Union-Jack-painted Minis. No joke has done its job until it's been thrashed into the ground and then stomped on – 'Shagadelic, baby!' The British love to send themselves up to the point of pain – and Myers loves to help.

USA, 1997
DIRECTOR:
Jay Roach
CAST INCLUDES:
Mike Myers, Elizabeth Hurley, Michael York, Mimi Rogers, Robert Wagner, Seth Green, Fabiana Udenio
SCREENPLAY:
Mike Myers
CINEMATOGRAPHY:
Peter Deming
**PRODUCERS/
PRODUCTION COMPANIES:**
Demi Moore, Mike Myers, Jennifer Todd, Suzanne Todd/Capella International, Moving Pictures, New Line Cinema [all US], KC Medien AG [GER], Eric's Boy, Juno Pix

The Big Lebowski

Jeff 'the Dude' Lebowski (Bridges) is an easy-going man. His life in LA is so laid-back as to be almost flat. His answer to most problems is 'Let's go bowling'. However, when his house is broken into by two gangsters who pee on his favourite rug, he finds himself becoming quite angry. Then, when he discovers that they think they are chasing Jeffrey Lebowski – 'the Big Lebowski' ('Big' as in millionaire), whose wife owes them a lot of money – he's furious. The Dude sets off to demand compensation (or at least rug-cleaning) from the Big Lebowski, only to find himself enmeshed in a series of events that span a kidnapping scenario, the art world and the porn industry.

The Coen Brothers' zany humour delights in weird characters – or characters so normal that they're weird. In this, their first (and possibly only) bowling movie, Dude's biggest bowling mate, Walter Sobchak (Goodman), is a Vietnam vet who attributes every cause and effect in life to the USA's involvement 'over there'. He does it when he's bowling, and he does it when he

USA/GB, 1998
DIRECTOR:
Joel Coen
CAST INCLUDES:
Jeff Bridges, John Goodman, Julianne Moore, Steve Buscemi, David Huddleston, Philip Seymour Hoffman, Tara Reid
SCREENPLAY:
Ethan Coen, Joel Coen
CINEMATOGRAPHY:
Roger Deakins
PRODUCERS/ PRODUCTION COMPANIES:
Ethan Coen/PolyGram Filmed Entertainment [US], Working Title Films [GB]

says he's not doing it. Donny (Buscemi), the other bowling mate, could be weird or 'normal', but we'll never know as the mere opening of his mouth provokes the order to "Shut the . . . . up". Another Coen-inspired weirdo is Jesus (Turturro), a Latino bowler with a rare door-to-door mission.

Like the Dude, the Coen's movie doesn't really want to get anywhere, but it makes sure we are happy to bowl along with it.

Le dîner de cons
The Dinner Game

FRANCE, 1998
DIRECTOR:
Francis Veber
CAST INCLUDES:
Thierry Lhermitte, Jacques Villeret,
Francis Huster, Daniel Prévost,
Alexandra Vandernoot,
Catherine Frot
SCREENPLAY:
Francis Veber – based on his play
CINEMATOGRAPHY:
Georges Klotz
PRODUCERS/
PRODUCTION COMPANIES:
Alain Poiré (Delegate
Producer)/EFVE, Gaumont, TF1 Films
Productions, TPS Cinéma

Pierre Brochant (Lhermitte) is one of Paris's sophisticated 'smart' set. Every week, he and a group of his professional friends play a nasty little game – 'the Dinner Game' – in which they compete in inviting to dinner the biggest idiot they can find. This week, Brochant has discovered a gem – the plump and child-like François Pignon (Villert) who proudly displays pictures of his model of the Eiffel Tower made from over 350,000 matches. Pignon arrives at Brochant's apartment to discover that his host's back has 'gone out' and that his wife has left him. Undeterred, Pignon sets out to help and, instead of the match-stick man being humiliated by Brochant's heartless cynicism, Brochant's life is devastated by Pignon's inept kindness.

Francis Veber is a master of the classic French farce – both as writer and director. Many of his plays and script collaborations have been translated into successful Hollywood comedies, including *Buddy, Buddy* (1981) and *The Birdcage* (1996). This French strain of screwball comedy has a cruel streak: usually there is a Pignon (indeed, Veber called his no-hoper 'François Pignon' in three of his plays) who is innocently unaware that he is a walking disaster area. The 'hero', on the other hand, mistakenly believes that reason can prevail – hence the farcical succession of misunderstandings and mishaps that follow. Veber's comic precision, timing and dialogue are all superb. *Le dîner de cons* is his biggest success to date: after, initially, over 900 performances on the Paris stage, it has gone on to make over $100 million (globally) at the box-office.

There's Something About Mary

USA, 1998
DIRECTORS:
Bobby Farrelly, Peter Farrelly
CAST INCLUDES:
Cameron Diaz, Matt Dillon,
Ben Stiller, Lee Evans,
Chris Elliott, Lin Shaye,
Jeffrey Tambor
SCREENPLAY:
Ed Decter, John J. Strauss,
Bobby Farrelly, Peter Farrelly,
from the story by Ed Decter,
John J. Strauss
CINEMATOGRAPHY:
Mark Irwin
PRODUCERS/
PRODUCTION COMPANIES:
Frank Beddor, Michael Steinberg,
Bradley Thomas, Charles B.
Wessler/20th Century Fox

Ted Stroehmann (Stiller) is a high-school geek with braces who is in love with Mary (Diaz), the loveliest girl in Rhode Island. After he helps her retarded brother (W. Earl Brown) out of an ugly corner, she invites him to the prom. Ted turns that into an unforgettable night by getting his dick caught in his tux-trousers zip. Thirteen years later Ted is still pining over Mary and, at the suggestion of friend Dom (Elliott), hires sleazy private detective Pat Healy (Dillon) to find her. Healy finds Mary living in Florida, but sends back a horrendous report of this beautiful and caring woman because he's fallen for her himself. In fact, he finds, every needy nerd in the state has discovered that there's something about Mary . . .

When it comes to bad taste, Mel Brooks could learn a thing or three from the Farrellys. They have been practising for a couple of films now, and they don't seem to have missed much. There are jokes about white-heads-on-the-eyeballs skin conditions, bodily fluids, the mentally handicapped, watering holes for gay men, the ugliness of the elderly (nude) and people in leg braces, and there are bucketfuls of semen. But somewhere behind (or underneath) all this are two very nice people called Ted and Mary who will be truly glad to know that they are part of what's making you laugh so hard.

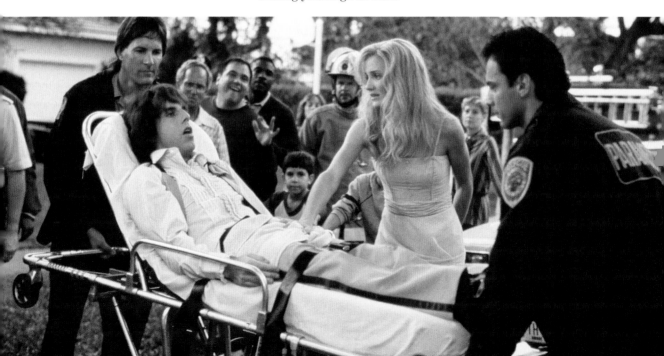

Meet the Parents

Cat-hating male nurse Greg Focker (Stiller) wishes to marry his girl-friend Pam (Polo). Pam takes Greg to visit her parents so that he can ask her father, cat-loving, macho, ex-CIA agent Jack Byrnes (De Niro), for her hand in marriage. Jack doesn't take to Greg, or his name, or the fact that he's a nurse, and Mr Jinx, the beloved family cat, also does his bit to make sure the weekend is a disaster.

Jack Byrnes is a superb role for De Niro. He has a humorous expression on his face almost all the time. He appears to be a humorous man who wants everyone to be happy and have a good time. However, just underneath the *bonhomie* are flashes of steel. Jack has been a CIA agent all his working life; nobody argues with Jack. Greg doesn't try to argue with Jack; instead he hurls himself into a quicksand of 'I'm honest and interesting' lies – and this for the benefit of a man who has a lie-detector in his basement. However, somewhere in Jack there is a pussycat, because he dotes on his children and has a very perceptive wife (Danner) who loves him.

USA, 2000
DIRECTOR:
Jay Roach
CAST INCLUDES:
Robert De Niro, Ben Stiller,
Teri Polo, Blythe Danner,
Nicole DeHuff, Jon Abrahams,
Owen Wilson, James Rebhorn,
Thomas McCarthy
SCREENPLAY:
James Herzfeld (as Jim Herzfeld) and
John Hamburg, from the story and
1992 screenplay by Greg Glienna and
Mary Ruth Clarke
CINEMATOGRAPHY:
Peter James
PRODUCERS/
PRODUCTION COMPANIES:
Robert De Niro, Jay Roach,
Jane Rosenthal, Nancy
Tenenbaum/Universal Pictures,
Tribeca Productions,
Nancy Tenenbaum Productions,
DreamWorks SKG
ACADEMY AWARD
NOMINATIONS (2001)
Best Music, Original Song:
Randy Newman, for the song
'A Fool In Love'

FRANCE/GERMANY, 2001
DIRECTOR:
Jean-Pierre Jeunet
CAST INCLUDES:
Audrey Tautou, Mathieu Kassovitz,
Rufus, Lorella Cravotta,
Serge Merlin
SCREENPLAY:
Guillaume Laurent (plus dialogue)
from the story by Jean-Pierre Jeunet
and Guillaume Laurent
CINEMATOGRAPHY:
Bruno Delbonnel
PRODUCERS/
PRODUCTION COMPANIES:
Arne Meerkamp van Embden [GER],
Jean-Marc Descham, Claudie Ossard
[FR]/Filmstiftung Nordrhein-Westfalen
[GER], France 3 Cinéma, La Sofica
Sofinergie 5, Le Studio Canal, MMC
Independent GmbH, Tapioca Films,
UGC Images, Victoires Productions
[all FR]
ACADEMY AWARD
NOMINATIONS (2002)
Best Art Direction-Set Decoration:
Aline Bonetto (art director),
Marie-Laure Valla (set decorator)
Best Cinematography:
Bruno Delbonnel
Best Foreign Language Film (France)
Best Sound:
Vincent Arnardi, Guillaume Leriche,
Jean Umansky
Best Writing, Screenplay Written
Directly for the Screen:
Guillaume Laurent, Jean-Pierre
Jeunet

Amélie
Amélie of Montmatre

Amélie (Tautou), an enchanting bubble of *joie-de-vivre* who lives in Paris, had a rather sad childhood: a mother who committed suicide and a father who couldn't cuddle. One day, a shocking piece of news causes her to drop something that dislodges a stone in the wall of her flat. She there discovers a rusty tin box full of a boy's childhood treasures. She finds the man that the boy has become, and is uplifted by the happiness she brings to him with the box. She realizes that bringing people happiness is her life's work and sets about doing this in a myriad of ways. Eventually, she is able to bring herself to her own happiness.

Jean-Pierre Jeunet, the director of the gruesomely yet exuberantly witty *Delicatessen* (1990), has, in *Amélie*, a truly unique achievement. When you mention *Amélie* to people who have seen it, their faces dissolve into the silliest smiles, and words such as 'wow', 'magical', 'wonderful', 'beautiful' and 'happy' fill the air. Jeunet, together with Audrey Tautou – a fairy with an alchemical wand – has produced a movie the like of which people haven't seen before. It is joyful, romantic and charming. It sprinkles colour everywhere. This little gem of a movie pulls from the viewer a new kind of laughter – naïve, not knowing – yet it never strays into whimsy. A flawless film graced by flawless performances.

Lost in Translation

Bob Harris (Murray) is a world-weary, past-his-prime actor who is in Tokyo to make whisky ads. He despises the job but is doing it for the money ($2 million) and to get away from a souring marriage. At the same hotel is Charlotte (Johansson), a 25-year-old philosophy graduate whose photographer-husband John (Ribisi) is making a video about an indie band – and doesn't really want her around. Bob and Charlotte, both feeling inwardly lost and outwardly strange in Tokyo, while away long hours together in strip clubs and karaoke bars, and spend charmed hours talking and listening. They know that these are really but short magical moments – but where there's magic, there's hope.

For this, her second movie, Sofia Coppola wrote the role of Bob for Bill Murray. When she finally tracked him down, all he would say was that he was 'inclined' to make the film – and then appeared on the day before shooting started in Tokyo. What followed was a new and wondrous Bill Murray. Both the acerbic grouch and unwilling romantic of *Groundhog Day* (1993) are there, but none of the Murray comic schtick. It's all available, however – that massive reservoir of comic talent lies just below this minimalist, romantic comedy of manners. Coppola creates a situation in which a sad Bob and a confused Charlotte can be safe with each other, where they can relax and find real laughter.

USA/JAPAN, 2003
DIRECTOR:
Sofia Coppola
CAST INCLUDES:
Scarlett Johansson, Bill Murray,
Akiko Takeshita
SCREENPLAY:
Sofia Coppola
CINEMATOGRAPHY:
Lance Acord
**PRODUCERS/
PRODUCTION COMPANIES:**
Sofia Coppola, Ross Katz/American
Zoetrope, Elemental Films [US],
Tohokashinsha Film Company Ltd.
**ACADEMY AWARD
NOMINATIONS (2004)**
Best Actor in a Leading Role:
Bill Murray
Best Director:
Sofia Coppola
Best Picture:
Ross Katz, Sofia Coppola
ACADEMY AWARDS
Best Writing, Screenplay Written
Directly for the Screen:
Sofia Coppola

DRAMA

Mr Smith Goes to Washington

USA, 1939
DIRECTOR:
Frank Capra
CAST INCLUDES:
Jean Arthur, James Stewart,
Claude Rains, Edward Arnold,
Guy Kibbee
SCREENPLAY:
Sidney Buchman (screenplay),
Lewis R. Foster (story)
CINEMATOGRAPHY:
Joseph Walker
PRODUCERS/
PRODUCTION COMPANIES:
Frank Capra/
Columbia Pictures Corporation
ACADEMY AWARD
NOMINATIONS (1940)
Best Actor in a Leading Role:
James Stewart
Best Actor in a Supporting Role:
Claude Rains
Best Actor in a Supporting Role:
Harry Carey
Best Art Direction: Lionel Banks
Best Director: Frank Capra
Best Film Editing:
Gene Havlick, Al Clark
Best Music, Scoring: Dimitri Tiomkin
Best Picture: Frank Capra
Best Sound, Recording:
John P. Livadary/Columbia SSD
Best Writing, Screenplay:
Sidney Buchman
ACADEMY AWARDS
Best Writing, Original Story:
Lewis R. Foster

When a congressional seat becomes available, the politicians are looking for someone who will play ball with the established regime, maintaining the status quo and keeping his personal views in check. While those in power think they have found the perfect man in Jefferson Smith (Stewart) it soon becomes clear that he is both a shrewd man and incorruptible.

Frank Capra's stirring insight into government and powers manages to fulfil its aims, whilst injecting a certain amount of humour into the proceedings. Master at bringing the trials of humanity to the big screen (*It's a Wonderful Life*), Capra uses his unique talent for dealing with big ideas in simple ways, to portray a man fighting for his ideals against the odds. Jefferson begins full of optimism for his new role of patriotic duty but soon discovers that, even at the top, the greed for power and wealth can corrupt moral ideals of service and duty to your country.

When it transpires that tycoon James Taylor (Arnold) is bolstering his real estate business with money that he's procured from public funds, it becomes Mr Smith's duty to expose this blatant corruption. The moral path is no easy walk however and cynical insiders try to ruin his career.

This film was a definite turning point for James Stewart, who won acclaim, from both the Academy and the audiences, for his heartfelt performance. Though it criticized the system this movie also proved that democracy held within it the means of its own redemption.

The Grapes of Wrath

Following one family's struggle to survive during the Great Depression, *The Grapes of Wrath* struck a real chord with audiences of the time and is gaining new-found acclaim, since its release on DVD a few years ago. Documenting real events, it is part historical document, part social observation, but above all a film that charts the strength and resilience of the farming families that suffered virtual devastation, as their livelihoods were lost and they faced starvation and homelessness.

Tom Joad (Fonda) returns to his Oklahoma farm from a stint in prison to find his family packing up and preparing to make the long journey to California, in search of work. They are representative of the thousands upon thousands of people who made the same difficult trek, having been forced from their smallholdings by the moneymen.

Based on the John Steinbeck novel of the same name, Ford's film doesn't attempt to dilute the message of the book or play to a Hollywood formula. Tom is still the same flawed hero, guilty of murder and far from perfect, but it's his everyman qualities that see him applauded as the voice of the common people, refusing to just roll over and die while those in power profit from his plight. The only real major deviation from the book is the ending, when Steinbeck's shocking and heart-rending climax is transformed into something a little more palatable for a cinema audience.

USA, 1940
DIRECTOR:
John Ford
CAST INCLUDES:
Henry Fonda, Jane Darwell,
John Carradine, Charley Grapewin,
Dorris Bowdon, Russell Simpson
SCREENPLAY:
Nunnally Johnson (screenplay),
John Steinbeck (novel)
CINEMATOGRAPHY:
Gregg Toland
PRODUCERS/
PRODUCTION COMPANIES:
Nunnally Johnson, Darryl F. Zanuck/
20th Century Fox
ACADEMY AWARD
NOMINATIONS (1941)
Best Actor in a Leading Role:
Henry Fonda
Best Film Editing: Robert L. Simpson
Best Picture: Darryl F. Zanuck,
Nunnally Johnson
Best Sound, Recording:
Edmund H. Hansen/ 20th Century-
Fox SSD
Best Writing, Screenplay:
Nunnally Johnson
ACADEMY AWARDS
Best Actress in a Supporting Role:
Jane Darwell
Best Director: John Ford

Citizen Kane

USA, 1941
DIRECTOR:
Orson Welles
CAST INCLUDES:
Orson Welles, Joseph Cotton,
Dorothy Comingore,
Agnes Moorehead, Ruth Warrick,
Ray Collins
SCREENPLAY:
Herman J Mankiewicz and
Orson Welles
CINEMATOGRAPHY:
Gregg Toland
**PRODUCERS/
PRODUCTION COMPANIES:**
Orson Welles/
Mercury Productions,
RKO Radio Pictures Inc.
**ACADEMY AWARD
NOMINATIONS (1942)**
Best Actor in a Leading Role:
Orson Welles
Best Art Direction-Interior Decoration,
Black-and-White:
Perry Ferguson, Van Nest Polglase,
A. Roland Fields, Darrell Silvera
Best Cinematography, Black-and-White:
Gregg Toland
Best Director:
Orson Welles
Best Film Editing:
Robert Wise
Best Music, Scoring of a
Dramatic Picture: Bernard Herrmann
Best Picture: Orson Welles
Best Sound, Recording: John Aalberg/
RKO Radio SSD
ACADEMY AWARDS
Best Original Screenplay: Herman J.
Mankiewicz, Orson Welles

Charles Foster Kane (Welles) utters the word 'Rosebud' with his dying breath and the film deals with the attempt by friends, acquaintances and colleagues to give meaning to these apparently innocuous and random syllables by means of flashbacks of his life.

Still regarded by many as the best film ever made, its reputation hasn't lessened with the passing of time and the accolades still pour in when any definitive list of movie greats is put together. The praise is deserved for many reasons, not least the fact that Orson Welles was only 25 years old when he co-wrote, starred in and directed *Citizen Kane*. This accomplishment was all the greater because, for its time, the film was highly innovative in many respects, particularly in revolutionizing cinematography.

As we dwell on the dying words of a lonely man, we are literally thrown into the middle of his life when he was a highly successful newspaper publisher, who built his up his empire from humble beginnings to become one of America's most powerful businessmen. However, success and happiness don't always go hand-in-hand, and this soon becomes apparent, as Kane begins to lose the power he has become accustomed to and his empire starts crumbling around him.

The film is said to have been based on real-life newspaper magnate, William Randolph Hearst, however it was difficult to prove as Welles created an amalgamation of various well-known paper men of the time. And what of Rosebud? The secret behind the word is revealed right at the end, but after so much searching and surmising, the truth is something of a surprise.

Children of Paradise

Les enfants du paradis

FRANCE, 1945
DIRECTOR:
Marcel Carné
CAST INCLUDES:
Arletty, Jean-Louis Barrault,
Pierre Brasseur, Pierre Renoir,
María Casares
SCREENPLAY:
Jacques Prévert
CINEMATOGRAPHY:
Marc Fossard, Roger Hubert
PRODUCERS/
PRODUCTION COMPANIES:
Raymond Borderie, Fred Orain/
Pathé Cinéma
ACADEMY AWARDS (1947)
Best Writing, Original Screenplay:
Jacques Prévert

Famous for being shot during the occupation of France in World War II, the crew included Jews who were forced to work in hiding. A lavish costume drama, set over a century beforehand, it offered a comparison to France at the time of filming, with poverty and desperation of wartime France as opposed to the opulence and the good life of the 19th century.

Despite the many characters we are introduced to over the course of the film, we become attached to the leads as we follow a simple love story. Garance (Arletty) is accused of being a pickpocket, but is reprieved by the silent re-enactment of events by mime artist Baptiste (Barrault). Baptiste subsequently becomes smitten by Garance, however, the worldly-wise lady has any number of suitors, all vying for her affections, some more successfully than others.

An epic, at over three hours in length, *Children of Paradise* nevertheless manages to justify its screentime with its lavish tour of the back streets, backrooms, theatres and bars of one of Paris' most glittering eras.

It has inevitably retained its accolade as one of the greatest of all French films, partly due to the astounding circumstances in which it was produced and the very fact that it was produced at all; a testament to the resilience and perseverance of all involved. It is also a wonderful piece of filmmaking that sees director Carné employing great skill in his manipulation of such a dramatic and extensive story.

The Lost Weekend

Charting one man's desperate battle with alcoholism, *The Lost Weekend* is probably the most honest and pragmatic study of this often misinterpreted and misunderstood disease ever produced. There is no romanticism or masculine bravado employed to excuse or to try and play down Don Birnnam's (Milland) frenzied nosedive for the bottle at every possible opportunity during this fateful 48 hours.

Displaying the telltale signs of many alcoholics, such as hiding booze around the house, lying, and sneaking into bars, we meet Don one particular weekend when he and his brother Wick (Terry) are supposed to be going down to stay with their parents. Having managed to stay dry for a while, it's more than Don can bear to be in the same room as a half-bottle of bourbon. The thought of it tortures him and tears him apart and, once he has given in, there's no going back; it's a downward spiral into the depths of human pain and despair. Don drinks his way around town, then sets out to try and pawn his belongings in order to continue to feed his addiction.

Milland manages to keep the film within the realms of reality with his truly agonizing performance. It's a subject that was crying out to be tackled but it was a brave choice and one that didn't sit easily with the original audience. Nevertheless, it remains a chilling insight into the realities faced by millions of people and demonstrates that alcoholism truly is a disease that drives people to forsake everything for one last drink.

USA, 1945
DIRECTOR:
Billy Wilder
CAST INCLUDES:
Ray Milland, Jane Wyman,
Phillip Terry, Howard Da Silva,
Doris Dowling
SCREENPLAY:
Charles Brackett and
Billy Wilder from the novel by
Charles R. Jackson
CINEMATOGRAPHY:
John F. Seitz
**PRODUCERS/
PRODUCTION COMPANIES:**
Charles Brackett/
Paramount Pictures
**ACADEMY AWARD
NOMINATIONS (1946)**
Best Cinematography,
Black-and-White: John F. Seitz
Best Film Editing: Doane Harrison
Best Music, Scoring of a Dramatic or
Comedy Picture: Miklós Rózsa
ACADEMY AWARDS
Best Actor in a Leading Role:
Ray Milland
Best Director: Billy Wilder
Best Picture: Charles Brackett
Best Writing, Screenplay: Charles
Brackett, Billy Wilder

The Best Years of Our Lives

USA, 1946
DIRECTOR:
William Wyler
CAST INCLUDES:
Myrna Loy, Fredric March,
Dana Andrews, Teresa Wright,
Virginia Mayo, Harold Russell
SCREENPLAY:
Robert E. Sherwood and MacKinlay
Kantor from the novel *Glory for Me*
CINEMATOGRAPHY:
Gregg Toland
**PRODUCERS/
PRODUCTION COMPANIES:**
Samuel Goldwyn/
Samuel Goldwyn Company
**ACADEMY AWARD
NOMINATIONS (1947)**
Best Sound, Recording:
Gordon Sawyer/ Samuel
Goldwyn SSD
Honorary Award:
Harold Russell
'For bringing hope and courage to his
fellow veterans through his
appearance in
The Best Years of Our Lives'
ACADEMY AWARDS
Best Actor in a Leading Role:
Fredric March
Best Actor in a Supporting Role:
Harold Russell
Best Director: William Wyler
Best Film Editing: Daniel Mandell
Best Music, Scoring of a Dramatic or
Comedy Picture: Hugo Friedhofer
Best Picture: Samuel Goldwyn
Best Writing, Screenplay:
Robert E. Sherwood

This film is as timeless as the subject it tackles; men returning from war. Just how do people cope with their reintegration into everyday life back home when they have seen and suffered so much? Wyler's three protagonists each has their own inner demons to deal with and they must somehow try to reconcile their World War II experiences with family life and the mundane normality of Boone City. Al (March) has to try and get to know the two children he left behind, both of whom have changed so much. He initially appears to adapt admirably to his previous life, even getting back his old job at the bank, but it seems the war has changed him irrevocably and his resolve is softened towards fellow ex-servicemen, to whom he approves loans without implementing all the necessary documentation.

Homer (Russell) lost both of his hands during the war and, on his return, finds it difficult to rekindle his relationship with his fiancée, Wilma. The obvious worries about his disability seem to encompass far more than simply a fear of rejection based on his physical appearance; he has changed and can no longer express his feelings. The third man, Fred (Andrews) can't even find his wife at first and, once he does, her flippancy drives them apart once more. This film is a poignant reminder of the hidden costs of war and the confusion of the men who fight for their country, only to find that they and the land for which they suffered have been altered irrevocably by the experience.

Great Expectations

Despite a number of later film and television interpretations of the famous work, Lean's is the one that is still remembered and referred to as the classic version. As with all Dickens' novels this work is rich in incidental charcters essential to the mood of the plot. The screenplay manages to preserve this texture in translating it to the screen. Pip is the protagonist in *Great Expectations* and is a boy essentially alone. Brought up by an older sister, Pip is invited to the house of the bitter Miss Havisham (Hunt) who was abandoned by her fiancé on their wedding day many years ago, and is yet to recover from the blow. The eccentric old lady lives with a young girl, Estella (Simmons), whom she adopted and for whom Pip is to be the playmate.

An anonymous benefactor soon sees Pip move to London, where his education and living costs will be met and, although he believes he is being made respectable enough to marry the beautiful Estella, it isn't, in fact, Miss Havisham who is paying. She has been rearing her young charge in the art of breaking hearts, as revenge for her own heartbreak at the hands of a man.

The film is an evocative and epic production which sets the standard for all future adaptations of Dickens for the screen. The opening scenes in which Pip meets the convict Magwitch will haunt you forever.

GB, 1946
DIRECTOR:
David Lean
CAST INCLUDES:
John Mills, Anthony Wager, Valerie Hobson, Jean Simmons, Bernard Miles. Martita Hunt
SCREENPLAY:
Anthony Havelock-Allan, David Lean, Cecil McGivern, Ronald Neame and Kay Walsh from the novel by Charles Dickens
CINEMATOGRAPHY:
Guy Green
PRODUCERS/ PRODUCTION COMPANIES:
Ronald Neame, Anthony Havelock-Allan/ Cineguild, The Rank Organisations Film Productions
ACADEMY AWARD NOMINATION (1948)
Best Director: David Lean
Best Picture: Ronald Neame
Best Writing, Screenplay: David Lean, Ronald Neame, Anthony Havelock-Allan
ACADEMY AWARDS
Best Art Direction-Set Decoration, Black-and-White: John Bryan, Wilfred Shingleton
Best Cinematography, Black-and-White: Guy Green

It's a Wonderful Life

USA, 1946
DIRECTOR:
Frank Capra
CAST INCLUDES:
James Stewart, Donna Reed,
Lionel Barrymore, Thomas Mitchell,
Henry Travers
SCREENPLAY:
Frances Goodrich, Albert Hackett,
Frank Capra, Jo Swerling (additional
scenes), Philip Van Doren Stern
from the story *The Greatest Gift*
CINEMATOGRAPHY:
Joseph F. Biroc, Joseph Walker
PRODUCERS/
PRODUCTION COMPANIES:
Frank Capra/ Liberty Films, RKO
Radio Pictures Inc.
ACADEMY AWARD
NOMINATIONS (1947)
Best Actor in a Leading Role:
James Stewart
Best Director: Frank Capra
Best Film Editing: William Hornbeck
Best Picture: Frank Capra
Best Sound, Recording: John Aalberg

In this now much lauded movie, Frank Capra explores the value and virtue of an 'ordinary' life of decency and integrity to the wider society of which it is a part. George Bailey (Stewart) dreamt of being a famous explorer when he was a boy, but the death of his father meant forsaking his dreams of travel and remaining in the town of Bedford Falls to take the helm of the family business. George is not really contented, but he slots into his niche, becoming much respected in the local community, particularly for his refusal to sell the business to local 'fat cat', Potter (Barrymore). This wily businessman practically owns the rest of the town and is prepared to do anything in order to complete his takeover. When misfortune strikes George despairs and contemplates suicide.

His guardian angel (Travers) appears to help him take stock, to see the value of his life. He asks him what the world would have been like if George hadn't been born and subsequently takes him on a tour of his life as if he had never existed,

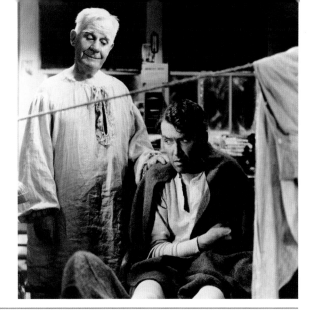

revealing the many ways in which George has contributed to the lives of those around him. Capra created a timeless piece of cinema that related so directly to the human psyche that it could not fail but to touch the hearts of audiences. However, it wasn't until long after the film was first released that it really gained in popularity and it still attracts new fans today.

Letter from an Unknown Woman

Recounting the demise of a woman scarred by love, *Letter from an Unknown Woman* was without a doubt the finest film of Ophüls' long career. A teenage girl becomes infatuated with a concert pianist and when they begin a relationship it seems that he shares the same feelings for her. However, when she falls pregnant, he abandons her and, despite rebuilding her life and marrying, she never recovers from the broken heart he inflicted upon her and the treatment meted out to her as a vulnerable young woman.

The film actually begins at the end of the story, when the pianist Brand (Jourdan) sits reading a letter from Lisa Berndl (Fontaine), apparently her last before she dies. We are told how years after their first tryst, they met again, only Brand made no connection between the grown woman and the shy girl he had abandoned years before.

It's a tale of unrequited love, told with beauty and passion, through the eloquent words of the spurned woman, who never stopped loving Brand and irrevocably changed the whole course of her life due to her passion for the man. By the end she has demystified the enigma of Brand and realized that he is far from worthy of the pain and suffering he has unconsciously caused her. However, she is powerless to change the feelings that consume her and must submit to the curse of loving him forever.

USA, 1948
DIRECTOR:
Max Ophüls
CAST INCLUDES:
Joan Fontaine, Louis Jourdan, Mady Christians, Marcel Journet, Art Smith
SCREENPLAY:
Howard Koch, Max Ophüls, and Stefan Zweig from the novel *Brief einer Unbekannten*
CINEMATOGRAPHY:
Franz Planer (as Frank Planer)
PRODUCERS/ PRODUCTION COMPANIES:
John Houseman, William Dozier/ Rampart Productions, Universal International Pictures

The Bicycle Thief
Ladri di Biciclette

ITALY, 1948
DIRECTOR:
Vittorio De Sica
CAST INCLUDES:
Lamberto Maggiorani, Enzo Staiola,
Lianella Carell, Gino Saltamerenda,
Vittorio Antonucci
SCREENPLAY:
Oreste Biancoli, Vittorio De Sica,
Gerardo Guerrieri, Suso Cecchi
d'Amico, Adolfo Franci, Cesare
Zavattini, Cesare Zavattini (story)
from the novel by Luigi Bartolini
CINEMATOGRAPHY:
Carlo Montuori
**PRODUCERS/
PRODUCTION COMPANIES:**
Giuseppe Amato/
Produzioni De Sica
**ACADEMY AWARD
NOMINATIONS (1950)**
Best Writing, Screenplay:
Cesare Zavattini
Honorary Award Italy:
Voted by the Academy Board of
Governors as 'the most outstanding
foreign language film released in the
United States during 1949'

A slice of life in poverty-stricken, post-war Rome, *The Bicycle Thief* is a simple tale that offers far more than its linear structure and uncomplicated characterizations suggest. Ricci (Maggiorani) queues at the same spot each morning with other men, hoping to gain work. When a job is offered one day he jumps at the chance to take it, only to discover that a bicycle is required. Despite saying that he owned a bicycle, Ricci had to pawn it in order to buy food for his family. There is a way round the predicament however, and Ricci's wife Maria (Carell) eagerly strips their bed of its sheets so that the bicycle can be retrieved from the pawnbrokers and Ricci can take the job.

Providing a rare insight into post war Italy at the time, there's a clever irony in play that sees Ricci putting up film posters as part of his job; the glamour of the silver screen staring down, larger than life, as the people below try to scrape a living and live their lives at the most basic level of existence. Needless to say, Ricci's bicycle is stolen from him and he scours the streets of Rome to no avail, looking for the thief. It's a cycle of poverty and desperation that he very nearly continues when he is tempted to steal another bicycle from someone else to replace his, in order to keep his job.

Often cited as one of the greatest films ever made, the simplicity of such a human tale hasn't been lost and a re-release of the film in 1999 earned a new audience and a renewed appreciation for the powerful sentiments dealt with by director Vittorio De Sica.

All About Eve

A rollercoaster ride through the glitzy world of 1950s American theatre, this classic film with its record-breaking haul of Oscars and star line-up, was always destined to remain a favourite. Its showbiz connotations still resonate today and its upfront behind-the-scenes analysis of the cynical yet all-encompassing theatrical milieu is a joy to watch.

The divine Bette Davis is engrossing in her portrayal of Margo Channing, an actress at the end of the line, but unsure how to go about doing anything else. When aspiring artiste Eve Harrington (Baxter) appears, Margo feels she be her mentor, as she herself was once in the very same position, struggling to get noticed and embark on her career. It's actually Margo, however, and not Eve, who really benefits from her generosity, Margo having lost sight of who she really is, after years of accolade, and acting parts. By taking Eve under her wing, she can experience a sense of autonomy, being proactive rather than having her every moved mapped out for her. As the film develops, however, Eve's ulterior motives begin to surface and we sense that she may be using every move in the book to simply pursue her own career.

Mankiewicz succeeded in recreating a world within a world, inhabited by characters so snappy and memorable that it's easy to be transported to the lights and greasepaint of the glittering stage.

USA, 1950
DIRECTOR:
Joseph L. Mankiewicz
CAST INCLUDES:
Bette Davis, Anne Baxter, George Sanders, Celeste Holm, Gary Merrill
SCREENPLAY:
Joseph L. Mankiewicz
CINEMATOGRAPHY:
Milton R. Krasner
PRODUCERS/
PRODUCTION COMPANIES:
Darryl F. Zanuck/
20th Century Fox
ACADEMY AWARD
NOMINATIONS (1951)
Best Actress in a Leading Role:
Anne Baxter
Best Actress in a Leading Role:
Bette Davis
Best Actress in a Supporting Role:
Celeste Holm
Best Actress in a Supporting Role:
Thelma Ritter
Best Art Direction-Set Decoration,
Black-and-White: Lyle R. Wheeler,
George W. Davis, Thomas Little,
Walter M. Scott
Best Cinematography, Black-and-
White: Milton R. Krasner
Best Film Editing: Barbara McLean
Best Music, Scoring of a Dramatic or
Comedy Picture: Alfred Newman
ACADEMY AWARDS
Best Actor in a Supporting
Role: George Sanders
Best Costume Design, Black-and-
White: Edith Head, Charles Le Maire
Best Director: Joseph L. Mankiewicz
Best Picture: Darryl F. Zanuck
Best Sound, Recording
Best Writing, Screenplay:
Joseph L. Mankiewicz

Sunset Boulevard

USA, 1950
DIRECTOR:
Billy Wilder
CAST INCLUDES:
William Holden, Gloria Swanson,
Erich von Stroheim, Nancy Olson,
Fred Clark, Lloyd Gough
SCREENPLAY:
Charles Brackett, Billy Wilder,
D.M. Marshman Jr.
CINEMATOGRAPHY:
John F. Seitz
PRODUCERS/
PRODUCTION COMPANIES:
Charles Brackett/
Paramount Pictures
ACADEMY AWARD
NOMINATIONS (1951)
Best Actor in a Leading Role:
William Holden
Best Actor in a Supporting Role:
Erich von Stroheim
Best Actress in a Leading Role:
Gloria Swanson
Best Actress in a Supporting Role:
Nancy Olson
Best Cinematography, Black-and-
White: John F. Seitz
Best Director: Billy Wilder
Best Film Editing: Arthur P. Schmidt,
Doane Harrison
Best Picture: Charles Brackett
ACADEMY AWARDS
Best Art Direction-Set Decoration,
Black-and-White:Hans Dreier,
John Meehan, Sam Comer,
Ray Moyer
Best Music, Scoring of a Dramatic or
Comedy Picture: Franz Waxman
Best Writing, Story and Screenplay:
Charles Brackett, Billy Wilder,
D.M. Marshman Jr.

Still regarded as the greatest film ever made on the subject of Hollywood, *Sunset Boulevard* charts the ill-fated meeting of faded star Norma Desmond (Swanson) and screenwriter on the make, Joe Gillis (Holden). Living in virtual isolation in a mansion, Norma spends her lonely days dreaming of how she could become a big name once again. Joe comes across the decrepit mansion and the lonely has-been by chance. Gillis is struggling to make it big and the dichotomy between the woman who's been at the top and the man who's scrabbling at the bottom, provides an interesting take on the asinine world of stardom and the film industry.

Norma not only employs Gillis to work on her comeback script, but she falls in love with him in the process, showering him with expensive gifts. Unbeknown to her, Gillis is also working with a young studio writer Betty (Olson) on a collaboration and, rather than returning any amorous feelings towards Norma, Gillis falls for Betty and things get complicated.

In an industry where youth and beauty are pretty much a prerequisite for continued employment, Norma struggles to come to terms with her fall from grace and for Gillis to go behind her back is an unqualified affront, after all the kindness she feels she has shown him. Norma believes she owns the young writer, as she has owned many people in the past, and this only serves to highlight the materialistic nature and egocentric view that presides over Norma's Hollywood. A warped outlook perhaps, but one that ends in murder and Norma Desmond's last great close-up. Erich von Stroheim gives an astounding performance as her former director/lover and now butler.

Ace in the Hole

Sacked from his job at a big newspaper, reporter Chuck Tatum (Douglas) resorts to taking a job on a small New Mexican paper. Whilst travelling to cover a local event, he literally stumbles across the story that could re-launch his career and goes to great lengths to ensure he gets exclusive access. The subject is the unfortunate Leo Minosa (Benedict) who has become trapped after a cave collapsed and he is unable to escape.

In a film that seems even more pertinent today than it did in the 1950s, the whole media institution is taken apart, examined and condemned, along with those who come along for the ride. When a good story is pursued to the detriment of its subject, the rules governing common decency are flouted and the news is no longer simply the news; it is a form of entertainment. This is the case in *Ace in the Hole*; the story has all the human interest elements that will guarantee it extended headlines but, in order to prolong the public interest and ensure his return to the big time, Chuck needs Leo to remain trapped in the cave for as long as possible. The relatively quick recovery option is therefore eschewed in favour of a much lengthier rescue plan, jeopardizing the man's health but keeping the assembled public and press more than happy.

Based on a true story in which the man actually died before being rescued, Wilder's film is a brave and blatant attack on the media, which, not surprisingly, won him little praise or acclaim at the time of its release.

USA, 1951
DIRECTOR:
Billy Wilder
CAST INCLUDES:
Kirk Douglas, Jan Sterling, Porter Hall, Robert Arthur, Frank Cady, Richard Benedict
SCREENPLAY:
Billy Wilder, Walter Newman, Lesser Samuels
CINEMATOGRAPHY:
Charles Lang
PRODUCERS/ PRODUCTION COMPANIES:
Billy Wilder, William Schorr/ Paramount Pictures
ACADEMY AWARD NOMINATIONS (1952)
Best Writing, Story and Screenplay: Billy Wilder, Walter Newman, Lesser Samuels

On the Waterfront

Loosely based on the real-life experiences of director Elia Kazan, *On the Waterfront* was essentially a justification for his actions during attempts in the 1950s to 'cleanse' America of its Communist elements. Kazan named contemporaries whom he believed to be involved with the Communist Party.

In the film Brando plays the part of Terry Malloy, errand boy for a notoriously corrupt docker's union, where workers are kept quiet and life is sweet for the men at the top. When he's unwittingly involved in a murder he decides it's time to re-evaluate his principles and make some tough decisions. Caught in the crossfire between his conscience and safety he must decide whether to put his life on the line to do what he believes to be right. History will decide whether the decision was the correct one for both Malloy and Kazan.

Marlon Brando was at the height of his career when he starred in this film, something which must have had a huge impact on its initial success and enduring popularity. However his performance was stand-alone and it was talent not fame that really drove home the message and still has people today talking about the film in terms of a classic. And with classic lines such as 'I coulda been a contender', its fate is undoubtedly sealed for many years to come.

USA, 1954
DIRECTOR:
Elia Kazan
CAST INCLUDES:
Marlon Brando, Karl Malden,
Lee J. Cobb, Rod Steiger, Pat
Henning, Eva Marie Saint
SCREENPLAY:
Budd Schulberg, Malcolm Johnson
(suggested by articles)
CINEMATOGRAPHY:
Boris Kaufman
**PRODUCERS/
PRODUCTION COMPANIES:**
Sam Spiegel/Columbia Pictures
Corporation, Horizon Pictures
**ACADEMY AWARD
NOMINATIONS (1955)**
Best Actor in a Supporting Role:
Lee J. Cobb
Best Actor in a Supporting Role:
Karl Malden
Best Actor in a Supporting Role:
Rod Steiger
Best Music, Scoring of a Dramatic or
Comedy Picture: Leonard Bernstein
ACADEMY AWARDS
Best Actor in a Leading Role:
Marlon Brando
Best Actress in a Supporting Role:
Eva Marie Saint
Best Art Direction-Set Decoration,
Black-and-White: Richard Day
Best Cinematography, Black-and-
White: Boris Kaufman
Best Director: Elia Kazan
Best Film Editing: Gene Milford
Best Picture: Sam Spiegel
Best Writing, Story and Screenplay:
Budd Schulberg

Rebel Without a Cause

Our first encounter with Jim Stark (Dean) is as he lies in the gutter, drunk. A fitting image for a film that predominantly deals with alienation and disquiet amongst the youth of 1950s America. Jim is by no means a wayward loser however; he is a symbol of the shifting dynamic of a country adapting to monumental social and political change.

Rebel Without a Cause follows Jim *et al.* as they purposefully misspend their youth, looking for answers to unanswerable questions. Parental indifference is offered up as one justification for the meaningless violence, as if a lack of love can be counteracted with acts of hate; attention seeking behaviour that will fill the void left by absent intimacy.

The 1950s was certainly a time when the generation gap was growing, as the Victorian values of a pre-war America began to be replaced by a more forward-thinking outlook and the youth found their voice but weren't yet sure how to use it. In the film, the bonds of friendship replace those of family and Jim, Judy and Plato come to represent a surrogate family unit, providing each other with a reassuring emotional support network. Jim is out to prove himself though, despite the security that his friendships provide, and the famous 'chicken run' scene really sums up the film. Stolen cars are revved up to race over the edge of a cliff, the drivers jumping out at the very last minute, thus demonstrating the universal and timeless display of male bravado and pride.

James Dean was the personification of this period in America's history. His moody screen dominance made him an overnight sensation and his untimely death made him a legend.

USA, 1955
DIRECTOR:
Nicholas Ray
CAST INCLUDES:
James Dean, Natalie Wood,
Sal Mineo, Jim Backus, Ann Doran
SCREENPLAY:
Stewart Stern, Irving Shulman from
the story by Nicholas Ray
CINEMATOGRAPHY:
Ernest Haller
**PRODUCERS/
PRODUCTION COMPANIES:**
David Weisbart/
Warner Bros.
**ACADEMY AWARD
NOMINATIONS (1956)**
Best Actor in a Supporting Role:
Sal Mineo
Best Actress in a Supporting Role:
Natalie Wood
Best Writing, Motion Picture Story:
Nicholas Ray

12 Angry Men

USA, 1957
DIRECTOR:
Sydney Lumet
CAST INCLUDES:
Martin Balsam, John Fiedler,
Lee J. Cobb, E.G. Marshall,
Jack Klugman, Ed Binns, Jack Warden,
Henry Fonda, Joseph Sweeney, Ed
Begley, George Voskovec,
Robert Webber
SCREENPLAY:
Reginald Rose.
CINEMATOGRAPHY:
Boris Kaufman
PRODUCERS/
PRODUCTION COMPANIES:
Henry Fonda, Reginald Rose,
George Justin/
Orion-Nova Productions
ACADEMY AWARD
NOMINATIONS (1958)
Best Director: Sidney Lumet
Best Picture:Henry Fonda,
Reginald Rose
Best Writing, Screenplay Based on
Material from Another Medium:
Reginald Rose

Twelve jury members are sent out to deliberate over the verdict of a murder trial. If the defendant is found guilty, he will be sentenced to death, so the life of a fellow human being hangs in the balance and these men must decide on his fate.

Almost the entire film is set in the jury room where the twelve white, male jurors ponder over the case that has been played out in court over the preceding six days. What initially appears to be a relatively clear-cut case of premeditated murder slowly becomes more complicated, and the discussion turns into a heated deliberation over the absolute certainty that the defendant is guilty.

Lumet is undoubtedly attacking the American legal system in this film and, despite the quite uniform gender, race and class make-up of the jury, a surprising number of prejudices and issues emerge within the confines of the room and the matter at hand. The defendant is non-white and racism is a key factor in many of the men's justifications of returning with a plea of 'guilty beyond reasonable doubt'. However, when juror number eight (Fonda) starts planting the seeds of doubt in their minds, there's a shift in the dynamic of the film.

By keeping the action contained in just one location, the audience is treated to a more genuine experience, becoming fully engrossed in the actual process involved in this monumental responsibility.

The Seventh Seal
Det sjunde inseglet

Set against the backdrop of 14th century Sweden, in the midst of the plague and the holy crusades, a knight (von Sydow) and his squire Jöns (Bjönstrand), return home. Having escaped death during his perilous travels, the knight enters a church and comes face to face with it, in the form of a hooded man. It transpires that the shadowy figure has been following the knight on his homeward journey.

Although dealing with a subject so dark and bleak, the film is thought-provoking and directed with such skill that the viewer is drawn in and forgets the depressing issues that are being played out on screen. Bergman was a master of this broody genre of film making, always exploring the complexities of human existence and religious beliefs.

Death is necessarily omnipresent in this country racked with plague and suffering but to feature it in such a tangible way is both shocking and obvious. The knight plays chess with Death, a significant imagery that Bergman employs to describe his own personal hypotheses about God and religion. By using the plague, he offers insights into peoples' personal religious beliefs, with the infected and doomed accepting their fate in differing ways, depending upon their spiritual leanings and relationship with the God they perceive as the creator and instigator of all worldly events and the devil, who must be cast out and banished.

SWEDEN, 1957
DIRECTOR:
Ingmar Bergman
CAST INCLUDES:
Gunnar Björnstrand, Bengt Ekerot,
Nils Poppe, Max von Sydow,
Bibi Andersson
SCREENPLAY:
Ingmar Bergman from his play
Trämålning
CINEMATOGRAPHY:
Gunnar Fischer
**PRODUCERS/
PRODUCTION COMPANIES:**
Allan Ekelund/Svensk Filmindustri

USA, 1957
DIRECTOR:
Alexander Mackendrick
CAST INCLUDES:
Burt Lancaster, Tony Curtis,
Susan Harrison, Martin Milner,
Sam Levene
SCREENPLAY:
Clifford Odets, Ernest Lehman from
the novelette by Ernest Lehman
CINEMATOGRAPHY:
James Wong Howe
**PRODUCERS/
PRODUCTION COMPANIES:**
James Hill, Tony Curtis, Harold Hecht,
Burt Lancaster/Hecht, Hill &
Lancaster, Hill-Hecht-Lancaster
Productions, Norma-Curtleigh
Productions

Sweet Smell of Success

J. J. Hunsecker (Lancaster) is a man who's used to being fawned over and treated like royalty. A famous newspaper columnist whose words send reverberations around Manhattan, he lives the playboy lifestyle, enjoying the good life as if it's his birthright. A small-fry publicity agent by the name of Falco (Curtis) is one of Hunsecker's sources, sifting through the proverbial dustbins of New York's small talk to dish the dirt and provide fodder for the famous column inches.

Director Mackendrick makes no real attempt to highlight any redeeming features that might be hidden in these two men. The film is about media sensationalism, entertainment procured at other peoples' expense and, as such, niceties would be superfluous. We are shown a world of greed and envy, two of the deadly sins that these men carry around with them like weights about their necks, imprisoning them in their shallow world with blinkered vision.

The fawning Falco is called upon to break up the relationship that has blossomed between Hunsecker's sister (Harrison) and a jazz musician; a further example of the vile egotism that fills every molecule of Hunsecker's being. As far as he's concerned, everyone can be bought, sold, bribed or destroyed; it's just a question of money and influence. Falco is far too eager to please, no doubt assuming that one good turn deserves another and that this can only mean positive things for his career prospects.

The Sweet Smell of Success is a parody of the careers of all those flitty hacks who based their very successful careers on gossip and lined their pockets with the fruits of sensationalism.

Vertigo

When his fear of heights starts to impinge on his effectiveness as a police officer, John Ferguson (Stewart) is compelled to leave the force. At a loose end, a friend asks a favour; he wants Ferguson to follow his wife, as she's been acting strangely. Ferguson obliges but it doesn't take long for him to become infatuated with the beautiful Madeleine (Novak). When eventually they meet, it's obvious that the feeling is mutual, however Ferguson's demons come back to haunt him once more, as he is unable to save Madeleine from a fatal fall from a bell tower.

Vertigo is a summation of all that Hitchcock did best; the suspense, the tension, the coercion of the camera to suit the mood and the almost remote female lead. In a plot that twists and retraces until we're not sure who is who any more, a tall tale of deception and intrigue is built up. When Ferguson meets a woman bearing a remarkable resemblance to Madeleine, soon after her death, the intrigue really starts to escalate and Hitchcock builds the notion of one man's obsession with obtaining perfection, as he tries to mould the lookalike into an exact replica of the love he lost prematurely.

Dealing with human neuroses in such a groundbreaking manner was part of the genius that earned Hitchcock his awesome reputation. You really don't know what his characters are going to have thrown at them next, but you know it will make sense, albeit strangely twisted, as soon as it happens.

USA, 1958
DIRECTOR:
Alfred Hitchcock
CAST INCLUDES:
James Stewart, Kim Novak,
Barbara Bel Geddes, Tom Helmore,
Henry Jones
SCREENPLAY:
Alec Coppel, Samuel A. Taylor, Pierre
Boileau and Thomas Narcejac from
the novel *d'Entre les Morts*
CINEMATOGRAPHY:
Robert Burks
**PRODUCERS/
PRODUCTION COMPANIES:**
James C. Katz/
Alfred J. Hitchcock Productions,
Paramount Pictures
ACADEMY AWARDS (1959)
Best Art Direction-Set Decoration,
Black-and-White or Color: Hal Pereira,
Henry Bumstead, Sam Comer,
Frank R. McKelvy
Best Sound: George Dutton/
Paramount SSD

To Kill a Mockingbird

USA, 1962
DIRECTOR:
Robert Mulligan
CAST INCLUDES:
Gregory Peck, Mary Badham,
Phillip Alford, Robert Duvall,
John Megna, Frank Overton,
Brock Peters, James Anderson
SCREENPLAY:
Horton Foote (screenplay),
Harper Lee (novel)
CINEMATOGRAPHY:
Russell Harlan
PRODUCERS/
PRODUCTION COMPANIES:
Alan J. Pakula/
Brentwood Productions,
Pakula-Mulligan, Universal
International Pictures
ACADEMY AWARD
NOMINATIONS (1963)
Best Actress in a Supporting Role:
Mary Badham
Best Cinematography, Black-and-
White: Russell Harlan
Best Director: Robert Mulligan
Best Music, Score - Substantially
Original: Elmer Bernstein
Best Picture: Alan J. Pakula
ACADEMY AWARDS
Best Actor in a Leading Role:
Gregory Peck
Best Art Direction-Set Decoration,
Black-and-White: Alexander Golitzen,
Henry Bumstead, Oliver Emert
Best Writing, Screenplay Based on
Material from Another Medium:
Horton Foote

Set in the American deep south in the 1930s, when racial intolerance was still the norm, *To Kill a Mockingbird* is the adaptation of Harper Lee's outstanding novel of the same name. In order to do justice to the book, it was imperative that Mulligan had the right cast and his choice of Peck for the part of lawyer Atticus Finch was clearly a stroke of genius. Finch takes on the case of Tom Robinson (Peters), a black man accused of rape. The law of being innocent until proven guilty seems lost on a prejudiced populace and this is a clear-cut tale of racism and injustice, as seen through the eyes of Finch's daughter, Scout (Badham).

Following lengthy court proceedings, Robinson is found guilty, a charge which we know to be incorrect and the flagrant racist undertones leave a nasty taste in your mouth. Robinson's most vocal accuser is the venom-filled Bob Ewell (Anderson), the father of the alleged victim, but he merely verbalizes what the majority of the white townsfolk are thinking.

Despite the tragic conclusion to the trial, the story offers some hope, not least in the portrait of Finch as a single parent, instilling principles of decency and morality into his children who can clearly see the inexcusable injustice for what it is. We are left with the facts, and the world is left with a film that reflects on a tainted period in history, but one which still has repercussions today.

8¹/₂

Ostensibly a film about a director at a creative impasse in his career, it has often been remarked that it was at least semi-autobiographical, reflecting many of the difficulties Fellini was experiencing in his own work and life.

Film director Guido (Mastroianni) is being hassled from all sides to begin production on his next film, but inspiration eludes him and personal crises fill his thoughts and, to a greater extent, his dreams. Indeed, it is during the dream sequences that we really learn about the true subject of the film. Sexual desire, frustration and a feeling of isolation as a human being, are just some of the issues he touches upon.

Guido has a wife and a mistress, both of whom want their fair share of the man. But, once he has divided himself amongst the hungry hopefuls waiting to pounce on the yet-to-be-confirmed film, there's not a whole lot left. It seems only in sleep is he free to explore the dark imaginings and desires of his mind and where Fellini has a creative free-reign to really push forward Guido's character.

Fellini's work was often misunderstood as being too highbrow for the average cinema audience but it was generally a lack of straightforward, linear structure in his films that forced people to interpret the stories for themselves. He doesn't make it easy for his audience but it's ultimately a more fulfilling experience.

ITALY/FRANCE, 1963
DIRECTOR:
Federico Fellini
CAST INCLUDES:
Marcello Mastroianni,
Claudia Cardinale, Anouk Aimée,
Rossella Falk, Sandra Milo
SCREENPLAY:
Ennio Flaiano, Tullio Pinelli,
Federico Fellini, Brunello Rondi. Story
by Federico Fellini and Ennio Flaiano
CINEMATOGRAPHY:
Gianni Di Venanzo
**PRODUCERS/
PRODUCTION COMPANIES:**
Angelo Rizzoli/
Cineriz, Francinex
**ACADEMY AWARD
NOMINATIONS (1964)**
Best Art Direction-Set Decoration,
Black-and-White: Piero Gherardi
Best Director: Federico Fellini
Best Writing, Story and Screenplay -
Written Directly for the Screen:
Federico Fellini, Ennio Flaiano,
Tullio Pinelli, Brunello Rondi
ACADEMY AWARDS
Best Costume Design, Black-and-
White: Piero Gherardi
Best Foreign Language Film (Italy)

A Man for all Seasons

GB, 1966
DIRECTOR:
Fred Zinnemann
CAST INCLUDES:
Paul Scofield, Wendy Hiller,
Leo McKern, Robert Shaw,
Orson Welles, Susannah York
SCREENPLAY:
Robert Bolt
CINEMATOGRAPHY:
Ted Moore
**PRODUCERS/
PRODUCTION COMPANIES:**
Fred Zinnemann, William N. Graf/
Open Road
**ACADEMY AWARD
NOMINATIONS (1967)**
Best Actor in a Supporting Role:
Robert Shaw
Best Actress in a Supporting Role:
Wendy Hiller
ACADEMY AWARDS
Best Actor in a Leading Role:
Paul Scofield
Best Cinematography, Color:
Ted Moore
Best Costume Design, Color:
Elizabeth Haffenden, Joan Bridge
Best Director: Fred Zinnemann
Best Picture: Fred Zinnemann
Best Writing, Screenplay Based on
Material from Another Medium:
Robert Bolt

King Henry VIII was used to getting his own way and, on those rare occasions that he didn't, he merely used a little persuasive pressure to bring those opposing him into line. The issue of marriage was no exception and, on discovering that his wife couldn't conceive, he wanted to remarry in order to produce heirs to the throne. This wasn't so straightforward in 16th century Catholic England, so Henry 'persuaded' his bishops to split from the church in Rome and form their own Church of England, over which he himself would preside, thus becoming a law unto himself. Only one man at court refused to openly accept the new church. Sir Thomas More (Scofield), the Lord Chancellor of England, showed his disapproval through his silence, earning him the King's disdain.

A Man for all Seasons charts the downfall of this great man who is prepared to give up everything he has worked for, in the name of his beliefs. His conscience persuades him to leave his office, spelling the end of the lavish lifestyle he enjoys. But this self-removal from public life isn't enough to assuage Henry's anger and More must eventually offer up his life in order to preserve the values he holds most precious. While those around him submitted to the King's all-encompassing domination, More gave up everything he had, yet kept that which should be most precious to every human being – his integrity. The skillful acting truly brings about a sense of the convictions of More and offers him up as the kind of person we all aspire to be.

Belle de jour

Séverine (Deneuve) is a breathtakingly beautiful young woman who has been married to her doctor husband (Sorel) for just a year. In that time they haven't slept together, Séverine preferring to stay in the guest bedroom, and herein lies the backbone of Buñuel's stunning exposition of sexual desires and frustrations. However, despite its gritty subject matter, Buñuel never allows the piece to stray into smutty territory and it remains tasteful and insightful.

Séverine has more than a passing interest in brothels and her curiosity eventually leads her to the front door of the establishment of Madame Anaïs (Page). We are aware that it's just a matter of time before she's on the payroll, as she has already made the biggest step simply by going there. Despite potentially humiliating treatment at the hands of some of her clients, Séverine is finally able to succumb to the urges that fill her sexually explicit dreams and the fact that this illicit, sordid side of her life is in absolute contrast to her home life, lends a greater element of excitement to the whole business. As she is only able to see customers in the afternoons while her husband works, Séverine is given the name Belle de Jour.

A truly perceptive look at some of the darker aspects of human desire, Buñuel's *Belle de Jour* emancipates its frustrated female lead in a way few films at the time dared. Of course, life cannot simply continue in such easy compartmentalized segments for Séverine and the complications threaten to bring about her downfall.

FRANCE/ITALY, 1967
DIRECTOR:
Luis Buñuel
CAST INCLUDES:
Catherine Deneuve, Jean Sorel,
Michel Piccoli, Geneviève Page,
Pierre Clémenti
SCREENPLAY:
Luis Buñuel, Jean-Claude Carrière
from the novel by Joseph Kessel
CINEMATOGRAPHY:
Sacha Vierny
PRODUCERS/
PRODUCTION COMPANIES:
Henri Baum, Raymond Hakim,
Robert Hakim/Five Film, Paris Film

USA, 1967
DIRECTOR:
Mike Nichols
CAST INCLUDES:
Anne Bancroft, Dustin Hoffman,
Katharine Ross, William Daniels,
Murray Hamilton
SCREENPLAY:
Calder Willingham,
Buck Henry from the novel
by Charles Webb
CINEMATOGRAPHY:
Robert Surtees
**PRODUCERS/
PRODUCTION COMPANIES:**
Lawrence Turman, Joseph E. Levine/
Embassy Pictures Corporation,
Lawrence Turman Inc.
**ACADEMY AWARD
NOMINATIONS (1968)**
Best Actor in a Leading Role:
Dustin Hoffman
Best Actress in a Leading Role:
Anne Bancroft
Best Actress in a Supporting Role:
Katharine Ross
Best Cinematography:
Robert Surtees
Best Picture: Lawrence Turman
Best Writing, Screenplay Based on
Material from Another Medium:
Calder Willingham, Buck Henry
ACADEMY AWARDS
Best Director: Mike Nichols

The Graduate

This iconic movie has any number of famous images and oft-repeated lines of dialogue associated with it. Suffice to say that the most memorable is when Mrs Robinson (Bancroft) purrs to Ben Braddock (Hoffman), 'Would you like me to seduce you?', having trapped him in her bedroom. Recent college graduate Ben is the son of Mr Robinson's business partner and family friend – all very cosy – and, having reached an indecisive crossroads in his life, he is ripe for the plucking by the sexually aware but unsatisfied Mrs Robinson.

The Graduate was a real film of the moment, speaking volumes about the America it represented, a populace uncertain and full of trepidation, rather like Ben, who makes a flustered refusal to Mrs Robinson's blatant offer of sex. It isn't long however, before her advances are more successful and Ben quickly loses his inhibitions, embarking on a crazy affair with this older, married woman. The adventure abruptly ends when Ben is introduced to the Robinson's daughter, Elaine (Ross) and decides that she's the girl for him. Already matched up with a suitable beau, this union is just as fraught with complications as that with her mother and Ben begins to learn that love is no easy path.

Nichols ensures that the audience is constantly in tune with Ben's awkward turmoil, as he tries to deal with all the complications that have suddenly entered his life. Having started the film berating the fact that he didn't know which direction his life was heading, he ends with at least one certainty; he wants Elaine and he'll go to great lengths to keep her.

Guess Who's Coming to Dinner

When the premise of a film is a girl bringing her fiancé home to meet her parents, it doesn't sound like much of a story. Make the girl white, the fiancé black and remember that it's 1960s America, and things start to look a little more interesting. Joanna Drayton (Houghton) has been brought up in a liberal household but her impending marriage to an African-American is set to test her parents' (Hepburn and Tracy) views to the limits. John Wade Prentice (Poitier) is a distinguished doctor so it seems likely that any reluctance to give their blessing to the impending union must be based solely upon the colour of his skin. This particular aspect of the script was originally criticized by many people, as there didn't appear to be any real dilemma. However, by basing any prejudices solely on colour, the potential for excuses over poor job prospects or differing social backgrounds was removed, leaving the real issue to be discussed.

In a topic that still has relevance today, people are asked to put their values on the line; it's all very easy to be a vocally progressive liberal but when the issues come walking through your front door, can you still stand by your beliefs with such heartfelt enthusiasm? Joanna's parents cite concerns for the couple's acceptance by society at large as their major issue, but is this a thin veil covering their own deep-rooted anxieties?

USA, 1967
DIRECTOR:
Stanley Kramer
CAST INCLUDES:
Spencer Tracy, Sidney Poitier,
Katharine Hepburn, Cecil Kellaway,
Beah Richards, Katharine Houghton
SCREENPLAY:
William Rose
CINEMATOGRAPHY:
Sam Leavitt
**PRODUCERS/
PRODUCTION COMPANIES:**
Stanley Kramer, George Glass/
Columbia Pictures Corporation
**ACADEMY AWARD
NOMINATIONS (1968)**
Best Actor in a Leading Role:
Spencer Tracy (Posthumously)
Best Actor in a Supporting Role:
Cecil Kellaway
Best Actress in a Supporting Role:
Beah Richards
Best Art Direction-Set Decoration:
Robert Clatworthy, Frank Tuttle
Best Director: Stanley Kramer
Best Film Editing: Robert C. Jones
Best Music, Scoring of Music,
Adaptation or Treatment:
Frank De Vol
Best Picture: Stanley Kramer
ACADEMY AWARDS
Best Actress in a Leading Role:
Katharine Hepburn
Best Writing, Story and Screenplay -
Written Directly for the Screen:
William Rose

Easy Rider

USA, 1969
DIRECTOR:
Dennis Hopper
CAST INCLUDES:
Peter Fonda, Dennis Hopper,
Antonio Mendoza, Phil Spector,
Mac Mashourian, Jack Nicholson
SCREENPLAY:
Peter Fonda, Dennis Hopper,
Terry Southern
CINEMATOGRAPHY:
László Kovács
PRODUCERS/
PRODUCTION COMPANIES:
Peter Fonda, William Hayward,
Bert Schneider
ACADEMY AWARD
NOMINATIONS (1970)
Best Actor in a Supporting Role:
Jack Nicholson
Best Writing, Story and Screenplay
Based on Material Not Previously
Published or Produced:
Peter Fonda, Dennis Hopper,
Terry Southern

The ultimate road movie that launched a thousand more, *Easy Rider* follows the journey of Wyatt (Fonda) and Billy (Hopper) as they rev up their motorbikes and leave L.A. for the narcotics-fuelled adventure they've risked everything to take. With drug references aplenty, hippy protagonists and a great score, this film was destined to be a hit with the misunderstood generation, all clamouring to be a part of the free and easy lifestyle it portrayed, living beyond the constraints of a law-abiding society.

It's not one big carefree orgy of cannabis and casual sex however, and tragedy strikes more than once, as the boys land themselves in trouble. They begin to realize that not everyone they meet appreciates their values and it's not such an easy ride after all; enter George Hanson (Nicholson), the lawyer who helps them out when they're arrested in redneck Middle America. George is intrigued and goes on to join them on their freedom crusade and he soon becomes infatuated with the lure of the open road, the antithesis of his own, sedentary life.

Chemical highs help him gain awareness of the wider world beyond his limited environs and experience, and he is one step closer to realizing his somewhat uninspired dream of visiting a famous brothel in New Orleans.

The cinematography is crafted to back up the whole essence of the film and it works wonderfully as a means of reiterating the central themes of freedom and escapism. However, when death is the ultimate price for a sense of freedom, the viewer is asked to question the ethics of opting out of the mainstream and going solo.

The Last Picture Show

Nothing much happens in the Texan town of Anarene, well nothing very different from thousands of other small towns scattered across America. But that's the beauty of this film; it's the quintessential uniformity and conformity that makes space for the growth of the quirky characters and the retelling of events in a certain place at a certain time; a snippet of history like any other, yet absolutely different.

Sam (Johnson) owns the town's only picture house, the Royal Theater, and this is the hub of much activity, not least the attempted seduction of Jacy Farrow (Shepherd) by the local adolescent boys. What the boys don't realize is that girls like Jacy take advantage by letting the boys take advantage and she is well aware of her sexuality and the way in which to use it to best further her plans. Two prospective beaux are friends Sonny (Bottoms) and Duane (Bridges) who are typical of high school boys across the generations in their predominant interest in cars and girls, but neither of them really has a genuine chance with Jacy who is on the lookout for her meal ticket.

As time slips by and life plods along in Anarene, the event of note is that the picture house is closed, rendered superfluous by the influx of the television set. In a town noticeably void of action or incident this in itself represents a changing era as people become even more insulated and housebound.

Bogdanovich was only thirty one when he directed this, his second feature film, and he really succeeds in creating just the right atmosphere, helped by a somewhat brave decision to choose relatively unknown actors.

USA, 1971
DIRECTOR:
Peter Bogdanovich
CAST INCLUDES:
Timothy Bottoms, Jeff Bridges,
Cybill Shepherd, Ben Johnson,
Cloris Leachman, Ellen Burstyn
SCREENPLAY:
Larry McMurtry,
Peter Bogdanovich from the novel
by Larry McMurtry
CINEMATOGRAPHY:
Robert Surtees
PRODUCERS/
PRODUCTION COMPANIES:
Stephen J. Friedman, Harold
Schneider, Bert Schneider/
BBS Productions, Columbia
Pictures Corporation
ACADEMY AWARD
NOMINATIONS (1972)
Best Actor in a Supporting Role:
Jeff Bridges
Best Actress in a Supporting Role:
Ellen Burstyn
Best Cinematography:
Robert Surtees
Best Director: Peter Bogdanovich
Best Picture: Stephen J. Friedman
Best Writing, Screenplay Based on
Material from Another
Medium:James Lee Barrett,
Peter Bogdanovich
ACADEMY AWARDS
Best Actor in a Supporting Role:
Ben Johnson
Best Actress in a Supporting Role:
Cloris Leachman

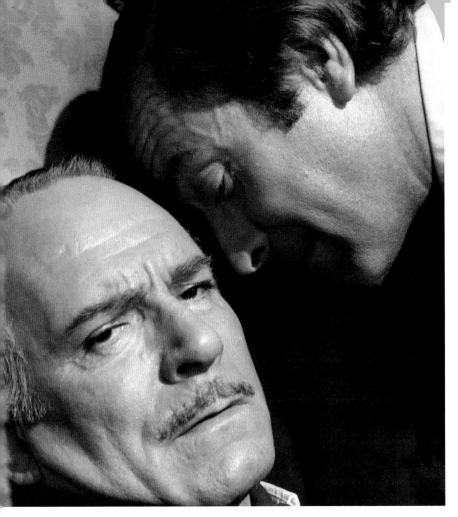

Sleuth

Sleuth is the story of an extravagant game played out over the course of a weekend between two men; Andrew Wyke (Olivier) and Milo Tindle (Caine). Wyke is an author with upper class leanings, whilst the working class Tindle is clawing his way up the business ladder with his chain of hair salons. What links these men beyond all else is Tindle's affair with Wyke's wife and, although Wyke has had his fun with her and is happy to grant a divorce, he is also slighted by the affair. On the initial premise of pulling off an insurance scam by setting up a mock burglary, the men soon become intent on outwitting each other and proving their worth so that, as the weekend wears on, the stakes become higher and the rules of the game are pushed ever forward.

Based on a play, the theatrical overtones are all too obvious as the majority of the film sees the two leads acting alone, against a simple backdrop, allowing both men to explore their characters in excruciating detail. The viewer benefits by witnessing a textbook acting lesson from the actors, as they are able to build their performances to a crescendo, with not a second of superfluous screen time.

It's a credit to director Mankiewicz that he keeps the minimalist elements intact, in terms of characters and locations. Great casting, a tight screenplay and sensitive directing all add up to produce a memorable film that the actors can count amongst their best work.

GB, 1972
DIRECTOR:
Joseph L. Mankiewicz
CAST INCLUDES:
Laurence Olivier, Michael Caine,
Alec Cawthorne, John Matthews,
Eve Channing, Teddy Martin
SCREENPLAY:
Anthony Shaffer
CINEMATOGRAPHY:
Oswald Morris
**PRODUCERS/
PRODUCTION COMPANIES:**
Morton Gottlieb, David Middlemas,
Edgar J. Scherick/Palomar Pictures
**ACADEMY AWARD
NOMINATIONS (1973)**
Best Actor in a Leading Role:
Michael Caine
Best Actor in a Leading Role:
Laurence Olivier
Best Director: Joseph L. Mankiewicz
Best Music, Original Dramatic Score:
John Addison

Nashville

With songs galore throughout the entire film, we are thrown
headfirst into America's country music capital, whilst witnessing
the machinations of the presidential candidate elections.
Comebacks, showdowns, backstabbing and heartbreak are all par
for the course in this all singing, all dancing epic that was
actually shot on location in Nashville, inevitably bringing a strong
sense of realism to the docu-style piece.

Robert Altman (*The Player*, *Gosford Park*), is the archetypal
large-cast director and *Nashville* is no exception. He seems to
relish the task of introducing as many characters as the plot can
physically handle, then giving them all the space to develop,
rather than having most of them blend into the backdrop as little
more than extras.

With a title that is as much statement as insight, *Nashville* is
an anomalous mix of music and politics; potentially strange
bedfellows but ones that produce an exceptional film at the
hands of this master craftsman. In a virtually unprecedented
move amongst directors, Altman made no changes to Joan
Tewkesbury's script, a
move which obviously
paid off and showed a
great deal of cinematic
altruism and a
perceptive eye. The
storylines interweave
naturally but the
separate strands and
relationships between
them are too intricate
to begin to analyze.
Needless to say,
everything comes
together to form a toe-
tapping story of great
magnitude, where the
characters are larger
than life and dish up a
real slice of America.

USA, 1975
DIRECTOR:
Robert Altman
CAST INCLUDES:
David Arkin, Barbara Baxley,
Ned Beatty, Karen Black,
Ronee Blakley, Timothy Brown
SCREENPLAY:
Joan Tewkesbury
CINEMATOGRAPHY:
Paul Lohmann
**PRODUCERS/
PRODUCTION COMPANIES:**
Robert Altman, Scott Bushnell,
Robert Eggenweiler, Martin Starger,
Jerry Weintraub/American
Broadcasting Company (ABC),
Paramount Pictures
**ACADEMY AWARD
NOMINATIONS (1976)**
Best Actress in a Supporting Role:
Ronee Blakley
Best Actress in a Supporting Role:
Lily Tomlin
Best Director: Robert Altman
Best Picture: Robert Altman
ACADEMY AWARDS
Best Music, Original Song: Keith
Carradine, for the song 'I'm Easy'

One Flew over the Cuckoo's Nest

When petty criminal R.P. McMurphy (Nicholson) opts for a stint in a pyschiatric hospital over a prison sentence, he believes he's getting off lightly. A natural free spirit and no passive accepter of authority, it isn't long before he is trying to rebel against the dominating and degrading atmosphere that is largely controlled by the austere Nurse Ratched (Fletcher).

In a film that clearly wears its heart on its sleeve when dealing with the difficult subject of mental health and its treatment, this is really only a sub-plot to the central theme; the subjugation of the individual and his or her enforced conformity to the rules of society. Nicholson plays the part of the subversive anarchist with suburb intuition, proving beyond reasonable doubt that if people have their identities removed and their problems pigeon-holed, they lose the very human traits that mould them as individuals. McMurphy provides an alternative path for some of the patients, showing them snippets of the life they deserve; a brief glimpse of the freedoms most of them will never enjoy.

In the end, McMurphy's undermining of the hospital rules leads to his own downfall as he is kept on as a patient and prescribed treatments that will inevitably take away his individuality and worse. *One Flew over the Cuckoo's Nest* was the first film in forty one years to win all five of the top Academy Awards which is a considerable feat considering that it very nearly didn't get made.

USA, 1975
DIRECTOR:
Milos Forman
CAST INCLUDES:
Jack Nicholson, Louise Fletcher,
William Redfield, Michael Berryman,
Peter Brocco
SCREENPLAY:
Bo Goldman and Lawrence Hauben
from the novel by Ken Kesey
CINEMATOGRAPHY:
Haskell Wexler
PRODUCERS/
PRODUCTION COMPANIES:
Michael Douglas, Saul Zaentz,
Martin Fink/Fantasy Films,
N.V. Zvaluw
ACADEMY AWARD
NOMINATIONS (1976)
Best Actor in a Supporting Role:
Brad Dourif
Best Cinematography:
Haskell Wexler, Bill Butler
Best Film Editing: Richard Chew,
Lynzee Klingman, Sheldon Kahn
Best Music, Original Score:
Jack Nitzsche
ACADEMY AWARDS
Best Actor in a Leading Role:
Jack Nicholson
Best Actress in a Leading Role:
Louise Fletcher
Best Director: Milos Forman
Best Picture: Saul Zaentz,
Michael Douglas
Best Writing, Screenplay Adapted
From Other Material:
Lawrence Hauben, Bo Goldman

All the President's Men

When junior reporters Carl Bernstein (Hoffman) and Bob Woodward (Redford) are sent to cover the trial of the burglary at National Democratic Headquarters, they end up exposing the biggest scandal in the history of American politics and one that eventually led to the resignation of President Nixon.

Penned by seasoned screenwriter William Goldman (*Butch Cassidy and the Sundance Kid*), *All the President's Men* is essentially a film that charts the perseverance and doggedness of the reporters, to try and discover the truth, despite the many obstacles placed in their path. As such, it sings the praises of investigative journalism as an essential and necessary public function, bringing to light corruption and high-level political scandal. Their progress is almost thwarted on a number of occasions, not least by the pedantic editor of the *Washington Post*, who is loathe to publish any accusations without full 'on the record' back-up. Salvation comes in the form of the dubiously-named 'Deep Throat' (Holbrook) whose true identity is kept a closely-guarded secret, but who points them in the right direction and provides them with enough information to be able to expose the Watergate scandal in the newspaper eventually.

Hoffman and Redford are both at the peak of their talents here, working off one another to produce an exciting, highly-charged race against time, as they try not only to ensure they collect enough evidence to break the story, but that another newspaper doesn't get there before them.

USA, 1976
DIRECTOR:
Alan J. Pakula
CAST INCLUDES:
Dustin Hoffman, Robert Redford,
Jack Warden, Martin Balsam,
Hal Holbrook
SCREENPLAY:
William Goldman from the book by
Carl Bernstein and Bob Woodward
CINEMATOGRAPHY:
Gordon Willis
**PRODUCERS/
PRODUCTION COMPANIES:**
Walter Coblenz,Jon Boorstin,
Michael Britton/ Warner Bros.,
Wildwood
ACADEMY AWARDS (1977)
Best Actor in a Supporting Role:
Jason Robards
Best Art Direction-Set Decoration:
George Jenkins, George Gaines
Best Sound: Arthur Piantadosi,
Les Fresholtz, Rick Alexander as
Dick Alexander, James E. Webb
Best Writing, Screenplay Based on
Material from Another Medium:
William Goldman

Rocky

USA, 1976
DIRECTOR:
John G. Avildsen
CAST INCLUDES:
Sylvester Stallone, Talia Shire,
Burt Young, Carl Weathers,
Burgess Meredith
SCREENPLAY:
Sylvester Stallone
CINEMATOGRAPHY:
James Crabe
PRODUCERS/
PRODUCTION COMPANIES:
Robert Chartoff,
Irwin Winkler, Gene Kirkwood/
Chartoff-Winkler Productions,
United Artists
ACADEMY AWARD
NOMINATIONS (1977)
Best Actor in a Leading Role:
Sylvester Stallone
Best Actor in a Supporting Role:
Burt Young
Best Actor in a Supporting Role:
Burgess Meredith
Best Actress in a Leading Role:
Talia Shire
Best Music, Original Song:
Bill Conti/music, Carol
Connors/lyrics, Ayn Robbins/ lyrics,
For the song 'Gonna Fly Now'
Best Sound: Harry W. Tetrick,
William L. McCaughey,
Lyle J. Burbridge, Bud Alper
Best Writing, Screenplay Written
Directly for the Screen:
Sylvester Stallone
ACADEMY AWARDS
Best Director: John G. Avildsen
Best Film Editing: Richard Halsey,
Scott Conrad
Best Picture: Irwin Winkler,
Robert Chartoff

When local boxer Rocky gets a once in a lifetime stab at the heavyweight championship, it's almost a given that he'll lose. Male pride and a misguided sense of possibility propel Rocky into one of the most famous workouts the big screen has ever known, with the underdog giving it his all for this one chance at the big time. It's a clichéd and much-used storyline that nevertheless manages to suspend our disbelief for the likeable guy who might, just might, be able to prove them all wrong.

Rocky is one of those archetypal feel-good films where, from the opening credits, you're cheering for the protagonist, and you know that in the end, everything's going to be alright. Sylvester Stallone wrote and starred in the film that secured his status as a household name and he did a such a great job of creating a character that he moulded into so perfectly, that it's difficult, even now, to separate the two.

Underlying the main boxing theme is the love story between Rocky and Adrian (Shire) and this adds a secondary emotional and human aspect to the hero, creating the sense that he's doing it all for love, to better himself for his girlfriend. It certainly gives Rocky a lot more depth to his character, elevating him from aspirational sportsman to all round Mr Nice Guy. It also implies that if everything goes wrong, there is emotional back-up for Rocky, that boxing is not his sole reason for getting up in the morning. The film requires this sub-plot to fully engage the viewer in more ways than simply building up to a great fight-scene finale.

Kramer vs. Kramer

Ted Kramer (Hoffman) is a workaholic. He has a great job in advertizing and, like many fathers, has sacrificed quality time with his only son, in order to pursue his career. When his wife Joanna (Streep) announces that she's leaving him, Ted is not only left with the devastation of a marriage break-up, but the added complication of becoming a single parent. It's back to basics for Ted who has to actually get to know his son at the same time as getting to know his way around the kitchen.

Kramer vs. Kramer is the definitive divorce film, tackling all the issues head on, with a gritty realism that really puts forward both painful sides of the argument. We feel for Ted, as he juggles work and home life, pretty unsuccessfully to begin with, clumsily finding his feet, only to be told by his son, 'Mommy doesn't do it like that'. But we equally appreciate the dilemma of a woman who feels she has been forgotten and that she must find some happiness for herself. As Ted finally learns what his priorities are, his career suffers and eventually he's demoted, unable to cut the mustard in a workplace that frowns upon the notion of a man as father first, worker second. When Joanna announces she wants custody of their son, Ted is adamant that he's proven himself capable of being a loving, caring parent and is loathe to give up the son he has grown to love beyond expression.

There is no simple conclusion to such a dilemma and Benton deals with it admirably. It's heartbreaking – should Ted be rewarded for breaking the mould and sacrificing everything to care for his son?

USA, 1979
DIRECTOR:
Robert Benton
CAST INCLUDES:
Dustin Hoffman, Meryl Streep,
Jane Alexander, Justin Henry,
Howard Duff
SCREENPLAY:
Robert Benton from the novel by
Avery Corman
CINEMATOGRAPHY:
Néstor Almendros
PRODUCERS/
PRODUCTION COMPANIES:
Stanley R. Jaffe, Richard Fischoff/
Columbia Pictures Corporation
ACADEMY AWARD
NOMINATIONS (1980)
Best Actor in a Supporting Role:
Justin Henry
Best Actress in a Supporting Role:
Jane Alexander
Best Cinematography:
Néstor Almendros
Best Film Editing:
Gerald B. Greenberg
ACADEMY AWARDS
Best Actor in a Leading Role:
Dustin Hoffman
Best Actress in a Supporting Role:
Meryl Streep
Best Director: Robert Benton
Best Picture: Stanley R. Jaffe
Best Writing, Screenplay Based on
Material from Another Medium:
Robert Benton

Raging Bull

Martin Scorsese's finest hour came about thanks to the real-life story of boxer Jake LaMotta (De Niro). Ostensibly a film charting the highs and lows of the boxer's tumultuous career, it is actually so much more. It could reasonably be argued that the boxing ring is simply a symbolic parallel for LaMotta's life outside it, a physical manifestation of the lifetime battle he fought with his personal demons.

The harrowing but visually stunning fight scenes were both inspired and gruelling, taking much longer to film than anticipated. However, both Scorsese and De Niro's pedantic attention to detail paid off, and they were rewarded with the greatest fight sequences to ever grace a cinema screen.

As LaMotta punches his way to supremacy in the ring, his acute jealousy over his wife consumes his very being and she ends up on the receiving end of his knockout blows. With no grounds for his suspicions, he is left with nothing but his own neuroses as a justification for his deplorable actions against the one constant in his life. As with so many greats, LaMotta's downfall is swift and unforgiving. He takes his beatings in a subservient way, accepting his punishment and his flawed character with a poignancy that doesn't demand sympathy but is deserving of pity.

Like many of the difficult roles De Niro has taken on in his career, he put everything he had into the preparation for *Raging Bull*, spending a lot of time with LaMotta, as he psyched himself up to play this mentally and physically draining part. He certainly did it justice.

USA, 1980
DIRECTOR:
Martin Scorsese
CAST INCLUDES:
Robert De Niro, Cathy Moriarty,
Joe Pesci, Frank Vincent,
Nicholas Colasanto, Theresa Saldana
SCREENPLAY:
Paul Schrader, Mardik Martin
from the book by
Jake LaMotta,
Joseph Carter and Peter Savage
CINEMATOGRAPHY:
Michael Chapman
**PRODUCERS/
PRODUCTION COMPANIES:**
Robert Chartoff, Irwin Winkler,
Hal W. Polaire, Peter Savage/
Chartoff-Winkler Productions
**ACADEMY AWARD
NOMINATIONS (1981)**
Best Actor in a Supporting Role:
Joe Pesci
Best Actress in a Supporting Role:
Cathy Moriarty
Best Cinematography:
Michael Chapman
Best Director: Martin Scorsese
Best Picture: Irwin Winkler,
Robert Chartoff
Best Sound: Donald O. Mitchell,
Bill Nicholson, David J. Kimball,
Les Lazarowitz
ACADEMY AWARDS
Best Actor in a Leading Role:
Robert De Niro
Best Film Editing:
Thelma Schoonmaker

The King of Comedy

Some people will do just about anything to get their fifteen minutes of fame and Rupert Pupkin (De Niro) is one of them. Absolutely convinced of his prowess as a stand-up comedian, Rupert is just looking for his one shot at the big time and he firmly believes that his talent will take him from there. To facilitate this introduction to fame and fortune, he has handpicked Jerry Langford's show as his forum and just needs to persuade the host (Lewis) to give him a slot. The fact that he has never actually performed in front of an audience before doesn't seem to perturb him, but being snubbed by Jerry obviously does. Desperate times call for desperate measures and Rupert decides the only solution is to kidnap Jerry and make him give him the precious slot on the show.

In a rare departure from their usual genre, the dynamic duo Scorsese and De Niro create an ingenious comedy that manages to entertain whilst looking at a genuine phenomenon. De Niro is wonderful as the desperate, starstruck Rupert, excusing his actions on the grounds of necessity and wowing the audience sufficiently when the time comes. Rupert does get his fifteen minutes and a whole lot more to boot, Scorsese clearly telling us what we already know about the crazy world of celebrity worship. Everyone's cheering for the insane kidnapping comic in the end, exactly as we're supposed to.

USA, 1983
DIRECTOR:
Martin Scorsese
CAST INCLUDES:
Robert De Niro, Jerry Lewis, Diahnne Abbott, Sandra Bernhard, Shelley Hack
SCREENPLAY:
Paul D. Zimmerman
CINEMATOGRAPHY:
Fred Schuler
PRODUCERS/ PRODUCTION COMPANIES:
Arnon Milchan, Robert F. Colesberry, Robert Greenhut/ 20th Century Fox, Embassy International Pictures

Fatal Attraction

USA, 1987
DIRECTOR:
Adrian Lyne
CAST INCLUDES:
Michael Douglas, Glenn Close,
Anne Archer, Ellen Hamilton Latzen,
Stuart Pankin
SCREENPLAY:
James Dearden, Nicholas Meyer
CINEMATOGRAPHY:
Howard Atherton
PRODUCERS/
PRODUCTION COMPANIES:
Stanley R. Jaffe, Sherry Lansing/
Paramount Pictures
ACADEMY AWARD
NOMINATIONS (1988)
Best Actress in a Leading Role:
Glenn Close
Best Actress in a Supporting Role:
Anne Archer
Best Director: Adrian Lyne
Best Film Editing: Michael Kahn,
Peter E. Berger
Best Picture: Stanley R. Jaffe,
Sherry Lansing
Best Writing, Screenplay Based on
Material from Another Medium:
James Dearden

Dan Gallagher (Douglas) is a happily married man with absolutely no reason to have a one-night stand. Of course, that's often reason enough in itself, but when combined with the sense of risk, the excitement and the flattery, and because he knows he can get away it, the temptation proves too great. Whatever the reason, it will be a decision he will live to regret for the rest of his life.

In a gripping reversal of the traditional male/female roles generally adhered to in this genre, the charismatic and sexually daring Alex (Close), becomes obsessed with Dan following their night together, eschewing all the unwritten rules that are taken as read between two people embarking upon one spontaneous, commitment-free night of passion. As her true unstable psyche becomes apparent, Dan's moment of reckless bravado results in a far more serious consequence than merely cheating on his wife. He has put her life in danger, as well as that of his daughter.

Lyne is blatant in his views on the whole scenario and the film's message is clear. However, the suspense transforms a relatively clean-cut premise into a layered film with Hitchcockian overtones and tense, character-driven moments. And who can possibly forget the rabbit scene?

Dangerous Liaisons

If you want to see the best example of an actor who is absolutely convincing and practically born to play a certain role, watch John Malkovich in *Dangerous Liaisons*. His potent mix of sensual provocateur and evil manipulator is truly mesmerizing and the crackling rapport between Malkovich and Close is exquisite.

Set in 18th Century France, the lavishly decadent backdrop provides a rich source of visual endorsement for the blatant innuendo and mischievous undertones of a script sharpened to a knife edge. Our bored leads get sadistic pleasure out of the corruption of relationships and, having once been in one together, they are now famously free from the constraints of love and bitter enough to destroy the happiness of others by whatever means they can.

The vicomte (Malkovich) is no classic oil painting, but his magnetism is hard to resist and he delights in his position of power as he takes on a bet to seduce the beautiful but naïve young Cecile (Thurman), stealing her virginity before her impending marriage. He almost finds the challenge beneath him, as she proves to be corrupted so easily. However, the arrival of Madame de Tourvel (Pfeiffer) throws a veritable spanner in the works, as the vicomte realizes that he isn't actually immune to the power of love.

You can't help but have a certain amount of reserved admiration for the brazen vicomte and his accomplice, as they swirl around in a grandiose manner amongst the pettiness of frivolous high society.

USA/GB, 1988
DIRECTOR:
Stephen Frears
CAST INCLUDES:
Glenn Close, John Malkovich,
Michelle Pfeiffer, Swoosie Kurtz,
Keanu Reeves, Mildred Natwick,
Uma Thurman
SCREENPLAY:
Christopher Hampton from his play
and the novel by Choderlos de Laclos
CINEMATOGRAPHY:
Philippe Rousselot
PRODUCERS/
PRODUCTION COMPANIES:
Norma Heyman, Hank Moonjean,
Christopher Hampton/Lorimar Film
Entertainment, NFH Productions,
Warner Bros. [us]
ACADEMY AWARD
NOMINATIONS (1989)
Best Actress in a Leading Role:
Glenn Close
Best Actress in a Supporting Role:
Michelle Pfeiffer
Best Music, Original Score:
George Fenton
Best Picture: Norma Heyman,
Hank Moonjean
ACADEMY AWARDS
Best Art Direction-Set Decoration:
Stuart Craig, Gérard James
Best Costume Design:
James Acheson
Best Writing, Screenplay Based on
Material from Another Medium:
Christopher Hampton

Rain Man

USA, 1988
DIRECTOR:
Barry Levinson
CAST INCLUDES:
Dustin Hoffman, Tom Cruise,
Valeria Golino, Gerald R. Molen,
Jack Murdock
SCREENPLAY:
Ronald Bass, Barry Morrow from
his story
CINEMATOGRAPHY:
John Seale
**PRODUCERS/
PRODUCTION COMPANIES:**
Mark Johnson, Gerald R. Molen,
David McGiffert, Gail Mutrux,
Peter Guber, Jon Peters/
Guber Peters Company,
Mirage Entertainment,
Star Partners II Limited
**ACADEMY AWARD
NOMINATIONS (1989)**
Best Art Direction-Set Decoration:
Ida Random, Linda DeScenna
Best Cinematography:
John Seale
Best Film Editing:
Stu Linder
Best Music, Original Score:
Hans Zimmer
ACADEMY AWARDS
Best Actor in a Leading Role:
Dustin Hoffman
Best Director: Barry Levinson
Best Picture: Mark Johnson
Best Writing, Original Screenplay:
Ronald Bass, Barry Morrow

When Charlie Babbit's (Cruise) father dies, he is left with more than he bargained for. In lieu of money or property, Charlie discovers instead that he has an older brother, Raymond (Hoffman) who he knew nothing about and who has been left the lion's share of the inheritance.

The film plots the initial determination of Charlie to avail himself of his entitled share of his father's estate, but matters are complicated by the discovery that his brother is autistic and he must first learn how to communicate with him, gain his trust and try to understand him, before he can wheedle the fortune away from him. The brilliance of the film is borne out more in its simplicity than any daring attempts at boundary breaking. For the most part, the audience and Charlie are simultaneously learning about Raymond's condition, becoming by turn shocked, amazed and distressed by the intricacies of this hitherto little understood affliction.

The irony occurs when it becomes apparent that Raymond has no appreciation of money and, from Charlie's perspective at least, this means he has no use for his inheritance. However, as they travel across the country together, a mutual understanding does develop between the two men and with it, a brotherly bond begins to emerge, putting a slight damper on Charlie's plan to simply relieve Raymond of his fortune. Dustin Hoffman takes character acting to a new level in this film and the rapport between the two leads is the ultimate secret of its success.

Do the Right Thing

Sal's Pizzeria has been trading for twenty years and now represents one of just a couple of white businesses in a black area. Tensions begin to surface in the most innocuous way, when local activist Buggin' Out (Esposito) berates the fact that owner Sal (Aiello), exclusively has photos of white people on his board of fame in the restaurant; where are the African-American heroes? History has proved time and again that the smallest incident can lead to the biggest confrontations and this is a great match to use to ignite the flame of racial violence.

This was one of the most open, honest and realistic discussions of race in America at its time of release. Spike Lee, known for courting controversy, didn't let the critics down with this film, in which violence erupts in a normally quiet Brooklyn neighbourhood. Without prophesying, condoning or condemning, Lee merely tells it like it is, leaving the viewer to put their own spin on the whys and wherefores of racial tension and integration in American inner cities. The story occurs against the backdrop of the hottest day of summer and there are definite symbolic overtones with regard to temperatures and tempers racing towards boiling point, both in this isolated incident and as a reflection of America in general. It's a clever metaphor that allows Lee to push people over the edge in a way that seems justified.

Do the Right Thing is a film that makes you sit up and pay attention, reflecting on its message long after the credits roll. And if that's not the mark of a great film, then nothing is.

USA, 1989
DIRECTOR:
Spike Lee
CAST INCLUDES:
Danny Aiello, Ossie Davis, Ruby Dee, Richard Edson, Giancarlo Esposito, Spike Lee
SCREENPLAY:
Spike Lee
CINEMATOGRAPHY:
Ernest R. Dickerson
PRODUCERS/ PRODUCTION COMPANIES:
Spike Lee, Monty Ross/40 Acres & a Mule Filmworks
ACADEMY AWARD NOMINATIONS (1990)
Best Actor in a Supporting Role: Danny Aiello
Best Writing, Screenplay Written Directly for the Screen: Spike Lee

Raise the Red Lantern
Da hong deng long gao gao gua

**CHINA/HONG KONG/
TAIWAN, 1991**
DIRECTOR:
Yimou Zhang
CAST INCLUDES:
Li Gong, Caifei He, Jingwu Ma,
Cuifen Cao, Qi Zhao
SCREENPLAY
Ni Zhen from the novel by Su Tong
CINEMATOGRAPHY
Zhao Fei, Lun Yang
**PRODUCERS/PRODUCTION
COMPANIES:**
Fu-Sheng Chiu, Hsiao-hsien Hou,
Wenze Zhang/ Century
Communications, China Film
Co-Production Corporation, ERA
International, Salon Films
ACADEMY AWARDS (1992)
Best Foreign Language Film
(Hong Kong)

When Songlian (Gong) arrives at her new home it is not with a sense of happy anticipation but one of resigned acceptance. The fourth wife of a wealthy Chinese man, Songlian had different ideas about where her future might take her, but her mother offered her as a concubine and she was unable to refuse. *Raise the Red Lantern* is dramatic in its scope, using cinematography and the limited locations it conveys the sense of a comfortable prison; this is basically how the four women live, each trying to curry favour with the master of the house, replicating that which occurs in everyday life within the confines of their quarters.

The film teaches us about the life of the concubine but it also illustrates human emotion and adaptability; these women have accepted their future and they learn to fight for their survival,

much as they would in the outside world, of which, incidentally, they know nothing. If they are antagonistic or ambivalent towards the newest addition to the household, it's because they fear for their own position in the miniature hierarchy that has been created amongst them.

The film takes its name from the red lantern – a device the master employs to signal which of his wives will be graced with his presence on any evening. As passing time is denoted by a change in the weather conditions, we are made painfully aware that life is trickling by, but then life trickles by whether you're a concubine or a free woman.

Glengarry, Glen Ross

Estate agents are often at the receiving end of ranting tirades about time wasting, money-grabbing and superficiality. Here we get to see behind the scenes of one particular agency and discover that the smiles are fake, the confidence erroneously bolstered and the big bucks elusive, to say the least.

Based on a play by David Mamet who based his play on his own experiences, *Glengarry, Glen Ross* is a sad tale of desperate men trying to sell real estate to people who don't want to buy it. The rules of supply and demand are disproportionately unbalanced against these pitiable individuals as they sell their very souls for the possibility of a commission. The leads are out of date, but it's all they have to go on, so they plod on with the cold-calling, hoping for a miracle. When Blake (Baldwin), the man with the silver sales tongue, arrives in the office to announce a new contest, they only sink lower into their mire of despondency as, this time, their jobs are on the line; win and you get a Cadillac, lose and you're out.

With its all-star cast, this film couldn't fail but to procure a certain positive following, however this doesn't necessarily result in timeless appreciation. What Foley and his cast have achieved is that perfect combination of talent and altruistic acting, which allows each man's ability to really shine and bring the piece together, without ever focusing too specifically on the stars behind the characters.

USA, 1992
DIRECTOR:
James Foley
CAST INCLUDES:
Jack Lemmon, Al Pacino, Ed Harris, Alan Arkin, Kevin Spacey, Alec Baldwin
SCREENPLAY:
David Mamet from his play
CINEMATOGRAPHY:
Juan Ruiz Anchía
PRODUCERS/ PRODUCTION COMPANIES:
Jerry Tokofsky, Stanley R. Zupnik, Nava Levin, Morris Ruskin, Karen L. Oliver /GGR, New Line Cinema, Zupnik Cinema Group
ACADEMY AWARDS (1993)
Best Actor in a Supporting Role: Al Pacino

The Player

USA, 1992
DIRECTOR:
Robert Altman
CAST INCLUDES:
Tim Robbins, Greta Scacchi,
Fred Ward, Whoopi Goldberg,
Peter Gallagher
SCREENPLAY:
Michael Tolkin
CINEMATOGRAPHY:
Jean Lépine
PRODUCERS/
PRODUCTION COMPANIES:
David Brown, Michael Tolkin,
Nick Wechsler, Cary Brokaw ,
William S. Gilmore, David Levy/
Avenue Pictures Productions,
Guild, Spelling Entertainment
ACADEMY AWARD
NOMINATIONS (1993)
Best Director: Robert Altman
Best Film Editing: Geraldine Peroni
Best Writing, Screenplay Based on
Material from Another Medium:
Michael Tolkin

Studio Executive Griffin Mill (Robbins) is the man-who-can when it comes to getting films made. However, hot on his heels is Larry Levy (Gallagher), whose alliterated name and shameful ambition prove him to be a dangerous contender for Mill's pole position. Larry's takeover bid is strengthened somewhat by Mill's distress at being hounded by a writer bearing a grudge, which leaves him shaken and not quite on top form. When he receives one malicious postcard too many, he personally goes after the scribe he believes to be the culprit, but ends up killing him and becoming the subject of a manhunt.

Often discussed and used as a learning tool, Robert Altman's scathing satirical exposé of the Hollywood machine deserves its cult-like status. With potentially the most star-studded cast ever to appear together in a film (many doing so for a paltry sum), he creates a vapid world of superficial characters and wannabes, all clamouring to step onto whichever rung of the ladder they can lift their waxed, tanned and toned legs onto.

As the film progresses we see Mill falling for his victim's girlfriend (Scacchi), whilst being chased by a police force that includes Whoopi Goldberg and Lyle Lovett. Hollywood is sent up big time, from the lowly screenwriter to the top dog, in all its glitzy, glamorous, back-stabbing glory and one has to wonder whether any other director could have got away with it.

Forrest Gump

Forrest Gump (Hanks) is a bit slow, the conventional anti-hero going nowhere and destined to melt into life's background. However, he has a talent; he can run like the wind and, as physical prowess is as admirable a gift as academic brilliance, it appears there's nothing to stop Forrest from becoming a success. And so he embarks on a rather accidental tour of the highs and lows of 1960s and 1970s America, meeting US presidents, and becomes a college football star and a Vietnam war hero in the process.

Forrest is essentially the embodiment of the ordinary man, showing that we can all do our bit to change the world. The film is a bit of a potted history of mid-twentieth century America, with a definite positive vibe being attributed to the country's various episodes, a feel-good, pat on the back for the stars and stripes. However, the amazing special effects elevate the film to something much greater than a simple re-telling of events, as archive footage is used to fantastic effect to place Forrest right in the thick of the action. Underlying the whole story are Forrest's feelings for Jenny (Wright), the girl who he's loved since childhood and it becomes apparent that he's doing everything for her.

Forrest Gump captured the hearts and imaginations of millions of cinema-goers, as the message made clear that everyone can be a hero, everyone can live their dreams.

USA, 1994
DIRECTOR:
Robert Zemeckis
CAST INCLUDES:
Tom Hanks, Robin Wright Penn, Gary Sinise, Mykelti Williamson, Sally Field
SCREENPLAY:
Eric Roth from the novel by Winston Groom
CINEMATOGRAPHY:
Don Burgess
PRODUCERS/ PRODUCTION COMPANIES:
Wendy Finerman, Steve Starkey, Steve Tisch/Paramount Pictures
ACADEMY AWARD NOMINATIONS (1995)
Best Actor in a Supporting Role: Gary Sinise
Best Art Direction-Set Decoration: Rick Carter, Nancy Haigh
Best Cinematography: Don Burgess
Best Effects, Sound Effects Editing: Gloria S. Borders, Randy Thom
Best Makeup: Daniel C. Striepeke, Hallie D'Amore, Judith A. Cory
Best Music, Original Score: Alan Silvestri
Best Sound: Randy Thom, Tom Johnson, Dennis S. Sands, William B. Kaplan
ACADEMY AWARDS
Best Actor in a Leading Role: Tom Hanks
Best Director: Robert Zemeckis
Best Effects, Visual Effects: Ken Ralston, George Murphy, Stephen Rosenbaum, Allen Hall
Best Film Editing: Arthur Schmidt
Best Picture: Wendy Finerman, Steve Starkey, Steve Tisch
Best Writing, Screenplay Based on Material from Another Medium: Eric Roth

The Shawshank Redemption

USA, 1994
DIRECTOR:
Frank Darabont
CAST INCLUDES:
Tim Robbins, Morgan Freeman,
Bob Gunton, William Sadler,
Clancy Brown
SCREENPLAY:
Frank Darabont, based on the short
story *Rita Hayworth* and *Shawshank
Redemption* by Stephen King
CINEMATOGRAPHY:
Roger Deakins
**PRODUCERS/
PRODUCTION COMPANIES:**
Niki Marvin, Liz Glotzer, David V.
Lester/Castle Rock Entertainment,
Columbia Pictures Corporation.
**ACADEMY AWARD
NOMINATIONS (1995)**
Best Actor in a Leading Role:
Tim Robbins
Best Cinematography: Roger Deakins
Best Film Editing:
Richard Francis-Bruce
Best Music, Original Score:
Thomas Newman
Best Sound: Robert J. Litt,
Elliot Tyson, Michael Herbick,
Willie D. Burton
Best Writing, Screenplay Based on
Material from Another Medium:
Frank Darabont
Best Picture: Niki Marvin

When Andy Dufresne's wife and her lover are found murdered, having been shot in bed, her husband (Robbins) is the prime suspect. This supposition swiftly becomes assumption, as it emerges that Andy had discovered the affair and the couple had a heated, alcohol-fuelled argument shortly before the murders took place. When circumstantial evidence is added to the obvious motive, the only possible outcome is a conviction. And so, as Andy begins his life sentence in Shawshank Jail, the film begins in earnest.

The Shawshank Redemption examines issues such as hope, despair, friendships in times of adversity and the harsh realities of a life sentence. However, it is human resilience that is lingered on throughout the film and, for this to be fully explored, Andy is paired up with the reflective 'Red' (Freeman) who provides the voice-over to Andy's silent initiation and eventual apparent resignation to his situation. Andy is the archetypal example of just how much physical and mental torment human beings can endure and, like everyone else in prison, Andy learns to get by. His business background and obvious education elevates him to a certain status, as he takes on the role of accountant to the prison's staff. Despite this surface display of equality, it isn't long before Andy is reminded, in no uncertain terms, that he will always be a con, inferior to all but fellow cons, regardless of his brain. However, it is Andy who has the last laugh.

The Shawshank Redemption arrived quietly then escalated as word spread and people fell in love with this simple tale of human traits.

Apollo 13

USA, 1995
DIRECTOR:
Ron Howard
CAST INCLUDES:
Tom Hanks, Bill Paxton, Kevin Bacon,
Gary Sinise, Ed Harris
SCREENPLAY:
William Broyles Jr., Al Reinert from
the book *Lost Moon* by Jim Lovell
and Jeffrey Kluger
CINEMATOGRAPHY:
Dean Cundey
**PRODUCERS/
PRODUCTION COMPANIES:**
Brian Grazer,
Todd Hallowell, Michael Bostick,
Aldric La'Auli Porte, Louisa Velis/
Imagine Entertainment,
Universal Pictures
**ACADEMY AWARD
NOMINATIONS (1996)**
Best Actor in a Supporting Role:
Ed Harris
Best Actress in a Supporting Role:
Kathleen Quinlan
Best Art Direction-Set Decoration:
Michael Corenblith, Merideth Boswell
Best Effects, Visual Effects:
Robert Legato, Michael Kanfer,
Leslie Ekker, Matt Sweeney
Best Music, Original Dramatic Score:
James Horner
Best Picture: Brian Grazer
Best Writing, Screenplay Based on
Material from Another Medium:
William Broyles Jr., Al Reinert
ACADEMY AWARDS
Best Film Editing: Mike Hill,
Daniel P. Hanley
Best Sound: Rick Dior,
Steve Pederson, Scott Millan,
David MacMillan

The subject of *Apollo 13* is exactly what the title suggests; the film charts the fraught thirteenth Apollo mission, undertaken in 1970. The very fact that the mission was unsuccessful immediately tells us that Howard was interested in the human story rather than any celebration of science and as this film is based on fact, he knew he had the basic structure and just needed to tackle it the right way.

By recreating the mission in excruciatingly accurate detail, the realism is accepted as a true representation and the audience can concentrate on the subject matter. Lovell (Hanks) takes the helm, accompanied by Haise (Paxton) and Swigert (Bacon), as they embark on their flight to the moon, only to have it abandoned partway when an oxygen tank explodes, leaving the three men in a desperate battle for their lives.

Despite the failure of the mission, the film is essentially a commendation of the space programme and a real American salute to the men and women who risk their lives to fulfil their dreams. We are exposed to the camaraderie, the rallying and the brave determination of these resolute individuals and we share their heartbreak when they realize it's not their turn to create history. Instead of walking on the moon they must gather their collective strength and do all they can to return to earth alive. They are helped by Gene Kranz (Harris) at Houston Mission Control and, as time ticks by, everyone becomes painfully aware that they are trapped in a volatile metal capsule that could become their coffin.

Shakespeare in Love

It seems fitting that a film about Shakespeare should be in the form of a comedy. After all, in his day, Shakespeare was a playwright for the masses, something that seems to have been forgotten with passing time. This is certainly a film for the masses, as its light-hearted look at fifteenth century writer's block humanizes Shakespeare as never before. It offers one interpretation of his life that certainly demystifies the often staid impressions we've conjured up of the great bard.

Will Shakespeare (Fiennes) is a dashing young playwright when we catch up with him, struggling to complete his latest work, *Romeo and Ethel, the Pirate's Daughter*. Viola de Lesseps (Paltrow) arrives on the scene to provide some much needed inspiration but she is betrothed to the Earl of Wessex (Firth), who is planning to whisk her off to America.

It's to its credit indeed that a film set in 1500s England can strike a chord today and this is certainly down to the well-structured and taut screenplay, co-penned by the hugely talented playwright, Tom Stoppard. There are numerous echoes of modern wit and we are shown that people essentially don't change all that much over the centuries. They laugh, they love, they work, they play and politics is omnipresent, albeit in the guise of an austere Queen Elizabeth I (Dench), who rules England's roost with an iron hand. It really is a charming feel-good film that will leave viewers with a fresh enthusiasm for the world's most famous wordsmith.

USA/GB, 1998
DIRECTOR:
John Madden
CAST INCLUDES:
Joseph Fiennes, Gwyneth Paltrow, Geoffrey Rush, Tom Wilkinson, Judi Dench, Colin Firth
SCREENPLAY:
Marc Norman and Tom Stoppard
CINEMATOGRAPHY:
Richard Greatrex
PRODUCERS/
PRODUCTION COMPANIES:
Donna Gigliotti, Marc Norman, David Parfitt, Harvey Weinstein, Edward Zwick, Bob Weinstein, Julie Goldstein/Bedford Falls Productions, Miramax Films, Universal Pictures
ACADEMY AWARD
NOMINATIONS (1999)
Best Actor in a Supporting Role: Geoffrey Rush
Best Cinematography: Richard Greatrex
Best Director: John Madden
Best Film Editing: Richard Gamble
Best Makeup: Lisa Westcott, Veronica Brebner
Best Sound: Robin O'Donoghue, Dominic Webber, Peter Glossop
ACADEMY AWARDS
Best Actress in a Leading Role: Gwyneth Paltrow
Best Actress in a Supporting Role: Judi Dench
Best Art Direction-Set Decoration: Martin Childs, Jill Quertier
Best Costume Design:Sandy Powell
Best Music, Original Musical or Comedy Score: Stephen Warbeck
Best Picture: David Parfitt, Donna Gigliotti, Harvey Weinstein, Edward Zwick, Marc Norman
Best Writing, Screenplay Written Directly for the Screen: Marc Norman, Tom Stoppard

The Truman Show

USA, 1998
DIRECTOR:
Peter Weir
CAST INCLUDES:
Jim Carrey, Laura Linney, Noah
Emmerich, Natascha McElhone,
Holland Taylor, Brian Delate
SCREENPLAY:
Andrew Niccol
CINEMATOGRAPHY:
Peter Biziou
PRODUCERS/
PRODUCTION COMPANIES:
Edward S. Feldman, Andrew Niccol,
Scott Rudin, Adam Schroeder,
Lynn Pleshette, Richard Luke
Rothschild/Paramount Pictures,
Scott Rudin Productions
ACADEMY AWARD
NOMINATIONS (2000)
Best Actor in a Supporting Role:
Ed Harris
Best Director: Peter Weir
Best Writing, Screenplay Written
Directly for the Screen:
Andrew Niccol

As the media pushed the boundaries of decency to their very limits, offering up the lives of other people as acceptable viewing fodder, along came *The Truman Show*. Although it didn't stop intrusive reality TV, it did at least make everyone sit up and start thinking about the need to enforce some limitations on just how far this form of 'entertainment' should be allowed to go.

Truman Burbank (Carrey) lives in a picture perfect world where he is surrounded by nice neighbours, a perfect wife (Linney) and the material trappings of a good job. What he isn't aware of however is that his every move is being broadcast to millions of viewers who put their own lives on hold as they sit down in front of the television to watch the mundane happenings in his. Adopted by the company that produces the show, Truman has only ever known the manufactured perfection of Seahaven and appears to be quite content with his lot until he falls for Sylvia (McElhone). Like all the other inhabitants of the town, apart from Truman, Sylvia is an actress, but when she starts to feel the same way about him she is swiftly removed from the set and a plausible excuse is concocted so that Truman isn't suspicious. When he isn't allowed to leave town, alarm bells start ringing and it isn't long before Truman realizes that things are amiss and the only reality he's ever known is about to be revealed as fake.

This is a truly original and extremely clever film that asks some pertinent questions about the world we live in. Carrey is wonderfully cast as Truman and is backed up by some great performances in the supporting cast.

All About My Mother
Todo Sobre mi Madre

Esteban (Azorin) has always wanted to learn the truth about the father he has never seen, but on the day his mother (Roth) finally decides to reveal the information, Esteban dies tragically before finding out what he has longed to know. A devastated Manuela embarks on a journey from Madrid to Barcelona in search of the missing man, befriending loners and misfits en route.

Almodóvar is the king of characterization and *All About My Mother* is no exception. The characters are quirky but realistically so. Who else could put a transvestite prostitute, a pregnant nun and a lesbian acting couple together in the same film and get away with it? It is the examination of the trials and tribulations of this disparate group and, more essentially, their experiences as women that form the crux of the story. As all the main characters necessarily have such different takes on the theme of womanhood, the film is never stilted or stereotypical. It is insightful, humorous and genuinely engaging.

Having once trodden the boards with Esteban's father, Manuela finds herself on stage once again, after procuring the part of understudy to a drug-addicted Nina. And so her life has come full circle and she is back in the theatre once more, childless again but full of both happy and bitter experiences that have caused her to develop into a different actress. All these women have suffered but we are led to believe that their experiences have shaped and moulded them into strong human beings and, more specifically, strong women.

SPAIN/FRANCE, 1999
DIRECTOR:
Pedro Almodóvar
CAST INCLUDES:
Cecilia Roth, Marisa Paredes, Candela Peña, Antonia San Juan, Penélope Cruz, Eloy Azorin
SCREENPLAY:
Pedro Almodóvar
CINEMATOGRAPHY:
Affonso Beato
PRODUCERS/
PRODUCTION COMPANIES:
Agustín Almodóvar, Michel Ruben/ El Deseo, France 2 Cinema, Renn Productions, Via Digital
ACADEMY AWARDS (2000)
Best Foreign Language Film (Spain)

American Beauty

When a film begins with the voice-over of a middle-aged man telling us that in a year from now he'll be dead, we know we are in for something different.

Lester Burnham (Spacey) is the quintessential middle-class white American, trapped in a life that has leached him of all passion and zeal. On the outside he has much to envy; great house, great lifestyle, attractive wife (Bening) and daughter, but, as we delve beneath the surface, we begin to realize that all is not roses in the Burnham household. His marriage has deteriorated into a campaign of snide comments and sarcasm, and his daughter is ambivalent towards him – an insult far greater than hate or rebellion. So when he catches the eye of her beautiful friend Angela, (Suvari), it's enough to give his sad existence a new lease of excitement and purpose.

Mendes' directorial debut was the archetypal nineties film that expressed the repressions of American suburbia, peering through the curtains like a raincoat-wearing voyeur and delving into the characters' lives in an intrusive manner. Lester's midlife sexual obsession is more wake-up call than realistic chase, giving him a whiff of the excitement he once experienced when life was more meaningful. Meanwhile, his unsatisfied wife embarks on an affair with a sleazy estate agent and his daughter becomes involved with the strange boy living across the road who videos her from his bedroom. Gradually the apparently quiet neighbourhood is revealed in all its quirky, ugly nakedness.

Although the premise of the film is to find out who murdered Lester, it's not really that important. The reason for his death and the road that takes each character towards a motive are the issues dealt with here.

USA, 1999
DIRECTOR:
Sam Mendes
CAST INCLUDES:
Kevin Spacey, Annette Bening,
Thora Birch, Wes Bentley,
Mena Suvari
SCREENPLAY:
Alan Ball
CINEMATOGRAPHY:
Conrad L. Hall
PRODUCERS/
PRODUCTION COMPANIES:
Dan Jinks, Bruce Cohen, Alan Ball,
Stan Wlodkowski/Dream Works SKG,
Jinks/Cohen Company
ACADEMY AWARD
NOMINATIONS (2000)
Best Actress in a Leading Role:
Annette Bening
Best Editing: Tariq Anwar
Best Music, Original Score:
Thomas Newman
ACADEMY AWARDS
Best Actor in a Leading Role:
Kevin Spacey
Best Cinematography:
Conrad L. Hall
Best Director: Sam Mendes
Best Picture: Bruce Cohen, Dan Jinks
Best Original Screenplay: Alan Ball

Traffic

Two narcotics cops intercept a huge drug delivery on the borders of Mexico, only to have the haul and glory taken from them by a General Salazar. Meanwhile, in America, Robert Wakefield (Douglas) is given the impossible but eagerly accepted task of clamping down on the drug problem. Throw into the mix a group of privileged kids getting high on cocaine and wealthy housewife Helena La Jolla (Zeta-Zones) unknowingly lunching on the proceeds of her husband's drug deals and you have a film that really delves into all sides of the seedy world of drugs, from every possible perspective.

Originally a mini-television series written by Simon Moore, *Traffik* was developed into a feature film at a time when western governments were unsuccessfully fighting real-life drug wars, in a very public manner. Here, Soderbergh relates some of the real stories behind the headlines, albeit through fictionalized characters and scenarios. Class, background or status does not limit drug dealing and usage and that essentially is the problem. The dichotomy between tackling the issue hands-on at street level and overseeing it from the comfort of a plush office, are all too obvious. Neither approach works, but we realize it can't. The institutionalised drugs phenomenon is too huge for anyone to even make a dent in the armour of the supply trade, or to curb demand even slightly. When it is revealed that Wakefield's daughter is one of the drug-taking teenagers and General Salazar is profiting from his position of power, it seems the war is all but lost. However, like all great battles, the wounded keep fighting until the bitter end.

USA, 2000
DIRECTOR:
Steven Soderbergh
CAST INCLUDES:
Benicio Del Toro, Michael Douglas,
Jacob Vargas, Catherine Zeta-Jones,
Erika Christensen
SCREENPLAY:
Stephen Gaghan based on the
original television series, *Traffik*
by Simon Moore
CINEMATOGRAPHY:
Steven Soderbergh
(as Peter Andrews)
PRODUCERS/
PRODUCTION COMPANIES:
Laura Bickford, Marshall Herskovitz,
Edward Zwick, Cameron Jones,
Graham King, Andreas Klein,
Mike Newell, Richard Solomon/
Bedford Falls Productions,
Compulsion Inc., Initial Entertainment
Group, Splendid Medien AG,
USA Films
ACADEMY AWARD
NOMINATIONS (2001)
Best Picture: Edward Zwick,
Marshall Herskovitz, Laura Bickford
ACADEMY AWARDS
Best Actor in a Supporting Role:
Benicio Del Toro
Best Director: Steven Soderburgh
Best Editing: Stephen Mirrione
Best Writing, Screenplay based on
Material Previously Produced or
Released: Stephen Gaghan

HORROR

Nosferatu, A Symphony of Terror

Nosferatu, Eine Symphonie des Grauens

GERMANY, 1922
DIRECTOR:
F.W. Murnau
CAST INCLUDES:
Max Schreck,
Gustav von Wangenheim,
Greta Schröder, Alexander Granach,
Georg H. Schnell
SCREENPLAY:
Henrik Galeen
CINEMATOGRAPHY:
Günther Krampf, Fritz Arno Wagner
PRODUCERS/
PRODUCTION COMPANIES:
Enrico Dieckmann, Albin Grau,
Wayne Keele/Jofa-Atelier Berlin-
Johannisthal, Prana-Film GmbH

Realtor Hutter (von Wangenheim) is driven mad by the vampire Count Orloc (Schreck), who then goes to Bremen to find Hutter's wife, Ellen (Schröder), with whom he has become infatuated.

For Count Orloc, read 'Count Dracula', as this is actually one of the earliest incarnations of Bram Stoker's famous creation in all but legal paperwork (which Murnau was unable to secure).

This version of Dracula presents The Count as more repulsive and wretched than the book's almost debonair figure, and it's certainly more politically charged. There is a potent theory that Orloc is actually a representation of Lenin, and the film a German propaganda piece warning of the Communist threat from Russia. The vampire's arrival at Bremen, in a black coffin and followed by hundreds of 'plague' carrying rats, isn't the most subtle of allegories, but there's much more to this film than fear of the Bolsheviks.

Murnau and his collaborators created possibly the most accomplished and beautiful film to that date, in any genre. Max Schreck is most impressive as The Count. Allegedly a student of 'the method' school of naturalistic acting, Schrek's performance was so believable many of the crew were apparently too scared to approach him. In fact, the first-rate film, *Shadow of the Vampire* (2000), hypothesizes that Schrek was a real vampire who struck a deal with Murnau for the leading lady's life – in exchange he would give the ultimate portrayal. Witnessing the power of Schrek's performance does make one wonder.

The Phantom of the Opera

USA, 1925
DIRECTOR:
Rupert Julian
CAST INCLUDES:
Lon Chaney, Mary Philbin,
Norman Kerry,
Arthur Edmund Carewe,
Gibson Gowland
SCREENPLAY:
Walter Anthony from the novel
by Gaston Leroux
CINEMATOGRAPHY:
Milton Bridenbecker, Virgil Miller,
Charles Van Enger (all uncredited)
PRODUCERS/
PRODUCTION COMPANIES:
Carl Laemmle/Universal Pictures [US]

A famous opera singer is forced to relinquish her role in a new production by a threatening Phantom (Chaney). She is replaced by the unknown Christine Daae (Philbin) a woman we soon discover the Phantom is in love with. But how will she respond to him?

There have been over a dozen screen versions of the famous tale, but this 1925 release is generally considered the definitive one. The legendary set is one of early cinemas great accomplishments, – it's a shame the technical limitations placed on the photographer prevents them being explored more comprehensively.

As beautiful as the sets are, the first and best reason to see *The Phantom of the Opera* is Lon Chaney's performance as the eponymous 'hero'. After cornering the market in lovelorn, physically deformed characters with *The Hunchback of Notre Dame* two years earlier, Chaney turns in a tragic performance as Erik, The Phantom (as the name appears in the credits). He brings such a carefully considered and well-balanced sensitivity to the ambiguous character that it's impossible to imagine anyone else in the role. Mary Philbin is also notable in the most famous role of her, all-too-brief, eight-year career. Any viewers who tend not to be scared by films of this age will have to think again, as the unmasking is guaranteed to leave even the most hardened of modern audiences aghast.

Freaks

USA, 1932
DIRECTOR:
Tod Browning
CAST INCLUDES:
Henry Victor, Harry Earles,
Daisy Earles, Olga Baclanova
SCREENPLAY:
Clarence Aaron, 'Tod' Robbins
CINEMATOGRAPHY:
Merritt B. Gerstad
**PRODUCERS/
PRODUCTION COMPANIES:**
Tod Browning/MGM

Cleopatra (Baclanova), a trapeze artist in a carnival, schemes with her lover, Hercules (Victor) to cheat midget Hans (Harry Earles) out of a large inheritance. Although his girlfriend, Frieda (Daisy Earles) is onto the scam, Hans is hopelessly in love with Cleopatra.

Tod Browning was already a renowned horror director after his *Dracula* (1931) starring Bela Lugosi created the western template for scary movies, but nobody was expecting *Freaks*. In *Freaks*, Browning created a vision made all the more real by his use of mainly non-professionals in his cast.

All Browning has to do to create his desired effect is show us the members of the carnival's freak show, a method he employs so comprehensively the film sometimes appears more like a documentary (in fact in some countries it was marketed as one to evade local censorship). Banned in numerous countries, it said much about these societies' attitude to people with physical disfigurements. Medical advances in the First World War allowed previously fatal injuries to be treated, and as a result, physical disfigurement became a more common sight, and one that was fascinating to American audiences in particular. Hollywood would not miss this opportunity and indirectly exploited it in many of its pioneering horror films (*The Phantom of the Opera* and *The Hunchback of Notre Dame* in particular), but *Freaks* is the most honest. It is uncompromising, challenging, and absolutely unique.

King Kong

A group of Americans, including beautiful actress Ann Darrow (Wray), discover a giant ape whilst exploring the remote Skull Island. After the monster is taken to New York for exhibition, it escapes and runs amok in search of Darrow.

Over 70 years old, King Kong remains one of the most popular mythical monsters of cinema. Unlike his contemporaries Frankenstein and Dracula, Kong hasn't yet been the subject of a worthy remake or sequel, leaving this vision the undisputed definitive, which is no bad thing.

Produced (like many other monster classics) in the early 1930s, Hollywood had just got to grips with sound and was ready to innovate in other areas of cinema, particularly visual effects. Although there was a large team working on the job, *Kong*'s impressive blending of live action and the innovative technique of stop-motion are attributed mainly to Willis H. O'Brien (who took the sole credit of Chief Technician on the film). By today's standards the ape may lack realism, but the personality expressed in his face cannot (yet) be mimicked so endearingly in CGI. At the time, it looked real enough to cause entire audiences to panic through sheer confusion, something else CGI is yet to do. But Kong is only one of the legends to appear in the film, credit must go to the lungs of Fay Wray, who will always be remembered as having the best scream in the movies, and should surely be given some kind of posthumous award to reflect this.

'The Most Awesome Thriller Of All Time' declared the promotional posters, in a dramatic manner of which promoter Carl Denham (Armstrong) would surely have approved. Perhaps it isn't quite true anymore, but it's certainly still impressive.

USA, 1933
DIRECTOR:
Merian C. Cooper,
Ernest B. Schoedsack
CAST INCLUDES:
Fay Wray, Robert Armstrong,
Bruce Cabot, Frank Reicher,
Sam Hardy
SCREENPLAY:
Merian C. Cooper, Edgar Wallace,
James Ashmore Creelman and
Ruth Rose
CINEMATOGRAPHY:
Edward Linden, J.O. Taylor,
Vernon L. Walker
**PRODUCERS/
PRODUCTION COMPANIES:**
Merian C. Cooper,
Ernest B. Schoedsack, David O.
Selznick/RKO Radio Pictures Inc.

Bride of Frankenstein

USA, 1935
DIRECTOR:
James Whale
CAST INCLUDES:
Boris Karloff, Colin Clive,
Valerie Hobson, Elsa Lanchester,
Ernest Thesiger
SCREENPLAY:
William Hurlbut, John L. Balderston,
Mary Shelley from the novel
Frankenstein
CINEMATOGRAPHY:
John J. Mescall
PRODUCERS/
PRODUCTION COMPANIES:
Carl Laemmle Jr./Universal Pictures
ACADEMY AWARD
NOMINATIONS (1936)
Best Sound, Recording: Gilbert
Kurland (sound director)

Following on directly from the 1931 version, we soon discover Doctor Henry Frankenstein (Clive) and his creation were not killed. With the monster on the loose again, and the mad Doctor Pretorius (Thesiger) attempting to create a bride for the monster, the townsfolk have never been in more danger.

Based on Mary Shelley's classic novel and directed by James Whale, the seminal 1931 masterpiece *Frankenstein* wouldn't seem to support a sequel (with the monster appearing to die at the end). But the *Bride of Frankenstein*'s inspired opening (an impossibly theatrical dramatisation of Mary Shelley revealing to Lord Byron and Percy Shelley that, 'the story doesn't end there') ensures its plausibility. Considered by many to be better than its predecessor, (certainly no less brutal, only a few minutes in and the grieving parents of the first film's child victim have been killed by the monster), *Bride of Frankenstein* is more personal. The monster, although previously presented to some extent as a victim, becomes a much more sympathetic character, and Frankenstein himself is less the selfish egomaniac and more a solemn, regretful figure. This leaves a gap in the screenplay for a cackling, psychotic

villain and the abhorrent Doctor Pretorius fills it with a ravenous zeal. His motives are never in doubt, from the moment you see his collection of tiny living humans in jars it's clear his only desire is to create a race of monsters to command. His presence is just one of many elements (special mentions for the lighting and photography are essential) which make *Bride of Frankenstein* probably the most important film of the era. It remains as spine chilling as any modern horror, but is generally more rewarding. So as Doctor Pretorius says, 'Let's raise a glass to the new world of Gods and monsters'.

Dead of Night

Walter Craig (Johns), an architect meeting a group of people for the first time, realizes he has dreamt the whole experience before. As each person recounts a tale of personal brushes with the supernatural, he begins to recall more, eventually remembering how the dream turns into a nightmare.

A successful compendium of spooky stories, this dry comic-horror is a joy to watch, and the credits read like a who's who of the 'up and comers' who would later shape British cinema. Segment directors include Robert Hamer (who later made *Kind Hearts and Coronets*), Basil Dearden (who went on to direct *The Captive Heart* and *The League of Gentleman*) and Charles Crichton (*The Lavender Hill Mob*). Whilst writers include T.E.B. Clarke (*Sons and Lovers*) and Angus MacPhail who, between them, were responsible for writing the majority of Ealing's better films. Also worthy of mention is cinematographer Douglas Slocombe, who shot the *Indiana Jones* films.

Each character brings something different to the film, making it a diverse but coherent exercise in storytelling. The five strangers each recount a spooky tale; one saw a vision of his own death and was able to avoid it, another bought a mirror that reflected a different image to the one it should, etc. Penned by H.G. Wells, the red herring of the bunch is particularly good. Two golfers play for the hand of a beautiful woman, the winner cheats and the loser chooses to commit suicide, later returning to haunt his old friend in the most agreeable manner possible. ('Just because a chap becomes a ghost, surely that doesn't mean he ceases to be a gentleman.')

The transition between tales is subtle and seamless, and the amiable group of storytellers are all a pleasure to watch, so much so it's possible to forget the film's a horror... until the grimly surreal conclusion.

GB, 1945
DIRECTORS:
Alberto Cavalcanti
(*Christmas Party* and *The Ventriloquist's Dummy*),
Charles Crichton
(*Golfing Story*),
Basil Dearden
(*Hearse Driver* and
Linking Narrative)
Robert Hamer (*The Haunted Mirror*)
CAST INCLUDES:
Mervyn Johns, Roland Culver,
Mary Merrall, Barbara Leake
SCREENPLAY:
John Baines, E.F. Benson,
T.E.B. Clarke, Angus MacPhail,
H.G. Wells
CINEMATOGRAPHY:
Jack Parker, Stanley Pavey,
Douglas Slocombe
**PRODUCERS/
PRODUCTION COMPANIES:**
Michael Balcon, Sidney Cole,
John Croydon/Eagle-Lion Films Inc.,
Ealing Studios, G.C.F., The Rank
Organisation Film Productions Ltd.

Les Diaboliques

FRANCE, 1955
DIRECTOR:
Henri-Georges Clouzot
CAST INCLUDES:
Simone Signoret, Véra Clouzot,
Paul Meurisse, Charles Vanel,
Jean Brochard
SCREENPLAY:
Pierre Boileau from the novel *Celle qui n'était*, Henri-Georges Clouzot,
Jérôme Géronimi
CINEMATOGRAPHY:
Armand Thirard
**PRODUCERS/
PRODUCTION COMPANIES:**
Henri-Georges Clouzot/Filmsonor
S.A., Vera Films

The wife and mistress of a tyrannical schoolmaster conspire to murder their tormentor. When the body inexplicably disappears they find it increasingly difficult to keep up their façade.

Shot and edited with a simplicity that makes it a pleasure to watch, this French classic of suspense was hugely influential. Its restrained style, rare but effective shocks and inventive ending clearly influenced Hitchcock when making *Psycho*, and subsequently created a template for the suspense thriller.

Paul Meurisse is suitably dastardly as the openly abusive 'victim,' Michel Delaselle. He intimidates everyone at the boarding school he runs (but is owned by his wife) including the other teachers, limiting their wine to two glasses per meal and berating their stupidity in front of the children. But it's the sympathetic killers who are centre stage for most of the film and under Henri-Georges Clouzot's delicate direction they are both superb. The more interesting character is the long-suffering and sickly wife, Christina (Clouzot, who was married to the director and making one of only three film appearances), trapped in the marriage by her religious convictions and aware Michel longs for her death so he can inherit her family fortune.

The most impressive aspect of the film, though, is the taut and inventive screenplay. Clouzot and Jérôme Géronimi's adaptation of Pierre Boileau's novel may be the perfect example of how to write a suspense thriller. The twists are never predictable and the shocks are devastating. Once started, it's impossible to turn away before the end, where the ultimate reward is more than generous.

Dracula

GB, 1958
DIRECTOR:
Terence Fisher
CAST INCLUDES:
Peter Cushing, Christopher Lee,
Michael Gough, Melissa Stribling,
Carol Marsh, John Van Eyssen
SCREENPLAY:
Jimmy Sangster, from the novel
by Bram Stoker
CINEMATOGRAPHY:
Jack Asher
**PRODUCERS/
PRODUCTION COMPANIES:**
Michael Carreras, Anthony Hinds,
Anthony Nelson Keys/Hammer Film
Productions Ltd.

Jonathan Harker arrives at a remote castle somewhere in Germany to catalogue the library of Count Dracula (Lee). We soon learn the profession of librarian is a cover for Harker's real identity – a student of vampirism, and that he is there to kill the Count. After his failure, Dracula leaves the castle in search of Harker's family and friends, none of whom are aware of the oncoming threat, with the exception of the eminent Doctor Van

Helsing (Cushing).

Also known as *The Horror of Dracula*, this is the first stab at the Vampire Count by legendary British studio, Hammer. Although the film takes considerable liberties with the novel, (mainly to tighten the pacing and focus on the salient points), it remains the most popular filmed version, largely due to the excellent perform-ances from the two leads. Christopher Lee is a commanding Dracula, the role for which he will always be remembered. His entrance (in shadow at the top of a staircase) is alarming even by modern standards, and the hospitable charm with which he immediately conducts himself is in stark contrast to the wretched, reclusive incarnations of some other features. Cushing's performance must carry the film (Lee is used very sparingly) and fortunately his dignity and determination move it along at a good pace, keeping it on the horror track in the face of several brilliant comedy asides – at one point, a mortician recounting an old man's fall down the mortuary steps quips, 'he came to pay his last respects... and remained to share them.' As effective as it is, this probably isn't the scariest horror movie ever made, nor is it the most technically impressive, but it might just be the most charming and enjoyable.

Psycho

USA, 1960
DIRECTOR:
Alfred Hitchcock
CAST INCLUDES:
Anthony Perkins, Janet Leigh,
Vera Miles, John Gavin,
Martin Balsam
SCREENPLAY:
Joseph Stefano from the novel by
Robert Bloch
CINEMATOGRAPHY:
John L. Russell
**PRODUCERS/
PRODUCTION COMPANIES:**
Alfred Hitchcock/Shamley
Productions
**ACADEMY AWARD
NOMINATIONS (1961)**
Best Actress in a Supporting Role:
Janet Leigh
Best Art Direction – Set Direction,
Black-and-White: John L. Russell
Best Director: Alfred Hitchcock

Secretary Marion Crane (Leigh) steals the $40,000 she has been instructed to bank. Immediately skipping town, she heads for her lover's California home. Stopping to spend the night at a quiet motel on the way, she finds a shy young man having problems with his mother.

Hitchcock's masterpiece of terror hasn't dated a bit in the years since its release. The ominous opening chords of Bernard Herrmann's now famous theme (set against the stylish credit design of Saul Bass) makes our hearts beat faster, as well as making it immediately clear that whatever lies ahead, it's not going to be agreeable to any of the characters...

But Hitchcock intended to mislead us from the start. For the first half hour the film is a straight crime thriller, featuring an

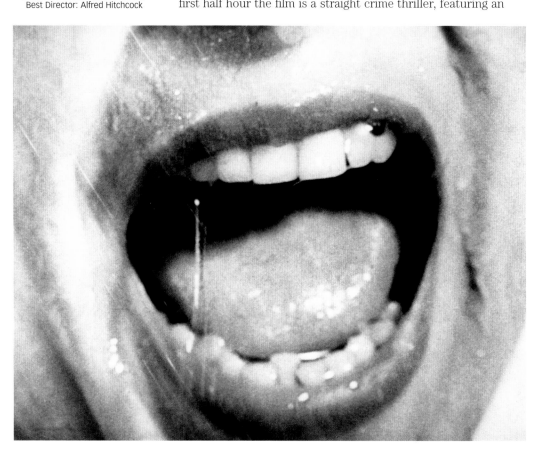

established star on the run for embezzlement -- classic Hitchcock material that comfortably fits the assumptions one might have had upon entering the cinema. *Psycho* was his first foray into horror, and even then it didn't happen until a third of the way through the film.

Shot in black and white (mainly to evade the censor's scissors) the film is stunning. Every shot is framed with subtle beauty, and every cut carefully considered to achieve precisely the intended effect. But none of this is news. The film appears in almost every 'all-time top 10' list devised, and for good reason. The interesting thing is just how unusual all this is for a horror film. Hitchcock lavished *Psycho* with at least as much care and attention as he did any of his films, and he did it at a time when the genre wasn't taken seriously. Horror (like sci-fi) was for drive-ins, existing only as exploitation B-movies since the demise of Universal's classic *Frankenstein*, *Dracula* and *Wolfman* pictures, while the British Hammer films had yet to make any impact in the States. What *Psycho* did was change the way cinema-goers thought about an entire genre. It made horror respectable again.

Peeping Tom

GB, 1960
DIRECTOR:
Michael Powell
CAST INCLUDES:
Karlheinz Böhm (as Carl Boehm),
Moira Shearer, Anna Massey,
Maxine Audley, Brenda Bruce
SCREENPLAY:
Leo Marks
CINEMATOGRAPHY:
Otto Heller
**PRODUCERS/
PRODUCTION COMPANIES:**
Michael Powell/Anglo-Amalgamated
Productions, Michael Powell

Mark (Karlheinz Böhm, credited here as Carl Boehm), a reclusive, voyeuristic focus puller and photography enthusiast forms an awkward friendship with a female neighbour that threatens to expose his secret obsession – murdering women in order to capture a record of their expression at the moment of death.

Michael Powell's sleazy horror-drama has aged remarkably well since it first baited the national newspapers with its provocative and upsetting presentation of a disturbed man's brutal hobby. Upon release it was effectively sunk by the critics, who were upset by the subject matter and the ruthless incrimination of the viewer with inventive camera work. The film eventually resurfaced thanks to a new generation of directors (including Martin Scorsese) who cited it as an influence.

Böhm excels in the lead, emotionally crippled he is an uncomfortable presence on screen, making the viewer squirm whenever he comes into contact with a woman. The explanation for his dysfunctional behaviour lies in his childhood. As we soon learn, his father forced him to grow up on camera as the subject of bizarre experiments, often engineering cruel and torturous circumstances in order to elicit a response. As a result, Mark is unable to relate to reality or people in the flesh, only through the camera lens he spends much of the film hiding behind.

"Do you know what the most FRIGHTENING thing in the world is...?"

PEEPING TOM

CERTIFICATE
X
ADULTS ONLY

CARL BOEHM
MOIRA SHEARER
ANNA MASSEY
MAXINE AUDLEY

IN EASTMAN COLOUR
Original Story and Screenplay by LEO MARKS
Produced and Directed by MICHAEL POWELL

Village of the Damned

All the residents of the English village of Midwitch briefly pass out at the same time and for the same duration. Some time later it's discovered all the women capable of bearing children are pregnant. Stranger still, when the children are born they all possess an eerie physical resemblance and age unusually quickly.

One of the best and last entries to the 1950s era paranoid horror/sci-fi series, *Village of the Damned*, (remade unsuccessfully in 1995 by fallen genre king John Carpenter), is a wonderfully crisp and subtle example of British cinema. The use of children is a chillingly effective device, particularly when they're totally devoid of emotion as they are here. Almost identical, they act as if they're component parts of one larger entity, eventually leading the kindly schoolteacher, Gordon Zellaby (Sanders) to believe they might be. Sanders is superb, his touching serenade to wife Anthea (Shelley) is both a career highlight and a wonderfully touching moment. Sadly his career came to a premature end twelve years later when he committed suicide through 'boredom'.

The photography of Geoffrey Faithful is beautiful throughout, and director Wolf Rilla keeps everything moving along at a brisk pace (the film is only 77 minutes long). The result is a modest, highly watchable little classic.

GB, 1960
DIRECTOR:
Wolf Rilla
CAST INCLUDES:
George Sanders, Barbara Shelley, Michael Gwynn, Laurence Naismith, John Phillips
SCREENPLAY:
Stirling Silliphant, Wolf Rilla, Ronald Kinnoch (as George Barclay) from the novel by John Wyndham
CINEMATOGRAPHY:
Geoffrey Faithfull
PRODUCERS/ PRODUCTION COMPANIES:
Ronald Kinnoch

Whatever Happened to Baby Jane?

USA, 1962
DIRECTOR:
Richard Aldrich
CAST INCLUDES:
Bette Davis, Joan Crawford, Victor Buono, Wesley Addy
SCREENPLAY:
Lukas Heller from the novel by Henry Farrell
PRODUCERS/ PRODUCTION COMPANIES:
Robert Aldrich, Kenneth Hyman/Aldrich, Seven Arts Pictures, Warner Bros.
ACADEMY AWARD NOMINATIONS (1963)
Best Actor in a Supporting Role: Victor Buono
Best Actress in a Leading Role: Bette Davis
Best Cinematography, Black-and-White: Ernest Haller
Best Sound: Joseph D. Kelly
ACADEMY AWARDS
Best Costume Design, Black-and-White: Norma Koch

Two middle-aged sisters, one a former child star, the other a now wheelchair-bound faded screen starlet, share a home and a bitter hatred of each other.

When director Robert Aldrich cast Bette Davis and Joan Crawford as the leads in this biting indictment of Hollywood and celebrity, he must have done so with a wry smile. Both actresses had been huge stars, almost forgotten by the 1960s, each bitterly hated the other, and both were hoping to revitalize their careers with the film (which they did).

Davis is 'Baby Jane Hudson,' an alcoholic riddled with bitterness and resentment. She is attempting an absurd comeback, desperately craving the attention her childhood success brought. Crawford's Blanche is the more sympathetic character, crippled in a car crash at the height of her success, she seems doomed to spend the rest of her years being cruelly tormented by her twisted sister.

Obvious comparisons with the similarly themed but better known *Sunset Boulevard* are valid, but this film is infinitely darker and gets right under the skin. The famous scene in which Jane serves Blanche a rat for dinner (and cackles hysterically at her horrified reaction), makes for uncomfortable viewing, while the ambiguous cause of Blanche's car crash brings into question Jane's basic sanity.

Although both actresses are a triumph in their roles, it's Davis' portrayal of Jane that is the more enjoyable, her vicious and mocking impressions of nemesis Crawford are almost as much fun to watch as they must have been to 'perform.'

The Birds

After a chance meeting in a pet shop, rich socialite Melanie Daniels (Hedren) decides to give Mitch Brenner (Taylor) a surprise visit at his family home in the quiet coastal town of Bodega Bay, but this is a Hitchcock movie, and the local birds seem to know it.

Although long associated with the genre, Hitchcock only actually made two horror movies (*Psycho* being the other) and, as is the way with Hitchcock movies, things are hardly done by the book. Hitchcock must have loved spending the first half hour pretending this was going to be a romantic comedy, but when he starts to drop in an increasing number of clues to the violence ahead it really begins to get interesting. Prophetic moments such as the seagull scratching Melanie's head and the bird crashing into the window of the Brenner's home become more frequent, brilliantly building the viewers' sense of unease and culminating in a chilling climax. One of the great achievements here is to make plausible most of the characters' relaxed and unsuspicious manner, while the audience is fed all the ominous events and touches required for the tension to mount and mount.

USA, 1963
DIRECTOR:
Alfred Hitchcock
CAST INCLUDES:
Tippi Hedren, Rod Taylor,
Jessica Tandy, Suzanne Pleshette,
Veronica Cartwright
SCREENPLAY:
Evan Hunter from the novella by
Daphne Du Maurier
CINEMATOGRAPHY:
Robert Burks
**PRODUCERS/
PRODUCTION COMPANIES:**
Alfred Hitchcock /Alfred J. Hitchcock
Productions, Universal Pictures
ACADEMY AWARDS (1964)
Best Effects, Special Visual Effects:
Ub Iwerks

The Haunting

GB, 1963
DIRECTOR:
Robert Wise
CAST INCLUDES:
Julie Harris, Claire Bloom,
Richard Johnson, Russ Tamblyn,
Fay Compton
SCREENPLAY:
Nelson Gidding from the novel by
Shirley Jackson
CINEMATOGRAPHY:
Davis Boulton
**PRODUCERS/
PRODUCTION COMPANIES:**
Denis Johnson, Robert Wise/Argyle
Enterprises, MGM

A huge, rambling mansion that has seen several mysterious deaths in its ninety-year history is leased to an eccentric British professor who is convinced that ghosts exist. Together with the skeptical Luke (Tamblyn), who stands to inherit the house, Psychic Theodora (Bloom) and insecure Eleanor (Harris), Doctor John Markway (Johnson) moves in to the building to test his theories.

On face value *The Haunting* could seem like any other haunted house movie to have graced the screen over the years, but that isn't so. Firstly, the characters are all hugely successful,

something generally not achieved in this usually cheap and cheerless sub-genre. Enthusiastic Dr. Markway (who inevitably finds a supernatural explanation for the most mundane event) is an infectious presence who has even the sceptical Luke doubting himself. Claire Bloom is excellent as the sophisticated Theodora, but the real achievement is Julie Harris' Eleanor, who must carry the film as the central character, and provide a voice-

over that runs throughout. She arrives at the house in a fragile emotional state and with no plans for the future (almost as if she intends to stay). Having left the home of her abusive sister and with her sickly mother having recently died, Eleanor attempts to be positive about her new lack of responsibility but the house seems to detect her insecurity and focuses it's ghostly attention upon her.

The film is also helped along by the large production values. The house is supposed to be immense and some beautiful lighting and camerawork show it off as such. The most likely explanation for the film's universal success is the presence of legendary director Robert Wise (who fitted it in between *West Side Story* and *The Sound of Music*), who is more than just a safe pair of hands. He lends creativity to the much copied and utterly terrifying night-time scenes when whatever presence the house harbours can be heard rumbling up and down the corridors hammering on the walls and doors.

Rosemary's Baby

USA, 1968
DIRECTOR:
Roman Polanski
CAST INCLUDES:
Mia Farrow, John Cassavetes,
Ruth Gordon, Sidney Blackmer,
Maurice Evans
SCREENPLAY:
Roman Polanski from the novel
by Ira Levin
CINEMATOGRAPHY:
William A. Fraker
**PRODUCERS/
PRODUCTION COMPANIES:**
William Castle, Dona
Holloway/Paramount Pictures
**ACADEMY AWARD
NOMINATIONS (1969)**
Best Writing, Screenplay Based on
Material from Another Medium:
Roman Polanski
ACADEMY AWARDS
Best Actress in a Supporting Role:
Ruth Gordon

Young newlyweds Guy and Rosemary (Cassavetes and Farrow) move into a New York apartment block and befriend the neighbours. When the elderly couple next door become a little too friendly for Rosemary, the warnings of a woman who recently committed suicide in the building come to mind.

Roman Polanski's (*Chinatown*, *The Pianist*) haunting gothic tale of devil worship is a well-crafted and surprisingly understated psychological horror. Using little more than the power of suggestion, Polanski first builds a horribly uncomfortable environment, attaching Rosemary's growing suspicions and concerns to the audience's and refusing the pieces of the puzzle necessary for its completion until the birth of the child. Farrow (married to Polanski at the time) is notable in the lead, a brittle but devoted wife who is pushed to one side when her husband's career takes off. But it's the ambiguous neighbour, Minnie Castevet (Gordon), who steals the show (and an Oscar). Gordon relished the opportunity of such a strong supporting role. Although over seventy at the time, she made more screen appearances after the film than before.

There are very few specific scary moments – instead the film follows the lead of Ira Levin's novel and devotes itself to the steady build-up of tension. But the scene in which the child is conceived, a surreal and bizarre dream sequence, is something that will stay with the most ardent horror buff for a long time.

Night of the Living Dead

A small group of people are trapped in a house when the dead rise up and walk again, hungry for human flesh.

Shot in grainy black-and-white on a miniscule budget, *Night of the Living Dead* surprised even its investors when it became the most successful independent film of its time, uniting audiences and (most) critics, leading one to famously dub it, 'The best film ever made in Pittsburgh.'

The first installment in director George A. Romero's 'Trilogy of the Dead', *Night of the Living Dead*, (*Dawn of the Dead* came next in 1978, followed by *Day of the Dead* in 1985), is his most successful social commentary, challenging some of the anachronistic beliefs still prevalent even in the late 1960s. One of the more obvious examples of this is the casting of African-American newcomer Duane Jones in the lead, particularly effective after a blonde actor is seemingly set up for the role and then killed early on. Jones is excellent, the dominant presence in every scene, he inevitably takes on the role of leader within the metaphorical society that develops inside the house. But it's not all politics, Romero is equally comfortable with the straight horror. Notable highlights include the half-eaten corpse that Barbara (O'Dea) stumbles upon when entering the house, its eye hanging out and face torn away. And the now famous scene of a sickly young girl suddenly recovering enough to lunge at her mother is one of horror cinema's great moments. *Night of the Living Dead* marked the debut for almost everyone involved, including Romero, but even without considering this fact it's still one of the genre's best examples.

USA, 1968
DIRECTOR:
George A. Romero
CAST INCLUDES:
Duane Jones, Judith O'Dea,
Karl Hardman, Marilyn Eastman,
Keith Wayne
SCREENPLAY:
John A. Russo, George A. Romero
CINEMATOGRAPHY:
George A. Romero
**PRODUCERS/
PRODUCTION COMPANIES:**
Karl Hardman, Russell Streiner/Image
Ten, Laurel, Market Square
Productions

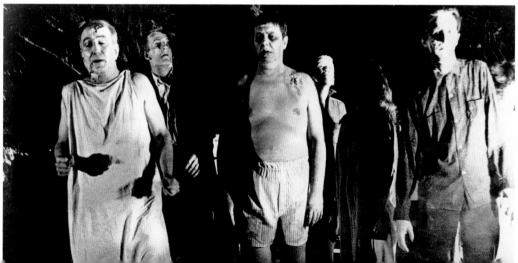

Deliverance

USA,1972
DIRECTOR:
John Boorman
CAST INCLUDES:
Jon Voight, Burt Reynolds,
Ned Beatty, Ronny Cox
SCREENPLAY:
James Dickey
CINEMATOGRAPHY:
Vilmos Zsigmond
**PRODUCERS/
PRODUCTION COMPANIES:**
John Boorman/Elmer Productions,
Warner Bros.
**ACADEMY AWARD
NOMINATIONS (1973)**
Best Director:John Boorman
Best Film Editing: Tom Priestly
Best Picture: John Boorman

In the Georgia backwaters, four city men set off on a canoe trip through beautiful countryside soon to be destroyed to make way for a dam. Dealing with the rapids is the biggest challenge they were expecting to face.

Notoriously fiery John Boorman (*Point Blank*) was not a popular choice to bring James Dickey's novel to the screen. Dickey (no pussycat himself) almost came to blows with the wild director before being banned from the set, but the result of their collaboration is arguably Boorman's greatest work. The environment comes to life as we leave civilization behind and plunge into some of the most isolated countryside in America. The sense of danger ominously creeping up on the four men pervades the following scenes.

Perhaps surprisingly, it is Burt Reynolds who steps forward and steals the show. He is magnificent as the highly physical, masculine Lewis, his performance avoiding all the landmines of caricature and stereotype so common in this type of character. This strong characterization is an essential component of the film's dynamic. As Lewis, he is the only one with any understanding of their surroundings and the potential ramifications of their first encounter with the mountain men. Their attack a third of the way through the film is one of the most memorable scenes ever created in cinema. Separated from Lewis, the helplessness of Ed (Voight) and Bobby (a never better Beatty) seems uncomfortably believable, while the shocking realism of the attackers' performances make the scene almost unwatchable. And then there's the second half of the film.

The Exorcist

In leafy Georgetown, Washington, successful actress Chris Macneil (Burstyn) begins to worry about her daughter, Regan (Blair) whose strange behaviour eventually becomes a matter for the church.

William Peter Blatty's novel had a difficult filming. Rumours still abound today of a curse on the production that caused at least two tragic deaths and a fire that burnt down much of the studio and production offices. Controversy and trouble even followed the film into release, with some church leaders declaring it a blasphemy, and many cinemagoers were sent into a moral outrage by the language and imagery employed. However, this didn't affect the film's success (at least not adversely). In spite of the structure (the slow build is very drawn-out compared to its contemporaries) and the harrowing finale, it was a massive success at the box office, proving that intelligent and demanding horror films had an audience. But the highlight of *The Exorcist* has to be the final half hour in which a battle of good versus evil is played out between the possessed child Regan, strapped to her bed, and the two priests, Father Merrin (von Sydow) and Father Karras (Miller) who is experiencing a crisis of faith that might influence the outcome. The child is a shocking presence, physically deformed and spitting obscenities. It is here that Blair achieves one of the most impressive performances by a child actor in the history of cinema.

Although two sequels followed, neither achieved the grim tone captured in this formidable and essential classic.

USA, 1973
DIRECTOR:
William Friedkin
CAST INCLUDES:
Ellen Burstyn, Max von Sydow,
Jason Miller, Lee J. Cobb, Linda Blair
SCREENPLAY:
William Peter Blatty
CINEMATOGRAPHY:
Owen Roizman
**PRODUCERS/
PRODUCTION COMPANIES:**
William Peter Blatty, Noel Marshall,
David Salven/Hoya Productions,
Warner Bros.
**ACADEMY AWARD
NOMINATIONS (1974)**
Best Actor in a Supporting Role:
Jason Miller
Best Actress in a Leading Role:
Ellen Burstyn
Best Actress in a Supporting Role:
Linda Blair
Best Art Direction – Set Decoration:
Bill Malley, Jerry Wunderlich
Best Cinematography:
Owen Roizman
Best Director: William Friedkin
Best Film Editing: John C. Broderick,
Bud S. Smith, Evan A. Lottman,
Norman Gay
Best Picture: William Peter Blatty
ACADEMY AWARDS
Best Sound: Robert Knudson,
Christopher Newman
Best Writing, Screenplay Based on
Material from Another Medium:
William Peter Blatty

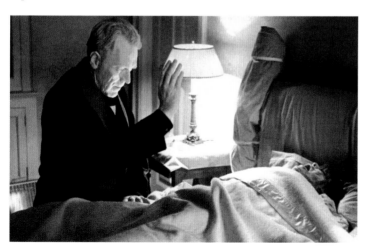

Don't Look Now

GB, 1973
DIRECTOR:
Nicholas Roeg
CAST INCLUDES:
Julie Christie, Donald Sutherland,
Hilary Mason, Clelia Matania
SCREENPLAY:
Allan Scott, Chris Bryant from a
story by Daphne Du Maurier
CINEMATOGRAPHY:
Anthony Richmond, Nicolas Roeg
PRODUCERS/
PRODUCTION COMPANIES:
Peter Katz, Frederick Muller, Anthony
B. Unger/Caset Productions Ltd.,
Eldorado Films, s.r.l.

After the tragic drowning of their young daughter, John and Laura Baxter (Sutherland and Christie) move to Venice where Laura meets two mysterious sisters, one of whom claims to be a psychic in contact with their daughter.

It is pedigree alone that makes this benchmark classic essential viewing. Directed by Nicholas Roeg (*Performance*, *Walkabout*), adapted from a short story by Daphne Du Maurier, and starring Donald Sutherland (*M*A*S*H*, *Ordinary People*) and Julie Christie (*Doctor Zhivago*), the film lives up to expectations. However the work of lesser-known contributors, like cinematographer Anthony Richmond, is not to be overlooked.

There are so many beautiful touches to this film. The striking vision of a child running in a red coat is an absolutely unforgettable image; the way in which Richmond's camera weaves through the dark Venetian alleyways beautifully mirrors the manner in which Roeg leads us through the psychological screenplay, never revealing what's around the next corner until it's upon us. This use of imagery both as a mirror for emotions and the psychological aspects of the screenplay is a prevalent theme. John's work as an architect sees him restoring one of the many gothic cathedrals shown throughout the film. Intellectuals can apply any of a dozen meanings to this but what strikes hardest is the sheer emotional clout this collective of talents have at their disposal. The grief over the girl's death is deeply disturbing, the love between John and Laura is beautiful but tinged with sadness, and most effective of all is the devastating terror brought on by the conclusion.

The Wicker Man

A letter detailing the abduction of a young girl brings police officer Sergeant Howie (Woodward) to a remote Scottish island. He is met with a complete lack of co-operation from the strange locals, who all claim the girl never existed.

Firmly established as one of Britain's greatest horror films, *The Wicker Man* sees career best performances from Edward Woodward (better known as TV's The Equalizer) as the deeply Religious Howie, and also Christopher Lee as the island's pagan Lord Summerisle. The two men spark fantastically off each other, Summerisle being a source of spiritual consternation for Howie. The scene in which they first meet has Howie (a virgin) witness a group of girls dancing naked around a fire. His blustering outrage at the scene is countered quite practically by Summerisle, 'Well, naturally they're naked. It's much too dangerous to jump through fire with their clothes on.'

Director Robin Hardy crafts the film beautifully. From the first frames, he instils the island with an air of authenticity that extends to the smallest detail, making the place and its inhabitants totally believable in spite of the peculiarities. When Howie arrives at the inn he finds the locals singing what first appears to be a song of adoration for the landlord's beautiful (and flattered) daughter Willow (Ekland), but we soon realize the song proclaims her a slut, yet she is still grateful. These small moments develop the islands quietly surreal personality very well, and provide numerous opportunities to outrage Howie, whose difficulty equating the island's Godless beliefs to his own deep Christian faith lies at the heart of the film.

GB, 1973
DIRECTOR:
Robin Hardy
CAST INCLUDES:
Edward Woodward, Christopher Lee,
Diane Cilento, Britt Ekland, Ingrid Pitt
SCREENPLAY:
Anthony Shaffer
CINEMATOGRAPHY:
Harry Waxman
PRODUCERS/
PRODUCTION COMPANIES:
Peter Snell

The Texts Chain Saw Massacre

The Texas Chain Saw Massacre

USA,1974
DIRECTOR:
Tobe Hooper
CAST INCLUDES:
Marilyn Burns, Allen Danziger,
Paul A. Partain, Edwin Neal,
Gunnar Hansen
SCREENPLAY:
Kim Henkel, Tobe Hooper
CINEMATOGRAPHY:
Daniel Pearl
PRODUCERS/
PRODUCTION COMPANIES:
Kim Henkel, Tobe Hooper, Jay
Parsley, Lou Peraino, Richard Saenz

A teenage girl, her wheelchair-bound brother and a few friends intend to spend a brief holiday in the family's rundown old summer house. In need of petrol, a nearby home seems an obvious source, but the neighbours aren't too friendly.

Based (very loosely) on the serial killer Ed Gene's brutal crimes, the story couldn't be simpler. One by one the kids wander into a neighbour's house and suffer a grizzly demise at the hands of Leatherface (Hansen), the only iconic horror psychopath whose threatening presence is undiminished by the over-exposure of his image in the popular media. But he's not the only psychopath in the film. Unusual (though not exclusive) is the use of an entire family as murderers. It might seem excessive, but it's perfectly in tune

with the rest of director Tobe Hooper's extreme and uncompromising vision, creating a numerical balance between the hunter and hunted (briefly anyway). But much more importantly, it announces, with authority, that there are places in America where inbred, deviant crackpots like this can carry out full lives in a structured social order. Escaped lunatics or serial killers must either remove themselves from society or conceal their true nature. Here Hooper creates a functional, open group, but so far removed from our idea of society as to have no awareness of its basic rules; therefore they have none of the weaknesses inherent in other killers such as the need to remain unidentified or to kill someone specific. But that's just one aspect of a much undervalued film, one that stands somehow alone, not really part of a particular cycle of horror movies, and though influential, not really responsible for starting one. Regardless of its technical deficiencies, it's still the most harrowing and terrifying film ever made.

Jaws

When a Great White Shark chooses the waters off peaceful holiday destination Amity Island for its feeding ground, the local population find themselves in a difficult position. Not wanting to deter the tourists that are so essential to local trade, the mayor initially tries to downplay the danger, but once it becomes apparent the shark is there to stay, police chief Brody (Scheider) must call on experts for help.

When Steven Spielberg began production on *Jaws* at the age of 27, he was already considered a bright hope for the future. He had turned out a similarly themed TV movie (*Duel* in 1971) to critical acclaim and with numerous other TV credits and even a feature film under his belt (*The Sugarland Express*, 1974) he had experience. However, running a multi-million dollar production with clashing stars, unpredictable weather and an unreliable mechanical monster would take its toll on even the most seasoned director and Spielberg was worried.

The first achievement of *Jaws* is that it contains no evidence of these problems. It stands as an audacious and masterful example of modern cinema, one of few films that can be described as absolutely perfect in every way. John Williams' indelible score, the sublime editing, gorgeous cinematography and perfect casting and acting all contribute to putting it streets ahead of contemporary mainstream cinema, let alone contemporary horror cinema. The bold decision to tease the viewer with tantalizing glimpses of the shark until the very end (Spielberg modestly jokes because it never worked) is hugely successful, making the phantom-like monster all the more of a threat. And the tension is worthy only of Hitchcock. The moment Hooper (Dreyfuss) discovers that the sunken boat of Ben Gardner (Kingsbury) isn't quite deserted provides one of the most notorious and effective shocks in cinema. And with the cheer inducing finale providing the ultimate in satisfaction, it's fair to say a better horror-thriller will probably never be made.

USA, 1975
DIRECTOR:
Steven Spielberg
CAST INCLUDES:
Roy Scheider, Robert Shaw,
Richard Dreyfuss, Lorraine Gary,
Murray Hamilton
SCREENPLAY:
Peter Benchley, Carl Gottlieb
CINEMATOGRAPHY:
Bill Butler
PRODUCERS/
PRODUCTION COMPANIES:
David Brown,
Richard D. Zanuck/Universal Pictures,
Zanuck/Brown Productions
ACADEMY AWARD
NOMINATIONS (1976)
Best Picture: Richard D. Zanuck,
David Brown
ACADEMY AWARDS
Best Film Editing: Verna Fields
Best Music, Original Score:
John Williams
Best Sound: Robert L. Hoyt,
Roger Heman Jr., Earl Madery,
John R. Carter

The Omen

When the child of the wealthy American ambassador to the UK, Robert Thorn (Peck), dies at birth, he substitutes another and avoids revealing the tragedy to his wife Katherine (Remick). Some years later the child has developed a fear of churches and is surrounded by a subtle web of quiet observers. But when some of these mysterious people begin to die under bizarre circumstances, Thorn begins to suspect his son may not be what he seems.

Richard Donner's epic is a deeply disturbing addition to the horror genre, exploring the traditional concept of good versus evil. It raises questions about faith and, depending on the viewers' own beliefs and opinions, will be interpreted in many different ways.

The subject and material is treated with respect throughout, and Donner was obviously aware that casting would be vital if he was to achieve the carefully considered performances he required. Peck's awesome stature provides substantial authority to both the film and character of Thorn, a somewhat sombre figure devoted to his wife and 'son'. Lee Remick is also impressive and the ever-dependable David Warner is superb as the ambiguous photographer Keith Jennings.

A film with such a dark tone also requires a carefully conceived visual style if it is to remain even, and acclaimed cinematographer Gilbert Taylor (who had previously worked with Polanski, Kubrick and Hitchcock and would later shoot *Star Wars*) created a harsh and uncompromising style that never permits the viewer to relax. Along with its similarly themed contemporary, *The Exorcist*, *The Omen* has stood the test of time well, retaining its curious ability to use fear in order to make us consider our own views on faith.

USA, 1976
DIRECTOR:
Richard Donner
CAST INCLUDES:
Gregory Peck, Lee Remick, David Warner, Billie Whitelaw, Harvey Stephens
SCREENPLAY:
David Seltzer
CINEMATOGRAPHY:
Gilbert Taylor
PRODUCERS/ PRODUCTION COMPANIES:
Harvey Bernhard, Mace Neufeld, Charles Orme/20th Century Fox
ACADEMY AWARD NOMINATIONS (1977)
Best Music, Original Song: Jerry Goldsmith for 'Ave Satani'
ACADEMY AWARDS
Best Music, Original Score: Jerry Goldsmith

Carrie

USA, 1976
DIRECTOR:
Brian De Palma
CAST INCLUDES:
Sissy Spacek, Piper Laurie,
Amy Irving, William Katt,
Betty Buckley, Nancy Allen
SCREENPLAY:
Lawrence D. Cohen from the novel
by Stephen King
CINEMATOGRAPHY:
Mario Tosi
**PRODUCERS/
PRODUCTION COMPANIES:**
Brian De Palma, Paul Monash,
Louis A. Stroller/Redbank Films
**ACADEMY AWARD
NOMINATIONS (1977)**
Best Actress in a Leading Role:
Sissy Spacek
Best Actress in a Supporting Role:
Piper Laurie

A frail teenage girl with psychic powers is bullied relentlessly by the girls at her high school, and browbeaten into a constant state of guilt by her fanatically religious mother.

Future A-list director Brian De Palma (*The Untouchables*, *Mission Impossible*) had spent fifteen years directing shorts and minor movies before adapting this Stephen King favourite.

Dealing directly with issues such as puberty and physical change (frequently alluded to via metaphor in horror) is an uncompromising but successful technique, and one that ensures *Carrie*'s place amongst the most emotionally powerful examples of the genre. Due to her ignorance, Carrie's (Spacek) first period is a distressing and public experience, seized upon by her tormentors, and also signifies the onset of her psychic capabilities; clearly the two events are linked. Carrie's mother, Margaret (Laurie), does little to support her daughter. More than a little mad, she is too busy harassing the neighbours with prophecies of eternal damnation and warnings to wicked non-believers. She is an oppressive presence, refusing Carrie privacy and preventing her from taking part in the normal activities of a teenage girl. She has inadvertently raised a disaffected, nervous daughter, who is no more able to understand relationships than she is her strange powers. Piper Laurie is excellent, but Spacek's astonishing turn in the lead is a frank and unselfconscious career-best performance more than worthy of her Academy Award nomination.

Eraserhead

Mary X (Stewart), the girlfriend of Henry Spencer (Nance) falls pregnant and delivers a very peculiar baby into a dark and troubled world.

The plot of *Eraserhead* – the epitome of David Lynch's challenging style – cannot be summed up in words. What is written above does technically happen, but we are deep into the realm of experimental surrealism here, and anything definable and explainable has no place.

Lynch has created a lifeless but noisy industrial world in which Henry lives a strange existence. He seems less interested in his girlfriend Mary (who is prone to physical fits) than he is the Lady in the Radiator, whose singing he likes to listen to. As with all Lynch's work there are bound to be red herrings, but it's hard to spot them in such an overstocked lake. Whether Henry's whole life is a dream or whether Lynch believes this bizarre and desolate world should be perceived as reality is not made clear, but neither is it important. What is important is the extent to which this surreal nightmare affects the audience. It's almost as if the film is working on our souls rather than our nerves, and without even a vague template of possible developments and scenarios, your mind is left dribbling in the corner of your throbbing skull.

USA, 1977
DIRECTOR:
David Lynch
CAST INCLUDES:
Jack Nance (as John Nance),
Charlotte Stewart, Allen Joseph,
Jeanne Bates, Judith Anna Roberts,
Laurel Near
SCREENPLAY:
David Lynch
CINEMATOGRAPHY:
Herbert Cardwell, Frederick Elmes
PRODUCERS/
PRODUCTION COMPANIES:
David Lynch/American Film
Institute (AFI)

Perhaps the best way to explain *Eraserhead* is to put it into the context of later Lynch works such as *Lost Highway* or *Mulholland Drive*, minus any sense of narrative. This film is an uncontrolled stream of Lynch's consciousness; bizarre, repulsive and upsetting – just as a horror should be.

Halloween

USA, 1978
DIRECTOR:
John Carpenter
CAST INCLUDES:
Donald Pleasence, Jamie Lee Curtis,
Nancy Kyes, P.J. Soles, Tony Moran
SCREENPLAY:
John Carpenter, Debra Hill
CINEMATOGRAPHY:
Dean Cundey
PRODUCERS/
PRODUCTION COMPANIES:
Moustapha Akkad, Debra Hill, Kool
Lusby, Irwin Yablans, John Carpenter

Over a decade after the six-year-old Michael Myers (Moran) murdered his sister on Halloween night, he escapes from the asylum in which he has spent his subsequent life and returns to his home town of Haddonfield.

John Carpenter's wildly creative *Halloween* is now well-established as one of the genre's greatest treasures as well as the film that created the slasher movie, a sub-genre that may yet have as many lives as its most prolific psychopaths.

The story is simple; bad guy wants to kill teenagers (ideally promiscuous ones). But the plot is not what makes *Halloween* so

scary. Michael Myers comes across as so remorselessly evil and detached that his back-story is effectively superseded by the hugely successful realization of the character. You don't need to know that he's an escaped lunatic who killed his sister, it's enough just to see him brazenly stalking Laurie (Lee Curtis) in the middle of the day. His lack of discretion convinces us it's all about that one night and damn the consequences. His blank face (actually a William Shatner mask painted white) gives away nothing, and it's all the more effective for being presented in the sunny suburbia of leafy Haddonfield (although Autumn, there's always plenty of foliage for Myers to step in and out of).

But Myers wouldn't exist without Carpenter (or co-writer Debra Hill). The five-minute, one take opening sequence, all seen through Myers' eyes, is bravura filmmaking that places us immediately and uncompromisingly in the shoes of a murderer. When we return to Haddonfield, Carpenter has the camera move through the quiet streets like an invisible voyeur selecting a target. The decision to set the last half entirely in two houses and the road between is highly effective, making the audience feel trapped even in what should be a comforting setting – it's almost as if Carpenter was challenging himself to avoid shortcuts like isolated farmhouses.

In short, *Halloween* is simply the most important horror film of the last forty years, and absolutely essential viewing.

Dawn of the Dead

The sequel to *Night of the Living Dead* starts where its predecessor left off, with zombies now outnumbering the living and the remnants of society in chaos. Two SWAT officers and a young couple set out in search of safety in a helicopter, eventually finding a shopping mall, that once cleared and barricaded, they decide will act as an ideal temporary safe haven. But it soon becomes apparent that help may not be coming any time soon.

George A. Romero, the godfather of zombie movies, had a lot to live up to when returning to the material of his hugely successful debut. Perhaps unexpectedly, Romero decides to take a swipe at consumerism. Unsubtle though it may be, it has stood the test of time magnificently. The numerous shots of zombies stumbling around aimlessly in the shopping centre will be familiar to anyone who has been to a supermarket on a Saturday morning. One of the underlying themes of greed rapidly leading to death is another effective message in a film that demands to be taken seriously as social commentary as well as a kick-ass zombie flick.

It's a popular view that this middle instalment in 'The Trilogy of the Dead' is a rare example of a sequel bettering the original. It certainly has more to say, perhaps more than any contemporary horror film, and it's certainly the best film ever made in a shopping mall.

USA, 1978
DIRECTOR:
George A. Romero
CAST INCLUDES:
David Emge, Ken Foree,
Scott H. Reiniger, Gaylen Ross
SCREENPLAY:
George A. Romero
CINEMATOGRAPHY:
Michael Gornick
PRODUCERS/
PRODUCTION COMPANIES:
Claudio Argento, Dario Argento,
Alfredo Cuomo, Richard P.
Rubinstein/Laurel Group

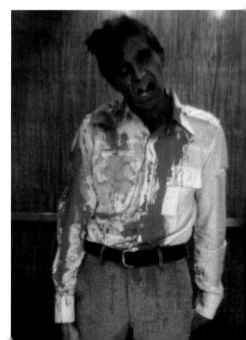

The Shining

USA, 1980
DIRECTOR:
Stanley Kubrick
CAST INCLUDES:
Jack Nicholson, Shelley Duvall,
Danny Lloyd, Scatman Crothers
SCREENPLAY:
Stanley Kubrick, Diane Johnson from
the novel by Stephen King
CINEMATOGRAPHY:
John Alcott
**PRODUCERS/
PRODUCTION COMPANIES:**
Robert Fryer, Jan Harlan,
Mary Lea Johnson, Stanley Kubrick,
Martin Richards/Hawk Films Ltd.,
Peregrine, Producers Circle,
Warner Bros.

Former teacher Jack Torrance (Nicholson) takes a job as the winter caretaker of a huge, isolated mountain hotel. He and his wife, Wendy (Duvall), and son Danny (Lloyd) are left alone in the place we soon learn to be haunted.

In 1980 Stanley Kubrick released his critically panned *The Shining* upon a very confused audience, most of whom found it too long, too slow and too hard to understand. Today the film is rightly considered one of the masterpieces of cinema, and the dialogue and imagery have become ingrained in popular culture. Jack Nicholson's showboating performance as the insane Torrance, at the time considered too over-the-top, is now his best known and beloved role. He chews his way through the countless scenes of twitching hysteria with such a demonic dedication it's impossible to take your eyes off him.

The remote and overbearing Overlook Hotel (casually established as being built on an Indian burial mound) takes on the second most potent personality of the film. The endless corridors weaving like arteries around the upper floors feel as if they could conceal any number of horrors (and do) while the gigantic halls have an eerie look to them, as if they remember the past horrors and anticipate their repetition. Without question one of the scariest films ever made, there are few sudden shocks, very little direct violence and no deaths until the last ten minutes. But the audience must withstand a huge amount of creeping psychological pressure brought on by a combination of qualities, any of which on its own would make the film a must-see – the performances, the smoothly hypnotic camera work, and particularly the disorienting dips into Jack's broken mind as he chats with a former caretaker or wanders through a huge ballroom filled with dancers.

Perhaps the most powerful quality is the film's totally unique nature. There is no reference in cinema, nothing even similar exists, so there's no way to predict what might happen next.

Friday the 13th

In the late 1950s, Camp Crystal Lake suffered a terrible tragedy when a boy was drowned and two revenge killings were carried out. For twenty years the summer camp remains deserted until a young couple arrive with a group of teenagers, planning to repair the camp and reopen for business. But they don't heed the warnings of the locals and the kids start dropping like flies.

When John Carpenter blew the horror genre wide open with *Halloween* in 1978, writer Victor Miller and director Sean S. Cunningham took their opportunity to jump on the bandwagon. At little expense they produced what looked like being a quirky rip-off, and whilst there is an element of truth in this assumption, *Friday the 13th* is a quality imitation. Essentially retelling *Halloween*'s story in a more remote environment, and adding a killer twist to the ending, this film is what really cemented the new 'slasher' style. As Wes Craven points out in *Scream* sixteen years later, 'There are certain rules to surviving a horror movie..' and *Friday the 13th* did as much to establish these rules as any contemporaries. Not only does the graphic violence make the audience feel like victims, we are also incriminated with the killer by the clever use of first person perspective camera shots. We are forced to see through his eyes as the teenagers are observed from the shadows. The twist at the end is one of the greatest in horror history, and the final scare is both unexpected and inspired, but make sure you stop there as the TV series and nine or so sequels are best avoided.

USA, 1980
DIRECTOR:
Sean S. Cunningham
CAST INCLUDES:
Betsy Palmer, Adrienne King,
Harry Crosby, Laurie Bartram,
Jeannine Taylor, Kevin Bacon
SCREENPLAY:
Victor Miller
CINEMATOGRAPHY:
Barry Abrams
PRODUCERS/
PRODUCTION COMPANIES:
Sean S. Cunningham, Alvin Geiler,
Steve Miner/Georgetown Productions
Inc., Paramount Pictures,
Sean S. Cunningham Films

The Fog

USA, 1980
DIRECTOR:
John Carpenter
CAST INCLUDES:
Adrienne Barbeau, Jamie Lee Curtis,
Janet Leigh, Tom Atkins
SCREENPLAY:
John Carpenter, Debra Hill
CINEMATOGRAPHY:
Dean Cundey
**PRODUCERS/
PRODUCTION COMPANIES:**
Barry Bernardi, Charles B. Bloch,
Pegi Brotman, Debra Hill/AVCO
Embassy Pictures, EDI

One hundred years after six townsfolk killed a group of wealthy lepers planning to settle just up the coast, the spirits of the murdered sailors return in a bank of glowing fog to kill the descendants of the six men and reclaim their gold.

Much has been written about how director John Carpenter changed the direction of horror with *Halloween* in 1978, but his next feature (he directed two TV movies in between) was to be an old fashioned ghost story. The quote that opens the film, 'Is all that we see or seem but a dream within a dream?' implies the director's intent to make the film's reality ambiguous. The scene that follows – a group of children around a late-night campfire listening to a story of sailors seeking vengeance – only reinforces this.

Although there are fairy-tale implications, the movie is not short on proper scares. The sailors are terrifying, and the fact that they are glimpsed only as shadows or through fog makes their presence all the more threatening and alarming. However, the film's great success lies primarily with the excellently conceived and realized characters. Such high levels of tension cannot be generated without caring for the imperilled townsfolk. One particularly effective device is the single mother and local DJ (one of three female leads) acting as the eyes and guiding voice for the town in her lighthouse-based radio station. From the lighthouse she can see the fog, but is agonizingly isolated and vulnerable. Like a good captain, we worry she might go down with the ship.

The Fog is a true classic of horror cinema. A sophisticated character structure marks it out as one of Carpenter's career highlights, and its effective simplicity ensures its place as one of the genre's too.

An American Werewolf in London

Two American students on a hitchhiking holiday around England fail to heed the words of the locals in a Yorkshire pub and find themselves lost at night on the moors. After being attacked by a strange beast, the lone survivor recuperates in London, but it's not long before he starts to realize his condition isn't improving in the way he had expected.

From the opening shot of the two naive boys (Naughton and Dunne) arriving in a cattle truck, surrounded by sheep on the way to the slaughterhouse, it's clear this is going to be an inventive and humorous affair. Indeed, director Landis is better known for his funny-bone than bloody-bones, with credits such as *Animal House*, *The Blues Brothers* and *Trading Places* making him a highly revered and influential comedy director. But whilst his tongue remains firmly in his cheek throughout, (after feeding one night, the werewolf wakes naked in human form and must queue for the bus home), you underestimate at your peril the utterly terrifying events which take place in between the smirks. One dream sequence in particular is guaranteed to leave you chilled, and the werewolf's attacks themselves are built with tension and finished with violence that seems strong even by today's standards.

Another aspect of the film that still deserves credit is the special makeup effects. Rick Baker did a stunning job, both in the werewolf transformation scene and with the dozens of lacerated and decomposing characters required, all of which had to be created with prosthetics and mechanics. There isn't a frame that doesn't stand up in the digital era.

An American Werewolf in London is a unique movie, as scary as any horror and as satirical as any comedy.

GB, 1981
DIRECTOR:
John Landis
CAST INCLUDES:
David Naughton, Jenny Agutter,
Griffin Dunne, John Woodvine
SCREENPLAY:
John Landis
CINEMATOGRAPHY:
Robert Paynter
PRODUCERS/
PRODUCTION COMPANIES:
George Folsey Jr., Peter Guber,
Jon Peters/ American Werewolf, Inc.,
Guber-Peters Company,
Lyncanthrope Films
PolyGram Filmed Entertainment
ACADEMY AWARDS (1982)
Best Makeup: Rick Baker

The Thing

In the Antarctic, an American scientific research base is invaded by an ancient alien capable of taking on the form of any human it comes into contact with.

This is the first of what director John Carpenter calls his 'Apocalypse Trilogy' (*The Thing* was followed by *They Live* and *Prince of Darkness*). In some ways though it's better to regard the film as the last of his 'Great Horror Trilogy' (after *Halloween* and *The Fog*) as they're more representative of the awesome skills Carpenter once wielded. This excellent adaptation of John W. Campbell's short story, *Who Goes There?* provides (like so many great horrors) a very simple situation and group dynamic on which the filmmakers can build tension. When we're introduced to the isolated men at the start, a tense atmosphere already exists. Later, when it must develop with the influence of The Thing itself, it becomes infinitely more threatening. Alongside *Halloween*, *The Thing* features Carpenter's best achievements in this area. But unlike *Halloween*, *The Thing* didn't kick-start a sub-genre, (though it did help dramatically in the advancement of special makeup effects technology), instead it almost deliberately bucks the slasher trend only four years after Carpenter started it. Part homage to 1950s sci-fi B-movies, part original creation, the film contains one of Carpenter's best characters, the surly helicopter pilot R.J. MacReady, a role Kurt Russell fits into magnificently.

Although not a huge success on release, (possibly a less demanding alien movie in the shape of *E.T.* was part of the reason), *The Thing* has since achieved a huge fan base and has become one of the best loved horror staples of late night TV.

USA, 1982
DIRECTOR:
John Carpenter
CAST INCLUDES:
Kurt Russell, Wilford Brimley,
T.K. Carter, David Clennon,
Keith David, Richard A. Dysart
SCREENPLAY:
Bill Lancaster from the story by
John W. Campbell Jr.
CINEMATOGRAPHY:
Dean Cundey
PRODUCERS/
PRODUCTION COMPANIES:
Stuart Cohen, David Foster,
Larry J. Franco, Wilbur Stark,
Lawrence Turman/Turman-Foster
Company, Universal Pictures

Poltergeist

USA, 1982
DIRECTOR:
Tobe Hooper
CAST INCLUDES:
Jo Beth Williams, Craig T. Nelson,
Beatrice Straight, Heather O'Rourke,
Zelda Rubinstein
SCREENPLAY:
Steven Spielberg, Michael Grais,
Mark Victor
CINEMATOGRAPHY:
Matthew F. Leonetti
**PRODUCERS/
PRODUCTION COMPANIES:**
Kathleen Kennedy, Frank Marshall,
Steven Spielberg/MGM
**ACADEMY AWARD
NOMINATIONS (1983)**
Best Effects, Sound Effects Editing:
Stephen Hunter Flick,
Richard L. Anderson
Best Effects, Visual Effects:
Richard Edlund, Michael Wood,
Bruce Nicholson
Best Music, Original Score:
Jerry Goldsmith

A young girl discovers she can communicate with a supernatural spirit through a dead channel on the family TV. Strange things soon start to happen in the Freeling home and after a while, the docile presence becomes more of a threat.

Although directed by Tobe Hooper (*The Texas Chain Saw Massacre*), the presence of producer Steven Spielberg has clearly tempered Hooper's violent and distressing style. But this is not necessarily a bad thing as this is a different kind of horror movie, one that cleverly circumvents the censors inflexible policies and has proved to be one of the most enduring and effective 'family horrors' (although it's certainly not recommended for young children). Spielberg has always had a skill for presenting upsetting details and events in a manner that can haunt children without being overtly threatening (*Jurassic Park,* for example). Apparently Tobe Hooper didn't realize any of this when he took the job and has always wanted to release his own, hardcore, version.

However, Hooper realizes the haunted house premise very successfully and (another Spielberg influence) a lot of time is spent establishing the characters and relationships that remain at the heart of the film. In particular, Carol Anne (O'Rourke), the youngest daughter and link to the spirits, provides a performance so rich and intelligent it's impossible to believe she was only six. Also watch out for Tangina Barrons (Rubinstein) in her scene-stealing appearance as a clairvoyant.

203

Gremlins

USA, 1984
DIRECTOR:
Joe Dante
CAST INCLUDES:
Zach Galligan, Phoebe Cates,
Hoyt Axton, Frances Lee McCain,
Polly Holliday
SCREENPLAY:
Chris Columbus
CINEMATOGRAPHY:
John Hora
**PRODUCERS/
PRODUCTION COMPANIES:**
Michael Finnell, Kathleen Kennedy,
Frank Marshall,
Steven Spielberg/Amblin
Entertainment, Warner Bros.

Billy Peltzer (Galligan) is thrilled when his father gives him an unusual furry pet for Christmas. But there are some peculiar rules Billy and his girlfriend Kate (Cates) must adhere to. Sunlight can be fatal, it can't get wet, and you must never feed it after midnight. It's only a matter of time before contact with some spilt water causes it to multiply, and then a late night snack turns most of the cute little furballs into vicious monsters.

In the mid-1980s Steven Spielberg was handed a promising and original script by the relatively unknown Chris Columbus. Too busy to direct (though he did eventually produce), he gave the job to 'up and comer' Joe Dante. When you consider the writer would later make *Home Alone* and the first two Harry Potter films, and the director would go on to make *Innerspace* and *The 'burbs*, it's no surprise that *Gremlins* has become one of the most fondly remembered cinema experiences for anybody now in their late twenties.

With this unparalled team of talents at the helm, *Gremlins* became the best 'horror film for kids' the cinema has ever produced. Although this is not an all-out horror movie, there are still plenty of scares, particularly the scene in which one of the cute little animals has been left at the local school to be examined. Without the teacher realizing, the sweet, harmless little animal has turned into a vile, savage Gremlin. This scene has more tension and suspense than you would expect from a redblooded slasher flick.

Throughout the film the scares are in all the right places, the score is superb, the gore is judged to perfection and the gags are as black as the chimney in which Kate's father gets stuck during the Christmas story she recounts to Billy. And for once the sequel is worth a look, too.

A Nightmare on Elm Street

Teenager Nancy (Langenkamp) is having vivid nightmares in which a sinister figure with knives for fingers and a hideously scarred face is attempting to kill her. When people start turning up dead and she discovers her friends are having the same dream, the local parents are forced to reveal a horrible secret from their past.

A Nightmare on Elm Street is probably the best known of the 1980s slasher movie wave. It spawned five straight sequels, a video game, a pop song, a franchise crossover movie, and a TV series before director Wes Craven returned to put a post-modern lid on the franchise with his 'dry run' for *Scream, New Nightmare* in 1994.

In spite of its age, it's the original *Nightmare* that packs the best punches. As David Lynch would do later in *Blue Velvet* and *Twin Peaks*, Craven delights in creating an impossibly perfect vision of small-town America, a transparent bubble of safety filled with fresh-faced teenagers (including a young Johnny Depp) who, once they start becoming victims of the town's nasty secret, are left helplessly vulnerable. All except Nancy that is, the plucky heroine, portrayed excellently by Langenkamp, who manages to stop short of the first trap in teenage slasher movies – being so aggravating that you start cheering for the killer!

If Craven has achieved one stroke of genius in the movie, it's pretty obvious... Freddy Krueger (Englund). He instantly became one of the most identifiable figures in film horror when unleashed in 1984, and twenty years on he's still giving people nightmares. If, for some reason, the mention of his name doesn't send a shiver down your spine, just repeat after me, 'One, two, Freddy's coming for you, three, four, better lock the door...'

USA, 1984
DIRECTOR:
Wes Craven
CAST INCLUDES:
John Saxon, Ronee Blakley,
Heather Langenkamp, Amanda Wyss,
Jsu Garcia, Robert Englund
SCREENPLAY:
Wes Craven
CINEMATOGRAPHY:
Jacques Haitkin
**PRODUCERS/
PRODUCTION COMPANIES:**
John Burrows, Stanley Dudelson,
Sara Risher, Robert Shaye,
Joseph Wolf/ Media Home
Entertainment, New Line Cinema,
Smart Egg Pictures

Manhunter

USA, 1986
DIRECTOR:
Michael Mann
CAST INCLUDES:
William L. Petersen, Kim Greist,
Joan Allen, Brian Cox, Tom Noonan
SCREENPLAY:
Michael Mann from the novel
by Thomas Harris
CINEMATOGRAPHY:
Dante Spinotti
**PRODUCERS/
PRODUCTION COMPANIES:**
Dino De Laurentiis, Richard A. Roth,
Bernard Williams/De Laurentiis
Entertainment Group (DEG),
Red Dragon Productions S.A.

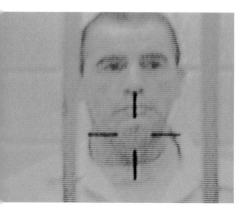

A pschopathic killer stumps the police and FBI and serial killer expert Will Graham (Peterson) is persuaded out of retirement to help. Graham soon seeks advice from his most notorious catch, one Hannibal Lecktor.

Using many of the same plot devices as the better known sequel *Silence of the Lambs, Manhunter* balances an excellent, taut detective story with brutal violence and horrific set-pieces. Dante Spinotti's (*Heat, LA Confidential*) stunning high-contrast cinematography, the core performances and director Mann's snappy style make this is a must-see.

William Peterson as the (possibly) psychic and certainly troubled former FBI agent Graham is totally convincing. Brian Cox is also underrated in the first screen version of the psychopathic serial killer Lecktor (not 'Lecter' as in other films). Anthony Hopkins' powerhouse performance in *Silence of the Lambs* may have been considered the definitive one, but viewed on its own merits, Cox's performance is every bit as impressive. Tom Noonan plays the ghoulish Francis Dollarhyde with creepy conviction. He has the power to make you shiver even when engaged in passive exchanges with other characters, and his presence on screen is guaranteed to prevent you feeling comfortable for even a second.

Evil Dead 2

USA, 1987
DIRECTOR:
Sam Raimi
CAST INCLUDES:
Bruce Campbell, Sarah Berry,
Dan Hicks, Kassie DePaiva, Ted
Raimi, Denise Bixler
SCREENPLAY:
Sam Raimi, Scott Spiegel
CINEMATOGRAPHY:
Peter Deming
**PRODUCERS/
PRODUCTION COMPANIES:**
Bruce Campbell, Alex De Benedetti,
Irvin Shapiro, Robert G. Tapert/De
Laurentiis Entertainment Group
(DEG), Renaissance Pictures.

In a remote woodland shack, young couple Ash and Linda (Campbell and Bixler) discover a tape recording left by a mysterious scientist claiming there is an evil, supernatural presence in the surrounding woods.

In the first *Evil Dead* movie, Raimi created a tense zombie classic as a tribute to hero George A. Romero. Although this superior sequel is essentially a remake, Romero has lost some ground to the 3 Stooges as Raimi's chief muse.

Evil Dead 2 has a truly unique tone, stemming from Raimi's appreciation of star Bruce Campbell's considerable gift for physical comedy. The scene in which Ash must defend himself from his own

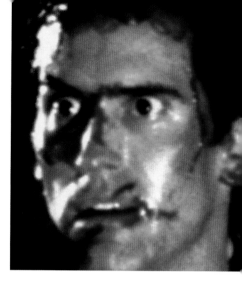

(possessed) right hand is a definitive moment. You know this is no ordinary zombie movie when the hand throws him into a wall and flips him head-over-heels before Ash gets the better of it and – ever resourceful – removes it with a chainsaw. After trapping the squirming hand under a bucket, a copy of *Farewell to Arms* is placed on top as a weight.

The movie was a success on release but with the passing of time it has become increasingly popular, and its star a certified legend of the genre. A third movie followed (*Army of Darkness*) and successfully recreated the spirit in a higher budget form, but it is this second installment that remains the best example of comedy-horror ever to be produced in the cinema.

Angel Heart

Harry Angel (Rourke) is a cynical private detective working small-time cases in 1950s New York. Wealthy client Louis Cyphre (De Niro) comes to him with a seemingly straightforward missing person case. Angel takes it, believing Cyphre is simply owed money by a man who disappeared twelve years previously. But then those involved begin turning up dead.

Comparisons with cynical private dicks like Philip Marlowe and Sam Spade are inevitable. But Angel's cynicism doesn't stem from a loss of faith in society, he never had any faith to begin with. And unlike the films Marlowe and Spade appeared in, *Angel Heart* is not a straight detective story, though it uses one as the framework for something original and terrifying. Just what the missing person owes Louis Cyphre is one of several alarming revelations that drag the viewer into the realm of psychological horror. One of director Alan Parker's (*Mississippi Burning*) clever touches is the way he peppers the film with obvious clues – we believe we know what's happening, and so we're continually caught off guard by the gruesome revelations that keep coming. Shot in a grainy and dirty style by cinematographer Michael Seresin, *Angel Heart* is unforgettable, engrossing and intelligent.

USA, 1987
DIRECTOR:
Alan Parker
CAST INCLUDES:
Mickey Rourke, Robert De Niro, Lisa Bonet, Charlotte Rampling, Stocker Fontelieu
SCREENPLAY:
Alan Parker from the novel by William Hjortsberg
CINEMATOGRAPHY:
Michael Seresin
PRODUCERS/ PRODUCTION COMPANIES:
Robert Dattila, Mario Kassar, Elliott Kastner, Alan Marshall, Andrew Vajna/Carolco Entertainment, Union, Winkast Film Productions Ltd.

Child's Play

USA, 1988
DIRECTOR:
Tom Holland
CAST INCLUDES:
Catherine Hicks, Chris Sarandon,
Alex Vincent, Brad Dourif,
Dinah Manoff
SCREENPLAY:
Don Mancini
CINEMATOGRAPHY:
Bill Butler
**PRODUCERS/
PRODUCTION COMPANIES:**
Elliot Geisinger, David Kirschner,
Laura Moskowitz, Barrie M.
Osborne/United Artists

Faced with certain death after a shoot-out in a toy store, serial killer Charles Lee Ray (Dourif) uses a voodoo curse to transfer his soul into a child's doll. Single mother Karen (Hicks) is unaware of this when she gives the doll to her son Andy (Vincent) on his birthday.

The reputation of *Child's Play* has been watered-down over the years with substandard sequels and parodies of its high-concept premise. The original (made by genre luminary Tom Holland) is possibly the last quality example of the vicious 1980s slasher.

Holland puts new spin on an already popular idea – the use of childhood icons as killers and psychopaths is extremely disturbing and effective. Famously, Stephen King used a clown in *It* (directed by Tommy Lee Wallace), and David Schmoelleris is one of many to use puppets in *Puppet Master*, but none of these films had the benefit of Brad Dourif's sleazy, threatening drawl and a distinctly satirical slant. His input is constantly electrifying but there are some great, original ideas that allow *Child's Play* to stand shoulder to shoulder with more lauded examples of the horror genre, particularly the moment of realization when the unused batteries fall from the already talkative Chucky's body.

Misery

Novelist Paul Sheldon (Caan) crashes his car on a remote New England road and is rescued by friendly nurse Annie Wilkes (Bates). Coincidentally she is a big fan of his books and in particular, the heroine Misery Chastaine. Recuperating in her house, Sheldon soon realizes Annie is more than a little unhinged and effectively he becomes a prisoner.

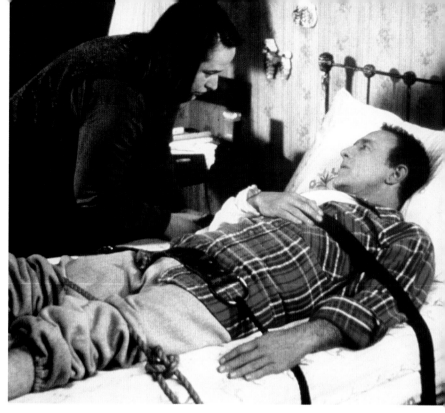

Stephen King's literary adaptations are notoriously hit-or-miss. The success of *Misery* stems from the experience and talent involved. Director Rob Reiner had an exceptional run up to *Misery*, successive hits including *Stand By Me*, *The Princess Bride* and *When Harry Met Sally* made him one of the hottest directors in Hollywood and gave him the power to pick his collaborators. Employing the talents of veterans like actor James Caan (*The Godfather*), Cinematographer Barry Sonnenfeld (*Miller's Crossing*) and screenwriter William Goldman (*Butch Cassidy and the Sundance Kid*), Reiner carefully composed a tense thriller, into which he injected Kathy Bates, the adrenalin shot to the film. She is magnificent as Sheldon's deranged super-fan and her impressive performance rightly earned her an Academy Award.

As with many of the genre's best examples, *Misery* doesn't assault the viewer prematurely. Instead, it carefully establishes the situation and then starts to build tension, making any act of violence seem all the more extreme and effective. The best example of this is the drastic measure Annie reasons must be taken to prevent Sheldon's escape. In King's book she removes his feet, but the alternative here is even more upsetting to witness.

USA, 1990
DIRECTOR:
Rob Reiner
CAST INCLUDES:
James Caan, Kathy Bates,
Richard Farnsworth
SCREENPLAY:
William Goldman from the novel
by Stephen King
CINEMATOGRAPHY:
Barry Sonnenfeld
**PRODUCERS/
PRODUCTION COMPANIES:**
Steve Nicolaides, Rob Reiner,
Andrew Scheinman,
Jeffrey Stott/Castle Rock
Entertainment, Nelson Entertainment
ACADEMY AWARDS (1991)
Best Actress in a Leading Role:
Kathy Bates

Tremors

USA, 1990
DIRECTOR:
Ron Underwood
CAST INCLUDES:
Kevin Bacon, Fred Ward, Finn Carter,
Michael Gross, Reba McEntire
SCREENPLAY:
S.S. Wilson, Brent Maddock from a
story by S.S. Wilson, Brent Maddock,
Ron Underwood
CINEMATOGRAPHY:
Alexander Gruszynski
PRODUCERS/
PRODUCTION COMPANIES:
Ellen Collett, Gale Anne Hurd,
Brent Maddock, S.S. Wilson/ No Frills
Film Production, Universal Pictures

A female seismologist working outside the small desert town of Perfection discovers inexplicable tremors. Before long she finds herself trapped with two idiot roughnecks and a scattering of locals when strange subterranean monsters lay siege.

Ron Underwood's (*City Slickers*) first theatrical outing as director is an inventive hotchpotch of 1950s sci-fi hokum, brimming with genre references, it proudly wears its B-movie badge all the way to the drive-in.

The gleefully stereotypical characters are a delight, particularly brainless cowboys Valentine (Bacon) and Earl (Ward) who possess a huge array of one-liners and a great chemistry. (Earl: 'Is this a job for an intelligent man?' Valentine: 'Well, show me one and I'll ask him'). The local survivalist, Burt (Gross), whose house is stocked with explosives, weapons and enough water to last five years, also deserves a special mention for comedy relief – cutting off a chunk of fuse, Earl: 'What kind of fuse is that?' Burt: 'Cannon fuse.' Earl: 'What the hell do you use it for?' Burt: 'My cannon.'

The monsters, or 'Graboids', are not exactly the scariest cinematic creation (they even have a sense of humour), and the fun most of the cast seem to be having trying to kill them doesn't exactly instil terror, but that's not the idea. There's no intention to scare, classic genre stereotypes are gently mocked for the viewers' amusement, without the film ever trying to be too clever. Charming and unpretentious fun.

The Silence of the Lambs

When the FBI fail to develop any leads as to the identity of a brutal serial killer operating in the mid-west, chief Jack Crawford (Glen) assigns trainee agent Clarice Starling (Foster) to interview convicted psychopath, Dr. Hannibal Lecter (Hopkins). Crawford hopes to wrong-foot the dangerous cannibal by sending an unworthy trainee and Starling must attempt to gain profiling information from Lecter without revealing too much of herself.

When it became only the third film to sweep the five most coveted Academy Awards (picture, director, actor, actress, adapted screenplay) at the 1992 Oscar ceremony, few people can have realized how different the film could have been. Originally to be directed by Gene Hackman, numerous people were above Anthony Hopkins, the film's trump card, on the list of potential Lecters that Hackman wanted. Brian Cox (Lecktor in Manhunter), Jeremy Irons, Robert Duvall and (inevitably) Robert De Niro are all said to have turned down the role before Hopkins, thankfully, accepted. He is the first reason to see the film, totally convincing in a role that makes the skin crawl, particularly the early prison scenes between him and Starling when the tension gets so extreme as to become stifling. The second reason is the huge achievement of disguising such a violent and upsetting horror as a thriller, and smuggling it into the theatres before anyone noticed, and all without having to compromise a single, brutal frame – and it is brutal. Buffalo Bill's (Levine) basement prison is the stuff of nightmares, and Lecter's eventual escape features some horrendous bloodletting and violence.

Slick, intelligent, stunningly photographed and suspenseful to the end, this is a horror film that earned its huge success, and mainstream audience.

USA, 1991
DIRECTOR:
Jonathan Demme
CAST INCLUDES:
Jodie Foster, Anthony Hopkins, Scott Glenn, Anthony Heald, Ted Levine
SCREENPLAY:
Ted Tally from the novel by Thomas Harris
CINEMATOGRAPHY:
Tak Fujimoto
PRODUCERS/ PRODUCTION COMPANIES:
Grace Blake, Ronald M. Bozman, Gary Goetzman, Edward Saxon, Kenneth Utt/Orion Pictures Corporation
ACADEMY AWARD NOMINATIONS (1992)
Best Film Editing: Craig McKay
Best Sound: Tom Fleischman, Christopher Newman
ACADEMY AWARDS
Best Actor in a Leading Role: Anthony Hopkins
Best Actress in a Leading Role: Jodie Foster
Best Director: Jonathan Demme
Best Picture: Edward Saxon, Kenneth Utt, Ronald M. Bozman
Best Writing, Screenplay Based on Material from Another Medium: Ted Tally

Scream

One year after the murder of teenager Sidney Prescott's (Campbell) mother, a serial killer starts carving his way through her friends in a sleepy American town.

Wes Craven's hugely inventive and amusing 'post-modern' slasher was so successful it both reinvigorated and changed the genre. Or rather, reverted it. John Carpenter wrote the rule book with *Halloween* in 1978, and nothing much changed until a wave of (arguably) more intelligent and serious

USA, 1996
DIRECTOR:
Wes Craven
CAST INCLUDES:
David Arquette, Neve Campbell,
Courteney Cox, Skeet Ulrich,
Rose McGowan, Matthew Lillard
SCREENPLAY:
Kevin Williamson
CINEMATOGRAPHY:
Mark Irwin
**PRODUCERS/
PRODUCTION COMPANIES:**
Stuart M. Besser, Dixie J. Capp,
Cathy Konrad, Marianne Maddalena,
Nicholas Mastandrea, Bob Weinstein,
Harvey Weinstein,
Cary Woods/Dimension Films,
Woods Entertainment

horror films became popular in the late 1980s (*Angel Heart*, *Silence of the Lambs*, *Misery*, etc.).

For *Scream*, Craven decided to dig out the old rule book, dust it down, add a few notes on self-referential mockery and throw all his skill and experience into a glossy and slightly watered-down slasher movie for a new generation. The result is a fantastically enjoyable film that works as both a sly comedy and an excellent addition to the slasher horror genre. Campbell's Sidney Prescott is a great substitute for Jamie Lee Curtis' Laurie Strode in *Halloween*, a sweet, delicate all-American girl who outlives her

friends through determination and the retention of her virginity –
an essential precaution if you want to survive in a slasher movie.
But the presence of horror legend Wes Craven ensures the film
doesn't stick so predictably to the generic blueprint as to lose its
ability to surprise and scare. The ingenious use of mobile phones is
an effective idea that provides great tension building potential,
particularly in the much copied and hugely successful opening
sequence in which a terrified young girl, home alone and receiving
prank phone calls from the killer, suddenly realizes she's being
watched by him, too.

Ringu
Ring

Rumours of a mysterious video tape that causes the death of
anybody who views it attracts the attention of a reporter. When her
son accidentally sees it, she must race against the clock to discover
its secret before his inevitable death.

Director Hideo Nakata found huge success in the west as well as
in his native Japan with this slick and highly original chiller. He uses
everything at his disposal to build a sense of fear. The dark and
moody visuals are particularly effective, with rain used to block out
light, while the incredible intensity of the video itself threatens to
reduce the audience to a collective of cowering wrecks every time
extracts are shown. The opening sequence is a minor masterpiece
in itself. Here, two schoolgirls discuss the rumour of a videotape
that kills when one reveals that she has not only seen it but also
received a phone call claiming that she would die in seven days
(something common to all the victims). As if that isn't enough,
exactly seven days have passed since the call. Strange things start
to happen in the house, culminating in the girl's unexplained death.
Her face stiff and disfigured by some unimaginable fear is as
disturbing as any image from the horror cinema portfolio.

Nakata's demanding and imaginative film is a harrowing watch,
but it's also rewarding, paying you back everything you've invested
– as long as you can bear to watch to the end. Don't bother with the
American remake, the Japanese original runs rings around it.

JAPAN, 1998
DIRECTOR:
Hideo Nakata
CAST INCLUDES:
Nanako Matsushima, Miki Nakatani,
Hiroyuki Sanada, Yuko Takeuchi,
Hitomi Sato
SCREENPLAY:
Hiroshi Takahashi from the novel
by Kôji Suzuki
CINEMATOGRAPHY:
Junichirô Hayashi
**PRODUCERS/
PRODUCTION COMPANIES:**
Masato Hara, Takashige Ichise,
Makoto Ishihara, Tatsuya Isomura,
Shinya Kawai, Takenori
Sento/Kadokawa Shoten Publishing
Co. Ltd., Omega Project

The Sixth Sense

USA, 1999
DIRECTOR:
M. Night Shyamalan
CAST INCLUDES:
Bruce Willis, Haley Joel Osment,
Toni Collette, Olivia Williams,
Trevor Morgan
SCREENPLAY:
M. Night Shyamalan
CINEMATOGRAPHY:
Tak Fujimoto
PRODUCERS/
PRODUCTION COMPANIES:
Kathleen Kennedy, Frank Marshall,
Barry Mendel, Sam Mercer
ACADEMY AWARD
NOMINATIONS (2000)
Best Actor in a Supporting Role:
Haley Joel Osment
Best Actress in a Supporting Role:
Toni Collette
Best Director: M. Night Shyamalan
Best Editing: Andrew Mondshein
Best Picture: Frank Marshall,
Kathleen Kennedy, Barry Mendel
Best Writing, Screenplay Written
Directly for the Screen:
M. Night Shyamalan

Malcolm Crowe (Willis), a child psychologist disillusioned by his tragic failure in an earlier case, and suffering a crumbling marriage, offers to help Cole Sear (Osment), a small boy with the troubling ability to see dead people.

Night Shyamalans' subtle and controlled ghost story is a triumph of more than just filmmaking. Shyamalan was a Hollywood nobody, having written and directed two largely unseen features. It was unlikely a major star would risk teaming up with him, even for an action movie or romantic comedy – traditionally safe genres. However, Shyamalan was peddling the most terrifying of screenplays for any established action star in need of a hit – a highly original, intelligent horror story. Fortunately Willis went for it and Shyamalans' inspired casting paid off. Audiences were comforted by a familiar face and flocked to see a demanding, slow paced horror film (it made $661 million and is eighteenth in the all-time worldwide box office chart. It is also the most rented video in America, eighty million in 2000 alone).

Although another large reason for the film's success is the

famous twist ending, it's more than a collection of gimmicks. Shyamalans' hypnotic and methodical style envelops us, the perfectly paced screenplay reveals plot points in carefully measured doses and a few good, solid scares are sprinkled over the top when necessary (Shyamalan has clearly learned a lot from Stanley Kubrick's *The Shining*). Willis' subtle and thoughtful performance is certainly a career highlight, but the revelation here is Haley Joel Osment's eerie and vulnerable Cole Sear, a role that won him an Academy Award nomination at the age of just twelve.

The Blair Witch Project

In 1994 the legend of the Blair Witch attracted three young documentary filmmakers to the small Maryland town of Burkittesville. After setting off into the woods, rumoured to be the spirits' home, they were never seen again. Five years on, *The Blair Witch Project* has been pieced together from the film and videotape found scattered throughout the forest in which they disappeared. But does it offer any evidence of a supernatural presence, and does it explain what happened to the three filmmakers?

In the early 1990s, glossy horror-thrillers such as *Misery* and *Silence of the Lambs* took horror out of the hands of 1970s and 1980s genre firebrands like Wes Craven and John Carpenter, making it mainstream in the process. Although Craven soon applied a twist to the slasher formula with *Scream* in 1996, it was Daniel Myrick and Eduardo Sánchez who made the greatest innovation since Carpenter's 1978 classic *Halloween*, when they released *The Blair Witch Project* in the midst of a bizarre marketing campaign. The story of the missing filmmakers was presented as true, and a huge amount of publicity was generated. In the face of this gimmick, it's easy to forget just how scary the film is. The shaky, handheld 16mm film and video creates such a (deliberately) stomach churning effect your body is on guard before we even get into the woods. This also helps build the tension, which is the cornerstone of the film's effectiveness. There are no monsters jumping out of the dark or knife-wielding maniacs with a grudge against teenagers. Instead there is a relentless, slow build of mystery and paranoia which the viewer must endure alongside the protagonists as we're forced to see it all through their eyes.

The scene in which Heather finally breaks down and (alone with a camera) confesses her belief that nobody will survive is almost unbearable – even though we've known from the start that she's right.

USA, 1999
DIRECTORS:
Daniel Myrick and Eduardo Sánchez
CAST INCLUDES:
Heather Donahue, Joshua Leonard, Mike Williams
SCREENPLAY:
Daniel Myrick and Eduardo Sánchez
CINEMATOGRAPHY:
Neal Fredericks
PRODUCERS/ PRODUCTION COMPANIES:
Robin Cowie, Bob Eick, Kevin J. Foxe, Gregg Hale, Michael Monello/Haxan Films
CANNES FILM FESTIVAL (1999)
Award of the Youth, Foreign Film: Daniel Myrick, Eduardo Sánchez

The Mummy

USA, 1999
DIRECTOR:
Stephen Sommers
CAST INCLUDES:
Brendan Fraser, Rachel Weisz,
John Hannah, Arnold Vosloo
SCREENPLAY:
Stephen Sommers
CINEMATOGRAPHY:
Adrian Biddle
PRODUCERS/
PRODUCTION COMPANIES:
Patricia Carr, Sean Daniel,
James Jacks, Kevin Jarre, Megan
Moran/Alphaville Films, Universal
Pictures
ACADEMY AWARD
NOMINATIONS (2000)
Best Sound: Leslie Shatz,
Chris Carpenter, Rick Kline,
Chris Munro

In ancient Egypt, the powerful priest Imhotep (Vosloo) is cursed and mummified alive after an affair with his Pharoah's mistress. Fast forward to 1923 and a group of explorers, including American adventurer Rick O'Connell (Fraser), who accidentally resurrect the Mummy. It's bad news all round as Imhotep wants to destroy the world, but it's a particular calamity for Rick's new love Evelyn (Weisz), who has been chosen as the substitute for Imhotep's lost love.

Director Stephen Sommers' intention was to make a rollicking, period adventure in the Indiana Jones mould, and like *Temple of Doom* the second Indy feature, he has laced the film liberally with supernatural scares.

The characters are pretty stock, but unavoidably likeable. With a

never-ending supply of one-liners, the dashing but egotistical Rick is a superb roguish hero, and the chemistry between him and the capricious scholar Evelyn is one of the film's great joys. But without a doubt the star of the show is the Mummy itself. One of the film's most intelligent ideas is to take it out of the restrictive bandages and (through some innovative CGI) present Imhotep as an emaciated and decomposing skeleton, capable of huge feats of agility as well as strength. As the film progresses, he becomes physically more human, allowing for a creative evolution in his disgusting appearance before actor Arnold Vosloo actually appears on screen.

A sequel followed, but, lacking the coherence of the original's tight and well-balanced screenplay it's best avoided. Although undeniably slick and modern, *The Mummy* also has an enchanting old-fashioned innocence that makes it perfect Saturday afternoon fodder.

Audition

Widowed for seven years, TV producer Shigeharu Aoyama (Ishibashi) lives with his teenage son, Shigehiko (Sawaki). Deciding it's time to remarry and realizing he has little idea how to go about finding a wife, he asks a friend for advice. At first he's not keen to take up his suggestion of sitting in on casting auditions for young actresses, but he soon succumbs to the pressure of loneliness and whilst leafing through candidates' resumés sets his heart on a girl even before the audition. A tentative courtship follows, but is the girl hiding something?

JAPAN, 2000
DIRECTOR:
Takashi Miike
CAST INCLUDES:
Ryo Ishibashi, Eihi Shiina,
Tetsu Sawaki, Jun Kunimura
SCREENPLAY:
Daisuke Tengan from the novel
by Ryu Murakami
CINEMATOGRAPHY:
Hideo Yamamoto
**PRODUCERS/
PRODUCTION COMPANIES:**
Satoshi Fukushima, Akemi Suyama,
Toyoyuki Yokohama/AFDF,
Omega Project

Prolific and challenging Japanese director Takashi Miike finally broke through in the west with this alternately touching and grueling 'romantic horror'. An emotionally wrenching opening (in which we witness the death of Aoyama's wife and the pain of his young son) gives way to a gentle, touching romance as two psychologically scarred people appear to find love. Eihi Shiina is superb as Asami Yamazaki, the *femme fatale* whose façade doesn't start to crumble until Aoyama has fallen hopelessly in love with her, in spite of the warnings of those close to him. Her recollections of a tortured childhood alert the viewer to the kind of excruciating violence that lies ahead when Miike destroys the film's narrative in a blaze of harrowing abhorrence that he seems to relish.

Shot in an edgy, over-saturated visual style, the viewer is never unaware of the inevitable sledgehammer blow that must come sooner or later – after all, this is a horror film. The tension built up during the extended middle section becomes almost unbearable even before Miike decides to show us any real evidence of the girl's twisted reality (a brief shot of her apartment, containing nothing but a telephone and a thrashing, growling sack comes out of the blue and scares you silly).

If David Lynch decided to make a cross between *Boxing Helena* and *Solaris*, it might look something like this.

The Others

1940s Jersey. A neurotic mother of two children, both allergic to daylight, battles to maintain a large house with the assistance of three increasingly suspicious servants, her husband seemingly having been killed in the war.

Essentially a modern reworking of assorted haunted house themes, writer/director Alejandro Amenábar adds some interesting ideas to the formula whilst abiding by strict genre rules.

The house in which almost the entire film takes place is suitably gothic and spooky. Isolated from a village we never see and permanently enveloped in fog, it's shot with an elegant, lingering style that helps it do what every haunted house must – take on a personality. This is aided by the children's allergy to light, an ingenious plot device that creates both a genuine threat to their lives and a good excuse for the terminal darkness that becomes part of the building's overbearing, interior identity. Moving the children from room to room requires huge feats of planning, interference or impediment could prove fatal as every inner door must be kept locked and curtains drawn wherever they go. Conversely, light becomes a refuge for Grace (Kidman), the heart of the film. Her struggle with loneliness and motherhood, and her neurotic fall into madness are portrayed perfectly by the excellent Kidman, who infuses the character with the same gothic elegance possessed by the house. The uncompromisingly dark twist ending is one of modern horror's best moments.

USA, 2001
DIRECTOR:
Alejandro Amenábar
CAST INCLUDES:
Nicole Kidman, Fionnula Flanagan, Christopher Eccleston, Alakina Mann, James Bentley, Eric Sykes
SCREENPLAY:
Alejandro Amenábar
CINEMATOGRAPHY:
Javier Aguirresarobe
**PRODUCERS/
PRODUCTION COMPANIES:**
Fernando Bovaira,
Eduardo Chapero-Jackson,
Tom Cruise, José Luis Cuerda,
Rick Schwartz, Park Sunmin,
Paula Wagner, Bob Weinstein,
Harvey Weinstein/Canal+ España,
Cruise-Wagner Productions,
Las Producciones del Escorpión S.L.,
Le Studio Canal+, Lucky Red,
Miramax Films, Sociedad General de
Cine (SOGECINE) S.A.

28 Days Later...

Twenty eight days after animal rights' activists release a virus that transforms people into wild zombie-like lunatics, an uninfected man (Murphy) wakes up in hospital. Together with a small group of survivors (including Gleeson), he starts on a long trek to find safety and the possibility of a new life. But in a crumbling society, it's not just the infected who pose a threat.

Danny Boyle (*Trainspotting*) turns his hand to zombie movies and succeeds in injecting new blood. Where Romero's classic zombies shuffle and stumble, Boyle's incarnations run like rabid, starving dogs.

This twist isn't entirely new, David Cronenberg has used many of the essential elements here before (and successfully), but these are the first cinema zombies that seem to launch themselves at you from the screen. Even when the characters are technically free, there is a feeling of claustrophobia and confinement brought about by the sense that there are no 'living' humans for miles. Garland's script conveys this in unusual places, a scene where Jim (Murphy) wanders across London's Westminster Bridge without a soul in sight is particularly striking. Boyle and cinematographer Anthony Dod Mantle get the most out of the digital cameras used, for financial reasons, changing colours slightly and leaving a soft-focus look usually associated with sentimental or romantic movies. This serves to increase the viewer's unease, and some frenetic and highly effective editing really hammer home the scares.

What sets *28 Days Later...* aside is its daring in all quarters – shooting on digital cameras, sticking to a UK setting, casting unknowns in lead roles and tackling a genre which doesn't tend towards crossover appeal whilst potentially deterring core fans with radical innovations. Fortunately, the gamble paid off – the film was a huge success in America and its place in the cult horror hall of fame is assured.

USA, 2001
DIRECTOR:
Danny Boyle
CAST INCLUDES:
Cillian Murphy, Naomie Harris, Noah Huntley, Brendan Gleeson, Christopher Eccleston
SCREENPLAY:
Alex Garland
CINEMATOGRAPHY:
Anthony Dod Mantle
PRODUCERS/
PRODUCTION COMPANIES:
Greg Caplan, Simon Fallon, Robert How, Andrew Macdonald/ British Film Council [GB], Canal+ [FR], DNA Films, Figment Films

MUSICAL

42nd Street

USA, 1933
DIRECTOR:
Lloyd Bacon
CAST INCLUDES:
Warner Baxter, Bebe Daniels,
George Brent, Ruby Keeler,
Guy Kibbee, Una Merkel, Ginger
Rogers, Ned Sparks, Dick Powell,
Allen Jenkins, Edward J. Nugent
SCREENPLAY:
Rian James, James Seymour and
Whitney Bolton (uncredited) from the
novel by
Bradford Ropes
CINEMATOGRAPHY:
Sol Polito
**PRODUCERS/PRODUCTION
COMPANIES:**
Darryl F. Zanuck (uncredited)/
Warner Bros.
**ACADEMY AWARD
NOMINATIONS (1934)**
Best Picture
Best Sound, Recording:
Nathan Levinson

The word goes up and down the street: producers Jones and Day are doing a new show – *Pretty Lady*. Rich business magnate Abner Dillon (Kibbee) is backing the musical to please leading lady Dorothy Brock (Daniels). Veteran director Julian Marsh (Baxter), though a sick man, signs up because he needs the money. He picks fifty girls by looking at their legs, including stage-worn showgirls Lorraine (Merkel) and Annie (Rogers) and wide-eyed newcomer Peggy (Keeler). Marsh drives the girls through tough rehearsals, off-stage relationships are in an uproar and, on the eve of first-night, Dorothy hurts her ankle. Peggy is sent on instead – and comes back a star.

42nd Street changed the direction of the backstage musical. It was a tale, not of glamour, but of the grim reality of theatre life, with its heartbreaks and grinding work schedules. It was also the film that saved Warner Brothers from bankruptcy and set it on course to become a major studio. Furthermore, in *42nd Street*, the Broadway choreographer Busby Berkeley came into his own on film. He contrasts real-life on *42nd Street* with his superb chorus-girl revue pieces and the extraordinary camera angles used to film them, creating kaleidoscopes, waves and chandeliers of exquisitely dressed girls. Warner Brothers promptly signed Berkeley to a seven-year contract. Ruby Murray was an exciting new kid on the block, too.

Gold Diggers of 1933

Three out-of-work chorus girls, Carol (Blondell), Trixie (MacMahon) and Polly (Keeler), learn that producer-friend Barney Hopkins (Sparks) hopes to be putting on a new show. Barney hears Brad Roberts (Powell) at the piano and discovers, on roping him in to the production, that he is also a fine singer-songwriter – and has money to back the show. Brad's wealthy family disapprove of his show-business tendencies and, when they hear he is engaged to Polly, brother Lawrence (William) arrives with a lawyer, Peabody (Kibbee) to put a stop to it. Carol and Trixie turn their 'gold digger' charms on the men and everyone gets married or engaged – and the show goes on.

Gold Diggers of 1933 was Busby Berkeley's second job as dance director for Warner Brothers, and it is even more elaborate than *42nd Street* (1933). The show blasts open with fifty four girls dressed in silver-coin costumes singing 'We're in the Money' with 'front girl' Ginger Rogers singing a chorus in Pig Latin. 'The Shadow Waltz' has seventy four girls in diaphanous crinolines playing neon-lit violins – some on a spiralling staircase, others forming the petals of a flower as seen from one of Berkeley's overhead crane shots. The film ends as unexpectedly as it begins, with Joan Blondell, echoed by Etta Moten, singing 'Remember My Forgotten Man' to the unthanked and unrecompensed heroes of World War I.

USA, 1933
DIRECTOR:
Mervyn LeRoy
CAST INCLUDES:
Warren William, Joan Blondell, Aline MacMahon,
Ruby Keeler, Dick Powell, Guy Kibbee,
Ned Sparks, Ginger Rogers
SCREENPLAY:
Erwin S. Gelsey, James Seymour,
David Boehm, Ben Markson from the
play by Avery Hopwood
CINEMATOGRAPHY:
Sol Polito
**PRODUCERS/
PRODUCTION COMPANIES:**
Robert Lord, Jack L. Warner/
Warner Bros.
**ACADEMY AWARD
NOMINATIONS (1934)**
Best Sound, Recording:
Nathan Levinson (sound director)

USA, 1934
UK TITLE:
The Gay Divorce
DIRECTOR:
Mark Sandrich
CAST INCLUDES:
Fred Astaire, Ginger Rogers,
Alice Brady, Edward Everett Horton,
Erik Rhodes, Eric Blore, Lillian Miles,
Charles Coleman,
William Austin, Betty Grable
SCREENPLAY:
George Marion Jr., Dorothy Yost,
Edward Kaufman, Robert Benchley
from the unproduced play by J.
Hartley Manners; musical adaptation
for play: Kenneth S. Webb, Samuel
Hoffenstein; musical book for the
play *The Gay Divorce*
by Dwight Taylor
CINEMATOGRAPHY:
David Abel
**PRODUCERS/PRODUCTION
COMPANIES**
Pandro S, Berman/RKO Radio
Pictures Inc.
**ACADEMY AWARD
NOMINATIONS (1935)**
Best Art Direction: Van Nest Polglase,
Carroll Clark
Best Music, Score: Max Steiner
Best Picture
Best Sound, Recording:
Carl Dreher
ACADEMY AWARDS
Best Music, Original Song:
Con Conrad (music), Herb Magidson
(lyrics) for the song 'The Continental'

The Gay Divorcee

The famous dancer, Guy Holden (Astaire) is travelling with his attorney-friend Egbert (Horton) in England when he meets and falls for Mimi (Rogers). Egbert is a friend of Mimi's Aunt Hortense (Brady), and the pair are trying to get Mimi divorced from her geologist husband, Cyril (Austin). They arrange for a hired correspondent to give Cyril reason to divorce Mimi. However, Mimi mistakes Guy for the correspondent and invites him to her room at midnight. When all is later explained, Mimi asks Cyril for a divorce so she can marry Guy, but Cyril says he forgives her. However, the waiter recognizes Cyril as a man who already has another wife. When Egbert and Hortense announce that they've married, Guy and Mimi respond by dancing.

Following their show-stopping 'Carioca' in *Flying Down to Rio* (1933) – the result of almost accidental pairing – RKO gave Astaire and Rogers star billing in *The Gay Divorcee*. Here they developed the elegant and sophisticated dance style most associated with them, and danced to two Cole Porter numbers: 'The Continental', which is a sensational song and dance routine that lasts for over twenty minutes. It also won the first Oscar for a song. The second is the memorable 'Night and Day'.

Top Hat

Two strangers, Jerry Travers (Astaire) and Dale Tremont (Rogers) meet by accident. Their budding romance is soon confused by a whole roster of mistaken identities. However, Jerry manages to win over the, by now, sceptical Dale with some romantic dances in delightful settings – 'Isn't This a Lovely Day' in a bandstand during a rainstorm in London and 'Cheek to Cheek' beside the canals of Venice.

Top Hat, RKO's biggest box-office hit of the thirties, is an exquisite production: the elegant costumes, art-deco sets, toe-tapping music and delightful lyrics (both by Irving Berlin) are all divine. This was the fourth film with Astaire and Rogers and it is possibly the best known and best loved. The dance sequences are the stuff of legend – who can forget Astaire practising his tap routine in his hotel late at night or when he puts on his 'Top Hat, White Tie, and Tails'? 'Cheek to Cheek' is without a doubt one of the duo's most romantic song and dance routines – Astaire nicknamed Rogers Feathers as her beautiful satin and ostrich feather gown moulted as she danced.

USA, 1935
DIRECTOR:
Mark Sandrich
CAST INCLUDES:
Fred Astaire, Ginger Rogers, Edward Everett Horton, Erik Rhodes, Eric Blore, Helen Broderick
SCREENPLAY:
Allan Scott, Dwight Taylor (also author of the story *The Gay Divorce*), Károly Nóti based on the play *The Girl Who Dared* by Alexander Faragó and Aladar Laszlo
CINEMATOGRAPHY:
David Abel
PRODUCERS/ PRODUCTION COMPANIES:
Pandro S. Berman/RKO Radio Pictures Inc.
ACADEMY AWARD NOMINATIONS (1936)
Best Art Direction: Carroll Clark, Van Nest Polglase
Best Dance Direction: Hermes Pan for 'Piccolino' and 'Top Hat'
Best Music, Original Song: Irving Berlin for the song 'Cheek to Cheek'
Best Picture

Show Boat

USA, 1936
DIRECTOR:
James Whale
CAST INCLUDES:
Irene Dunne, Allan Jones,
Charles Winninger, Paul Robeson,
Helen Morgan, Helen Westley,
Queenie Smith, Sammy White,
Donald Cook, Hattie McDaniel,
Francis X. Mahoney,
Marilyn Knowlden, Sunnie O'Dea
SCREENPLAY:
Oscar Hammerstein from the novel
by Edna Ferber
CINEMATOGRAPHY:
John J. Mescall
**PRODUCERS/
PRODUCTION COMPANIES:**
Carl Laemmle Jr./Universal Pictures

Julie LaVerne (Morgan) is the leading lady on the Mississippi showboat under the helm of Cap'n Andy Hawks (Winninger). When a local sherrif accuses Julie of being a mulatto, she and husband Steve (Cook) have to leave the boat. Hawks' daughter Magnolia 'Nola' (Dunne) replaces her and falls in love with the new leading man, Gaylord Ravenal (Jones). They marry, have a daughter, Kim (Knowlden), and then go to Chicago where Gaylord's gambling ruins them. He leaves in shame, and Nola goes back to the stage. When she retires, Kim (O'Dea) goes on to sing on Broadway – where they meet Gaylord again.

Most of the cast had been in one or other of the stage productions of Edna Ferber's story. The unexpected choice was to use classic horror-film maker James Whale as the director. However, it certainly works: people speak of the 1936 *Show Boat* as the one with soul, and also that it's more than a musical – it's a film. Furthermore, it has Helen Morgan singing 'Can't Help Lovin' That Man' o Mine', and the incomparable Robson singing the charming 'I Still Suits Me' and his soul-searing 'Ol' Man River'.

Alexander's Ragtime Band

It's prohibition-era New York. Young Roger Grant (Power) has abandoned his classical music training to form his own 'Alexander's Ragtime Band'. He hires Stella Kirby (Faye) as his singer and soon finds he is in love with her – but so is pianist Charlie Dwyer (Ameche). Roger and Charlie battle over the love of Stella for some twenty five years. In the meantime, Roger meets Jerry (Merman) another vocalist, and Stella opts for Broadway and marries Charlie. After many more mix-ups and adventures – including World War I – everyone meets up again and settles down with the right partner.

This lavish musical is a sumptuous all-star showcase for twenty eight of Irving Berlin's songs. The movie took its title from Berlin's hit of 1911 – a song which, ironically, was not in ragtime. 'Easter Parade', 'Heat Wave', 'A Pretty Girl Is Like a Melody' – they're all here. Jerome Kern said 'Irving Berlin has no place in American music. He is American music'. Berlin himself said 'I'd rather have Alice Faye introduce my songs than any other singer I know'. However, the young Ethel Merman certainly did justice to 'My Walking Stick' and 'Blue Skies'.

USA, 1938
DIRECTOR:
Henry King
CAST INCLUDES:
Tyrone Power, Alice Faye,
Don Ameche, Ethel Merman,
Jack Haley, Jean Hersholt,
Helen Westley, John Carradine
SCREENPLAY:
Kathryn Scola, Richard Sherman,
Lamar Trotti from the story by
Irving Berlin
CINEMATOGRAPHY:
J. Peverell Marley
**PRODUCERS/
PRODUCTION COMPANIES:**
Darryl F. Zanuck/Twentieth Century
Fox Film Corp.
**ACADEMY AWARD
NOMINATIONS (1939)**
Best Art Direction: Bernard Herzbrun,
Boris Leven
Best Film Editing:
Barbara McLean
Best Music, Original Song:
Irving Berlin, for the song
'Now It Can Be Told'
Best Picture: Darryl F. Zanuck,
Harry Joe Brown
Best Writing, Original Story:
Irving Berlin
ACADEMY AWARDS
Best Music, Scoring:
Alfred Newman

The Wizard of Oz

USA, 1939
DIRECTOR:
Victor Fleming, King Vidor
CAST INCLUDES:
Judy Garland, Frank Morgan,
Ray Bolger, Bert Lahr, Jack Haley,
Billie Burke, Margaret Hamilton,
Charley Grapewin,
Pat Walshe, Clara Blandick and Terry
as Toto
SCREENPLAY:
Noel Langley, Florence Ryerson and
Edgar Allan Woolf from the novel *The
Wonderful Wizard of Oz* by L. Frank
Baum
CINEMATOGRAPHY:
Harold Rosson
**PRODUCERS/
PRODUCTION COMPANIES:**
Mervyn LeRoy/Metro-Goldwyn-Mayer
(MGM)
**ACADEMY AWARD
NOMINATIONS (1940)**
Best Art Direction: Cedric Gibbons,
William A. Horning
Best Cinematography, Color:
Harold Rosson
Best Effects, Special Effects:
A. Arnold Gillespie (photographic),
Douglas Shearer (sound)
Best Picture: Mervyn LeRoy
ACADEMY AWARDS
Best Music, Original Score:
Herbert Stothart
Best Music, Original Song:
Harold Arlen (music), E.Y. Harburg
(lyrics) for the song
'Over the Rainbow'
CANNES FILM FESTIVAL (1939)
Palme d'Or Nomination:
Victor Fleming

Kansas farm-girl Dorothy (Garland) is feeling very sad because a nasty neighbour wants to have her dog Toto – her only friend – put to sleep. She is planning to run away when a tornado blows away the farm-house. When it comes to ground, Dorothy finds she's in the Land of Oz. She sets off to find the Wizard, who will help her to get home. On the way she meets a Scarecrow who needs a brain, a Tin Man who wants a heart, a Cowardly Lion who desperately needs courage, the Good Fairy of the North (who, she hopes, will save her from the Wicked Witch of the West) and lots of Munchkins. Her many adventures show her that magical is wonderful, but home is best.

Once you see *The Wizard of Oz*, ideas and images such as The Yellow Brick Road, the heartless Tin Man, the scaredy Lion, and 'Somewhere Over the Rainbow' will be with you forever. The songs (by Harold Arlen and E.Y. Harburg) fitted perfectly into the plot, advancing the surprise-a-minute story-line. The role of the Wizard was originally written with W.C. Fields in mind but, when MGM didn't offer enough money, he apparently told them he was too busy writing the script for *You Can't Cheat an Honest Man*!

Strike Up the Band

USA, 1940
DIRECTOR:
Busby Berkeley
CAST INCLUDES:
Mickey Rooney, Judy Garland,
Paul Whiteman and Orchestra,
June Preisser, William Tracy,
Larry Nunn, Margaret Early
SCREENPLAY:
John Monks Jr., Fred F. Finklehoffe (as
Fred Finklehoffe)
CINEMATOGRAPHY:
Ray June
**PRODUCERS/PRODUCTION
COMPANIES:**
Arthur Freed/Loew's Inc., Metro-
Goldwyn-Mayer (MGM)
**ACADEMY AWARD
NOMINATIONS (1941)**
Best Music, Original Song:
Roger Edens, George E. Stoll for the
song 'Our Love Affair'
Best Music, Score: George E. Stoll,
Roger Edens
ACADEMY AWARDS
Best Sound, Recording:
Douglas Shearer (M-G-M SSD)

When their high school won't donate the funds to enable the kids to enter Paul Whiteman's high-school band radio contest, Jimmy (Rooney) – drums and piano – and Mary (Garland) – vocals – determine that they and their fellow band-members will raise the necessary cash themselves. They put on a show which earns the money they need, but then Jimmy gives it all to band-member Willie (Nunn) whose mother is very ill. However, who should arrive in town? Yes, none other than Paul Whiteman himself, who offers a helping hand.

'The merriest pair on the screen' are here directed, for the second of four times, by Busby Berkeley. Rooney, at his most irrepressible, is beautifully contrasted with a maturing, blooming Garland whose singing (particularly of 'Nobody') is beautiful. Berkeley's 'fruit orchestra' set-piece is memorably stunning.

Yankee Doodle Dandy

The composer, singer and dancer George M. Cohan (Cagney) has been invited to meet President Franklin D. Roosevelt whom he has recently 'spoofed' in a musical comedy called 'I'd Rather Be Right'. He tells the president his rags-to-riches life story. In his childhood, Cohan travelled in vaudeville with his parents (Huston & DeCamp) and sister (Jeanne Cagney). He broke with the family act and headed for Broadway with another young hopeful called Mary (Leslie) whom he eventually marries. It takes a long time for his career to take off but, now, he has dozens of shows to his name and many well-loved published songs. The president gives him a congressional medal, after which he goes out to join in a WWII parade where young soldiers are singing his WWI song 'Over There'.

George Cohan's life and career were firmly tidied up and sanitized for this musical; however both his amazing output of music – especially such heartfelt patriotic numbers as 'Grand Old Flag' and 'Over There' – and Cagney's 300% input into the movie role (earning him a well-deserved Oscar) did give the USA a much-needed tonic at that miserable point in World War II. Cagney also needed the tonic as he had recently been threatened with black-listing by the House of Un-American Activities Committee. This was the first black-and-white film to be colourized digitally for its re-release in 1985.

USA, 1942
DIRECTOR:
Michael Curitz
CAST INCLUDES:
James Cagney, Joan Leslie,
Walter Huston, Richard Whorf,
Irene Manning, George Tobias, Rosemary
DeCamp, Jeanne Cagney, Frances
Langford, George Barbier, S.Z. Sakall,
Walter Catlett,
Douglas Croft, Eddie Foy Jr.
SCREENPLAY:
Robert Bruckner and Edmund Joseph
from a story by Robert Bruckner
CINEMATOGRAPHY:
James Wong Howe
**PRODUCERS/
PRODUCTION COMPANIES:**
Hal B. Wallis, Jack L.Warner/Warner Bros.
**ACADEMY AWARD
NOMINATIONS (1943)**
Best Actor in a Supporting Role: Walter
Huston
Best Director: Michael Curtiz
Best Film Editing: George Amy
Best Picture: Jack L. Warner,
Hal B. Wallis, William Cagney
Best Writing, Original Story:
Robert Buckner
ACADEMY AWARDS
Best Actor in a Leading Role:
James Cagney
Best Music, Scoring of a Musical Picture:
Ray Heindorf,
Heinz Roemheld
Best Sound, Recording:
Nathan Levinson (Warner Bros. SSD)

You Were Never Lovelier

USA, 1942
DIRECTOR:
Willian A, Seiter
CAST INCLUDES:
Fred Astaire, Rita Hayworth,
Adolphe Menjou, Isobel Elsom,
Leslie Brooks, Adele Mara,
Gus Schilling, Barbara Brown,
Douglas Leavitt, Xavier Cugat,
Xavier Cugat Orchestra
SCREENPLAY:
Michael Fessier, Ernest Pagano,
Delmer Daves from a story by
Carlos A. Olivari and
Sixto Póndal Ríos
CINEMATOGRAPHY:
Ted Tetzlaff
PRODUCERS/
PRODUCTION COMPANIES:
Louis F. Edelman/Columbia Pictures
Corporation
ACADEMY AWARD
NOMINATIONS (1943)
Best Music, Original Song: Jerome
Kern (music), Johnny Mercer (lyrics)
for the song 'Dearly Beloved'
Best Music, Scoring of a Musical
Picture: Leigh Harline
Best Sound, Recording:
John P. Livadary (Columbia SSD)

Eduardo Acuna (Menjou), a wealthy Argentinian hotel magnate, believes that daughters should be married in order of age. However, his third and fourth daughters (Brooks & Mara) can't get hitched because daughter number two, Maria (Hayworth), appears to have no interest in men. Dancer Bob Davis (Astaire) meets Maria while trying to get a job from Eduardo, but she cold-shoulders him. Eduardo starts sending Maria flowers and love-letters, hoping she'll think they come from a 'respectable' suitor, but she assumes they are from Bob. Eduardo offers Bob a dance contract on condition he leaves Argentina afterwards. However, the problems for Eduardo of getting Maria married to the man of his dreams have only just begun.

The pairing of Hollywood's most elegant dancer and most enticing love goddess (seldom has Hayworth been lovelier) has to be good news – and it is. The on-again, off-again relationship between Astaire's Bob and Hayworth's Maria, permits dance director Val Raset plenty of opportunities to raise the passion level or to glide through cooler encounters. Jerome Kern and Johnny Mercer provide a glorious array of songs – Hayworth's numbers were sung by Nan Wynn.

The Gang's All Here

Rich, young Andy Mason (Ellison) is on leave from the army when he meets and falls for beautiful showgirl Edie (Faye). By the time morning comes, he's won her heart and her hand – although he hasn't given her his real name. He then has to leave to report for active duty in the Pacific. In due course Andy completes his term of duty and comes home – with a medal. To celebrate his return, his parents have arranged to put on a benefit show in which Edie's troupe will be performing. Their meeting will be unavoidable, as will her discovery of his true identity – and of Vivian, who is another lady for whom he seems to be coming home.

The plot of a Busby Berkeley movie is never much to marvel at but, for *The Gang's All Here*, it sinks to the level of a conversation stopper. It's only purpose is to give Alice Faye the opportunity to sing some lovely songs, to let Benny Goodman swing, to enable Pallette, Greenwood and Horton to be, as always, deliriously funny, to give Busby Berkeley the opportunity to create some wondrously outrageous chorus-line numbers – and to allow spike-heeled Carmen Miranda to wear her nine-foot-high Tutti Frutti Hat. The number involving the Hat, the Strawberries and the Banana Girls is the crowning moment of Technicolor, movie-musical kitsch.

USA, 1943
UK TITLE:
The Girls He Left Behind
DIRECTOR:
Busby Berkeley
CAST INCLUDES:
Alice Faye, Carmen Miranda,
Phil Baker, Benny Goodman,
Eugene Pallette, Charlotte
Greenwood, Edward Everett
Horton,Tony De Marco, James Ellison,
Dave Willock
SCREENPLAY:
Walter Bullock from a story by
Nancy Wintner, George Root Jr. and
Tom Bridges
CINEMATOGRAPHY:
Edward Cronjager
**PRODUCERS/
PRODUCTION COMPANIES:**
William LeBaron/Twentieth Century
Fox Film Corporation
**ACADEMY AWARD
NOMINATIONS (1944)**
Best Art Direction-Interior
Decoration, Color: James Basevi,
Joseph C. Wright, Thomas Little

Meet Me in St. Louis

The Smith family lives at 5135 Kensington, St. Louis: Anna (Astor) and Alonzo (Ames), their son Lon (Daniels) and their four daughters – Rose (Bremer), Esther (Garland), Agnes (Carroll) and Tootie (O'Brien). In the spring, Esther falls in love with the new boy next door John Truett (Drake). Then, father announces that he has received a position in New York and they will be moving after Christmas.

At the winter dance, Esther tells John about having to leave St. Louis and he asks her to marry him. Tootie waits at the window for Santa to arrive; she is worried that he won't be able to find her next year. Esther comforts her little sister and sings 'Have Yourself a Merry Little Christmas', but Tootie runs out into the snow and smashes her snowmen. The doctor is called to help calm her, and father decides that his family needs to stay in St. Louis. The last scene shows the Smith family and John at the World's Fair which has come to town.

This was only Minnelli's third film, yet his ability to work with the songs, which slip seamlessly into the story, is masterly. Indeed, the film didn't follow a putting-on-a show formula; instead, Minnelli took a suburban-life story and, without letting it get sentimental, told of simple, family things in superb colour. The songs include 'The Boy Next Door', 'The Trolley Song' and 'You Are For Loving'. The producer Arthur Freed dubbed the singing voice of Leon Ames.

USA, 1944
DIRECTOR:
Vincente Minnelli
CAST INCLUDES:
Judy Garland, Margaret O'Brien,
Mary Astor, Lucille Bremer,
Leon Ames, Tom Drake,
Marjorie Main, Harry Davenport,
June Lockhart, Henry H. Daniels Jr.,
Joan Carroll, Hugh Marlowe,
Robert Sully, Chill Wills
SCREENPLAY:
Fred F. Finklehoffe and Irving Brecher
from a novel by Sally Benson
CINEMATOGRAPHY:
George (J.) Folsey
PRODUCERS/
PRODUCTION COMPANIES:
Arthur Freed/Metro-Goldwyn-Mayer
(MGM)
ACADEMY AWARD
NOMINATIONS (1945)
Best Cinematography, Colour:
George J. Folsey
Best Music, Original Song:
Ralph Blane, Hugh Martin for the
song 'The Trolley Song'.
Best Music, Scoring of a Musical
Picture: George E. Stoll
Best Writing, Screenplay: Irving
Brecher, Fred F. Finklehoffe

Easter Parade

One minute Don Hewes (Astaire) is singing 'It Only Happens When I Dance With You' to his beautiful dance partner Nadine Hale (Miller) and, in the next, she tells him she's leaving him for a high-prestige solo job headlining a much bigger show. A couple of moments later, while still bitter at being dumped both professionally and personally, and swearing that he'll pick any girl off the street and turn her into a dancer to rival Nadine – along comes Hannah Brown (Garland). Before long, he has to accept that Hannah is quite a different sort of talent, and has to adjust his own style to blend with hers. Meanwhile, Don's buddy, Johnny (Lawford), falls for Hannah, while Hannah, of course, falls for Don, although Don can't seem to get over Nadine, but Nadine has her eye on Johnny – and they're all looking forward to the Easter Parade.

When Gene Kelly broke his ankle on the eve of production, the 'retired' Fred Astaire stepped in to the role of Don Hewes – and so began his next twenty years as a movie star. However, Cyd Charisse – also signed up – had broken a leg, so Astaire's new Nadine was the vibrant Ann Miller who, in more than one scene, stole the show. Fred and Judy doing 'We're a Couple of Swells' is an all-time favourite, and the other great Irving Berlin numbers include 'Easter Parade' itself, Astaire's 'Drum Crazy', Steppin' Out With My Baby', and Miller's stunning 'Shakin' My Blues Away'.

USA, 1948
DIRECTOR:
Charles Walters
CAST INCLUDES:
Judy Garland, Fred Astaire,
Peter Lawford, Ann Miller,
Jules Munshin, Clinton Sundberg,
Richard Beavers
SCREENPLAY:
Sidney Sheldon, Frances Goodrich,
Albert Hackett from a story by
Frances Goodrich and Albert Hackett
CINEMATOGRAPHY:
Harry Stradling Sr.
PRODUCERS/
PRODUCTION COMPANIES:
Arthur Freed/MGM
ACADEMY AWARDS (1949)
Best Music, Scoring of a Musical
Picture: Johnny Green,
Roger Edens

GB, 1948
DIRECTOR:
Michael Powell, Emeric Pressburger
CAST INCLUDES:
Anton Walbrook, Marius Goring,
Moira Shearer,
Robert Helpmann, Léonide Massine,
Albert Bassermann,
Ludmilla Tchérina,
Esmond Knight
SCREENPLAY:
Michael Powell,
Emeric Pressburger from the fairy
tale by
Hans Christian Andersen
CINEMATOGRAPHY:
Jack Cardiff
**PRODUCERS/
PRODUCTION COMPANIES:**
Michael Powell,
Emeric Pressburger/Independent
Producers, J. Arthur Rank Films,
The Archers
**ACADEMY AWARD
NOMINATIONS (1949)**
Best Film Editing: Reginald Mills
Best Picture: Michael Powell,
Emeric Pressburger
Best Writing, Motion Picture Story:
Emeric Pressburg
ACADEMY AWARDS
Best Art Direction-Set
Decoration, Color:
Hein Heckroth, Arthur Lawson
Best Music, Scoring of a Dramatic or
Comedy Picture: Brian Easdale

The Red Shoes

Ballerina Vicky Page (Shearer) and composer Julian Craster (Goring) join the famous Lermontov (Walbrook) ballet company. Vicky falls in love with Julian and is groomed for the lead in his ballet *The Red Shoes*, which is a great success. But Lermontov demands that she choose between her career and her lover. For Vicky, the strain is too great . . .

One of Powell and Pressburger's best-loved films; for many, seeing it is an eye-opening and inspirational cinematic moment. It is also ranked, by British Film Institute members, as the ninth best British film ever made. Not so for studio boss J. Arthur Rank (the dominant force in British film-making) who walked out during the gala performance. The special effects used to heighten the drama of the ballet sequence are still sensational, and the Technicolor photography, production design and score are all perfect.

On the Town

Three sailors, Gabey (Kelly), Chip (Sinatra) and Ozzie (Munshin) – who are on 24-hour shore leave – want to find some 'good-looking broads' with whom to taste the Big Apple. Gabey falls for the current 'Miss Turnstiles' – the monthly calendar girl featured on the subway who, this month, is Ivy Smith (Vera-Ellen). Chip is pounced on by Hildy (Garrett), a 'let's get physical' taxi driver, and Ozzie is snapped up by museum researcher Claire (Miller) who sees him as her missing link to Neanderthal Man. Once Gabey finds Ivy, the three couples set out to have a good time – which they do, judging by the number of New York City cops who end up chasing after them.

A ballet by Jerome Kern led to a 1944 Broadway hit by Betty Comden and Adolph Green (who also played Claire and Ozzie in it) who went on to write the screenplay after MGM bought the play. Much of the movie was filmed on location (unheard of at that time) in New York, including the scenes in the old Brooklyn Navy Yard and those on top of the Empire State Building – tough on Munshin who was afraid of heights. Great numbers from Leonard Bernstein's score include 'New York, New York', 'On the Town', 'Prehistoric Man' and 'Main Street'.

USA, 1949
DIRECTOR:
Stanley Donen, Gene Kelly
CAST INCLUDES:
Gene Kelly, Frank Sinatra,
Betty Garrett, Jules Munshin,
Vera-Ellen, Florence Bates,
Alice Pearce, George Meader,
Judy Holliday
SCREENPLAY:
Adolph Green, Betty Comden from a
play by Adolph Green
and Betty Comden
CINEMATOGRAPHY:
Harold Rosson
PRODUCERS/
PRODUCTION COMPANIES:
Arthur Freed/MGM
ACADEMY AWARDS (1950)
Best Music, Scoring of a Musical
Picture: Roger Edens,
Lennie Hayton

An American in Paris

USA, 1951
DIRECTOR:
Vincente Minnelli
CAST INCLUDES:
Gene Kelly, Leslie Caron,
Oscar Levant, Georges Guétary,
Nina Foch
SCREENPLAY:
Alan Jay Lerner (and story)
CINEMATOGRAPHY:
John Alto, Alfred Gilks
PRODUCERS/
PRODUCTION COMPANIES:
Arthur Freed/Metro-Goldwyn-Mayer
(MGM)
ACADEMY AWARD
NOMINATIONS (1952)
Best Director: Vincente Minnelli
Best Film Editing:
Adrienne Fazan
ACADEMY AWARDS
Best Art Direction-Set Decoration, Color:
Cedric Gibbons, E. Preston Ames,
Edwin B. Willis, F. Keogh Gleason
Best Cinematography, Color:
Alfred Gilks, John Alton
Best Costume Design, Color:
Orry-Kelly, Walter Plunkett,
Irene Sharaff
Best Music, Scoring of a Musical Picture:
Johnny Green,
Sally Chaplin
Best Picture: Arthur Freed
Best Writing, Story and Screenplay:
Alan Jay Lerner

Before being called up for World War I, Jerry Mulligan (Kelly) was an artist. Now that the war is over, he's decided to continue painting in Paris. Life in Paris is good: painting, meeting his pianist-friend Adam (Levant) in sidewalk cafés, and attempting to sell his paintings on sunny street corners. Furthermore, he has attracted the attentions of an elegant older woman, Milo Roberts (Foch), who purports to be an art patron. But now Jerry has seen the girl of his dreams, Lisa (Caron). In spite of Milo's obvious jealousy and Lisa's existing boyfriend, Jerry knows he must follow his heart.

The elements of *An American in Paris* that people still speak of with rapture are the little French nymph that is Leslie Caron, the glorious dancer that is Gene Kelly, and the closing 13-minute ballet sequence, the like of which many viewers have never seen before. Gene Kelly had seen something like it before; when trying to persuade MGM to back this film, he showed them the 15-minute ballet sequence from *The Red Shoes* (1949). Vincente Minnelli was a groundbreaking director of musicals and the perfect partner for Kelly on this project. It's often said that it is the ballet that won the film its six Oscars.

Singin' in the Rain

It's 1927 and *The Jazz Singer* has been seen – and heard. However, silent stars are still worshipped, none more so than Don Lockwood (Kelly) and his beautiful on-screen partner Lina Lamont (Hagen). Their fans believe them to be a 'hot' off-screen item, too. Unfortunately, Lina's voice is so dreadful that, once they have heard her in a sound movie, no fan will ever swoon again. However, Don has met a lovely studio hopeful called Kathy Seldon (Reynolds) who has a charming voice. The plan is to hide Kathy on set, behind the scenery, and have her speak for Lina – but Lina is not amused!

Before becoming a big-time musical producer, Arthur Freed wrote song lyrics with composer Nacio Herb Brown. He thought there was still mileage in those songs, and commissioned scriptwriters Comden and Green to write a movie round them. However, when the resulting film, *Singin' in the Rain*, first appeared, it was mostly greeted with indifference. Not even Jean Hagen's Oscar nomination or Donald O'Connor's Golden Globe had them queuing round the block. The compilation film *That's Entertainment* (1974) is often credited with showing many people what they were missing.

USA, 1952
DIRECTOR:
Stanley Donen, Gene Kelly
CAST INCLUDES:
Gene Kelly, Donald O'Connor,
Debbie Reynolds, Jean Hagen,
Millard Mitchell, Cyd Charisse,
Douglas Fowley, Rita Moreno
SCREENPLAY:
Betty Comden, Adolph Green
CINEMATOGRAPHY:
Harold Rosson
**PRODUCERS/PRODUCTION
COMPANIES:**
Arthur Freed/Metro-Goldwyn-Mayer
(MGM)
**ACADEMY AWARD
NOMINATIONS (1953)**
Best Actress in a Supporting Role:
Jean Hagen
Best Music, Scoring of a Musical
Picture: Lennie Hayton

The Band Wagon

Has-been Hollywood-musical star Tony Hunter (Astaire) is in New York to try and revive his dying career. His old friends, Lester and Lily Marton (Levant and Fabray), have an idea for a light-hearted pop musical and have asked Tony to star in it. They ask Jeffrey Cordova (Buchanan) to direct it because his Broadway successes will attract backers. However, Jeffrey decides to turn the show into 'meaningful' theatre and hires top ballerina Gaby Gerard (Charisse) as Tony's co-star. This is a disastrous move: she thinks he's too old, he thinks she's too tall, their styles don't blend and, at the off-Broadway try-out, the backers withdraw. However, washed-up Tony takes the helm, and things start to come right.

For serious musical lovers, if *An American in Paris* (1951) or *Singin' in the Rain* (1952) is not top of their list, then *The Band Wagon* almost certainly is. It has the Minnelli magic, a great score, an Astaire who's probably never been better and a Charisse who's at the peak of her perfection. On top of all that, there is the elegant Jack Buchanan, revelling in a part that enables him to scene-steal more than once. Minnelli, once again, revealed his genius in the closing dance sequence. Here the 'Girl Hunt Ballet' is a Mickey-Spillane-type take-off with Astaire in cream suit and black shirt and Charisse in red dress and black mesh tights – and seduction oozing from every step.

USA, 1953
DIRECTOR:
Vincente Minnelli
CAST INCLUDES:
Fred Astaire, Cyd Charisse,
Oscar Levant, Nanette Fabray,
Jack Buchanan, James Mitchell,
Robert Gist
SCREENPLAY:
Betty Comden, Adolph Green
CINEMATOGRAPHY:
Harry Jackson
**PRODUCERS/
PRODUCTION COMPANIES:**
Arthur Freed/Metro-Goldwyn-Mayer
(MGM)
**ACADEMY AWARD
NOMINATIONS (1954)**
Best Costume Design, Color:
Mary Ann Nyberg
Best Music, Scoring of a Musical
Picture: Adolph Deutsch
Best Writing, Story and Screenplay:
Betty Comden, Adolph Green

Gentlemen Prefer Blondes

'Two Little Girls From Little Rock', lounge singers Lorelei (Monroe) and Dorothy (Russell), are setting off on a transatlantic cruise to (as Lorelei reminds us) 'Europe France'. Dorothy wants to meet a nice, manly man, though she's not averse to luxury. Lorelei wants to meet rich men – though she already has, at home, one rich beau whom she's encouraging, by her absence, to marry her. Lorelei settles for the elderly Sir Francis 'Piggy' Beekman, who owns diamond mines, but Lady Beekman rocks the boat when she discovers her diamond tiara has been given to Lorelei. Dorothy is smitten with Ernie Malone (Reid), but discovers he's been hired by Lorelei's beau's father to spy on her. Then it's time to disembark for Paris, and the game gets more challenging as the stakes get higher . . .

Marilyn Monroe's musical comedies are exquisitely funny because she is the perfect straight person. Marilyn is sometimes sexy-funny in her on-stage role within the musical, but other than that, she's as straight as a die. She's also an excellent female buddy; her relationships with other women (or 'women', in *Some Like It Hot*, 1959), are both honest and realistic. Then, there is the joy of the musical numbers – even if only five songs do barely a musical make. The fact that she is an entertainer on a cruise ship means that all the stops can be pulled out: the 'Diamonds are a Girl's Best Friend' dress is stunningly pink, and 'When Love Goes Wrong' is full-blown after-dinner decadence. And Jane is very good, too.

USA, 1953
DIRECTOR:
Howard Hawks
CAST INCLUDES:
Jane Russell, Marilyn Monroe, Charles Coburn, Elliott Reid, Tommy Noonan, George Winslow, Marcel Dalio, Taylor Holmes, Norma Varden, Howard Wendell
SCREENPLAY:
Charles Lederer from the novel by Anita Loos and the play by Joseph Fields and Anita Loos
CINEMATOGRAPHY:
Harry J. Wild
PRODUCERS/ PRODUCTION COMPANIES:
Sol C. Siegel/20th Century Fox

Seven Brides for Seven Brothers

USA, 1954
DIRECTOR:
Stanley Donen
CAST INCLUDES:
Jane Powell, Howard Keel,
Jeff Richards, Russ Tamblyn,
Tommy Rall, Marc Platt, Matt Mattox,
Jacques d'Amboise, Julie Newmar
(Newmeyer), Nancy Kilgas, Betty Carr,
Virginia Gibson, Ruta Lee (Kilmonis),
Norma Doggett, Ian Wolfe, Mr. Bixby
SCREENPLAY:
Albert Hackett, Frances Goodrich,
Dorothy Kingsley from the story *The
Sobbin' Women* by
Stephen Vincent Benet
CINEMATOGRAPHY:
George (J.) Folsey
**PRODUCERS/
PRODUCTION COMPANIES:**
Jack Cummings/Metro-Goldwyn-Mayer
(MGM)
**ACADEMY AWARD
NOMINATIONS (1955)**
Best Cinematography, Colour:
George J. Folsey
Best Film Editing: Ralph E. Winters
Best Picture: Jack Cummings
Best Writing, Screenplay:
Albert Hackett, Frances Goodrich,
Dorothy Kingsley
ACADEMY AWARDS
Best Music, Scoring of a Musical Picture:
Adolph Deutsch, Saul Chaplin

Oregon farmer Adam Pontipee (Keel) goes off to town to find himself a wife. He espies the lovely Milly (Powell), marries her and takes her home – where she finds six more Pointipee boys. Milly gives them all a bath and a proper dinner and starts teaching them how to be courteous to ladies. One night, between tending the farm and dancing up a storm, the boys listen to Adam's story of the 'Sobbin' (Sabine) Women. Inspired by this, they head into town to carry off their own women. Milly is furious and bars the men from the house, but spring comes, and things start to blossom . . .

Seven Brides for Seven Brothers was a mystifyingly (to the studio) massive success when it opened, and has remained enormously popular ever since. The choreography, say the critics, or the superb score. Nonsense. *Seven Brides* is pure Mills and Boon: women being carried off against their will by handsome, virile men who then are given a rough time before the women give in. It's romantic bliss. It's probably also the first time, in a musical, that boys really danced like boys. The putting-up-a-house competition between the girls' former town beaux and their new farmyard suitors is one of the most vigorous and energetic boots-and-braces dance routines on film. Gloriously politically incorrect.

A Star is Born

A 'Night of Stars' benefit is being held at Hollywood's Shrine Theatre. Norman Maine (Mason), once a huge star, but now washed up by a steady stream of alcohol, arrives – drunk. He shambles on to the stage during a song-and-dance act Esther Blodgett (Garland) is performing. Esther does a brilliant job of lightening the situation and getting him off the stage. When Maine wakes up, sober, he remembers Esther and sets out to find her. He encourages her and arranges for her first small breaks. As Esther – now Vicki Lester and Mrs Norman Maine – goes from strength to strength, Norman's downhill path escalates. He sees that he is damaging her career and her life, and realizes that this can't go on.

Judy Garland sang superbly in *A Star Is Born*, and Cukor's direction enabled her to show her full range of acting talents. Judy, by this time was thirty two and, given the stresses in her life and her nerves and the pills and the booze, the fact that she managed to play a very young woman who lovingly cherishes her wreck of a star (an excellent Mason) – a path she found herself on more and more frequently – was an amazing achievement. The 'delight' spot is her 'Born in a Trunk' sequence, which is more or less her own mini-biography.

USA, 1954
DIRECTOR:
George Cukor
CAST INCLUDES:
Judy Garland, James Mason, Jack Carson, Charles Bickford, Tommy Noonan, Lucy Marlow, Amanda Blake, Irving Bacon, Hazel Shermet, Lotus Robb
SCREENPLAY:
Moss Hart from 1937 screenplay by Dorothy Parker, Alan Campbell, William A. Wellman and 1937 story by William A. Wellman and Robert Carson, inspired by Adela Rogers St. John's story *What Price Hollywood?*
CINEMATOGRAPHY:
Sam Leavitt
PRODUCERS/
PRODUCTION COMPANIES:
Sidney Luft/Transcona Enterprises, Warner Bros.
ACADEMY AWARD
NOMINATIONS (1955)
Best Actor in a Leading Role: James Mason
Best Actress in a Leading Role: Judy Garland
Best Art Direction-Set Decoration, Color: Malcolm C. Bert, Gene Allen, Irene Sharaff, George James Hopkins
Best Costume Design, Color: Jean Louis, Mary Ann Nyberg, Irene Sharaff
Best Music, Original Song: Harold Arlen (music); Ira Gershwin (lyrics) for the song 'The Man that Got Away'
Best Music, Scoring of a Musical Picture: Ray Heindorf

Oklahoma!

USA, 1955
DIRECTOR:
Fred Zinnemann
CAST INCLUDES:
Gordon MacRae, Gloria Grahame,
Gene Nelson, Charlotte Greenwood,
Shirley Jones, Eddie Albert,
James Whitmore, Rod Steiger
SCREENPLAY:
Sonya Levien, William Ludwig from
the play *Green Grow the Lilacs* by
Lynn Riggs and Oscar Hammerstein
CINEMATOGRAPHY:
Floyd Crosby, Robert Surtees
**PRODUCERS/
PRODUCTION COMPANIES:**
Arthur Hornblow Jr./Magna
Corporation, Rodgers & Hammerstein
Productions
**ACADEMY AWARD
NOMINATIONS (1956)**
Best Cinematography, Color:
Robert Surtees
Best Film Editing: Gene Ruggiero,
George Boemler
ACADEMY AWARDS
Best Music, Scoring of a Musical
Picture: Robert Russell Bennett,
Jay Blackton, Adolph Deutsch
Best Sound, Recording: Fred Hynes
(Todd-AO Sound Dept.)

Curly McLain (MacRae) is a cowboy in the territory of Oklahoma (shortly to become a state). He is courtin' Laurey (Jones), a sweet strawberry-blonde farm girl who's been raised by her Aunt Eller (Greenwood). He's invited her to a 'social'. She wants to go, but thinks he'll get big-headed if he realizes how much she likes him. To make Curly jealous, she agrees to go with the hired hand, Jud (Steiger), but he's so mean and moody she wishes she hadn't. She should be worried, because Judd has been in love with Laurey for a good while – and would kill to stop anyone else getting her . . .

This delightful Rogers and Hammerstein operetta was, not surprisingly, a big hit on Broadway before director Fred Zinnemann turned it into an exuberant film. It is replete with such favourites as 'Oh What a Beautiful Mornin', 'I'm Just a Girl Who Can't Say No' and 'Surrey With the Fringe on Top'. Gordon MacRea and Shirley Jones have beautiful voices that blend effortlessly and phrase lyrics superbly. Even Rod Steiger's 'Poor Judd is Dead' is a very pleasant surprise. The story goes that he always had a naturally operatic voice – he just couldn't hold a key. Agnes De Mille's choreography ranges from boisterous to ballet.

High Society

There are three men in the life of Tracy Lord (Kelly). The first is C. K. Dexter-Haven (Crosby), or 'Dex', who was her childhood sweetheart and from whom she is now divorced. Dex, a successful jazz musician, now lives nearby and wants Tracy back. The second is George Kittredge, a safe, sound (but dull) businessman whom she is about to marry. The third is Mike Connor (Sinatra) a reporter for *Spy* magazine which is threatening to run an exposé on Tracy's playboy father (Blackmer) unless given an 'exclusive' on her wedding. Mike, however, has also fallen in love with Tracy. Is Tracy caught in a terrible dilemma, or is she just spoilt for choice?

High Society is a reworking of Philip Barry's play *The Philadelphia Story*, already filmed in 1940. John Patrick's instructions were to re-work it just enough to make room for nine Cole Porter songs. As a result, *High Society* offers Crosby singing 'Now You Has Jazz' with Louis Armstrong and Sinatra and Crosby's 'Well, Did You Evah!' a song which had previously been sung in *DuBarry Was a Lady*, in 1939 on Broadway, by Betty Grable and Charles Walters – *High Society*'s director. This was Kelly's last film before becoming Princess of Monaco, and her engagement ring in the film is her own!

USA, 1956
DIRECTOR:
Charles Walters
CAST INCLUDES:
Bing Crosby, Grace Kelly,
Frank Sinatra, Celeste Holm,
John Lund, Louis Calhern,
Sidney Blackmer, Louis Armstrong,
Margalo Gillmore, Lydia Reed, Gordon
Richards, Richard Garrick
SCREENPLAY:
John Patrick from the play, *The Philadelphia Story* by Philip Barry
CINEMATOGRAPHY:
Paul Vogel
**PRODUCERS/
PRODUCTION COMPANIES:**
Sol C. Siegel/Bing Crosby
Productions, Metro-Goldwyn-Mayer
(MGM), Sol C. Siegel Productions
**ACADEMY AWARD
NOMINATIONS (1957)**
Best Music, Original Song: Cole
Porter, for the song 'True Love'
Best Music, Scoring of a Musical
Picture: Johnny Green,
Saul Chaplin
Best Writing, Motion Picture Story:
Edward Bernds,
Elwood Ullman
(The screenwriters graciously and
voluntarily declined the nomination.
The Academy had inadvertently
confused their quickly made Bowery
Boys series entry called *High Society*
with the similarly titled Cole Porter
musical *High Society*, which came
out the following year).

The King and I

USA, 1956
DIRECTOR:
Walter Lang
CAST INCLUDES:
Deborah Kerr,
Yul Brynner, Rita Moreno,
Martin Benson, Terry Saunders,
Rex Thompson, Carlos Rivas,
Patrick Adiarte, Alan Mowbray,
Geoffrey Toone
SCREENPLAY:
Ernest Lehman, from the play by Oscar
Hammerstein II and the book, *Anna and
the King of Siam*, by Margaret Landon
CINEMATOGRAPHY:
Leon Shamroy
**PRODUCERS/
PRODUCTION COMPANIES:**
Charles Brackett/
20th Century Fox
**ACADEMY AWARD
NOMINATIONS (1957)**
Best Actress in a Leading Role:
Deborah Kerr
Best Cinematography, Color:
Leon Shamroy
Best Director: Walter Lang
Best Picture: Charles Brackett
ACADEMY AWARDS
Best Actor in a Leading Role:
Yul Brynner
Best Art Direction-Set Decoration,
Color: Lyle R. Wheeler, John DeCuir,
Walter M. Scott, Paul S. Fox
Best Costume Design, Color:
Irene Sharaff
Best Music, Scoring of a Musical
Picture: Alfred Newman, Ken Darby
Best Sound, Recording: Carl Faulkner
(20th Century-Fox SSD)

After the death of her husband, an Englishwoman, Anna (Kerr), travels to Siam (Thailand) with her son Louis (Thompson) to become English teacher to the many children of King Mongkut of Siam. She has some initial clashes of wills with the King (but adores the children) before realizing that, although very proud, he has an alert and curious mind and wishes to learn. She finds the notion of polygamy unacceptable but, nevertheless, king and governess view each other with affection and respect. When he dies, she stays on to help young Prince Chulalongkorn take over his father's throne.

The King and I is a feast of costumes, settings, drama, forbidden romance, delicious children and wonderful songs, including 'Hello Young Lovers', 'We Kiss in a Shadow' and 'Something Wonderful'. There is also a very fine performance by Deborah Kerr as a brave, firm but warm-hearted woman. However, *The King and I* belongs to Yul Brynner. No one has ever made a role so much their own. He began with it on stage, took it into film and then onto television. In the course of thirty four years, he played it over 4,600 times. His powerful stance, his piercing eyes and his beautiful voice combine to produce the King of Kings. Brynner kept the Buddhist monk hairstyle as his trademark.

Funny Face

One day, Jo Stockton (Hepburn), a young intellectual who works in a Greenwich Village bookstore, is descended on by one of *Quality* magazine's photo shoots. She appears in some of the pictures taken by fashion-photographer Dick Avery (Astaire), and the editor, Maggie Prescott (Thompson), realizes they've found their new '*Quality* girl'. Jo agrees to go to Paris for a big fashion shoot, but only so that she can meet her guru, 'emphatheticalism' founder Professor Flostre (Auclair). Once in Paris, Dick and Jo find their budding attraction for each other has 'bumpy ride' written all over it.

Audrey Hepburn goes, in a flash, from being a mousey frump in shapeless sack to being a vision of extraordinary elegance and loveliness in Givenchy. In addition, she does her own singing (lovely voice, most are agreed, but is it strong enough?) and her own graceful dancing (ballet trained), and she and Astaire did manage to put a sizzle into their dances and romantic moments together – despite his being twice her age and Paris having its wettest-ever summer. Beautiful Gershwin songs and exquisite settings, costumes and photography make *Funny Face* a feast for the senses.

USA, 1957
DIRECTOR:
Stanley Donen
CAST INCLUDES:
Audrey Hepburn, Fred Astaire,
Kay Thompson, Michel Auclair,
Robert Flemyng, Dovima,
Suzy Parker, Sunny Hartnett,
Jean Del Val, Virginia Gibson,
Sue England, Ruta Lee, Alex Gerry,
Iphigenie Castiglioni
SCREENPLAY:
Leonard Gershe
CINEMATOGRAPHY:
Ray June
PRODUCERS/
PRODUCTION COMPANIES:
Roger Edens/Paramount Pictures
ACADEMY AWARD
NOMINATIONS (1958)
Best Art Direction-Set Decoration: Hal
Pereira, George W. Davis, Sam Comer,
Ray Moyer
Best Cinematography: Ray June
Best Costume Design:
Edith Head, Hubert de Givenchy
Best Writing, Story and Screenplay -
Written Directly for the Screen:
Leonard Gershe

Pal Joey

USA, 1957
DIRECTOR:
George Sidney
CAST INCLUDES:
Rita Hayworth, Frank Sinatra,
Kim Novak, Barbara Nichols,
Bobby Sherwood, Hank Henry,
Elizabeth Patterson
SCREENPLAY:
Dorothy Kingsley from the play by
John O'Hara
CINEMATOGRAPHY:
Harold Lipstein
**PRODUCERS/
PRODUCTION COMPANIES:**
Fred Kohlmar/Columbia Pictures
Corporation, Essex Distributing,
George Sidney Productions
**ACADEMY AWARD
NOMINATIONS (1958)**
Best Art Direction-Set Decoration:
Walter Holscher, William Kiernan,
Louis Diage
Best Costume Design: Jean Louis
Best Film Editing: Viola Lawrence,
Jerome Thoms
Best Sound: John P. Livadary
(Columbia SSD)

Renowned ladies man Joey Evans (Sinatra) arrives in San Francisco looking for nightclub-entertainment work and lands a job at The Barbary Coast Club. Almost at once, he meets Linda English (Novak), a chorine who is as genuine as she is lovely, and Vera Simpson (Hayworth), a burlesque queen who retired after making a rich marriage and who is now widowed but still very rich. Joey starts romancing both of them, one for his heart and one for his bank balance (he wants to open his own nightclub), but will he get away with it?

After the tremendous success of *Cover Girl* in 1944, starring Rita Hayworth and Gene Kelly, Harry Cohn of Columbia bought the rights to the Broadway musical, *Pal Joey* (in which Kelly had also starred), intending to unite the pair on screen again. However, Louis B. Mayer owned Kelly's contract, and his price for the loan-out was too high. It was seventeen years before Cohn did manage to film *Pal Joey*. By that time, Hayworth was ready to play woman-of-the-world Vera, rather than Linda, the *ingénue* – and Sinatra's Joey had become much less of a heel. Hayworth sings 'Bewitched, Bothered and Bewildered' beautifully, and 'The Lady is a Tramp' became one of Sinatra's signature tunes.

South Pacific

The year is 1943. The place is the Solomon Islands in the South Pacific. The US armed forces want to set up a naval base in readiness for the invasion of New Guinea which is held by the Japanese. For this, they need the help of French plantation owner Emile de Becque (Brazzi). Nurse Nellie Forbush (Gaynor) and Becque have become very close, but she refuses to marry him because he has children by a Polynesian woman (now dead). Lt. Joseph Cable (Kerr) is also on the islands on a dangerous mission. He has met and fallen for a Polynesian girl, Liat (Nuyen), but he has difficulty proposing because of her ethnic background. Lots of difficult decisions must be made in this war-torn time.

Joshua Logan cast a wide net when looking for Nellie: Elizabeth Taylor, Audrey Helpurn, and Doris Day were all considered – but Mitzi Gaynor did the best screen test. Leon Shamroy was Oscar nominated for the general excellence of his work and also for a system of coloured camera filters that he devised, whereby various scenes could be tinted in the colours that portrayed specific feelings. The songs include 'Some Enchanted Evening', 'Younger than Springtime', 'There is Nothing Like a Dame' and 'Bali Hai'.

USA, 1958
DIRECTOR:
Joshua Logan
CAST INCLUDES:
Rossano Brazzi, Mitzi Gaynor, John Kerr, Ray Walston, Juanita Hall, France Nuyen, Russ Brown, Jack Mullaney, Ken Clark, Floyd Simmons, Candace Lee, Warren Hsieh, Tom Laughlin
SCREENPLAY:
Paul Osborn, from the play by Oscar Hammerstein and Joshua Logan, and the novel, *Tales of the South Pacific* by James Michener
CINEMATOGRAPHY:
Leon Shamroy
PRODUCERS/ PRODUCTION COMPANIES:
Buddy Adler/20th Century Fox, Magna Corporation, Rodgers & Hammerstein Productions, South Pacific Enterprises
ACADEMY AWARD NOMINATIONS (1959)
Best Cinematography, Color: Leon Shamroy
Best Music, Scoring of a Musical Picture: Alfred Newman, Ken Darby
ACADEMY AWARDS
Best Sound: Fred Hynes (Todd-AO SSD)

West Side Story

The streets of New York's West Side are home to two warring gangs: the Puerto Rican Sharks, whose leader is Bernardo (Chakiris) and the 'Anglo' Jets, led by Riff (Tamblyn). However, Bernardo's sister, Maria (Wood) and Tony (Beymer), an ex-member of the Jets, have fallen in love. The streets of New York begin to rumble with the anger of both gangs, and soon, death is stalking those streets.

West Side Story, the movie, is still one of the best-ever film adaptations of a stage musical. Jerome Robbins, director and choreographer of the hit Broadway version, shared directing credits with Robert Wise. This appears to have been a troubled relationship, with Robbins insisting on levels of perfection that the budget and schedule couldn't absorb. Although stylized, the dance routines fit the energy and language of Leonard Bernstein's ground-breaking score so well that they still have street-cred today. The opening sequence – the camera panning over Manhattan till it closes in on a playground and a close-up of the Jet's main-man Riff, snapping his fingers to the rhythm of the music and action that's about to begin – could qualify for all ten Oscars on its own.

USA, 1961
DIRECTOR:
Jerome Robbins, Robert Wise
CAST INCLUDES:
Natalie Wood, Richard Beymer,
Russ Tamblyn, Rita Moreno,
George Chakiris, Simon Oakland,
Ned Glass, William Bramley
SCREENPLAY:
Ernest Lehman, from the play by
Arthur Laurents, based on the play
Romeo and Juliet by
William Shakespeare; staging by
Jerome Robbins
CINEMATOGRAPHY:
Daniel L. Fapp
PRODUCERS/
PRODUCTION COMPANIES:
Robert Wise/Beta Productions,
Mirisch Films [GB], Seven Arts
Productions [GB]
ACADEMY AWARD
NOMINATIONS (1962)
Best Writing, Screenplay Based on
Material from Another Medium:
Ernest Lehman
ACADEMY AWARDS
Best Actor in a Supporting Role:
George Chakiris
Best Actress in a Supporting Role:
Rita Moreno
Best Art Direction-Set Decoration,
Colour: Boris Leven,
Victor A. Gangelin
Best Cinematography, Colour:
Daniel L. Fapp
Best Costume Design, Colour:
Irene Sharaff
Best Director: Robert Wise,
Jerome Robbins
(The first time a directing award was
shared)
Best Film Editing:
Thomas Stanford
Best Music, Scoring of a Musical
Picture: Saul Chaplin, Johnny Green,
Sid Ramin, Irwin Kostal
Best Picture: Robert Wise
Best Sound: Fred Hynes (Todd-AO
SSD), Gordon Sawyer
(Samuel Goldwyn SSD)

Viva Las Vegas

Racing-car driver Lucky Jackson (Presley) has come to Las Vegas for the Grand Prix, but currently lacks an engine. While being a waiter at a casino to earn the engine money, he meets Rusty (Ann-Margret), a swimming instructor at his hotel. While they are having a really good time together, he loses the money he has saved. Lucky has also been having problems with rival driver, Elmo (Danova). In the end, how lucky will he be?

It was unusual for Elvis to share the limelight with anyone, but here Ann-Margret gets equal billing and on-screen time. This certainly worked well on-screen because this was Elvis' most successful film on release to the theatres, and he and Ann-Margret were, apparently, as hot an item off-screen as they were on. Las Vegas (not yet ruined by commercialism) was a lovely venue, the songs were good, and Rusty and Lucky danced their little socks off (a talent contest was introduced to give them maximum opportunity). Elvis seemed more involved, acting-wise, than he had been for some time. A sage critic has described him, in movies, as being 'The Jedi master of emoting without bothering with facial expressions'.

USA, 1964
DIRECTOR:
George Sidney
CAST INCLUDES:
Elvis Presley, Ann-Margret,
Cesare Danova, William Demarest,
Nicky Blair
SCREENPLAY:
Sally Benson
CINEMATOGRAPHY:
Joseph Biroc
**PRODUCERS/
PRODUCTION COMPANIES:**
Jack Cumming, George Sidney/
Metro-Goldwyn-Mayer (MGM)

A Hard Day's Night

GB, 1964
DIRECTOR:
Richard Lester
CAST INCLUDES:
John Lennon, Paul McCartney,
George Harrison, Ringo Starr,
Wilfrid Brambell, John McCartney
(Paul's grandfather),
Norman Rossington, John Junkin,
Victor Spinetti, Anna Quayle
SCREENPLAY:
Alun Owen
CINEMATOGRAPHY:
Gilbert Taylor
**PRODUCERS/
PRODUCTION COMPANIES:**
Walter Shenson/Proscenium Films
**ACADEMY AWARD
NOMINATIONS (1965)**
Best Music, Scoring of Music,
Adaptation or Treatment:
George Martin
Best Writing, Story and Screenplay –
Written Directly for the Screen:
Alun Owen

The Beatles (John, Paul, George and Ringo) have just finished a gig and are racing for a train, pursued by screaming girls, bewildered policemen and reporters asking the customary inane questions. Waiting on the train for them is Paul's grandfather (Brambell) who causes all kinds of trouble by giving them very bad advice. The gang then travels on, with their road crew, to a television studio to prepare for a TV special. The boys don't like rehearsals and run-throughs and take every chance to split or goof around. However, the show itself is a great success.

A Hard Day's Night is the Beatles' own look at the phenomenon of Beatlemania and how, by clowning, joshing, acting crazy and working very hard, they combined being Beatles with staying sane. The four chose Richard Lester to direct because they thought his *The Running Jumping & Standing Still Film* from 1959 (about British radio comedians, The Goons) was brilliant. Liverpool playwright Alun Owen worked with them on the script. Lester takes the movie at a tremendous pace, which echoes the boys' wackiness and their *joie de vivre*. The humour was their own – 'What do you call that hairstyle you're wearing?' 'Arthur'.

Mary Poppins

USA, 1964
DIRECTOR:
Robert Stevenson
CAST INCLUDES:
Julie Andrews, Dick Van Dyke,
David Tomlinson, Glynis Johns,
Hermione Baddeley, Reta Shaw,
Karen Dotrice, Jane Banks,
Matthew Garber, Elsa Lanchester,
Arthur Treacher, Reginald Owen
SCREENPLAY:
Bill Walsh, Don DaGradi from the
Mary Poppins books by P. L. Travers
CINEMATOGRAPHY:
Edward Colman
PRODUCERS/
PRODUCTION COMPANIES:
Walt Disney, Bill Walsh/Walt
Disney Pictures
ACADEMY AWARD
NOMINATIONS (1965)
Best Art Direction-Set Decoration,
Color: Carroll Clark,
William H. Tuntke, Emile Kuri,
Hal Gausman
Best Cinematography, Color:
Edward Colman
Best Costume Design, Color:
Tony Walton
Best Director: Robert Stevenson
Best Music, Scoring of Music,
Adaptation or Treatment: Irwin Kostal
Best Picture: Walt Disney, Bill Walsh
Best Sound: Robert O. Cook
(Walt Disney SSD)
Best Writing, Screenplay Based on
Material from Another Medium:
Bill Walsh, Don DaGradi
ACADEMY AWARDS
Best Actress in a Leading Role:
Julie Andrews
Best Effects, Special Visual Effects:
Peter Ellenshaw, Hamilton Luske,
Eustace Lycett
Best Film Editing: Cotton Warburton
Best Music, Original Song:
Richard M. Sherman, Robert B.
Sherman for the song
'Chim Chim Cher-ee'
Best Music, Score - Substantially
Original: Richard M. Sherman,
Robert B. Sherman

London, 1910. When Mary Poppins (Andrews) floats down into the lives of the boisterous but rather unappreciated Banks children, Jane (Dotrice) and Michael (Garber), things take a magical turn for the better. Their many amazing outings include a visit to her friend Bert (Van Dyke). Bert's a chimney sweep and a street artist, so they all take a holiday inside the wondrous world of one of his pavement drawings. However, although supercalifragilistic, Mary Poppins is a nanny who is lovingly firm, and so fussy that Mr Banks (Tomlinson) does come to appreciate her – and to enjoy his children.

Walt Disney had wanted to make this film since his young daughters told him about P. L. Travers' books, but it took twenty years for him to overcome her objections. Even then, after seeing the finished film, she produced a list of changes she wanted the studio to make. Disney cast Andrews as Mary Poppins (her film debut) after seeing her in *Camelot* on Broadway, but had to delay shooting till baby Emma arrived. Fortunately, Andrews got the author's seal of approval after Ms Travers heard her voice on the phone.

USA, 1964
DIRECTOR:
George Cukor
CAST INCLUDES:
Audrey Hepburn, Rex Harrison,
Stanley Holloway, Wilfrid Hyde-White,
Gladys Cooper, Jeremy Brett,
Theodore Bikel, Mona Washbourne,
Isobel Elsom
SCREENPLAY:
Alan Jay Lerner from the musical play
by Alan Jay Lerner and the play
Pygmalion by George Bernard Shaw
CINEMATOGRAPHY:
Harry Stradling Sr.
**PRODUCERS/
PRODUCTION COMPANIES:**
Jack L. Warner/Warner Bros.
**ACADEMY AWARD
NOMINATIONS (1965)**
Best Actor in a Supporting Role:
Stanley Holloway
Best Actress in a Supporting Role:
Gladys Cooper
Best Film Editing: William H. Ziegler
Best Writing, Screenplay Based on
Material from Another Medium:
Alan Jay Lerner
ACADEMY AWARDS
Best Actor in a Leading Role:
Rex Harrison
Best Art Direction-Set Decoration,
Colour: Gene Allen, Cecil Beaton,
George James Hopkins
Best Cinematography, Color:
Harry Stradling Sr.
Best Costume Design, Color:
Cecil Beaton
Best Director: George Cukor
Best Music, Scoring of Music,
Adaptation or Treatment:
André Previn
Best Picture: Jack L. Warner
Best Sound: George Groves
(Warner Bros. SSD)

My Fair Lady

Phonetics Professor Henry Higgins (Harrison) accepts a bet from fellow academic Colonel Pickering (Hyde-White). The bet is that Higgins, in six months, cannot turn Cockney flower-seller Eliza Doolittle (Hepburn) into a lady, whose 'common' origins would not be spotted – not even at such a prestigious occasion as the Embassy Ball. He succeeds, but omits to give Eliza any of the credit for their success. She storms off, threatening to accept the proposal from one of her new young beaux. Can Higgins undo the mistakes he has made?

Warner Brothers beautifully staged musical was their most expensive film to date ($17 million), but it recouped its expenses by being one of the year's five most successful films. The songs are unforgettable: 'I Could Have Danced All Night', 'I'm Getting Married in the Morning', 'All I Want is a Room Somewhere'. Hepburn was disappointed that, after singing in *Funny Face* (1957), the studio insisted on Marnie Dixon dubbing her songs. Julie Andrews, too, had been very disappointed – at not playing Eliza (her role on Broadway), but, at the Oscars ceremony, she thanked Jack Warner for leaving her free to win Best Actress for *Mary Poppins*. Cecil Beaton's inspirational clothes won another of the movie's eight Awards.

Les parapluies de Cherbourg
The Umbrellas of Cherbourg

Guy Foucher (Castelnuovo) and Geneviève Emery (Deneuve) are in love. He is a motor-mechanic and gas station attendant; she lives with her mother (Vernon) and works in her mother's umbrella shop. They sneak away and meet whenever they can. When it's time for guy to do his national service he is shipped out to join the army in Algeria. Geneviève discovers she is pregnant. The umbrella shop gets into financial difficulties but is saved by Roland Cassard (Michel), a suave and handsome man of means. He proposes to Geneviève, knowing she is carrying another man's child. Geneviève now has to decide between love and security.

For many, Jacques Demy's musical is a magical movie. Its simple, bittersweet love story is treated as an operetta: every word is sung. Furthermore, the theme tune sweeps across the heart-strings, and every scene is tuned with chords of colour: a sweater here will be echoed by a van there; the luminous tint of a flower will be reflected in an umbrella. This wonderful panoply of colours had begun to fade in the original film, but it was lovingly restored in 1994.

FRANCE, 1964
DIRECTOR:
Jacques Demy
CAST INCLUDES:
Catherine Deneuve, Nino Castelnuovo, Anne Vernon, Marc Michel, Ellen Farner, Mireille Perrey, Jean Champion, Pierre Caden, Jean-Pierre Dorat
SCREENPLAY:
Jacques Demy
CINEMATOGRAPHY:
Jean Rabier
PRODUCERS/ PRODUCTION COMPANIES:
Mag Bodard/Parc Film [FR], Madeleine Films [FR], Beta Film GmbH [GER]
ACADEMY AWARD NOMINATIONS (1966)
Best Music, Original Song: Michel Legrand (music), Jacques Demy (lyrics) for the song 'I Will Wait for You'
Best Music, Score - Substantially Original: Michel Legrand, Jacques Demy
Best Music, Scoring of Music, Adaptation or Treatment: Michel Legrand
Best Writing, Story and Screenplay - Written Directly for the Screen: Jacques Demy

USA, 1965
DIRECTOR:
Robert Wise
CAST INCLUDES:
Julie Andrews, Christopher Plummer,
Eleanor Parker, Richard Haydn,
Peggy Wood, Charmian Carr,
Heather Menzies,
Nicholas Hammond, Duane Chase,
Angela Cartwright, Debbie Turner,
Kym Karath
SCREENPLAY:
Ernest Lehman, Howard Lindsay
(book) and Russel Crouse (book),
from Maria Augusta Trapp's novel
based on the Trapp Family Singers
CINEMATOGRAPHY:
Ted (D.) McCord
**PRODUCERS/
PRODUCTION COMPANIES:**
Robert Wise/20th Century Fox,
Argyle Enterprises
**ACADEMY AWARD
NOMINATIONS (1966)**
Best Actress in a Leading Role:
Julie Andrews
Best Actress in a Supporting Role:
Peggy Wood
Best Art Direction-Set Decoration,
Color: Boris Leven, Walter M. Scott,
Ruby R. Levitt
Best Cinematography, Color:
Ted D. McCord
Best Costume Design, Color:
Dorothy Jeakins
ACADEMY AWARDS
Best Director: Robert Wise
Best Film Editing: William Reynolds
Best Music, Scoring of Music,
Adaptation or Treatment: Irwin Kostal
Best Picture: Robert Wise
Best Sound: James Corcoran (20th
Century-Fox SSD), Fred Hynes
(Todd-AO SSD)

The Sound of Music

Maria (Andrews), who is a postulant in an abbey in Austria, is told by Mother Superior (Wood) that she doesn't have the decorum to become a full-time nun. She's sent to do the work of God with the Von Trapp family near Salzburg. Baron Von Trapp (Plummer), an ex-naval officer, is still grieving for his wife, and the house is not a happy place. However, everything changes when Maria encourages the children to sing. Von Trapp and Maria fall in love and get married, and the whole family enters a singing contest. Just at that moment, however, Germany occupies Austria, and Von Trapp is called on to serve in the German Navy . . .

The Sound of Music could have been very different. The director was nearly William Wyler, who spent some time working on the script and looking at locations. Von Trapp could have been Yul Brynner, Sean Connery or Richard Burton; Doris Day and Audrey Hepburn both turned down the role of Maria. The opening shot nearly didn't happen: every time the helicopter carrying the camera flew over her, the downdraft knocked Julie Andrews off her feet. Would-be Von Trapp children included Kurt Russell, Richard Dreyfuss and the four eldest Osmond Brothers (Alan, Jay, Merrill and Wayne).

Funny Girl

Would-be show girl Fanny Brice (Streisand), born in 1891 and raised in the Jewish slums of New York City, meets and subsequently marries handsome gambler Nick Arnstein (Sharif) who brings her to the attention of musical impresario Florenz Ziegfeld (Pidgeon). Ziegfeld hires her for his new Ziegfeld Follies show. Her comic flair has great appeal and soon she is one of the Follies' biggest stars. Yet, while the star of her ambition is rising, her marriage is moving into rocky waters.

Streisand had already starred in the Broadway production but, as so often happens, the producers were anxious that a Broadway star wouldn't have the box-office appeal to turn a costly project into a massive profit. Streisand, in conjunction with the venerable William Wyler's direction, gave Columbia it's highest-grossing production of the sixties – and she won the Best Actress Oscar. It was noted in reviews on its release that the energy, power, excitement and magnificence of the film's finale, 'Don't Rain on My Parade', falls not far short of the impact of the chariot race in Wyler's *Ben-Hur* (1959).

USA, 1968
DIRECTOR:
William Wyler
CAST INCLUDES:
Barbra Streisand, Omar Sharif, Kay Medford, Anne Francis, Walter Pidgeon, Lee Allen, Mae Questel, Gerald Mohr
SCREENPLAY:
Isobel Lennart based on the play by Isobel Lennart
CINEMATOGRAPHY:
Harry Stradling Sr.
**PRODUCERS/
PRODUCTION COMPANIES:**
Ray Stark/Columbia Pictures Corporation, Rastar Pictures
ACADEMY AWARD NOMINATIONS (1969)
Best Actress in a Supporting Role: Kay Medford
Best Cinematography: Harry Stradling Sr.
Best Film Editing: Robert Swink, Maury Winetrobe, William Sands
Best Music, Original Song: Jule Styne (music), Bob Merrill (lyrics) for the song 'Funny Girl'
Best Music, Score of a Musical Picture (Original or Adaptation): Walter Scharf
Best Picture: Ray Stark
Best Sound
ACADEMY AWARDS
Best Actress in a Leading Role: Barbra Streisand; tied with Katharine Hepburn for *The Lion in Winter*

Hello, Dolly!

USA, 1969
DIRECTOR:
Gene Kelly
CAST INCLUDES:
Barbra Streisand, Walter Matthau,
Michael Crawford, Marianne
McAndrew, Danny Lockin, E.J. Peaker,
Joyce Ames, Tommy Tune,
Louis Armstrong
SCREENPLAY:
Ernest Lehman, Michael Stewart
from the play *The Matchmaker* by
Thornton Wilder
CINEMATOGRAPHY:
Harry Stradling Sr.
PRODUCERS/
PRODUCTION COMPANIES:
Ernest Lehman/20th Century Fox,
Chenault Productions, Inc.
ACADEMY AWARD
NOMINATIONS (1970)
Best Cinematography:
Harry Stradling Sr.
Best Costume Design: Irene Sharaff
Best Film Editing: William Reynolds
Best Picture: Ernest Lehman
ACADEMY AWARDS
Best Art Direction-Set Decoration:
John DeCuir, Jack Martin Smith,
Herman A. Blumenthal,
Walter M. Scott, George James
Hopkins, Raphael Bretton
Best Music, Score of a Musical
Picture (Original or Adaptation):
Lennie Hayton, Lionel Newman
Best Sound: Jack Solomon,
Murray Spivack

Dolly Levi (Streisand) is (at the beginning of the last century) a highly regarded professional matchmaker. She has been hired by Horace Vandergelder (Matthau), a 'well-known, unmarried half-a-millionaire', to find him a wife. Dolly, however, decides she wishes to marry him herself. Her complicated scheming enmeshes and confuses many of the people in Vandergelder's life, but she eventually gets everyone satisfactorily matched.

Hello, Dolly didn't flow quite so easily from Broadway to cinema box-office hit as *Funny Girl* had the year before. Explanations included: Streisand was far too young to play Dolly convincingly; off-stage animosity between Matthau and Streisand carried over into their on-screen relationship; and Dolly was not a character that anyone could warm to – just a woman on the make. On the plus side, Streisand was peaking in her combined talents as singer, actress and comedienne, Michael Kidd's dance routines are still wonderful, and the 'Hello Dolly' sequence, filmed in the Harmonia Gardens, is inspirational. It seems that the appetite for big-budget musicals was simply on the wane; however, retrospectively, it's a top-notch studio extravaganza.

Woodstock

It's the summer of 1969 and, in the Far East, the Vietnam War is being fought. In the USA, a three-day rock festival is being held at Woodstock, a 600-acre farm near Bethel, New York. This is the age of the hippie, of the Flower Power Generation, of 'Make love, not war'. The twelve cameras filming the event record the mud, the skinny-dipping, the flower-painted faces and thousands of arms swaying in unison. They monitor those on coke, acid, grass, hash and LSD – which include many of the performers as someone had laced all the back-stage drinks with acid. There is an interview with Port-a-San man, who has one son somewhere at the festival and the other flying helicopters in Vietnam. Home-based helicopters drop food and blankets for the 500,000-strong Woodstock Nation. Those that can't get in knock the fences down. Traffic on the incoming roads is so dense that the musicians perform in order of arrival. After the cameras have filmed everyone leaving, the editors slowly reverse the film so that the Woodstock Nation once again fills the fields.

The Woodstock movie nearly didn't happen. At the last moment, Michael Wadleigh and his partner, producer Bob Maurice, threw together a production team – just in case Woodstock turned out to be more than just another rock concert. They shot 120 miles of film that was edited down to roughly three hours by Thelma Schoonmaker and Martin Scorsese. A surprising number of bands asked not to be included because they didn't feel their performances were good enough. In 1995, a Director's Cut was issued featuring previously missing sets by Janis Joplin and Jefferson Airplane, and Jimi Hendrix's 'The Star Spangled Banner'. *Woodstock* is still the definitive rock-festival movie, and possibly unparalleled as a summary of a generation.

USA, 1970
DIRECTOR:
Michael Wadleigh
CAST INCLUDES:
Richie Havens, Joan Baez, Joe Cocker, Arlo Guthrie, Lawrence Ferlinghetti, Members of: The Who, Sha-Na-Na, Country Joe and the Fish, Crosby, Stills and Nash, Ten Years After, Santana
SCREENPLAY:
None - Documentary
CINEMATOGRAPHY:
Don Lenzer, David Myers, Richard Pearce, Michael Wadleigh, Al Wertheimer
PRODUCERS/
PRODUCTION COMPANIES:
Bob Maurice/Wadleigh-Maurice Ltd.
ACADEMY AWARD
NOMINATIONS (1971)
Best Film Editing:
Thelma Schoonmaker
Best Sound: Dan Wallin, L.A. Johnson
ACADEMY AWARDS
Best Documentary, Features:
Bob Maurice

USA, 1972
DIRECTOR:
Bob Fosse
CAST INCLUDES:
Liza Minnelli, Michael York,
Helmut Griem, Joel Grey, Fritz
Wepper, Marisa Berenson,
Elisabeth Neumann-Viertel
SCREENPLAY:
Jay Presson Allen from the book
Berlin Stories by Christopher
Isherwood, the play *I Am a Camera*
by John Van Druten, and the musical
Cabaret by Joe Masteroff
CINEMATOGRAPHY:
Geoffrey Unsworth
PRODUCERS/
PRODUCTION COMPANIES:
Cy Feuer/ABC Circle Films, American
Broadcasting Company (ABC)
ACADEMY AWARD
NOMINATIONS (1973)
Best Picture: Cy Feuer
Best Writing, Screenplay Based on
Material from Another Medium: Jay
Presson Allen
ACADEMY AWARDS
Best Actress in a Leading Role:
Liza Minnelli
Best Actor in a Supporting Role:
Joel Grey
Best Art Direction-Set Decoration:
Rolf Zehetbauer, Hans Jürgen
Kiebach, Herbert Strabel
Best Cinematography:
Geoffrey Unsworth
Best Director: Bob Fosse
Best Film Editing: David Bretherton
Best Music, Scoring Original Song
Score and/or Adaptation: Ralph Burns
Best Sound: Robert Knudson,
David Hildyar

Cabaret

Berlin, 1930, and the strength of the Nazis is on the rise. Brian Roberts (York) comes to Berlin. He meets Sally Bowles (Minnelli), the daughter of a US diplomat, who earns her living at the Kit-Kat club where the tone of the cabaret is set by the very decadent Master of Ceremonies (Grey). Sally wants to be an actress, and 'anything goes' to achieve that aim. Rich aristocrat Maximilian von Heune (Griem) moves into both their lives while, elsewhere, rich Jewish heiress Natalia Landauer (Berenson) is having to make a stealthy escape. Brian, too, decides Berlin is probably no longer a safe place to be.

Bob Fosse's masterpiece of a musical will be forever timeless, despite all the 1930s events and accessories. The characters are contemporary and always fashionable. The hopelessness and gloom lurking around every corner is historically immediate and archetypal. The brilliant routines in the Kit-Kat Club are both a shaft of much-needed fun and a clear warning of the approach of something dreadful. Minnelli's performance is perfect; what a tragedy that no-one was truly able to catch that brilliance again. Few musicals bear watching as often as this one.

The Rocky Horror Picture Show

Denton, Ohio. Janet (Sarandon) and Brad (Bostwick) have just got engaged and are driving off to share the good news when their car breaks down in a thunderstorm. Looking for help, they stumble across the castle of doctor Frank-N-Furter (Curry), a transvestite who is entertaining alien transsexual guests from the galaxy of Transylvania. The Dr. invites the young couple to witness the unveiling of blonde, bemuscled Rocky Horror (Hinwood), his artificially created love-toy for the relieving of sexual tension. Frank-N-Furter makes Brad and Janet his 'guests' for the night, after which Denton will never seem the same again.

Richard O'Brien's play, *The Rocky Horror Show*, had done very well on the London stage, but the filmed version bombed both with the critics and at the box-office. Then, word got around that the film was in the wrong slot, that it was a midnight movie, and slowly the tide turned. Now, some thirty years later, *The Rocky Horror Picture Show* has been on continuous release in various cinemas all over the world. Nor is it just a word-of-mouth success and a cult movie: it's a full-blown event, a ritual. Not only do people come dressed for the occasion (usually as Curry's inimitable Frank-N-Furter), but there is a 'scripted' interchange of dialogue with the screen, plus dances, actions, props and sing-a-longs. There are even audience-participation packs available for newcomers.

USA, 1975
DIRECTOR:
Jim Sharman
CAST INCLUDES:
Tim Curry, Susan Sarandon, Barry Bostwick, Richard O'Brien, Nell Campbell, Jonathan Adams, Peter Hinwood, Meat Loaf, Charles Gray
SCREENPLAY:
Jim Sharman, Richard O'Brien from his play *The Rocky Horror Show*
CINEMATOGRAPHY:
Peter Suschitzky
PRODUCERS/ PRODUCTION COMPANIES:
Michael White/20th Century Fox

Saturday Night Fever

USA, 1977
DIRECTOR:
John Badham
CAST INCLUDES:
John Travolta, Karen Lynn Gorney,
Barry Miller, Joseph Cali, Paul Pape,
Donna Pescow, Bruce Ornstein,
Julie Bovasso, Martin Shakar,
Sam J. Coppola, Nina Hansen,
Val Bisoglio
SCREENPLAY:
Norman Wexler from magazine
article 'Tribal Rites of the New
Saturday Night' by Nik Cohn
CINEMATOGRAPHY:
Ralf D. Bode
**PRODUCERS/
PRODUCTION COMPANIES:**
Robert Stigwood/Paramount Pictures,
Robert Stigwood Organization (RSO)
**ACADEMY AWARD
NOMINATIONS (1978)**
Best Actor in a Leading Role:
John Travolta

Tony Manero (Travolta) has a dreary job in a Brooklyn paint shop during the day, but on Saturday night, in the 2001 Odyssey disco, he's king of the dance floor. The disco is where he's popular and admired, unlike home where he's mocked by his father and unflatteringly compared to his brother Frank (Shakar), a priest. Then he meets Stephanie (Gorney) at the club. She's beautiful, from Manhattan, has a nice apartment and is a great dancer – but they both want more out of life. The first step is to see if, together, they can win the up-coming disco dance contest.

Saturday Night Fever has a magic and an energy that exceed the sum of its parts. John Badham's film tells of no-hoper Brooklyn kids escaping the grind at the disco. These particular kids are, however, not easy to like: they're sexist, racist, selfish and charmless. Tony is really no better, except that Travolta's Tony does charm you into thinking: 'If only that kid really believed in himself, he could go places.' In addition, Travolta dancing – or even just swaggering along – to the Bee Gees soundtrack (the all-time biggest-seller until Jackson's 'Thriller') is seventies feel-good.

New York, New York

USA, 1977
DIRECTOR:
Martin Scorsese
CAST INCLUDES:
Liza Minnelli, Robert De Niro,
Lionel Stander, Barry Primus,
Mary Kay Place, Georgie Auld,
George Memmoli, Dick Miller
SCREENPLAY:
Earl Mac Rauch, Mardik Martin from
a story by Earl Mac Rauch
CINEMATOGRAPHY:
László Kovács
**PRODUCERS/
PRODUCTION COMPANIES:**
Robert Chartoff, Irwin
Winkler/Chartoff-Winkler Productions

Jimmy Doyle (De Niro), a saxophone player, and Francine Evans (Minnelli), a lounge singer, meet in Times Square on V-J Day and decide they're meant for each other. Slightly further down the line, Jimmy's controlling, selfish nature is well to the fore, and Francine has turned into a doormat. Then, when she's accompanying him to an audition, her sensational voice is discovered. Her career begins to eclipse his – but at a high cost to their relationship.

Martin Scorsese has meticulously recreated the musical scene in post-World War II New York – the late-night atmosphere (those smoky browns), a whole new interweaving of poverty and wealth, and the big-band numbers themselves. He also deals with the tough realism, for musicians, of life on the move: the tedium of the travelling and the one-night stands, with happier moments to be found in companionship, a card game or a comfortable room for

the night. He also deals with the reality that, not even in musicals, is there always a happy ending. De Niro gets neatly under Jimmy's skin, and, other than *Cabaret* (1972), this is the closest anyone's got to finding Minnelli.

The Last Waltz

This record of The Band's last concert – after sixteen years on the road – was shot on Thanksgiving Day, 1976, at the Winterland Ballroom in San Francisco. Apart from the five band members – Levon Helm, Robbie Robertson, Richard Manuel, Garth Hudson and Rick Danko – a wealth of musical talent was there, both for support and to perform. Concert footage was interspersed with a few studio sessions plus Scorsese's interviews with Band members, mostly asking them about life on the road.

For *The Last Waltz*, Martin Scorsese chose to shoot in 35mm, a first for a music documentary. At times, a great sadness and weariness seems to hang over everything, then to be transcended by such moments as The Band and the Staple Singers singing 'The Weight', and by Muddy Waters' 'Mannish Boy' and Joni Mitchell's 'Coyote'. The Band themselves do what is probably their best-ever gig: 'Up on Crickle Creek', 'The Shape I'm In', 'It Makes No Difference', 'Ophelia' – they're all there and all glorious. Scorsese chooses to go for the spectacular finish with everyone singing 'I Shall Be Released'.

USA, 1978
DIRECTOR:
Martin Scorsese
CAST INCLUDES:
Paul Butterfield, Eric Clapton, Rick Danko, Neil Diamond, Dr. John, Bob Dylan, Lawrence Ferlinghetti, Emmylou Harris, Ronnie Hawkins, Levon Helm, Garth Hudson, Howard Johnson, Richard Manuel, Michael McClure, Joni Mitchell, Van Morrison, Pinetop Perkins, Robbie Robertson, Martin Scorsese, Roebuck 'Pops' Staples, Ringo Starr, Muddy Waters, Ron Wood, Neil Young, Bill Graham
CINEMATOGRAPHY:
Michael Chapman, Michael W. Watkins, Vilmos Zsigmond
**PRODUCERS/
PRODUCTION COMPANIES:**
Robbie Robertson, Joel Chernoff (uncredited)/FM Productions, Last Waltz Inc.

Grease

USA, 1978
DIRECTOR:
Randal Kleiser
CAST INCLUDES:
John Travolta, Olivia Newton-John,
Stockard Channing, Jeff Conaway,
Barry Pearl, Michael Tucci,
Kelly Ward, Didi Conn, Jamie
Donnelly, Dinah Manoff, Eve Arden,
Frankie Avalon, Joan Blondell,
Sid Caesar
SCREENPLAY:
Bronte Woodard; adaptation by
Allan Carr from the musical by Jim
Jacobs and Warren Casey
CINEMATOGRAPHY:
Bill Butler
PRODUCERS/
PRODUCTION COMPANIES:
Allan Carr, Robert
Stigwood/Paramount Pictures
ACADEMY AWARD
NOMINATIONS (1979)
Best Music, Original Song: John Farrar
for the song
'Hopelessly Devoted to You'

Southern California, 1950s. It's school vacation and, while away on holiday, Danny Zuko (Travolta) meets, and has a short, sweet summertime romance with, lovely Australian Sandy Olsson (Newton-John). School starts up again – and there's Sandy who's on a student-exchange programme. Romance is trickier this time round. Danny is the leader of the leather-jacketed, slick-haired, tough T-Birds. Sandy is so cute, pretty, clean and wholesome that not even the Pink Ladies gang wants her. Danny has his image to think about – and Rizzo (Channing) wants Danny back. Both Danny and Sandy have to find a way to win the other. The way Sandy finds is electric!

The producers claimed to want new faces for *Grease* the movie, but most of the cast had been in productions of the stage musical – including Travolta as Doody. Travolta, here, is as sizzling as in *Saturday Night Fever* (1972), plus showing he can sing as well as dance. Newton-John plays both goody-goody and hot-stuff girl with equal charm, and her slinky, high-heeled, black-clad power-babe is the *Grease* clip most-often shown. Knock-out success though it was, *Grease* did virtually nothing for the careers of anyone involved.

All That Jazz

Joe Gideon (Scheider) is feeling the strain. With one hand, he's auditioning the dancers and working on the choreography for his new show; with the other, he's editing his film about a stand-up comedian – which doesn't leave much for ex-wife Audrey (Palmer), girl-friend Kate (Reinking) or daughter Michelle (Foldi). Not even the start-the-day selection of tried-and-tested uppers and downers is working as it should. Joe is also ignoring symptoms of heart disease and having regular sessions with his Angel of Death (Lange) during which they travel through many painful old memories. Heart surgery time comes along – but is he ready to die?

It's not a completely autobiographical piece, but Bob Fosse has based quite a bit of *All That Jazz* on his own life. Although not a dancer, Roy Scheider was chosen as Joe/Fosse because of his great dancer's body. Ann Reinking is both a perfect and a bizarre choice: she was Fosse's mistress for years, and won a Tony for her choreography of the 1990 version of Fosse's Broadway musical *Chicago: A Musical Vaudeville* – from whence comes 'All That Jazz'. Fosse has left nothing out of this movie – except restraint. Nevertheless, this love song to theatre and show business is far more brilliant than over-the-top.

USA, 1979
DIRECTOR:
Bob Fosse
CAST INCLUDES:
Roy Scheider, Jessica Lange,
Leland Palmer, Ann Reinking, Cliff
Gorman, Ben Vereen, Erzsebet Foldi
SCREENPLAY:
Robert Alan Aurthur, Bob Fosse
CINEMATOGRAPHY:
Giuseppe Rotunno
PRODUCERS/
PRODUCTION COMPANIES:
Robert Alan Aurthur/20th Century
Fox, Columbia Pictures Corporation
ACADEMY AWARD
NOMINATIONS (1980)
Best Actor in a Leading Role:
Roy Scheider
Best Cinematography:
Giuseppe Rotunno
Best Director: Bob Fosse
Best Picture: Robert Alan Aurthur
Best Writing, Screenplay Written
Directly for the Screen:
Robert Alan Aurthur, Bob Fosse
ACADEMY AWARDS
Best Art Direction-Set Decoration:
Philip Rosenberg, Tony Walton,
Edward Stewart, Gary J. Brink
Best Costume Design: Albert Wolsky
Best Film Editing: Alan Heim
Best Music, Original Song Score and
Its Adaptation or Best Adaptation
Score: Ralph Burns

The Blues Brothers

USA, 1980
DIRECTOR:
John Landis
CAST INCLUDES:
John Belushi, Dan Aykroyd,
James Brown, Cab Calloway,
Ray Charles, Aretha Franklin, Steve
Cropper, Carrie Fisher, John Candy,
Henry Gibson
SCREENPLAY:
Dan Aykroyd, John Landis
CINEMATOGRAPHY:
Stephen M. Katz
**PRODUCERS/
PRODUCTION COMPANIES:**
Robert K. Weiss/Universal Pictures

On being released from prison, Joliet 'Jake' Blues is met by brother Elwood and, together, they visit the home where they were raised by nuns. The 'Penguin' tells them that the home is in debt and that $5000 is needed within eleven days to keep it open. What to do? Re-form their Blues band and stage a lucrative concert! The boys set about their 'mission from God'. Tracking down erstwhile band members does seem to involve upsetting a lot of people and crashing a lot of cars, but the boys struggle bravely on . . .

Facts about *The Blues Brothers* read like answers to 'Trivial Pursuit'. What are Elwood and Jake when they're not the Blues Brothers? Two cities south west of Chicago. How many film directors appear in the film? Five: John Landis, Dan Aykroyd, Frank Oz, John Candy and Stephen Spielberg. What record did the film break? The world record for the number of cars crashed. John Landis has achieved a rare thing with *The Blues Brothers*: he's taken a slot from *Saturday Night Live* and made it work as a movie. Not that it appeared to work to start with: it was trashed by critics and ignored by audiences. Gradually, however, the video sales rose and rose . . . and they keep on rising.

Fame

A new school year has started at the New York City High School for the Performing Arts, and a new batch of hopefuls is ready and waiting, each with a burning desire to succeed. Eight of them begin to get to know one another and to share in each other's triumphs and failures, happiness and heartbreaks – knowing that not all of them are going to make it.

Alan Parker likes the combination of music, film and kids, or so his films would seem to suggest: there's *Bugsy Malone* (1976), *Fame*, *Pink Floyd: The Wall* (1982), *The Commitments* (1991), plus, of course, the less-youthful *Evita* (1996). As a teen movie, *Fame* is much more focused than the bulk of the Brat Pack genre that would be projected onto kids in the 1980s, and the energy, enthusiasm and creativity of *Fame*'s whole young cast is awesome. A quarter of a century later, the big show numbers still work. Moreover, if you look carefully you'll see the erstwhile nasty Dr. Romano from *ER* is very much in there – with hair!

USA, 1980
DIRECTOR:
Alan Parker
CAST INCLUDES:
Irene Cara, Lee Curreri, Laura Dean,
Antonia Franceschi, Boyd Gaines,
Albert Hague, Tresa Hughes,
Steve Inwood, Paul McCrane,
Anne Meara, Joanna Merlin,
Maureen Teefy, Gene Anthony Ray
SCREENPLAY:
Christopher Gore
CINEMATOGRAPHY:
Michael Seresin
PRODUCERS/
PRODUCTION COMPANIES:
David De Silva, Alan Marshall/
Metro-Goldwyn-Mayer (MGM)
ACADEMY AWARD
NOMINATIONS (1981)
Best Film Editing: Gerry Hambling
Best Music, Original Song:
Michael Gore (music), Lesley Gore
(lyrics) for the song
'Out Here on My Own'
Best Sound: Michael J. Kohut,
Aaron Rochin, Jay M. Harding
Christopher Newman
Best Writing, Screenplay Written
Directly for the Screen:
Christopher Gore
ACADEMY AWARDS
Best Music, Original Score:
Michael Gore
Best Music, Original Song:
Michael Gore (music), Dean Pitchford
(lyrics) for the song 'Fame'

Little Shop of Horrors

USA, 1986
DIRECTOR:
Frank Oz
CAST INCLUDES:
Rick Moranis, Ellen Greene,
Vincent Gardenia, Steve Martin,
Tichina Arnold, Michelle Weeks,
Tisha Campbell, Levi Stubbs (voice of
Audrey II), James Belushi,
John Candy, Christopher Guest, Bill
Murray, Stan Jones (narrator/voice)
SCREENPLAY:
Howard Ashman (also musical);
Charles B. Griffith (1960 screenplay)
CINEMATOGRAPHY:
Robert Paynter
PRODUCERS/
PRODUCTION COMPANIES:
David Geffen/The Geffen Company
ACADEMY AWARD
NOMINATIONS (1987)
Best Effects, Visual Effects:
Lyle Conway, Bran Ferren,
Martin Gutteridge
Best Music, Original Song:
Alan Menken (music), Howard
Ashman (lyrics) for the song 'Mean
Green Mother from Outer Space'

Poor orphaned, nerdy Seymour (Moranis) works in the flower shop belonging to old Mr Mushnik (Gardenia) – as does Audrey (Greene), with whom Seymour is in love. Audrey, however, has a boyfriend, Orin Scrivello (Martin), an obnoxious and sadistic motor-bike-riding dentist. One day, just after an eclipse of the moon, Seymour finds a strange plant. He names it Audrey II. The plant starts to grow, and soon it is enormous. Seymour becomes famous and popular but is beginning to think he must give up his new-found fame as the plant feeds on blood, and now it's big enough to eat whole corpses. . .

Rick Moranis has, here, leapt from being a rather easy-to-ignore actor to being the heart and soul of *Little Shop of Horrors*. He makes us believe in Audrey II (he's the one it talks to) and we feel for him in his blossoming love affair with Audrey I. Furthermore – he can sing! In addition, Frank Oz's laid-back, 'If it's fun, we'll do it' directing style is warm and easy, and there are the hilarious and scene-stealing guest turns – including Bill Murray as a masochistic patient. The film was shot on the largest soundstage in Western Europe – the 007 stage at England's Pinewood studios. The original script called for Audrey and Seymour to be eaten by Audrey II. Bad idea.

Dirty Dancing

It's the summer of 1963. Frances 'Baby' Houseman (Grey) is on holiday with her family in a Catskills resort. The activities on offer seem very tame until she hears pulsating music coming from the staff lodge. Inside, there's some steamy dancing going on, and the steamiest dancer is Johnny Castle (Swayze), the resort dance instructor. When Johnny's partner has to rest up – after an unwanted pregnancy (not Johnny's fault) and a botched abortion, Baby offers to help him out, dance-wise, and the two get close – and steamy. Baby's father then gets Johnny fired, but will he find a way to return before the big dance contest?

Dirty Dancing's soundtrack really took off. '(I've Had) The Time of My Life', 'Hungry Eyes', and 'She's Like the Wind' could be responsible for Karaoke. Swayze and Grey certainly have chemistry – and she manages to convince the world she, as Baby, is only 17 (not 27). For girls, this is a deeply romantic film, and one to watch over and over again. The most romantic moment is when Johnny says to Baby, 'Nobody puts Baby in the corner!'. Then, if you're a girl, you burst into tears.

USA, 1987
DIRECTOR:
Emile Ardolino
CAST INCLUDES:
Jennifer Grey, Patrick Swayze,
Jerry Orbach, Cynthia Rhodes,
Jack Weston, Jane Brucker,
Kelly Bishop, Lonny Price,
Max Cantor
SCREENPLAY:
Eleanor Bergstein
CINEMATOGRAPHY:
Jeff Jur
**PRODUCERS/
PRODUCTION COMPANIES:**
Linda Gottlieb/Great American Films
Limited Partnership, Vestron Pictures
ACADEMY AWARDS (1988)
Best Music, Original Song: Frankie
Previte (music), John DeNicola
(music), Donald Markowitz (music),
Frankie Previte (lyrics) for the song
'(I've Had) The Time of My Life'

Moulin Rouge!

USA, 2001
DIRECTOR:
Baz Luhrmann
CAST INCLUDES:
Nicole Kidman, Ewan McGregor,
John Leguizamo, Jim Broadbent,
Richard Roxburgh, Garry McDonald,
Jacek Koman, Matthew Whittet,
Kerry Walker, Caroline O'Connor,
Christine Anu, Natalie (Jackson)
Mendoza, Lara Mulcahy,
David Wenham, Kylie Minogue
SCREENPLAY:
Baz Luhrmann, Craig Pearce
CINEMATOGRAPHY:
Donald (M.) McAlpine
**PRODUCERS/
PRODUCTION COMPANIES:**
Fred Baron, Martin Brown,
Baz Luhrmann/Bazmark Films
**ACADEMY AWARD
NOMINATIONS (2002)**
Best Actress in a Leading Role:
Nicole Kidman
Best Cinematography:
Donald McAlpine
Best Editing: Jill Bilcock
Best Makeup: Maurizio Silvi,
Aldo Signoretti
Best Picture: Fred Baron,
Martin Brown, Baz Luhrmann
Best Sound: Andy Nelson, Anna
Behlmer, Roger Savage, Guntis Sics
ACADEMY AWARDS
Best Art Direction-Set Decoration:
Catherine Martin (art director),
Brigitte Broch (set decorator)
Best Costume Design:
Catherine Martin, Angus Strathie

Montmartre, Paris, 1889; Christian (McGregor) is a penniless young writer who comes to Paris to pursue the Bohemian life of truth, beauty, freedom and love. He meets Toulouse-Lautrec (Leguizamo) who invites Christian to help him write a show they can sell to the Moulin Rouge. Zidler (Broadbent), the impresario of the Moulin Rouge (a bordello, burlesque show and dance hall, and a den of all hedonistic pleasures), wants to turn it into a real theatre. To this end he needs a patron. The Duke of Worcester (Roxburgh) agrees to foot the bills in exchange for the exclusive favours of the club's star dancer, Satine (Kidman). However, although a professional courtesan, Satine has fallen in love – with Christian.

Baz Luhrmann pulls out all the stops for *Moulin Rouge!* – indeed, he has a whole battery of new stops. This Australian director, with a background in opera, has the cast sing their own songs – songs that were not around in 1889. Everything from Elton John's 'Your Song' via 'All You Need Is Love' and 'Like a Virgin' to 'Roxanne' is in there, but it all fits beautifully around the velvet curtains and the elegant boudoir. All the senses are fed, as richly as they would have been in its heyday, by the Moulin Rouge itself. Sound, music, colour, texture, voluptuousness, movement, dance, flavours, tragedy, love – it's all here in this 21st-century musical.

Chicago

Chicago in the 1920s and Roxie Hart (Zellweger) will do anything to be famous. To this end, she has an affair with a man who claims to know people 'in the business'. When she realizes he doesn't – she kills him. Already on Death Row is Velma Kelly (Zeta-Jones) who caught her husband with her sister, and murdered both of them. Velma was making all the newspaper headlines until Roxy pushed her off. Enter Billy Flynn (Gere) a smooth-talking attorney – hired by Roxie's ever-loving husband Amos (Reilly) – who knows how to 'arrange' these matters for lady clients. Roxie is now headline news and could be an even bigger star if she plays the court-room scene right.

Moulin Rouge! (2001) announced the return of the screen musical, and *Chicago* moved in to carry on the flame. Chicago had done well on Broadway, first in 1975 and again in 1997 – there is always a production of it going on somewhere. Bob Fosse, the main man behind the original *Chicago*, had grown up in that city in the 1920s and 1930s and knew the mobsters, the murders, the cops on the make and the heated headlines. Fortunately, all that energy, drama, gloss and sleaze is still there on the screen. *Chicago* works well for the 21st-century audience, as the dialogue and action are slotted in between the musical numbers rather than the classic formula – 'And then he/she felt moved to burst into song' – which is already yesterday's news.

USA, 2002
DIRECTOR:
Rob Marshall
CAST INCLUDES:
Taye Diggs, Clive Saunders,
Catherine Zeta-Jones,
Renée Zellweger, Richard Gere,
Lucy Liu, Christine Baranski, Dominic
West, Sean McCann, John C. Reilly,
Chita Rivera, Queen Latifah
SCREENPLAY:
Bill Condon, from the play *Chicago* by
Maurine Dallas Watkins and the
musical *Chicago* by Bob Fosse and
Fred Ebb
CINEMATOGRAPHY:
Dion Beebe, James Chressanthis
(additional photography)
**PRODUCERS/
PRODUCTION COMPANIES:**
Martin Richards/Loop Films [CAN],
Miramax Films,
The Producers Circle Co.
**ACADEMY AWARD
NOMINATIONS (2003)**
Best Actor in a Supporting Role:
John C. Reilly
Best Actress in a Leading Role:
Renée Zellweger
Best Actress in a Supporting Role:
Queen Latifah
Best Cinematography: Dion Beebe
Best Director: Rob Marshall
Best Music, Original Song:
John Kander (music), Fred Ebb (lyrics)
for the song 'I Move On'
Best Writing, Screenplay Based on
Material Previously Produced or
Published: Bill Condon
ACADEMY AWARDS
Best Actress in a Supporting Role:
Catherine Zeta-Jones
Best Art Direction-Set Decoration:
John Myhre (art director), Gordon Sim
(set decorator)
Best Costume Design:
Colleen Atwood
Best Editing: Martin Walsh
Best Picture: Martin Richards
Best Sound: Michael Minkler,
Dominic Tavella, David Lee

ROMANCE

Sunrise

USA, 1927
DIRECTOR:
F.W. Murnau
CAST INCLUDES:
George O'Brien, Janet Gaynor,
Margaret Livingston, Bodil Rosing,
J. Farrell McDonald, Ralph Sipperly,
Jane Winton, Arthur Housman,
Eddie Boland
SCREENPLAY:
Carl Mayer from the novella
Die Reise nach Tilsit by
Hermann Sudermann. Titles by
Katherine Hilliker and H.H. Caldwell
CINEMATOGRAPHY:
Charles Rosher, Karl Struss
PRODUCERS/
PRODUCTION COMPANIES:
William Fox/Fox Film Corporation
ACADEMY AWARD
NOMINATIONS (1929)
Best Art Direction: Rochus Gliese
ACADEMY AWARDS
Best Actress in a Leading Role:
Janet Gaynor
Also for *Seventh Heaven* (1927) and
Street Angel (1928).
Best Cinematography:
Charles Rosher, Karl Struss
Best Picture, Unique and Artistic
Production

A city woman (Livingston), on holiday in the country, has an affair with a young married farmer. She wants him to murder his wife (Gaynor) and go with her. The husband plans a boating 'accident' but can't go through with it. In a state of anguish, he and his wife take a tramcar to the city, and reaffirm their vows in a church where a wedding is taking place. On the way home in the boat, a tremendous storm blows up. He is washed ashore, but it appears she is lost. The city woman re-appears, thinking he has followed her plan and he all but strangles her in his despair as he waits for news of his wife.

Murnau is one of the great silent directors, indeed, one of the great men of cinema. Cinema buffs and cameramen still can't figure out how he accomplished half the things he did, but are unanimous in affirming the brilliance of his camera-work, lighting, framing, back-screen projection – the lot. It is a tragedy that he made only three more films before being killed in a car crash at the age of 42. In the first year of Academy Award presentations, Janet Gaynor won the very first Best Actress Oscar for *Sunrise* (and two previous films); *Sunrise* won the first Oscar for 'Unique and Artistic Picture'.

It Happened One Night

When spoilt young Ellie Andrews (Colbert) weds a mercenary playboy, her rich banker father (Connolly) whisks her away on the family yacht until he can have the marriage annulled. Ellie dives overboard and sets off to join her husband. On a night bus she meets hung-over, just-been-fired reporter Peter Warne (Gable). He recognizes her and, in exchange for his not telling papa, she agrees to give him her story. To avoid discovery, they take to hitch-hiking and manage to spend two blameless days and nights together while falling in love. Then Peter sneaks off to borrow enough money to propose to her, Ellie wakes up and thinks she's been abandoned, papa sends conciliatory messages, and another round of complications begins.

Nobody wanted to make *It Happened One Night*, the first of many wonderful 1930s screwball comedies – no one, that is, except Frank Capra and his scriptwriter Robert Riskin. At last, Harry Cohn, of Columbia grudgingly gave it the go-ahead – but then no one wanted to star in it. Eventually, they got Gable on loan from MGM because Louis B. Mayer was annoyed with him and thought a 'bus' movie would be fitting punishment, and Claudette Colbert on the agreement that they paid her twice her usual fee and didn't expect her to work for more than four weeks. This was the first film to win the Oscars Grand Slam: Best Picture, Director, Actor, Actress and Screenplay

USA, 1934
DIRECTOR:
Frank Capra
CAST INCLUDES:
Clark Gable, Claudette Colbert,
Walter Connolly, Roscoe Karns,
Jameson Thomas, Alan Hale,
Arthur Hoyt, Blanche Frederici,
Charles C. Wilson
SCREENPLAY:
Robert Riskin from the story *Night Bus* by Samuel Hopkins Adams
CINEMATOGRAPHY:
Joseph Walker
**PRODUCERS/
PRODUCTION COMPANIES:**
Frank Capra, Harry Cohn
(uncredited)/Columbia Pictures
Corporation
ACADEMY AWARDS (1935)
Best Actor in a Leading Role:
Clark Gable
Best Actress in a Leading Role:
Claudette Colbert
Best Director: Frank Capra
Best Picture
Best Writing, Adaptation:
Robert Riskin

Camille

USA, 1936
DIRECTOR:
George Cukor
CAST INCLUDES:
Greta Garbo, Robert Taylor,
Lionel Barrymore, Elizabeth Allan,
Jessie Ralph, Henry Daniell,
Lenore Ulric, Laura Hope Crews,
Rex O'Malley
SCREENPLAY:
Zoe Akins, Frances Marion, James
Hilton from the novel and the play
La Dame aux camélias by Alexandre
Dumas fils
CINEMATOGRAPHY:
William (H.) Daniels, Karl Freund
PRODUCERS/
PRODUCTION COMPANIES:
Bernard H. Hyman, Irving
Thalberg/Metro-Goldwyn-Mayer
(MGM) (controlled by Loew's Inc.)
ACADEMY AWARD
NOMINATIONS (1938)
Best Actress in a Leading Role:
Greta Garbo

Paris, 1847. Beautiful Marguerite 'Camille' Gautier, currently the mistress of the Baron de Varville (Daniell), is one of the most sought-after women in Paris. She is content with her life of parties and soirées until she meets the charming and honest Armand Duval (Taylor) and falls in love with him. Unfortunately, he can't afford to support her, so she must continue to depend on the baron while meeting Armand in secret. However, their happiness is threatened and not only by the baron's suspicions: Armand's family is expressing strong disapproval and Camille herself is seriously ill with tuberculosis. This woman, who has had her every wish gratified, must decide if she loves Armand enough to let him go.

Alexandre Dumas fils created, in his original novel and play, the symbol of the camellia to represent illicit sexual love. It was the badge of the mistress, and it is very fitting that Garbo, the brightest star in the Hollywood firmament, should take on the role of the definitive movie mistress. Between them, Garbo and Cukor (the 'women's director'), plus a very sensitive contribution from Robert Taylor, turn what could easily have been a tear-jerker into a classic.

Wuthering Heights

Mr. Earnshaw (Kellaway), a kind gentleman farmer, who lives with his children Cathy and Hindley at Wuthering Heights on the Yorkshire moors, decides to take in a starving gypsy child named Heathcliff. As they grow up, Heathcliff (Olivier) is accepted by all except Hindley (Williams) who, when his father dies, condemns Heathcliff to a life of servitude in the stables. Heathcliff only stays at the house because of Cathy (Oberon). Although she loves him, too, Cathy decides to marry the more prosperous Edgar Linton (Niven). Heathcliff leaves for the Americas, but when he returns, life on the moors becomes very stormy.

For many, *Wuthering Heights* is the ultimate tale of doomed love, unrequited passions and revenge. Samuel Goldwyn certainly considered it to be his favourite Goldwyn production. It also garnered much critical acclaim. In that hotly contested year of 1939 – described more than once as the 'greatest year in motion-picture history' – it earned eight Academy Award nominations and won one. Being dragged away from London and his new fiancée, Vivien Leigh, was hard for Olivier. However, it must have been even harder to be passed over for the Best Actor Oscar while she was awarded Best Actress for *Gone with the Wind*.

USA, 1939
DIRECTOR:
William Wyler
CAST INCLUDES:
Merle Oberon, Laurence Olivier, David Niven, Flora Robson, Donald Crisp, Geraldine Fitzgerald, Hugh Williams, Leo G. Carroll, Miles Mander, Cecil Kellaway
SCREENPLAY:
Charles MacArthur, Ben Hecht, John Huston (uncredited), from the novel by Emily Brontë
CINEMATOGRAPHY:
Gregg Toland
PRODUCERS/ PRODUCTION COMPANIES:
Samuel Goldwyn/Samuel Goldwyn Company
ACADEMY AWARD NOMINATIONS (1940)
Best Actor in a Leading Role: Laurence Olivier
Best Actress in a Supporting Role: Geraldine Fitzgerald
Best Art Direction: James Basevi
Best Director: William Wyler
Best Music, Original Score: Alfred Newman
Best Picture: Samuel Goldwyn
Best Writing, Screenplay: Ben Hecht, Charles MacArthur
ACADEMY AWARDS
Best Cinematography, Black-and-White: Gregg Toland

The Shop Around the Corner

USA, 1940
DIRECTOR:
Ernst Lubitsch
CAST INCLUDES:
James Stewart, Margaret Sullavan,
Frank Morgan, Joseph Schildkraut,
Sara Haden, Felix Bressart,
William Tracy
SCREENPLAY:
Samson Raphaelson, Ben Hecht
(uncredited), from the play
Parfumerie by Miklós László
CINEMATOGRAPHY:
William H. Daniels
PRODUCERS/
PRODUCTION COMPANIES:
Ernst Lubitsch/Loew's Inc.,
Metro-Goldwyn-Mayer (MGM)

Budapest, Hungary in the 1930s. Alfred Kralik (Stewart) works at Matuschek & Co the gift shop around the corner. Alfred has been telling his fellow shop assistants about the dream girl with whom he is currently having a pen-pal correspondence, when in walks Miss Klara Novak (Sullavan), a young woman who is looking for a job. Alfred and Klara hit it off badly almost immediately. Six months later, things are worse – although the pen-pal relationship grows ever-more loving. Then, one day, Alfred and Klara both arrange to meet their pen-pals after work. Which Alfred will meet which Klara?

Having a pen pal, with whom you could be the charming, intelligent, successful person you would like to be, has been a

popular way for people to keep their spirits up during a recession – be that national, global or merely personal. Margaret Sullavan had many down patches in her short life, and there was a general lament that this glorious actress made so few films. Sullavan had a great fondness for Stewart, encouraging him and helping him get parts, and the chemistry between them, here, in Lubitsch's subtle, polished, timeless romantic comedy, is delightful. Miklós László's tale was used again for pen pals Judy Garland and Van Johnson in *In the Good Old Summer Time* (1949) and by email pals Meg Ryan and Tom Hanks in *You've Got Mail* (1998).

Waterloo Bridge

An ageing Col. Roy Cronin (Taylor), on the eve of World War II, stands on London's Waterloo Bridge remembering the beautiful girl he met there during World War I – Myra Lester (Leigh), a ballet dancer – and how they fell wildly in love. They can't find a way to get married before he leaves for the front, so she misses a performance in order to say goodbye to him and is fired from the ballet company. Poverty, and the news that he is believed dead, drive her to prostitution. Then, while working one night, she sees him. Their passionate reunion is marred for her by what she has become, and she realizes – for his sake – their love must end.

Waterloo Bridge had poignant war connections of its own. It went into production in 1939 as Hitler was invading Poland and it premièred in New York on the day (14 May, 1940) that Nazi bombs flattened Rotterdam. It is certainly a weepie, but in the hands of Mervyn LeRoy and its two stars, it was a lyrical weep rather than a soggy one. Both Leigh and Taylor said *Waterloo Bridge* was their favourite film and, for Taylor, it marked the first appearance of what was to become his trademark moustache.

GB, 1940
DIRECTOR:
Mervyn LeRoy
CAST INCLUDES:
Vivien Leigh, Robert Taylor,
Lucile Watson, Virginia Field,
Maria Ouspenskaya, C. Aubrey Smith
SCREENPLAY:
S.N. Behrman, Hans Rameau,
George Froeschel, from the play by
Robert E. Sherwood
CINEMATOGRAPHY:
Joseph Ruttenberg
**PRODUCERS/
PRODUCTION COMPANIES:**
Sidney Franklin/
Mervyn LeRoy/Loew's Inc.,
Metro-Goldwyn-Mayer (MGM)
**ACADEMY AWARD
NOMINATIONS (1941)**
Best Cinematography, Black-and-
White: Joseph Ruttenberg
Best Music, Original Score:
Herbert Stothart

The Philadelphia Story

USA, 1940
DIRECTOR:
George Cukor
CAST INCLUDES:
Cary Grant, Katharine Hepburn,
James Stewart, Ruth Hussey,
John Howard, Roland Young,
John Halliday, Mary Nash,
Virginia Weidler, Henry Daniell
SCREENPLAY:
Donald Ogden Stewart, Waldo Salt
(uncredited), from the play by
Philip Barry
CINEMATOGRAPHY:
Joseph Ruttenberg
PRODUCERS/
PRODUCTION COMPANIES:
Joseph L. Mankiewicz/Metro-
Goldwyn-Mayer (MGM)
ACADEMY AWARD
NOMINATIONS (1941)
Best Actress in a Leading Role:
Katharine Hepburn
Best Actress in a Supporting Role:
Ruth Hussey
Best Director: George Cukor
Best Picture: Joseph L. Mankiewicz
ACADEMY AWARDS
Best Actor in a Leading Role:
James Stewart
Best Writing, Screenplay:
Donald Ogden Stewart

On the eve of the wedding of Philadelphia heiress Tracy Samantha Lord (Hepburn) to wealthy and worthy George Kitteridge (Howard), her first husband appears – the wealthy and deliciously unworthy C.K. Dexter Haven (Grant). Another uninvited 'guest' that morning is a scandal concerning her errant father Seth Lord (Halliday) – who also hasn't been invited but turns up anyway. The next non-invitees are Mike Connor (Stewart) and Liz Imrie (Hussey), two reporters from *Spy* magazine who are chasing the Seth scandal, but will hold back on it in exchange for the wedding exclusive. Having, under the same roof, a playboy father and three men who fancy her drives Tracy to the champagne bottle. She does, however, end up at the wedding marrying the right man.

This was the fourth (and final) time for Grant and Hepburn as a comedy pair. Their ease with each other brought a fine resonance to Tracy and Dex's divorced status in *The Philadelphia Story*, allowing a very apt and rare level of intimacy, even as barbed insults fly back and forth. Stewart gives an excellent portrayal of the blue-collar reporter who has no truck with all this money-driven power – but who is nevertheless there to produce a mouth-watering account of it for his readers. George Cukor directs a fine script with great style and the result is a classic romantic screwball, remade as the Kelly/Crosby/Sinatra musical, *High Society*, in 1956.

The Lady Eve

Jean Harrington (Stanwyck), aboard an ocean liner, introduces herself to millionaire Charles Pike (Fonda) by ensuring that he trips over her foot. Jean and her father 'Colonel' Harrington (Coburn) are, in fact, card sharps on board to 'work' the ship. She finds herself falling in love with Charles, but promises her father not to announce her feelings until the end of the voyage. Meantime, someone else warns Charles and he then cuts her dead. Jean swears revenge. On next appearance, she is seen arriving at the Pike mansion as Lady Eve Sidwich from England. She charms everyone and, after some confused moments, Charles rejects the idea that she looks like Jean. He falls in love with her and they get married – but Jean's revenge isn't over yet.

Preston Sturges' directorial debut, *The Great McGinty* (1940), so impressed the critics that the studio encouraged him to make another film (*Christmas in July*, 1940) straight away. By the time he got to *The Lady Eve*, his third, he was being offered front-line stars. Both critics and audiences greatly approved of Stanwyck and Fonda's comic talents, and further comedy vehicles were lined up for them. Sturges usually based his scripts on his own stories, although this one is attributed to (Oscar nominated) Monckton Hoffe. However, he does tell the story of once opening the door to his first wife and talking to her for quite a while without recognizing her.

USA, 1941
DIRECTOR:
Preston Sturges
CAST INCLUDES:
Barbara Stanwyck, Henry Fonda, Charles Coburn, Eugene Pallette, William Demarest, Eric Blore, Melville Cooper, Martha O'Driscoll, Janet Beecher, Robert Greig, Dora Clement, Luis Alberni
SCREENPLAY:
Preston Sturges from the story by Monckton Hoffe
CINEMATOGRAPHY:
Victor Milner
**PRODUCERS/
PRODUCTION COMPANIES:**
Paul Jones/Paramount Pictures
**ACADEMY AWARD
NOMINATIONS (1942)**
Best Writing, Original Story: Monckton Hoffe

281

Casablanca

USA, 1942
DIRECTOR:
Michael Curtiz
CAST INCLUDES:
Humphrey Bogart, Ingrid Bergman,
Paul Henreid, Claude Rains,
Conrad Veidt, Sydney Greenstreet,
Peter Lorre, S.Z. Sakall,
Madeleine LeBeau, Dooley Wilson
SCREENPLAY:
Julius J. Epstein, Philip G. Epstein,
Howard Koch, Casey Robinson
(uncredited), from the play *Everybody
Comes to Rick's* by Murray Burnett
and Joan Alison
CINEMATOGRAPHY:
Arthur Edeson
**PRODUCERS/
PRODUCTION COMPANIES:**
Hal B. Wallis/Loew's Inc., Warner Bros.
**ACADEMY AWARD
NOMINATIONS (1944)**
Best Actor in a Leading Role:
Humphrey Bogart
Best Actor in a Supporting Role:
Claude Rains
Best Cinematography, Black-and-
White: Arthur Edeson
Best Film Editing: Owen Marks
Best Music, Scoring of a Dramatic or
Comedy Picture: Max Steiner
ACADEMY AWARDS
Best Director: Michael Curtiz
Best Picture: Hal B. Wallis
Best Writing, Screenplay:
Julius J. Epstein, Philip G. Epstein,
Howard Koch

Casablanca, December 1941. Wartime refugees heading for freedom come to Casablanca, desperately seeking the necessary documents. Most of them find their way to Rick's Café Américain, run by Richard 'Rick' Blaine, a cynical expatriate and former soldier of fortune. Rick deals in such papers. He acquires two invaluable letters just before underground leader Victor Laszlo (Henreid) and his wife Ilsa (Bergman) arrive. Rick and Ilsa had been lovers, and he still bears the scars of her leaving. Now, he has the chance to turn Victor over to the SS and flee Casablanca with Ilsa. What will Mr. 'I don't stick my neck out for anyone' choose to do?

Surely the best loved of all the Hollywood classics and certainly one of the favourites of all time, *Casablanca* had everything going for it. Bogart is at his enigmatic best playing the anti-hero for all he's worth, Bergman is beautiful and there are some great performances from the likes of Claude Rains and Sydney Greenstreet in the supporting cast. Even now, you only have to hear the opening bars of 'As Time Goes By' by Herme Hupfeld and you are immediately transported to exotic Casablanca – which was in fact the back lot of the Warner Brothers studio.

As to *Casablanca*'s famous lines, a sure sign of a picture's cult status, the usually misquoted closing line is 'Louie, I think this is the beginning of a beautiful friendship' (a last-minute dub-in), while 'Play it again, Sam' comes from the Marx Brothers' *A Night in Casablanca* (1946).

Now, Voyager

USA, 1942
DIRECTOR:
Irving Rapper
CAST INCLUDES:
Bette Davis, Paul Henreid,
Claude Rains, Gladys Cooper,
Bonita Granvill, John Loder,
Ilka Chase, Lee Patrick,
Franklin Pangborn, Katharine
Alexander, James Rennie,
Mary Wickes, Janis Wilson
SCREENPLAY:
Casey Robinson from the novel by
Olive Higgins Prouty
CINEMATOGRAPHY:
Sol Polito
**PRODUCERS/
PRODUCTION COMPANIES:**
Hal B. Wallis/Warner Bros.
**ACADEMY AWARD
NOMINATIONS (1943)**
Best Actress in a Leading Role:
Bette Davis
Best Actress in a Supporting Role:
Gladys Cooper
ACADEMY AWARDS
Best Music, Scoring of a Dramatic or
Comedy Picture: Max Steiner

Charlotte Vale (Davis) is a depressed and frumpish young woman, completely dominated by her heartlessly selfish mother (Cooper). A well-wisher introduces her to Dr. Jaquith (Rains) who persuades her to come to his sanatorium for analysis and treatment. When she leaves, she's an elegant and confident woman. She goes on a cruise and falls in love with kind and attentive Jerry Durrance (Henreid), but he's already married. When she returns home, her refusal to comply so frustrates her mother that she dies of a heart attack. Charlotte's guilt drives her back to the sanatorium but she isn't there for long.

Now, Voyager is one of the women's pictures – one with a five-hankie rating. Davis was very brave to agree to looking so deeply unattractive during the opening scenes. Barbara Stanwyck had started the movement of female stars not always looking like stars with *Stella Dallas* (written by *Now, Voyager's* author), but Davis went the whole way – shapeless dress; hair scraped back in a bun; thick, coarse eyebrows; unbecoming glasses and no makeup. Fortunately, by the end of the film, she gets to leave audiences with a very different impression. She also has one of the best-ever last lines – 'Oh Jerry, don't let's ask for the moon. We have the stars.'

Random Harvest

John 'Smithy' Smith (Colman) is found in the trenches, during World War II, shell-shocked and suffering from amnesia. He is rescued from an asylum on Armistice night by Paula Ridgeway (Garson). They marry and settle down happily. Then, on a trip to Liverpool, Smithy is knocked down in the street, at which point his immediate past vanishes and memory of his pre-war life – as Charles Rainier – returns. Charles goes back to his family estates and becomes a wealthy businessman. However, Paula is still with him – now disguised as Margaret Hansen, his elegant and efficient secretary – patiently waiting for his whole memory to be restored.

Random Harvest's weepie credentials are impeccable. Few movie heroines have ever made such a staggering sacrifice for their man as Garson does here. The romantic details are impeccable, too, down to the roses around the door of Paula and Smithy's idyllic country cottage. *Random Harvest* was also an example of Hollywood's favouring May-September story-lines at this time for the simple reason that the young Gables and Taylors had gone off to war. Though it failed to win an Oscar, *Random Harvest* was a great success at the box-office and, for many years, held the longest-run record at New York's Radio City Music Hall.

USA, 1942
DIRECTOR:
Mervyn LeRoy
CAST INCLUDES:
Ronald Colman, Greer Garson,
Philip Dorn, Susan Peters,
Henry Travers, Reginald Owen,
Bramwell Fletcher, Rhys Williams
SCREENPLAY:
Claudine West, George Froeschel,
Arthur Wimperis from the novel by
James Hilton
CINEMATOGRAPHY:
Joseph Ruttenberg
PRODUCERS/
PRODUCTION COMPANIES:
Sidney Franklin/Metro-Goldwyn-
Mayer (MGM)
ACADEMY AWARD
NOMINATIONS (1943)
Best Actor in a Leading Role:
Ronald Colman
Best Actress in a Supporting Role:
Susan Peters
Best Art Direction-Interior
Decoration, Black-and-White:
Cedric Gibbons, Randall Duell, Edwin
B. Willis, Jack D. Moore
Best Director: Mervyn LeRoy
Best Music, Scoring of a Dramatic or
Comedy Picture:
Herbert Stothart
Best Picture: Sidney Franklin
Best Writing, Screenplay:
George Froeschel, Claudine West,
Arthur Wimperis

Brief Encounter

GB, 1945
DIRECTOR:
David Lean
CAST INCLUDES:
Celia Johnson, Trevor Howard,
Stanley Holloway, Joyce Carey,
Cyril Raymond, Everley Gregg,
Marjorie Mars, Margaret Barton
SCREENPLAY:
Anthony Havelock-Allan, David Lean,
Ronald Neame (all uncredited), from
the play *Still Life* by Noel Coward
(also uncredited)
CINEMATOGRAPHY:
Robert Krasker
**PRODUCERS/
PRODUCTION COMPANIES:**
Noel Coward, Anthony Havelock-
Allan , Ronald Neame/Cineguild [GB],
G.C.F., The Rank Organisation Film
Productions Ltd. [GB]
**ACADEMY AWARD
NOMINATIONS (1947)**
Best Actress in a Leading Role:
Celia Johnson
Best Director: David Lean
Best Writing, Screenplay:
Anthony Havelock-Allan, David Lean,
Ronald Neame
CANNES FILM FESTIVAL (1946)
Grand Prize of Festival: David Lean

Mrs. Laura Jesson (Johnson) and Dr. Alec Harvey (Howard) meet at Milford Junction railway station when he gently removes some grit from her eye. They meet again by accident, go to the cinema, and arrange to meet the following week. When they go to a restaurant, Laura is deeply embarrassed when they run into old friends. Alec takes her to a friend's flat but, when the friend comes back unexpectedly, she runs away. Alec finds her at the station and tells her he loves her and that he has accepted a job abroad. Can she really be about to say goodbye to him, for the last time, at their station?

A superb five-hankie movie, thanks in no small part to Rachmaninov's 'Second Piano Concerto', *Brief Encounter* was a courageous undertaking for Lean – as shown by it's rather mediocre on-release box-office returns. In choosing Noel Coward's very middle-class story with a somewhat middle-aged cast (even Trevor Howard, in his first starring role, was 29), with non-star names and without a happy ending, he wasn't embarking on a profitable route. However, the honesty and sensitivity with which he depicted those events has stood the test of time well. *Brief Encounter* is a classic.

La belle et la bête
Beauty and the Beast

A merchant (André), for whom business is not going well, lives with his daughters – Belle (Day) and her two sisters – and a son whose friend wishes to marry Belle. She, however, feels she must look after her father. One day on his way home, the merchant stumbles into the extraordinary castle of a mysterious Beast (Marais). The Beast tells him he must die – or send one of his three daughters in his place. The loyal Belle sets off immediately. Every day, the Beast asks her: 'Will you be my wife?' At first she is horrified by the Beast, then she finds herself sympathizing and feeling warmly towards him. When he begins to metamorphose before her eyes, she isn't sure that she wouldn't rather he returned to being her Beast.

Cocteau's film of this famous fairy tale is a ripe choice for psychosexual interpretations. This was his first feature film embodying all of his gifts as an artist: as a poet, writer and painter, and his many years of studying the art of film. He was persuaded to make this movie by his long-term lover Jean Marais who played the triple role of Beast, the Prince and Avenant (Belle's suitor). 'Genius' was the word used to describe Cocteau the filmmaker from the outset. No one, before, had used a film to express so many artistic media. Current DVDs of the film include an additional audio track of a *La Belle et la bête* opera, written by Phillip Glass in 1995, which can be run concurrently. Not only do the voices sync well with the actors' lips, but Glass' music adds yet another dimension to this already magical experience.

FRANCE, 1946
DIRECTOR:
Jean Cocteau,
René Clément (uncredited)
CAST INCLUDES:
Jean Marais, Josette Day, Marcel André, Mila Parély, Nane Germon, Michel Auclair, Raoul Marco
SCREENPLAY:
Jean Cocteau (also story and dialogue), Jeanne-Marie Leprince de Beaumont (story)
CINEMATOGRAPHY:
Henri Alekan
PRODUCERS/ PRODUCTION COMPANIES:
André Paulvé/DisCina [FR]

The Ghost and Mrs. Muir

USA, 1947
DIRECTOR:
Joseph L. Mankiewicz
CAST INCLUDES:
Gene Tierney, Rex Harrison,
George Sanders, Edna Best,
Vanessa Brown, Anna Lee,
Robert Coote, Natalie Wood,
Isobel Elsom, Victoria Horne
SCREENPLAY:
Philip Dunne from the novel by
R.A. Dick
CINEMATOGRAPHY:
Charles Lang Jr.
**PRODUCERS/
PRODUCTION COMPANIES:**
Fred Kohlmar/20th Century Fox
**ACADEMY AWARD
NOMINATIONS (1948)**
Best Cinematography, Black-and-
White: Charles Lang

London/Cornwall, at the turn of the 20th century. Recently widowed, Lucy Muir (Tierney) is struggling with a bossy but well-meaning family. She decides to move with daughter Anna (Wood) to a house in Cornwall. She meets the house ghost, the crotchety Captain Daniel Gregg (Harrison). As their friendship grows, and her money dwindles, he persuades her to write a book about his seafaring life and it becomes a bestseller. Then, she meets the charming Miles Fairly (Sanders), and the Captain sadly says goodbye to her before wiping the memory of him from her mind. However, Mr. Fairly isn't really charming, and Gregg hasn't really left her forever.

A wonderful score by Bernard Hermann, full of soft gentleness and sweeping passion, perfectly complements this deeply romantic movie. Hollywood, as always, takes care of the romantic details – this time a cliff-top cottage (albeit not hugging a cliff in Cornwall but one in California, which was more budget-friendly). In Tierney's hands, the lovely Lucy's assertiveness grows until she is a woman of feisty resolve. Harrison never lets the Captain become sugary; however, he does play Captain Gregg at full stretch throughout which is, sometimes, slightly over the top – for a dead man. One of the joys of *The Ghost and Mrs. Muir* is that there are plenty of surprises along the way – including a really romantic ending.

Adam's Rib

Mr. and Mrs. Bonner, Adam and Amanda (Tracy and Hepburn), are legal professionals. Each of them lands a new job, which happens to be prosecuting (him) and defending (her) the accused woman in an attempted-murder trial. Doris Attinger (Holliday) tried (but failed) to shoot her husband on catching him with a floozie (Hagen). Hepburn makes the trial an equality-of-the sexes battle, claiming that the husband, Warren Attinger (Ewell), wouldn't be found guilty of the same crime. She turns the courtroom into a circus. Husband Adam, already needled by Amanda's encouragement of an ingratiating suitor (Wayne), finds himself increasingly angry. The Bonner marriage is looking a little strained.

Adam's Rib was the sixth of nine Tracy-Hepburn pairings, and many consider it to be their best. Their good friends, the scriptwriting Kanins (Garson Kanin and Ruth Gordon), had written *Adam's Rib* especially for them. Furthermore, all four were so impressed with Judy Holliday's film debut that they made sure she got the starring role in *Born Yesterday* (1950). In spite of the intensity of the battle played out here, the Kanins' point was that there is very little difference between the sexes – and as Tracy states at the end, 'Viva la difference – hurrah for that little difference.' And the romance? Well, if the Bonners hadn't been such a loving couple, there would have been no point in having a fight.

USA, 1949
DIRECTOR:
George Cukor
CAST INCLUDES:
Spencer Tracy, Katharine Hepburn,
Judy Holliday, Tom Ewell,
David Wayne, Jean Hagen,
Hope Emerson, Eve March,
Clarence Kolb
SCREENPLAY:
Ruth Gordon, Garson Kanin
CINEMATOGRAPHY:
George J. Folsey
**PRODUCERS/
PRODUCTION COMPANIES:**
Lawrence Weingarten/Metro-
Goldwyn-Mayer (MGM)
**ACADEMY AWARD
NOMINATIONS (1951)**
Best Writing, Story and Screenplay:
Ruth Gordon, Garson Kanin

The Quiet Man

USA, 1952
DIRECTOR:
John Ford
CAST INCLUDES:
John Wayne, Maureen O'Hara,
Barry Fitzgerald, Ward Bond,
Victor McLaglen, Mildred Natwick,
Francis Ford
SCREENPLAY:
Frank S. Nugent from the story
Green Rushes by Maurice Walsh
CINEMATOGRAPHY:
Winton C. Hoch
PRODUCERS/
PRODUCTION COMPANIES:
Merian C. Cooper, G.B. Forbes,
John Ford, L.T. Rosso/Argosy
Productions Corporation, Republic
Pictures Corporation
ACADEMY AWARD
NOMINATIONS (1953)
Best Actor in a Supporting Role:
Victor McLaglen
Best Art Direction-Set Decoration,
Colour: Frank Hotaling,
John McCarthy Jr.,
Charles S. Thompson
Best Picture: John Ford,
Merian C. Cooper
Best Sound, Recording:
Daniel J. Bloomberg
(Republic Sound Department)
Best Writing, Screenplay:
Frank S. Nugent
ACADEMY AWARDS
Best Cinematography, Colour:
Winton C. Hoch, Archie Stout
Best Director: John Ford

In America, Sean Thornton (Wayne) was a boxer, but he retired from this career after accidentally killing a man in the ring. Now, he has returned to his Irish home town of Innisfree, a place, he hopes, where he can finally be at peace. Sean's first move is to buy the cottage in which he was born. This alienates the town bully, Squire 'Red' Will Danaher, who wanted that land for his own use. Sean then meets and falls for Danaher's sister, Mary Kate (O'Hara) a red-haired colleen with a spunky will and a passionate heart. Getting Danaher's permission for the marriage is a thankless task, but when Danaher refuses to hand over his sister's dowry and Sean refuses to fight him for it, Mary thinks he's a coward and walks out. The romance in their relationship (and there is plenty of romance) is off to a slow start.

The director John Ford, while working away on westerns, was trying to drum up the backing for *The Quiet Man*, a homage to the Emerald Isle of his roots. The big studios said 'No thank you'. Eventually Ford went to Republic, the westerns and B-movies studio. Republic said 'OK – if you make us a western first'. Ford made them *Rio Grande*, and they funded *The Quiet Man*. The romance between Sean and Mary takes on much of a *The Taming of the Shrew* theme: deep understanding of the worth and strengths of each other grows while the sparks fly. A rockin' romance.

Roman Holiday

Ann (Hepburn), a very young princess visiting Rome on a goodwill tour, with all its ceremonies, speeches and interviews, suddenly reaches the end of her tether and bolts – just as the de-stressing sedative her doctor gave her takes effect. She wakes up on the sofa of Joe Bradley (Peck), an American journalist who recognizes her. She wants someone to show her some fun, and he wants an exclusive story, so off they set. She gets a haircut, they go on a wild scooter ride through the streets of Rome and they dance on a barge on the Tiber while his paparazzi friend, Irving (Albert), tries to take pictures. Too soon, she has to decide whether duty to her country comes before freedom and newly kindled love, and he has to discover whether he can put his heart and his honour before his scoop.

Most of the people who saw Hepburn in *Roman Holiday* were seeing her for the first time. She'd had some very minor roles in mostly minor films, but this was the moment when this slender, innocent, impish Gigi of a girl walked elegantly into the centre of the screen. With Peck as her stalwart, manly and honourable escort, the romance of unrequited love reaches its peak in their deliciously bittersweet final moment on screen together.

The writer, Dalton Trumbo, was blacklisted as one of the legendary Hollywood Ten due to allaged un-American activities, so when *Roman Holiday* won the Academy Award for Best Screenplay his friend, Ian McLellan Hunter, took credit for the story and accepted the Oscar.

USA, 1953
DIRECTOR:
William Wyler
CAST INCLUDES:
Gregory Peck, Audrey Hepburn, Eddie Albert, Hartley Power, Harcourt Williams, Margaret Rawlings, Tullio Carminati, Paolo Carlini, Claudio Ermel
SCREENPLAY:
Ian McLellan Hunter, John Dighton, story by Dalton Trumbo (credited to Ian McKellan Hunter)
CINEMATOGRAPHY:
Henri Alekan, Franz (F.)Planer
PRODUCERS/
PRODUCTION COMPANIES:
William Wyler/Paramount Pictures
ACADEMY AWARD
NOMINATIONS (1954)
Best Actor in a Supporting Role: Eddie Albert
Best Art Direction-Set Decoration, Black-and-White: Hal Pereira. Walter H. Tyler
Best Cinematography, Black-and-White: Franz Planer, Henri Alekan
Best Director: William Wyler
Best Film Editing: Robert Swink
Best Picture: William Wyler
Best Writing, Screenplay: Ian McLellan Hunter. John Dighton
ACADEMY AWARDS
Best Actress in a Leading Role: Audrey Hepburn
Best Costume Design, Black-and-White: Edith Head
Best Writing, Motion Picture Story: Ian McLellan Hunter. Dalton Trumbo

To Catch a Thief

USA, 1955
DIRECTOR:
Alfred Hitchcock
CAST INCLUDES:
Cary Grant, Grace Kelly, Jessie Royce
Landis, John Williams, Charles Vanel,
Brigitte Auber, Jean Martinelli,
Georgette Anys
CINEMATOGRAPHY:
Robert Burks
**PRODUCERS/
PRODUCTION COMPANIES:**
Alfred Hitchcock
(uncredited)/Paramount Pictures
**ACADEMY AWARD
NOMINATIONS (1956)**
Best Art Direction-Set Decoration,
Colour: Hal Pereira, J. McMillan
Johnson, Sam Comer, Arthur Krams
Best Costume Design, Colour:
Edith Head
ACADEMY AWARDS
Best Cinematography, Colour:
Robert Burks

John Robie (Grant) was a cat burglar – specializing in expensive gems, and known by the respectful title of 'The Cat' – until he took up comfortable retirement on the Riviera. Now there's a 'copy Cat' about and, as Robie is under suspicion, he feels that, to prove his innocence, he must catch the jewel thief himself. In this detective work he is assisted by the beautiful and wealthy playgirl Frances Stevens (Kelly). Initially, she believes he's guilty but thinks no less of him for that. Thrilled by the idea that he may be a master thief, her main interest is in catching him – for herself. As he's a bit distracted at the moment, she sets out to seduce him with her own diamonds.

Alfred Hitchcock was a stickler for order and control in his films so, when he found congenial and trustworthy collaborators, he liked to hang on to them. Grace Kelly and Cary Grant were two of his favourite actors. On this occasion he coaxed Grant out of his threatened retirement by offering him the chance of playing opposite Grace Kelly, the new movie sensation, as a suave and sexy hero in a sophisticated and romantic comedy drama – with Riviera locations thrown in. Moreover, the role would be especially attractive to Grant because the film was a genuine who-dunnit – and Grant could keep everyone guessing till the end. The title comes from the proverb 'Set a thief to catch a thief'.

All That Heaven Allows

Stoningham, New York. When Cary Scott (Wyman) falls in love with Ron Kirby (Hudson), all the prosperous suburban tongues in Stoningham start to wag. She is a wealthy widow who is part of their social set; he is a gardener and fifteen years her junior. Even her grown-up children are scandalized; they want her to marry Harvey (Nagel), who is decent and older and just looking for companionship and affection. Cary must choose between all the known bonuses of convention and the unknown territory that will be love.

Douglas Sirk's films were usually melodramas and, as such, were not taken very seriously, even though they were, in melodrama terms, excellent passion-boilers. However, Sirk is, through his films, commenting in perceptive detail on American life, very often subtly pointing out how crippled are the lives of the bourgeoisie. In *All That Heaven Allows* we see his natural world versus her 'city' world, his casual clothes versus her formal outfits, dinner with friends instead of dinner at the country club, a bottle of wine versus a tray of cocktails. All these clues help viewers to see how imprisoned Cary is, and how difficult is her choice.

USA, 1955
DIRECTOR:
Douglas Sirk
CAST INCLUDES:
Jane Wyman, Rock Hudson, Agnes Moorehead, Conrad Nagel, Virginia Grey, Gloria Talbott, William Reynolds, Charles Drake, Hayden Rorke
SCREENPLAY:
Peg Fenwick, Edna (L.) Lee from the story by Harry Lee
CINEMATOGRAPHY:
Russell Metty
PRODUCERS/ PRODUCTION COMPANIES:
Ross Hunter/Universal International Pictures

An Affair to Remember

USA, 1957
DIRECTOR:
Leo McCarey
CAST INCLUDES:
Cary Grant, Deborah Kerr,
Richard Denning, Neva Patterson,
Cathleen Nesbitt, Robert Q. Lewis,
Charles Watts, Fortunio Bonanova,
George Winslow
SCREENPLAY:
Leo McCarey, Delmer Daves,
Donald Ogden Stewart (originally
uncredited) from the story by
Leo McCarey and Mildred Cram
CINEMATOGRAPHY:
Milton (R.) Krasner
PRODUCERS/
PRODUCTION COMPANIES:
Leo McCarey, Jerry Wald/20th
Century Fox
ACADEMY AWARD
NOMINATIONS (1958)
Best Cinematography:
Milton R. Krasner
Best Costume Design:
Charles Le Maire
Best Music, Original Song:
Harry Warren (music),
Harold Adamson (lyrics),
Leo McCarey (lyrics) for the song
'An Affair to Remember'
Best Music, Scoring: Hugo Friedhofer

Charming, handsome Nicky Ferrante (Grant) and glamorous night-club singer Terry McKay (Kerr) are on the same cruise from Europe to New York where they will both be meeting up with their fiancés. However, it's love at first sight for Nicky and Terry. They spend every wonderful moment together and, when they stop off in the south of France, Terry even visits Nicky's grandmother Janou (Nesbitt) with him. Before they reach their destination, they decide to test their love. They will meet at the top of the Empire State Building in six months time and, if they are still in love, they will get married. However, Fate stops Terry getting there on time.

McCarey and Cram's story is a good one – good enough to have been made more than once. Leo McCarey made it himself, first, as *Love Story* in 1939, starring Irene Dunne and Charles Boyer. In 1994, Glenn Gordon Caron directed it with a very starry cast – Warren Beatty, Annette Bening, Katherine Hepburn and 'More (other) Stars than there are in Heaven' as MGM would say. Bollywood lovers can see it as *Mann* (1999), directed by Indra Kumar, starring Aamir Jhan and Manisha Koirala and with Sharmilla Tagore as Grandma. The scriptwriters of *Sleepless in Seattle* (1993) have clearly seen it, and the ultimate accolade – a spoof – comes courtesy of The Muppets in *The Muppets Take Manhattan* (1984).

The Long, Hot Summer

Ben Quick (Newman) has a reputation for barn burning which keeps him on the move. This summer finds him in the Southern town of Frenchman's Bend, being given a lift in their automobile by two young ladies Clara Varner (Woodward) and Eula Varner (Remick). Clara is the daughter of Will Varner (Welles) who owns most of the town, and Eula is the wife of his son Jody (Franciosa). When Will Varner gets back to town, he's not amused to learn that there's a barn burner about but, on meeting Ben, Varner decides he likes Ben enough to give him Jody's job in the store and to encourage him to marry Clara – at 23, already a spinster. Clara is cool with Ben until he nettles her enough to get her temperature rising – and then how the sparks do fly!

Among Martin Ritt's students at the Actors' Studio in New York (where he taught for many years) were Paul Newman, Joanne Woodward, Anthony Franciosa and Lee Remick – all of whom were offered parts in *The Long, Hot Summer*. A rich vein of sexual tension was added to their on-screen pairing by Newman and Woodward's off-screen love affair. They had known one another for a while, but couldn't get married until Newman's wife agreed to a divorce. Within a week of that divorce being finalized, they were married. They are still married and are still starring in films together.

USA, 1958
DIRECTOR:
Martin Ritt
CAST INCLUDES:
Paul Newman, Joanne Woodward,
Anthony Franciosa, Orson Welles,
Lee Remick, Angela Lansbury,
Richard Anderson
SCREENPLAY:
Irving Ravetch and Harriet Frank Jr.
from the stories *Barn Burning* and *The Spotted Horses*, and the novel *The Hamlet* by William Faulkner
CINEMATOGRAPHY:
Joseph LaShelle
PRODUCERS/
PRODUCTION COMPANIES:
Jerry Wald/Jerry Wald Productions, Inc.
CANNES FILM FESTIVAL (1958)
Best Actor: Paul Newman

Pillow Talk

USA, 1959
DIRECTOR:
Michael Gordon
CAST INCLUDES:
Rock Hudson, Doris Day,
Tony Randall, Thelma Ritter,
Nick Adams, Julia Meade, Allen
Jenkins, Marcel Dalio
SCREENPLAY:
Maurice Richlin, Stanley Shapiro,
Russell Rouse, (story),
Clarence Greene (story)
CINEMATOGRAPHY:
Arthur E. Arling
PRODUCERS/
PRODUCTION COMPANIES:
Ross Hunter, Martin Melcher/Arwin
Productions, Universal
International Pictures
ACADEMY AWARD
NOMINATIONS (1960)
Best Actress in a Leading Role
Doris Day
Best Actress in a Supporting Role:
Thelma Ritter
Best Art Direction-Set Decoration,
Colour: Richard H. Riedel,
Russell A. Gausman, Ruby R. Levitt
Best Music, Scoring of a Dramatic or
Comedy Picture: Frank De Vol
ACADEMY AWARDS
Best Writing, Story and Screenplay -
Written Directly for the Screen:
Russell Rouse, Clarence Greene,
Stanley Shapiro, Maurice Richlin

Jan Morrow (Day) is a successful interior designer whose business and personal life are interrupted by songwriter Brad Allen (Hudson) with whom she shares a party line. All day long he sings his songs down the phone to his various girl friends. Brad's work is being financed by a millionaire Broadway producer, Jonathan Forbes (Randall), who, as it happens, is trying to persuade Jan to be his third wife. One day, Brad sees Jan and recognizes her from Jonathan's description – and then recognizes her voice from hearing it so often on the phone. He assumes an outrageous alter ego, and sets about getting to know her. When Jan finds out, she exacts her own mortifying revenge.

The romantic comedies of the fifties are wittily romantic – because romance and wit was all that was on offer and any pillow talk had to be done over the phone. At the heart of these glossy comedies is candyfloss.

However, for this kind of film, Hudson and Day are a perfect pairing. She was America's fifties sweetheart: bubbly and cutely rebellious but as wholesome as apple pie. Hudson's extraordinary good looks took him into brooding roles in tormented melodramas. *Pillow Talk* gave them both the chance of something new. Hudson got to deliver snappy, stinging lines, and Day got the chance to remind people that she was a great comedienne and a sexy lady. The film was a box-office smash and she got nominated for both an Oscar and a Golden Globe.

À bout de souffle

Michel (Belmondo) thinks of himself as a young Humphrey Bogart, but he's really just a small-time hood. While stealing a car, out in the country, he shoots a policeman who is following him. He goes back to Paris to hide out in the room of his American girlfriend, Patricia (Seberg), who's a student and wants to be a journalist. She tells him she may be pregnant. They then spend time fooling around, making love and talking – and making 'getaway' money by stealing and selling more cars. Michel wants to leave the country, but Patricia is uncertain. She'd rather be an American intellectual in Paris. Michel's name and picture are now on the front pages of newspapers. The police are everywhere and they are closing in . . .

'Modern movies begin here' say the critics. Godard's film was the start of the French New Wave – a reaction against the existing structure and narrative of French film. The young couple here are having a very sixties relationship, one that reflects all the existential 'I am alone' angst that was being blotted out by the drugs which turned everything into 'I'm all right, Jack'. However, Godard does spend twenty-five minutes of the film on the bedroom scene. In this time, Michel and Patricia get as affectionate, as close and as 'rounded out' as it's possible for them to be, given their fundamental emptiness. Michel says to Patricia: 'When we talked, I talked about me, you talked about you, when we should have talked about each other.'

FRANCE, 1960
USA/UK TITLE:
Breathless/By a Tether (informal)
DIRECTOR:
Jean-Luc Godard
CAST INCLUDES:
Jean-Paul Belmondo, Jean Seberg, Daniel Boulanger, Jean-Pierre Melville, Henri-Jacques Huet, Van Doude, Claude Mansard, Jean-Luc Godard
SCREENPLAY:
Jean-Luc Godard from a story by François Truffaut
CINEMATOGRAPHY:
Raoul Coutard
PRODUCERS/ PRODUCTION COMPANIES:
Georges de Beauregard/Impéria [FR], Les Films Georges de Beauregard, Société Nouvelle de Cinématographie

The Apartment

USA, 1960
DIRECTOR:
Billy Wilder
CAST INCLUDES:
Jack Lemmon, Shirley MacLaine,
Fred MacMurray, Ray Walston,
Jack Kruschen, David Lewis,
Hope Holiday, Joan Shawlee
SCREENPLAY:
Billy Wilder and I.A.L. Diamond
CINEMATOGRAPHY:
Joseph LaShelle
**PRODUCERS/
PRODUCTION COMPANIES:**
Billy Wilder/The Mirisch Corporation
**ACADEMY AWARD
NOMINATIONS (1961)**
Best Actor in a Leading Role:
Jack Lemmon
Best Actor in a Supporting Role:
Jack Kruschen
Best Actress in a Leading Role:
Shirley MacLaine
Best Cinematography, Black-and-
White: Joseph LaShelle
Best Sound: Gordon Sawyer
(Samuel Goldwyn SSD)
ACADEMY AWARDS
Best Art Direction-Set Decoration,
Black-and-White: Alexandre Trauner,
Edward G. Boyle
Best Director: Billy Wilder
Best Film Editing ; Daniel Mandell
Best Picture: Billy Wilder
Best Writing, Story and Screenplay -
Written Directly for the Screen: Billy
Wilder, I.A.L. Diamond

The life of Manhattan insurance clerk C.C. Baxter (Lemmon) is a nightmare. It shouldn't be; he has all his superiors writing glowing reports about him, but the price is the key to his apartment for their extramarital affairs. Baxter, himself, isn't having an affair, but he is in love with elevator girl Fran Kubelik (MacLaine). However, he's distressed to discover that Fran has been visiting his apartment with Sheldrake (MacMurray) the company boss. Fran is similarly distressed to learn that Sheldrake is having other extramarital affairs, and Baxter subsequently finds, in his apartment, Fran – who has tried to kill herself. Baxter must try to turn things around so that he can keep Fran and his apartment.

Billy Wilder very skilfully sets up the funny side of *The Apartment*'s scenario before peeling the humour away, layer by layer, till we see the bleakness beneath. An optimistic streak, however, is maintained by the honestly cheerful Miss Kubelik until her own world becomes too grim. Jack Lemmon seems to have been liberated by his portrayal as Daphne in *Some Like It Hot* (1959). He finds new depths, as C.C. Baxter, that allow him to forge the perfect balance between the film's comic top layer and its darker implications. Shirley MacLaine was perfectly cast as his co-star, and ended a run of disappointing movies with an Oscar nomination.

Breakfast at Tiffany's

USA, 1961
DIRECTOR:
Blake Edwards
CAST INCLUDES:
Audrey Hepburn, George Peppard,
Patricia Neal, Buddy Ebsen,
Martin Balsam, José Luis de
Villalonga, John McGiver, Alan Reed
SCREENPLAY:
George Axelrod from the novel by
Truman Capote
CINEMATOGRAPHY:
Franz (F.) Planer
**PRODUCERS/
PRODUCTION COMPANIES:**
Martin Jurow, Richard
Shepherd/Jurow-Shepherd,
Paramount Pictures
**ACADEMY AWARD
NOMINATIONS (1962)**
Best Actress in a Leading Role:
Audrey Hepburn
Best Art Direction-Set Decoration,
Colour: Hal Pereira, Roland Anderson,
Sam Comer, Ray Moyer
Best Writing, Screenplay Based on
Material from Another Medium:
George Axelrod
ACADEMY AWARDS
Best Music, Original Song: Henry
Mancini (music), Johnny Mercer
(lyrics) for the song 'Moon River'
Best Music, Scoring of a Dramatic or
Comedy Picture: Henry Mancini

Holly Golightly won't thank you for referring to her origins in Texas – not since she came to New York and found ways to allow grateful men to fund her glamorous existence. Any time Holly is feeling blue, she takes a trip to Tiffany's – the only jewellery store worth browsing in. Her new neighbour, Paul (Peppard) doesn't judge her: he has his own rich lady friend, in 2-E (Neal). Little by little, Holly and Paul are getting closer, but any kind of 'real' relationship terrifies Holly. She won't own or be owned by anyone – even to the extent that her cat is only called 'Cat', and she sets the poor animal free in the rain when she feels she's getting too fond of it. What hope, then, for Paul?

Audrey Hepburn, that beautiful creature in the Givenchy dress and the pearls and the huge sunglasses, is Holly Golightly, and everyone's instant call-up image of *Breakfast at Tiffany's*. However, she nearly wasn't. The novel's author, Truman Capote, had always seen Marilyn Monroe in that role, but her drama coach, Lee Strasburg vetoed the idea. As Monroe was in the process of changing her image, he explained, the role of a call girl wouldn't be suitable. In the novel, Holly is very free-spirited and, for instance, even has a 'fling' with another woman. The film's producers thought that such attributes didn't fit well with Hepburn's image and they were omitted. Nevertheless, Hepburn always said she felt that, as Holly Golightly, she was miscast.

Un homme et une femme

FRANCE, 1966
USA/UK TITLE:
A Man and a Woman
DIRECTOR:
Claude Lelouch
CAST INCLUDES:
Anouk Aimée, Jean-Louis Trintignant,
Pierre Barouh, Valérie Lagrange,
Antoine Sire, Souad Amidou,
Henri Chemin, Yane Barry
SCREENPLAY:
Claude Lelouch,
Pierre Uytterhoeven
CINEMATOGRAPHY:
Claude Lelouch
PRODUCERS/
PRODUCTION COMPANIES:
Claude Lelouch/Les Films 13 [FR]
ACADEMY AWARD
NOMINATIONS (1967)
Best Actress in a Leading Role:
Anouk Aimée
Best Director: Claude Lelouch
ACADEMY AWARDS
Best Foreign Language Film (France)
Best Writing, Story and Screenplay -
Written Directly for the Screen:
Claude Lelouch, Pierre Uytterhoeven
CANNES FILM FESTIVAL (1966)
Palme d'Or: Claude Lelouch
Tied with *Signore & Signori* (1965).
In 1966 the Grand Prize was given as
'Grand prix du vingtième anniversaire
du Festival international du film'
(20th Anniversary Grand Prize).
OCIC Award: Claude Lelouch

Anne Gauthier (Aimée) is a widowed production assistant in the movie business. Her young daughter, Françoise (Amidou), attends a boarding school in Deauville. There, Anne meets racing-car driver Jean-Louis Duroc (Trintignant), a widower, whose son, Antoine (Sire), also boards at the school. When she misses her train, Jean-Louis offers her a lift back to Paris. As the two become increasingly attracted to one another, they slowly begin to reveal their feelings and the painful and tragic elements in their pasts that locked them into themselves. Indeed, they are performing the age-old ritual of falling in love.

When Lelouch's *A Man and a Woman* appeared it was as if a small cyclone tore through all the awards ceremonies and film festivals the world over – winning everything as it went. It also, having been so cheaply made (Lelouch did nearly everything on the movie) made a good-sized fortune. For all it's stylistic innovations, including a complicated timetable for when colour and when black-and-white, it is the sensual romance of two powerfully attractive stars – French ones, too! – that made it such a hit. Lelouche has made many other successful (and often romantic) films including a variation on *A Man and a Woman – Another Man, Another Chance* (1977), and a sequel to it – *A Man and a Woman: 20 Years Later* (1986).

Barefoot in the Park

USA, 1967
DIRECTOR:
Gene Saks
CAST INCLUDES:
Robert Redford, Jane Fonda,
Charles Boyer, Mildred Natwick,
Herb Edelman, Mabel Albertson,
Fritz Feld, James Stone, Ted Hartley,
Paul E. Burns
SCREENPLAY:
Neil Simon from his own play
CINEMATOGRAPHY:
Joseph LaShelle
PRODUCERS/
PRODUCTION COMPANIES:
Hal B. Wallis/Nancy Productions,
Paramount Pictures
ACADEMY AWARD
NOMINATIONS (1968)
Best Actress in a Supporting Role:
Mildred Natwick

Newly married Paul (Redford) and Corie (Fonda) start wedded life in their bijou but problem-riddled fifth-floor (no elevator) flat. Paul is a sensible and dedicated young lawyer while Corie is a bubbly free spirit who wants him to stay home and play. To her, he seems completely unspontaneous; for his part, Corie is beginning to give him a headache. Meantime, Corie's mother (Natwick) is lonely, and regularly staggers up the five flights – and on up to the sixth, after meeting the charming Mr Velasco (Boyer). Paul, feeling totally worn down by work, Corie and a head-cold, consoles himself with a lot of whisky, and soon he and Corie are in the middle of a full-scale newlywed crisis.

Adapted by Neil Simon from his own hilarious Broadway hit, *Barefoot in the Park* transferred to the screen with Redford and Natwick reprising their original roles. The stars of the film, however, are probably the stairs. Anyone entering the flat (little more than one room – and the setting for 75% of the film) is out of breath – including all the reluctant workmen who are trying to tame the flat's eccentricities. Redford and Fonda are a charismatic couple, and Mildred Natwick, – as Ethel, Corie's mother – brilliantly delivers her very funny lines and well deserves her Oscar nomination.

Love Story

USA, 1970
DIRECTOR:
Arthur Hiller
CAST INCLUDES:
Ali MacGraw, Ryan O'Neal,
John Marley, Ray Milland,
Russell Nype, Katharine Balfour,
Sydney Walker, Robert Modica,
Walker Daniels, Tommy Lee Jones
SCREENPLAY:
Erich Segal
CINEMATOGRAPHY:
Richard (Dick) C. Kratina
PRODUCERS/
PRODUCTION COMPANIES:
Howard G. Minsky/Love Story
Company, Paramount Pictures [us]
ACADEMY AWARD
NOMINATIONS (1971)
Best Actor in a Leading Role:
Ryan O'Neal
Best Actor in a Supporting Role:
John Marley
Best Actress in a Leading Role:
Ali MacGraw
Best Director: Arthur Hiller
Best Picture: Howard G. Minsky
Best Writing, Story and Screenplay
Based on Factual Material or Material
Not Previously Published or
Produced: Erich Segal
ACADEMY AWARDS
Best Music, Original Score:
Francis Lai

Oliver Barrett IV (O'Neal) is studying law at Harvard while Jenny Cavalleri (MacGraw) is majoring in music at Radcliffe. They meet and quarrel a lot until, in a long kiss, they find undying love. Jenny is going to Paris to further her music studies, but shelves this plan when Oliver proposes marriage. Enter the fathers-in-law. Wealthy Oliver Barrett III is far from pleased because Jenny is from the wrong social background, and cuts off the pair without a penny. Phil Cavalleri, on the other hand, is delighted, though not happy with a non-conformist wedding ceremony. The young couple goes from strength to loving strength until they decide it's time for children. Then, a shock awaits them that they couldn't have imagined.

Paramount was very grateful for *Love Story*. They were lamenting a seriously disappointing year for hit films when this modestly budgeted little movie blew the roofs of box offices everywhere. *Love Story* was one of the first movies to gross $100 million on first release – and a good deal more after that. It was also one of the first times that an author wrote a best-selling book from a screenplay. Francis Lai's Oscar-winning theme music has become a classic, and the two veteran Hollywood actors, Milland and Marley, are superb. Five hankies, minimum!

A New Leaf

Ageing, snobbish, bachelor playboy Henry Graham (Matthau) has run out of money. He reluctantly takes his butler's advice to get himself a rich wife. After a few false starts, he stumbles upon millionairess Henrietta Lowell (May) – myopic, clumsy, awkward, usually covered in crumbs, a frump and a botanist. Henry intends to marry and then murder her because he doesn't want to be married or to share her wealth with anyone. Henrietta's dream is to find a new plant – which she does. She shows Henry a leaf and says she's named it after him. Henry is touched, but not enough to cancel the murder plan. He agrees to go with her on a field trip, and the perfect murder moment arrives when their canoe overturns in rapids (she can't swim) – but what does he see on the bank . . . ?

A New Leaf is an exquisitely funny film. It's scripted by Elaine May and is her debut as a director. It was the subject of a court battle with Paramount: May's version was nearly three hours long with a dark sub-plot, in which Henry did murder a couple of blackmailers and she wanted her name removed. She didn't succeed, and what is left of the film is certainly as much as one could want. Matthau has probably never been better than as this arrogant, heartless, selfish, insensitive, greedy and homicidal man. May is incomparable as a disaster zone who still manages to be sweet and naïvely sexy. Henry's redemption – which he fights to the last – is the more funny and delightful because it's engineered by a woman who has no idea that anything's changed.

USA, 1971
DIRECTOR:
Elaine May
CAST INCLUDES:
Walter Matthau, Elaine May, Jack Weston, George Rose, James Coco, Doris Roberts, Renée Taylor, William Redfield, Graham Jarvis
SCREENPLAY:
Elaine May, from the story *The Green Heart* by Jack Ritchie
CINEMATOGRAPHY:
Gayne Rescher
PRODUCERS/
PRODUCTION COMPANIES:
Hillard Elkins, Howard W. Koch, Joseph Manduke/Aries Productions, Elkins Productions International Corporation

USA, 1973
DIRECTOR:
Sydney Pollack
CAST INCLUDES:
Barbra Streisand, Robert Redford,
Bradford Dillman, Lois Chiles,
Patrick O'Neal, Viveca Lindfors,
Allyn Ann McLerie, Murray Hamilton,
Herb Edelman, Diana Ewing,
Sally Kirkland
SCREENPLAY:
Arthur Laurents, David Rayfiel
(uncredited)
CINEMATOGRAPHY:
Harry Stradling Jr.
**PRODUCERS/
PRODUCTION COMPANIES:**
Ray Stark/Columbia Pictures
Corporation, Rastar Productions
**ACADEMY AWARD
NOMINATIONS (1974)**
Best Actress in a Leading Role:
Barbra Streisand
Best Art Direction-Set Decoration:
Stephen B. Grimes, William Kiernan
Best Cinematography:
Harry Stradling Jr.
Best Costume Design:
Dorothy Jeakins, Moss Mabry
ACADEMY AWARDS
Best Music, Original Dramatic Score:
Marvin Hamlisch
Best Music, Original Song:
Marvin Hamlisch (music),
Alan Bergman (lyrics), Marilyn
Bergman (lyrics) for the song
'The Way We Were'

The Way We Were

It's the late 1930s, and Katie Morosky and Hubbell Gardner meet at university. They are from very different backgrounds: she's Jewish, outspoken and a political activist; he's from a WASP family and wants to be a writer. There's a mutual underlying attraction that neither of them follows up. However, some years later, when they meet up again, they embark on a wonderful romance despite their ideological differences. They get married and, by the time they move out to California where he will adapt one of his novels as a screenplay, it's the early 1950s and people are being blacklisted as Communist sympathizers. Katy (now pregnant) is still as vocal as ever and she and Hubbell decide they must part. Years later, they bump into each other again, and the magic is still there . . .

The critics mauled *The Way We Were*, but the public loved it. Perhaps it was the theme song – which went on to be a monumental hit; perhaps it was the unexpectedly strong on-screen chemistry between Redford and Streisand; perhaps it was the strength of the plot that was heart-wrenching without being sentimental; perhaps it was the five-hankie ending – whatever it was, it worked.

Annie Hall

Successful New York comedian Alvy Singer (Allen) is introduced by his manager, Rob (Roberts), to would-be singer Annie Hall (Keaton). The couple begin an affair and move in together, with Alvy encouraging Annie to 'go for it' both in her career and in her attempts at further education. Nevertheless, they are both still seeing their analysts. Alvy becomes jealous of record-producer Tony Lacey's (Simon) attentions to Annie, and Alvy and Annie split up for a while. They are reconciled in time to fly to Hollywood and pursue career possibilities for Alvy. They attend a party given by Lacey, and that seems to herald the right time to split up once and for all. However, their affair still has more to offer Alvy.

Annie Hall was advertised as a 'nervous romance', and finds Allen expanding his range of cinematic comedy ingenuity. There is, for instance, Alvy and Annie's opening exchange in which, counter-pointing their rather banal conversational exchange, title boards show what they are really thinking. Allen also gives strong indications as to where his work is now: when, for instance, Alvy's in bed with Annie he says that 'this is the most fun I've ever had without laughing', showing his readiness to move beyond the protective laughter of his all-out comedies into the world of direct feeling. This is first and foremost a love story, and a very interesting record of love in the 1970s. And Ralph Lauren's clothes for Annie caused a fashion revolution.

USA, 1977
DIRECTOR:
Woody Allen
CAST INCLUDES:
Woody Allen, Diane Keaton,
Tony Roberts, Carol Kane,
Paul Simon, Shelley Duvall,
Janet Margolin, Colleen Dewhurst,
Christopher Walken
SCREENPLAY:
Woody Allen and Marshall Brickman
CINEMATOGRAPHY:
Gordon Willis
PRODUCERS/
PRODUCTION COMPANIES:
Charles H. Joffe, Jack Rollins/Rollins-Joffe Productions
ACADEMY AWARD
NOMINATIONS (1978)
Best Actor in a Leading Role:
Woody Allen
ACADEMY AWARDS
Best Actress in a Leading Role:
Diane Keaton
Best Director: Woody Allen
Woody Allen was not present at the
awards ceremony.
Co-presenter King Vidor accepted
the award on his behalf.
Best Picture: Charles H. Joffe
Best Writing, Screenplay Written
Directly for the Screen:
Woody Allen, Marshall Brickman

10

USA, 1979
DIRECTOR:
Blake Edwards
CAST INCLUDES:
Dudley Moore, Julie Andrews,
Bo Derek, Robert Webber,
Dee Wallace (Stone), Sam J. Jones,
Brian Dennehy, Max Showalter
SCREENPLAY:
Blake Edwards
CINEMATOGRAPHY:
Frank Stanley
PRODUCERS/
PRODUCTION COMPANIES:
Tony Adams, Blake Edwards/Geoffrey
Productions Inc., Orion Pictures
Corporation
ACADEMY AWARD
NOMINATIONS (1980)
Best Music, Original Score:
Henry Mancini
Best Music, Original Song:
Henry Mancini (music), Robert Wells
(lyrics) for 'The Song from 10
(It's Easy to Say)'

George Webber (Moore) is a writer of hit songs who's going through a mid-life crisis. He has a lovely home, a fulfilling career, a nice car and Samantha (Andrews), his beautiful and intelligent girlfriend. But he's feeling the onset of age, and his lust for life seems to be diminishing. Then, on the beach, he sees an angel in white. It's Jenny (Derek), a blonde, perfectly proportioned goddess of a girl – who happens to be about to get married. She's not just a perfect '10' (the top of George's beauty scale), she's an '11'. She represents his youth, and he pursues her, uphill and down. Will he catch her? Will she be the answer to his dreams?

Blake Edwards uses *10* to remind us that 40 is a dangerous age. At 40, men are much more at home with fantasy than reality, and George is not really at all comfortable with the actual free spirit of sexual revolution that Jenny represents. The male menopause is upon him; old age itself seems like a dreaded disease and the only way to put it off is with a last fling. Dudley Moore was able to remind the world, in *10*, how very funny he is, Julie Andrews got to play a role – very effectively – that was elegant and sexy, and Bo Derek was responsible for a new hairstyle.

The French Lieutenant's Woman

Anna (Streep) and Mike (Irons) are starring in the film of a story set in Lyme Regis in 19th century England. It tells of the infatuation of Charles Smithson (Irons) with the strangely fascinating Sarah Woodruff (Streep), even though he is engaged to Ernestina (Baxter), a charming young lady of good family and a considerable dowry. Sarah, on the other hand, is supposedly a 'wronged' and, therefore, tainted woman. So involved does Charles become, that he feels obliged to break his engagement to Ernestina. He then finds that Sarah has vanished, and resolves to try to find her. Meanwhile, Anna and Mike are carrying on an illicit affair that bears extraordinary similarities to the parts they are playing.

John Fowles' magnificent novel was not an easy undertaking for Harold Pinter to adapt for the screen. It has, for example, a narrator, and it also has alternative endings. Pinter chose to put the original story within a film so that the detachment of the filmmaking process would echo the function of the narrator. Contemporary insight on the plight of the Victorian characters would also be provided by the observations of the film-within-a-film actors playing the parts. Interestingly, Charles and Sarah's affair is a lot more passionate than Anna and Mike's.

GB, 1981
DIRECTOR:
Karel Reisz
CAST INCLUDES:
Meryl Streep, Jeremy Irons,
Hilton McRae, Emily Morgan,
Charlotte Mitchell, Lynsey Baxter,
Jean Faulds, Peter Vaughan,
Colin Jeavons, Liz Smith,
Patience Collier John Barrett,
Leo McKern, Arabella Weir
SCREENPLAY:
Harold Pinter, from the novel by John
Fowles
CINEMATOGRAPHY:
Freddie Francis
PRODUCERS/
PRODUCTION COMPANIES:
Leon Clore/Juniper Films
ACADEMY AWARD
NOMINATIONS (1982)
Best Actress in a Leading Role:
Meryl Streep
Best Art Direction-Set Decoration:
Assheton Gorton, Ann Mollo
Best Costume Design: Tom Rand
Best Film Editing: John Bloom
Best Writing, Screenplay Based on
Material from Another Medium:
Harold Pinter

An Officer and a Gentleman

USA, 1982
DIRECTOR:
Taylor Hackford
CAST INCLUDES:
Richard Gere, Debra Winger,
David Keith, Robert Loggia,
Lisa Blount, Lisa Eilbacher,
Louis Gossett Jr., Tony Plana,
Harold Sylvester, David Caruso
SCREENPLAY:
Douglas Day Stewart
CINEMATOGRAPHY:
Donald (E.) Thorin
PRODUCERS/
PRODUCTION COMPANIES:
Martin Elfand/Capitol Equipment
Leasing, Lorimar Film Entertainment
ACADEMY AWARD
NOMINATIONS (1983)
Best Actress in a Leading Role:
Debra Winger
Best Film Editing: Peter Zinner
Best Music, Original Score:
Jack Nitzsche
Best Writing, Screenplay Written
Directly for the Screen:
Douglas Day Stewart
ACADEMY AWARDS
Best Actor in a Supporting Role:
Louis Gossett Jr.
Best Music, Original Song:
Jack Nitzsche (music),
Buffy Sainte-Marie (music),
Will Jennings (lyrics) for the song 'Up
Where We Belong'.

Loner Zack Mayo (Gere) decides he's getting too like the alcoholic father he was stuck with when his mother died. He decides to shake off escalating delinquency by signing up for Naval Officer's Candidate School with the aim of becoming a Navy pilot – a long-held dream. Once there, he falls foul of his tough drill instructor, Gunnery Sergeant Emil Foley (Gossett Jr.), who puts Mayo through every test known to drill sergeants. Gossett warns the recruits about the local girls who are desperate to catch a pilot husband; however, when Paula (Winger) catches him, he thinks he might want to stay caught. Foley and Paula may find the way to turn Mayo into an officer and a gentleman.

An Officer and a Gentleman contained a very compelling central romance of the 'will he, won't he' and 'can she, can't she' order. When you're left on tenterhooks for that long, anything seems like a happy ending. However, Mayo's development, though predictably inspirational, is worth watching because this is Gere at his very best. Deborah Winger, too, is excellent, making more than the most of a very underwritten part, and Louis Gossett Jr. was Oscar-winning. John Travolta was originally slated for the part of Mayo. That would have been interesting, too.

Out of Africa

Dane Karen Blixen (Streep), despairing of being a spinster forever, goes to Kenya to enter a marriage of convenience with Baron Bror Blixen-Finecke (Brandauer). Together, they start a coffee plantation. When World War I breaks out, Bror joins a provisional army and Karen runs the plantation by herself. When Bror returns, and she feels his philandering ways have gone too far, she throws him out. She herself has met big-game hunter Denys Hatton (Redford). They are soon having a passionate affair and Denys moves his few belongings into her home. Their romance continues, becoming ever more turbulent. She, wanting a mate as strong as herself, is desperate to keep him. He, with the wildness of Africa rooted within him, won't be tied down.

The Kenyan scenery photographed for *Out of Africa* is staggering. It's beautiful and it's vast. The sweeping aerial shots are breathtaking and accompanied by the Oscar-winning score by John Barry, stay with you long after the cinema lights are back on.

This is an epic tale; based on Isak Dinesen's memoirs of life and love in colonial Africa at the beginning of the 20th century. The chemistry between Streep and Redford is tangible; all in all a beautifully obseved and skilfully directed picture.

USA, 1985
DIRECTOR:
Sydney Pollack
CAST INCLUDES:
Meryl Streep, Robert Redford,
Klaus Maria Brandauer,
Michael Kitchen, Malick Bowens,
Joseph Thiaka, Stephen Kinyanjui,
Michael Gough, Suzanna Hamilton,
Rachel Kempson, Graham Crowden,
Leslie Phillips, Mike Bugara
SCREENPLAY:
Kurt Luedtke from the memoirs of
Isak Dinesen and
the book *Silence Will Speak* by
Errol Trebinski. Also A. E. Houseman,
for the poem 'To an Athlete,
Dying Young'
CINEMATOGRAPHY:
David Watki
PRODUCERS/
PRODUCTION COMPANIES:
Sydney Pollack/Mirage
Entertainment, Universal Pictures
ACADEMY AWARD
NOMINATIONS (1986)
Best Actor in a Supporting Role:
Klaus Maria Brandauer
Best Actress in a Leading Role:
Meryl Streep
Best Costume Design:
Milena Canonero
Best Film Editing: Fredric Steinkamp,
William Steinkamp,
Pembroke J. Herring, Sheldon Kahn
ACADEMY AWARDS
Best Art Direction-Set Decoration:
Stephen B. Grimes, Josie MacAvin
Best Cinematography: David Watkin
Best Director: Sydney Pollack
Best Music, Original Score:
John Barry
Best Picture: Sydney Pollack
Best Sound: Chris Jenkins,
Gary Alexander, Larry Stensvold,
Peter Handford
Best Writing, Screenplay Based on
Material from Another Medium:
Kurt Luedtke

Nine 1/2 Weeks

John (Rourke) buys and sells money on Wall Street. Elizabeth (Basinger) works at a SoHo art gallery. Their eyes lock in a Chinese Grocery store in Manhattan and then meet again in a flea market. He buys her a mink stole and takes her to his houseboat on the Hudson. He changes his sheets – to Billy Holliday's 'Strange Fruit' - and offers her an erotic affair. They play every kind of sex game, usually with him in control. He seduces her with endearments and expensive gifts, while insisting on an ever-more debasing sexual itinerary. Soon, Elizabeth has to decide whether the hedonistic pleasure is worth the total annihilation of her self, or whether she can find a way to cut free from her sensual imprisonment.

When Adrian Lyne's *Nine 1/2 Weeks* opened, there hadn't been a mainstream movie quite as open about lust'n'sex since *Last Tango in Paris* (1972). Lyne creates an enormous amount of sexual tension by making it a foreplay movie. The orgasms are in the build-up, the ideas, John's commands, and are further heightened, for the viewer, by the scenes of (mainly her) everyday life. On one level, he and she are deeply aroused while, on another, they are frozen, as much objects as are their clothes and sex toys. This is Rourke 'while he was still hot'. The beautiful Basinger had, apparently, body doubles for all the 'heavy' stuff.

USA, 1986
DIRECTOR:
Adrian Lyne
CAST INCLUDES:
Mickey Rourke, Kim Basinger, Margaret Whitton, David Margulies, Christine Baranski
SCREENPLAY:
Sarah Kernochan, Zalman King, Patricia Louisianna Knop from the novel by Elizabeth McNeill
CINEMATOGRAPHY:
Peter Biziou
**PRODUCERS/
PRODUCTION COMPANIES:**
Keith Barish, Mark Damon, Antony Rufus Isaacs, Sidney Kimmel, Zalman King/Galactic Films, Jonesfilm, Metro-Goldwyn-Mayer (MGM), Producers Sales Organization, Triple Ajaxxx

The Princess Bride

A grandfather (Falk) settles down to read a bedtime story to his sick grandson (Savage). The story tells of Westley (Elwes), a farm hand who works for – and loves – the beautiful Buttercup (Wright). When she realises she loves him too, he sets out to earn his fortune so they can be married. After a time, she learns that he has been killed by pirates. Broken-hearted, Buttercup offers no resistance when Prince Humperdinck decides he wishes to marry her. In fact, he really wishes to murder her, thus causing a war from which he can profit. However, just in time, a dark stranger appears, bent on rescuing her.

Rob Reiner came to this fairy tale with the same attitude that made his *This Is Spinal Tap* (1984) such a brilliantly funny film.

USA, 1987
DIRECTOR:
Rob Reiner
CAST INCLUDES:
Cary Elwes, Mandy Patinkin, Chris Sarandon, Christopher Guest. Wallace Shawn, André the Giant, Fred Savage, Robin Wright (Penn), Peter Falk, Peter Cook, Mel Smith, Carol Kane, Billy Crystal
SCREENPLAY:
William Goldman, from his own book
CINEMATOGRAPHY:
Adrian Biddle
**PRODUCERS/
PRODUCTION COMPANIES:**
Rob Reiner, Andrew Scheinman/Act III Communications, Buttercup Films Ltd., The Princess Bride Ltd.
**ACADEMY AWARD
NOMINATIONS (1988)**
Best Music, Original Song: Willy De Ville, for the song 'Storybook Love'

That worked because every element of the rock documentary was treated with consummate respect – before showing how easy it is to let all those elements slip over from the reasonable, through the looking glass, into a world which is the wrong way round, and then some. Here, the matter-of-fact logic of a child's fairytale world is spun around Fezzik the Giant, Miracle Max, the Screaming Eels and the Cliffs of Insanity. For the children, Reiner preserves the magic; for the grown-ups, he reminds them of the magic and leaves them helpless with laughter. Oh, and they all lived happily ever after.

The Fabulous Baker Boys

Piano duo Jack (Jeff Bridges) and Frank (Beau Bridges) Baker have been playing smaltzy music in small clubs for many years. Just recently, however, gigs have been getting scarce and the brothers feel a female vocalist could keep the act going. After a run of dispiriting interviews, Susie Diamond (Pfeiffer), a former 'escort', appears – and, boy, can she put over a song! The new act takes off in a big way but, seeing themselves though Susie's eyes, each of the Baker Boys is having to re-evaluate what he's doing and where he's going. Then, when Jack and Susie also become an off-stage item, all three find tensions coming to the surface.

Both Bridges boys are fine actors, and they project a superb sense, here, of how tight the discipline has to be behind such a laid-back-seeming duo – a real theatrical double act. Michelle Pfeiffer, in her red dress, 'Makin' Whoopee' on top of a grand piano, has all the seductiveness of a Gilda – and a great voice. Madonna, apparently, turned the role down as too mushy.

USA, 1989
DIRECTOR:
Steven Kloves
CAST INCLUDES:
Jeff Bridges, Michelle Pfeiffer,
Beau Bridges, Ellie Raab,
Xander Berkeley, Dakin Matthews
SCREENPLAY:
Steven Kloves
CINEMATOGRAPHY:
Michael Ballhaus
**PRODUCERS/
PRODUCTION COMPANIES:**
Mark Rosenberg, Paula Weinstein,
Courtney Silberberg/Gladden
Entertainment, Mirage, Tobis
Filmkunst
**ACADEMY AWARD
NOMINATIONS (1990)**
Best Actress in a Leading Role:
Michelle Pfeiffer
Best Cinematography:
Michael Ballhaus
Best Film Editing: William Steinkamp
Best Music, Original Score:
Dave Grusin

When Harry Met Sally

USA, 1989
DIRECTOR:
Rob Reiner
CAST INCLUDES:
Billy Crystal, Meg Ryan, Carrie Fisher,
Bruno Kirby, Steven Ford, Lisa Jane
Persky, Michelle Nicastro
SCREENPLAY:
Nora Ephron
CINEMATOGRAPHY:
Barry Sonnenfeld
PRODUCERS/
PRODUCTION COMPANIES:
Rob Reiner, Andrew
Scheinman/Castle Rock
Entertainment, Nelson Entertainment
ACADEMY AWARD
NOMINATIONS (1990)
Best Writing, Screenplay Written
Directly for the Screen: Nora Ephron

Harry and Sally meet when sharing a car trip from graduation at Chicago University to post-college life in New York City. This quickly turns into eighteen hours of bickering and they conclude they have nothing in common. One important discussion point was 'Can women and men be friends without sex getting in the way?' 'No', said Harry. 'Yes' said Sally. Five years pass before their paths cross again and arguing resumes. Sally now has a businessman boyfriend and Harry is engaged to be married. Another five years pass; Sally's boyfriend has gone, and Harry's wife has left him for another man. This time they sleep together. Can two friends sleep together and still love each other in the morning?

When Harry Met Sally is a family affair. Rob Reiner and Nora Ephron cheerfully admit that there's a lot of Rob in Harry and a good deal of Nora in Sally. Ephron reveals that the 'I'll have what she's having' line, after Ryan's immortalized fake-an-orgasm-in-a-restaurant moment, was suggested by Billy Crystal and performed by Rob Reiner's mother. Reiner inter-slots the various stages of Harry and Sally with short interviews in which elderly couples talk about how, long ago, they met (real stories, although performed by actors), thus lending much more gravitas to the issues of coupledom. The film looks at a relationship that takes a long while to grow, with all the perils and pleasure of first being friends.

Pretty Woman

Out-of-towner Edward Lewis (Gere) is a ruthless, high-powered young businessman. While driving down Sunset Boulevard, he decides to pick up a prostitute – Vivian (Roberts). After a night with Viv, he asks her to stay on at his hotel: he enjoys her company and he needs a partner for social events. He gives her money to get some 'decent' clothes, but the fashion stores ignore her. However, Barney (Elizondo), the hotel manager, comes to her aid and soon she's 'lookin' good.' After a delightful week of events and togetherness which is full of surprises for both, commitment-phobe Edward pays Viv off – and then finds he misses her badly. Even his ruthlessness has softened since knowing her. But can he find her, and will she have him?

Pretty Woman tells of a callous man played by a mega-sex-symbol who hires a hooker – for a week! – and then dumps her, and yet it's no more licentious or vicious than a warm, Cinderella fairy-tale (without the wicked step-family). Yet, at the same time, in Garry Marshall's hands, there's a completely straightforward element to their business dealings that merely makes them all the more accessible and friendly. Romance seldom comes in as good a package.

USA, 1990
DIRECTOR:
Garry Marshall
CAST INCLUDES:
Richard Gere, Julia Roberts,
Ralph Bellamy, Jason Alexander,
Laura San Giacomo, Alex Hyde-White,
Amy Yasbeck, Elinor Donahue,
Hector Elizondo
SCREENPLAY:
J.F. Lawton
CINEMATOGRAPHY:
Charles Minsky
PRODUCERS/
PRODUCTION COMPANIES:
Arnon Milchan, Steven Reuther,
Nancy Gros (uncredited)/Silver
Screen Partners IV,
Touchstone Pictures
ACADEMY AWARD
NOMINATIONS (1991)
Best Actress in a Leading Role:
Julia Roberts

Ghost

USA, 1990
DIRECTOR:
Jerry Zucker
CAST INCLUDES:
Patrick Swayze, Demi Moore,
Whoopi Goldberg, Tony Goldwyn
SCREENPLAY:
Bruce Joel Rubin
CINEMATOGRAPHY:
Adam Greenberg
**PRODUCERS/
PRODUCTION COMPANIES:**
Howard W. Koch, Lisa
Weinstein/Paramount Pictures
**ACADEMY AWARD
NOMINATIONS (1991)**
Best Film Editing: Walter Murch
Best Music, Original Score:
Maurice Jarre
Best Picture: Lisa Weinstein
ACADEMY AWARDS
Best Actress in a Supporting Role:
Whoopi Goldberg
Best Writing, Screenplay Written
Directly for the Screen:
Bruce Joel Rubin

Sam (Swayze) and Molly (Moore) are very much in love. On their way home one night, a mugger shoots him. On regaining consciousness, he discovers that there are a lot of strange people about, and some of them walk through walls. Gradually, the 'people' he meets show him that he's a) dead, b) a ghost and c) still about because he's got a job to do. By skulking around he learns that he was intentionally murdered because he was about to uncover a crime committed by his friend Carl (Goldwyn), and now Molly is in danger. He finds pseudo-psychic Oda Mae (Goldberg), and has to discover a way to show her that she can understand him – and help Molly.

Ghost is a very sensual movie. Both Moore and Swayze have had some goodly experience doing 'sensual', and it very much pays off here. The Twilight World of ghosts is great fun. There are clever ghosts, evil ghosts, well-meaning ghosts, beginner ghosts, and ghosts that are just as useless at it as they have ever been. *Ghost* allows Whoopi Goldberg to be hilariously and Oscar-winningly splendid, and there is a to-die-for romantic ending.

Green Card

Brontë Mitchell (MacDowell) and Georges Faure (Depardieu) have been brought together by Fate (in the guise of a friend of both). Brontë, an inner-city horticulturist, needs a husband in order to get a wonderful apartment-with-greenhouse but for couples only in Manhattan. Georges needs a green card visa that will allow him to stay and work in the USA. They decide they will get married for these reasons only and then go their separate ways. Unfortunately, more is required: they must be seen to be living together. For a whole weekend, Georges has to run the gauntlet of her parents, boyfriend and fussiness, while she has to endure smoking and garlic. Perhaps getting married is not the easiest way to start a romance.

Green Card was launched on the suggestion that 'If you liked Pretty Woman, give Green Card a try.' Andie MacDowell was even cover-featured under the strapline: 'This year's Pretty Woman?' The people who did go to see Green Card because they loved Pretty Woman were probably disappointed. Both films

focus on a very unlikely pair of people finding their way in the early days of a relationship. Pretty Woman, however, has Julia Roberts doing an Eliza Doolittle amid the top echelons of society, with all the glamour that entails. Green Card, on the other hand, has Depardieu's boundless French charm and the cheery understanding that he is 'too oaf' for Brontë – but 'oaf' is exactly what she needs.

AUSTRALIA/FRANCE/USA, 1990
DIRECTOR:
Peter Weir
CAST INCLUDES:
Gérard Depardieu, Andie MacDowell, Bebe Neuwirth, Gregg Edelman, Robert Prosky, Jessie Keosian, Ethan Phillips, Mary Louise Wilson
SCREENPLAY:
Peter Weir
CINEMATOGRAPHY:
Geoffrey Simpson
PRODUCERS/ PRODUCTION COMPANIES:
Peter Weir/Australian Film Finance Corporation (AFFC), DD Productions [FR], Greencard Productions, Lam Ping, Sédif Productions [FR], Touchstone Pictures [US], Union Générale Cinématographique (UGC)
ACADEMY AWARD NOMINATIONS (1991)
Best Writing, Screenplay Written Directly for the Screen: Peter Weir

Age of Innocence

USA, 1993
DIRECTOR:
Martin Scorsese
CAST INCLUDES:
Daniel Day-Lewis, Michelle Pfeiffer,
Winona Ryder, Alexis Smith,
Geraldine Chaplin, Mary Beth Hurt,
Alec McCowen, Richard E. Grant,
Miriam Margolyes, Robert Sean
Leonard, Siân Phillips,
Jonathan Pryce, Michael Gough,
Joanne Woodward
SCREENPLAY:
Jay Cocks, Martin Scorsese from the
novel by Edith Wharton
CINEMATOGRAPHY:
Michael Ballhaus
PRODUCERS/
PRODUCTION COMPANIES:
Barbara De Fina/Cappa Production,
Columbia Pictures Corporation
ACADEMY AWARD
NOMINATIONS (1994)
Best Actress in a Supporting Role:
Winona Ryder
Best Art Direction-Set Decoration:
Dante Ferretti, Robert J. Franco
Best Music, Original Score:
Elmer Bernstein
Best Writing, Screenplay Based on
Material from Another Medium:
Jay Cocks, Martin Scorsese
ACADEMY AWARDS
Best Costume Design:
Gabriella Pescucci

New York; late 19th century. Newland Archer (Day-Lewis) is happily engaged to the pretty and eligible Miss May Welland (Ryder), when Countess Ellen Olenska (Pfeiffer), May's cousin, appears on the New York scene. She left America to marry a dashing Polish count but, having found him unfaithful and abusive, has now returned in order to divorce him. Ellen is a disturber of the status quo and, therefore, something of a social outcast. When this upper layer of New York society realizes that Newland has fallen in love with Ellen (in fact, with her intelligence and courageous independence as much as her beauty), they silently close ranks, determined to save Newland from himself.

Nothing could be a less-obvious entry in Scorsese's filmography than this Merchant-Ivory film subject with its glorious attention to the trappings and accessories of the people under scrutiny. Indeed, the classic paintings, everywhere on walls, are $200,000-worth of superb reproductions. However, Scorsese's main interest is the structure of this society and how Mafia-like it is. Its restrictive rules and codes are set in stone and its retributions are forged in steel. Yet, heartless and claustrophobic though this appears, Newland comes to realize how much care went into his 'preservation', and how many sacrifices others also made.

Sleepless in Seattle

Sam (Hanks), a recent young widower, and his son Jonah (Malinger) are still grieving for their wife and mother when they move to Seattle for a fresh start. After a while, Jonah decides Sam is no better and what they need is a new wife and mom. Jonah phones Dr Marcia's national radio talk show, and Sam finds himself on the air baring his soul. Millions of women listen in and know they are the answer to Sam's problems – including Annie (Ryan), an engaged journalist in Baltimore. Jonah likes Annie's letter; he feels she's the one, and sets up the ultimate make-or-break meeting.

Often slated as a woman's movie, the comedic performances of Hanks and Ryan, not to mention the cute Jonah, save this feel-good picture from pure schmaltz. The romance flys off in all the wrong directions, as do the protaganists.

However, this is a full-scale, no-holds-barred romantic screwball (which acknowledges *An Affair to Remember*, 1957) with not just a novel twist at the end but with everything at the end. If you like Meg Ryan, you'll cry your eyes out in the closing scene; if you don't, then you may cry your eyes out for poor little Jonah and Sam.

USA, 1993
DIRECTOR:
Nora Ephron
CAST INCLUDES:
Tom Hanks, Meg Ryan, Bill Pullman,
Ross Malinger, Rosie, O'Donnell,
Gaby Hoffmann, Victor Garber,
Rob Reiner
SCREENPLAY:
Nora Ephron, David S. Ward,
Jeff Arch, from the story by Jeff Arch
CINEMATOGRAPHY:
Sven Nykvist
PRODUCERS/
PRODUCTION COMPANIES:
Gary Foster/TriStar Pictures
ACADEMY AWARD
NOMINATIONS (1994)
Best Music, Original Song: Marc
Shaiman (music)
Ramsey McLean (lyrics), for the song
'A Wink and a Smile'
Best Writing, Screenplay Written
Directly for the Screen: Nora Ephron,
David S. Ward, Jeff Arch

While You Were Sleeping

USA, 1995
DIRECTOR:
Jon Turteltaub
CAST INCLUDES:
Sandra Bullock, Bill Pullman,
Peter Gallagher, Peter Boyle,
Jack Warden, Glynis Johns
SCREENPLAY:
Daniel G. Sullivan, Fredric LeBow
CINEMATOGRAPHY:
Phedon Papamichael
**PRODUCERS/
PRODUCTION COMPANIES:**
Roger Birnbaum, Joe Roth/Caravan
Pictures, Hollywood Pictures

Lonely orphaned Lucy (Bullock), a toll-booth fares collector for the Chicago subway, is in love with regular commuter Peter Callaghan (Gallagher) who hasn't noticed her yet. When Peter is mugged and falls onto the line, Lucy jumps down and saves his life. While she is sitting by his bed in hospital, waiting for Peter to come out of his coma, the rest of his family arrive. They've been told she's his fiancée, and so they're doubly pleased to see her. She keeps up this charade because she likes the idea of having a family, particularly one that includes Peter's handsome, charming brother Jack (Pullman).

Sandra Bullock started up the stardom ladder as the break-neck bus driver in her previous movie, *Speed* (1994). The outcome of *While You Were Sleeping*, as with most romantic comedies, is pretty predictable. The dialogue and the acting have to carry the rather ludicrous plotline and this is achieved effortlessly. Peter's family move and act as one and introduce a black comedy element that is the perfect backdrop for Bullock. She's an actress whom the camera loves: it laps up her kookiness, her face, her gangly gracefulness and her warmth – all perfect elements of a really feel-good romance.

Romeo + Juliet

A television anchorwoman (Moore), on the news, is announcing the tragic death of two star-crossed lovers and the incidents that led up to it. The gang war between the Montagues and the Capulets has been bad recently, resulting in a huge shoot-out at a gas station. Around that time, the parents of Juliet Capulet arrange a party at which they hope Juliet (Danes) will become engaged to the very eligible Dave Paris (Rudd). However Romeo Montague arrives, after which he and Juliet can't take their eyes off each other. They are secretly married by Father Laurence (Postlethwaite), and hope this will bring about a truce between the families. Alas, this is not to be.

For some, Baz Luhrmann's take on Romeo and Juliet will be lost in a muddle of furniture and objects, a mass of jangling sounds and a whirlwind of visuals. For others, it will be visually stunning and highly entertaining. We first meet the lovers in a scene, as erotic as it is unusual, when their eyes meet through a crowded fish-tank before Juliet is swept away to dance with her intended. They make love with their eyes, with their body language, with their smiles and through the fire-field of passion between them. Even impending tragedy can't dilute this moment. The youth and undoubted talents of DiCaprio and Danes make this movie a huge success with the young. The timeless story of teenage love ruined by family strife had not been told for a new generation since Zeffirelli's masterpiece in 1968.

USA, 1996
DIRECTOR:
Baz Luhrmann
CAST INCLUDES:
Leonardo DiCaprio, Claire Danes, Diane Venora, Miriam Margolyes, John Leguizamo, Harold Perrineau, Edwina Moore, Carlos Martín Manzo Otálora, Paul Sorvino, Brian Dennehy, Pete Postlethwaite, Paul Rudd
SCREENPLAY:
Craig Pearce, Baz Luhrmann from the play by William Shakespeare
CINEMATOGRAPHY:
Donald (M.) McAlpine
PRODUCERS/
PRODUCTION COMPANIES:
Baz Luhrmann, Gabriella Martinelli/20th Century Fox, Bazmark Films
ACADEMY AWARD
NOMINATIONS (1997)
Best Art Direction-Set Decoration: Catherine Martin, Brigitte Broch

319

The English Patient

USA, 1996
DIRECTOR:
Anthony Minghella
CAST INCLUDES:
Ralph Fiennes, Juliette Binoche,
Willem Dafoe, Kristin Scott Thomas,
Naveen Andrews, Colin Firth,
Julian Wadham, Jürgen Prochnow
SCREENPLAY:
Anthony Minghella, from the novel by
Michael Ondaatje
CINEMATOGRAPHY:
John Seale
PRODUCERS/
PRODUCTION COMPANIES:
Saul Zaentz/J&M Entertainment,
Miramax Films, Tiger Moth
Productions
ACADEMY AWARD
NOMINATIONS (1997)
Best Actor in a Leading Role:
Ralph Fiennes
Best Actress in a Leading Role:
Kristin Scott Thomas
Best Writing, Screenplay Based on
Material from Another Medium:
Anthony Minghella
ACADEMY AWARDS
Best Actress in a Supporting Role:
Juliette Binoche
Best Art Direction-Set Decoration:
Stuart Craig, Stephanie McMillan
Best Cinematography:
John Seale
Best Costume Design:
Ann Roth
Best Director:
Anthony Minghella
Best Film Editing:
Walter Murch
Best Music, Original Dramatic Score:
Gabriel Yared
Best Picture: Saul Zaentz
Best Sound: Walter Murch,
Mark Berger, David Parker,
Christopher Newman

Italy, in the last days of World War II. A badly burned man, 'the English patient', can travel no further with a hospital convoy, so nurse Hanna (Binoche) sets up a make-shift camp in which to stay and tend to him. Gradually, his memory returns. He is not English but the Hungarian Count Laszlo de Almasy (Fiennes). Before the war, he took flights over the desert to make maps that were later used by English troops in North Africa. Based in Cairo, he met Katharine Clifton (Scott Thomas), a young woman disappointed by her husband, and soon Laszlo and Katharine are in the throes of a passionate affair. Meanwhile Hanna has developed a very tender love for Laszlo, and a romantic love for a soldier who is staying at their camp.

Love and tragedy, passion and violence come together in Anthony Minghella's masterful reworking of Ondaatje's 1992 Booker-Prize-winning novel. Although this is a romantic epic, his characters are not allowed to get too overblown; they remain believable. *The English Patient* is an exquisitely produced film with more than enough to hold the viewer's eye and plenty to help it shed a tear or two. As Minghella says: 'Everyone is interested in pain, passion and war.'

USA, 1997
DIRECTOR:
James Cameron
CAST INCLUDES:
Leonardo DiCaprio, Kate Winslet,
Billy Zane, Kathy Bates, Bill Paxton,
Gloria Stuart, Frances Fisher,
Bernard Hill
Jonathan Hyde, David Warner,
Victor Garber
SCREENPLAY:
James Cameron
CINEMATOGRAPHY:
Russell Carpenter
PRODUCERS/
PRODUCTION COMPANIES:
James Cameron/20th Century Fox,
Lightstorm Entertainment,
Paramount Pictures
ACADEMY AWARD
NOMINATIONS (1998)
Best Actress in a Leading Role:
Kate Winslet
Best Actress in a Supporting Role:
Gloria Stuart
Best Makeup: Tina Earnshaw,
Greg Cannom, Simon Thompson
ACADEMY AWARDS
Best Art Direction-Set Decoration:
Peter Lamont (art director),
Michael Ford (set decorator)
Best Cinematography:
Russell Carpenter
Best Costume Design:
Deborah Lynn Scott
Best Director: James Cameron
Best Effects, Sound Effects Editing:
Tom Bellfort, Christopher Boyes
Best Effects, Visual Effects:
Robert Legato, Mark A. Lasoff,
Thomas L. Fisher, Michael Kanfer
Best Film Editing: Conrad Buff IV,
James Cameron, Richard A. Harris
Best Music, Original Dramatic Score:
James Horner
Best Music, Original Song: James
Horner (music), Will Jennings (lyrics)
for the song 'My Heart Will Go On',
performed by Céline Dion.
Best Picture: James Cameron,
Jon Landau
Best Sound: Gary Rydstrom, Tom
Johnson, Gary Summers, Mark Ulano

Titanic

A treasure hunter (Paxton), looking for a diamond in the wreck of the Titanic, discovers in a safe the nude picture of a young woman. After it is shown on television, Rose Dawson (Stuart), aged 101, comes forward. She, Rose (Winslet), was that young girl on the ship. She was travelling with her mother (Fisher) and a wealthy man (Zane) whom she desperately didn't want to marry. She was about to throw herself over the rails when she was stopped by Jack (DiCaprio), a young man who had won his steerage ticket in a poker game. They fell in love and spent every moment together until the iceberg broke the ship apart. Even then, they determined to stay together.

James Cameron spent $200,000 million and five extra months on perfecting his *Titanic*. Most people know the story and many of the statistics. His aim, therefore, was to show that this disaster was far more vast and more unbelievable than could be imagined by anyone who hadn't been there. He takes us there: into the state rooms, the dining rooms, the cabins and the engine rooms – first kitted out and decorated as they should be, and then with everything undone by water. Having got the outer scale of this tragedy in place, he tells the inner story through the heartbreak of a third-class boy and a first-class girl.

As Good As It Gets

USA, 1997
DIRECTOR:
James L. Brooks
CAST INCLUDES:
Jack Nicholson, Helen Hunt,
Greg Kinnear, Cuba Gooding Jr.,
Skeet Ulrich, Shirley Knight,
Yeardley Smith
SCREENPLAY:
Mark Andrus, James L. Brooks from
the story by Mark Andrus
CINEMATOGRAPHY:
John Bailey
PRODUCERS/
PRODUCTION COMPANIES:
James L. Brooks, Bridget Johnson,
Kristi Zea/Gracie Films,
TriStar Pictures
ACADEMY AWARD
NOMINATIONS (1998)
Best Actor in a Supporting Role:
Greg Kinnear
Best Film Editing: Richard Marks
Best Music, Original Musical or
Comedy Score: Hans Zimmer
Best Picture: James L. Brooks,
Bridget Johnson, Kristi Zea
Best Writing, Screenplay Written
Directly for the Screen: Mark Andrus
(also story), James L. Brooks
ACADEMY AWARDS
Best Actor in a Leading Role:
Jack Nicholson
Best Actress in a Leading Role:
Helen Hunt

Melvin Udall (Nicholson) is a famous writer of romantic fiction, although the 'real' Melvin is a rude, selfish, obsessive-compulsive misanthrope with not one romantic spot in his aura. However, at the only restaurant where he will eat (using his own plastic cutlery), waitress Carol (Hunt) does tolerate him fondly. When gay neighbour Simon (Kinnear) is beaten up one night, Melvin is prevailed upon to look after Melvin's dog Verdell, and his icy, previously dogophobic heart begins to thaw a little. Then, when Carol leaves the restaurant to look after her asthmatic son, he's shocked to discover how upset he is – and not just about this change to his routine. Mean Melvin could be about to make some moves.

Jack Nicholson is at his best when he's at his nastiest, and Melvin is a perfect (and Oscar-winning) Nicholson part. Directors can put the sins of the world into his mouth because the world will meekly listen. It may be the charm; it may be that we don't protest because we might miss what he's going to say next. However, thanks to Simon and Carol and Verdell, he is getting nicer and his one-step forward, three steps back relationship with Carol is beginning to pay off. Fortunately, these improvements don't put an end to his great one-liners.

Hua yang nian hua

In the Mood for Love

Hong Kong, 1962. Two couples have just rented rooms next-door to each other in a cramped apartment building. First, there is newspaper-editor Chow Mo-Wan (Leung) and his wife. The second couple are Su Li-zhen (Cheung), a beautiful secretary who is now Mrs Chan, and her executive husband. With their spouses often away, Chow and Li-zhen spend most of their time together as friends. They have everything in common from noodle shops to martial arts. Then, they are shocked to discover that their spouses are having an affair. Hurt and angry, they find comfort in their growing friendship even as they resolve to remain true to their marriage vows, even if their spouses are not.

Wong Kar Wai is noted for shooting without a script and for visuals that are dripping with colour and moods of all kinds. Maggie Cheung and Tony Leung are two of the biggest stars in Asia. The combination results in a stunning movie. Drawn to each other first out of lust and then from escalating desire, this honourable pair faces, every day, the double pain of rejection by their spouses and the new, unrequited-love scenario into which they've put themselves. Together, director and actors eroticize this sexual tension to a point where it seems impossible that their resolve can hold.

HONG KONG/FRANCE, 2000
DIRECTOR:
Kar Wai Wong
CAST INCLUDES:
Maggie Cheung, Tony Leung, Siu Ping-lam, Tung Cho 'Joe' Cheung (as Cheun Tung Joe), Rebecca Pan, Lui Chun
SCREENPLAY:
Kar Wai Wong
CINEMATOGRAPHY:
Christopher Doyle, Mark Lee
(Li Pingbin)
PRODUCERS/
PRODUCTION COMPANIES:
Wong Kar Wai/Block 2 Pictures Inc.
[HK], Jet Tone Production Co.,
Paradis Films [FR]
CANNES FILM FESTIVAL
NOMINATIONS (2000)
Palme d'Or: Kar Wai Wong
CANNES FILM FESTIVAL (2000)
Best Actor: Tony Leung
Technical Grand Prize: Christopher Doyle, Mark Lee (Li Pingbin),
William Chang

SCIENCE FICTION & FANTASY

Metropolis

GERMANY, 1927
DIRECTOR:
Fritz Lang
CAST INCLUDES:
Alfred Abel, Gustav Fröhlich,
Brigitte Helm, Rudolf Klein-Rogge,
Fritz Rasp
SCREENPLAY:
Fritz Lang from the novel
by Thea von Harbou
CINEMATOGRAPHY:
Karl Freund, Günther Rittau
PRODUCERS/
PRODUCTION COMPANIES:
Erich Pommer, Giorgio Moroder
(1984 restoration)/Universum Film
A.G. (UFA)

Some time in the future, society has split into two distinct groups. The thinkers, who live in luxurious penthouses, and the workers who toil in mines. The leader's son, Freder Frederson (Fröhlich) visits the mines to witness first-hand the roots of his society, but discovers a people on the verge of revolution.

Georges Méliès may have traveled to the moon in 1914, but *Metropolis* marks the birth of the true science fiction film, laying down a framework of themes and stylistic concepts that have changed very little in nearly 80 years. Virtually all of the genre's worthwhile additions have been influenced in some way by Fritz

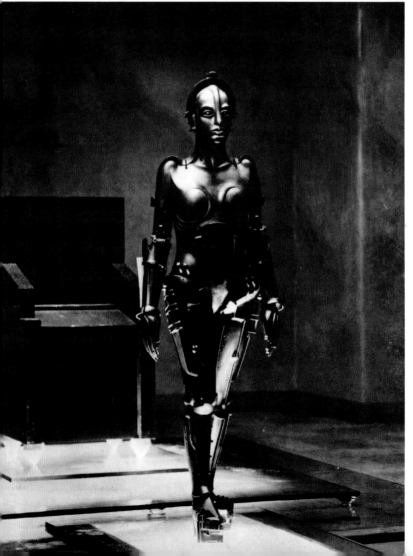

Lang's inspired and ambitious film.

As with many classics from the silent era, numerous cuts have appeared on home video and DVD over the years, varying hugely in picture quality, but even the murkiest transfer can't obscure the film's rich, gothic production design and incredible visual style. Beautiful skyscrapers reach above the clouds while claustrophobic mine shafts burrow into the ground. *Metropolis* is a film of none too subtle comparisons (the thinkers occupy their days playing sports and socializing whilst the workers are marched in and out of lifts with militaristic co-ordination).

The potent visuals stay in the mind long after the film has ended. The army of workers shuffling to and fro, the Tower of Babel and the giant clock all leave indelible images, and there are countless other impressive achievements to discover upon watching this truly spectacular film.

Lost Horizon

Famous British diplomat Bob Conway (Colman) is kidnapped and taken to the surreal Tibetan settlement of Shangri-La. At first, he and his four companions are intent on mounting an unlikely escape from the remote colony, but its strange, supernatural appeal begins to win them over.

One of the most impressive and spectacular films of the era, Frank Capra's rare foray out of middle America is a true masterpiece.

Made and released between world wars, the more complicated themes of James Hilton's novel are refined to a simple message of peace. Conway is a man dedicated to ending war, early on in the film he hypothesizes that when made foreign secretary he will lay down Britain's arms and others will follow his lead. In Shangri-La, he and his companions find a place where just such a thing has happened. Beautiful and enchanting, virtual immortality is assured, as is the complete absence of disputes, needs and problems of any kind – something that appeals immediately to Conway. Colman seems to be a cross between Clark Gable and David Niven – a magnificently charming presence – and he portrays the character's private fear, that peace is ultimately unobtainable, with subtle emotion.

The message of peace is so successfully conveyed that for the 1943 re-release, much of its pacifist message was cut, sadly resulting in the loss of some material. A restoration project undertaken by the AFI has managed to replace most of it, though seven minutes of image are lost forever. In the most complete print available, the seven minutes of (complete) soundtrack are accompanied by appropriate stills.

USA, 1937
DIRECTOR:
Frank Capra
CAST INCLUDES:
Ronald Colman, Jane Wyatt,
John Howard, Margo,
Thomas Mitchell
SCREENPLAY:
Robert Riskin from the novel
by James Hilton
CINEMATOGRAPHY:
Joseph Walker
**PRODUCERS/
PRODUCTION COMPANIES:**
Frank Capra/Columbia Pictures
Corporation
**ACADEMY AWARD
NOMINATIONS (1937)**
Best Actor in a Supporting Role:
H.B. Warner
Best Assistant Director:
Charles C. Coleman
Best Music, Score:
Dimitri Tiomkin
Best Picture:
Frank Capra
Best Sound, Recording:
John P. Livadary (Columbia SSD)
ACADEMY AWARDS
Best Art Direction:
Stephen Goosson
Best Film Editing:
Gene Havlick, Gene Milford

The Man in the White Suit

GB, 1951
DIRECTOR:
Alexander Mackendrick
CAST INCLUDES:
Alec Guinness, Joan Greenwood,
Cecil Parker, Michael Gough,
Ernest Thesiger
SCREENPLAY:
John Dighton, Roger MacDougall,
Alexander Mackendrick
CINEMATOGRAPHY:
Douglas Slocombe
**PRODUCERS/
PRODUCTION COMPANIES:**
Michael Balcon, Sidney Cole/Ealing
Studios, J. Arthur Rank Films,
Universal International Pictures
**ACADEMY AWARD
NOMINATIONS (1951)**
Best Writing, Screenplay:
Roger MacDougall, John Dighton,
Alexander Mackendrick

An eccentric scientist develops a fabric that can never get dirty and will never wear out. Unfortunately, both the textile industry establishment and the unions fail to see the benefit.

Satirizing in equal measures both the antiquated capitalist management of a north of England mill town, and its reactionary union, *The Man in the White Suit* makes a successful farce of the relationship between labour and capital.

Every character is fully-rounded and convincing – even by the end, the film hasn't resorted to providing us with a 'boo-hiss' villain or a hero to cheer for, and the narrative would certainly support both. It is more interested in showing humanity that the squabbling between society's disparate classes benefits nobody, and selfishness exists in equal measures in all walks of life.

Sidney Stratton's (Guinness) invention should change the world for the better, yet it's not in the interests of the mill owners or labourers, who can both see the long-term problem of an everlasting fabric. Normally, the audience would expect to support a lone radical, a genius whose incredible innovation could save the ordinary people a fortune... but at the expense of the little old lady who does a bit of washing to make ends meet? That makes things more interesting, and the film's ambiguous presentation lets us decide for ourselves.

As with most of Ealing's comedy output from the early 1950s, *The Man in the White Suit* is brilliantly written, directed and performed. Ealing regular Mackendrick (*The Ladykillers*) clearly had a special relationship with the sublime Guinness, whose subtle touch is an almost unparalleled joy.

The Day the Earth Stood Still

A flying saucer lands in Washington, sending the world into a state of paranoia. Its two occupants are Klaatu (Rennie), a humanoid, and Gort (Martin), his robot. Their warnings to mankind of the dangers of atomic power prove difficult to accept.

Robert Wise's impeccably produced classic differs substantially from standard 1950s sci-fi hokum. Based on a short story by Harry Bates, the film largely avoids the exploitation of America's cold war paranoia, opting instead to issue a warning of mankind's potential for atomic self-destruction. The alien visitor charged with relaying this message of peace hardly receives a warm welcome. Justifying his races concerns about us, Klaatu is met with violence and distrust upon his arrival. After being shot and arrested by the jittery military authorities, our society receives some redemption at the hands of an imaginative young boy, Bobby (Gray), and his liberal mother Helen (Neal). It's the open-minded who are presented as our potential saviours, whilst the petty ignorance and reactionary approach of the media and government prove to be our greatest liability.

The film's success in illustrating its despair over our unfounded fear of the unknown was noted by the Golden Globes. In 1952, America's second biggest cinema awards ceremony named it 'Best Film Promoting International Understanding'.

The Day the Earth Stood Still is probably the best and most rewarding of the 1950s political sci-fi movie cycle. Featuring an excellent score from Hitchcock collaborator Bernard Herrmann, impressive effects and great performances, the film is as enjoyable and relevant today as it must have been on its release.

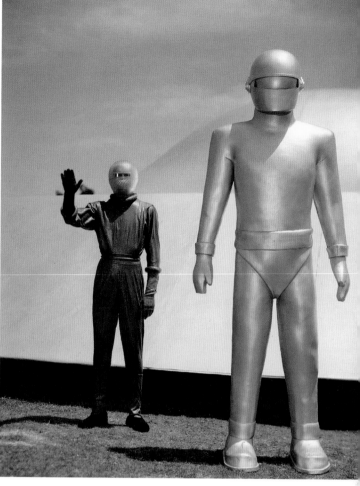

USA, 1951
DIRECTOR:
Robert Wise
CAST INCLUDES:
Michael Rennie, Patricia Neal,
Billy Gray, Lock Martin
SCREENPLAY:
Edmund H. North from Harry Bates
story *Farewell to the Master*
CINEMATOGRAPHY:
Leo Tover
**PRODUCERS/
PRODUCTION COMPANIES:**
Julian Blaustein/20th Century Fox

War of the Worlds

Aliens from Mars seek to colonize Earth by means of invasion and the total annihilation of the human race. When the military prove to be inadequate, a group of Californian scientists battle against the odds to find a solution.

Writer Barré Lyndon's adaptation changes much of H.G. Wells' classic novel while maintaining the important themes. A small town in America's midwest is now the destination for the first Martian pod, and a scientist caught up on a fishing trip is the new hero.

Given the subject and the timing, one might expect *War of the Worlds* to be a flagship of 1950s Cold War paranoia movies, but at times it seems keen to convince us otherwise. There are many references to nations uniting against a common foe, with information and ideas constantly exchanged between countries. Although no Communist nations are evident in the international alliance that forms, the extent of our awareness of other nations within the story is unusual for the time, as are the numerous shots of international landmarks being destroyed. America's military are presented as woefully inadequate, and its greedy, selfish citizens destroy the best hope for survival – hardly propaganda filmmaking. As a result of this more even-handed approach, it's easier to enjoy the film in its own right, rather than as a curiosity of politically motivated scare mongering. Lead characters Dr. Clayton Forrester and Sylvia Van Buren (Barry and Robinson) are charming and believable, while the Academy Award winning special effects are most impressive, providing a plethora of alien ships and large battles.

USA, 1953
DIRECTOR:
Byron Haskin
CAST INCLUDES:
Gene Barry, Ann Robinson,
Les Tremayne, Robert Cornthwaite
SCREENPLAY:
Barré Lyndon from the novel
by H.G. Wells
CINEMATOGRAPHY:
George Barnes
**PRODUCERS/
PRODUCTION COMPANIES:**
Frank Freeman Jr., George Pal,
Cecil B. DeMille/Paramount Pictures
**ACADEMY AWARD
NOMINATIONS (1954)**
Best Film Editing:
Everett Douglas
Best Sound, Recording:
Loren L. Ryder (Paramount Sound
Department)
ACADEMY AWARDS
Best Effects, Special Effects:
Gordon Jennings

Forbidden Planet

After contact with the colonists of distant planet Altair 4 is lost, a spaceship captained by Commander John J. Adams (Nielson) is dispatched to investigate. The crew find only two survivors, scientist Dr. Morbius (Pidgeon), and his daughter, Altaira (Francis). The others have apparently been killed by a strange creature, but the planet holds more surprises than a simple monster.

A sci-fi movie with a substantial budget was an unusual thing in the 1950s, even more unusual was the decision to shoot in colour. Basing the story on William Shakespeare's *The Tempest* completes the film's trilogy of baffling facts. But it all makes sense when you consider MGM made *Forbidden Planet* to take advantage of the massive popularity of sci-fi B-movies, reasoning that a lavishly produced colour epic, partly-written by the definitive star writer, would be even more successful than the cheap exploitation movies so popular at drive-ins. As a result, the film avoids the era's genre clichés. There is no real manipulation of Cold War fears, the alien creature's appearance is far from typical, and its origins certainly prove to be an original twist. Instead the intention seems to be to make a glossy but intelligent family adventure movie within the liberating framework of science fiction. The presence of director Fred Wilcox (better known for making *Lassie* films) is further testament to the fact.

But *Forbidden Planet* will always be remembered for two things above all else. Firstly, it features Leslie Nielson's best known straight performance (before being typecast as comedy buffoon Detective Frank Drebbin in the 1980s), and secondly, it marks the first appearance of now legendary Robby the Robot, so popular he is even endowed with his own actor filmography on The Internet Movie Database. Robby has appeared in over a dozen films and TV shows since his auspicious début, but has sadly been even less fortunate than Nielson when it comes to typecasting.

USA, 1956
DIRECTOR:
Fred M. Wilcox
CAST INCLUDES:
Walter Pidgeon, Anne Francis, Leslie Nielsen, Robby the Robot
SCREENPLAY:
Irving Block, Allen Adler, Cyril Hume, based on William Shakespeare's play, *The Tempest*
CINEMATOGRAPHY:
George J. Folsey
PRODUCERS/ PRODUCTION COMPANIES:
Nicholas Nayfack/ Metro-Goldwyn-Mayer (MGM)
ACADEMY AWARD NOMINATIONS (1957)
Best Effects, Special Effects: A. Arnold Gillespie, Irving G. Ries, Wesley C. Miller

Invasion of the Body Snatchers

USA, 1956
DIRECTOR:
Don Siegel
CAST INCLUDES:
Kevin McCarthy, Dana Wynter,
Larry Gates, King Donovan
SCREENPLAY:
Richard Collins, Jack Finney,
Daniel Mainwaring
CINEMATOGRAPHY:
Ellsworth Fredericks
PRODUCERS/
PRODUCTION COMPANIES:
Walter Wanger/Allied Artists Pictures
Corporation, Walter Wanger
Productions Inc.

Local doctor Miles Bennell (McCarthy) returns to his hometown of Santa Mira to find numerous patients claiming their relatives have been replaced by imposters. His suspicions aroused, it's not long before he discovers the horrible truth.

Shot in 19 days for just $300,000, Don Siegel's potent Cold War classic is one of the era's defining movies. Irrelevant to the way in which the ambiguous allegories are interpreted (anti-McCarthyist, anti-communist, anti-conformity, etc.), it remains a highly effective exercise in paranoia. The film's great success lies primarily in its observations of everyday life. The simple act of a man mowing the lawn becomes hugely sinister when it's nothing more than a charade.

An invader mimicking normal human activity in order to go unnoticed, but with an indefinable uniformity to its mannerisms, is just enough to chill the spine, making for more uneasy viewing than any number of monsters in flying saucers attacking American landmarks. Of course, achieving your scares this way is also easier on the budget.

It's notable, too, that unlike most other 1950s paranoia movies, it's never established whether the Invaders attack Earth specifically. Seeds floating through space land in fields and then grow pods, so adding yet another potential allegory to the list – the spreading of disease by outsiders.

Invasion of the Body Snatchers is a good old-fashioned B-movie with an unusually potent concoction of classic genre allegory and social commentary. After watching it, close study of friends and family is unavoidable.

The Incredible Shrinking Man

After being doused in a radioactive powder while out at sea, Scott Carey (Williams) begins to shrink. After losing his job he finds a brief respite from his bizarre disorder in the friendship of a circus midget, but he soon finds himself trapped in his own basement facing all manner of problems.

Genre fan Richard Matheson effectively launched his career when he adapted this curio from his own novel for director Jack Arnold (*It Came From Outer Space*). Going on to write numerous sixties B-movies and *Twilight Zone* episodes, as well as the book, *I am Legend* (later adapted to Charlton Heston vehicle *The Omega Man*), Matheson was interested in exploring the theme of everyday objects and circumstances unexpectedly taking on a threatening nature. He demonstrates it best here, though his belligerent truck driver in Steven Spielberg's *Duel* is also a highly successful creation.

Shrinking your lead character down to less than the length of a match allows for all manner of dangerous situations. A house spider and Carey's own cat become deadly adversaries, while the simple task of moving between the many surfaces and levels in his basement is a painstaking task. Although the oversized scissors and pens inevitably seem amusing when juxtaposed with Carey (appealing to the playful aspect of our character in the same way as kids' shows like *The Borrowers* and *Planet of the Giants*) the film touches on serious themes of metaphysics, emasculation and humanity.

USA, 1957
DIRECTOR:
Jack Arnold
CAST INCLUDES:
Grant Williams, Randy Stuart, April Kent, Paul Langton
SCREENPLAY:
Richard Matheson
CINEMATOGRAPHY:
Ellis W. Carter
PRODUCERS/ PRODUCTION COMPANIES:
Albert Zugsmith/Universal International Pictures

Jason and the Argonauts

USA, 1963
DIRECTOR:
Don Chaffey
CAST INCLUDES:
Todd Armstrong, Nancy Kovack,
Gary Raymond, Laurence Naismith,
Niall MacGinnis
SCREENPLAY:
Beverley Cross, Jan Read
CINEMATOGRAPHY:
Wilkie Cooper
**PRODUCERS/
PRODUCTION COMPANIES:**
Ray Harryhausen,
Charles H. Schneer/
Columbia Pictures Corporation,
Morningside Worldwide

The son of a fallen king, Jason gathers the best athletes and warriors in Greece. Supposedly aided by the gods, he sets sail for the end of the world where he hopes to find the magical Golden Fleece that will bring him to power.

The name of a special effects artist isn't something one expects to see above a film's title, but to genre fans Ray Harryhausen's unprecedented success means his name has been a byword for fantasy and imaginative stop-motion for fifty years. Although he would make more films (*Clash of the Titans*, *One Million Years BC*, the *Sinbad* movies, etc.), Harryhausen considers *Jason* to be the culmination of his technique and career.

Intended as the first of a series, the film uses Greek mythology as a backdrop, allowing for a succession of impressive monster themed set-pieces, (the winged Harpies who harass a blind man, Talos, the giant bronze statue woken by Hercules, etc.), and the presence of the gods themselves, here depicted as playfully omnipotent (almost sadistic) beings who pull the strings of mankind from Mount Olympus. The highlight of the film, and Harryhausen's definitive creation, are the skeleton warriors Jason must defeat in the film's finale. A triumph of creativity over available technology, they appear from the ground before drawing swords and launching into hand-to-hand combat with the real actors. It was nearly thirty years before CGI could render such imaginative animation in a more technically convincing manner, and even now there is no way to replicate the charm.

Dr. Strangelove or: How I Learned to Stop Worrying and Love the Bomb

Insane Air Force Brigadier General Jack D. Ripper (Hayden) issues the go code to his bomber wing through fear of an eventual communist invasion. While the planes armed with nuclear bombs head for their Russian targets, US President Merkin Muffley tries to find a way to minimize the inevitable international carnage.

Whilst trying to adapt Peter George's *Red Alert*, a serious novel about a holocaust caused by inflexible military and political policy, Kubrick realized it was impossible to make a straight movie of the ridiculous scenario. A switch to satire proved much more successful, and allowed for a second collaboration between Kubrick and Peter Sellers (the first being their auspicious partnership on *Lolita* two years earlier).

Sellers is awesome, playing three of the film's five main roles; the British Group Captain Lionel Mandrake, the President, and the eponymous doctor, perhaps his most accomplished performance. Stangelove (a former Nazi scientist now researching weapon systems for the Americans) is a fantastic comic creation, a man completely unable to control a bizarre affliction which causes him to refer to the President as 'mein Führer' and randomly perform Nazi salutes.

The film treads a dangerously fine line between horrific bad taste and powerful satire. Fortunately the judgement is consistently spot on. The scene in the war room where President Muffley must attempt to communicate the impending disaster via telephone to a drunk Russian premier at a noisy party is played perfectly, the potentially horrifying confrontation immediately defused by the Russian's accusation that Muffley never calls for a friendly chat anymore. One of the best lines of the film sums up the absurdity of its premise perfectly – upon seeing a general wrestling with the Soviet ambassador, the President informs them, 'You can't fight in here! This is the war room.'

GB, 1964
DIRECTOR:
Stanley Kubrick
CAST INCLUDES:
Peter Sellers, George C. Scott, Sterling Hayden, Slim Pickens, Peter Bull
SCREENPLAY:
Stanley Kubrick, Terry Southern and Peter George from his novel *Red Alert*, aka *Two Hours to Doom*
CINEMATOGRAPHY:
Gilbert Taylor
PRODUCERS/ PRODUCTION COMPANIES:
Stanley Kubrick, Victor Lyndon, Leon Minoff/Hawk Films Ltd
ACADEMY AWARD NOMINATIONS (1965)
Best Actor in a Leading Role: Peter Sellers
Best Director: Stanley Kubrick
Best Picture: Stanley Kubrick
Best Writing, Screenplay Based on Material from Another Medium: Stanley Kubrick, Peter George, Terry Southern

Fahrenheit 451

USA, 1966
DIRECTOR:
François Truffaut
CAST INCLUDES:
Oskar Werner, Julie Christie,
Cyril Cusack, Anton Diffring,
Jeremy Spenser
SCREENPLAY:
Jean-Louis Richard, David Rudkin,
Helen Scott, François Truffaut from
the novel by Ray Bradbury
CINEMATOGRAPHY:
Nicolas Roeg
**PRODUCERS/
PRODUCTION COMPANIES:**
Lewis M. Allen, Miriam Brickman,
Michael Dalamar,
Jane C. Nusbaum/Anglo Enterprises,
Vineyard

In a future fascist state, a fireman called Montag (Werner) starts to read the illegal books he is supposed to be incinerating, while his wife, Linda (Christie) wastes away in front of the television.

Francois Truffaut's (*Jules et Jim, La Nuit Americaine*) adaptation of Ray Bradbury's novel has long been the subject of debate. Although the film does deviate from its source material, and is inevitably challenging to watch, the real cause of such diverse reactions might be its potent subject matter, still touching raw nerves after so many years.

The future population is presented as a mass of conformist zombies, intellectually deadened by undemanding television and formulaic consumerism. Although extreme in its presentation, this theme has never been more relevant than it is today. In 1966, Linda's refusal to miss even a moment of her interactive soap opera must have seemed far-fetched, now it isn't even satire.

This bland and sterile future society is in stark contrast to the secret world of the freethinkers Montag is compelled to join. A makeshift campsite in the forest is home to dozens of 'books' – people who have opted out of society and settled far from it, each having memorized a book that then becomes their identity. They spend their time reciting to one another, passing on their knowledge so that the stories may live forever.

With hindsight, it's fair to say the basic hypothesis of the film has proved uncomfortably accurate. The government may not yet control everything we see on television, but it's dumbed down quite nicely on its own. And with politically correct pressure groups removing more and more books from the school curriculum, the nightmare vision of *Fahrenheit 451* seems increasingly close to reality.

Planet of the Apes

Astronaut George Taylor (Heston) crash lands on an unknown planet. He is soon captured by its dominant inhabitants, an advanced society of apes capable of speech and with a rudimentary grasp of technology.

An extravagant adaptation of the novel by Pierre Boulle, *Planet of the Apes* quickly became a sensation when it was released in 1968. It was the first film to generate widespread merchandising, in addition to spawning four direct sequels and spin-off television and cartoon shows. But before the formula was impoverished, *Planet of the Apes* had some very salient points to make about 1960s concerns.

USA, 1968
DIRECTOR:
Franklin J. Schaffner
CAST INCLUDES:
Charlton Heston, Roddy McDowall,
Kim Hunter, Maurice Evans,
Linda Harrison
SCREENPLAY:
Michael Wilson, Rod Serling from the
novel by Pierre Boulle
CINEMATOGRAPHY:
Leon Shamroy
PRODUCERS/
PRODUCTION COMPANIES:
Mort Abrahams,
Arthur P. Jacobs/20th Century Fox,
APJAC Productions
ACADEMY AWARD
NOMINATIONS (1969)
Best Costume Design:
Morton Haack
Best Music, Original Score for a
Motion Picture (not a Musical):
Jerry Goldsmith
ACADEMY AWARDS
Honorary Award for outstanding
make-up achievement:
John Chambers

Effectively holding a mirror up to mankind, the ape society is a slightly exaggerated reflection of our own. Segregated into strict classes (gorillas make up the military, orang-utans the intellectuals and chimpanzees the rest), the apes treat the indigenous, speechless humans like animals. The arrival of Taylor shocks them as much as a talking chimp would shock modern scientists. Faced with the unknown, the apes respond in a typically human manner, reacting with fear, lobotomizing Taylor's shipmate and attempting to do the same to him. The post-nuclear holocaust environment also plays on the concerns of 1960s America, and here the film differs from its source in order to be a little more topical. Boulle's novel depicts a more advanced ape society, essentially like modern man's, but considering the famous twist ending, it was clearly decided a barren landscape would be more arresting, not to mention cheaper.

2001: A Space Odyssey

USA, 1968
DIRECTOR:
Stanley Kubrick
CAST INCLUDES:
Keir Dullea, Gary Lockwood,
William Sylvester, Douglas Rain
SCREENPLAY:
Stanley Kubrick, Arthur C. Clarke
(from his short story)
CINEMATOGRAPHY:
Geoffrey Unsworth
PRODUCERS/
PRODUCTION COMPANIES:
Stanley Kubrick/
Metro-Goldwyn-Mayer (MGM), Polaris
ACADEMY AWARD
NOMINATIONS (1969)
Best Art Direction-Set Decoration:
Anthony Masters, Harry Lange,
Ernest Archer
Best Director:
Stanley Kubrick
Best Writing, Story and Screenplay -
Written Directly for the Screen:
Stanley Kubrick, Arthur C. Clarke
ACADEMY AWARDS
Best Effects, Special Visual Effects:
Stanley Kubrick

A monolith, previously seen to stimulate the evolution of primitive apes, is discovered buried on the moon. Once uncovered, it sends a radio signal towards Jupiter. In an attempt to learn more about it, the spaceship *Discovery* is dispatched to the signals destination.

Starting with the origin of man, and ending with the next stage of our evolution, Kubrick could hardly have anticipated how ambitious the project would become when he first met author Arthur C. Clarke and suggested they collaborate on, 'the proverbial good science fiction picture'. After ransacking Clarke's oeuvre, they settled on a short story, *The Sentinel*, that would form the basis of the film. Clarke immediately started work on a novel, while Kubrick simultaneously adapted it into a screenplay – a highly unusual method, but one that allowed for each to contribute to the other's work.

The completed screenplay presented numerous challenges to the filmmakers. Aside from the technical difficulty of constructing a giant centrifuge (to achieve the appearance of weightlessness), the story called for a total absence of dialogue in the first and last half hour, while the bulk of the film features

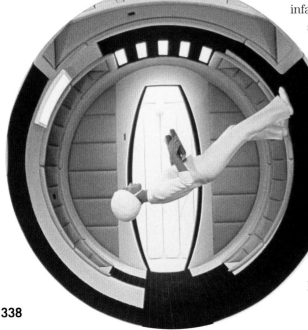

just three characters, one of which is a computer – the infamous HAL9000 (Rain). This minimalist narrative style only serves to emphasize the enormous themes Clarke and Kubrick set out to tackle – where are we going, and what is our place in the universe? Although the film can initially seem frustratingly ambiguous, repeated viewings do start to reveal the vernacular of its message, and the unprecedented rewards to be gained make for an incredibly satisfying experience.

The turn of the millennium, and the centenary of film have seen a lavish proliferation in the number of 'Top 100 Films' and 'Greatest Ever Movie' polls carried out, in which *2001: A Space Odyssey* generally features. But its rightful place always has been, and always will be, on the top spot.

A Clockwork Orange

GB, 1971
DIRECTOR:
Stanley Kubrick
CAST INCLUDES:
Malcolm McDowell, Patrick Magee,
Michael Bates, Warren Clarke,
John Clive
SCREENPLAY:
Stanley Kubrick from the novel
by Anthony Burgess
CINEMATOGRAPHY:
John Alcott
**PRODUCERS/
PRODUCTION COMPANIES:**
Stanley Kubrick, Si Litvinoff,
Max L. Raab, Bernard Williams/Hawk
Films Ltd., Polaris
Productions, Warner Bros.
**ACADEMY AWARD
NOMINATIONS (1972)**
Best Director:
Stanley Kubrick
Best Film Editing:
Bill Butler
Best Picture:
Stanley Kubrick
Best Writing, Screenplay Based on
Material from Another Medium:
Stanley Kubrick

In a violent future, society is on the verge of crumbling. A revolutionary new process, designed to reform criminals in the minimum time possible, is tested on convicted murderer Alex (McDowell) with mixed results.

Stanley Kubrick never made a film that didn't court controversy, but *A Clockwork Orange* caused more than all his previous work combined. Blamed (initially by *The Daily Mail*) for almost every crime of the day, the film was eventually withdrawn from release in the UK at the request of the director, but only after his family received death threats (technically it was never banned as urban legend claims). Accusations that the film endorses violence are laughable, though the attire and dialogue of the protagonist may have been adopted by self-conscious sociopaths of the time, the film's 136 minutes of gruelling violence (much of it suffered by Alex) is hard to accept as incitement. However, such indictments haven't affected the film's true purpose and power. Novelist Anthony Burgess' warning of a dystopian future in which criminal gangs and violent yobs maraud freely, with little concern for prosecution, has proved more prophetic than he could have imagined (similarly, the violence depicted in the film doesn't seem extreme by modern cinema standards). This ensures the film's primary themes of social commentary resonate just as well today.

Stylish, terrifying, influential, brutal, there are few adjectives one cannot apply to *A Clockwork Orange*.

Silent Running

In the future, all plant life on Earth has died out and the only remaining specimens orbit in giant glass globes attached to spaceships. Lowell Freeman (Dern) is a botanist responsible for maintaining one of the vessels, a devoted naturalist, he is devastated when instructions come through ordering the destruction of the globes.

In 1972, Douglas Trumbull, a renowned special effects artist, who had worked with Stanley Kubrick on *2001: A Space Odyssey* and Robert Wise on *The Andromeda Strain*, was ready to step behind the camera himself. With environmental concerns more prominent in the post 1960s era, he chose to marry ecological themes with his own innovative special effects techniques, simultaneously making a potent statement and creating the aesthetic juxtapositions that define the film's visual style. The sight of his (totally convincing) spaceships, each with visible forests and gardens safely contained within enormous glass bubbles, is one of the most inspiring visions of the genre.

USA, 1972
DIRECTOR:
Douglas Trumbull
CAST INCLUDES:
Bruce Dern, Cliff Potts, Ron Rifkin, Jesse Vint
SCREENPLAY:
Deric Washburn, Michael Cimino, Steven Bochco
CINEMATOGRAPHY:
Charles F. Wheeler
**PRODUCERS/
PRODUCTION COMPANIES:**
Michael Gruskoff, Marty Hornstein, Douglas Trumbull/Michael Gruskoff Productions, Universal Pictures

The simple story revolves around the character of Freeman. Dedicated to his forests, he is in a state of constant anticipation, waiting for the instruction to return to Earth for re-propagation. But he is clearly a little unhinged; the image of him frantically digging up plants whilst illuminated by the nuclear detonations of nearby globes is unforgettable, his wide eyes betraying the madness that will lead him to commit murder. The powerful central performance, contrasting style (heightened by folk queen Joan Baez's soundtrack) and compelling message make it one of the most unusual and valuable films of the time.

Solaris
solyaris

Psychologist Kris Kelvin (Banionis) is sent to Solaris, a space station monitoring a planet of the same name. The ocean world has many strange, unexplained properties, and as Kelvin soon discovers, it seems to be affecting the crew onboard the station.

Tarkovsky's meditation on guilt, desire, religion and the nature of the human conscience is a powerful and ambitious vision. Intellectually gruelling and hugely demanding, it is often compared to Stanley Kubrick's *2001: A Space Odyssey*, sharing a hypnotic pace, incredible atmosphere, and determination to tackle the most ambitious subjects, though *Solaris* possibly makes more use of metaphor to establish its themes. The planet can be seen as a representation of God, something the scientists are unable to understand by the mere application of established theories. Kelvin's eventual acceptance of its influence requires him to relinquish his scientific beliefs and embrace something that he can never understand. The planets' emotionally tortuous influence on the crew is to impose a deceased loved one upon them (it's not clear whether the entities' motives are malevolent or misjudged). In Kelvin's case, his guilt and regret over the death of former wife Hari (Bondarchuk) is interpreted, and the woman materializes on the station, courtesy of Solaris. We witness Kelvin's changing reaction to her, along with the change in his own personality, portrayed with a detailed, well-judged and ambiguous performance from Banionis. Tarkovsky's film cleverly mirrors the eponymous planet by probing the viewer, eliciting different reactions based on the individuals own beliefs.

U.S.S.R., 1972
DIRECTOR:
Andrei Tarkovsky
CAST INCLUDES:
Natalya Bondarchuk,
Donatas Banionis, Jüri Järvet,
Nikolai Grinko, Vladislav Dvorzhetsky
SCREENPLAY:
Stanislaw Lem (novel),
Fridrikh Gorenshtein,
Andrei Tarkovsky
CINEMATOGRAPHY:
Vadim Yusov
**PRODUCERS/
PRODUCTION COMPANIES:**
Viacheslav Tarasov/Creative Unit of
Writers & Cinema Workers,
Mosfilm, Unit Four
CANNES FILM FESTIVAL (1972)
FIPRESCI Prize:
Andrei Tarkovsky
Grand Prize of the Jury:
Andrei Tarkovsky (who was also
nomiated for the Palme d'Or)

Sleeper

In 2173, Miles Monroe, a clarinet player and owner of a New York health food store, is brought out of cryogenic suspension by radical scientists in order to carry out a mission that will hopefully lead to the toppling of the oppressive government state. Unfortunately, he becomes separated from the militants and wanders around lost in a bizarre future.

Woody Allen's only real excursion into sci-fi (despite *Zelig* and numerous other flirtations with the genre) is also one of his most popular films. Deciding the visual freedom afforded by an imaginary, futuristic reality would suit a more physical performance, Allen employs many tricks used in the silent era by the likes of Harold Lloyd and Keystone Kops, adding to the plethora of comedy styles he experiments with throughout the film. Whilst relying on the sci-fi comedy cornerstone – the premise that nothing works in the future – he also pokes fun at the ignorance of our future selves. When asked for his help in identifying historical figures, Monroe claims actor Bela Lugosi was mayor of New York and French President Charles De Gaulle was a TV chef!

The fascist government of *Sleeper* bears some similarity to those of *Brazil, Fahrenheit 451* and *Metropolis* (amongst many others), but Allen's approach to its ridicule is very different here. Instead of cleverly exposing the flaws of an overbearing state, Allen just mocks it, presenting the authorities as a bunch of buffoons, repeatedly bungling chances to capture Monroe and not worthy of a more intelligent or satirical assault. In one of the best sight gags, the guards at a farm that grows unfeasibly large fruit repeatedly slip on a banana skin the size of a canoe.

Sleeper is one of the most accessible films of Allen's early career. Concise and consistently funny, like John Carpenter's *Dark Star* it's a benchmark of sci-fi comedy.

USA, 1973
DIRECTOR:
Woody Allen
CAST INCLUDES:
Woody Allen, Diane Keaton,
John Beck, Mary Gregory
SCREENPLAY:
Woody Allen, Marshall Brickman
CINEMATOGRAPHY:
David M. Walsh
**PRODUCERS/
PRODUCTION COMPANIES:**
Marshall Brickman, Jack Grossberg,
Charles H. Joffe, Ralph Rosenblum,
Jack Rollins/Rollins-Joffe Productions

Westworld

USA, 1973
DIRECTOR:
Michael Crichton
CAST INCLUDES:
Yul Brynner, Richard Benjamin,
James Brolin
SCREENPLAY:
Michael Crichton
CINEMATOGRAPHY:
Gene Polito
**PRODUCERS/
PRODUCTION COMPANIES:**
Paul Lazarus III, Michael I.
Rachmil/Metro-Goldwyn-Mayer
(MGM)

An enormous theme park recreates three historic environments, complete with robotic characters and extraordinary attention to detail. Two wealthy visitors (Benjamin and Brolin) to Westworld inadvertently offend the meanest robot gunslinger in town (Brynner), who embarks on a vendetta when the machines go haywire.

Dealing with almost exactly the same subject as his later film adaptation, *Jurassic Park*, Michael Crichton makes his point in a more subtle and simple manner here in *Westworld*. As in his subsequent dino-thriller, Crichton meditates on the ramifications

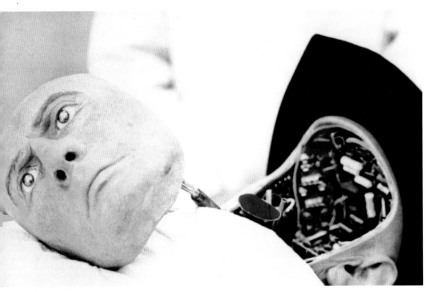

of mankind's ability to play God, but there are some interesting changes. Where Jurassic Park was a romantic optimist's dream, Westworld is a commercially motivated corporate resort. This crucial difference allows the film to play with more intellectually satisfying (though perhaps less exhilarating and astounding) themes like consumerism and capitalism. The technicians who service the robots have no particular enthusiasm for what they do, and the patron's omnipotence can often expose some of society's worst traits. A scene set in neighbouring Romanworld, in which a visitor lies around being fed and entertained by concubines, is an uncomfortable sight, money having bought him the ultimate phoney fantasy.

Westworld's greatest success, though, lies in its second half and the Gunslinger's protracted and relentless pursuit of Benjamin's character, Peter Martin. Crichton (making his feature directorial debut) draws every last bit of tension imaginable from the basic premise, his successful treatment clearly inspiring James Cameron's *Terminator*.

Dark Star

Four very bored men have been travelling through deep space for twenty years. Their job is to destroy unstable planets, making the area safe for settlement.

Starting life as a student film, Carpenter later found funding to expand his 'hippie sci-fi' short into a feature length comedy. Spoofing *2001: A Space Odyssey* (a tagline was cheeky enough to proclaim it, 'A Spaced-Out Odyssey'), one of the film's cleverest aspects is the spoofing of *2001*'s themes as well as the format. Where Kubrick and others use man's reliance on fundamentally flawed technology to draw attention to our dehumanization, Carpenter uses it as a comedic device. The eponymous space ship has been clattering about the universe for twenty years and is riddled with malfunctions. The sleeping quarters are blown away, the commander was killed by a faulty seat, and, now, all the toilet roll has been destroyed! But the best example is the desperate, existential argument that takes place between the crew and bomb number 20, which has received (false) instructions to detonate under the ship, and is at first unwilling to accept the possibility that nothing exists. After pondering the very meaning of life, the bomb is eventually satisfied by the concept that it exists but that everything else is false data.

It's a shame Carpenter has seldom returned to comedy – based on this evidence his gift is immense. In *Dark Star*, he and collaborator Dan O'Bannon have made the most intelligent and influential sci-fi comedy of them all.

USA, 1974
DIRECTOR:
John Carpenter
CAST:
Brian Narelle, Cal Kuniholm,
Dre Pahich, Dan O'Bannon
SCREENPLAY:
John Carpenter, Dan O'Bannon
CINEMATOGRAPHY:
Douglas Knapp
**PRODUCERS/
PRODUCTION COMPANIES:**
John Carpenter, J. Stein Kaplan,
Jack H. Harris/University of Southern
California

Close Encounters of the Third Kind

USA, 1977
DIRECTOR:
Steven Spielberg
CAST INCLUDES:
Richard Dreyfuss, François Truffaut,
Teri Garr, Melinda Dillon, Bob Balaban
SCREENPLAY:
Steven Spielberg
CINEMATOGRAPHY:
William A. Fraker, Douglas Slocombe,
Vilmos Zsigmond
PRODUCERS/
PRODUCTION COMPANIES:
Clark L. Paylow, Julia Phillips,
Michael Phillips/Columbia Pictures
Corporation, EMI Films Ltd.
ACADEMY AWARD
NOMINATIONS (1978)
Best Actress in a Supporting Role:
Melinda Dillon
Best Art Direction-Set Decoration:
Joe Alves, Daniel A. Lomino, Phil
Abramson
Best Director:
Steven Spielberg
Best Effects, Visual Effects:
Roy Arbogast, Douglas Trumbull,
Matthew Yuricich, Gregory Jein,
Richard Yuricich
Best Film Editing:
Michael Kahn
Best Music, Original Score:
John Williams
Best Sound:
Robert Knudson, Robert J. Glass,
Don MacDougall,
Gene S. Cantamessa,
ACADEMY AWARDS
Best Cinematography:
Vilmos Zsigmond
Special Achievement Award:
Frank Warner for sound
effects editing.

An Indiana everyman is one of a small group of people to witness a group of UFOs. The encounter leaves him obsessively attempting to mould a shape implanted in his mind, as he becomes increasingly disengaged from his family.

'We are not alone', ran the tagline for *Close Encounters*, the film in which Steven Spielberg laid down his manifesto for popular cinema domination. He had already had a huge hit with *Jaws* two years earlier, but here we see all his trademark beats together for the first time. A difficult father-son relationship (as well as an absent father/lost child scenario), shadowy authorities, and a plucky mother coping with it all – Spielberg has never been afraid to tell personal stories. Yet, as with many of his films, it's also quite dark. Roy Neary's (Dreyfuss) descent into madness doesn't short-change the viewer,

it's every bit as real and disturbing as one might expect, eventually costing him his family. But ultimately Roy doesn't care, he is a man on a mission (another recurring theme for Spielberg). His determination to find out more about the strange ships is the film's driving force, and is mirrored by mother Jillian Guiler's (Dillon) search for her abducted son. But they aren't the only ones trying to discover what's going on. Claude Lacombe (Truffaut), a French scientist charged with making first contact, has the same childlike optimism as Neary – a scene of Lacombe enthusiastically chasing a giant, rolling globe is a nice counter to Neary's mashed potato sculpting.

Close Encounters may not be perfect, but one would need ice for blood not to be touched by its innocent charm and infectious sense of wonder.

Star Wars: Episode IV – A New Hope

A naive young farm boy (Hamill), a mystical old sage (Guinness), and a smuggler (Ford) get caught up in an intergalactic rebellion.

After directing *THX1138* and the hugely successful *American Graffiti*, George Lucas found himself in great demand in 1974. *Apocalypse Now* looked to be next on his slate, having been prepped by collaborator Francis Ford Coppola, and suitably in keeping with the young director's previous mature and intelligent work. Instead, he surprised everyone by heading off to England to make a Flash Gordon movie with tin robots, space wizards and a seven-foot dog.

The film's success at the box office (and in exploiting its promotional and merchandizing potential) is now legendary. If you adjust for inflation, the worldwide gross stands at nearly $2 billion, and that doesn't include revenue from sequels, video games and merchandize. Nor does it reflect the large proportion of the populace who consider the film an abomination. Quite why it remains so divisive is hard to understand. There are certainly flaws, particularly in the dialogue and performances, but these are generally no more relevant to the film's critics than to its fans, detractors preferring to cite vague concerns over the film's influence on Hollywood's increasing commercialism. But that is to miss the point entirely. It is inevitable that success will bring about change in any industry; we should be grateful the film which became the medium's most popular offspring is one of such charm, innocence and all round quality. The score is one of the greatest ever recorded, the effects are photo-real, the production design is timeless and the whole thing is stuck together with a masterly ability for storytelling.

For most of the generation lucky enough to discover *Star Wars* before its formula was imitated and diluted, it remains the shared, innocent and fantastical experience we remember from childhood, and nothing can change that.

USA, 1977
DIRECTOR:
George Lucas
CAST INCLUDES:
Mark Hamill, Harrison Ford, Carrie Fisher, Alec Guinness, David Prowse
SCREENPLAY:
George Lucas
CINEMATOGRAPHY:
Gilbert Taylor
PRODUCERS/ PRODUCTION COMPANIES:
Gary Kurtz, George Lucas, Rick McCallum/Lucasfilm Ltd.
ACADEMY AWARD NOMINATIONS (1978)
Best Actor in a Supporting Role: Alec Guinness
Best Director: George Lucas
Best Picture: Gary Kurtz
Best Writing, Screenplay Written Directly for the Screen: George Lucas
Special Achievement Award For Sound Effects: Ben Burtt
ACADEMY AWARDS
Best Art Direction-Set Decoration: John Barry, Norman Reynolds, Leslie Dilley, Roger Christian
Best Costume Design: John Mollo
Best Effects, Visual Effects: John Stears, John Dykstra, Richard Edlund, Grant McCune, Robert Blalack
Best Film Editing: Paul Hirsch, Marcia Lucas, Richard Chew
Best Music, Original Score: John Williams
Best Sound: Don MacDougall, Ray West, Bob Minkler, Derek Ball

Superman

A small boy is sent to Earth from a dying alien world. Blessed with superpowers, he becomes a crime-fighter in the city of Metropolis whilst his alter-ego works as a newspaper reporter.

In 1973, 28-year-old Ilya Salkind pitched the idea of a Superman movie to his producer father Alexander. Although popular as cartoons, television shows and serials, comic books weren't considered suitable for feature film adaptation, but the Salkinds were convinced it would work. Eventually gaining finance from Warners (who were to distribute but not produce), the film started shooting in March, 1977 with Richard Donner (in demand after *The Omen*) at the helm. But a troubled pre-production (original director, James Bond legend Guy Hamilton, was forced to drop out at the last minute) rolled straight into a troubled shoot, with a titanic power struggle between the Salkinds and Donner. The European producers weren't interested in Superman the American icon, envisioning instead a campy, kitsch hero closer to the Batman series. Although Donner prevailed, his insistence on taking his time and doing it properly caused the abandonment of *Superman 2* (being shot simultaneously).

Donner's bullish perseverance would certainly pay dividends, his excellent judgement allowing for plenty of comedy without the loss of dignity. Reeve is superb as both Superman and alter-ego Clark Kent, while the clever casting of Brando and Hackman adds a legitimacy to the film's claims of sophistication and sincerity. The success in realizing this claim is probably *Superman*'s most lasting influence – the comic book adaptation golden rule: Respect the characters at all costs! After all, who remembers *Dick Tracy*?

USA, 1978
DIRECTOR:
Richard Donner
CAST INCLUDES:
Christopher Reeve, Marlon Brando, Gene Hackman, Margot Kidder, Ned Beatty
SCREENPLAY:
Mario Puzo, David Newman, Leslie Newman, Robert Benton, Tom Mankiewicz, from Jerry Siegel & Joe Shuster's comic
CINEMATOGRAPHY:
Geoffrey Unsworth
PRODUCERS/ PRODUCTION COMPANIES:
Charles F. Greenlaw, Alexander Salkind, Ilya Salkind, Pierre Spengler/Alexander Salkind, Dovemead Films, Film Export A.G., International Film Production
ACADEMY AWARD NOMINATIONS (1979)
Best Film Editing: Stuart Baird
Best Music, Original Score: John Williams
Best Sound: Gordon K. McCallum, Graham V. Hartstone, Nicolas Le Messurier, Roy Charman
ACADEMY AWARDS
Special Achievement Award For Visual Effects:
Les Bowie, Colin Chilvers, Denys N. Coop, Roy Field, Derek Meddings, Zoran Perisic

Alien

GB, 1979
DIRECTOR:
Ridley Scott
CAST INCLUDES:
Tom Skerritt, Sigourney Weaver,
Harry Dean Stanton, John Hurt,
Ian Holm, Yaphet Kotto
SCREENPLAY:
Dan O'Bannon, Ronald Shusett
CINEMATOGRAPHY:
Derek Vanlint
PRODUCERS/
PRODUCTION COMPANIES:
Gordon Carroll, David Giler,
Walter Hill, Ivor Powell,
Ronald Shusett/20th Century Fox,
Brandywine Productions Ltd
ACADEMY AWARD
NOMINATIONS (1980)
Best Art Direction-Set Decoration:
Michael Seymour, Leslie Dilley,
Roger Christian, Ian Whittaker
ACADEMY AWARDS
Best Effects, Visual Effects:
H.R. Giger, Carlo Rambaldi,
Brian Johnson, Nick Allder,
Denys Ayling

The deep-space mining ship *Nostromo* responds to a distress call from an uncharted planet. Some of the crew go aboard an ancient alien vessel on the surface, but after discovering the distress signal is actually a warning they leave. However, one of them has already become host to a gestating alien.

Coming just two years after George Lucas released *Star Wars*, Ridley Scott's bold decision to focus on suspense and strong characterization was highly successful, and did much to aid the sci-fi genre's credibility at a time when it seemed lost in the domain of children's fantasy adventure. Much time is spent establishing a social structure between the crewmembers of the *Nostromo*, an element that is handled exceptionally well by Scott and his cast. Tension between officers and engineers is exposed with great authenticity, as is the misogyny suffered by the film's superbly conceived and realized central character, Ellen Ripley (Weaver), whose perceived vulnerability makes her scenes of confrontation more interesting, even after her

formidable character and superior endurance skills have become evident.

But the film's rich characterization is just one side of the coin. The awesome production design is breathtaking, and H.R. Gigers vision for the alien itself is amongst the most memorable cinematic creations of its kind. Dripping aqueous slime and with acid for blood, the monster is terrifying, providing Scott with fantastic material on which to build the tension – possibly the film's greatest success. The scenes of the crew searching the ship's cavernous chambers would have Alfred Hitchcock watching through his fingers.

Mad Max 2: The Road Warrior

After the death of his family in the first film, Max (Gibson) continues to roam the post-apocalyptic wastelands of Australia. Civilization has broken down still further and fuel is now the most valuable commodity. After discovering an encampment under threat from a gang of thugs, he pledges to help the inhabitants.

With the dark tone and brutal character of the eponymous anti-hero already established in the original film, returning co-writer/ director George Miller is able to spend the first half of *Mad Max 2* illustrating the desperate situation in which society now finds itself. The desolate environment stifles all optimism, but Max is well equipped for life here – he is as much a part of the landscape as the opportunistic thieves and marauding gangs he encounters.

AUS, 1981
DIRECTOR:
George Miller
CAST INCLUDES:
Mel Gibson, Bruce Spence,
Michael Preston, Max Phipps
SCREENPLAY:
Terry Hayes, George Miller,
Brian Hannant
CINEMATOGRAPHY:
Dean Semler
**PRODUCERS/
PRODUCTION COMPANIES:**
Byron Kennedy/Kennedy Miller
Productions

But it's obvious a man like Max needs a mission, and the desert encampment he discovers provides him with one. The film's fantastic second half is essentially a protracted and violent car chase that sees Max attempt to drive a tanker truck, containing the only known fuel reserves, to safety. With a specific (and wonderfully simple) aim, Max and the film come alive. Shot and edited with a loose creativity that makes the audience really feel a part of the action, Miller is highly successful in wringing every last gruesome idea out of the simple concept.

Anyone who can stomach the first film's brutality will find the sequel at least as satisfying, but avoid the third at all costs. It has Tina Turner in it. And that's not the worst thing about it. . .

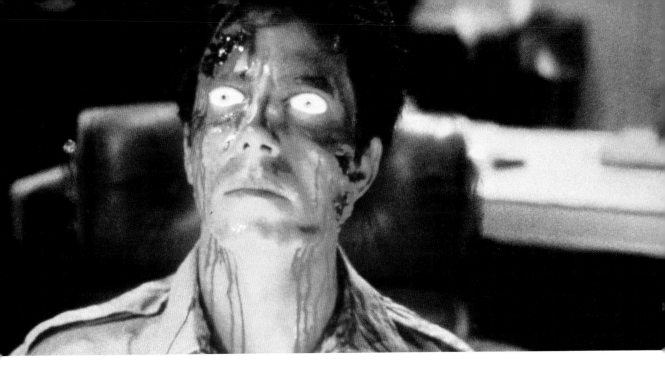

Scanners

CANADA, 1981
DIRECTOR:
David Cronenberg
CAST INCLUDES:
Jennifer O'Neill, Stephen Lack,
Patrick McGoohan, Lawrence Dane,
Michael Ironside
SCREENPLAY:
David Cronenberg
CINEMATOGRAPHY:
Mark Irwin
**PRODUCERS/
PRODUCTION COMPANIES:**
Pierre David, Claude Héroux,
Victor Solnicki/Canadian Film
Development Corporation (CFDC),
Filmplan

A secret subculture of powerful telepaths led by Darryl Revok (Ironside) is intent on destroying society, whilst another wants to live in peace. Scientist Paul Ruth (McGoohan) hopes the unaffiliated telepath Cameron Vale (Lack) will infiltrate Revok's organization and help destroy it.

Cronenberg is on familiar territory in *Scanners,* arguably the best film to emerge from his late 1970s/early 1980s obsession with disease and mutation. A concept that clearly inspired Bryan Singer's *X-Men,* the Scanners are presented as human mutants whose gifts have left them ostracized by society and, conversely, fought over by rival factions of their own subculture. As in *X-Men,* most have spent their lives as social outcasts with their new-found popularity bringing little comfort. But Cronenberg doesn't waste much time over the sociological aspects of his film, it is a sci-fi B-movie at heart and isn't ashamed to admit it. *Scanners* was one of those videos that was omnipresent during the 1980s rental boom. Cronenberg would probably be proud to know that his film features (according to one survey) the 'most paused moment' in the decade's prolific rental history - the shot of a Scanners head exploding after going up against Revok in a psychic power struggle.

Time Bandits

A young boy is kidnapped by a gang of time-travelling dwarf thieves in possession of a stolen map showing gateways in time and reality. Pursued by the Supreme Being, the gang embark on a series of adventures including meetings with Napoleon and an ogre.

Terry Gilliam's only true children's movie is one of the most imaginative and daring fairy tales ever filmed. The director's insistence on casting all the lead roles with dwarves – with the exception of young Kevin (Warnock) – was a serious handicap in finding finance. Gilliam was expecting to be short of money from the start. He was apparently used to this, (the character of Agamemnon was described in the screenplay as, 'someone of equal but cheaper stature than Sean Connery'), and he realized that he needed some star cameos if he was to get his hands on real money. Fortunately, Connery happened to see the script and agreed to play the role of Agamemnon (and the fireman at the end of the film) for a cut rate, and with Gilliam cronies Cleese and Palin already on board, they were away.

A triumph of imagination over mathematical formula and financial frugality, Gilliam takes the opportunity to twist history around his own crazed sense of humour. Sherwood forest is still home to the impossibly polite Robin Hood (Cleese), but we discover he actually robs from the poor. Napoleon (Holm) has a height complex and the Vicious Ogre the gang run into suffers from terrible back pain.

The result is both bewitching and hilarious, a true classic that should be preserved, if for no other reason than to show how creative and imaginative kids' films can be when the rights aren't sold to fast food chains before the cameras have even started rolling.

GB, 1981
DIRECTOR:
Terry Gilliam
CAST INCLUDES:
Craig Warnock, David Rappaport,
Sean Connery, John Cleese,
Michael Palin
SCREENPLAY:
Michael Palin, Terry Gilliam
CINEMATOGRAPHY:
Peter Biziou
PRODUCERS/
PRODUCTION COMPANIES:
Terry Gilliam, George Harrison,
Denis O'Brien, Neville C.
Thompson/Handmade Films Ltd

Blade Runner

USA, 1982
DIRECTOR:
Ridley Scott
CAST INCLUDES:
Harrison Ford, Rutger Hauer,
Sean Young, Daryl Hannah,
William Sanderson
SCREENPLAY:
Hampton Fancher,
David Webb Peoples from
Philip K. Dick's novel, *Do Androids
Dream of Electric Sheep?*
CINEMATOGRAPHY:
Jordan Cronenweth
**PRODUCERS/
PRODUCTION COMPANIES:**
Michael Deeley, Hampton Fancher,
Brian Kelly, Jerry Perenchio,
Ivor Powell, Run Run Shaw,
Bud Yorkin/Blade Runner Partnership,
The Ladd Company
**ACADEMY AWARD
NOMINATIONS (1983)**
Best Art Direction-Set Decoration:
Lawrence G. Paull, David L. Snyder,
Linda DeScenna
Best Effects, Visual Effects:
Douglas Trumbull, Richard Yuricich,
David Dryer

Rick Deckard (Ford) is a retired police officer, once responsible for finding and killing renegade 'replicants' — man-made servants and soldiers almost indistinguishable from humans. A highly sophisticated and murderous gang lead by the enigmatic Roy Batty (Hauer) is on the loose, and Deckard is persuaded to take the case.

The first and possibly best Philip K. Dick adaptation, *Blade Runner* is an arresting triumph of design, atmosphere and storytelling. Ridley Scott's self-assured approach lends a convincing air to the year 2019, making the city's neon-lit streets seem as real as those walked by Deckard's spiritual grandfather, Philip Marlowe. In fact, the influence of Raymond Chandler and his famous P.I. is evident throughout Dick's novel and particularly the film. Deckard is a similarly hard-bitten and morally ambiguous character, making a living amongst the sleaziest dregs of society. There is even a scene in which Deckard plays a gawky fool to gain the trust of an incidental character, his mannerisms and voice identical to an impression performed by Bogart's Marlowe in *The Big Sleep*. From character to narrative, to the shadowy visual style, *Blade Runner* is riddled with film noir references.

Fortunately, powerful performances all round prevent the stylized aesthetic from swamping the story. Ford is great, but it's Rutger Hauer who is the real revelation here. A stalwart of sci-fi and horror B-movies, Batty is the most high-profile and successful role to date for the Dutch actor, who makes him a threatening and electrifying presence.

Available in two versions, the superior is the 1991 director's cut which removes a dreadful commentary – insisted upon by the distributor – begrudgingly and lazily recorded by Ford.

E.T. the Extra-Terrestrial

An alien botanist is befriended by a young boy when accidentally marooned on Earth.

The pinnacle of Spielberg's filmmaking adolescence, *E.T.* is one of the best-known and most beloved movies of all time. It represents an innocence all too often overlooked by modern family cinema, choosing to revel in innocuous sentimentality, successfully appealing to our imaginative and affectionate better nature. Perhaps it's a little too sentimental for some tastes, over-exposure and excessive merchandising in the 1980s certainly haven't helped the film's saccharine image, but even the most cynical moviegoer should give it another chance. After more than twenty years it can finally stand on its own, devoid of the hype, marketing and media saturation that made up as much of E.T.'s identity as the film itself; it's now just a simple, beautifully told story.

Spielberg loves to build his films around fractured families, generally featuring lonely kids lacking a patriarchal figure. *E.T.* is essentially a story about two lost children embarking on a therapeutic and symbiotic friendship. Elliot (Thomas) is clearly a troubled child at the start of the film, appearing emotionally stilted. Through his friendship with E.T., he seems to learn how to communicate and form relationships. It's no wonder that people have speculated that Spielberg intended the story to be an allegory, and that the little alien is a messianic prophet!

It has been a long time since movies like this have been made with such skill. Filmmakers of Spielberg's calibre come along all too infrequently, and when they do, they don't tend to make family movies. *E.T.* should be appreciated as the rare gem that it is, and after the recent spit and polish supplied for the DVD special edition, there are more reasons than ever to revisit this classic.

USA, 1982
DIRECTOR:
Steven Spielberg
CAST INCLUDES:
Henry Thomas, Dee Wallace-Stone, Robert MacNaughton, Drew Barrymore
SCREENPLAY:
Melissa Mathison
CINEMATOGRAPHY:
Allen Daviau
**PRODUCERS/
PRODUCTION COMPANIES:**
Kathleen Kennedy, Melissa Mathison, Steven Spielberg/Amblin Entertainment, Universal Pictures
**ACADEMY AWARD
NOMINATIONS (1983)**
Best Cinematography: Allen Daviau
Best Director: Steven Spielberg
Best Film Editing: Carol Littleton
Best Picture:
Steven Spielberg, Kathleen Kennedy
Best Writing, Screenplay Written Directly for the Screen:
Melissa Mathison
ACADEMY AWARDS
Best Effects, Sound Effects Editing:
Charles L. Campbell, Ben Burtt
Best Effects, Visual Effects:
Carlo Rambaldi, Dennis Muren, Kenneth Smith
Best Music, Original Score:
John Williams
Best Sound:
Robert Knudson, Robert Glass, Don Digirolamo, Gene S. Cantamessa

Star Trek: The Wrath of Khan

USA, 1982
DIRECTOR:
Nicholas Meyer
CAST INCLUDES:
William Shatner, Leonard Nimoy,
DeForest Kelley, Ricardo Montalban,
Kirstie Alley, James Doohan,
SCREENPLAY:
Jack B. Sowards from a story by,
Harve Bennett & Jack B. Sowards,
based on the television series by
Gene Roddenberry
CINEMATOGRAPHY:
Gayne Rescher
PRODUCERS/
PRODUCTION COMPANIES:
Harve Bennett, William F. Phillips,
Robert Sallin/Paramount Pictures

Khan (Montalban), an old adversary of Admiral James T. Kirk, seizes control of a federation starship and seeks revenge. Meanwhile, the mysterious Genesis project is also garnering attention.

For the second movie featuring the original crew of the U.S.S. *Enterprise*, seasoned filmmaker Robert Wise (*West Side Story*, *The Sound of Music*) makes way for second time director Nicholas Meyer, who turns in an exceptional sci-fi adventure, easily bettering his predecessor.

As in virtually all the original *Star Trek* movies, Kirk and his crew are retired as the film starts, but a training mission (or similar excuse) requires them to be onboard when some catastrophe calls the

Enterprise into action. In this case, it's the threat Khan poses to a team of scientists, including Kirk's former partner and estranged son, working on a project that could become hugely dangerous in the wrong hands. The remote research station becomes the location for a fantastic game of cat and mouse between the crippled spaceships of Kirk and Khan, who steals every scene in which he appears. In fact, Montalban's gloriously extravagant performance and flamboyant dialogue ('From hells heart I stab at thee!') prove to be amongst the film's best trump cards. But it's no 'one man show'. *The Wrath of Khan* is the most complete of the ten *Star Trek* movies. The sharp script successfully deals with the lead's age, providing plenty of banter between Kirk, Spock (Nimoy) and McCoy (Kelly). It also avoids the sort of action scenes that Roger Moore's James Bond was embarrassing himself with at about the same time.

Aside from the film's individual successes over the rest of the series, it is the only one that stands up on its own merit. There is no need to be a fan, or even a casual viewer, it is not just a great *Star Trek* movie but a great sci-fi movie.

Tron

Computer hacker Kevin Flynn (Bridges) is turned into a software programme by the malevolent computer of ENCOM, an abhorrent manufacturer of hugely successful video games for whom Flynn once worked. Meanwhile, an independent programme, Tron (Boxleitner), is attempting to disable the Master Control Program (MCP) that runs the entire company.

The hugely imaginative premise of *Tron* is based on the idea that every computer programme is a conscious entity with the physical characteristics of its writer. They exist within the spacious environment of ENCOM's computer system and are subject to the same basic laws of physics as we are. The genius of the film is the incredible visual style developed for the software characters and their environment – where we spend about eighty per cent of the film's running time. Although it uses a combination of special effects techniques, (including rotoscoping and compositing), the most striking achievement of *Tron* is the extent to which computer animation is used, unprecedented at the time. In fact, although *Tron* was Academy Award nominated for costume and sound, it was refused a nomination for special effects because the use of CGI was considered to be cheating!

Director and creative driving force Steve Lisberger is interested in more than just flashy effects, although he recognizes the concept's potential for allegory and exploits it to the full, playing on themes of dehumanization and liberty. Illustrating the danger of society becoming too reliant on computers, the MCP is so powerful it no longer serves man. Company president Ed Dillinger (Warner) must take its orders and retrieve files for it, (the most basic role of a computer), and in a religious reference, many of the programs under its sadistic control have ceased to believe in 'The Users'. Tron is the messiah, bringing hope to the downtrodden. He must destroy the MCP to bring freedom to all and fulfill the purpose for which he was created.

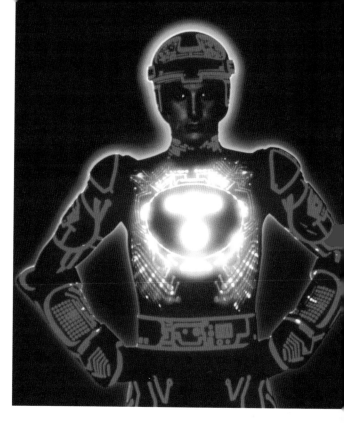

USA, 1982
DIRECTOR:
Steven Lisberger
CAST INCLUDES:
Jeff Bridges, Bruce Boxleitner,
David Warner, Cindy Morgan,
Barnard Hughes
SCREENPLAY:
Steven Lisberger, Bonnie MacBird
CINEMATOGRAPHY:
Bruce Logan
**PRODUCERS/
PRODUCTION COMPANIES:**
Harrison Ellenshaw, Donald Kushner,
Ron Miller/Lisberger/Kushner,
Walt Disney Pictures
**ACADEMY AWARD
NOMINATIONS (1983)**
Best Costume Design:
Eloise Jensson, Rosanna Norton
Best Sound:
Michael Minkler, Bob Minkler,
Lee Minkler, James LaRue

Ghost Busters

A New York apartment building is subjected to a tidal wave of paranormal activity. Meanwhile a group of scientists go into business as ghost catchers.

A ragtag group of eccentrics and losers must somehow defeat an ancient demon intent on destroying the world – what concept could better lend itself to the extravaganza of ideas, characters, special effects and one-liners thrown at it by the writers?

Thought up by *Saturday Night Live* alumni Aykroyd and Ramis (who would play failed scientists Stantz and Spengler), the film took advantage of a new generation of more demanding and media-savvy kids. Aiming the comedy somewhere between their and their parents' sense of humour, the film was able to attract the children without deterring adults, making it the biggest grossing comedy of all time. It also took advantage of the immense talents of Bill Murray, the film's resident scene stealer. His Peter Venkman is a fantastically sardonic opportunist, just falling short of both sleazy and nasty (he spends half the film trying to get Weaver's Dana Barrett into bed, the other half victimizing Stantz and Spengler), but ultimately he's just lazy. The lethargic, laid-back manner with which he greets unimaginable confrontations provides some of the film's best moments, particularly first contact with 'Slimer' and the showdown with the ancient Sumerian God, Gozer (Jovan).

Brimming over with memorable moments and characters (the giant marshmallow man, the scary library ghost, Moranis' Louis Tully), but perhaps the film's most lasting gift to popular culture comes from theme tune writer Ray Parker Jr. – now who you gonna call?

USA, 1984
DIRECTOR:
Ivan Reitman
CAST:
Bill Murray, Dan Aykroyd, Sigourney Weaver, Harold Ramis, Rick Moranis
SCREENPLAY:
Dan Aykroyd, Harold Ramis
CINEMATOGRAPHY:
László Kovács
PRODUCERS/ PRODUCTION COMPANIES:
Bernie Brillstein, Michael C. Gross, Joe Medjuck, Ivan Reitman/ Black Rhino Productions, Columbia Pictures Corporation
ACADEMY AWARD NOMINATIONS (1985)
Best Effects, Visual Effects: Richard Edlund, John Bruno, Mark Vargo, Chuck Gaspar
Best Music, Original Song: Ray Parker Jr. for the song 'Ghostbusters'

The Terminator

A sophisticated android (Schwarzenegger) is sent from the future to kill Sarah Connor (Hamilton). Her only protector is the intense rebel soldier, Reese (Biehn), who followed the Terminator back in time.

Opening in a future scorched by nuclear holocaust, giant robots (or 'Hunter-Killers') pursue the scattered remnants of mankind through the desolate landscape. A subtitle reveals, 'The machines' war to exterminate mankind has raged for decades', then Brad Fiedel's dramatic score crashes in. So begins James Cameron's far from subtle debut for Cyberdine Systems model 101, better known as the Terminator, one of sci-fi's most iconic creations. Although impossible to imagine anyone else in the role, Schwarzenegger wasn't the first choice. Originally Lance Henriksen (who appears as police officer Vukovich, instead) was to play the part, but when Cameron saw the Austrian bodybuilder he was convinced his stature would lend a more intimidating quality to his robotic killing machine. The film launched Schwarzenegger's career and the relentless android became his signature character.

Essentially a series of pursuits and shootouts the film lacks the overblown scale and pomposity of its sequels and stays true to its B-movie roots. This more linear form better suits the clear concept and characters, most of whom have simple motivations and avoid stepping outside their remit. But the film still has an intelligent point to make, its intention to highlight fears of dehumanization and the dangers of our reliance on machines is frighteningly successful.

USA, 1984
DIRECTOR:
James Cameron
CAST INCLUDES:
Arnold Schwarzenegger,
Michael Biehn, Linda Hamilton,
Paul Winfield, Lance Henriksen
SCREENPLAY:
Harlan Ellison, James Cameron,
Gale Anne Hurd, William Wisher
CINEMATOGRAPHY:
Adam Greenberg
**PRODUCERS/
PRODUCTION COMPANIES:**
John Daly, Derek Gibson, Gale Anne
Hurd/Hemdale Film Corporation,
Cinema 84, Euro Film Fund,
Pacific Western

Back to the Future

USA, 1985
DIRECTOR:
Robert Zemeckis
CAST INCLUDES:
Michael J. Fox, Christopher Lloyd,
Lea Thompson, Crispin Glover,
Thomas F. Wilson, Claudia Wells
SCREENPLAY:
Robert Zemeckis, Bob Gale
CINEMATOGRAPHY:
Dean Cundey
**PRODUCERS/
PRODUCTION COMPANIES:**
Neil Canton, Bob Gale,
Kathleen Kennedy, Frank Marshall,
Steven Spielberg/Amblin
Entertainment, Universal Pictures
**ACADEMY AWARD
NOMINATIONS (1986)**
Best Music, Original Song:
Chris Hayes (music), Johnny Colla
(music), Huey Lewis (lyrics), for the
song 'The Power of Love'
Best Sound:
Bill Varney, B. Tennyson Sebastian II,
Robert Thirlwell, William B. Kaplan
Best Writing, Screenplay Written
Directly for the Screen:
Robert Zemeckis, Bob Gale
ACADEMY AWARDS
Best Effects, Sound Effects Editing:
Charles L. Campbell,
Robert R. Rutledge

Teenager Marty McFly (Fox) inadvertently goes thirty years back in time and interrupts his mother and father's first meeting. To avoid fading out of existence he must convince his future parents that they're meant to be together.

A staple for anybody who grew up in the eighties, *Back to the Future*'s mix of sci-fi, comedy and action proved a huge hit, and turned its star into a household name.

Directed and co-written by Robert Zemeckis (*Forrest Gump*) and produced by Steven Spielberg, the film is a high point of the hugely successful cycle of glossy, high concept kids' movies that were so prolific in the mid 1980s - *Ghostbusters*, *Inner Space*, *Gremlins*, *The Goonies* etc. Like most of these, *Back to the Future*'s appeal lies partly in not talking down to its young audience, something which explains its longevity and popularity amongst adults. The immense charm Fox lends to lead character Marty is another success. His skateboarding, guitar-playing cool is tempered nicely by his confused manner and diminutive stature, making him the template non-threatening teen male for the rest of the decade. Avoiding his pushover father and alcoholic mother, Marty spends most of his time with girlfriend Jennifer (Wells) and eccentric Doc Brown, (the excellent Lloyd), who offers precisely the kind of wild-eyed mad inventor kids love, even though it's his mistake that acts as the catalyst for Marty's disastrous retreat into the past.

Brazil

In an officious future bureaucracy, a man is wrongly arrested and a browbeaten civil servant (Pryce) longs for a simple life with the woman from his dreams.

When director Terry Gilliam completed *Brazil*, an attack on oppressive and stifling authority, he presented it to his backers at Universal who promptly told him to chop half an hour and give it a happy ending. Bewildered by the irony of such an instruction, and with no intention of abiding by it, Gilliam went into battle. He took out adverts in trade papers, held secret screenings for U.S. critics (with a print smuggled back from Europe), and generally made an absolute nuisance of himself until Universal eventually relented.

But to call the film simply an attack on authority is an under-estimation. Gilliam's frustration with all aspects of western culture, politics and society are poured into this therapy session of a movie. Our obsession with vanity, (evident in the ridiculous fashions and omnipresent celebrity plastic surgeons), the petty-minded officials who won't turn off a tap without the correct forms, the over-engineered appliances that never work, the mountains of paper that (quite literally) swamp people – everything the director finds abhorrent is roundly mocked and satirized. Gilliam's success in creating this depressing society is nicely tempered by his equally successful comic creations. The likes of Jim Broadbent (a bizarre plastic surgeon) and Michael Palin (an oily civil servant) are on-hand, as is Robert De Niro, wonderful as Harry Buttle, a terrorist plumber who intercepts ignored maintenance requests and does the work himself – dressed in SAS fatigues and heavily armed. Orwell never created a better dystopian future, and he certainly wasn't this much fun!

GB, 1985
DIRECTOR:
Terry Gilliam
CAST INCLUDES:
Jonathan Pryce, Robert De Niro,
Katherine Helmond, Ian Holm,
Bob Hoskins, Michael Palin
SCREENPLAY:
Terry Gilliam, Tom Stoppard,
Charles McKeown
CINEMATOGRAPHY:
Roger Pratt
**PRODUCERS/
PRODUCTION COMPANIES:**
Patrick Cassavetti,
Arnon Milchan/Embassy International
Pictures, Universal Pictures
**ACADEMY AWARD
NOMINATIONS (1986)**
Best Art Direction-Set Decoration:
Norman Garwood, Maggie Gray
Best Writing, Screenplay Written
Directly for the Screen:
Terry Gilliam, Tom Stoppard,
Charles McKeown

GB, 1986
DIRECTOR:
James Cameron
CAST INCLUDES:
Sigourney Weaver, Carrie Henn,
Michael Biehn, Lance Henriksen,
Paul Reiser, Bill Paxton
SCREENPLAY:
James Cameron, David Giler,
Walter Hill
CINEMATOGRAPHY:
Adrian Biddle
PRODUCERS/
PRODUCTION COMPANIES:
Gordon Carroll, David Giler, Walter
Hill, Gale Anne Hurd/20th Century
Fox, Brandywine Productions Ltd
ACADEMY AWARD
NOMINATIONS (1987)
Best Actress in a Leading Role:
Sigourney Weaver
Best Art Direction-Set Decoration:
Peter Lamont, Crispian Sallis
Best Film Editing:
Ray Lovejoy
Best Music, Original Score:
James Horner
Best Sound:
Graham V. Hartstone,
Nicolas Le Messurier,
Michael A. Carter, Roy Charman
ACADEMY AWARDS
Best Effects, Sound Effects Editing:
Don Sharpe
Best Effects, Visual Effects:
Robert Skotak, Stan Winston,
John Richardson, Suzanne M. Benson

Aliens

Ripley (Weaver), the sole survivor of the previous film, returns to Earth after fifty seven years in the suspended animation chamber of an escape pod. She discovers the planet that played host to the alien's eggs has been colonized, and contact with the pioneering families there has been lost. The sinister 'company' convinces Ripley to return as advisor to a detachment of marines.

James Cameron cleverly changes direction for his sequel to Ridley Scott's 1979 masterpiece, *Alien*. Realizing there is no sense in attempting to recreate the subtleties and tension of the original, he opts for the gung-ho approach and floods the screen with heavily armed space marines and literally dozens of aliens. On paper it sounds worryingly like the classic sequel to a classic film (a faster, bigger disappointment), but Cameron pulls it off. Where Scott seemed to sit behind you in the cinema audience and carefully massage your neck while cracking the occasional muscle, Cameron hits you over the head with a club and steals your seat.

But that's not to say *Aliens* is dumb. Picking up on its predecessor's theme of motherhood, we are introduced to an orphaned girl, Newt (Henn) with whom Ripley forms an immediate bond (she lost a daughter on her journey back to Earth), and also the alien queen, allowing for a fantastic confrontation between two matriarchal figures.

Ripley emerges as an even more densely layered character this time around. Tenacious, resourceful and sympathetic, Weaver plays the part with a mesmerizing conviction that helps establish Ripley as the genre's greatest female character.

The Fly

Seth Brundle (Goldblum), an eccentric scientist experimenting in the field of matter transportation, is amalgamated with a house fly at the genetic level. At first unaware, he gradually mutates into a deranged beast.

Differing dramatically from the 1958 original, Cronenberg's version of *The Fly* is a gruesome meditation on disease and deformity, both subjects with which his obsession was established in earlier films such as *Rabid*, *Shivers* and *Scanners*. But *The Fly* is more accessible than his previous work, which may go some way to explaining its crossover success, becoming a box office hit and ubiquitous presence in the video collections of eighties teenagers.

Goldblum is perfectly cast as the brilliant but doomed young scientist. Already an expert in idiosyncratic mannerisms and intonation, here he displays a surprisingly touching chemistry with Davis (in the role of Veronica Quaife, a journalist with whom Brundle starts a relationship), though this may be a result of their off-screen attraction. The repugnant development of the fly itself is the most memorable aspect of the film. Subtly manifesting at first through strangely stubborn hairs, Brundle's body eventually collapses as the mutation spreads through his genes. Teeth, fingers and other appendages detach, while skin and scalp peel away in the most revolting way imaginable. Cronenberg clearly relishes the excuse (and budget) to be as repugnant as possible, turning in one of his best films, and one of the best horror/sci-fi crossovers to date.

USA, 1986
DIRECTOR:
David Cronenberg
CAST INCLUDES:
Jeff Goldblum, Geena Davis,
John Getz, Joy Boushel
SCREENPLAY:
David Cronenberg,
Charles Edward Pogue (based on
George Langelaan's story)
CINEMATOGRAPHY:
Mark Irwin
**PRODUCERS/
PRODUCTION COMPANIES:**
Marc Boyman, Stuart Cornfeld, Kip
Ohman/Brooksfilms
ACADEMY AWARDS (1987)
Best Makeup:
Chris Walas, Stephan Dupuis

RoboCop

USA, 1987
DIRECTOR:
Paul Verhoeven
CAST INCLUDES:
Peter Weller, Nancy Allen,
Dan O'Herlihy, Ronny Cox,
Kurtwood Smith
SCREENPLAY:
Michael Miner, Edward Neumeier
CINEMATOGRAPHY:
Sol Negrin, Jost Vacano
**PRODUCERS/
PRODUCTION COMPANIES:**
Jon Davison, Stephen Lim,
Edward Neumeier, Arne Schmidt,
Phil Tippett/Orion Pictures
Corporation
**ACADEMY AWARD
NOMINATIONS (1988)**
Best Film Editing:
Frank J. Urioste
Best Sound:
Michael J. Kohut, Carlos DeLarios,
Aaron Rochin, Robert Wald
ACADEMY AWARDS
Special Achievement Award for
Sound Effects Editing:
Stephen Hunter Flick, John Pospisil

In the near future, Detroit is gripped by a crime wave. OCP (a giant corporation now in charge of policing the city) initiates its RoboCop program, a radical new law enforcement concept that will make a cyborg supercop of deceased police officer Alex Murphy (Weller).

Paul Verhoeven's visceral, violent and excellent movie is truly a product of its time. It takes a shot at almost anything that moved in the Reagan 1980s; corporate business practice, a cynical media, vicious yuppies and law enforcement that verges on fascism. The Dutch director's image of America, as an outsider, allows for a more objective view, and with such an uncompromising visual and thematic style, it's no wonder *RoboCop* comes across as such an aggressive film. Verhoeven's insistence on showing the effect of each bullet makes for a pretty graphic and extreme experience. Probing satire is eschewed in favour of the sledgehammer approach the director made his own in subsequent films like *Total Recall* and *Starship Troopers*. In fact, the satire is so extreme it enters the realm of black comedy (the outcome of a hostage negotiation might depend on which brand of stereo the getaway car features, hospital adverts boast of the new 'Yamaha hearts').

RoboCop has been described as, 'fascism for liberals,' a natural extension of the Reaganomics that inspire it. RoboCop is just as much a child of the era as the criminals he pursues, or the sinister corporation that created him. Don't write this one off as an exploitation flick, it's just too good.

Batman

A millionaire who, as a child, witnessed his parents' brutal slaying, turns his resources against the criminals of Gotham City, and in particular a sociopathic killer called The Joker.

Tim Burton's *Batman* is the first big screen treatment to translate the comic's dark style and complicated hero intact, thankfully abstaining from the gaudy, camp approach of the television show (and later, the dire third and fourth films in the series). Keaton is brilliant in the title role, emotionally and physically convincing; his casting was originally controversial amongst fans but he remains the strongest Batman filmed so far. Yet it's Nicholson's Joker that (perhaps unsurprisingly) steals the show. He struts outrageously through the part like a cross between Mick Jagger and his own Jack Torrence, turning in the most gleefully over-the-top performance of his career.

The symbiotic relationship of the two characters, both suffering issues of duality in their personalities, lends the film great emotional depth. Bruce Wayne is compelled to do what he does even though it gives him little satisfaction. Likewise, The Joker is driven by his madness and desire for vengeance. Such complicated characters had never before been seen in a comic book adaptation (which at the time were usually relegated to serials or television). We can thank – or curse – *Batman*'s huge success for the wave of comic book movies that have dominated the summer blockbuster season for the last fifteen years. *Batman* was, and still is, their template.

USA, 1989
DIRECTOR:
Tim Burton
CAST INCLUDES:
Michael Keaton, Jack Nicholson, Kim Basinger, Robert Wuhl, Pat Hingle
SCREENPLAY:
Bob Kane (Batman characters), Sam Hamm, Warren Skaaren
CINEMATOGRAPHY:
Roger Pratt
PRODUCERS/ PRODUCTION COMPANIES:
Peter Guber, Barbara Kalish, Chris Kenny, Benjamin Melniker, Jon Peters, Michael E. Uslan/Guber-Peters Company, PolyGram Filmed Entertainment, Warner Bros.
ACADEMY AWARDS (1989)
Best Art Direction-Set Decoration: Anton Furst, Peter Young

Total Recall

In the future, Douglas Quaid (Schwarzenegger) is a construction worker who dreams of visiting Mars. When he decides to have a holiday implanted directly into his brain by a specialist company, a whole host of memories start to resurface and he must follow a series of clues while evading various attempts on his life.

Familiar territory for author Philip K. Dick,

USA, 1990
DIRECTOR:
Paul Verhoeven
CAST INCLUDES:
Arnold Schwarzenegger, Rachel Ticotin, Sharon Stone, Ronny Cox, Michael Ironside
SCREENPLAY:
Philip K. Dick (short story), Ronald Shusett, Dan O'Bannon, Jon Povill, Gary Goldman
CINEMATOGRAPHY:
Jost Vacano
PRODUCERS/ PRODUCTION COMPANIES:
Buzz Feitshans, Robert Fentress, Mario Kassar, Elliot Schick, Ronald Shusett, Andrew G. Vajna/Carolco International N.V., Carolco Pictures Inc., TriStar Pictures
ACADEMY AWARD NOMINATIONS (1991)
Best Effects, Sound Effects Editing: Stephen Hunter Flick
Best Sound:
Nelson Stoll, Michael J. Kohut, Carlos DeLarios, Aaron Rochin
ACADEMY AWARDS
Special Achievement Award (for Visual Effects):
Eric Brevig, Rob Bottin, Tim McGovern, Alex Funke

(confused realities, ambiguous personalities, flawed technology), and director Verhoeven, (twisty plot, fascist society), *Total Recall* is a successful combination of the two men's talents, just as much intelligent mystery thriller as it is crowd pleasing blockbuster.

Providing Schwarzenegger with one of the best and most demanding roles he's ever had, requiring a performance ranging in emotion and character due to Quaid's multiple personality, is a pretty risky move. He pulls it off just fine, but this being a Verhoeven movie, everything is painted with huge, fat brush strokes and subtle performances don't feature on the palette. In fact, subtlety has been dispensed with in all areas, allowing for a refreshingly simple and honest movie within a genre that has produced more than its fair share of pretentious films. At one point, cartoonish arch villain Cohaagen actually says, 'I'll blow this place up and be home in time for corn flakes!' You don't get one-liners like that in *Alien*.

To be fair, it's not exactly a dumb movie. The plot requires some concentration and Verhoeven does spoon in some political opinion, but, as with his other work, (most notably *RoboCop* and *Starship Troopers*) there is no need to pay attention to his ham-fisted explorations of fascism and authority when there are such big explosions on offer.

Naked Lunch

After accidentally killing his wife, drug addict William Lee (Weller) goes to the strange and hallucinatory Interzone. Once there, he writes reports for the insects who provide him with an array of bizarre drugs.

Cronenberg's adaptation of the classic William S. Burroughs novel may be even less coherent than its famously unintelligible source. Ditching much of the material in the book and incorporating elements from Burroughs' own life (and other stories), Lee is developed into a still more obvious pseudonym for the author. Cronenberg is even brave enough to make Burroughs' accidental shooting of his wife, whilst drunkenly performing a William Tell routine, a major narrative device. Not that the film is seemingly big on conventional narrative. The surreal story is difficult to follow at first, blending reality, hallucinations and literature, then revelling in the mind-twisting freedom this approach provides. Interzone (actually supposed to be Tangiers) is home to duplicitous secret agent bugs, that double as typewriters, paranoid monsters, physics defying metallurgists and the, mainly homosexual, hedonistic authors whose insane writings appear to be the cause of it all. Lee's brief moments of clarity find him back in his own 1950s America, apparently in the middle of writing a novel. His heroic narcotic intake seems to cause him to hallucinate the story right onto the page, where he then finds himself living out an imaginary and horrifying new life.

Naked Lunch is an incredibly impressive and original film, and one that makes no compromises to the viewer over its ambiguous meaning. It is amongst the most imaginative works of modern cinema.

CANADA, GB, JAPAN, 1991
DIRECTOR:
David Cronenberg
CAST INCLUDES:
Peter Weller, Judy Davis, Ian Holm, Julian Sands, Roy Scheider
SCREENPLAY:
David Cronenberg from the novel by William S. Burroughs
CINEMATOGRAPHY:
Peter Suschitzky
PRODUCERS/PRODUCTION COMPANIES:
Gabriella Martinelli, Jeremy Thomas/Film Trustees Ltd., Naked Lunch Productions, Nippon Film Development and Finance, Inc., Recorded Picture Company (RPC), The Ontario Film Development Corporation, Téléfilm Canada

Jurassic Park

USA, 1993
DIRECTOR:
Steven Spielberg
CAST INCLUDES:
Sam Neill, Laura Dern, Jeff Goldblum,
Richard Attenborough
SCREENPLAY:
Michael Crichton, David Koepp
CINEMATOGRAPHY:
Dean Cundey
**PRODUCERS/
PRODUCTION COMPANIES:**
Kathleen Kennedy, Gerald R. Molen,
Lata Ryan, Colin Wilson/Universal
Pictures, Amblin Entertainment
ACADEMY AWARDS (1994)
Best Effects, Sound Effects Editing:
Gary Rydstrom, Richard Hymns
Best Effects, Visual Effects:
Dennis Muren, Stan Winston,
Phil Tippett, Michael Lantieri
Best Sound:
Gary Summers, Gary Rydstrom,
Shawn Murphy, Ron Judkins

On a remote tropical island, an eccentric billionaire has built a safari park populated by genetically recreated dinosaurs. Not yet open for business, he invites palaeontologists, Alan Grant (Neill) and Ellie Sattler (Dern), chaos theorist Ian Malcolm (Goldblum) and his grandchildren for a sneak preview. Unsurprisingly, things don't go smoothly.

'An adventure 65 million years in the making'. *Jurassic Park*'s tagline could refer to time spent developing technology for the monstrous hit that finally showed what CGI can do. Directed by Steven Spielberg and starring... well, dinosaurs; make no mistake, even if the story didn't work so well and the cast wasn't so good, it wouldn't have made any difference in 1993. After nearly a century of cartoons, miniatures, stop-motion, and men in suits, photo-real dinosaurs had hit the screens.

Time has been surprisingly kind to *Jurassic Park*. The

proliferation of CG technology in modern cinema means the dinosaurs don't have quite the same impact, but considering their age they stand up admirably to contemporary computer creations. The real revelation on re-watching the film is the quality of everything else that, at the time, was overshadowed by the huge monsters. Spielberg is on such familiar ground here that he relaxes a little, allowing his core cast a free run. Loopy dino-keeper John Hammond (Attenborough) is clearly just there for the fun of it all, his enjoyment being infectious, while Goldblum's turn as a quirky mathematician is brilliantly entertaining. But the real fun is set to one side for the T. Rex and velociraptor scenes in which Spielberg expertly jacks up the tension, and gore. There may not be any new attractions, but *Jurassic Park* is worth revisiting for those that were missed on the first trip.

Twelve Monkeys

By 2035 only one per cent of the population is still alive, the rest having been wiped out by an unknown virus. Convict James Cole (Willis) is sent back in time on a mission to discover the origins of the virus.

The most commercial film of Gilliam's career provides the auteur with a rare box office hit that manages to retain a characteristic visual flair and offbeat narrative structure. The film sees both male leads grappling with madness. Cole's sanity is in question from the start. When he is selected for the mission it is unclear whether he is deemed insane by the authorities who have incarcerated him. He starts to wonder himself when locked up in a present day asylum with 'crazy as a loon' Jeffrey Goines (Pitt). Gilliam enjoys keeping the state of both men's mental health ambiguous, twisting and turning the plot and time-line in order to confuse the viewer, even throwing in the odd red herring. Willis excels in one of the most layered and intelligent performances of his career, once again proving how good he can be when well cast by a competent director (*Pulp Fiction*, *The Sixth Sense*). He holds the film together but has the odd scene stolen by Pitt, clearly relishing the freedom inherent in the portrayal of a lunatic.

As original and interesting as his best work, *Twelve Monkeys* is a great 'entry level' Gilliam movie for those who are yet to be converted. More polished than *Brazil*, more coherent than *The Adventures of Baron Munchausen* and more mature than *Time Bandits*, it is an inventive and demanding addition to the Gilliam repertoire.

USA, 1995
DIRECTOR:
Terry Gilliam
CAST INCLUDES:
Bruce Willis, Madeleine Stowe, Brad Pitt, Christopher Plummer
SCREENPLAY:
Chris Marker (film *La Jetee*), David Webb Peoples, Janet Peoples
CINEMATOGRAPHY:
Roger Pratt
PRODUCERS/ PRODUCTION COMPANIES:
Robert Cavallo, Mark Egerton, Robert Kosberg, Gary Levinsohn, Lloyd Phillips, Charles Roven, Kelley Smith-Wait/Atlas Entertainment, Classico, Universal Pictures
ACADEMY AWARD NOMINATIONS (1996)
Best Actor in a Supporting Role: Brad Pitt
Best Costume Design: Julie Weiss

Independence Day

USA ,1996
DIRECTOR:
Roland Emmerich
CAST INCLUDES:
Bill Pullman, Jeff Goldblum,
Will Smith, Bill Pullman, Mary
McDonnall, Judd Hirsch, Brent Spiner
SCREENPLAY:
Dean Devlin, Roland Emmerich
CINEMATOGRAPHY:
Karl Walter Lindenlaub
PRODUCERS/
PRODUCTION COMPANIES:
Dean Devlin, Roland Emmerich,
Ute Emmerich, William Fay,
Peter Winther/20th Century Fox,
Centropolis Entertainment [us]
ACADEMY AWARD
NOMINATIONS (1997)
Best Sound:
Chris Carpenter, Bill W. Benton,
Bob Beemer, Jeff Wexler
ACADEMY AWARDS
Best Effects, Visual Effects:
Volker Engel, Douglas Smith,
Clay Pinney, Joe Viskocil

Huge alien spaceships take up position above Earth's major cities, causing panic and confusion. After a period of silence it becomes clear that they intend to invade.

Surfing a huge sci-fi tidal wave kicked up by the television tsunami that was *The X-Files*, *Independence Day* took great advantage of slick new visual effects and hoary old science fiction themes to become one of the biggest grossing films in history. Sticking surprisingly closely to H.G. Wells' *War of the Worlds*, (updating mankind's saviour from cold virus to computer virus – you know, for the kids), co-writer/director Roland Emmerich crafts a good old-fashioned Cold War paranoia movie, with added bells and whistles.

Choosing an ensemble cast rather than using a straightforward hero figure is a nice idea, allowing for a balance of serious and comedic characters that helps lighten the film

without losing the dramatic impact. It may be using some 1950s sci-fi tricks but, as Emmerich successfully demonstrates, a 1990s audience is very different. So President Whitmore (Pullman) does the frowning while computer expert David Levinson (Goldblum) gets to lark about with Air Force pilot Steve Hiller (Smith). There are also excellent cameos from Judd Hirsch and Brent Spiner. The cast come second to the effects, though. Finally able to destroy international landmarks convincingly, Emmerich sets out to make up for all those poorly shot miniatures that tumbled into Big Ben and the Eiffel Tower in the 1950s, one of the film's best moments is the very impressive obliteration of the White House.

The plot may be full of holes, some of the dialogue might make your ears bleed, and the President's 'rousing' speech is sure to offend anyone brighter than a glass of water. But there is plenty of quality on show here, and the sheer spectacle and fun on offer makes *Independence Day* worth 145 minutes of anybody's life.

Men in Black

A wisecracking New York cop (Smith) is recruited to a secret agency responsible for keeping Earth's numerous extra-terrestrial citizens in check. Partnered with a grouchy old-timer (Jones) together they must prevent an interplanetary diplomatic incident that could end the world.

The tagline, 'Protecting the earth from the scum of the universe', is a good indication of the simple, honest and unpretentious fun to be had with *Men in Black*. Not taking things too seriously, Sonnenfeld relishes the creative opportunity handed him by Lowell Cunningham's comic, filling the film's concise ninety minutes with quality gags, imaginative aliens and brilliantly conceived action scenarios.

The teaming of Smith and Jones is an inspired piece of casting, their enjoyable chemistry lying at the heart of the film's appeal. Smith (who is given the moniker 'J') is repeatedly shocked, befuddled and rattled by his encounters with the bizarre alien communities that apparently exist right under our noses, while the deadpan Jones, or 'K', expresses a laconic lack of interest in them. Together they are set against a powerful alien Bug inhabiting the (decomposing) body of a farmer, D'Onofrio. Here Sonnenfeld's comedy gift is evident again, drawing a superb comic performance from D'Onofrio. Every creative and technical role on the film is carried out with the utmost professionalism, each contributor working in perfect harmony to create a super-slick, top-notch family movie.

USA 1997
DIRECTOR:
Barry Sonnenfeld
CAST INCLUDES:
Tommy Lee Jones, Will Smith,
Linda Fiorentino, Vincent D'Onofrio,
Rip Torn
SCREENPLAY:
Ed Solomon from the comic by
Lowell Cunningham
CINEMATOGRAPHY:
Donald Peterman
PRODUCERS/
PRODUCTION COMPANIES:
Laurie MacDonald, Steven R. Molen,
Walter F. Parkes, Graham Place,
Steven Spielberg/Amblin
Entertainment, Columbia Pictures
Corporation, MacDonald/Parkes
Productions Anderson
ACADEMY AWARD
NOMINATIONS (1998)
Best Art Direction-Set Decoration:
Bo Welch (art director), Cheryl
Carasik (set decorator)
Best Music, Original Musical or
Comedy Score:
Danny Elfman
ACADEMY AWARDS
Best Makeup:
Rick Baker, David LeRoy

The Matrix

A computer hacker, Anderson (Reeves), discovers mankind is actually held captive by alien machines who feed us an artificial, computer created perception of reality while draining the electrical current produced by our brains.

Some of the pseudo-religous concepts and philosophy contained within *The Matrix* may seem slightly misjudged, the excessive product placement is a valid gripe and the dreadful sequels have undoubtedly tainted the film's reputation – but none of that matters. In *The Matrix*, writer-director brothers Larry and Andy Wachowski created the most original and exciting action movie since *The Terminator*.

Setting the film in a world where the rules of physics can be bent, or even broken, allows not only for spectacular visual effects, (most obviously the much lauded 'bullet-time' which allows the camera to move around an object in three dimensions – and slow motion), but imaginative, computer game-like scenarios impossible in any normal environment. The highlight for any true action fan isn't the revolutionary photographic technique, but the moment Neo (Anderson's alter-ego) requests quite simply, 'Guns, lots of guns', allowing him and Trinity (Moss) to march into the reception hall of the machines' HQ and start one of the most excessive and balletic gunfights in modern film.

While the plot doesn't quite stand up to close scrutiny, (can each human mind really generate enough electricity to run the huge human storage halls and growing fields as well as the matrix itself, while leaving enough over to be worth harvesting?), the film is at least stretching its legs on the huge running track of possibility afforded by its flawed concept.

USA, 1999
DIRECTORS:
Andy Wachowski, Larry Wachowski
CAST INCLUDES:
Keanu Reeves, Laurence Fishburne,
Carrie-Anne Moss, Hugo Weaving
SCREENPLAY:
Andy Wachowski, Larry Wachowski
CINEMATOGRAPHY:
Bill Pope
PRODUCERS/
PRODUCTION COMPANIES:
Bruce Berman, Dan Cracchiolo,
Carol Hughes, Andrew Mason,
Richard Mirisch, Barrie M. Osborne,
Joel Silver, Erwin Stoff,
Andy Wachowski,
Larry Wachowski/Groucho II Film
Partnership, Silver Pictures, Village
Roadshow Pictures
ACADEMY AWARDS (2000)
Best Editing:
Zach Staenberg
Best Effects, Sound Effects Editing:
Dane A. Davis
Best Effects, Visual Effects:
John Gaeta, Janek Sirrs,
Steve Courtley, Jon Thum
Best Sound:
John T. Reitz, Gregg Rudloff,
David E. Campbell, David Lee

X-Men

In the near future, evolution has taken a massive step forward, creating tension between mutants and the world's normal citizens. Favouring integration between the two societies, Professor Charles Xavier (Stewart) and his followers must defend mankind from a band of more aggressive mutants.

Bryan Singer's stylish comic-book adaptation is one of the most interesting and intelligent so far filmed. Though *Superman* successfully upped the ante by introducing a more developed and less camp tone

than previous screen superheroes, it was arguably the troubled and ambiguous dual personality of Tim Burton's *Batman* that first applied 'serious' themes to the formula. With *X-Men*, the idea is expanded still further.

The prevalent theme throughout the film is prejudice. Singer successfully taps into the potential of the comic's premise. Fear and distrust between the public and the mutants is expertly whipped up by self-serving politicians, in a manner reminiscent of 1950s anti-Communist McCarthyism. This is a nice reference to (and indictment of) one of sci-fi's founding principles.

No matter how talented the filmmakers, it's very difficult to pull off serious concepts in a movie with characters named Cyclops, Wolverine and Sabretooth. Singer's determination to cast the best actors possible is the film's master stroke. The likes of Ian McKellen and Patrick Stewart lend an authoritative presence, whilst from the younger generation, Famke Janssen and Hugh Jackman are particularly impressive.

X-Men is the most satisfying superhero movie since *Batman*, and like *Batman*, the sequel's up to scratch, too.

USA, 2000
DIRECTOR:
Bryan Singer
CAST INCLUDES:
Hugh Jackman, Patrick Stewart,
Ian McKellen, Famke Janssen,
James Marsden
SCREENPLAY:
Tom DeSanto, Bryan Singer,
David Hayter
CINEMATOGRAPHY:
Newton Thomas Sigel
PRODUCERS/PRODUCTION COMPANIES:
Avi Arad, Tom DeSanto,
Richard Donner, Matthew Edelman,
Kevin Feige, Stan Lee, Scott Nimerfro,
Lauren Shuler Donner, Joel Simon,
Bill Todman Jr., Ralph Winter/20th
Century Fox, Bad Hat Harry
Productions, Donner/Shuler-Donner
Productions, Genetics Productions,
Marvel Enterprises, Springwood
Productions

A.I. Artificial Intelligence

USA, 2001
DIRECTOR:
Steven Spielberg
CAST INCLUDES:
Haley Joel Osment, Jude Law,
Frances O'Connor, Brendan Gleeson,
Sam Robards, William Hurt
SCREENPLAY:
Ian Watson, Steven Spielberg,
Brian Aldiss (short story)
CINEMATOGRAPHY:
Janusz Kaminski
PRODUCERS/
PRODUCTION COMPANIES:
Jan Harlan, Kathleen Kennedy,
Walter F. Parkes,
Steven Spielberg/Warner Bros.,
DreamWorks SKG, Amblin
Entertainment, Stanley Kubrick
Productions
ACADEMY AWARD
NOMINATIONS (2002)
Best Effects, Visual Effects:
Dennis Muren, Scott Farrar,
Stan Winston, Michael Lantieri
Best Music, Original Score:
John Williams

In a future where lifelike robots are commonplace, a married couple, whose young son is in a coma, take delivery of David (Osment), the first of a new generation of robot children capable of real emotions. When David's love for his foster mother is not reciprocated, he is compelled to make a dangerous journey in search of The Blue Fairy, whom he believes can make him human.

Based loosely on a short story by Brian Aldiss (*Supertoys Last All Summer Long*) the film was originally conceived by Stanley Kubrick, but fearing he lacked the sentimentality required to direct the film, he offered to produce for his friend Steven Spielberg. Sadly Kubrick died before the unprecedented collaboration of two such titans could take place, though he does receive a joint production credit and his fingerprints are clearly visible throughout the film – particularly in the production design, which is, in many places, based on Kubrick's original concept art.

The biggest stumbling block was how to render their lead character, a boy of eleven, convincingly. Believing it impossible for any child to have the necessary skills for the demanding role of David, CGI, robots and even midgets were considered as a substitute in the early days of planning. But when *The Sixth Sense* exposed Haley Joel Osment's talents he was cast, much to the benefit of the film. His performance is hugely impressive and the chemistry between him and Jude Law (portraying Gigolo Joe, a fugitive android who becomes David's guide) allows for a genuinely touching relationship that, in a way, is the real heart of the film.

Harry Potter and the Philosopher's Stone

Harry Potter (Radcliffe) is an orphaned eleven-year-old boy living with his neglectful aunt and uncle. However, life soon takes an unexpected turn for Harry as he discovers he is a wizard and, much to his delight, is sent away to Hogwarts School of Witchcraft and Wizardry. Once there, he and his newfound friends must battle an evil wizard to prevent him from stealing the titular gem, capable of providing immortality.

It was inevitable that the immense success of J.K. Rowling's books would bring Hollywood calling. Warner Brothers picked up the rights, predictably calling on Steven Spielberg to direct, they were turned down – 'It would be like shooting fish in a barrel'. Terry Gilliam was considered, but apparently uneasy about the direction he would take, Warner Brothers turned to the safe pair of hands of Chris Columbus (*Home Alone*, *Mrs Doubtfire*) to launch the franchise. After nailing the biggest opening weekend in history, and eventually grossing more than any movie except *Titanic*, it's likely the Warner executives gave themselves a pat on the back for their decision.

Although unlikely to convert critics of the book, the first *Harry Potter* film is a lovingly produced feast for the eyes and ears. The production design of Stuart Craig and photography of John Seale are simply stunning, while John Williams (*Star Wars*, *Jaws*) turns in his best score since the *Indiana Jones* films, capturing the spirit of the subject with a majestic, full-bodied central theme tune. Harry and his friends Ron (Grint) and Hermione (Watson) are all adequate in their roles, but the assorted adult witches and wizards draw on an awesome pool of British acting talent. Most successful are the ambiguous Snape (Rickman) and school groundskeeper Hagrid (Coltrane).

This film is essential viewing for more than just the kids and converted – any film fan should appreciate one of the greatest assortments of talent ever assembled.

USA, 2001
DIRECTOR:
Chris Columbus
CAST:
Richard Harris,
Robbie Coltrane, Daniel Radcliffe,
Emma Watson, Rupert Grint,
Alan Rickman
SCREENPLAY:
Steven Kloves from the novel by
J.K. Rowling
CINEMATOGRAPHY:
John Seale
**PRODUCERS/
PRODUCTION COMPANIES:**
Todd Arnow, Michael Barnathan,
Chris Columbus,
Paula DuPré Pesman,
Duncan Henderson,
David Heyman, Mark Radcliffe,
Tanya Seghatchian/Warner Bros.
**ACADEMY AWARD
NOMINATIONS (2002)**
Best Art Direction-Set Decoration:
Stuart Craig (art director),
Stephanie McMillan (set decorator)
Best Costume Design:
Judianna Makovsky
Best Music, Original Score:
John Williams

Minority Report

In 2054, homicide is a thing of the past in Washington D.C. thanks to the Precrime Initiative, a scheme which uses psychics to identify murderers in advance of the crime. When the police officer in charge (Cruise) is implicated in the killing of a man he has never met, he must go on the run in order to piece together the puzzle.

Dealing with issues of paranoia, the removal of personal liberty and even creeping totalitarianism, Spielberg has made a dazzling, tense thriller of Philip K. Dick's short story. Cruise is well cast as Detective John Anderton, secretly addicted to drugs and emotionally broken after the disappearance of his son and collapse of his marriage. In public he is a confident and successful 'supercop,' the protegé of Precrime architect Lamar Burgess (von Sydow), they both have complete faith in the apparently infallible system. That faith is not shared by the ambiguous Detective Danny Witwer (Farrell), brought in to assess Precrime's viability for expansion, but inevitably spearheading the search for Anderton once he goes on the lam.

Like previous Dick adaptations *Blade Runner* and *Total Recall*, *Minority Report* boasts an impressive visual style. The washed out, de-saturated colours lend a classic film noir feel to the gorgeous production design, which is then shot with a graceful, flowing style by Kaminski.

While administering healthy doses of action and pathos to the 'intellectual thriller' premise, Spielberg doesn't overlook the light-hearted moments so necessary in a film with such a dark tone. A scene in which Cruise is pursued along a factory production line has a wonderful comedy payoff; becoming trapped as components are added to a car under construction, he is eventually able to drive his completed prison right out of the factory and to safety.

USA, 2002
DIRECTOR:
Steven Spielberg
CAST INCLUDES:
Tom Cruise, Colin Farrell, Steve Harris, Max von Sydow, Samantha Morton
SCREENPLAY:
Scott Frank, Jon Cohen from the short story by Philip K. Dick
CINEMATOGRAPHY:
Janusz Kaminski
PRODUCERS/ PRODUCTION COMPANIES:
Jan de Bont, Bonnie Curtis, Michael Doven, Gary Goldman, Sergio Mimica-Gezzan, Gerald R. Molen, Walter F. Parkes, Ronald Shusett/20th Century Fox , DreamWorks SKG, Amblin Entertainment, Blue Tulip
ACADEMY AWARD NOMINATIONS (2003)
Best Sound Editing:
Richard Hymns, Gary Rydstrom

Spider-Man

Troubled student Peter Parker (Maguire) is bitten by a spider and takes on some of the arachnid's characteristics. Deciding to use his new powers for good, he becomes a web-slinging, wall-walking superhero.

The last major comic book character to evade big screen treatment, a potential Spider-Man man movie was the subject of speculation and rumour for two decades before Sam Raimi (the *Evil Dead* trilogy) brought him to the cinema, raking in a massive $821 million in the process.

The enormous financial success of *Spider-Man* is largely due to Raimi cleverly retaining enough of the comic's themes and style to satisfy its established fanbase, while coating the whole thing in box office gloss to attract the multiplex crowd. But now the dust has settled, does all this mean the film's any good? Maguire is certainly impressive in the lead, believable as both nerdy schoolboy Parker and the eponymous hero. The rest of the cast are all spot-on, particularly Dunst, as love interest Mary Jane Watson, and Willem Dafoe as Spidey's schizophrenic nemesis, The Green Goblin, a scientist sent mad after using himself as guinea-pig in a military experiment. Raimi keeps things light and swift, achieving unusual emotional diversity and depth for a blockbuster, and the technical aspects are all up to scratch, too. In truth there isn't really anything to satisfy the critics who lined up ready to find fault with what looked like being another shoddy comic adaptation. The character development (usually the bane of these films) is probably the greatest success of all. Maguire's orphaned but optimistic Peter Parker is immensely likable, his vulnerability exposed in a tentative romance with 'M.J.' that's surprisingly touching. The relationship with his Aunt and Uncle also packs a powerful emotional punch, particularly when they both become victims.

USA, 2002
DIRECTOR:
Sam Raimi
CAST INCLUDES:
Tobey Maguire, Willem Dafoe, Kirsten Dunst, James Franco, Cliff Robertson, Rosemary Harris
SCREENPLAY:
David Koepp from the comic book by Stan Lee and Steve Ditko
CINEMATOGRAPHY:
Don Burgess
PRODUCERS/ PRODUCTION COMPANIES:
Avi Arad, Ian Bryce, Grant Curtis, Heidi Fugeman, Stan Lee, Steven P. Saeta, Laura Ziskin/Columbia Pictures Corporation, Marvel Enterprises, Laura Ziskin Productions
ACADEMY AWARD NOMINATIONS (2003)
Best Sound:
Kevin O'Connell, Greg P. Russell, Ed Novick
Best Visual Effects:
John Dykstra, Scott Stokdyk, Anthony LaMolinara, John Frazier

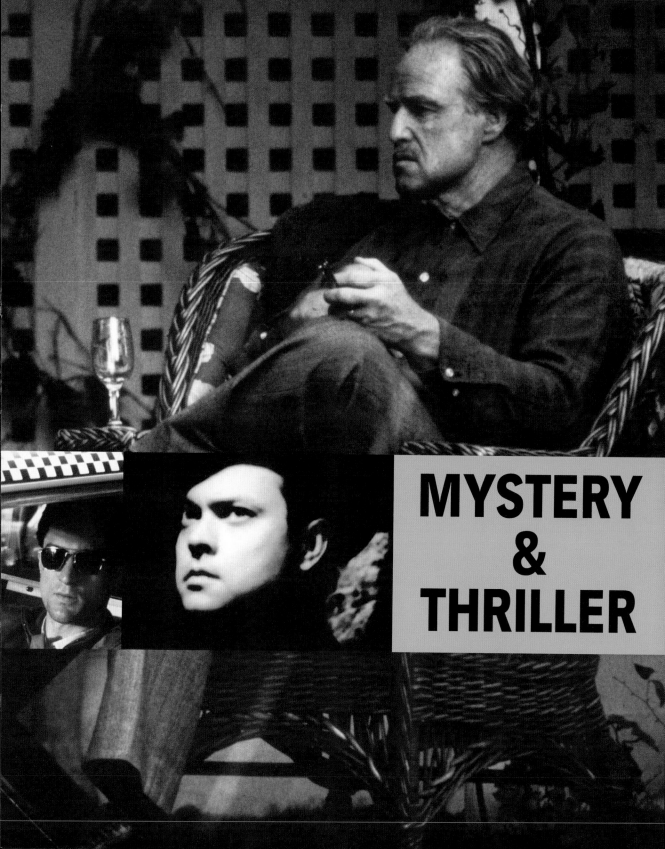

MYSTERY & THRILLER

Little Caesar

USA, 1931
DIRECTOR:
Mervyn LeRoy
CAST INCLUDES:
Edward G. Robinson,
Douglas Fairbanks Jr., Glenda Farrell,
William Collier Jr., Sidney Blackmer
SCREENPLAY:
W.R. Burnett (novel),
Francis Edward Faragoh,
Robert N. Lee
CINEMATOGRAPHY:
Tony Gaudio
PRODUCERS/
PRODUCTION COMPANIES:
Hal B. Wallis/
First National Pictures Inc
ACADEMY AWARD
NOMINATIONS (1931)
Best Writing, Adaptation:
Francis Edward Faragoh,
Robert N. Lee

Little Caesar, often called the grandfather of the gangster movie, was produced at the beginning of the sound era and while in some areas it shows its age it is still an efficient and well-paced thriller. The film charts the rise of Rico (Robinson) from small-time crook up through the gangster hierarchy. His naked ambition and brutality enable him to supplant one crime boss after another, but he seems insatiable in his quest for power and the dubious respect of the demi-monde.

Robinson is convincing as the rising gangster boss with no humanity, only ruthless determination to climb to the top of the tree, no matter who he has to kill on the way. With his 'ugly mug', Robinson was an unlikely screen star, but in this film he found his forté as the short hood looking for respect and he gives an expressive and entertaining performance.

Technically *Little Caesar* is quite basic by modern standards but the fast moving pace and gritty subject matter was new to audiences of the time. So much so that it effectively launched the gangster genre, even without the explicit violence and colourful slang that would later become such vital components. Despite the lack of on-screen violence there is no doubting how dangerous and amoral Rico actually is. This seminal mob flick is a must for all fans of the gangster movies, and if vintage flicks aren't normally your thing, it's worth watching just to see where all those clichés started.

The Public Enemy

The public enemy of the title is Tom Powers (Cagney) and the film charts his rise from shoplifting street urchin to ruthless, bootlegging gangster boss. Similar in many respects to *Little Caeser* which was released in the same year, *The Public Enemy* differs in that it is more concerned with exploring the social environment that creates criminals. The film begins with Tom and Matt (Woods) as children working for the Fagin like character, Putty-Nose (Kinnel) who teaches them to steal, and as they get older, gives them their first guns. The relationship sours when, after a robbery goes wrong, Putty-Nose lies low rather than providing the promised support for the pair.

Based on the real-life mobster Earl Weiss, it is the context of the film which makes it important. One of the first 'talkies', the gritty, violent themes were particularly suited to the depression era; spoken dialogue and sound brought the gangster flick to life. The Production Code was not yet in force and the opening of the film included a disclaimer from the studio that it was not trying to glamorize violence and criminal activity. Indeed the Code was brought in as a direct response to films such as *The Public Enemy*.

However, despite the disclaimer, violent it is. Cagney swaggers, spits and shoots and in the process creates a legend. The most famous scene is when Tom rubs half a grapefruit into the face of his moll, but for the most part the violence is off-camera and the wonderful direction makes this more effective than many of its latter day, more graphic equivalents.

USA, 1931
DIRECTOR:
William A. Wellman
CAST INCLUDES:
James Cagney, Edward Woods,
Jean Harlow, Joan Blondell,
Beryl Mercer
SCREENPLAY:
Harvey F. Thew from the story by
Kubec Glasmon and John Bright
CINEMATOGRAPHY:
Devereaux Jennings
**PRODUCERS/
PRODUCTION COMPANIES:**
Darryl F. Zanuck/ Warner Bros
**ACADEMY AWARD
NOMINATIONS (1931)**
Best Writing, Original Story:
John Bright, Kubec Glasmon

Rebecca

USA, 1940
DIRECTOR:
Alfred Hitchcock
CAST INCLUDES:
Laurence Olivier, Joan Fontaine,
George Sanders, Judith Anderson,
Gladys Cooper
SCREENPLAY:
Philip MacDonald, Michael Hogan
from the novel by
Daphne Du Maurier
CINEMATOGRAPHY:
George Barnes
PRODUCERS/
PRODUCTION COMPANIES:
David O. Selznick/
Selznick International Pictures
ACADEMY AWARD
NOMINATIONS (1941)
Best Actor in a Leading Role:
Laurence Olivier
Best Actress in a Leading Role:
Joan Fontaine
Best Actress in a Supporting Role:
Judith Anderson
Best Art Direction, Black-and-White:
Lyle R. Wheeler
Best Director: Alfred Hitchcock
Best Effects, Special Effects:
Jack Cosgrove (photographic),
Arthur Johns (sound)
Best Film Editing: Hal C. Kern
Best Music, Original Score:
Franz Waxman
Best Writing, Screenplay:
Robert E. Sherwood, Joan Harrison
ACADEMY AWARDS
Best Cinematography,
Black-and-White: George Barnes
Best Picture: David O. Selznick

Hitchcock's *Rebecca*, based on the novel of the same name by Daphne Du Maurier, is a brooding, melodramatic thriller. It follows the tale of a young woman (Fontaine) who is introduced to a rich widower, Maxim de Winter (Olivier) while in Monte Carlo. De Winter is travelling to get over the loss of his wife Rebecca, whose tragic death continues to haunt him. They fall in love, though with little hint of romance, and then marry. The previously unnamed young woman now becomes 'the second Mrs de Winter', interestingly as the film is named after the dead and unseen first wife. Once the newlyweds return to Max's estate, however, it is clear that through Rebecca's memory, her grip on the staff and house has not diminished since her death.

With a story by Du Maurier, direction by Hitchcock and starring Laurence Olivier you know you are going to get something special. *Rebecca* does not disappoint; the story is enthralling, Hitchcock's camera work is, as usual, flawless and Olivier's de Winter is by turns pitiable, charming and cold. Joan Fontaine is also excellent as the beautiful but shy young bride who undergoes something of a transformation during the film. However, both are eclipsed by Judith Anderson as the manipulative and menacing housekeeper, Mrs Danvers.

The atmosphere and feel of the film are built up through some moody cinematography; the black and white film is full of deep, bold images and clear black shadows. The message is clear this is a dark, psychological thriller; the suspense will keep you watching, the mystery will keep you guessing.

The Maltese Falcon

Sam Spade (Bogart) is a San Francisco private eye who becomes immersed in a violent mystery when he starts to investigate the murder of his partner. One strange character after another appears as he gets closer to solving the crime. Each character has one thing in common; a desire to get their hands on the golden, jewel-encrusted statue of the Maltese Falcon. The falcon inspires greed, fear and violence, but in itself, however, it is relatively unimportant; it is merely the hook on which to hang the characters who are the substance of the film.

Bogart's performance as Spade was to have an incredible impact on his career; the cold, tough-guy with a world-weary grin would set him up for his classic roles in *Casablanca* and *The African Queen*. The myth was born. *The Maltese Falcon* was also to be a turning point for its director John Huston. In this, his debut, he shows his obvious talent even at the time when Hitchcock was creating *Rebecca* and Welles was filming *Citizen Kane*, the quality of his camera work is clear.

The style of the movie has everything to do with making it a success. The plot and action are tight but the main attraction is the characters. The way in which the actors bring them to life is sublime to watch. Violence is implicit but it is not seen, instead every nuance of the hard men's speech and attitude is imbued with their strength and brutality.

USA, 1941
DIRECTOR:
John Huston
CAST INCLUDES:
Humphrey Bogart, Mary Astor,
Gladys George, Sydney Greenstreet,
Peter Lorre, Barton MacLane
SCREENPLAY:
Dashiell Hammett (novel),
John Huston (screenplay)
CINEMATOGRAPHY:
Arthur Edeson
PRODUCERS/
PRODUCTION COMPANIES:
Henry Blanke, Hal B. Wallis/
First National Pictures Inc.,
Warner Bros.
ACADEMY AWARD
NOMINATIONS (1942)
Best Actor in a Supporting Role:
Sydney Greenstreet
Best Picture: Hal B. Wallis
Best Writing, Screenplay: John Huston

Double Indemnity

USA, 1944
DIRECTOR:
Billy Wilder
CAST INCLUDES:
Fred MacMurray, Barbara Stanwyck,
Edward G. Robinson, Porter Hall,
Jean Heather,
SCREENPLAY:
Billy Wilder, Raymond Chandler
based on the novel by James M. Cain
CINEMATOGRAPHY:
John Seitz
PRODUCERS/
PRODUCTION COMPANIES:
Buddy G. DeSylva, Joseph Sistrom/
Paramount Pictures
ACADEMY AWARD
NOMINATIONS (1945)
Best Actress in a Leading Role:
Barbara Stanwyck
Best Cinematography,
Black-and-White: John F. Seitz
Best Director: Billy Wilder
Best Music, Scoring of a Dramatic or
Comedy Picture: Miklós Rózsa
Best Picture: Joseph Sistrom
Best Sound, Recording:
Loren L. Ryder (Paramount SSD)
Best Writing, Screenplay:
Raymond Chandler, Billy Wilder

'I killed him for money – and for a woman. I didn't get the money. And I didn't get the woman.' So runs the opening line of this fascinating film as Walter Neff (MacMurray) begins his confession into a Dictaphone. Told in flashback with Neff narrating, we learn that he is an insurance rep who begins an affair with Phyllis (Stanwick) when he visits her house to renew her husband's car insurance. They sign up her husband with a life policy, which has a double indemnity, and then murder him and make it look like an accident.

The opening confession leads us nicely into the movie, but rather than being the end of the story it immediately follows the crime and so points towards a man who does not expect to escape justice. Stanwyck gives one of her best performances and casts the mould for the *femme fatale* character in many successive films. As befits the time, she is not overtly sexy, but her seductive manipulation of Neff is thoroughly believable. MacMurray plays Neff to perfection, but it is Robinson, as Barton Keyes the claims investigator, who sets the film alight.

The screenplay was based on a James M. Cain novel adapted

by Raymond Chandler who made the original material even more evocative and as sharp as broken glass. The dialogue gives the characters a smartness and presence on screen that is hugely entertaining. Billy Wilder's direction is precise and the way he combines elements of romance with cynicism, suspense with humour gives an interesting take on film noir.

The Big Sleep

The adaptation of a Raymond Chandler novel, this film is notoriously difficult to understand. This is not just because of the amazingly complex plot, but also because the author himself admitted that he did not know who had committed one of the seven murders in his book. Philip Marlowe (Bogart) is the Private detective hired by General Sternwood to investigate the blackmail of his younger daughter, Carmen (Vickers). This apparently straightforward case leads Marlowe into a maze of killers and blackmail, gamblers and sex, and ultimately into the arms of the general's other daughter, Vivian (Bacall).

During filming, Bogart and Bacall were the talk of Hollywood due to their off-screen marriage and especially their age difference; he was forty four while she was only twenty. On-screen the two sparkled and some of the highlights of the film are their shared scenes when they bring real chemistry into some fabulously flirty dialogue. Bogart, of course, was at the top of his game here; he was a huge star and gives an assured performance as the suave but world-weary tough guy. The fact that he has such presence in front of the camera makes Marlowe's spell over women all the more believable.

Despite the convoluted plot, *The Big Sleep* is a classic noir and a thoroughly enjoyable movie. The cast are excellent, in particular, Martha Vickers is a pleasure to watch as the sex mad younger sister. The dialogue is wickedly witty and littered with double entendres while the subject matter is bold for the era. While murder was a common subject, it is rare to find nymphomania and drug use dealt with in this way during the 1940s.

USA, 1946
DIRECTOR:
Howard Hawks
CAST INCLUDES:
Humphrey Bogart, Lauren Bacall,
John Ridgely, Martha Vickers,
Dorothy Malone
SCREENPLAY:
William Faulkner, Jules Furthman,
Leigh Bracket from the novel by
Raymond Chandler
CINEMATOGRAPHY:
Sidney Hickox
**PRODUCERS/
PRODUCTION COMPANIES:**
Howard Hawks, Jack L. Warner/
First National Pictures Inc.,
Warner Bros.

Kiss of Death

USA, 1947
DIRECTOR:
Henry Hathaway
CAST INCLUDES:
Victor Mature, Brian Donlevy,
Coleen Gray, Richard Widmark,
Taylor Holmes
SCREENPLAY:
Ben Hecht, Charles Lederer from the
story by Eleazar Lipsky
CINEMATOGRAPHY:
Norbert Brodine
PRODUCERS/
PRODUCTION COMPANIES:
Fred Kohlmar/20th Century Fox
ACADEMY AWARD
NOMINATIONS (1948)
Best Actor in a Supporting Role:
Richard Widmark
Best Writing, Original Story:
Eleazar Lipsky

Kiss of Death is widely remembered for one scene in particular; when an old lady in a wheelchair is sent tumbling down the stairs. Shocking and senseless, it is a perfect illustration of the nature of the psycho-villain of the film, Tommy Udo (Widmark). Tommy has been betrayed by a former accomplice, Nick Bianco (Mature), who was captured when a robbery at a jewellery shop went amiss. By turning in his partners in crime, Nick is paroled while they are imprisoned. However when Tommy is released from prison, he is out for revenge against Nick and his new family.

Widmark was nominated for an Oscar for his debut role as the sadistic and psychotic Tommy. In an era when bad guys were rarely evil, his portrayal was interesting for its extremes; one moment mercilessly brutal and another manically giggling. Complementing this is Mature's performance which is excellently balanced between stool-pigeon and family man, his warmth creating sympathy for his character which is essential to the story.

In *Kiss of Death*, Hathaway has created a classic film noir; his taut direction creates moody unrelenting pace. The black-and-white photography adds a fine tone to the film, the use of light and shadows in the New York locations adds a sense of foreboding and tension. It is however, Widmark's film; the warped humour and the terrifying brutality form the hook on which the rest of the movie hangs.

The Third Man

The Third Man is set in post-war Vienna, a shattered city, divided between the allies and ruled by shady bureaucrats. Holly Martins (Cotton) arrives to take a job working for his friend Harry Lime (Welles), but when he gets to Vienna he discovers that Harry is dead. The death seems suspicious so Holly begins to investigate, despite being warned off by everyone he meets. The puzzle seems to hinge on a third man seen at the scene when Harry died, but who is he and what is his connection to Harry?

This film is cited by many as the best ever made, and whether you agree or not it is difficult to criticize. Wonderful moments such as the chase in the sewers, the balloon seller, the cuckoo clock speech and Harry's entrance are all sublime. Harry himself is one of cinema's great characters; smooth and lethal, at the same time, charming and repellent.

The cinematography casts Vienna in a surreal light, a lopsided place, full of unnatural angles as though the normal rules of perspective do not apply. This is so completely in keeping with the action; the rubble, ruins and craters are a perfect backdrop to the intrigue of the politicians, plotters and black marketeers.

The tone is completed with the score, played on a zither by Anton Karas; it manages to be joyless but strangely upbeat. It is almost a subversive presence; so important to the mood and only obvious when it pauses to build tension in a scene. So much of the credit must go to director, Carol Reed, who was Oscar nominated for *The Third Man*. The vision, tone and pace of the film are superb; the result is a genuinely timeless classic.

GB, 1949
DIRECTOR:
Carol Reed
CAST INCLUDES:
Joseph Cotton, Alida Valli,
Orson Welles, Trevor Howard,
Paul Hörbiger
SCREENPLAY:
Graham Greene from the story by
Graham Greene and
Alexander Korda
CINEMATOGRAPHY:
Robert Krasker
PRODUCERS/
PRODUCTION COMPANIES:
Hugh Perceval, Carol Reed/
British Lion Film Corporation,
London Film Productions
ACADEMY AWARD
NOMINATIONS (1951)
Best Director: Carol Reed
Best Film Editing:
Oswald Hafenrichter
ACADEMY AWARDS
Best Cinematography,
Black-and-White: Robert Krasker

The Asphalt Jungle

USA, 1950
DIRECTOR:
John Huston
CAST INCLUDES:
Sterling Hayden, Louis Calhern,
Jean Hagen, James Whitmore,
Sam Jaffe, Marilyn Monroe,
Anthony Caruso
SCREENPLAY:
Ben Maddow, John Huston from
the novel by W.R. Burnett
CINEMATOGRAPHY:
Harold Rosson
PRODUCERS/
PRODUCTION COMPANIES:
Arthur Hornblower Jr. /MGM
ACADEMY AWARD
NOMINATIONS (1951)
Best Actor in a Supporting Role:
Sam Jaffe
Best Cinematography,
Black-and-White: Harold Rosson
Best Director: John Huston
Best Writing, Screenplay:
Ben Maddow, John Huston

In *The Asphalt Jungle* John Huston created a classic film noir which would influence many later heist movies, not least *The Ladykillers* (1955), *Rififi* (1954), *Ocean's Eleven* (1960) and *Reservoir Dogs* (1992). Doc Riedenschneider (Jaffe), a criminal mastermind, is just out of prison and has a brilliant plan for a million-dollar jewellery heist. He recruits Louis (Caruso) as a safecracker, Gus (Whitmore) as the driver, and Dix (Hayden) as a strong-arm man to help with the raid. Initially the plan runs like clockwork but each member of the gang proves to have his own fatal flaw and each contributes to his own downfall.

Unlike many of the movies which drew inspiration from *The Asphalt Jungle*, this film is less concerned with the cunning plan or brilliant heist. Instead it is more character driven, exploring deception, relationships and human weakness. The lack of action in the film gave the cast plenty of opportunity to develop their

characters. Despite being largely unknown, the cast was no less talented for it, most had wide experience in supporting roles and each showed a deft touch in revealing his or her character's taints. Monroe is worthy of note, not simply because this was her big break but also because she is excellent as the bimbo niece.

As a director, Huston is at the top of his game, getting the most out of the screenplay and the cast. The film is beautifully shot in gloriously ominous black and white. The opening shots take in a bleak inner city, decaying and polluted – giving the film an almost documentary style. A sense of unease and apprehension builds up through the use of interiors with only glimpses of a dark urban exterior hinting at impending doom.

Strangers on a Train

Based on a novel by Patricia Highsmith, *Strangers on a Train* is a classic piece of Hitchcockian ingenuity. All the elements are there; an ordinary man caught in an impossible situation, some marvellous cinematic set pieces and the creeping, sinister build up of tension.

The plot is delightfully straightforward and quickly revealed. Guy (Granger) is a professional tennis player whose marital problems have been well reported in the press. Bruno (Walker) meets Guy on a train and suggests that they help each other out; Bruno will murder Guy's wife if Guy will murder Bruno's father in return. With prior knowledge of the crime both can establish an airtight alibi and can never be linked to the crime. So ends what Guy thinks is a harmless conversation until his wife is murdered and Bruno insists that he keep to his end of the deal.

Once again, in this movie, Hitchcock shows the quality of his film making. His use of lighting and camera work is outstanding and adds to the atmosphere and suspense. In particular, Bruno's un-moving face in a sea of tennis spectators, all turning their heads back and forth in unison is wonderful, as is the reflection of the murder in his victim's glasses. Walker is a splendid villain – smooth, creepy and amoral, and at times it is hard not to identify more with Bruno than with the weaker Guy.

Exhilarating, fast-moving and, together with his characteristically wicked approach, this is one of Hitchcock's most resourceful and cold-blooded thrillers, and the climactic runaway roundabout provides one of his most exciting endings.

USA, 1951
DIRECTOR:
Alfred Hitchcock
CAST INCLUDES:
Farley Granger, Ruth Roman, Robert Walker, Leo G. Carroll, Patricia Hitchcock
SCREENPLAY:
Raymond Chandler, Whitfield Cook, Czenzi Ormonde from the novel by Patricia Highsmith
CINEMATOGRAPHY:
Robert Burks
PRODUCERS/
PRODUCTION COMPANIES:
Alfred Hitchcock, Barbara Keon/ Warner Bros.
ACADEMY AWARD
NOMINATIONS (1952)
Best Cinematography, Black-and-White: Robert Burks

The Big Heat

On the surface, this film is a classic tale of one good cop and his search for justice and revenge in a corrupt town. Detective Banion (Ford) is as straight as they come. A suicide investigation seems straightforward enough until the victim's mistress is murdered and Banion's boss orders him off the case. When he refuses, and starts shaking down the local gang boss, the response is quick, violent and ultimately tragic.

With his performance as a maverick cop, barely able to suppress his rage, Ford brings intensity to the film and shows what an excellent actor he is.

USA, 1953
DIRECTOR:
Fritz Lang
CAST INCLUDES:
Glenn Ford, Gloria Grahame,
Jocelyn Brando, Alexander Scourby,
Lee Marvin
SCREENPLAY:
Sydney Boehm, William P. McGivern
CINEMATOGRAPHY:
Charles Lang
**PRODUCERS/
PRODUCTION COMPANIES:**
Robert Arthur/Columbia Pictures
Corporation

However it is Lee Marvin and the female roles that bring an extra dimension to the film and it is this that makes *The Big Heat* much more than a regular revenge flick. Stone (Marvin) is a cold, menacing brute and the scene where he throws a coffee pot at Debby (Graham) is truly shocking and probably the film's most famous moment.

The director, Lang, also uses the female roles to hint at a darker side to the movie. In his determination to bring the criminals down, Banion seems almost careless of the cost and, even worse, he actively involves and endangers those in his care. Three women murdered and one who is very scared is a high price for Banion's revenge, although he seems oblivious to the fact.

It is, however, the pace and tension that Lang has wrought from the tight script and excellent cast that makes this gritty noir such a standout film. From an era before violence was commonplace in filmmaking, *The Big Heat* is an excellent example of how it can be used to add impact to a clever plot and depth to sharply drawn characters.

Rear Window

This highly-charged suspense classic from Hitchcock shows all his flair for original and intelligent story telling. L. B. 'Jeff' Jeffries (Stewart), is a much travelled photographer, confined to a wheelchair with his leg in a cast. The rear window of his apartment looks out into the courtyard which he shares with his neighbours. Jeff amuses himself by watching the comings and goings outside and uses his telephoto lens to see through the open windows into his neighbours' apartments. This innocent voyeurism takes a dark turn when Jeff becomes increasingly sure that one of his neighbours, Lars Thorwald (Burr), has murdered his wife.

The theme of voyeurism is central to this film; we, the audience, impotently watch as Jeff helplessly watches the world through his window. Hitchcock places the audience in Jeff's shoes through his camerawork; all of the action takes place either in Jeff's apartment or is viewed from his wheelchair through the window. Whatever Jeff sees through the lens the audience also sees and this breaks the need for much dialogue to tell the story; instead the plot unfolds visually.

Grace Kelly gives a fine performance as Jeff's girlfriend Lisa who is a daily visitor to the flat and she becomes his legs when he sends her to investigate his suspicions. This highlights, once again, Jeff's impotence as he cannot go to her aid when she is in danger and this inability to move is another diabolical tool which Hitchcock uses to incessantly notch up the tension. And of course we, the audience, are as helpless as Jeff and must sit passively and wait for the gripping finale, we know it's coming, and we're right.

USA, 1954
DIRECTOR:
Alfred Hitchcock
CAST INCLUDES:
James Stewart, Grace Kelly, Wendell Corey, Thelma Ritter, Raymond Burr
SCREENPLAY:
John Michael Hayes, Cornell Woolrich
CINEMATOGRAPHY:
Robert Burks
PRODUCERS/ PRODUCTION COMPANIES:
Alfred Htchcock/ Paramount Pictures, Patron Inc.
ACADAMY AWARD NOMINATIONS (1955)
Best Cinematography, Color: Robert Burks
Best Director: Alfred Hitchcock
Best Sound, Recording: Loren L. Ryder (Paramount)
Best Writing, Screenplay: John Michael Hayes

The Night of the Hunter

USA, 1955
DIRECTOR:
Charles Laughton
CAST INCLUDES:
Robert Mitchum, Shelley Winters,
Lillian Gish, James Gleason,
Evelyn Varden, Peter Graves
SCREENPLAY:
James Agee, Davis Grubb
CINEMATOGRAPHY:
Stanley Cortez
PRODUCERS/
PRODUCTION COMPANIES:
Paul Gregory/Paul Gregory
Productions, United Artists

Ben Harper (Graves) is in prison awaiting execution for murder. His cell mate, Rev. Powell (Mitchum), tries unsuccessfully to persuade him to reveal where he has stashed $10,000 – the fruits of his crime. When Powell is released from prison he makes a bee-line for Ben's home and the newly widowed Willa (Winters). Powell marries her for the money without realizing that her two children are the only ones who know the location of the cash. Not one to be deterred, Powell does not hold back and reveals his true, evil self in his search for the riches.

Robert Mitchum played one of the most memorable villains in cinema with his portrayal of the preacher and manages to get the perfect balance between oily charmer and walking nightmare. The cinematography is highly stylized and almost gothic at times and sets the theme of the film as a fable or bad dream. In particular the shot where we see Willa dead is strangely compelling; she is sitting serenely at the wheel of her car which is at the bottom of the river, her hair drifting around her face in the current.

In *The Night of the Hunter* Laughton has produced a film which is both original and frightening. It combines elements of horror and fantasy and many of the techniques he uses here would later inspire other more obvious horror flicks. Not everyone will like this film however; it is surreal in places and has an unconventional style and mood.

Rififi

Du rififi chez les hommes

Rififi was made in France after the director was blacklisted in the anti-Communist witch-hunt in post-war Hollywood. This low-budget, film noir went on to become a classic; the main robbery sequence has inspired many imitators, although few can match it for pace and tension.

Tony (Servais) has just been released from a prison sentence and is bent on taking his revenge on his ex-girlfriend who is now involved with a small-time police informer and night club boss. Joe (Möhner) and Mario (Manuel) are planning a smash and grab on a jewellery store and want Tony to join them. He does, but persuades them to up the stakes and to try for the safe instead. They call on the services of Cesar (Dassin) an impeccably turned-out, woman-chasing, professional safe cracker.

This film is beautifully shot; no set could ever match these streets, cafes and bars. The black-and-white photography creates a wonderful style and captures the moody, smoky Paris of the 1950s. The actual heist is a great piece of film making; for almost thirty minutes the thieves work in soft shoes and in silence. No music, dialogue or effects interrupt the on-screen visual feast; a creaking floorboard and dropped screwdriver are the only noises and simply add to the tension. After the heist, the film changes pace and reaches its inevitable bloody conclusion. *Rififi* can be roughly translated as 'pitched conflict' and that is certainly an apt title.

FRANCE, 1955
DIRECTOR:
Jules Dassin
CAST INCLUDES:
Jean Servais, Carl Möhner,
Robert Manuel, Jules Dassin,
Marie Sabouret
SCREENPLAY:
Jules Dassin, René Wheeler
from the novel by Auguste Le Breton
CINEMATOGRAPHY:
Philippe Agostini
PRODUCERS/
PRODUCTION COMPANIES:
René Bezard, Henri Bérard,
Pierre Cabaud, René Gaston
Vuattoux/Indusfilms, Prima Film,
Société Nouvelle Pathé Cinéma

The Killing

USA, 1956
DIRECTOR:
Stanley Kubrick
CAST INCLUDES:
Sterling Hayden, Coleen Gray,
Vince Edwards, Jay C. Flippen,
Marie Windsor
SCREENPLAY:
Stanley Kubrick, Jim Thompson
from the novel by Lionel White
CINEMATOGRAPHY:
Lucien Ballard
PRODUCERS/
PRODUCTION COMPANIES:
James B. Harris, Alexander Singer/
Harris-Kubrick Productions

The title here refers not to a death, but rather to a big payday; in this case two million dollars. When Johnny Clay (Hayden) is released from prison he is planning one last big heist before he retires. He recruits a group of willing helpers to ensure that his complex plan can be pulled off without anyone getting hurt. However, he doesn't plan on one of his gang spilling the beans, a fact which leads to some unexpected results.

This film was quite a breakthrough for Kubrick both in terms of budget, class of the cast and the attention which it received in Hollywood. The film itself is a testament to the quality of direction. At a time when non-linear time-lines were mainly seen in flashback alone, Kubrick shows a deft touch in editing the film which tells a version of the story from each character's perspective. This enables the story to be told both through flashbacks and in jumps forward and allows the various strands of the plot to be developed simultaneously.

The black-and-white cinematography adds an extra dimension to this classic gritty noir. However, the film relies on the cast to carry the multiple perspective technique that is used so well and while they all turn in great performances, Hayden is the stand out actor. By having such an insight into each character, Kubrick exposes both the gangs' blind greed and their foibles; it is these weaknesses that will eventually lead to their downfall.

Touch of Evil

Touch of Evil opens with a classic piece of film making; the shot follows a bomb in the boot of a car as it travels along. As the timer ticks down, the camera soars overhead, taking in the sleazy bars, music, cafés and people that the car passes. After over three minutes on this single shot the camera settles on a couple walking by, the car explodes and they join the other witnesses who rush over to see what has happened. The couple are newlyweds on honeymoon; he is Mike Vargas (Heston), Mexico's leading narcotics policeman, who puts the honeymoon on ice to help investigate the bombing and comes into conflict with the local police.

Orson Welles plays Captain Quinlan the huge, sweating, embittered chief of police, who regularly plants evidence to support his intuition. Mike's wife, Susan, played by Janet Leigh, is excellent as the innocent who gets dragged into the middle of the conflict. Heston is restrained and controlled as the principled Mexican cop, although his makeup does make him stand out from the 'Latino' actors rather than fit in with them. However, it is Welles who shines, both in front of and behind the camera as director.

The cinematography and Welles' virtuoso camera work make *Touch of Evil* a taut and well-paced thriller. The subtlety of his direction gives the film an intimate feel and nervous atmosphere. *Touch of Evil* was Welles' last film as a director in Hollywood, and as one of the highlights of his career it is as unforgettable and spectacular as the climax of the film itself.

USA, 1958
DIRECTOR:
Orson Welles
CAST INCLUDES:
Charlton Heston, Janet Leigh, Orson Welles, Joseph Calleia, Akim Tamiroff, Marlene Deitrich
SCREENPLAY:
Orson Welles from the novel by Whit Masterson
CINEMATOGRAPHY:
Russell Metty
PRODUCERS/ PRODUCTION COMPANIES:
Albert Zugsmith/Universal Pictures

Charade

The fascinating thing about *Charade* is that it doesn't really fit into any one genre, part romance, part screwball comedy, throw in a heavy dose of Hitchcock suspense and you're getting close. Regina (Hepburn) is on the verge of divorcing her husband when he is murdered. The shock is compounded when she finds he had converted everything they owned into cash and it's gone missing. Her husband's criminal associates think she's got the cash stashed and they want it back. What follows is a romp in, under and over Paris as Regina and her new romantic interest, Peter (Grant), try to keep one step ahead of the bad guys who have a nasty habit of turning up dead.

When Stanley Donen, the director of *Singing in the Rain*, teams up with Cary Grant and Audrey Hepburn you know you're going to get something special. *Charade* does not disappoint; the plot is nicely developed with false identities, double crosses and a great twist, but the main attraction will always be the stars. In their only movie together Grant and Hepburn sizzle. Helped along by a witty script, there is a genuine chemistry that shines through the banter.

In support, Walter Matthau, James Coburn, and George Kennedy are all in fine form and show the quality which would see them all win Oscars for supporting roles in other films. Henry Mancini's score helps to build the tension alongside some excellent action sequences which combine in an exciting climax to the cat-and-mouse chase.

USA, 1963
DIRECTOR:
Stanley Donen
CAST INCLUDES:
Cary Grant, Audrey Hepburn, Walter Matthau, James Coburn, George Kennedy
SCREENPLAY:
Peter Stone (story), Marc Behm (story), Peter Stone (screenplay)
CINEMATOGRAPHY:
Charles Lang
PRODUCERS/ PRODUCTION COMPANIES:
Stanley Donen, James H. Ware, Universal Pictures
ACADEMY AWARD NOMINATIONS (1964)
Best Music Original Song Henry Mancini (music), Johnny Mercer (lyrics), for the song 'Charade'

Goldfinger

Goldfinger, the third film in the Bond franchise, is considered by many aficionados to be the best of the lot. This time around, James Bond (Connery), the suave, sophisticated, spy about town has to foil Auric Goldfinger (Fröbe) who plans to contaminate the gold reserves at Fort Knox. The story, as usual, takes Bond around the world via the beds of any number of young ladies, before he saves the day in the nick of time.

This Bond film was the first to make those fantastic gadgets an integral part of the movie and introduced us to the Aston Martin DB5 – one of the most popular 007 cars. It also marked a departure from the earlier films in that it introduced more humour and didn't take itself so seriously. Love them or hate them, this is when the really corny one-liners became firmly embedded into Bond culture.

Auric Goldfinger is a more low-key villain than many others but his mute hat-throwing henchman Oddjob (Sakata) must surely rate as one of the most memorable sidekicks in the series. Even forty years after its release, *Goldfinger* is still pretty risqué as seen in the nudity, sex and some sparkling exchanges between Bond and Pussy Galore (Blackman). Pussy Galore was one of the few Bond girls to really have much in the way of character and intelligence. While most are simply required to look great and sigh 'Oh James!' on cue, Blackman's charm, and some neat writing, made her strong character unforgettable.

Of course, the real draw is Bond himself. Connery is an outstanding and utterly convincing 007. With a twinkle in his eye and a fine chest of hair he manages to pull off that most difficult of balancing acts; he is fancied by the women and cheered on by the men.

GB, 1964
DIRECTOR:
Guy Hamilton
CAST INCLUDES:
Sean Connery, Honor Blackman,
Gert Fröbe, Shirley Eaton,
Tania Mallet, Harold Sakata
SCREENPLAY:
Richard Maibaum, Paul Dehn from
the novel by Ian Fleming
CINEMATOGRAPHY:
Ted Moore
**PRODUCERS/
PRODUCTION COMPANIES:**
Albert R. Broccoli, Harry Saltzman/
Danjaq Productions,
Eon Productions Ltd.
ACADEMY AWARDS (1965)
Best Effects, Sound Effects:
Norman Wanstall

Bonnie and Clyde

USA, 1967
DIRECTOR:
Arthur Penn
CAST INCLUDES:
Warren Beatty, Faye Dunaway,
Michael J. Pollard, Gene Hackman,
Estelle Parsons
SCREENPLAY:
David Newman, Robert Benton
CINEMATOGRAPHY:
Burnett Guffey
PRODUCERS/
PRODUCTION COMPANIES:
Warren Beatty/Tatira-Hiller
Productions, Warner Brothers,
Seven Arts
ACADEMY AWARD
NOMINATIONS (1968)
Best Actor in a Leading Role:
Warren Beatty
Best Actor in a Supporting Role:
Michael J. Pollard
Best Actor in a Supporting Role:
Gene Hackman
Best Actress in a Leading Role:
Faye Dunaway
Best Costume Design:
Theadora Van Runkle
Best Director: Arthur Penn
Best Picture: Warren Beatty
Best Writing, Story and Screenplay -
Written Directly for the Screen:
David Newman, Robert Benton
ACADEMY AWARDS
Best Actress in a Supporting Role:
Estelle Parsons
Best Cinematography:
Burnett Guffey

Clyde Barrow (Beatty) is a small-time bank robber, just out of prison, who hooks up with Bonnie Parker (Dunaway) a girl bored with her small-town life. Together they embark upon a string of violent bank robberies throughout the 1930s Midwest, pursued by incompetent cops and extravagant headlines. This is a classic story loosely based on the real-life exploits of two of America's most famous anti-heroes.

In *Bonnie and Clyde*, Penn has created a film that is by turns funny, tragic, subtle and, for its time, extremely violent. At first, the film is very up-beat with almost the feel of a 'caper' as Bonnie and Clyde turn over banks, get into scrapes and then show a pair of clean heels to the law. This all changes however when Clyde accidentally kills someone during a getaway. The mood of the film becomes more serious and although the robberies continue, the violence increases and the humour becomes darker.

Beatty and Dunaway give wonderful performances as the lovers on the run, but it is the supporting cast members that really shine. Michael J. Pollard plays the dependable, but bored side-kick to perfection. Gene Hackman is excellent as Clyde's delightful older brother, and Estelle Parsons was deservedly rewarded by the Academy for her portrayal as the shrewish Blanche.

The result is an interesting study of violence and celebrity where the stunning cinematography makes the folk-story into a legend. The climax of the movie is stylized in the extreme and the almost elegant arrangement captures both the tragedy of the pair and their release.

In the Heat of the Night

This film, set in the Deep South of the 1960s, has been widely praised for its treatment of racism in a story of a black cop visiting a bigoted town. When the body of a wealthy industrialist is found on the street of a small town, the local police think they have solved the murder when they arrest Tibbs (Poitier), a black man waiting at the nearby station. However, it becomes apparent that they have the wrong man when Tibbs is revealed as a hot-shot police investigator, in town to visit his mother. Tibbs agrees to stay on and help local Police Chief Gillespie (Steiger) and, with some fancy police work, shows the local cops how it's done.

Director Jewison provides marvellous direction in this character study camouflaged as a thriller. Steiger truly deserved his Oscar for his role as the lazy, prejudiced cop who learns a grudging respect for Tibbs. Reportedly a method actor, he seems fully immersed in the life and world of the police chief. Poitier's customary dignity and quiet authority is a perfect counterpoint. The two make a fascinating pair and their quietly developing relationship is one of the central themes of the film.

Ray Charles' unforgettable, bluesy vocals add just the right touch to complement the fine score, all of which adds to the atmosphere of the hot and humid ambience of the Deep South. *In the Heat of the Night* can be seen as a forceful, social commentary or simply a classic murder mystery, either way it is a thoughtful and entertaining movie.

USA, 1967
DIRECTOR:
Norman Jewison
CAST INCLUDES:
Sidney Poitier, Rod Steiger, Warren Oates, Lee Grant, Larry Gates
SCREENPLAY:
Stirling Silliphant from the novel by John Ball
CINEMATOGRAPHY:
Haskell Wexler
**PRODUCERS/
PRODUCTION COMPANIES:**
Walter Mirisch/The Mirisch Corporation
**ACADEMY AWARD
NOMINATIONS (1968)**
Best Director: Norman Jewison
Best Effects, Sound Effects: James Richard
ACADEMY AWARDS
Best Actor in a Leading Role: Rod Steiger
Best Film Editing: Hal Ashby
Best Picture: Walter Mirisch
Best Sound: Richard Carruth
Best Writing Screenplay Based on Material from Another Medium: Stirling Silliphant

Point Blank

Lee Marvin plays Walker, who is persuaded by an old friend to take part in robbing money from a criminal gang on the island of Alcatraz. Walker's wife joins them, but when the friend kills the gang members, Walker flees the scene and settles in an old prison cell. His wife finds him, and when the friend appears it is clear that both he and the wife were in on it together. The friend shoots him and they leave him for dead. However, he does not die and is approached by a man called Yost, who agrees to tell Walker where his cut of the money is if Walker will despatch the criminal outfit called the Organization. Many members of the Organization are duly disposed of, and Walker's search for the money leads him full circle, and to a startling discovery.

There are many aspects to this movie that take it outside the realms of the standard revenge flick. Marvin excels as a cold-blooded ruthless man out for not so much revenge as his money, something he will do anything to secure. Boorman's dream-like direction is firmly rooted in the art house; combined with a number of flashbacks, the viewer is invited to consider whether what he watches unfolding is in fact happening at all. Is it all a dream? Did Walker actually die in the cell? These questions become more compelling when one realizes that Walker does not kill anyone in the film; while various members of the Organization do meet untimely ends when Walker appears, the deaths are not actually his doing. Poorly and pointlessly remade by Mel Gibson as *Payback*, this is a compelling movie which has dated a little, in no small part because of the soundtrack.

USA, 1967
DIRECTOR:
John Boorman
CAST INCLUDES:
Lee Marvin, Angie Dickinson,
Keenan Wynn, Carroll O'Connor,
Lloyd Bochner
SCREENPLAY:
Alexander Jacobs, David Newhouse,
Rafe Newhouse from the novel by
Donald E. Westlake
CINEMATOGRAPHY:
Philip H. Lathrop
**PRODUCERS/
PRODUCTION COMPANIES:**
Judd Bernard, Robert Chartoff/
Metro-Goldwyn-Mayer

Bullitt

Frank Bullitt (McQueen) and two other cops are assigned the task of protecting a mob witness by a shady politician. Each policeman agrees to take a shift in the small room overlooking the freeway. During the second shift, gunmen shoot the witness and the guard, and the police discover that the door to the room had been opened to the gunmen. The witness is rushed to hospital and Bullitt asks that the fact of the shooting be covered up. A further attempt at a hit is made on the witness in the hospital, and the gunmen begin following Bullitt. After an explosive finale to a spectacular car chase, Bullitt discovers that the witness may not be who he seems.

Praised as one of the greatest police dramas of all time, much of *Bullitt's* fame comes from 'that' car chase. It is remembered as one of the seminal early, perhaps first, examples of the craft and the film won an Oscar for best editing. However, judged by today's standards of *Matrix*-style CGI fests, the sight of a couple of cars speeding around the steep hills of San Francisco does not perhaps hold the appeal it once did. Movie nerds can amuse themselves by counting the number of hubcaps falling off the same car and watching out for the number of times the cars pass the same VW. There are a few interesting early cameos to look out for, and the film is more intelligent than most of its genre. Car chase aside, however, the plot is slow and a little pedestrian, although McQueen shines as the rugged cop who will do whatever is necessary to find out the truth.

USA, 1968
DIRECTOR:
Peter Yates
CAST INCLUDES:
Steve McQueen, Robert Vaughn, Jacqueline Bisset, Don Gordon, Robert Duvall
SCREENPLAY:
Alan Trustman, Harry Kleiner from the novel by Robert L. Fish
CINEMATOGRAPHY:
William A. Fraker
PRODUCERS/ PRODUCTION COMPANIES:
Philip D'Antoni, Robert E. Relyea/Solar Productions
ACADEMY AWARD NOMINATIONS (1969)
Best Sound: Seven Arts Studio Sound Department
ACADEMY AWARDS
Best Film Editing: Frank P. Keller

The Thomas Crown Affair

USA, 1968
DIRECTOR:
Norman Jewison
CAST INCLUDES:
Steve McQueen, Faye Dunaway,
Paul Burke, Jack Weston,
Biff McGuire
SCREENPLAY:
Alan Trustman
CINEMATOGRAPHY:
Haskell Wexler
PRODUCERS/
PRODUCTION COMPANIES:
Hal Ashby, Norman Jewison/
Simkoe, Solar Productions,
The Mirisch Corporation
ACADEMY AWARD
NOMINATIONS (1969)
Best Music, Original Score for a
Motion Picture (not a Musical):
Michel Legrand
ACADEMY AWARDS
Best Music, Original Song:
Michel Legrand (music),
Alan Bergman (lyrics),
Marilyn Bergman (lyrics)

Norman Jewison, the director of *The Thomas Crown Affair*, described it as a film 'of style over content'. While it is undoubtedly highly styled it is also a powerful study of sexual chemistry set within the bounds of an entertaining caper. Thomas Crown (McQueen) is a jet set millionaire, who keeps himself amused by masterminding the perfect bank robbery. Vicky Anderson (Dunaway) is the insurance investigator who is called in to help the bank recover their money. While Vicky suspects that Thomas was behind the robbery she has no proof. She socializes with him to try and trick him into giving something away, but their growing attraction is more than she was counting on.

The highlight of the film is, without doubt, the romantic tension between the two leads. This is almost tangible at times and does not rely on dialogue to accentuate it; indeed, both characters tend to keep their cards close to their chest. Both, of course, look great; Mcqueen is the stylish and cool playboy around town, Dunaway

looks every inch the glamorous model (which of course she was). The chess scene is a great example of how the director heightens the mood; pieces are toyed with, close ups are drawn-out and sexual imagery abounds. After over six minutes with almost no dialogue the kiss is a wonderful conclusion to a highly charged piece of film-making.

The use of multiple screens during the heist was innovative at the time and together with the award-winning score makes this a thoroughly enjoyable film. While some of the styling does look dated compared to modern films this adds to the overall effect. The cars, the clothes and the lifestyle of the 1960s, together with two of Hollywood's hottest stars, come together nicely in this chic, stylish flick.

The Italian Job

Charlie Croker (Caine) has just been released from prison but far from going straight he is planning his next big robbery. To finance the heist he approaches Mr Bridger (Coward), an aristocratic gang boss currently serving time himself. The planning of the robbery and the escape give car chase fans plenty to get excited about and some of the one-liners have passed into history – 'You're only supposed to blow the bloody doors off!'. And no-one can ever forget the ultimate cliff-hanger of an ending.

This was Michael Caine's second film and certainly helped to propel him to stardom. As the cockney wide boy criminal he displays a charisma and charm that fits in well with the cheeky chases through the streets of Turin. The film harks back to more innocent times, when criminals could pull off a heist with a cosh and a smart mouth. Adding to this sense of nostalgia is Noel Coward's brief performance as the crime lord Mr Bridger in this, his last film. A small nod of recognition and a half wave is all the response needed when he gets an enthusiastic ovation from his fellow inmates; this is a dignified curtain call to a distinguished career. Any review of this film would be incomplete without mention of Benny Hill, whose performance is simply a reprise of his television show. His humour is as quintessentially British as the Mini Cooper and he is perfectly cast as a professor with a liking for the larger lady.

Product placement or stylish use of a British motoring icon? Whichever you decide, there is no getting away from it, the Mini Coopers are the real stars of this great British caper.

UK, 1969
DIRECTOR:
Peter Collinson
CAST INCLUDES:
Michael Caine, Noel Coward, Benny Hill, Raf Vallone,
Tony Beckley
SCREENPLAY:
Troy Kennedy-Martin
CINEMATOGRAPHY:
Douglas Slocombe
**PRODUCERS/
PRODUCTION COMPANIES:**
Stanley Baker, Michael Deeley/
Oakhurst Productions,
Paramount Pictures

USA, 1971
DIRECTOR:
Don Siegel
CAST INCLUDES:
Clint Eastwood, Harry Guardino,
Reni Santoni, John Vernon,
Andrew Robinson
SCREENPLAY:
Harry Julian Fink, Rita M. Fink,
Dean Riesner
CINEMATOGRAPHY:
Bruce Surtees
PRODUCERS/
PRODUCTION COMPANIES:
Robert Daley, Carl Pingitore,
Don Siegel/The Malpaso Company,
Warner Bros.

Dirty Harry

'…ask yourself one question: Do I feel lucky? Well, do ya punk?' So asks Inspector Harry Callaghan in one of Eastwood's most memorable roles and one of cinema's most memorable quotes. In this first film of the *Dirty Harry* series we are introduced to the dangerous and violent side of San Francisco which is Callaghan's work place. After thwarting a bank robbery and a suicide attempt, Callaghan is faced with his main challenge – a deranged sharpshooter killing innocent civilians and holding the city to ransom. After an illegal search causes the case against the killer to collapse, Callaghan falls back on less orthodox methods to get his man.

After success in westerns and war films this was one of Eastwood's first major roles in a contemporary movie. Despite playing the part of a policeman, Callaghan is for Eastwood, essentially a reprise of his role as the man with no name; a maverick solving his problems with a Colt. Callaghan is insensitive, unsociable, and any humanity is largely left unspoken. This role confirmed Eastwood as a major star and set him firmly on the path to Hollywood legend.

While cited as a forerunner to later cop-based action movies, director Don Siegel has produced a film which is more than that. This is a morality piece or, if you like, a liberal backlash. In *Dirty Harry*'s San Francisco the criminals are protected while the law abiding public is not. The only role for city lawyers and politicians in this film is to try and hold back the one man who can save the city from the over-the-top, wild-eyed psychopath (Robinson). Of course, they don't succeed and in the final shot (taken from *High Noon*), Callaghan discards his badge and walks away.

The French Connection

The documentary style of the camera work and the fact that the story was based on the exploits of two real police officers gives *The French Connection* a gritty, real-life feel. The story centres on Popeye Doyle (Hackman) and Buddy Russon (Scheider), two New York policemen on the trail of a large shipment of heroin from France. As the police close in, Alain Charnier (Rey), one of the importers, decides to kill the cops who have the gang under surveillance to give them time to complete the deal.

Gene Hackman won an Oscar for his portrayal of Popeye Doyle and rightly so, for he gave us one of cinema's most enduring characters. Far from being a typical hero, Popeye is a quick-tempered, hard-drinking bigot and neither the screenplay nor Hackman try to make us have much sympathy for him. Yes, he is a hard working, tough cop but it is his adversary Charnier who is far more refined and likeable.

The French Connection was primarily filmed on location in France and New York and the latter in particular is grimy and run-down, showing us a glimpse of the true dark side of the city. One of the most famous scenes in the movie is when the cops are chasing a runaway elevated train through the city and this is a classic piece of cinema. However it is not the action sequences alone which make this movie. Instead, it is a lesson in the use of quality actors and patient directing to build characters and then use them to tell the story with pace and tension.

USA, 1971
DIRECTOR:
William Friedkin
CAST INCLUDES:
Gene Hackman, Fernando Rey,
Roy Scheider, Tony Lo Bianco,
Marcel Bozzuffi
SCREENPLAY:
Robin Moore (novel), Ernest Tidyman
(screenplay)
CINEMATOGRAPHY:
Owen Roizman
**PRODUCERS/
PRODUCTION COMPANIES:**
Philip D'Antoni, G. David Schine,
Kenneth Utt/20th Century Fox,
D'Antoni Productions,
Schine-Moore Productions
**ACADEMY AWARD
NOMINATIONS (1972)**
Best Actor in a Supporting Role:
Roy Scheider
Best Cinematography:
Owen Roizman
Best Sound: Theodore Soderberg,
Christopher Newman
ACADEMY AWARDS
Best Actor in a Leading Role:
Gene Hackman
Best Director: William Friedkin
Best Film Editing:
Gerald B. Greenberg
Best Picture: Philip D'Antoni
Best Writing, Screenplay Based on
Material from Another Medium:
Ernest Tidyman

The Godfather

USA, 1972
DIRECTOR:
Francis Ford Coppola
CAST INCLUDES:
Marlon Brando, Al Pacino,
James Caan, Richard S. Castellano,
Robert Duvall, Sterling Hayden
SCREENPLAY:
Francis Ford Coppola,
Mario Puzo from his novel
CINEMATOGRAPHY:
Gordon Willis
**PRODUCERS/
PRODUCTION COMPANIES:**
Gray Frederickson, Albert S. Ruddy/
Paramount Pictures
**ACADEMY AWARD
NOMINATIONS (1973)**
Best Writing, Screenplay Based on
Material from Another Medium:
Mario Puzo,
Francis Ford Coppola
Best Actor in a Supporting Role:
James Caan
Best Actor in a Supporting Role:
Robert Duvall
Best Actor in a Supporting Role:
Al Pacino
Best Costume Design:
Anna Hill Johnstone
Best Director:
Francis Ford Coppola
Best Film Editing: William Reynolds,
Peter Zinner
Best Sound: Charles Grenzbach,
Richard Portman,
Christopher Newman
ACADEMY AWARDS
Best Actor in a Leading Role:
Marlon Brando
Best Picture: Albert S. Ruddy

At its simplest, *The Godfather* is a film about a conflict within the Mafia, in fact, though, that conflict is simply the stage that Coppola uses to set out what he is really interested in; loyalty, family and, most importantly, power. Don Corleone (Brando) is the leader of a Mafia family, in dispute with the rest of the Mafia over a proposal to sell drugs. When he survives an assassination attempt it sparks a gang war and brings his eldest son Michael (Pacino) back into the family business.

One of Coppola's neatest tricks is how he creates sympathy for the heroes and makes us care about them. No mean feat given the nature of their business, but this is achieved through limiting the scope of the film, most of which takes place in a family setting; wedding, baptism, home and business. The only crime is to take sides against the family. The Mafia, which runs protection and gambling rackets, is replaced with a more benevolent, paternal organization worthy of respect. The violence which touches the family is real but their own victims are never the blameless or innocent, but rather the treacherous and unworthy.

The whole cast is wonderful but Brando, in particular, is faultless – powerful and utterly compelling. Pacino is also at the top of his game here; Michael is his father's son, quietly assured and confident of what he has to do, not necessarily liking it, but never hesitating. Add in to the mix a fine supporting cast and dark, rich cinematography and you have a film worthy of all the popular and critical acclaim.

Mean Streets

USA, 1973
DIRECTOR:
Martin Scorsese
CAST INCLUDES:
Robert De Niro, Harvey Keitel,
David Proval, Amy Robinson, Richard
Romanus
SCREENPLAY:
Martin Scorsese, Mardik Martin
CINEMATOGRAPHY:
Kent L. Wakeford
PRODUCERS/
PRODUCTION COMPANIES:
E. Lee Perry, Martin Scorsese,
Jonathan T. Taplin

In his debut, *Mean Streets*, Scorsese demonstrates the depth and originality of his film-making which would go on to become his trademark. The mean streets in question are those of Little Italy, New York. Charlie (Keitel) is a small time hood working for his uncle. His friend Johnny (De Niro) seems bent on self destruction, running up debts, blowing up mail boxes and more seriously, disrespecting the local Mafia. Charlie has to try and keep Johnny out of trouble (a seemingly impossible task) while hiding the fact that he's in love with Amy, Johnny's cousin.

While not in quite the same league as *Taxi Driver*, *Mean Streets* is still an amazing first film. The writing and characters illustrate what life was like on the grimier side of life in Manhattan for New York's first generation Italian-Americans. Keitel shines in his role of nice-guy hood, but the star of the film is undoubtedly De Niro in what was, for him, a real career breakthrough. His portrayal of the near-psychopath Johnny is entirely convincing; he brings an energy and restlessness to the role that is in turn endearing and irritating.

Smart use of a cracking soundtrack is something that Scorsese always does well. Here he doesn't disappoint, and the bar fight with 'Hey Mr Postman' as a backing track is inspired. The result is a gritty movie which draws on all the Italian-American influences from Scorsese's early years and it sets De Niro on the path to superstardom. The use of hand-held cameras adds a sense of realism to the film, putting the action and the violence in the face of the viewer.

Serpico

Based on the true life exploits of a real cop, *Serpico* follows one man's stand against police corruption. The film opens with Serpico (Pacino), covered with blood, being rushed to hospital. In flashback we see his early life as a street cop when his colleagues turn a blind eye to misdemeanours in return for food, drink and payoffs. As his career continues the corruption around him gets progressively worse, causing him to make official complaints which leads to the obvious conclusion.

The story is held together by the characters on the street and in the force and it is Pacino's performance in particular that cements it. Pacino is in virtually every scene and handles the transition from rookie to beardy plainclothes cop with his usual skill. The film has received a fair amount of criticism for being overlong and paced too slowly. This is probably fair comment and with any other actor it might be a serious flaw. With Pacino however, it is a delight to see him on screen; his presence is magnetic and he keeps your interest even when the plot dawdles.

Lumet adopts an almost documentary style for the film which certainly helps to give it a gritty, real-life edge. While he wants to create an empathy with Serpico, there is little or no sentimentality involved. The decaying urban backgrounds in New York add more than just style, giving the film impact. When these elements come together what we see is a genuine cynicism about the bureaucratic corruption and while that topic is familiar to us today, it would certainly have been more of an exposé thirty-odd years ago.

USA, 1973
DIRECTOR:
Sidney Lumet
CAST INCLUDES:
Al Pacino, John Randolph, Jack Kehoe, Biff McGuire, Barbara Eda-Young
SCREENPLAY:
Waldo Salt, Norman Wexler from the novel by Peter Maas
CINEMATOGRAPHY:
Arthur J. Ornitz
**PRODUCERS/
PRODUCTION COMPANIES:**
Martin Bregman, Dino De Laurentiis, Roger M. Rothstein/ Paramount Pictures, Produzion De Laurentis
**ACADEMY AWARD
NOMINATIONS (1974)**
Best Actor in a Leading Role: Al Pacino
Best Writing, Screenplay Based on Material from Another Medium: Waldo Salt, Norman Wexler

The Sting

USA, 1973
DIRECTOR:
George Roy Hill
CAST INCLUDES:
Paul Newman, Robert Redford,
Robert Shaw, Charles Durning,
Ray Walston
SCREENPLAY:
David S. Ward
CINEMATOGRAPHY:
Robert Surtees
**PRODUCERS/
PRODUCTION COMPANIES:**
Tony Bill, Robert L. Crawford,
Julia Phillips, Michael Phillips/
Universal Pictures
**ACADEMY AWARD
NOMINATIONS (1974)**
Best Actor in a Leading Role:
Robert Redford
Best Cinematography:
Robert Surtees
Best Sound: Ronald Pierce,
Robert R. Bertrand
ACADEMY AWARDS
Best Art Direction-Set Decoration:
Henry Bumstead, James W. Payne
Best Costume Design: Edith Head
Best Director: George Roy Hill
Best Film Editing:
William Reynolds
Best Music, Scoring Original Song
Score and/or Adaptation:
Marvin Hamlisch
Best Picture: Tony Bill,
Michael Phillips, Julia Phillips
Best Writing, Story and Screenplay
Based on Factual Material or Material
Not Previously Published or
Produced: David S. Ward

Redford and Newman reprise their partnership from *Butch Cassidy and the Sundance Kid* as two Chicago conmen brought together by the murder of a mutual friend. They plan revenge against the culprit, mob leader Lonnegan (Shaw), who is himself a master conman. Their revenge is the only type they are capable of –a sting. To carry out the sting, they set up a fake gambling den in which the unexpected climax takes place. However, it's not only Lonnegan they have to deal with; they also have the police breathing down their necks. It's an elaborate and tightly plotted film, full of so many twists and turns that we are barely able to keep up with them on first viewing.

A film as much remembered for the design and music as the plot, few who watch it forget Redford's red suit or the recurring piano theme of 'The Entertainer'. A real example of how 'they don't make them like they used to'; likeable, loveable rogues get their revenge on the gangland boss through a combination of quick talking, a certain cheeky chappiness and their cunning and guile.

The movie swept the board at the Oscars, and has certainly stood the test of time, to the extent that almost every film or programme about con men, including recent examples like *Confidence* and the TV Show *Hustle*, are inevitably and unfavourably compared to it. It's best not to talk about the disappointing and frankly pointless sequel ten years later or these pale imitators.

Chinatown

Robert Towne deservedly won an Oscar for his screenplay of this masterly, complex mystery. It all starts off on a familiar footing. Jake Gittes (Nicholson), a Los Angeles private eye, is hired by Evelyn Cross Mulwray (Dunaway) to investigate the adultery of her husband. From there Jake is led through a world of intrigue, corruption and double cross as the husband turns up dead and every lead he has points to a connection with water.

Although, the plot is convoluted, the quality of the script provides a clear path through the maze of events. Add in some wonderful dialogue and the journey is a fascinating one. Nicholson is magical, in Gittes we can see the superstar he will become, and his face can tell a thousand stories, with or without the plaster on the nose. His wicked grin softens the world-weary cynicism and adds a sympathetic side to his hard, somewhat aloof character. Dunaway is enchanting as the enigmatic, classy blonde and Huston is the perfect foil as her disturbing and pitiless father. The gorgeous cinematography and varied score by Jerry Goldsmith adds the final touches to a classic piece of filmmaking by Polanski.

The inspiration for the film was the Southern Californian land grab in the early part of the twentieth century, where water supplies were manipulated by various magnates to acquire land for redevelopment. In addition, this was the first film Polanski made after the murder of his wife, Sharon Tate, by the Manson gang. These events go some way to explaining the tragic conclusion of the film and certainly must have contributed to the feeling of despair it leaves you with.

USA, 1974
DIRECTOR:
Roman Polanski
CAST INCLUDES:
Jack Nicholson, Faye Dunaway,
John Huston, Perry Lopez,
John Hillerman
SCREENPLAY:
Robert Towne
CINEMATOGRAPHY:
John A. Alonzo
**PRODUCERS/
PRODUCTION COMPANIES:**
Robert Evans, C.O. Erickson/
Long Road, Paramount Pictures,
Penthouse
**ACADEMY AWARD
NOMINATIONS (1975)**
Best Actor in a Leading Role: Jack
Nicholson
Best Actress in a Leading Role:
Faye Dunaway
Best Art Direction-Set Decoration:
Richard Sylbert, W. Stewart
Campbell, Ruby R. Levitt
Best Cinematography:
John A. Alonzo
Best Costume Design:
Anthea Sylbert
Best Director: Roman Polanski
Best Film Editing: Sam O'Steen
Best Music, Original Dramatic Score:
Jerry Goldsmith
Best Picture: Robert Evans
Best Sound: Charles Grenzbach,
Larry Jost
ACADEMY AWARDS
Best Writing. Original Screenplay:
Robert Towne

USA, 1974
DIRECTOR:
Francis Ford Coppola
CAST INCLUDES:
Gene Hackman, John Cazale,
Allen Garfield, Frederic Forrest,
Cindy Williams
SCREENPLAY:
Francis Ford Coppola
CINEMATOGRAPHY:
Bill Butler
**PRODUCERS/PRODUCTION
COMPANIES:**
Francis Ford Coppola, Fred Roos,
Mona Skager/American Zoetrope,
Paramount Pictures, The Coppola
Company, The Directors Company
**ACADEMY AWARD
NOMINATIONS (1975)**
Best Picture:
Francis Ford Coppola
Best Sound: Walter Murch,
Art Rochester
Best Writing, Original Screenplay:
Francis Ford Coppola

The Conversation

Hackman plays Harry, a paranoid and reclusive professional surveillance man who is instructed to spy upon a young couple. After taping a crucial conversation, he suspects that his work may lead to their murder. Recalling a previous tragedy in which he became implicated, he becomes obsessed with finding out the truth behind the conversation he has heard.

This film is a real gem, but one that is often overlooked in Coppolla's canon, coming as it did between *Godfather*s *I* and *II*, and well before *Apocalypse Now*. However, both director and leading man are at their best in this taut psychological thriller. The themes of surveillance, paranoia and eavesdropping were fresh in the minds of the American people when this film was released; coming out shortly after the Watergate scandal broke. While the film has certainly dated, these themes are no less relevant today, in an age of CCTV, fidelity cards and monitored e mails. However, this is far more than a sociological document; this is a character study of a reclusive loner who, over the course of the film, realizes that his job has real, and deadly, consequences for his subjects, and the ensuing crisis of conscience that this realization brings.

Technically superb, it is hardly surprising given its subject that the sounds are just as important as the pictures; it deserves loud home cinema treatment, particularly in the opening sequence and in the scene where Harry attempts to decipher the all-important missing phrase from the recording.

The themes have been repeated often in films since, perhaps most memorably when Hackman reprised and updated his role in the disappointing *Enemy of the State*. No subsequent film has captured its brooding sense of paranoia and claustrophobia, however.

Dog Day Afternoon

Al Pacino plays Sonny, a man who hatches a plan to rob a bank. With an inept accomplice, he bungles the bank job and the police and news crews are alerted when a siege ensues. Over the next twelve hours, Sonny finds himself at the centre of a media circus. The crowds that gather initially regard him as a hero (in keeping with the anti-authoritarian mood in the US, post-Vietnam) but when the reason for the robbery becomes clear, they begin to lose sympathy for Sonny.

Allegedly based on a true story, this film can be viewed as a biting satire on the media's infatuation with crime and criminals a long time before the more obvious and brutal *Natural Born Killers* – witness, particularly, the delivery boy taking a pizza to Sonny mid-siege. While there are comic elements, there is a real sense of tragedy in the way in which loser Sonny briefly becomes the centre of attention before the movie's perhaps inevitable end. This is in no small part due to Pacino's brilliant portrayal of a character that could not be further removed from his previous role, Michael Corleone, in the criminal food chain. It's perhaps a moot point now whether he or Nicholson was more deserving of the best actor Oscar, which went to the latter for *One Flew Over The Cuckoo's Nest*. Certainly Pacino deserved it more for this movie than his eventual recognition for the over-acted *Scent of a Woman*. The direction of Sidney Lumet (who teamed up previously with Pacino for *Serpico*) and the cinematography contribute to the edgy atmosphere, as the golden hues make the viewer almost feel the sweltering heat of that long, sticky Brooklyn afternoon.

USA, 1975
DIRECTOR:
Sidney Lumet
CAST INCLUDES:
Al Pacino, John Cazale,
Charles Durning, James Broderick,
Beulah Garrick
SCREENPLAY:
Frank Pierson from the articles by
P.F. Kluge and Thomas Moore
CINEMATOGRAPHY:
Victor J. Kemper
**PRODUCERS/
PRODUCTION COMPANIES:**
Martin Bregman, Martin Elfand,
Robert Greenhut/Artists
Entertainment Complex
**ACADEMY AWARD
NOMINATIONS (1976)**
Best Actor in a Leading Role:
Al Pacino
Best Actor in a Supporting Role:
Chris Sarandon
Best Director: Sidney Lumet
Best Film Editing: Dede Allen
Best Picture: Martin Bregman,
Martin Elfand
ACADEMY AWARDS
Best Writing, Original Screenplay:
Frank Pierson

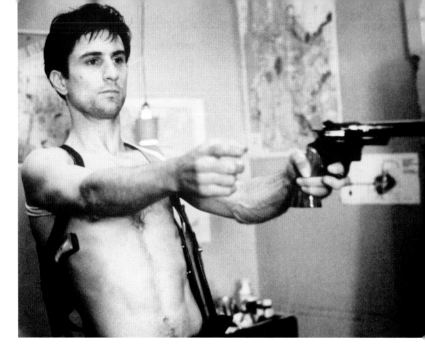

USA, 1976
DIRECTOR:
Martin Scorsese
CAST INCLUDES:
Robert De Niro, Cybill Shepherd,
Peter Boyle, Jodi Foster,
Harvey Kietel
SCREENPLAY:
Paul Schrader
CINEMATOGRAPHY:
Michael Chapman
**PRODUCERS/PRODUCTION
COMPANIES:**
Phillip M. Goldfarb, Julia Phillips,
Michael Phillips, Bill Phillips/Columbia
Pictures Corporation, Italo/Judeo
Productions
**ACADEMY AWARD
NOMINATIONS (1977)**
Best Actor in Leading Role:
Robert De Niro
Best Actress in a Supporting Role:
Jodi Foster
Best Music, Original Score:
Bernard Herrmann
Best Picture: Michael Phillips,
Julia Phillips

Taxi Driver

Travis Bickle (De Niro) drives his cab around the dingy streets of New York, witnessing the underbelly of the city and becoming consumed by it. We know it will only be a matter of time before it facilitates his downfall.

Bickle flaunts his frustrated isolation like a fallen good Samaritan, inflicting his loneliness on those around him in the shape of unwanted attention and overzealous help. The apparent salvation of a 12-year-old prostitute (Foster) is blinkered by the self-satisfaction that is obviously derived by Bickle from his far from altruistic act of kindness. This is a man crushed by the grim memories and experiences of the Vietnam War, a man with nothing in his life barr his sexist world view of the helpless woman in need of liberation. Of course, Scorsese points out the obvious; Bickle is the one who searches for redemption, his actions reflecting his own deep-rooted belief in his own superfluous existence.

Taxi Driver was, and still is, a seminal work that maintains a position of great importance in cinematic history. The absolute internal struggle played out with such conviction by De Niro, allows the audience to see one man's struggle with his tortured life. It's a character study unrivalled since and shows an actor at his peak and screenwriting and directing at their very best.

Scarface

Tony Montana (Pacino) is a Cuban refugee who tries to go straight on his arrival in the US. When that doesn't work out, he turns to crime and over time, and numerous bloody and violent deaths, comes to run the Miami cocaine underworld. What goes up must come down, however, and the film charts Tony's inevitable paranoid decline.

Written by a young Oliver Stone and directed by Brian De Palma after a number of critical flops, *Scarface* has become one of the iconic gangster movies. So much so, that many forget that it was itself a remake of the 1932 classic, which was perhaps as controversial at that time as this was when first released. Eschewing the poetic beauty and themes of family ties, the honour and respect of the *Godfather* films, this is an altogether different beast; one where people meet their end by chainsaw and where the protagonist is clearly insane from the beginning.

To that extent, it's what *Goodfellas* would have been had Scorcese concentrated on Pesci's character rather than Liotta's. Not a thinking man's gangster movie, we feel little sympathy or attachment for Tony Montana during his rise to power and miserable descent. Perhaps that is the point; surely better that than an admiration for the murderers in the Corleone family. The destruction of Pfieffer and Mastrantonio is certainly not pleasant, although in other respects the film is riotously enjoyable, full of eighties' excess and brutal, almost comic book, violence. From the enormous pad complete with room-sized sunken bath, the scene with Tony burying his face is an enormous bowl of cocaine to the final ultra-violent shootout on the staircase, this film contains scene after scene of decadent, guilty pleasure.

USA, 1983
DIRECTOR:
Brian De Palma
CAST INCLUDES:
Al Pacino, Steven Bauer, Michelle Pfeiffer, Mary Elizabeth Mastrantonio, Robert Loggia
SCREENPLAY:
Oliver Stone
CINEMATOGRAPHY:
John A. Alonzo
PRODUCERS/ PRODUCTION COMPANIES:
Martin Bregman, Peter Saphier, Louis A. Stroller/Universal Pictures

Witness

USA, 1985
DIRECTOR:
Peter Weir
CAST INCLUDES:
Harrison Ford, Kelly McGillis,
Josef Sommer, Lukas Haas,
Jan Rubes, Danny Glover
SCREENPLAY:
William Kelley, Earl W. Wallace,
Pamela Wallace
CINEMATOGRAPHY:
John Seale
PRODUCERS/
PRODUCTION COMPANIES:
David Bombyk, Edward S. Feldman,
Wendy Stites/ Paramount Pictures
ACADEMY AWARD
NOMINATIONS (1986)
Best Actor in a Leading Role:
Harrison Ford
Best Art Direction-Set Decoration:
Stan Jolley,
John H. Anderson
Best Cinematography: John Seale
Best Director: Peter Weir
Best Music, Original Score:
Maurice Jarre
Best Picture: Edward S. Feldman
ACADEMY AWARDS
Best Film Editing: Thom Noble
Best Writing, Screenplay Written
Directly for the Screen: William
Kelley, Pamela Wallace,
Earl W. Wallace

While travelling with his mother Rachel (McGillis), Samuel, a young Amish boy, is witness to the mens' room murder of an undercover cop. As in all the best films, the killers are soon on his trail, forcing mother, son and hard-bitten cop John Book (Ford) to take refuge within the Amish community. Once there, Book has to adapt to a completely new way of life and deal with his growing attraction to the widow, Rachel.

Director Peter Weir does a wonderful job in turning a simple good cop, bad cop witness-protection movie into something much more. He explores the conflicts of two opposite lifestyles coming into contact and how a good man, such as Book, can unintentionally bring violence into a previously peaceful world. To illustrate this he uses a range of imagery and techniques, not least of all with regard to wheat and bread. The opening of the movie is a beautiful shot of a wheat field, in the closing sequence a grain silo is used as a weapon; Book, for all the right reasons, has tainted the Amish world.

On a different level, this is a simple and beautifully understated love story. The chemistry of Ford and McGillis virtually crackles and the tension that builds between them is a

treat to watch. Both turn in career-high performances; McGillis is captivating as the young widow torn between her upbringing and her desire, Ford is great in one of his first serious roles as the unassuming hero. The cinematography and use of music is outstanding, and the barn-raising scene, in particular, is a lesson in filmmaking.

The Untouchables

Sean Connery won an Academy Award for his role of a veteran Chicago cop in this gangster movie set in the 1930s. Federal Agent Elliot Ness (Costner) is determined to bring down Chicago crime lord Al Capone (De Niro) despite the fact that Capone runs the city and controls the police force. To aid him, Ness recruits George Stone (Garcia) a rookie sharpshooter straight out of the academy, Malone (Connery) a tough old-school beat cop, and Oscar (Smith) a Treasury accountant. Together, this team takes the title role and sets about indicting Capone for tax evasion. What follows is a stylish cops-and-robbers movie with excellent camera work from Burum and some remarkable set pieces.

De Niro turns in an excellent, if short, performance as Capone. He faultlessly switches between showboating media star and brutal mobster – his baseball themed 'pep-talk' is classic stuff. Costner, in one of his best performances, gives a fine depiction of the initially honourable and innocent Ness. His performance perfectly captures the changes that Ness experiences as he faces the consequences of the increasingly dirty war that he is waging on Capone. It is Connery however who gives the outstanding performance of the film, his on-screen presence dominates his scenes and he is utterly believable as the grizzled, hard-talking, streetwise cop Malone.

With *The Untouchables*, De Palma has created a wonderfully entertaining film that's stylish and directed with flair. The scene where Malone is murdered is a lesson to all filmmakers in how to build up tension. The climactic baby carriage scene at Union Station is a superb example of how the interaction of music, sound effects and slow motion can create one of cinema's greatest shoot outs.

USA, 1987
DIRECTOR:
Brian De Palma
CAST INCLUDES:
Kevin Costner, Sean Connery, Charles Martin Smith, Andy Garcia, Robert De Niro
SCREENPLAY:
David Mamet from the novel by Oscar Fraley, Eliot Ness and Paul Robsky
CINEMATOGRAPHY:
Stephen H. Burum
PRODUCERS/ PRODUCTION COMPANIES:
Raymond Hartwick, Art Linson/ Paramount Pictures
ACADEMY AWARD NOMINATIONS (1988)
Best Art Direction-Set Decoration: Patrizia von Brandenstein, William A. Elliott, Hal Gausman
Best Costume Design: Marilyn Vance
Best Music, Original Score: Ennio Morricone
ACADEMY AWARDS:
Best Actor in a Supporting Role: Sean Connery

Goodfellas

USA, 1990
DIRECTOR:
Martin Scorsese
CAST INCLUDES:
Robert De Niro, Ray Liotta, Joe Pesci,
Lorraine Bracco, Paul Sorvino
SCREENPLAY:
Martin Scorsese from the book *Wise Guy* by Nicholas Pileggi
CINEMATOGRAPHY:
Michael Ballhaus
**PRODUCERS/
PRODUCTION COMPANIES:**
Barbara De Fina, Bruce S. Pustin,
Irwin Winkler/Warner Bros.
**ACADEMY AWARD
NOMINATIONS (1991)**
Best Actress in a Supporting Role:
Lorraine Bracco
Best Director: Martin Scorsese
Best Film Editing:
Thelma Schoonmaker
Best Picture: Irwin Winkler
Best Writing, Screenplay Based on
Material from Another Medium:
Nicholas Pileggi,
Martin Scorsese
ACADEMY AWARDS
Best Actor in a Supporting Role:
Joe Pesci

Goodfellas is based on the true story of one man's life in the New York Mafia. Liotta plays Henry Hill the central character of the film, with De Niro and Pesci making up the other 'Goodfellas'. As Henry Hill grows up, he progresses from running errands for the local Mafia to become a fully-fledged member of the gang. Henry is half-Italian, half-Irish and as such will never be accepted into the higher echelons of the Mafia as a 'name'. This, however, does not prevent him from living the good life; status, cars, cash and mistresses are all to be enjoyed. The focus is firmly on the camaraderie however, and the Goodfellas are rarely apart – family parties, gambling and carousing are as much a part of this life as the violence, extortion and robbery. The story really gets interesting when the bonds and loyalty that tie the Goodfellas together start to unravel.

From the director that made such classics as *Taxi Driver* and *Raging Bull*, it is high praise to rate *Goodfellas* as one of Scorsese's finest films, but it is completely justified. Scorsese provides an insight into the mob but without losing the audience's sympathy with, and interest in, the characters. Add to that some outstanding performances from actors such as De Niro, Liotta and especially Pesci, and you have a brilliant movie.

As with many Mafia films there is a fair amount of violence, however, more worthy of note is the tension which Scorsese builds and it is the threat of impending violence that makes this movie stand out. This film also has humour; I challenge anyone watching the 'You think I'm funny?' scene not to feel the hairs stand up on the back of their neck before laughing out loud in relief. And if that's not enough, there are a couple of great recipes – just remember to slice your garlic with a razor blade.

Miller's Crossing

For fans of gangster movies, the Coen brothers have produced a classic film, full of sharp-suited spivs, corrupt cops, long-suffering molls and the best use of hats in any movie. The only things that smoke more than our hero Tom Regan (Byrne) are the Tommy guns. Regan is the right-hand man of Leo (Finney) a big-time gangster during the prohibition. When Leo falls for Verna (Harden) he refuses to let rival boss Johnny Caspar (Polito) kill Verna's brother Berni (Turturro), a cheating snivelling bookie. Confused? You will be, the plot twists and turns with double and triple crosses as the characters all work the angles. Keeping up with the shifting allegiances is not made any easier by the dialogue, which is pure Coen brothers; a blend of slang, obscure nicknames and 1930s gangster rap.

In addition to the snappy dialogue, the Coen stamp can be seen in the feel of the locations. The illicit bars are glitzy and vibrant but the rest of the city is often under-lit, grey and washed out, the perfect backdrop to some classic set pieces. Perhaps the most memorable of which is when a surprisingly athletic Finney turns the tables on some would-be assassins and dispatches a carload of heavies with a Tommy gun to the strains of 'Danny Boy' from his bedside gramophone.

Byrne glowers and broods on-screen; his soft brogue nicely balances the uncompromising and often cruel side of his character. For me however, Polito, as rival boss Johnny Caspar, steals the movie with his 'ethical' approach to gangsterism and some wonderful dialogue. The overall result is a complex but hugely entertaining pastiche of the gangster movie – watch it, then watch it again.

USA, 1990
DIRECTOR:
Joel Coen, Ethan Coen
CAST INCLUDES:
Gabriel Byrne, Marcia Gay Harden,
John Turturro, Jon Polito,
Albert Finney
SCREENPLAY:
Joel Coen, Ethan Coen
CINEMATOGRAPHY:
Barry Sonnenfeld
**PRODUCERS/
PRODUCTION COMPANIES:**
Ben Barenholtz, Ethan Coen,
Graham Place, Mark Silverman/
20th Century Fox, Circle Films Inc.

Basic Instinct

USA, 1992
DIRECTOR:
Paul Verhoeven
CAST INCLUDES:
Michael Douglas, Sharon Stone,
George Dzundza, Jeanne Tripplehorn,
Denis Arndt
SCREENPLAY:
Joe Eszterhas
CINEMATOGRAPHY:
Jan de Bont
PRODUCERS/
PRODUCTION COMPANIES:
William S. Beasley, Louis D'Esposito,
Mario Kassar, Alan Marshall/ Carolco
Pictures Inc., Le Studio Canal+,
TriStar Pictures
ACADEMY AWARD
NOMINATIONS (1993)
Best Film Editing: Frank J Urioste
Best Music, Original Score:
Jerry Goldsmith

Nick Curran (Douglas) is a wily San Francisco detective who gets out of his depth while investigating the murder of an aging rocker. Already under investigation himself for being too handy with his gun, Curran finds himself relentlessly drawn into the world (and bed) of the prime suspect, Catherine Tramell (Stone). As the film unfolds it becomes apparent that Tramell is involved in the murder but is she too obvious a suspect and is Curran going to be the next victim or killer?

In *Basic Instinct*, Verhoeven succeeded in bringing a strong cast to what is essentially a high quality erotic thriller, a genre in which you would not normally expect to see the Hollywood élite. In fact, the hype which surrounded the release was due more to the combination of violence, sex and, let's be honest, that leg crossing scene, than the sight of Michael Douglas (naked or

otherwise). Sharon Stone is sexy as hell and Verhoeven allows her character, and not her not insignificant charms, to dominate her scenes. Whether she is off-camera or on, Stone is the centre of attention and this can be seen in the naked lust in the eyes of all those men (and women) around her. Interestingly, though, Stone is often directed straight to camera, a neat trick which further emphasizes her character's ability to manipulate those around her.

Basic Instinct keeps you guessing all the way and the action and style make this movie stand out from the crowd of cheaper and poorer imitations that it has spawned.

Reservoir Dogs

This amazing debut film came about when Quentin Tarantino, then one of LA's many struggling actor-writers, met Harvey Keitel's wife at a screenwriting class. She read the script, passed it to Harvey and the rest is cinematic history.

Five strangers, known only by pseudonym colours, are recruited to rob a diamond merchant. When the heist goes bad, the suspicious dogs try to identify the rat in the pack. Unlike most heist movies, the actual robbery is not central to the plot and is not shown until near the end of the film. In what has become trademark Tarantino style, some wonderful writing and editing shows the action, not chronologically, but in flashbacks and cuts forward. This technique of simultaneously developing different strands of the plot makes what is actually a very simple story seem vastly more complex. Amid the accusations and increasingly violent recriminations that follow the heist, the tension builds to a wonderful standoff and shocking climax.

Some critics vilified Tarantino for packaging as *über*-cool a film with so much sadism, bloodshed and depravity. However, while parts of the film are undeniably shocking, much of the gore is so over-stylized as to be unbelievable. A career defining performance from Michael Madsen, alongside the talents of Harvey Keitel and Steve Buscemi, give this film a weight that most independent filmmakers can only dream of. The sharp dialogue and a too-cool-for-school soundtrack combine to give an originality and style which would inspire countless copies and set Tarantino on his way to becoming one of Hollywood's big players.

USA, 1992
DIRECTOR:
Quentin Tarantino
CAST INCLUDES:
Harvey Keitel, Tim Roth,
Michael Madsen, Steve Buscemi,
Chris Penn
SCREENPLAY:
Roger Avary, Quentin Tarantino
CINEMATOGRAPHY:
Andrzej Sekula
PRODUCERS/
PRODUCTION COMPANIES:
Lawrence Bender,
Richard N. Gladstein, Monte Hellman,
Harvey Keitel, Ronna B. Wallace/
Live Entertainment,
Dog Eat Dog Productions Inc.

Pulp Fiction

USA, 1994
DIRECTOR:
Quentin Tarantino
CAST INCLUDES:
John Travolta, Samuel L. Jackson,
Uma Thurman, Bruce Willis,
Ving Rhames, Tim Roth
SCREENPLAY:
Roger Avary (stories),
Quentin Tarantino (screenplay)
CINEMATOGRAPHY:
Andrzej Sekula
**PRODUCERS/
PRODUCTION COMPANIES:**
Lawrence Bender,
Danny DeVito, Richard N. Gladstein,
Michael Shamberg, Stacey Sher,
Bob Weinstein, Harvey Weinstein/
A Band Apart, Jersey Films,
Miramax Films
**ACADEMY AWARD
NOMINATIONS (1995)**
Best Actor in a Leading Role:
John Travolta
Best Actor in a Supporting Role:
Samuel L. Jackson
Best Actress in a Supporting Role:
Uma Thurman
Best Director: Quentin Tarantino
Best Film Editing: Sally Menke
Best Picture: Lawrence Bender
ACADEMY AWARDS
Best Writing, Screenplay Written
Directly for the Screen:
Quentin Tarantino, Roger Avary

Pulp Fiction is a skilful collection of interconnecting stories, with overlapping and interwoven plots, the main characters of which inhabit a world of drugs, crime and damage limitation. The main link in each story is Vincent Vega, brother of Mr Blonde from *Reservoir Dogs* and played by the once-again-cool John Travolta. Vincent and his partner Jules (Jackson) are killers working for Marcellus Wallace (Rhames); the film tells the story of what happens when simple things like a date, a fixed fight, a diner robbery and returning your boss's dirty laundry do not go according to plan.

There are so many aspects of *Pulp Fiction* that are worthy of praise. The screenplay is incredibly tight and makes it a pleasure to watch the varied stories unfold. The all-star cast is notable for including perennial favourites Keitel and Walken, bringing Thurman and Jackson into the mainstream and reinvigorating the careers of Travolta and Willis. The result is some memorable performances not only due to the interesting mix of stars but, more importantly, because of the cracking dialogue. The writing is extravagant and clever; each character has a distinct personal style which leads to some wonderful scenes, with engaging dialogue that is included not to advance the plot, but simply to entertain.

Tarantino apparently worked in a video shop and was inspired to write *Pulp Fiction* by his love of old films. Most viewers will not understand all of the obscure references or get the nods to cult movies and you don't need to. *Pulp Fiction* stands apart as a fantastic film in its own right – quirky, funny and with (literally) heart-stopping moments.

Léon

FRANCE, 1994
DIRECTOR:
Luc Besson
CAST INCLUDES:
Jean Reno, Gary Oldman, Natalie
Portman, Danny Aiello
SCREENPLAY:
Luc Besson
CINEMATOGRAPHY:
Thierry Arbogast
PRODUCERS/
PRODUCTION COMPANIES:
Claude Besson, Luc Besson, Bernard
Grenet, Patrice Ledoux/
Buena Vista, Gaumont, Dauphin

Léon tells the tale of Mathilda (Portman) a twelve-year-old girl living in a family without love. Her father is involved in drug dealing for some bent cops led by the terrifying Agent Stansfield (Oldman). When Stansfield discovers he is being cheated by Mathilda's father, he takes revenge by executing the entire family apart for Mathilda who escapes and seeks refuge in a neighbour's flat. Léon (Reno), the neighbour, is more than he seems however, and when Mathilda discovers he is a contract killer she begs him to teach her how to settle her own scores.

Luc Besson, writer and director, puts together a stylish and riveting thriller, which doesn't take itself too seriously. The pace is fast moving and the action sequences are enjoyable. Jean Reno gives a solid performance in the title role and manages to balance the conflicting elements of his character well. It is, however, Portman, as Mathilda, who steals the show with a combination of lost waif meets driven avenger. Oldman is excellent as the psychopathic cop and if he overplays the part he can be forgiven as he is a pleasure to watch.

Placing a twelve-year-old girl so firmly in the centre of such a violent and adult-themed film was a brave move by Besson and he was criticized for it. Some of the themes are similar to his earlier release *La Femme Nikita* (1992) except that in that film the would-be assassin is a young women and not a young girl. That aside, *Léon* is well directed, it is entertaining and full of tension and has a dynamic visual flair.

Se7en

USA, 1995
DIRECTOR:
David Fincher
CAST:
Morgan Freeman, Brad Pitt,
Kevin Spacey, Gwyneth Paltrow
SCREENPLAY:
Andrew Kevin Walker
CINEMATOGRAPHY:
Darius Khondji, Harris Savides
PRODUCERS/
PRODUCTION COMPANIES:
Stephen Brown, Phyllis Carlyle, William
C. Gerrity, Nana Greenwald, Lynn Harris,
Dan Kolsrud, Anne Kopelson, Arnold
Kopelson, Gianni Nunnari, Sanford
Panitch, Michele Platt, Richard
Saperstein/New Line Cinema
ACADEMY AWARD
NOMINATIONS (1996)
Best Film Editing: Richard Francis-Bruce

Se7en was a turning point in director David Fincher's career; prior to this he made *Alien 3*, after this he made *Fight Club*. In *Se7en*, Fincher has made a film that is original and stylish, add in Brad Pitt, Morgan Freeman and a fantastic twist and you have something definitely worth seeing. The plot is diabolically straightforward. Detectives Somerset (Freeman) and Mills (Pitt) are investigating a series of brutal murders where the killer (Spacey) is, quite literally, making the seven sins deadly.

The style of the movie fits the subject; the lighting is dark, often torch lit at the crime scenes, outside the rain is almost constant and the atmosphere is depressing. Pitt and Freeman are convincing as the unlikely partners, the script gives them enough space to stamp their not inconsiderable talents on the roles. Spacey, however, as the killer, runs away with the film as the supremely arrogant and intelligent psycho – his final smile is perfection.

Not for the faint-hearted, *Se7en* is uncompromising and at times stomach-churning, however the details of the crimes are entirely necessary to balance the simplicity of the plot. The violence is never gratuitous, as with the rest of the film, Fincher displays a delicate, stylish touch which is all the more effective. The pace of the film is brilliantly controlled; the tension rises as the chase heats up, each addition to the body-count raises the bar another level. The end, when it comes, is unexpected, a truly shattering climax to a film that thinks out of its box.

The Usual Suspects

USA, 1995
DIRECTOR:
Bryan Singer
CAST INCLUDES:
Stephen Baldwin, Gabriel Byrne,
Benicio Del Toro, Kevin Pollak,
Kevin Spacey
SCREENPLAY:
Christopher McQuarrie
CINEMATOGRAPHY:
Newton Thomas Sigel
PRODUCERS/
PRODUCTION COMPANIES:
Hans Brockmann, François Duplat,
Art Horan, Robert Jones,
Kenneth Kokin, Michael McDonnell,
Bryan Singer/PolyGram Filmed
Entertainment, Spelling Films
International, Blue Parrot, Bad Hat
Harry Productions, Rosco Film GmbH
ACADEMY AWARDS (1996)
Best Actor in a Supporting Role:
Kevin Spacey
Best Writing, Screenplay
Written Directly for the Screen:
Christopher McQuarrie

Bryan Singer's *The Usual Suspects* received widespread acclaim and commercial success when it was released in 1995. By drawing together a stellar cast to tell a convoluted tale, he created an entertaining take on the heist movie. Five criminals, McManus (Baldwin), Keaton (Byrne), Fenster (Del Toro), Hockney (Pollak) and Verbal (Spacey), are pulled in by the cops for a line up. Subsequently released, it becomes apparent that they were drawn together for a reason, when a spokesman for the elusive criminal mastermind Keyser Soze approaches them. Soze is a sinister and widely-feared gangster who wants them to raid a ship containing a drug shipment, kill everyone on-board and collect a large sum of cash.

Told primarily through flashback, by Verbal as the police interrogate him after the event, the mystery deepens and the tension builds to a surprising twist. It is this revelation that is the film's crowning glory, and its weakest point. The surprise is so unexpected that you could kick yourself for not seeing it coming. However, with the benefit of hindsight there are few clues that would enable you to work it out and hence the effect is rather contrived.

All the main actors do a great job in portraying their varied characters although it has to be said that none really inspire much sympathy. Spacey, in particular, is especially effective and gives the most memorable performance of the film; the Academy obviously agreed. The result is a baffling but entertaining story worth watching for the climax and the on-screen connection of some of Hollywood's most versatile and distinctive actors.

Fargo

With wide open scenery, snowy fields, and some really strange accents, surely this film is set in some far-flung corner of Scandanavia? No, the location is actually the Coen Brothers' home state of Minnesota. William H. Macey stars as Jerry Lundegaard, a sleazy second-hand car dealer who hires a couple of hoods to kidnap his wife to get a ransom from her rich father-in-law. Unfortunately for them, Marge Gunderson (McDormand), a police chief from a sleepy town in the American Mid-West, picks up their trail, a task not made any easier by the fact that she is hugely pregnant.

Like all of the Coen brothers' films, *Fargo* looks great and sounds better. The scenery and landscapes are bleak but you sense that the Coens retain a fondness for the open spaces of their childhood home. McDormand's character and her pregnancy add a warmth and humanity to balance the brutality and violence of the kidnappers. That said, the Coens don't pull any punches, the locals are narrow-minded and even the heroine seems a bit of a bumpkin when she strays out of uniform and dines out in town.

The comedy is black, as you'd expect from the Coens, and the irony is thick. Some may find the humour harder to understand than the accents, but it is definitely worth persevering, as this is a wonderful film. Not often do filmmakers get the right balance between comedy and cruelty, humanity and irony, but this film is spot on. The story is not the most original, but the storytelling is delightful and most definitely deserved its two Oscars.

USA, 1996
DIRECTORS:
Joel Coen, Ethan Coen
CAST INCLUDES:
Frances McDormand,
William H. Macy, Steve Buscemi,
Harve Presnell, Peter Stormare
SCREENPLAY:
Ethan Coen, Joel Coen
CINEMATOGRAPHY:
Roger Deakins
PRODUCERS/
PRODUCTION COMPANIES:
Tim Bevan, John Cameron,
Ethan Coen, Eric Fellner/ Gramercy
Pictures, PolyGram Filmed
Entertainment, Working Title Films
ACADEMY AWARD
NOMINATIONS (1997)
Best Actor in a Supporting Role:
William H. Macy
Best Cinematography:
Roger Deakins
Best Director: Joel Coen
Best Film Editing: Ethan Coen
(as Roderick Jaynes)
Joel Coen (as Roderick Jaynes)
Best Picture: Ethan Coen
ACADEMY AWARDS
Best Actress in a Leading Role:
Frances McDormand
Best Writing, Screenplay Written
Directly for the Screen: Ethan Coen,
Joel Coen

L. A. Confidential

USA, 1997
DIRECTOR:
Curtis Hanson
CAST INCLUDES:
Kevin Spacey, Russell Crowe,
Guy Pearce, James Cromwell,
Kim Basinger, Danny DeVito
SCREENPLAY:
Brian Helgeland, Curtis Hanson from
the novel by James Ellroy
CINEMATOGRAPHY:
Dante Spinotti
**PRODUCERS/
PRODUCTION COMPANIES:**
Curtis Hanson, Brian Helgeland,
Dan Kolsrud, Arnon Milchan, Michael
G. Nathanson, David L.
Wolper/Monarchy Enterprises B.V.,
Regency Enterprises, Warner Bros.
**ACADEMY AWARD
NOMINATIONS (1998)**
Best Art Direction-Set Decoration:
Jeannine Claudia Oppewall, Jay Hart
Best Cinematography:
Dante Spinotti
Best Director: Curtis Hanson
Best Film Editing: Peter Honess
Best Music Original Dramatic Score:
Jerry Goldsmith
Best Picture: Arnon Milchan,
Curtis Hanson, Michael G. Nathanson
Best Sound: Andy Nelson,
Anna Behlmer, Kirk Francis
ACADEMY AWARDS
Best Actress in a Supporting Role:
Kim Basinger
Best Writing, Screenplay Based on
Material from Another Medium: Brian
Helgeland, Curtis Hanson

The seedy side of 1950s Los Angeles is the setting for this complex tale of Hollywood sleaze and police corruption. An investigation into a series of unexplained murders draws together three very different cops. Ed Exley (Pearce) is the high-flyer of the police force, honest, straight-laced and bespectacled. Jack Vincennes (Spacey) is urbane and suave, a cop by day and TV personality by night and always on the lookout for a quick buck. Bud White (Crowe) is the maverick, willing to bend the rules in his passionate quest for justice but his brutal temper is always simmering just below the surface.

With such an array of stars as this film boasts there is always the worry that egos will be bruised, directors bullied and the whole will not be equal to the sum of the individual parts. In *L.A. Confidential* however, Hanson has created a film which dispels any such doubt. All the cast are on wonderful form; none more so than Basinger, as the high class hooker and 'ringer' for Veronika Lake, and Crowe, as the brooding Bud White.

While *L.A. Confidential* is imbued with much of the mood and tradition of film noir, it doesn't have the feel of a period piece. Hanson weaves a tangled storyline, but razor-sharp characters and excellent timing mean that following the plot is a great ride. As you watch the film it is difficult not to be drawn into the lush sights and sounds of Ellroy's Los Angeles, which is at times cynical but always seductive.

Run Lola Run

Lola rennt

Lola's boyfriend, a minor criminal, is supposed to deliver some money to an associate. Unfortunately, however, he leaves the bag containing the cash on a train. He calls Lola from a phone box in a blind panic asking her to replace the money as soon as possible in order to save his life. Lola thinks about her bank manager father. From this simple premise, the film shows three different outcomes to the predicament, depending upon certain events.

So what we have is a hip version of *Sliding Doors*. This German film is short (clocking in at 80 minutes) but hugely enjoyable. There is very little dialogue and a pumping techno soundtrack, almost throughout. This is clearly a movie pitched at the MTV generation; the viewer is treated to animated sequences, black-and-white and stills footage, split screens and all manner of speeding up and slowing down.

And has a film ever been more literally titled? Lola does indeed run, and run, but never once does this become monotonous or boring, in part due to the various techniques and styles used to tell the story. It is also in part due to the number of (necessarily recurrent) visual gags. So, in each version of the story, we see two men carrying a sheet of glass across the road. What happens to that glass depends in each case upon what has happened prior to the viewer seeing it. The quirkiness and skewed logic used to contrive various situations brings to mind Jeunet at his best and the visceral, kinetic energy will keep viewers hooked. Ridiculous, but brilliant, cinema.

GERMANY, 1998
DIRECTOR:
Tom Tykwer
CAST INCLUDES:
Franka Potente, Moritz Bleibtreu, Herbert Knaup, Nina Petri, Armin Rohde
SCREENPLAY:
Tom Tykwer
CINEMATOGRAPHY:
Frank Griebe
PRODUCERS/ PRODUCTION COMPANIES:
Stefan Arndt, Gebhard Henke, Maria Köpf, Andreas Schreitmüller/X-Filme Creative Pool, Westdeutscher Rundfunk, arte

Memento

USA, 2000
DIRECTOR:
Christopher Nolan
CAST INCLUDES:
Guy Pearce, Carrie-Anne Moss,
Joe Pantoliano, Mark Boone Junior,
Russ Fega
SCREENPLAY:
Christopher Nolan,
Jonathan Nolan (story)
CINEMATOGRAPHY:
Wally Pfister
PRODUCERS/
PRODUCTION COMPANIES:
Christopher Ball, Elaine Dysinger,
Aaron Ryder, Emma Thomas, Jennifer
Todd, Suzanne Todd, William Tyrer/
I Remember Productions, Llc
Newmarket Capital Group LLC
Team Todd
ACADEMY AWARD
NOMINATIONS (2002)
Best Editing: Dody Dorn
Best Writing, Screenplay Written
Directly for the Screen:
Christopher Nolan,
Jonathan Nolan (story)

In a cinematic world full of re-makes, re-imaginings and all out copies, it is rare to find a movie as original and thought provoking as *Memento*. Guy Pearce plays Leonard Shelby, a man searching for the man who raped and murdered his wife. Shelby has a problem however; since his wife's death he suffers from a rare disorder that means that he cannot retain new memories. As a result, he must make copious notes, take photos of people he meets, and even tattoo his body with hints in order to keep track of the on-going investigation.

Christopher Nolan lays out what he has in store for us from the opening shot when we see a Polaroid fading from fully developed to completely blank. Nolan plunges the viewer into Shelby's shoes with a neat trick; while each scene is played chronologically, they are ordered in reverse. Hence the film starts at the story's conclusion and fills in the gaps as it 'progresses' to the beginning. This makes watching the film a

confusing experience and there is no neat payoff after the climax. All of the characters seem to have some level of duplicity and it is unclear who can be trusted; Shelby himself manipulates his own memories through the notes he makes.

To write-off the film as unfathomable, however, is to understate its intelligence and inventiveness. Solid performances by the cast as well as taut and stylish direction bring out the most from the rightly acclaimed screenplay. And if you are frustrated by the labyrinthine editing, the DVD of the film allows the scenes to be played chronologically.

City of God
Cidade de Deus

Shot using a hand held camera, *City of God* is a vibrant and dynamic glimpse of life in the slums of Rio de Janeiro through the 1960s, 1970s and 1980s. The story is told from the point of view of Rocket (Rodrigues) a quiet boy with no intention of falling into the cesspit of petty crime, drugs and violence that surrounds him. Instead he takes photos of his surroundings in order to try and escape them. Li'l Ze (Firmino) however, grows up leading a gang and is a ruthless, cold-hearted killer who builds up an empire that controls the City of God. Shocking and violent, this film pulls no punches; murder and robbery are everyday events for even the youngest child and when gang warfare breaks out, everyone is pulled in.

The opening shot of the film is wonderfully imaginative and a signal to the audience that they are in for a great ride. The camera chases a horde of screaming, laughing kids who are, in turn, chasing a chicken. In a moment the whole mood changes, the kids become Li'l Ze's gang; draw their guns and square up to a group of cops. Rocket finds himself caught in the middle; the camera begins a mad circle around him before setting us down twenty years earlier.

The inventive camera work and use of fast editing gives the film a vibrancy and energy like no other. In addition, some wonderful characters and a sprinkling of humour give the whole movie a balance that shows the filmmakers' compassion for their subject.

BRAZIL, 2002
DIRECTOR:
Fernando Meirelles,
Kátia Lund (co-director)
CAST INCLUDES:
Alexandre Rodrigues,
Leandro Firmino, Phellipe Haagensen,
Douglas Silva, Jonathan Haagensen
SCREENPLAY:
Bráulio Mantovani from the novel
by Paulo Lins
CINEMATOGRAPHY:
César Charlone
**PRODUCERS/
PRODUCTION COMPANIES:**
Andrea Barata Ribeiro,
Marc Beauchamps, Daniel Filho,
Hank Levine, Vincent Maraval,
Mauricio Andrade Ramos, Donald
Ranvaud, Juliette Renaud,
Walter Salles, Elisa Tolomelli/
O2 Filmes, VideoFilmes, Globo Filmes,
Lumiere Productions, Studio Canal
Wild Bunch
**ACADEMY AWARD
NOMINATIONS (2004)**
Best Cinematography:
César Charlone
Best Director:
Fernando Meirelles
Best Editing: Daniel Rezende
Best Writing, Screenplay Based on
Material Previously Produced or
Published: Bráulio Mantovani

WAR

Shoulder Arms

USA, 1918
DIRECTOR:
Charles Chaplin
CAST INCLUDES:
Charlie Chaplin, Albert Austin,
Henry Bergman, Sydney Chaplin,
Edna Purviance
SCREENPLAY:
Charles Chaplin
CINEMATOGRAPHY:
R. H. Totheroh
**PRODUCERS/
PRODUCTION COMPANIES:**
Charles Chaplin/First National

Chaplin is a private in the army at a training camp at the time of World War I. Although his drilling squad is not very capable, he outshines the others in incompetence. After being on his feet all day, he gets into his bunk and falls asleep. He dreams of what he'll do on the battlefield. In enemy-held territory, he covers himself in a tree trunk in order to move around undetected until a French girl (Purviance) gives him refuge. When she is arrested by German soldiers, Charlie rescues her and captures the Kaiser, Hindenburg and the Crown Prince. Then he is woken up by two soldiers who tell him to get on with training.

One of the greatest of Charlie Chaplin's films was released only a few weeks before the armistice, drawing howls of protest from those who thought that one shouldn't make fun of trench warfare so fresh in the memory. Yet, it was Chaplin's biggest triumph up to that time, proving that audiences needed a good laugh and release after the tragic war. Abandoning his baggy trousers, cane and bowler hat for the first time since he devised the character of the tramp, Charlie, in uniform, is just as funny as before, especially camouflaged as a tree trunk.

Wings

Two pals, Jack Powell (Rogers) and David Armstrong (Arlen) are vying for the same girl, Sylvia Lewis (Ralston). Mary Preston (Bow) is the doting girl-next-door with her eye on Powell. After they join up as airmen when America enters World War I, Mary joins the war effort as an ambulance driver in France. Having seen action in the air, the two rather disillusioned pilots go on a drunken

furlough in Paris where they meet up with Mary again, before returning to battle.

Dedicated 'to those young warriors of the sky whose wings are folded about them forever', *Wings* was the first winner of the Best Picture Oscar award, the only silent film to have that honour. With its superb pictorial qualities, and the spectacular dog fights balanced with a tender love triangle, it is one of the best flying films of any period. William Wellman's experiences as a much-decorated airman with the crack Lafayette Flying Corps in France during World War I, and later as a stunt pilot, lent authority to the breath-taking aerial sequences, all filmed without faking or process shots. This was done by mounting cameras on the front of the planes, the actors going aloft with the pilot, who would duck down as they struck the right heroic attitudes. The film was shot with the co-operation of the US government, which supplied thousands of soldiers, hundreds of planes, and pilots as extras. One of the stunt flyers ended up in hospital with a broken neck after a crash. Paramount Studios was flooded with fan letters for the young actor who played a pilot who leaves a half-eaten candy bar before going to his death in the sky. On the strength of the reaction to his 20-second appearance, the studio offered Gary Cooper a contract.

USA, 1927
DIRECTOR:
William Wellman
CAST INCLUDES:
Clara Bow, Charles 'Buddy' Rogers,
Richard Arlen, Jobyna Ralston,
Gary Cooper
SCREENPLAY:
Hope Loring, Louis D.Lighton from a
story by John Monk Saunders
CINEMATOGRAPHY:
Harry Perry
**PRODUCERS/
PRODUCTION COMPANIES:**
Adolph Zukor/Paramount
ACADEMY AWARDS (1929)
Best Picture
Best Engineering Effects:
Roy Pomeroy

All Quiet on the Western Front

USA, 1930
DIRECTOR:
Lewis Milestone
CAST INCLUDES:
Lew Ayres, Louis Wolheim, John Wray,
Raymond Griffith, Gerard Duval
SCREENPLAY:
Del Andrews, Maxwell Anderson,
George Abbott
CINEMATOGRAPHY:
Arthur Edeson
**PRODUCERS/
PRODUCTION COMPANIES:**
Carl Laemmle Jr/ Universal
**ACADEMY AWARD
NOMINATIONS (1930)**
Best Writing Achievement:
George Abbot, Maxwell Anderson,
Del Andrews
ACADEMY AWARDS
Best Picture
Best Director: Lewis Milestone
Best Cinematography: Arthur Edeson

In Germany, at the start of World War I, a group of schoolboys is inspired to join up by their chauvinistic schoolmaster. The film then follows seven boys, full of patriotic fervour, who are thrown into the horror of trench warfare, mainly the initially enthusiastic recruit Paul Baumer (Ayres). At one stage, he finds a Frenchman (Griffith) in a shell-hole, stabs him and then agonizes about what he has done. One by one, his comrades are maimed or killed in action, and Paul gets more and more disillusioned by the futility of war, until he too, when reaching for a butterfly, is fatally shot by a sniper's bullet.

Based on Erich Maria Remarque's novel, this devastating film was a milestone in anti-war movies, particularly as it is an American movie seen from the German side. The penultimate scene, when the young soldier sees the beauty of a butterfly amidst the carnage, is justly celebrated. Particularly effective were the tracking shots of the soldiers attacking the enemy lines and the counter-attacks with death on both sides. So realistic were these sequences that they have often been used in documentary films of the war. Skilful use is made of the early sound system, crane shots, music and photography by Arthur Edeson. The leading player, Ayres, would become a conscientious objector during World War II. First released in a 140-minute version, it was cut to around 110 minutes without losing much of its initial impact.

La Grande Illusion

The Grand Illusion

During World War I, three French soldiers, the working class Maréchal (Gabin), the middle-class Jew Rosenthal (Dalio) and the aristocratic Boieldieu (Fresnay), after attempting to escape from various German POW camps, are held prisoner in a fortress run by the Commandant Von Rauffenstein (von Stroheim). Boieldieu dies so that Maréchal and Rosenthal can escape. They make their way to a farm, where a German war widow (Parlo) gives them refuge before they can get across the border to Switzerland.

Jean Renoir's most popular film, based on a true story, is not only a moving anti-war statement (though none of the war is seen), but a rich exploration of class loyalties and transcending friendships. Von Rauffenstein believes he has more in common with Boieldieu than they have with their fellow countrymen because of class. The fluid deep-focus photography (Renoir tried to keep people in frame at the same time giving them equal status), the set-pieces like the singing of 'La Marseillaise' during theatricals by prisoners in drag, and the extraordinarily sensitive performances, make *La Grande Illusion* one of cinema's most enduring masterpieces.

FRANCE, 1937
DIRECTOR:
Jean Renoir
CAST INCLUDES:
Jean Gabin, Pierre Fresnay,
Erich von Stroheim, Marcel Dalio,
Dita Parlo, Julien Carette
SCREENPLAY:
Charles Spaak, Jean Renoir
CINEMATOGRAPHY:
Christian Matras, Claude Renoir
**PRODUCERS/
PRODUCTION COMPANIES:**
Albert Pinkovitch, Frank Rollmer
(both uncredited)/R.A.C. (Réalisation
d'art Cinématographique)

Sergeant York

USA, 1941
DIRECTOR:
Howard Hawks
CAST INCLUDES:
Gary Cooper, Joan Leslie,
Walter Brennan, Margaret Wycherly,
Ward Bond
SCREENPLAY:
Abem Finkel, Harry Chandlee,
Howard Koch, John Huston from *The War Diary of Sergeant York* by
Alvin C York and biographies by
Sam K. Cowan and Tom Skeyhill
CINEMATOGRAPHY:
Sol Polito, Arthur Edeson
**PRODUCERS/
PRODUCTION COMPANIES:**
Hal B. Wallis/Warner Bros.
**ACADEMY AWARD
NOMINATIONS (1942)**
Best Picture: Jesse L. Lasky,
Hal B. Wallis
Best Actor in a Supporting Role:
Walter Brennan
Best Actress in a Supporting Role:
Margaret Wycherly
Best Art Direction-Interior
Decoration, Black-and-White:
Fred M. MacLean, John J. Hughes
Best Cinematography,
Black-and-White: Sol Polito
Best Director: Howard Hawks
Best Music, Scoring of a Dramatic
Picture: Max Steiner
Best Sound, Recording:
Nathan Levinson
Best Writing, Original Screenplay:
Abem Finkel, John Huston,
Harry Chandlee, Howard W. Koch
ACADEMY AWARDS
Best Actor in a Leading Role:
Gary Cooper
Best Film Editing: William Holmes

Alvin C. York is an irresponsible Tennessee mountain farmer trying to scratch a living out of the rocky earth. He finds religion after lightning strikes his rifle during a land dispute, forcing him to take a pacifist stance at the beginning of World War I. However, he gradually adapts his Christian beliefs to the circumstances. In one of the most heroic actions of the war, the soldier with born-again belligerence and armed with a Springfield rifle, wipes out thirty five German machine gunners and captures 132 prisoners almost single-handed. He returns to his mother (Wycherly) and girlfriend (Leslie) as a hero.

The film, based on the true story of World War I's most decorated American soldier, was meant as an inspiration to American audiences emerging from isolationism to enter World War II. The real Alvin C. York, who only gave his permission to film his story if Gary Cooper played him, supervised every phase of the production. As a result, it is chronicled with exemplary fidelity, offering the perfect framework for Cooper's sincerity and underplaying which exuded the goodness and piety of the character. Cooper's York, as the poet Carl Sandburg wrote, 'is one of the most beloved illiterates this country has ever known'. The director manages to balance an almost Fordian view of rural America with more Hawksian battle scenes.

In Which We Serve

HMS *Torrin*, a Royal Navy destroyer, is dive-bombed during the Battle of Crete and sinks. The surviving crew members, including Captain Kinross (Coward), Chief Petty Officer Walter Hardy (Miles) and Ordinary Seaman Shorty Blake (Mills), manage to reach a float. As they await rescue – or death – each of them remembers the events leading up to that moment, and the homes and families they have left behind. The Captain thinks of his wife and children, Hardy of his wife and mother-in-law, and Shorty remembers meeting his wife-to-be on a train. A young stoker (Attenborough) recalls his fear when the ship prepared to launch a torpedo attack, and how he deserted his post. HMS *Torrin* was involved in the evacuation of troops from Dunkirk. The float suffers another machine gun attack, and more of the crew are killed.

This 'story of a ship', mostly told in flashback, has Noel Coward giving a characteristically clipped performance as the captain based on Lord Louis Mountbatten, freely re-enacting his naval exploits. Permeating this moving wartime propaganda epic is the deep love for the ship which symbolizes the nation, without too many false heroics or flagwaving. The film is also significant in giving David Lean, who edited the film, his first chance to direct. Other first timers were Celia Johnson, Richard Attenborough, Daniel Massey and an 11-week-old Juliet Mills.

GB, 1942
DIRECTOR:
David Lean, Noel Coward
CAST INCLUDES:
Noel Coward, Michael Wilding,
John Mills, Bernard Miles, Celia Johnson
SCREENPLAY:
Noel Coward
CINEMATOGRAPHY:
Ronald Neame
PRODUCERS/
PRODUCTION COMPANIES:
Noel Coward/ Two Cities Films Ltd.,
British Lion Film Corporation
ACADEMY AWARD
NOMINATIONS (1944)
Best Picture: Noel Coward
Best Writing, Original Screenplay:
Noel Coward
ACADEMY AWARDS
Noel Coward received a special
Oscar for his 'outstanding
production achievement'

Five Graves To Cairo

USA, 1943
DIRECTOR:
Billy Wilder
CAST INCLUDES:
Franchot Tone, Erich von Stroheim,
Anne Baxter, Akim Tamiroff,
Peter Van Eyck
SCREENPLAY:
Charles Brackett, Billy Wilder
(from the play by Lajos Biró)
CINEMATOGRAPHY:
John F Seitz
**PRODUCERS/
PRODUCTION COMPANIES:**
Charles Brackett/ Paramount
**ACADEMY AWARD
NOMINATIONS (1944)**
Best Cinematograpraphy, Black-and-
White: John F. Seitz
Best Art Direction-Interior
Decoration, Black-and-White: Hans
Dreier, Ernst Fegté, Bertram Granger
Best Film Editing: Doane Harrison

A British tank commander (Tone), caught behind the lines during the North African Campaign, stumbles into a resort hotel at a desert oasis. While the hotel is occupied by the advancing Field-Marshall Rommel (von Stroheim), the soldier poses as a club-footed waiter in order to unravel the meaning of the mysterious 'Five Graves'. He is helped by a French maid (Baxter), with whom he falls in love.

Although a comparatively minor Billy Wilder movie, it is hugely enjoyable, with the war mainly acted out inside an oasis hotel. The script manages to inject wit and humour into a tense cat-and-mouse war drama, played out by Tone and the magnificent von Stroheim, who would later appear in Wilder's *Sunset Boulevard* (1950). Here he plays Rommel as a brutal Hun, not the noble soldier as portrayed later by James Mason in *The Desert Fox* (1951). The first shot of him is the back of his heavily-creased neck bursting out of his high military collar. Also excellent is Fortunio Bonanova as an opera-loving Italian, and Akim Tamiroff as the wily hotel owner.

The Life and Death of Colonel Blimp

A portrait, over forty years, of an archetypal British officer, Clive Wynne-Candy (Livesey) during the Boer War, World War I and the beginning of World War II, when he is seen as an old has-been who still believes he can win any fight with honour and maintain 'gentlemanly conduct'. Throughout, he keeps his friendship with a 'good' German officer (Walbrook) with whom he had fought a duel in Berlin in 1902. It takes his old German friend to point out how much the rules have been changed when fighting the Nazis.

Winston Churchill ordered the film to be banned from export because he felt it gave the wrong impression of the British soldier, and also it stressed, unusually for the times, Anglo-German friendship. However, Michael Powell and Emeric Pressburger tried to enshrine the ambiguity of the British national character in General Candy (played with wit and sincerity by Roger Livesey, expertly ageing throughout the film). It was the first Technicolor film made by the brilliant British writing-directing team, and it is truly sumptuous. A very young Deborah Kerr plays three parts across the three eras, embodying Wynne-Candy's vision of feminine charms.

GB, 1943
DIRECTOR:
Michael Powell, Emeric Pressburger
CAST INCLUDES:
Roger Livesey, Anton Walbrook,
Deborah Kerr, Roland Culver
SCREENPLAY:
Michael Powell, Emeric Pressburger
from the cartoon character created
by David Low
CINEMATOGRAPHY:
Georges Périnal
**PRODUCERS/
PRODUCTION COMPANIES:**
Michael Powell, Emeric Pressburger/
The Archers, Independent Producers

Rome, Open City

Roma, città aperta

ITALY, 1945
DIRECTOR:
Roberto Rossellini
CAST INCLUDES:
Anna Magnani, Aldo Fabrizi,
Marcello Pagliero, Maria Michi,
Harry Feist
SCREENPLAY:
Sergio Amidei, Federico Fellini
CINEMATOGRAPHY:
Ubaldo Arata
PRODUCERS/
PRODUCTION COMPANIES:
Giuseppe Amato, Ferruccio De
Martino, Roberto Rossellini
(all uncredited)/Minerva Film,
Excelsa Film
ACADEMY AWARD
NOMINATIONS (1947):
Best Writing, Screenplay:
Sergio Amidei, Federico Fellini
CANNES FILM FESTIVAL (1946)
Grand Prize of the Festival

In 1944, in the last days of the German occupation of Italy, Resistance leader Manfredi (Pagliero), fleeing the Gestapo, is given refuge by the pregnant Pina (Magnani). When she is shot, he takes shelter with a good-time girl (Michi), who betrays him. Manfredi and a priest (Fabrizi) are arrested. However, the film offers some hope for the future and victory.

The film that brought the Italian Neo-Realist movement to fruition was concerned with capturing, as directly as possible, the experiences of ordinary people caught up in political events. Using a documentary approach and filming with minimum resources in the actual streets and apartments of Rome, Roberto Rossellini achieved an immediacy and intensity that audiences had never previously witnessed. Two of the few professionals in the cast, Magnani and Fabrizi, give extremely moving performances. Emerging from the ashes of World War II, *Rome, Open City* is one of Europe's first post-war masterpieces.

The Story of G.I. Joe

A small group from the 18th Infantry is followed by war correspondent Ernie Pyle (Meredith) from North Africa to Italy. The group includes an understanding captain (Mitchum), who has risen from the ranks, a tough sergeant (Steele) who carries a phonograph record of his child's voice around with him, and a Brooklyn Romeo (Cassell).

Journalist Ernie Pyle, on whose book and experiences the film was based, died just before the picture was released. He was among a group of experienced war reporters who acted as technical consultants on the film, and it was thus one of the most authentic of war movies. Unlike the usual war saga, it concentrated on the fatigue, discomfort and anxiety that the common soldier must suffer. Director William Wellman, himself an active participant in World War I, used an effective semi-documentary style in his attempt to tell it how it was. Robert Mitchum, quietly impressive in his first substantial role, gained an Oscar nomination.

USA, 1945
DIRECTOR:
William Wellman
CAST INCLUDES:
Burgess Meredith, Robert Mitchum, Freddy Steele, Wally Cassell, Jimmy Lloyd
SCREENPLAY:
Leopold Atlas, Guy Endore, Philip Stevenson based on the war memoirs *Here Is Your War* and *Brave Men* by Ernie Pyle
CINEMATOGRAPHY:
Russell Metty
**PRODUCERS/
PRODUCTION COMPANIES:**
Lester Cowan/United Artists
**ACADEMY AWARD
NOMINATIONS (1946)**
Best Actor in a Supporting Role: Robert Mitchum
Best Writing, Screenplay: Leopold Atlas, Guy Endore, Philip Stevenson
Best Music, Original Song: Ann Ronell for the song 'Linda'
Best Music, Scoring of a Dramatic or Comedy Picture: Louis Applebaum, Ann Ronell

They Were Expendable

USA, 1945
DIRECTOR:
John Ford
CAST INCLUDES:
Robert Montgomery, John Wayne,
Donna Reed, Jack Holt, Ward Bond
SCREENPLAY:
Frank W. Wead from the book by
William L. White
CINEMATOGRAPHY:
Joseph August
**PRODUCERS/
PRODUCTION COMPANIES:**
John Ford /MGM
**ACADEMY AWARD
NOMINATIONS (1946)**
Best Sound, Recording:
Douglas Shearer
Best Special Effects: Donald Jahraus,
R.A. MacDonald, A. Arnold Gillespie,
Michael Steinmore

Just before the outbreak of World War II, Lieutenant John Brickley (Montgomery) is assigned to take his Motor Torpedo Boat Squadron to Manila Bay to assist in the defence against a possible Japanese attack in the Philippines. However, once there, he finds that the top brass has relegated the small PT craft to messenger duty. But when war breaks out, Brickley and his crew shoot down three Japanese planes during an attack on their base. Again, when the squadron is reassigned to Bataan, they are ordered to run messages, until they prove their worth and that of the PT boat.

An elegiac portrait of the American navy in the Philippines just before the islands fell to the Japanese in 1942, *They Were Expendable* was also a tribute to Lieutenant John D. Bulkeley

(later Vice Admiral) who pioneered the use of the PT boat in combat, played under the different name of Lieutenant John Brickley by a superb Robert Montgomery. The conviction of Montgomery's performance can be partly put down to the fact that he had just completed four years as a naval officer. John Ford, too, had served in the navy, making several notable documentaries. This experience also added to the film's realism and poignancy, one of the finest of all WWII movies.

Battleground

Members of the US army infantry unit are trapped during the siege at the Belgian town of Bastogne in December 1944. Among the motley group are a skirt-chaser (Johnson), who falls for a local girl (Darcel); a small-town journalist (Hodiak), a young Mexican (Montalban) and a veteran (Murphy) waiting for his discharge. They hold their ground against the Nazis, despite being surrounded and outnumbered. When all seems lost, Allied tanks begin to move into the area and save the battered group.

'The guts, gags and glory of a lot of wonderful guys' read the posters, without revealing that the film depicts the misery, agony and grief of soldiers, with no glorification of individual servicemen. Grimly honest, with a small amount of love interest to leaven the seriousness, it steered away from the usual romantic view of war. This may be because the director, Wellman, a former pilot during World War I, knew what war was all about. Bastogne was brilliantly recreated on MGM's backlot.

USA, 1949
DIRECTOR:
William A. Wellman
CAST INCLUDES:
Van Johnson, John Hodiak,
Ricardo Montalban, George Murphy,
Marshall Thompson,
James Whitmore
SCREENPLAY:
Robert Pirosh
CINEMATOGRAPHY:
Paul C. Vogel
**PRODUCERS/
PRODUCTION COMPANIES:**
Dore Schary/ MGM
**ACADEMY AWARD
NOMINATIONS (1950)**
Best Picture: Dore Schary
Best Director: William A. Wellman
Best Actor in a Supporting Role:
James Whitmore
Best Film Editing: John D. Dunning
ACADEMY AWARDS
Best Cinematography, Black-and-
White: Paul Vogel
Best Writing, Story and Screenplay:
Robert Pirosh

Sands of Iwo Jima

USA, 1949
DIRECTOR:
Allan Dwan
CAST INCLUDES:
John Wayne, John Agar,
Forrest Tucker, Arthur Franz,
Richard Jaekel, Adele Mara
SCREENPLAY:
James Edward Grant, Harry Brown
CINEMATOGRAPHY:
Reggie Lanning
**PRODUCERS/
PRODUCTION COMPANIES:**
Edmund Grainger/ Republic
**ACADEMY AWARD
NOMINATIONS (1950)**
Best Actor in a Leading Role:
John Wayne
Best Film Editing:
Richard L. Van Enger
Best Sound Recording
Best Writing, Motion Picture Story:
Harry Brown

Tough marine sergeant John Stryker (Wayne) seems a martinet and a bully as he trains young Marines for combat in the Pacific war. As he leads them into battle to capture the strategic island of Iwo Jima, held by the Japanese, the troops begin to appreciate the importance of trust and friendship, especially in dangerous situations. On the way to glory are two women, a good New Zealand girl (Mara) and one who, it would seem, is less good, from Honolulu.

Filmed at Fort Pendleton with the full help of the Marines, this gung-ho classic, nowadays offensive to Japanese sensibilities, is considered *the* John Wayne war movie, and was a huge hit. Wayne, who was never near a war, gives one of his most convincing performances. The use of authentic combat footage is striking, and the three surviving Marine veterans who raised the American flag on Mount Suribachi in the iconic gesture, repeated here, have small parts. The final battle on the island is excitingly realized, and the relationships between the men are well explored.

Twelve O'Clock High

At the height of World War II, a US bomber squadron based in England, is demoralized having suffered many losses on dangerous raids over Germany. Brigadier General Frank Savage (Peck) has taken over command from Colonel Keith Davenport (Merrill). Davenport, a popular leader who has been relieved of his post because, appalled by the casualty rates, he had become too emotionally involved with the pilots he sent over to bomb Germany. Davenport and other officers begin to cast doubts on the value of daylight precision bombing which was still in the experimental stage.

The pilots resent the new man, who is a disciplinarian and keeps his distance, gradually cracking under the strain and responsibility of command. But as they continue to fly dangerous missions over Germany, the group and their new leader develop mutual respect and admiration, until the once-alienated commander feels that his men are part of a family.

One of the best films about the pressures which war imposes at the top. The anti-heroic, realistic approach to warfare was unusual so soon after the actual events. Although there are exciting aerial sequences, it is on the ground that the film really gets tense. Despite Gregory Peck standing out in one of his finest performances, the picture offers a splendid example of ensemble acting. The film's climax, in which the general waits patiently for his squad to return to base – painfully aware that they may not return at all – is one of the most subtle yet emotionally intense scenes of any World War II drama.

USA, 1949
DIRECTOR:
Henry King,
CAST INCLUDES:
Gregory Peck, Dean Jagger,
Hugh Marlowe, Gary Merrill,
Millard Mitchell
SCREENPLAY:
Sy Bartlett, Beirne Lay Jr. from
their novel
CINEMATOGRAPHY:
Leon Shamroy
**PRODUCERS/PRODUCTION
COMPANIES:**
Darryl F. Zanuck/20th Century-Fox
**ACADEMY AWARD
NOMINATIONS (1950)**
Best Actor in a Leading Role:
Gregory Peck
Best Picture: Darryl F. Zanuck
ACADEMY AWARDS
Best Actor in a supporting Role:
Dean Jagger
Best Sound Recording: 20th Century-
Fox Sound Department

The Desert Fox

USA, 1951
DIRECTOR:
Henry Hathaway
CAST INCLUDES:
James Mason, Cedric Hardwicke,
Jessica Tandy, Luther Adler,
Everett Sloane, Leo G. Carroll,
George Macready, Richard Boone,
Eduard Franz
SCREENPLAY:
Nunnally Johnson from the biography
by Brigadier Desmond Young
CINEMATOGRAPHY:
Norbert Brodine
PRODUCERS/
PRODUCTION COMPANIES:
Nunnally Johnson/20th Century-Fox

Field Marshall Rommel, the Desert Fox, is the commander of the crack Afrika Korps, whose brilliant tactics have earned him the respect of both friend and foe. When the tide is turning at El Alamein, Rommel disobeys Hitler's orders and pulls his men out of battle. Returning to Germany, he is torn between loyalty to his country and his own better judgment. He is forced to take drastic measures to save his wife and son from possible danger.

This is not only a war film but the tragedy of a man who waited too long before acting on his better instincts. As interpreted by James Mason, Rommel is competent, self-assured, loyal, and aggressive, and the movie treats him as a wonderful soldier who is, unfortunately, on the wrong side. Rommel's home life is expertly sketched, making his final action understandable. Many of the scenes are filmed in a quasi-documentary style by Henry Hathaway, avoiding romantic heroics and sentimentality. California stands in brilliantly for the North African desert. Mason repeated his sensitive impersonation of Rommel again in *The Desert Rats* (1953).

The Red Badge of Courage

During the American Civil War, Henry (Murphy), a raw recruit, loses his illusions of heroism during his first skirmish, a baptism of fire that makes him desert prior to engaging the enemy for the second time. While spending an idyllic time in the forest, he witnesses his friend's death and receives an accidental wound from a retreating soldier. Henry gradually comes to terms with the realities of warfare and emerges as a hero.

Few films have pondered so acutely the feelings of anxiety and finally outright fear in a young man preparing for battle. John Huston has caught the feeling of fright and awe in Stephen Crane's classic war novel, using remarkable documentary-style photography, although the film is renowned for having been butchered by MGM. A narration delivered by James Whitmore fills in some of the gaps created by the studio's scissor-happy editors. Paradoxically, Audie Murphy, America's most decorated soldier in World War II, plays the inexperienced young soldier.

USA, 1951
DIRECTOR:
John Huston
CAST INCLUDES:
Audie Murphy, Bill Maudlin,
Douglas Dick, Arthur Hunnicut,
Royal Dano, Andy Devine
SCREENPLAY:
John Huston, Albert Band from the
Stephen Crane novel
CINEMATOGRAPHY:
Harold Rosson
**PRODUCERS/
PRODUCTION COMPANIES:**
Gottfried Reinhardt/MGM

The Cruel Sea

GB, 1953
DIRECTOR:
Charles Frend
CAST INCLUDES:
Jack Hawkins, Donald Sinden,
Denholm Elliott, Stanley Baker,
Virginia McKenna
SCREENPLAY:
Eric Ambler from a novel by
Nicholas Monsarrat
CINEMATOGRAPHY:
Gordon Dines
PRODUCERS/
PRODUCTION COMPANIES:
Leslie Norman/Ealing Studios
ACADEMY AWARDS
NOMINATIONS (1954)
Best Writing, Screenplay: Eric Ambler

The story follows the Royal Navy Corvette *Compass Rose* and her Captain (Hawkins), who moulds an inexperienced crew into an effective and disciplined fighting force, from the dark days before Dunkirk through to final victory. Shortly after the outbreak of World War II the *Compass Rose*, under Captain Ericson leaves harbour for sea trials and three weeks of training for her inexperienced crew. This proves a baptism of fire, as they are battered by storms. They later encounter their first U-Boat. As the war rages, the ship and crew succeed, with many losses of life, in helping to defeat the U-Boat threat.

Eight years after the end of World War II, Michael Balcon's Ealing Studios brought Nicholas Monsarrat's best-selling novel *The Cruel Sea* to the screen, launching the careers of Donald Sinden, Denholm Elliott and Virginia McKenna and also

establishing Jack Hawkins as a star. The screenplay doesn't avoid showing the futility of war, and emphasises the emotional and psychological damage inflicted by war: several officers turn to drink, an officer has a breakdown, a rating calls the Captain a "Bloody murderer!", and Ericson himself cries when his decision to depth-charge a U-Boat results in the death of British sailors. In fact, this was a rare reaction to the usual 'stiff-upper-lip' heroics of British war films. It is also a prime example of a documentary style lending authenticity to the fictional story.

From Here to Eternity

On a Hawaiian military base just before Pearl Harbor, Private 'Prew' Prewitt (Clift) is a stubborn soldier who transfers into a new unit. He immediately makes enemies with the captain of the unit when he refuses to participate in the Army boxing tournament, and becomes the butt of his aggression. However, he finds comfort in the arms of a hooker (Reed). Prew's friend Private Maggio (Sinatra) is picked on by sadistic Fatso (Borgnine) and dies in a knife fight. Meanwhile, First Sergeant Warden (Lancaster), is carrying on an affair with the wife of the captain. Then, the bombing of Pearl Harbor changes everything.

Based on James Jones' hefty, 859-page steamy 1951 novel of the same name, it was skilfully boiled down, and toned down, for American audiences of the early 1950s, while still tackling controversial subjects such as prostitution, adultery, military injustice, corruption and violence, alcohol abuse, and murder. Shot with almost documentary realism, it was a huge success, winning the most Oscars since *Gone With The Wind* (1939). It was also notable for the casting against type of the usually lady-like Deborah Kerr as the adulterous wife – her sex scene with Burt Lancaster on the beach has become an anthology piece – and for reviving Sinatra's flagging career.

USA, 1953
DIRECTOR:
Fred Zinnemann
CAST INCLUDES:
Burt Lancaster, Deborah Kerr, Montgomery Clift, Frank Sinatra, Donna Reed, Ernest Borgnine
SCREENPLAY:
Daniel Taradash from the James Jones novel
CINEMATOGRAPHY:
Burnett Guffey
PRODUCERS/ PRODUCTION COMPANIES:
Buddy Adler/Columbia
ACADEMY AWARD NOMINATIONS (1954)
Best Actor in a Leading Role: Burt Lancaster, Montgomery Clift
Best Actress in a Leading Role: Deborah Kerr
Best Music, Scoring of a Dramatic or Comedy Picture: George Duning
Best Costume Design, Black-and-White: Jean Louis
ACADEMY AWARDS
Best Picture: Buddy Adler
Best Actor in a Supporting Actor: Frank Sinatra
Best Actress in a Supporting Role: Donna Reed
Best Director: Fred Zinnermann
Best Cinematography, Black-and-White: Burnett Guffey
Best Writing, Screenplay: Daniel Taradash
Best Sound, Recording: John P. Livadary
Best Film Editing: William Lyon

Stalag 17

USA,1953
DIRECTOR:
Billy Wilder
CAST INCLUDES:
William Holden, Don Taylor,
Otto Preminger, Robert Strauss,
Neville Brand, Peter Graves,
Sig Rumann
SCREENPLAY:
Billy Wilder, Edwin Blum from the
play by Donald Bevan and
Edmund Trzcinski
CINEMATOGRAPHY:
Ernest Laszlo
**PRODUCERS/
PRODUCTION COMPANIES:**
Billy Wilder/Paramount
**ACADEMY AWARD
NOMINATIONS (1954)**
Best Director: Billy Wilder
Best Actor in a Supporting Role:
Robert Strauss
ACADEMY AWARDS
Best Actor in a Leading Role:
William Holden

Stalag 17 is an unruly World War II POW camp run by an arrogant and cruel camp commandant Von Scherbach (Preminger), who advises the American officer inmates about the impossibility of escape. In fact, every time someone has attempted it, the Germans seem to be aware of it and they are caught. A feeling grows that there must be a spy among the prisoners in the camp and the suspicion falls on Sefton (Holden), a cynical, cocky loner, a scheming and wheeling sergeant whose only interest in their escape plans is laying odds on their chances of succeeding or failing.

Stalag 17 is a rousing, biting depiction of the raw and tense conditions among American servicemen in a prisoner of war camp. It shows all the cruel ironies, the jousting and scheming and upmanship games, the temporary loyalties and feuds and the accumulated tensions of a group of men in confinement. William Holden gives one of his most versatile and full-bodied performances as the shifty Sefton. Otto Preminger is wonderful casting as the sadistic camp commander, an in-joke on a director known for his martinet methods.

Mister Roberts

On a small cargo ship, the USS *Reluctant* (aka the Bucket), floating somewhere in the Pacific during World War II, Lieutenant Roberts (Fonda), the gentle cargo officer, who fears he will miss seeing action before the war is over, mollifies a long-suffering crew, including the resourceful, lazy and boastful Ensign Pulver (Lemmon) and the world-weary doctor (Powell) against the machinations of their tyrannical captain (Cagney). After the crew wreaks havoc ashore, the captain inflicts a demanding work schedule on them. Driven beyond his breaking point, Mr. Roberts avenges himself upon the hated symbol of the captain's authority, a jealously guarded and much-watered palm tree. Ensign Pulver also finds the strength to make his own stand against the Captain's tyranny.

There was a great deal of drama off-screen in the making of *Mister Roberts* when John Ford and Henry Fonda, recreating his Broadway role, clashed resulting in Ford walking off the picture. Ironically, Jack Warner wanted Marlon Brando or William Holden but Ford had held out for Fonda. Nevertheless, the film turned out to be a big box-office and critical hit, mainly because of the trenchant script and the performances of Fonda, returning to the screen after seven years, Cagney in one his most unsympathetic roles, Powell in his last screen appearance and Lemmon, whose Oscar-winning portrayal set the seal on the type of role he would soon be making his own. Although not a shot is fired in the film, it makes a strong statement about men at war.

USA, 1955
DIRECTOR:
John Ford, Mervyn Leroy,
Joshua Logan (uncredited)
CAST INCLUDES:
Henry Fonda, James Cagney,
William Powell, Jack Lemon,
Nick Adams
SCREENPLAY:
Joshua Logan and
Frank S. Nugent from the play by
Logan and the novel by
Thomas Heggen
CINEMATOGRAPHY:
Winton C. Hoch
**PRODUCERS/
PRODUCTION COMPANIES:**
Leland Hayward/Warner Bros.
**ACADEMY AWARD
NOMINATIONS (1956)**
Best Picture: Leland Heyward
Best Sound: William A. Mueller
ACADEMY AWARDS
Best Actor in a Supporting Role:
Jack Lemmon

Attack!

USA, 1956
DIRECTOR:
Robert Aldrich
CAST INCLUDES:
Jack Palance, Eddie Albert,
Lee Marvin, Robert Strauss,
Buddy Ebsen
SCREENPLAY:
James Poe from the play
The Fragile Fox by Norman Brooks
CINEMATOGRAPHY:
Joseph Biroc
**PRODUCERS/
PRODUCTION COMPANIES:**
Robert Aldrich/United Artists

During World War II's Battle of the Bulge, a cowardly captain (Albert) and a conniving colonel (Marvin), who ignores his inferior's mistakes, risk the lives of a platoon, diligently led by Lieutenant Costa (Palance), who suffers a smashed arm in the battle. The platoon has to fight its way back from the front line, where it has been stranded without cover. Costa then confronts the captain...

Few punches are pulled in this chillingly ambiguous depiction of the attitude of certain officers during World War II, the main targets of the screenplay's scorn. No wonder the US Defense Department declined to co-operate on the production, a bold film to make during the Eisenhower era. The all-male cast, headed brilliantly by Jack Palance, in one of his most demanding roles, demonstrate Robert Aldrich's central theme of 'man's efforts to prevail against impossible odds'. The powerful ending has Eddie Albert having a mental breakdown and Palance becoming an avenging monster.

The Burmese Harp

Biruma no tategoto

By July 1945, the war was nearing its end for the Japanese forces in Burma. Among the many units crossing the mountains of Burma to escape into Thailand was one in which the men sang songs to the accompaniment of a strange handmade instrument resembling a Burmese harp. One of these soldier-musicians, the young Private Mizushima (Yasui), decides to become a Buddhist monk and attempts to bury as many bodies of Japanese soldiers as he can.

Kon Ichikawa's first film on what he termed 'the pain of the age', is a non-naturalistic odyssey in visionary black-and-white images throbbing with the anguish that war brings. Adapted from Michio Takeyama's novel by the director's wife, it was one of the first of a number of Japanese films concerned with pacifist themes related to the defeat of Japan in 1945, and is almost an act of atonement made by the postwar Japanese film industry. It not only indicts militarism, but is a cry of anguish for those who suffered during World War II. *The Burmese Harp* achieves its power and poignancy through the juxtaposition of the horror of war with the beauty of nature.

JAPAN, 1956
DIRECTOR:
Kon Ichikawa
CAST INCLUDES:
Shôji Yasui, Rentaro Mikuni,
Tatsuya Mihashi, Taketoshi Naîto,
Jun Hamamura
SCREENPLAY:
Natto Wada based on the novel by
Michio Takeyama
CINEMATOGRAPHY:
Minoru Yokoyama
**PRODUCERS/
PRODUCTION COMPANIES:**
Masayuki Takaki/Nikkatsu
Corporation
**ACADEMY AWARD
NOMINATIONS (1957)**
Best Foreign Language Film

The Bridge on the River Kwai

GB, 1957
DIRECTOR:
David Lean
CAST INCLUDES:
William Holden, Alec Guinness,
Jack Hawkins, Sessue Hayakawa,
Geoffrey Horne
SCREENPLAY:
Carl Forman, Michael Wilson
(Pierre Boulle credited for the
blacklisted writers above) from the
novel by Boulle
CINEMATOGRAPHY:
Jack Hildyard
PRODUCERS/
PRODUCTION COMPANIES:
Sam Spiegel/Columbia-Horizon
ACADEMY AWARD
NOMINATIONS (1958)
Best Actor in a Supporting Role:
Sessue Hayakawa.
ACADEMY AWARDS
Best Picture: Sam Spiegel
Best Actor in a Leading Role:
Alec Guinness
Best Director: David Lean
Best Screenplay Based on Material
from Another Medium: Pierre Boulle
(fronting for Carl Foreman and
Michael Wilson)
Best Cinematography: Jack Hildyard
Best Film Editing: Peter Taylor
Best Music, Scoring: Malcolm Arnold
Best Actor in a Supporting Role:
Sessue Hayakawa.

British POW's in Burma are ordered to build a bridge across the River Kwai by camp commander Colonel Saito (Hayakawa), which will be used to transport Japanese munitions. Colonel Nicholson (Guinness) refuses, despite all the various 'persuasive' devices at Saito's disposal. Finally, Nicholson agrees, not so much to co-operate with his captor as to provide a morale-boosting project for the military engineers under his command. Meanwhile British and American intelligence officers, led by American Shears (Holden) and Major Warden (Hawkins) conspire to blow up the structure, but Nicholson has acquired a sense of pride in his creation and tries to foil their plans.

The Bridge on the River Kwai was based on the best-selling novel by Pierre Boulle, out of which David Lean fashioned a spectacle of brilliant set-pieces, at the same time forcing audiences to question their received ideas about individual courage and responsibility. Such is the film's cunning that we have been encouraged to identify with Guinness's character to the point that we, too, resist the demolition of the bridge, a structure that can only aid the enemy. Superbly cast, especially Guinness, who is a personification of courage and stubbornness, the film was distinguished by a narrative and visual sweep. It took a gruelling three months to shoot in Ceylon.

Paths of Glory

USA, 1957
DIRECTOR:
Stanley Kubrick
CAST INCLUDES:
Kirk Douglas, Ralph Meeker,
Adolph Menjou, George Macready,
Wayne Morris
SCREENPLAY:
Stanley Kubrick, James Thompson,
Calder Willingham from the novel by
Humphrey Cobb
CINEMATOGRAPHY:
Georg Krause
**PRODUCERS/
PRODUCTION COMPANIES:**
James B. Harris/United Artists

Based on an actual incident in World War I that was hushed up by the French authorities at the time, *Paths of Glory* is set at the front, in France, in 1916. A general (Macready), with the complicity of another scheming general (Menjou), orders Colonel Dax (Douglas) to fire on his own troops because some of them refused to go over the top. Dax defies the orders; three men are chosen at random and executed after a court martial. The furious colonel resigns his commission.

The anti-militarist stance of *Paths of Glory* was so powerful that the film was banned in parts of Europe (especially France) and in US military movie theatres for some years. It came opportunely in the aftermath of the Korean War and after Senator McCarthy's fall. The bitterly ironic and moving film established Stanley Kubrick as an important figure in American cinema. Much of the graphic description of trench warfare must be attributed to the camerawork of Georg Krause, but the cross-cutting, the savage view of the officers, and the harsh awareness of death were all Kubrick's. A particularly poignant scene is towards the end when a young German woman (played by Kubrick's wife Susanne Christian) stills a crowd of rowdy French veterans with a song in a café. It is perhaps significant that this outspoken movie never won a major award.

Ballad of a Soldier

Ballada o soldate

A naïve young soldier, refuses a medal and instead takes four days leave from the front to visit his mother at the height of the Nazi invasion. En route, by train, truck, and on foot, he meets various people affected by the war, a crippled veteran, a comic sentry, faithful and faithless wives, and a girl with whom he falls in love. We know from the outset that he will be killed in battle and buried by strangers, far from home, known to them only as 'a Russian soldier'.

This simple and moving view of everyday life in wartime Russia helped the move away from Soviet Socialist Realism towards a more humanistic cinema With its ballad-like structure and unrhetorical style, the film drew on the director's own experiences of the misery and waste of war and the confusion of the aftermath. It continued the trickle of Soviet films welcomed in the West in the late fifties. In fact, it was the first film from the USSR to enter an American film festival – in San Francisco – which it won.

USSR, 1959
DIRECTOR:
Grigori Chukhraj
CAST INCLUDES:
Vladimir Ivashov,
Zhanna Prokhorenko,
Antonina Maksimova,
Nikolai Kryuchkov
SCREENPLAY:
Grigori Chukhrai, Valentin Yezhov
CINEMATOGRAPHY:
Vladimir Nikolayev, Era Saveleya
PRODUCERS/
PRODUCTION COMPANIES:
M. Chernova/Ministry of Culture of
the USSR
ACADEMY AWARD
NOMINATIONS (1962)
Best Writing, Story and Screenplay –
Written Directly for the Screen:
Valentin Yezhov and Grigori Chukhraj

The Guns of Navarone

USA/GB, 1961
DIRECTOR:
J. Lee Thompson
CAST INCLUDES:
Gregory Peck, David Niven,
Stanley Baker, Anthony Quinn,
Anthony Quayle, Irene Papas,
Gia Scala
SCREENPLAY:
Carl Foreman from the novel by
Alistair MacLean
CINEMATOGRAPHY:
Oswald Morris
PRODUCERS/
PRODUCTION COMPANIES:
Carl Foreman/ Columbia
ACADEMY AWARD
NOMINATIONS (1962)
Best Writing,Screenplay Based on
Material from Another Medium:
Carl Foreman
Best Director: J. Lee Thompson
Best Music, Scoring of a Dramatic
or Comedy Picture: Dimitri Tiomkin
Best Film Editing: Alan Osbiston
Best Picture: Carl Foreman
Best Sound: John Cox
ACADEMY AWARDS
Best Special Effects: Bill Warrington
(visual) and Chris Greenham (audible)

A group of commandos, made up of Allied and Greek soldiers, each with a specialist talent, is assembled by British intelligence in an attempt to achieve the impossible – destroying the seemingly impregnable German artillery cannons concealed deep within solid rock on the Greek island of Navarone. The six-man commando team consists of mountaineer Captain Mallory (Peck), humanitarian explosive's expert Corporal Miller (Niven), Greek resistance fighter Andrea Stravos (Quinn), British Major Franklin (Quayle), young marksman Private Pappadimos (Darren) and ruthless killer CPO Brown (Baker). Meeting them along the way are resistance leader Maria (Papas), who is Pappadimos' older sister, and Anna (Scala), a beautiful Greek girl who was reportedly tortured by the Germans. Although they are captured by the Germans, they manage to escape, and disguised in stolen Nazi uniforms the group finally arrives at the town of Navarone to carry out the mission.

A rip-roaring adventure yarn which includes bloody hand-to-hand conflicts between the good guys and the Nazis, an

enormous tidal wave, and our heroes scaling treacherously steep cliffs, most of it spectacularly filmed on Rhodes in the Aegean Sea. This made *The Guns of Navarone* a tremendous box-office hit and it remains one of the best films of its type. The action spoke louder than words, although Carl Foreman's script had a great deal to say about the various loyalties and motivations of the assorted characters played by a terrific cast with Niven almost stealing the show as a cynical and cowardly commando. The film led to many imitations including an inferior sequel called *Force Ten From Navarone* (1978).

The Longest Day

On June 6, 1944, the Allied Invasion of France marked the end of Nazi domination over Europe. The attack involved 3,000,000 men, 11,000 planes and 4,000 ships. This epic recreation of the Allied invasion of Normandy is seen from the viewpoints of the French, English, German, and American soldiers, and features an all-star cast, who speak in their own languages. The massive preparations, mistakes and random events that determined the outcome are shown and add to the realism.

Producer Darryl F. Zanuck's three-hour epic takes on the daunting task of covering that fateful day from all perspectives – from the German high command and front-line officers to the French Resistance and all the key Allied participants. The screenplay by Cornelius Ryan, based on his own authoritative book, is as factually accurate as possible. The endless parade of stars (John Wayne, Henry Fonda, Robert Mitchum, Sean Connery, and Richard Burton, to name a few) makes for an astute mix of realism and Hollywood star-power. The set-piece battles are spectacular.

USA, 1962
DIRECTOR:
Ken Annakin (British scenes)
Andrew Marton (American scenes)
Bernhard Wicki (German scenes)
CAST INCLUDES:
Richard Burton, Sean Connery,
Henry Fonda, Curt Jurgens,
Robert Mitchum, Robert Ryan,
John Wayne
SCREENPLAY:
Romain Gary, James Jones,
David Pursall, Jack Seddon,
Cornelius Ryan (from his book)
CINEMATOGRAPHY:
Jean Bourgoin, Walter Wottitz
PRODUCERS/
PRODUCTION COMPANIES:
Darryl F. Zanuck /20th Century-Fox
ACADEMY AWARD
NOMINATIONS (1963)
Best Art Direction-Set Decoration,
Black-and-White: Vincent Korda,
Gabriel Béchir, Ted Haworth,
Léon Barsacq
Best Film Editing: Samuel E. Beetley
Best Picture: Darryl F. Zanuck
ACADEMY AWARDS
Best Cinematography, Black- and-
White: Walter Wottitz, Jean Bourgoin
Best Special Effects: Robert A.
MacDonald (visual),
Jacques Maumont (audible)

The Great Escape

In Stalag Luft III in Upper Silesia in March 1944, the German high command has selected a group of the most talented British, American, and Canadian escape artists and placed them in a POW camp specifically designed to foil any attempts at escape. But as soon as they arrive, the prisoners, led by Steve McQueen as the rebellious Virgil Hilts, begin work on a series of tunnels under the direction of Roger "Big X" Bartlett (Attenborough). He assigns the POWs to jobs according to their specialities. For more than a year, 600 prisoners, most of whom won't be leaving, work toward an escape that will temporarily disrupt the operations of the German army. More than seventy men get away, and the film then follows their attempts to get out of Germany.

The Great Escape was the longest (173 minutes), most expensive and biggest money-making POW picture of all. Though the plot was similar to many other barbed-wire-tunnel-digging pictures, this was directed with greater gusto and offered some ingenious variations on the familiar theme. Filmed in Germany, the picture starts light-heartedly, and ends in a tragic but uplifting manner. Out of the host of big-name stars, it was McQueen, commandeering a Nazi motorbike and teaching it to jump fences, who contributed most to the film's vast appeal.

USA, 1963
DIRECTOR:
John Sturges
CAST INCLUDES:
Steve McQueen, James Garner, Richard Attenborough, James Coburn, Charles Bronson, Donald Pleasence, James Donald
SCREENPLAY:
W.R. Burnett, James Clavell from the book by Paul Brickhill
CINEMATOGRAPHY:
Daniel Fapp
PRODUCERS/ PRODUCTION COMPANIES:
John Sturges/ United Artists
ACADEMY AWARD NOMINATIONS (1964)
Best Film Editing: Ferris Webster

The Train

During the last days of the German occupation of Paris, von Waldheim (Scofield), an art-obsessed German colonel, arranges to steal all of the city's great art treasures and send them on a train to Germany. When the French Resistance discovers the plan, Labiche (Lancaster), a French railway engineer, is ordered to stop the train. Not wishing to risk lives or the paintings, which are part of the French national heritage, Labiche concocts an elaborate scheme to keep the train in France. Both Labiche and von Waldheim become obsessed with their missions.

The Train begins with a dedication 'to those French railway men, living and dead, whose magnificent spirit and whose courage inspired this story'. The film also seems a tribute to Burt Lancaster's athletic prowess. He leaps over walls and on and off trains. Even when he's shot in the leg, he moves faster than anyone else in the mostly genuine French cast. The fast-paced action is very well handled by John Frankenheimer, replacing Arthur Penn after several days shooting. Real trains, not models, were used throughout, with multiple cameras capturing as much action with as few takes as possible. During one crash sequence, a locomotive came in too fast and destroyed six of seven cameras at one blow. The film also raises the question whether any work of art is worth anyone's life.

FRANCE/ITALY/USA, 1964
DIRECTOR:
John Frankenheimer
CAST INCLUDES:
Burt Lancaster, Paul Scofield,
Jeanne Moreau, Michel Simon,
Suzanne Flon
SCREENPLAY:
Franklin Coen, Frank Davis,
Walter Bernstein, Albert Husson
based on
Le Front de l'Art by Rose Valland
CINEMATOGRAPHY:
Jean Tournier, Walter Wottitz
**PRODUCERS/
PRODUCTION COMPANIES:**
Jules Bricken/United Artists
**ACADEMY AWARD
NOMINATIONS (1966)**
Best Writing, Story and
Screenplay – Written Directly for the
Screen: Franklin Coen, Frank Davis

The Bedford Incident

USA, 1965
DIRECTOR:
James B. Harris
CAST INCLUDES:
Donald Sutherland, James MacArthur,
Richard Widmark, Sidney Poitier,
Martin Balsam
SCREENPLAY:
James Poe, based on a novel by
Mark Rastovich
CINEMATOGRAPHY:
Gilbert Taylor
PRODUCERS/
PRODUCTION COMPANIES:
James B. Harris, Richard
Widmark/Columbia

The USS *Bedford*, on a routine NATO patrol, ends up in a showdown with a Russian submarine. Captain Eric Finlander (Widmark), the maniacal commander, obsessed with hunting down the sub, regardless of the risks involved, drives his tense crew to the brink of nervous exhaustion. Ben Munceford (Poitier), a photojournalist aboard, is assigned to record a 'typical' mission. His moral indignation is put to the test by the captain's obsession with forcing the sub to the surface. Several crew members are at their breaking points as Finlander continues his prowl. Especially affected is a former German U-boat commander (Portman), now aboard the *Bedford* as a NATO observer.

The director, James B. Harris, managed to capture the claustrophobia of the confined setting, and maintained dramatic tension throughout. Although the cat-and-mouse chase is

reminiscent of the earlier World War II film with Robert Mitchum chasing a Nazi sub in *The Enemy Below* (1957) and the later *Hunt For Red October* (1990), there is the unspoken racism in Finlander's animosity towards Munceford, and the battle of wits on board the American destroyer reflects the battle outside it. It is also a reflection on the madness that could have ignited the Cold War into a hot one at any moment. It also played on the public anxiety about nuclear war, as seen in other films such as *Dr. Strangelove*, the year before.

Von Ryan's Express

An American Air Force pilot, Colonel Joseph Ryan (Sinatra), is shot down and placed in an Italian POW camp, mainly housing British troops. Because Ryan is now the highest ranking officer, he takes over command from Major Eric Fincham (Howard), thus creating animosity between them. When Italy surrenders to the Allies, the Italian jailers desert and the prisoners are left on their own. Under Ryan's command, the prisoners escape from Italy by stealing a German prisoner of war train heading for a German concentration camp and divert it northward to neutral Switzerland and freedom. When the Germans realize what has happened, the chase is on.

A really rousing World War II yarn, excellently handled by Mark Robson and his expert team. There are several exciting sequences such as the escapees disguised in German uniforms trying to get past the checkpoints, an encounter with a double-dealing Gestapo agent, and an attack on the central railway control tower in Milan. The concluding battle, set in the Alps, has the prisoners attempting to clear the tracks while fighting off attacking German aircraft and also their oncoming German pursuers. It is as much fun as an old-fashioned serial.

USA, 1965
DIRECTOR:
Mark Robson
CAST INCLUDES:
Frank Sinatra, Trevor Howard,
James Brolin, Raffaela Carra,
Brad Dexter
SCREENPLAY:
Wendell Mayes,
Joseph Landon from the novel by
David Westheimer
CINEMATOGRAPHY:
William H. Daniels
PRODUCERS/
PRODUCTION COMPANIES:
Saul David/20th Century-Fox
ACADEMY AWARD
NOMINATIONS (1966)
Best Effects, Sound Effects:
Walter Rossi

The Dirty Dozen

USA/GB, 1967
DIRECTOR:
Robert Aldrich
CAST INCLUDES:
Lee Marvin, Ernest Borgnine,
Charles Bronson, Jim Brown,
John Cassavetes, Robert Ryan,
Donald Sutherland
SCREENPLAY:
Lukas Heller, Nunnally Johnson from
the novel by E.M. Nathanson
CINEMATOGRAPHY:
Edward Scaif
PRODUCERS/
PRODUCTION COMPANIES:
Kenneth Hyman/MGM
ACADEMY AWARD
NOMINATIONS (1968)
Best Actor in a Supporting Role:
John Cassavetes
Best Film Editing: Michael Luciano
Best Sound
ACADEMY AWARDS
Best Effects, Sound Effects:
John Poyner

A group of twelve hardened American military prisoners –
murderers, rapists, thieves and assorted misfits – most of whom
are facing death sentences, are given the chance to redeem
themselves by going on a suicide mission behind Nazi lines. They
are whipped into a crack army unit by tough Major Reisman
(Marvin), who initially uses them to best the troops of his by-the-
book superior officer, Colonel Breed (Ryan), in war games. The
'dirty dozen' includes a sex pervert (Savalas), a psycho
(Cassavetes) and a retarded killer (Sutherland). They then lead a
perilous assault on a well-guarded chateau and kill the Nazi
officials vacationing there, becoming somewhat dubious heroes.

Robert Aldrich, who by the time of *The Dirty Dozen* had been
delving into the darker side of life for more than a decade, scored
a huge hit with this rousing thriller laced with a stinging cynicism
perfectly in tune with the increasingly sceptical tenor of the times.
Though condemned for its excessive violence, this much-imitated
war movie was the most popular film of 1967. The ironic side is
that these criminals are redeemed by committing acts that are
more barbaric than the ones they were condemned for – because
anything is acceptable in war. As in Aldrich's *Attack!*, it gives the
impression that officers were hypocritical and stupid and only the
ordinary soldier is worth anything.

Hell in the Pacific

Set in the Pacific in 1944, the film focuses on two combatants stranded on the same barren atoll: a Japanese naval officer (Mifune) and a U.S. marine pilot (Marvin). At first the two men warily stalk each other, both revealing something by refusing to kill the other when the opportunity arises. At length the Japanese officer captures the American, who ultimately escapes, returns, and ties up his opponent. The American finally releases his prisoner as both men grasp the pointlessness of their behaviour, and a truce develops between them, since neither can understand the other's language. They soon become aware that co-operation would help speed their departure and increase their odds of survival.

USA, 1968
DIRECTOR:
John Boorman
CAST INCLUDES:
Lee Marvin, Toshirô Mifune
SCREENPLAY:
Alexander Jacobs, Eric Bercovici
CINEMATOGRAPHY:
Conrad Hall
PRODUCERS/
PRODUCTION COMPANIES:
Reuben Bercovitch/American
Broadcasting Company (ABC), Henry
G. Saperstein Enterprises Inc.,
Selmur Productions

In what is virtually a silent film, Boorman invokes his recurring 'man against nature' theme, here seen as a plea for human solidarity. Marvin shows a psychological complexity rarely seen in his other work, while Mifune displays the kind of physical dynamism that brought him fame in the films of Akira Kurosawa. The two actors respected each other with Marvin calling Mifune 'just about the most gutsy, honourable chunk of talent in the whole frigging world'. According to Marvin's widow, 'Of all the movies of Lee's career, *Hell in the Pacific* was undoubtedly the most important to him on a personal level. In it he was reliving, exploring and resolving his feelings about his war, and putting the results on the screen.'

Conrad Hall's camerawork does justice to the spectacular beauty of the Micronesian islands where the film was shot. The drama of enemies forced to share their lives makes a powerful statement.

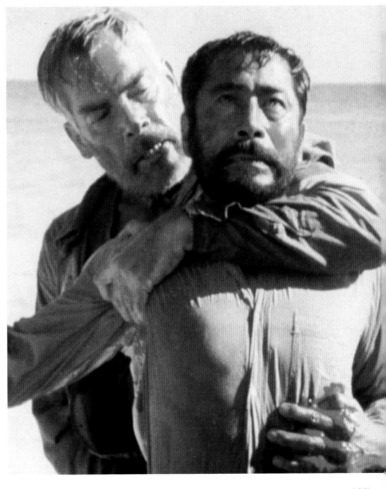

Where Eagles Dare

GB, 1968
DIRECTOR:
Brian G. Hutton
CAST INCLUDES:
Clint Eastwood, Richard Burton,
Mary Ure, Michael Horden,
Anton Diffring
SCREENPLAY:
Alistair MacLean from his novel
CINEMATOGRAPHY:
Arthur Ibbetson
PRODUCERS/
PRODUCTION COMPANIES:
Elliott Kastner/MGM

In 1944, Major John Smith (Burton), a British agent, is in charge of a group of six Allied soldiers given the task of rescuing an American general – who is reportedly in possession of the plans for D-Day – from a seemingly impregnable German fortress located high in the Bavarian Alps. The general must be freed before being made to reveal Allied plans for an invasion of France. Assisting Smith is an American, Lieutenant Morris Schaffer (Eastwood), a fierce soldier with an array of deadly weapons. As the men penetrate the fortress, facing an endless supply of German soldiers, it becomes apparent that there are double and triple agents in the ranks of the rescue team.

Where Eagles Dare has all the elements of a stirring war adventure story, and makes spectacular use of the location high in the Alps for scenes such as the thrilling fight on top of a cable car. No need to ask for much deep characterization, though there is a sparky chemistry between the contrasting Richard Burton and Clint Eastwood, and there is the presence of one of the nastiest Nazis in the business, the sneering Anton Diffring. The plot, too, is more complex than many of the cliff-hanging serials the film resembles.

Catch-22

The film centres on a group of World War II fliers in the Mediterranean and the insanity of war. The catch-22 of the title deals with a military snafu that results when a bombardier, the highly neurotic and paranoid Captain Yossarian (Arkin), attempts to get out of the military by feigning insanity – however, completing the paperwork for this proves him sane. No matter how 'crazy' he behaves, the Army Air Corps is crazier. His superiors and peers are all buffoons and maniacs. Indeed, the insanity of the war only seems to feed their personal aberrations, especially those of Milo Minderbinder (Voight), a wheeler-dealer who soon has the entire war effort working for his personal profit.

Eventually Yossarian is psychologically isolated.

Shot at a cost of $18 million in Mexico, the film is mounted on a giant scale, with at least a dozen B-25 airplanes enlisted to provide an appropriately grandiose bombing campaign. *Catch-22* is a funny, bizarre, satirical black comedy, with serious undertones, which was still relevant nine years after the Joseph Heller bestselling anti-war novel was published. It also has a terrific all-star cast led by Arkin, whose deadpan performance refuses to provide Yossarian with any sentimentality. It takes the craziness of war to its logical conclusion when Yossarian is seen as the only sane member of the company. David Watkin's camerawork is brilliant, capturing the feel of the bright sunlight of the location, and Nichols' direction captures the paradoxes and surrealism that pervade military life.

USA, 1970
DIRECTOR:
Mike Nichols
CAST INCLUDES:
Alan Arkin, Orson Welles, Anthony Perkins, Martin Balsam, Richard Benjamin, Jon Voight
SCREENPLAY:
Buck Henry from the novel by Joseph Heller
CINEMATOGRAPHY:
David Watkin
PRODUCERS/ PRODUCTION COMPANIES:
John Calley, Martin Ransohoff/Paramount

Tora! Tora! Tora!

USA/JAPAN, 1970
DIRECTOR:
Richard Fleischer, Toshio Masuda,
Kinji Fukasaku
CAST INCLUDES:
Martin Balsam, Jason Robards,
Sô Yamamura, Joseph Cotton,
E.G Marshall, Tatsuya Mihashi
SCREENPLAY:
Larry Forrester, Hideo Oguni, Ryuzo
Kikushima from the books *Tora! Tora!*
Tora! by Gordon W. Prange and *The*
Broken Seal: Operation Magic and
the Secret Road to Pearl Harbor
by Ladislas Farago
CINEMATOGRAPHY:
Charles F. Wheeler
PRODUCERS/
PRODUCTION COMPANIES:
Elmo Williams/20th Century-Fox
ACADEMY AWARD
NOMINATIONS (1971)
Best Art Direction-Set Decoration:
Richard Day, Walter M. Scott,
Norman Rockett, Carl Biddiscombe,
Yoshirô Muraki, Jack Martin Smith,
Taizô Kawashima
Best Cinematography: Charles F.
Wheeler, Osamu Furuya, Sinsaki
Himeda, Masamichi Satoh
Best Film Editing: James E. Newcom,
Pembroke J. Herring, Inoue Chikaya
Best Sound: Herman Lewis,
Murray Spivack
ACADEMY AWARDS
Best Effects, Special Visual Effects:
L.B. Abbott, A.D. Flowers

The bombing of Pearl Harbor is presented from the perspectives of both the Japanese and American sides. The first half shows the collapse of diplomacy between the nations as tension rises. While the Japanese military plans its attack on American military installations, the American forces, due to a series of blunders, leaves the naval and air forces sitting ducks for the impending attack. The second half is the devastating battle itself.

Despite audiences knowing the result of the build up towards Pearl Harbor, the tension that leads up to it is palpable and the climactic 30-minute battle, a massive feat of cinematic engineering, still excites as well as surprises. What makes this epic war film stand out from previous chronicles of World War II, is that *Tora! Tora! Tora!* was an American-Japanese co-production giving an equitable view of the historic battle. Richard Fleisher oversaw the complicated production, having to work with two Japanese directors (after Akira Kurosawa withdrew from the film), turning the story, with dozens of characters, into a coherent whole.

M*A*S*H

This is life in a Mobile Army Surgical Hospital – a Korean War field hospital. Between gory operations to save soldiers' lives, anarchic medics Hawkeye (Sutherland) and Trapper John (Gould) play practical jokes and pursue nurses, under the nose of their nemesis Major Burns (Duvall).

When *M*A*S*H* appeared in 1970, audiences – caught up in rebellion generated by the civil rights movement, feminism, the drug culture, and the demonstration against the Vietnam War – revelled in the film's iconoclastic humour, its joyous deflation of patriotism, religion, heroism and other values cherished by the establishment. It wasn't lost on them that Korea was standing in for Vietnam. The outrageous black comedy became an immediate box-office success, and spawned a popular long-running TV series. It also was the first financial and critical success for Robert Altman, who said he was offered *M*A*S*H* because 'fourteen more acceptable directors turned it down.' Altman's experimental use of sound is evident with simultaneous conversations and loudspeaker announcements.

USA, 1970
DIRECTOR:
Robert Altman
CAST INCLUDES:
Donald Sutherland, Elliott Gould,
Tom Skerritt, Sally Kellerman,
Robert Duvall
SCREENPLAY:
Ring Lardner Jr. from the novel by
Richard Hooker
CINEMATOGRAPHY:
Harold E. Stine
PRODUCERS/
PRODUCTION COMPANIES:
Ingo Preminger/20th Century-Fox
ACADEMY AWARD
NOMINATIONS (1971)
Best Director: Robert Altman
Best Actress in a Supporting Role:
Sally Kellerman
Best Film Editing: Danford B. Greene
Best Picture: Ingo Preminger
ACADEMY AWARDS
Best Writing, Screenplay Based on
Material from Another Medium:
Ring Lardner Jr.
CANNES FILM FESTIVAL (1970)
Palme d'Or: Robert Altman

Patton

USA, 1970
DIRECTOR:
Franklin J. Schaffner
CAST INCLUDES:
George C. Scott, Karl Malden,
Stephen Young, Michael Strong,
Morgan Paull
SCREENPLAY:
Francis Ford Coppola and
Edmund H. North from the books
A Soldier's Story by Omar N. Bradley
and *Patton: Ordeal and Triumph* by
Ladislas Farago
CINEMATOGRAPHY:
Fred Koenekamp
**PRODUCERS/
PRODUCTION COMPANIES:**
Frank McCarthy/20th Century-Fox
**ACADEMY AWARD
NOMINATIONS (1971)**
Best Cinematography:
Fred J. Koenekamp
Best Music, Original Score:
Jerry Goldsmith
Best Effects, Special Visual Effects:
Alex C. Weldon
ACADEMY AWARDS
Best Picture: Frank McCarthy
Best Actor in a Leading Role:
George C. Scott
Best Director: Franklin J. Schaffner
Best Original Screenplay:
Francis Ford Coppola,
Edmund H. North
Best Art Direction-Set Decoration:
Urie McCleary, Gil Parrondo,
Antonio Mateos, Pieere-Louis Thévenet
Best Sound: Douglas Williams,
Don Bassman
Best Film Editing: Hugh S. Fowler

The biopic follows the campaigns of US Commander General George S. Patton (Scott), from Tunis to the conquest of Sicily – where he slaps a fatigued soldier and is relieved of his command – later to England and to Normandy in charge of the Third Army. He lifts the siege of Bastogne during the Battle of the Bulge, then pushing into Czechoslovakia and sniffing glorious victory, he is forced by Eisenhower to make way for Montgomery's Northern Front. After the war, Patton's forces occupy Bavaria, but his unconcealed resentment of the Russians and his refusal to dismiss Nazis from civil office leads to his downfall and bitter departure.

One of the most intelligent of war epics of its period, the film hinges on George C. Scott's gargantuan performance – conceived like a tragic Shakespearean hero. Scott, his head shaved, his craggy features cast in expressions of contempt or rage, took the role because Patton 'was a professional and I admire professionalism'. Yet Scott refused to pick up his Oscar, considering the award ceremony to be a 'meat market'. The script represents Patton as a huge, ebullient warlord – a driven man to whom war and victory are all – but also as an enigma of flawed humanity. Although there are only eleven minutes of battle scenes in the film, it illustrates much about modern warfare.

Cross of Iron

Set in 1943, the film focuses on Corporal Steiner (Coburn), an accomplished but war-weary combat veteran, leading a doomed German platoon facing annihilation on the Russian Front. While the enemy attacks, Steiner's authority is undermined when Captain Stransky (Schell) takes over the command of his troops. A Prussian aristocrat, Stransky has one goal in mind: to win the coveted Iron Cross, Germany's highest medal, at any cost. There follows an intense battle of wills.

'Men on the front lines of Hell' screamed the posters for *Cross of Iron*, Sam Peckinpah's only war film, which proved to be just as disturbing and compelling as many of his Westerns. *Variety* commented that 'pacifism, Peckinpah style, means mayhem is the message'. But the director's characteristic graphic style is wedded to the violence of the subject of war, seen from the German perspective. He presents a male ethos wherein moral certainty is collapsing. There's usually little room for women in Peckinpah's world, though an encounter with female guerillas shows them exacting revenge with dreadful results.

GB/W. GERMANY, 1977
DIRECTOR:
Sam Peckinpah
CAST INCLUDES:
James Coburn, Maximilian Schell,
James Mason, David Warner
SCREENPLAY:
Julius Epstein, James Hamilton,
Walter Kelley from the novel
The Willing Flesh by Willi Heinrich
CINEMATOGRAPHY:
John Coquillon
**PRODUCERS/
PRODUCTION COMPANIES:**
Wolf C. Hartwig, Arlene Sellers,
Alex Winitsky/EMI Films Ltd.,
Incorporated Television Company
(ITC), Jadran Film, Radiant Film
GmbH, Rapid Film, Terra Filmkunst

The Deer Hunter

The film explores the experiences shared by a group of young men growing up in a small Pennsylvania industrial town, whose lives are dominated by the gruelling labour in the steel mills. Mike (De Niro), Nick (Walken), and Stevie (Savage) are just about to depart for military training, having volunteered to go to Vietnam together. Stevie gets married before he leaves, and Mike and Nick go on a hunting trip. They are then thrown into the hell of war, which affects their lives forever. Stevie ends up in a wheelchair, Nick who survives capture is traumatized by the experience, and Mike learns the dangers of the macho code he lived by.

This was the first major American movie about the Vietnam War, and one of the most controversial. The controversy derived from the harrowing sequence in which American POWs are forced to play Russian roulette by their captors. Although Russian-roulette gambling games were not a common occurrence during the Vietnam War, they're used here as a metaphor for the futility of the war itself. Also to be taken metaphorically is the untriumphal singing of 'God Bless America' at the end. The film's principal theme of friendship and the personal impact of war, packs a devastating dramatic punch and exactly caught the mood of the time. The set-pieces such as the wedding (almost a production number) and the hunt are epically conceived. Michael Cimino's second film was also his last success.

USA, 1978
DIRECTOR:
Michael Cimino
CAST INCLUDES:
Robert De Niro, John Cazale, John Savage, Christopher Walken, Meryl Streep
SCREENPLAY:
Michael Cimino, Deric Washburn, Louis Garfinkle, Quinn K. Redeker
CINEMATOGRAPHY:
Vilmos Zsigmond
PRODUCERS/ PRODUCTION COMPANIES:
EMI Films
ACADEMY AWARD NOMINATIONS (1979)
Best Actor in a Leading Role: Robert De Niro
Best Actress in a Supporting Role: Meryl Streep
Best Cinematography: Vilmos Zsigmond
Best Writing, Screenplay Written Directly for the Screen: Michael Cimino, Deric Washburn, Louis Garfinkle, Quinn K. Redeker
ACADEMY AWARDS
Best Picture:Barry Spikings, Michael Deeley, Michael Cimino John Peverall
Best Director: Michael Cimino
Best Actor in a Supporting Role: Christopher Walken
Best Film Editing: Peter Zinner
Best Sound: Richard Portman, William L. McCaughey, Aaron Rochin, C. Darin Knight

Apocalypse Now

Loosely based on *Heart of Darkness* by Joseph Conrad, it tells the story of Captain Willard (Sheen), a special agent sent into Cambodia to assassinate the renegade American Green Beret Colonel Kurtz (Brando), who has set himself up as a god to the local tribe. Willard is assigned a navy patrol boat operated by Chief (Hall) and three young 'rock 'n' rollers with one foot in the grave' (Forrest, Bottoms, and Fishburne). They are escorted on part of their journey by an air cavalry unit led by Lt. Colonel Kilgore (Duvall), a gung-ho commander, who carries out a helicopter bombing raid on a peasant village. After witnessing a surreal USO show featuring Playboy playmates and an anarchic battle with the Vietcong at a bridge, Willard reaches Colonel Kurtz's compound. A crazed photo journalist (Hopper) welcomes the crew, and Willard begins to question his orders to 'terminate the colonel's command'.

The gruelling making of this film in the Filipino jungles is almost as famous as the film as it led to vast budget overruns and physical and emotional breakdowns. *Apocalypse Now* assaults the senses with some extraordinary set-pieces. Coppola certainly achieved his aim of wanting to give the audience the sense of 'the horror, the madness, the sensuousness and the moral dilemma of the Vietnam War'. The opening scene is a perfect illustration of how Coppola combines vision and sound when the sight of helicopter blades dissolves into those of an electric fan on the ceiling above Willard. The combined brilliance of the cinematography, editing and sound montage (Walter Murch) makes the bombing sequence one of the most celebrated in cinema history. After they have blasted the village to the sound of 'The Ride of the Valkyries', Duvall announces, 'I love the smell of napalm in the morning'. In August 2001, *Apocalypse Now Redux* a restored and updated version of the 1979 film was released, including forty nine minutes of never-before-seen footage, a Technicolor enhancement, and a six-channel soundtrack.

USA, 1979
DIRECTOR:
Francis Ford Coppola
CAST INCLUDES:
Marlon Brando, Martin Sheen,
Robert Duvall, Fred Forrest,
Sam Bottoms, Albert Hall,
Dennis Hopper, Larry Fishburne
SCREENPLAY:
John Milius, Francis Ford Coppola
loosely based on *Heart of Darkness*
by Joseph Conrad
CINEMATOGRAPHY:
Vittorio Storaro
**PRODUCERS/PRODUCTION
COMPANIES:**
Francis Coppola/United Artists
**ACADEMY AWARD
NOMINATIONS (1980)**
Best Picture: Francis Ford Coppola,
Fred Roos, Gray Frederickson,
Tom Sternberg
Best Director: Francis Ford Copolla
Best Actor in a supporting Role:
Robert Duvall
Best Art Direction-Set Decoration:
Dean Tavoularis, Angelo P. Graham,
George R. Nelson
Best Film Editing: Richard Marks,
Walter Murch, Gerald B. Greenberg,
Lisa Fruchtman
Best Writing, Screenplay Based on
Material from Another Medium:
John Milius, Francis Ford Coppola
ACADEMY AWARDS
Best Cinematography:
Vittorio Storaro
Best Sound: Walter Murch, Mark
Berger, Richard Beggs, Nathan Boxer.
CANNES FILM FESTIVAL (1979)
FIPRESCI Prize: Francis Ford Coppola
Palme d'Or: Francis Ford Coppola

The Big Red One

USA, 1980
DIRECTOR:
Sam Fuller
CAST INCLUDES:
Lee Marvin, Mark Hamill,
Robert Carradine, Bobby DiCicco,
Kelly Ward Johnson
SCREENPLAY:
Samuel Fuller
CINEMATOGRAPHY:
Adam Greenberg
**PRODUCERS/
PRODUCTION COMPANIES:**
Gene Corman/United Artists

The film follows the fortunes and misfortunes of a squad from the 1st US Infantry Division (The Big Red One) through World War II, from a beachhead assault on North Africa, to France, Sicily, Belgium and on to the liberation of a concentration camp in Czechoslovakia. A nameless battle-hardened sergeant (Marvin), and four young recruits, are the only members of the squad who survive the war.

Director Sam Fuller had carried the story of *The Big Red One*, his first film in seven years, around in his head since his experiences as a GI in Europe during World War II. There are hardly any heroics – the final line is 'Survival is the only glory in war' – only a stark yet poetic description of incidents. War is reduced to its bloody essentials in Fuller's direct, no-holds-barred method, and although his screenplay makes no effort to delve too deeply into the characters, through whose eyes a series of battles are seen, we gradually get to know their desires and fears. The film, shot almost entirely on location in Israel, was two years in the making.

Das Boot

In 1941, the German submarine fleet is heavily engaged in the Battle of the Atlantic to harass and destroy English shipping. One such U-boat goes on a dangerous mission from La Rochelle to Spain and back, threatened by Allied depth charges and air raids.

Das Boot (The Boat) is the most popular foreign language film ever released in the United States. The film examines, in almost documentary detail, how these submariners maintained their professionalism, attempting to accomplish impossible missions, while all the time attempting to understand and obey the ideology of the government under which they served. At $12 million, the most expensive German film to date is a compendium of every submarine movie ever made, with all the expected claustrophobic horrors.

The main interest is not only in seeing the war from the German point-of-view, although most of the crew are 'good' Germans – there is only one despised Nazi on board – but also in the spectacular handheld camerawork, accurately depicting conditions under water. It lives up to the director's desire 'to show the gritty and terrible reality of war and to combine it with a highly entertaining story and fast-paced action style that would pull audiences into the experience of these young men'.

W.GERMANY, 1981
DIRECTOR:
Wolfgang Petersen
CAST INCLUDES:
Jürgen Prochnow, Herbert Grönemeyer, Klaus Wennemann, Hubertus Bengsch, Martin Semmelrogge
SCREENPLAY:
Wolfgang Petersen from the novel by Lothar G. Buchheim
CINEMATOGRAPHY:
Jost Vacano
PRODUCERS/ PRODUCTION COMPANIES:
Michael Bittins, Mark Damon, Ortwin Freyermuth, John W. Hyde, Edward R. Pressman, Günter Rohrbach/Bavaria Film, Radiant Film GmbH, Süddeutscher Rundfunk (SDR), Twin Bros. Productions (Director's cut), Westdeutscher Rundfunk (WDR)
ACADEMY AWARD NOMINATIONS (1983)
Best Cinematography: Jost Vacano
Best Director: Wolfgang Petersen
Best Effects, Sound Effects Editing: Mike Le Mare
Best Film Editing: Hannes Nikel
Best Sound: Milan Bor, Trevor Pyke, Mike Le Mare
Best Writing, Screenplay Based on Material from Another Medium: Wolfgang Petersen

The Killing Fields

GB, 1984
DIRECTOR:
Roland Joffe
CAST INCLUDES:
Sam Waterston, Haing S. Ngor,
John Malkovich, Julian Sands,
Craig T. Nelson, Spalding
Gray, Bill Paterson, Athol Fugard
SCREENPLAY:
Bruce Robinson
CINEMATOGRAPHY:
Chris Menges
**PRODUCERS/
PRODUCTION COMPANIES:**
David Putnam/Goldcrest
**ACADEMY AWARD
NOMINATIONS (1985)**
Best Actor in a Leading Role:
Sam Waterston
Best Director: Roland Joffé
Best Picture: David Puttnam
Best Writing, Screenplay Based on
Material from Another Medium:
Bruce Robinson
ACADEMY AWARDS
Best Actor in a Supporting Role:
Haing S. Ngor
Best Cinematography: Chris Menges
Best Film Editing: Jim Clark

It is Year Zero when Pol Pot's Khmer Rouge entered the capital Phom Penh, turned the population into serfs and slaughtered two million of them. The story is told from the perspective of Pulitzer-prize winning American journalist Sidney Schanberg (Waterston) whose friendship with his interpreter Dith Pran (Ngor), forms the basis of the film. Pran saves the lives of Schanberg and his fellow journalists, and is then left to save himself from the labour camps and certain death by obliterating all traces of his education. He escapes into Thailand and is finally reunited with Schanberg, who, in his turn, had been searching for him.

The Killing Fields has a scale and humanity seldom seen these days, especially in British films, and the evocation of the suffering of the people, especially that of Dith Pran has an unparalleled emotional force. The fact that he was portrayed by first-time actor Haing S. Ngor, a Cambodian gynaecologist whose own family had been wiped out by the Khmer Rouge, adds to the potency of the film. Unhappily, the Oscar-winning Dr Haing S. Ngor was brutally murdered by a street gang for no reason at all several years later. The whole atmosphere of the period is brilliantly captured by the camera of Chris Menges.

Come and See

Idi i smotri

Teenaged Florya (Kravchneko) is taken off by a group of anti-German partisans, fighting in the woods of Byleorussia in 1943. They disappear and he is left to wander, gun in hand, until he rejoins them as a hardened and active participant as a result of the horrors he has witnessed.

Drawn from three different books by Ales Adamovich, *Come and See* has been reconstructed as a surreal tragedy, described as 'an epic of derangement'. This sense of derangement is heightened by the film's soundtrack, most significantly when the bombing of a village damages Florya's hearing. Florya's ordeal, which turns his hair grey and wrinkles his young face, is undeniably moving. From the moment, early on in the film, when the boy discovers his village is destroyed and his family dead, the viewer joins him in witnessing an unbroken series of Nazi atrocities. Some of the images are unforgettable – such as the agonizing struggle through a swamp to reach an encampment of lamenting women, and the journey to find food, accompanied by a death's head effigy of Hitler.

USSR, 1985
DIRECTOR:
Elem Klimov
CAST INCLUDES:
Aleksei Kravchenko, Olga Mironova,
Liubomiras Lauciavicius,
Vladas Bagdonas
SCREENPLAY:
Ales Adamovich, Elem Klimov based
on the works of Ales Adamovich
CINEMATOGRAPHY:
Aleksei Rodionov
**PRODUCERS/PRODUCTION
COMPANIES**
Byelarusfilm, Mosfilm, Sovexportfilm

479

Platoon

USA, 1986
DIRECTOR:
Oliver Stone
CAST INCLUDES:
Tom Berenger, Willem Dafoe,
Charlie Sheen, Forest Whitaker,
Francesco Quinn
Kevin Dillon, Reggie Johnson,
Keith David, Johnny Depp
SCREENPLAY:
Oliver Stone
CINEMATOGRAPHY:
Robert Richardson
**PRODUCERS/PRODUCTION
COMPANIES:**
Arnold Kopelson/Hemdale Film
Corporation
**ACADEMY AWARD
NOMINATIONS (1987)**
Best Actor in a Supporting Role:
Tom Berenger, Willem Dafoe
Best Cinematography:
Robert Richardson
Best Original Screenplay: Oliver Stone
ACADEMY AWARDS
Best Picture: Arnold Kopelson
Best Director: Oliver Stone
Best Sound: John Wilkinson,
Richard Rogers, Charles Grenzbach,
Simon Kaye
Best Film Editing: Claire Simpson

In Vietnam, Chris (Sheen), a raw recruit, or 'new meat', at first wonders whether he'll ever be able to survive in the jungle conditions. But he gradually adapts and, as time goes by, begins to see that the platoon is divided into two groups. On the one side is the evil, literally, battle-scarred vet Sergeant Barnes (Berenger), who believes in total war, and on the other is the good, battle-weary veteran Sergeant Elias (Dafoe), who believes in compassion and humanity. Both struggle in the words of young Chris 'for possession of my soul'.

After a lull of seven years since *Apocalypse Now*, the last serious film to depict the Vietnam war directly, *Platoon* forcefully returned the war to the Hollywood agenda. It slammed the spectator with spectacular sights and sounds, portraying the mindless jingoism, the brutality, the torture and killing of Vietnamese peasants, and the dependency on booze and drugs of the average American soldier or 'grunt'. This is counterbalanced by the use of Samuel Barber's 'Adagio for Strings' on the soundtrack. Loosely autobiographical, the hell of Vietnam is made more real by Stone's own vivid memories of his time in Vietnam. Shot in the Philippines in 54 days, on a low budget, it grossed over $127.5 million.

Full Metal Jacket

Full Metal Jacket begins at Parris Island in South Carolina for one platoon's recruit training. We meet Sergeant Hartman (Ermey), the senior drill instructor, and several privates he decides to pick out and nickname: Joker (Modine), witty and sarcastic; Cowboy (Howard), a true marine who goes by the book, and Gomer Pyle (D'Onofrio), who's fat and foolish. After boot camp, the new Marines are shipped to Vietnam. Involved in battles, Cowboy is killed by a sniper, whom the Marines discover is a young Vietnamese girl. Joker, now a military journalist, shoots her.

Stanley Kubrick's penultimate film is a cynical, cold-as-steel, often stylized view of the Vietnam War, revealing the ritualized debasement of men in the name of patriotism in the first half, and the horrific results of this patriotism in the second. The boot-camp section goes further than any film before it in showing the sadistic brutality of the training, here in the person of Sergeant Hartman (brilliantly played by real-life drill sergeant R. Lee Ermey.) The film is full of wonderful set-pieces: the opening montage of the recruits being shaved bald, the recruits vulgar introduction to Hartman, Pyle's brutal beating by his fellow troops or Pyle's homicidal/suicidal showdown in the barracks head, and the sniper scene in the Vietcong village (almost from the enemy's perspective) and the Mickey Mouse sing-along at the climax of the film. The film is successful in personalizing war with the selective trials of soldiers, somewhere between the realism of *Platoon* and the surrealism of *Apocalypse Now*. Joker sums up the ironic approach to the war when asked why he came to Vietnam: 'I wanted to meet interesting and stimulating people of an ancient culture – and kill them.'

USA, 1987
DIRECTOR:
Stanley Kubrick
CAST INCLUDES:
Matthew Modine, R. Lee Ermey, Arliss Howard, Vince D'Onofrio, Adam Baldwin
SCREENPLAY:
Stanley Kubrick, Michael Herr and Gustav Hasford, based on the novel *The Short Timers* by Gustav Hasford
CINEMATOGRAPHY:
Douglas Milsome
PRODUCERS/ PRODUCTION COMPANIES:
Stanley Kubrick, Jan Harlan/ Warner Bros.
ACADEMY AWARD NOMINATIONS (1988)
Best Writing, Screenplay Based on Material from Another Medium: Stanley Kubrick, Michael Herr, Gustav Hasford

Good Morning, Vietnam

Adrian Cronauer (Williams) is an airman disc jockey who is brought from Crete to Saigon in 1965 to entertain the troops and boost their morale. His morning programme on the Armed Forces Network is an inventive mix of outrageous comic routines, controversial political humour, and loud rock music. While many at the station celebrate this breath of fresh air, his immediate superiors, including a straight-laced lieutenant and an uptight sergeant major, are angered by his unconventional and unpredictable behaviour.

USA, 1987
DIRECTOR:
Barry Levinson
CAST INCLUDES:
Robin Williams, Forest Whitaker,
Tung Thanh Tran, J.T. Walsh,
Robert Wuhl, Bruno Kirby
SCREENPLAY:
Mitch Markovich
CINEMATOGRAPHY:
Peter Sova
PRODUCERS/
PRODUCTION COMPANIES:
Mark Johnson, Larry Brezner/
Buena Vista
ACADEMY AWARD
NOMINATIONS (1988)
Best Actor in a Leading Role:
Robin Williams

Based on the case of a US armed forces DJ, the film, if one discounts *M*A*S*H* – ostensibly about the Korean War – was the first Vietnam comedy and one of the first to treat the Vietnamese as real people. Robin Williams gives what virtually amounts to an extremely funny virtuoso stand-up (though he's at the turntable) comedy solo. This part, much of which was ad-libbed, is mostly remembered about the film, but it also captures the tensions and misunderstandings of the war. Adrian's pursuit of a beautiful Vietnamese girl, and his friendship with her brother, eventually get him into deep trouble with those who see all Vietnamese as the enemy.

Schindler's List

At the start of World War II, Oskar Schindler (Neeson), a wealthy businessman who owns a munitions factory, while a member of the Nazi Party, quickly learns to manipulate the corrupt and cruel system to his own purposes. The drinking, gambling and womanizing Schindler becomes moved by the plight of the Jews, and he risks his own life and fortune by rescuing more than one thousand of them from the gas chambers by employing them in his factory.

This long (185 minutes) and ambitious movie finally brought Steven Spielberg one of the top Academy Awards after trying for nearly twenty years. With an intelligent script, a superb cast, and by shooting in Poland in many of the authentic backgrounds, in a restrained manner and in powerful black-and-white images – hand-held camera footage gives it a documentary style resonance – Spielberg came closer than most directors to filming the impossible – the Holocaust. Possibly the most moving moment in the film is the epilogue (in colour) of the actual survivors and their families, including his widow, filing past Oskar Schindler's grave in Israel.

USA, 1993
DIRECTOR:
Steven Spielberg
CAST INCLUDES:
Liam Neeson, Ralph Fiennes,
Ben Kingsley, Caroline Goodall,
Jonathan Sagalle
SCREENPLAY:
Steven Zaillian based on the novel
Schindler's Ark by Thomas Keneally
CINEMATOGRAPHY:
Janusz Kaminski
**PRODUCERS/
PRODUCTION COMPANIES:**
Steven Spielberg, Gerald R. Molen,
Branko Lustig/ Amblin-Universal
**ACADEMY AWARD
NOMINATIONS (1994)**
Best Actor in a Leading Role:
Liam Neeson
Best Actor in a Supporting Role:
Ralph Fiennes
Best Costume Design:
Anna Sheppard
Best Makeup: Matthew W. Mungle,
Christina Smith, Judith A. Cory
Best Sound: Andy Nelson, Ron
Judkins, Scott Millan, Steve Pederson
ACADEMY AWARDS
Best Picture: Steven Spielberg,
Gerald R. Molen, Branko Lustig
Best Director: Steven Spielberg
Best Writing, Screenplay Based on
Material from Another Medium:
Steven Zaillian
Best Cinematography:
Janusz Kaminski
Best Film Editing: Michael Kahn
Best Art Direction-Set Decoration:
Allan Starski, Ewa Braun
Best Music, Original Score:
John Williams

Saving Private Ryan

American soldiers land on Omaha Beach during the D-Day landings in World War II, with multiple deaths from enemy fire. An army captain (Hanks) has been assigned to take his squad of seven men into France to find Private Ryan (Damon), whose three brothers have been killed in combat, and get him home to his grieving mother. To this end, they have to travel through treacherous German held territory. They find Ryan and a small group of Paratroopers trying to hold onto a key bridge about to be attacked by a German Panzer Group.

The film opens with some of the most devastating footage of combat ever committed to film. For twenty minutes the audience is assailed by subjective sight and sound in an attempt to recreate the feeling of being in the midst of a battle. Much of this terrifying effect is due to the camerawork of Janusz Kaminski. Having established that war is hell, the film moves into a complex examination of heroism, much of it seen through the eyes of Corporal Upham (Davies), the frightened translator, who speaks excellent German and French, but is really a civilian and the audience's surrogate. The final spectacular battle sequence is shot more objectively than the graphic opening sequence so that we can see that war is not all chaos, but tactics. Tom Hanks and the rest of the cast effectively play down any heroics.

USA, 1998
DIRECTOR:
Steven Spielberg
CAST INCLUDES:
Tom Hanks, Edward Burns,
Tom Sizemore, Jeremy Davies,
Vin Diesel, Matt Damon
SCREENPLAY:
Robert Rodat
CINEMATOGRAPHY:
Janusz Kaminski
PRODUCERS/
PRODUCTION COMPANIES:
Steven Spielberg, Ian Bryce,
Mark Gordon, Gary Levinsohn/ Amblin-
Dreamworks
ACADEMY AWARD
NOMINATIONS (1999)
Best Picture: Steven Spielberg,
Ian Bryce, Mark Gordon, Gary Levinsohn
Best Actor in a Leading Role:
Tom Hanks
Best Art Direction-Set Decoration:
Tom Sanders,
Lisa Dean Kavanaugh
Best Music, Original Dramatic Score:
John Williams
Best Makeup: Lois Burwell, Conor
O'Sullivan, Daniel C. Striepeke
Best Original Screenplay:
Robert Rodat
ACADEMY AWARDS
Best Director: Steven Spielberg
Best Cinematography:
Janusz Kaminski
Best Film Editing: Michael Kahn
Best Effects, Sound Effects Editing:
Gary Rydstrom, Richard Hymns
Best Sound: Gary Rydstrom, Gary
Summers, Andy Nelson, Ron Judkins

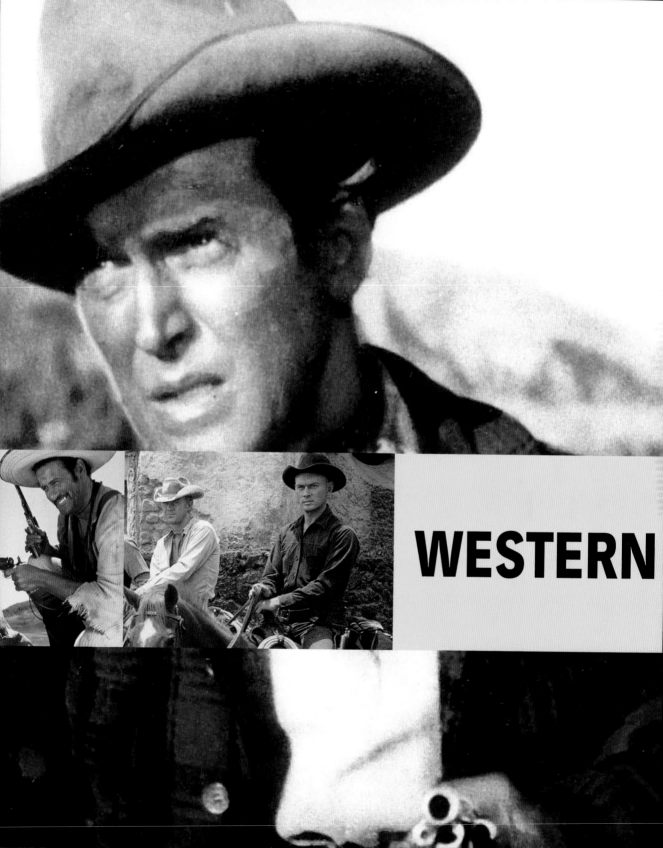

WESTERN

Union Pacific

USA, 1939
DIRECTOR:
Cecil B DeMille
CAST INCLUDES:
Barbara Stanwyck, Joel McCrea,
Robert Preston, Brian Donlevy,
Akim Tamiroff, Anthony Quinn,
Henry Kolker, George Bancroft,
Berton Churchill, Louise Platt
SCREENPLAY:
Walter DeLeon, C. Gardner Sullivan,
Jesse Lasky Jr. from the novel *Trouble
Shooters* by Ernest Haycox
CINEMATOGRAPHY:
Victor Milner
**PRODUCERS/
PRODUCTION COMPANIES:**
Cecil B. DeMille/Paramount
**ACADEMY AWARD
NOMINATIONS (1940)**
Best Special Effects:
Gordon Jennings, Loren L. Ryder,
Farciot Edouart
CANNES FILM FESTIVAL (1939)
Winner of the Palme d'Or

In 1862, in the midst of the American Civil War, two rival railroad companies decide to undertake the construction of an American transcontinental railroad that will stretch from the East to West coasts. Engineer Jeff Butler (McCrea) is hired to ensure that the Union Pacific is completed and arrives at its destination on time. But financial opportunist Asa Barrows (Kolker) hopes to profit from obstructing it. Butler has his hands full fighting Barrows' agent, gambler Sid Campeau (Donlevy), and faces enormous odds, including derailments, an old Civil War army buddy (Preston) who is working for the bad guys, and hostile Indians.

The name of Cecil B. DeMille almost always guaranteed action on an epic scale and this does not disappoint. The film includes an uncomplex upright hero, an irredeemable villain, a spectacular trainwreck, Indian attacks and a cavalry rescue. Like a few other DeMille movies of his best period (1937-1947), including *The Plainsman*, *North West Mounted Police* and *Unconquered*, it is an energetic, colourful, patriotic celebration of frontiersmen, extolling strength, perseverance and forthright manliness. Among all this shooting and fisticuffs, Barbara Stanwyck as a fiery Irish postmistress more than holds her own. DeMille effortlessly manages to alternate between studio sound stages and outdoor location work.

Stagecoach

Nine people are making a coach trip through dangerous Indian territory: an outlaw under arrest called the Ringo Kid (Wayne), the marshal accompanying him (Bancroft), Dallas, a woman of ill-repute (Trevor), a timid liquor salesman (Meek), a shifty gambler (Carradine), an embezzling banker (Churchill), an alcoholic doctor (Mitchell), a pregnant woman (Platt) and the driver (Devine). En route, loves and hates develop among them, a baby is born, and there are deaths during an attack by Apaches at the climax.

Stagecoach was a landmark in the history of the Western. It raised the genre to artistic status, bringing about a revival, stamped John Ford as one of the great Hollywood directors, and rocketed John Wayne from B pictures to stardom. Beautifully shot in the now familiar Monument Valley, it was Ford's first Western for thirteen years. Much of the second unit work was directed by the legendary stunt man Yakima Canutt who also played a cavalry scout. It is he who falls under the wagon wheels and horses' hoofs and can be just glimpsed getting to his feet after the shot. While preparing for *Citizen Kane*, Orson Welles is said to have watched *Stagecoach* around forty times, especially the scenes with a low-angle camera requiring the sets to have ceilings.

USA, 1939
DIRECTOR:
John Ford
CAST INCLUDES:
John Wayne, Claire Trevor,
Thomas Mitchell, John Carradine,
Andy Devine, Donald Meek
SCREENPLAY:
Dudley Nichols from the Ernest
Haycox story *Stage to Lordsburg*
CINEMATOGRAPHY:
Bert Glennon
PRODUCERS/
PRODUCTION COMPANIES:
Walter Wanger/United Artists
ACADEMY AWARD
NOMINATIONS (1940)
Best Picture: Walter Wanger
Best Director: John Ford
Best Cinematography, Black-and-
White: Bert Glennon
Best Art Direction: Alexander Toluboff
Best Film Editing: Dorothy Spencer
ACADEMY AWARDS
Best Actor in a Supporting Role:
Thomas Mitchell
Best Music, Scoring:
Richard Hageman, Frank Harling,
John Liepold, Leo Shuken

The Ox-Bow Incident

Saddle tramps Gil Carter (Fonda) and Art Croft (Morgan) ride into a small Nevada town in 1885 just as an illegal posse gets up to track down the suspected killers of a popular rancher. Out for blood are the victim's best friend Jeff Farnley (Lawrence) and the bigoted local bigshot 'Major' Tetley (Conroy), who sees a vigilante killing as a way of imposing manliness on his cowardly son Gerald (Eythe). Carter goes along with the mob, partly to keep them from suspecting him. The mob arrests three drifters (Andrews, Quinn, Ford), tries them by a kangaroo court, and lynches them. Carter, meanwhile, realizes too late that the men were innocent.

There have been few better examples of the dangers of mob hysteria than this powerful Western directed with intensity and precision by William Wellman. It is even more remarkable for being released during World War II when most Hollywood fare was of a patriotic nature. Henry Fonda's liberal persona is not over exploited, portraying him as an ordinary good-hearted guy caught up in ugly events. By obscuring Fonda's eyes as he reads a final letter written by one of the victims, none of whom are presented as saints, Wellman allows audiences to focus on the message instead of the personality.

USA, 1943
DIRECTOR:
William Wellman
CAST INCLUDES:
Henry Fonda, Dana Andrews, Anthony Quinn, Henry Morgan, Jane Darwell, Marc Lawrence, Frank Conroy, Francis Ford, William Eythe
SCREENPLAY:
Lamar Trotti from the novel by Walter Van Tilburg Clark
CINEMATOGRAPHY:
Arthur Miller
PRODUCERS/ PRODUCTION COMPANIES:
Lamar Trotti/20th Century-Fox
ACADEMY AWARD NOMINATIONS (1944)
Best Picture: Lamar Trotti

Duel in the Sun

Orphaned when her father is condemned for murdering his Indian wife and her lover, Pearl Chavez (Jones) goes to live with Texan Senator McCanles (Barrymore), his wife (Gish) and two sons. Both of the latter, upright Jesse (Cotten) – who is banished for contesting his father's opposition to the railroad – and arrogant and amoral Lewton (Peck), are attracted to her. After Lewton guns down her husband-to-be on the eve of the wedding, and escapes into exile, Pearl joins him at Squaw's Head Rock where the two engage in an agonized shootout before dying in a final embrace.

This demented, delirious Western of sibling rivalry for the love of a tempestuous half-breed is Hollywood High Romanticism at its peak. Played mostly against blood-red skies, it was producer David O. Selznick's challenge to his own *Gone With The Wind*. He gave it one of the biggest publicity campaigns in US film history and it grossed around $17 million. Its eroticism, rare in a Western, earning the movie the nickname 'Lust In The Dust', had it condemned by The Legion of Decency, it was denounced from the pulpit by Catholics and Protestants alike, and banned by some local councils. All this should be enough to tempt audiences to see this flamboyant and visually resplendent melodrama.

USA, 1946
DIRECTOR:
King Vidor
CAST INCLUDES:
Gregory Peck, Jennifer Jones,
Joseph Cotton, Walter Huston,
Herbert Marshall, Lionel Barrymore,
Lillian Gish
SCREENPLAY:
David O Selznick, Oliver Garrett from
the novel by Niven Busch
CINEMATOGRAPHY:
Lee Garmes, Harold Rossen,
Ray Rennahan
**PRODUCERS/
PRODUCTION COMPANIES:**
David O Selznick/Selznick
**ACADEMY AWARD
NOMINATIONS (1947)**
Best Actress in a leading Role:
Jennifer Jones
Best Actress in a Supporting Role:
Lillian Gish

My Darling Clementine

USA, 1946
DIRECTOR:
John Ford
CAST INCLUDES:
Henry Fonda, Linda Darnell,
Victor Mature, Cathy Downs,
Walter Brennan
SCREENPLAY:
Winston Miller, Samuel G. Engel from
the story by Sam Hellman from the
novel *Wyatt Earp, Frontier Marshal*
by Stuart N. Lake
CINEMATOGRAPHY:
Joseph MacDonald
**PRODUCERS/
PRODUCTION COMPANIES:**
Samuel G Engel/20th Century-Fox

In 1882, Wyatt Earp (Fonda) and his brothers are driving their cattle towards California. Leaving James, the youngest brother, to guard the livestock, they go into town for some relaxation. On their return, the Earps discover the cattle gone and James killed. Wyatt agrees to become marshal of Tombstone and makes his brothers his deputies. They suspect the Clanton clan headed by the ruthless patriarch Old Man Clanton (Brennan) and set about to prove their guilt, setting the stage for the celebrated gunfight at the OK Corral. Along the way, Earp falls in love with a schoolteacher named Clementine (Downs), who is the fiancée of the consumptive, heavy-drinking Doc Holiday (Mature).

Although rich in period detail, *My Darling Clementine* does not pretend to be realistic but is a mystic poetic masterpiece haunted by romantic imagery of paradise lost. The town of Tombstone was meticulously recreated in Monument Valley for the film and it provides some very striking images.

Take the wonderful sequence of the founding of the town's new church and the square dance to celebrate it, or Henry Fonda famously silhouetted on a porch, his foot up against a post, or Doc Holiday's drunken carriage ride. As the latter, Victor Mature gives perhaps his best performance as an educated man – he is able to prompt a Shakespearean actor stumbling through a soliloquy – who has wasted a promising life. Fonda is soberly impressive as his antithesis.

Fort Apache

Captain Kirby York (Wayne) knows the Indians well and seeks to make peace with the local tribes. Owen Thursday (Fonda), an arrogant lieutenant colonel from the East takes command of the fort. His daughter Philadelphia (Temple) is courted by the son (Agar) of the sergeant major (Bond), a liaison bitterly opposed by Thursday. Despising Indians and hoping to advance his career, he breaks York's agreement with Cochise, and launches a Custer-like charge that wipes out his entire force. York tells reporters that Thursday died gloriously.

This was the first of John Ford's magnificent calvary trilogy (the others were *She Wore a Yellow Ribbon* and *Rio Grande*), made within two years, all starring John Wayne, all about the US cavalry's battles with the Indians and all beautifully filmed at Ford's favourite location – Monument Valley on the Arizona-Utah border. However, it is the life at the fort that is so vividly captured: the reunions and separations of loved ones, the waiting women, the carousing of the soldiers, the singing interludes, the formal dances including a Grand March at a non-commissioned officers' ball. Henry Fonda is superb as the unyielding commander, stiff in bearing and in behaviour, and John Wayne is the perfect contrast.

USA, 1948
DIRECTOR:
John Ford
CAST INCLUDES:
John Wayne, Henry Fonda,
Shirley Temple, John Agar,
Ward Bond, Victor MacLaglen
SCREENPLAY:
Frank S. Nugent from the story
Massacre by James Warner Bellah
CINEMATOGRAPHY:
Archie Stout
**PRODUCERS/
PRODUCTION COMPANIES:**
John Ford, Merian C. Cooper/RKO

Red River

The end of the Civil War finds Thomas Dunson (Wayne), master of a vast cattle domain in Texas, having to drive his livestock over the Chisholm Trail into Missouri, hoping to benefit from the huge market created by the new railroad. Dunson is a martinet who creates his own laws, alienating some of his men, his long-time friend, the wagon-train cook (Brennan) and, more significantly, his adopted son Matthew Garth (Clift). They quarrel bitterly, with Garth going his own way, deserting Dunson, who has lost control of the drive. The picture ends with a showdown between Wayne and Clift, using fists not guns, and a reconciliation.

Red River is full of striking Fordian elements – silhouetted covered wagons, people posing against sunset skies, songs on the sound track – but it is purely Hawksian in its fascination with masculine by-play. The exploration of the Freudian subtext of the script – a dual character study in which the patriarchal John Wayne is faced with Montgomery Clift, fighting to prove his independence and 'kill the father' – gives the Western an added depth. This succeeds brilliantly because of the contrast between Wayne's muscular macho security and Clift's nervy angularity, creating a special tension.

Although this was Clift's first film, the public had already seen him in the previously released *The Search*.

USA, 1948
DIRECTOR:
Howard Hawks
CAST INCLUDES:
John Wayne, Montgomery Clift,
Joanne Dru, Walter Brennan,
John Ireland
SCREENPLAY:
Borden Chase, Charles Schnee from
the novel *The Chisholm Trail* by
Borden Chase
CINEMATOGRAPHY:
Russell Harlan
PRODUCERS/
PRODUCTION COMPANIES:
Howard Hawks/United Artists
ACADEMY AWARD
NOMINATIONS (1949)
Best Film Editing: Christian Nyby
Best Writing, Motion Picture Story:
Borden Chase

She Wore a Yellow Ribbon

Captain Nathan Brittles (Wayne), a Cavalry officer about to retire, must carry out one last mission: to escort two women to the safety of a military fort. The younger of the women (Dru), flirts and causes trouble between two young cavalrymen (Agar, and Carey Jr.) though she will fall in love with the former. They reach the fort, only to find it decimated by Indian marauders. Brittles makes a desperate attempt to negotiate peace between the Indians and the cavalry before his term is up.

The second of the three cavalry films with John Wayne, is the only one in colour. And what colour! The ochre hues of Monument Valley, the blue and gold uniforms, the saturated colours of wagons lit up during a spectacular storm, red sunsets on a desert cemetery where widower Wayne talks to his dead wife. A homage to the Western paintings of Frederic Remington, Ford subtly shows us the results of a massacre, a stagecoach burning, wounded soldiers, but not the actions that caused them. Amidst the drama is the romance of the young lovers and the comedy of the drinking and brawling of Victor McLaglen and his friendly sparring with Wayne. Wayne, only 33 at the time, is marvellous as a man near retirement. There is a moving moment when he wishes to read the inscription on a watch his troops have given him as a farewell gift and he shyly reaches for a pair of reading spectacles.

USA, 1949
DIRECTOR:
John Ford
CAST INCLUDES:
John Wayne, Joanne Dru, John Agar,
Ben Johnson, Harry Carey Jr.,
Victor McLaglen
SCREENPLAY:
Frank S. Nugent, Laurence Stallings
from the stories *War Party* and *The
Big Hunt* by James Warner Bellah
CINEMATOGRAPHY:
Winton C. Hoch
**PRODUCERS/
PRODUCTION COMPANIES:**
John Ford, Merian C. Cooper/RKO
ACADEMY AWARDS (1950)
Best Cinematography, Color:
Winton C. Hoch

The Gunfighter

USA, 1950
DIRECTOR:
Henry King
CAST INCLUDES:
Gregory Peck, Helen Westcott, Millard Mitchello, Karl Malden, Skip Homeier, Richard Jaeckel, B.G. Norman
SCREENPLAY:
William Bowers, William Sellers from a story by Bowers and André de Toth
CINEMATOGRAPHY:
Arthur Miller
PRODUCERS/ PRODUCTION COMPANIES:
Nunnally Johnson/20th Century-Fox
ACADEMY AWARD NOMINATIONS (1951)
Best Writing, Motion Picture Story: William Bowers, André de Toth

Ageing gunfighter Jimmy Ringo (Peck) regrets his criminal past, and is tired of travelling from town to town. But he finds there is no such thing as a retired gunslinger. Everywhere he goes he is regularly challenged by cocky young gunmen hoping to make names for themselves, such as Eddie (Jaeckel). Forced to shoot him, Ringo is now tailed by Eddie's three brothers. Ringo rides to yet another dusty Western town to see the wife (Westcott) and young son Jimmie (Norman) he abandoned. Meanwhile, Eddie's brothers arrive in town. A local aspiring gunman (Homeier) also wants to kill Ringo, to establish his reputation.

The Gunfighter is not a traditional Western in that there is very little action, being more of a character study and morality play. It was also rare in painting an authentic picture of the late 19th century West suggesting the sepia photographs of the period. Sporting a heavy moustache for the first time, Peck brings gravitas to the role of a man who cannot escape his past. When the film failed at the box-office, the studio moguls blamed the moustache. *The Gunfighter*, the second of six films that Peck made with director Henry King, the first being *Twelve O'Clock High* (1949), has gained in critical appreciation over the years and is now considered one of the great westerns.

Winchester '73

Frontiersman Lin McAdam (Stewart) rides into town on the trail of Dutch Henry Brown (McNally), only to find himself in a Dodge City marksmanship contest. McAdam wins a precious Winchester model '73 rifle, but Dutch steals it and leaves town. McAdam is bent on tracking down his murderous antagonist, who happens to be his brother, while the rifle keeps changing hands. It passes to an Indian chief (Hudson), a gun trader (Drake), a bank robber (Duryea), back to Dutch, and finally, at a shoot-out on a rocky mountain precipice, into the hands of its rightful owner.

Winchester '73 is the film which established Anthony Mann as a Western auteur, and the first of several collaborations with James Stewart and the writer Borden Chase. This 'story of a rifle' provided Mann with the possibility of covering many aspects of the genre: cavalry, Indians, settlers, badmen, etc. It also revealed a new Stewart, more bitter and uncompromising than had been seen before his collaboration with Mann. The scene where Stewart smashes Dan Duryea's head on the bar shows him to be an equal when it comes to sadism. Beautifully photographed by William Daniels, this exceptional Western was responsible for a renewal of the genre, its demise is often announced prematurely.

USA, 1950
DIRECTOR:
Anthony Mann
CAST INCLUDES:
James Stewart, Dan Duryea, Stephen McNally, Millard Mitchell, John McIntire, Shelley Winters, Charles Drake, Rock Hudson
SCREENPLAY:
Robert L. Richards, Borden Chase from the story by Stuart N. Lake
CINEMATOGRAPHY:
William Daniels
PRODUCERS/ PRODUCTION COMPANIES:
Aaron Rosenberg/Universal

Bend of The River

USA, 1952
DIRECTOR:
Anthony Mann
CAST INCLUDES:
James Stewart, Arthur Kennedy, Julia
Adams, Rock Hudson
SCREENPLAY:
Borden Chase from the novel *Bend
of the Snake* by Bill Gulick
CINEMATOGRAPHY:
Irving Glassberg
**PRODUCERS/
PRODUCTION COMPANIES:**
Aaron Rosenberg/Universal

Glyn McLyntock (Stewart), an ex-Missouri raider, now a reformed character trying to hide his criminal past, is working as a scout to a wagon train heading for farming land in Oregon. Along the way, he rescues former partner Cole Garett (Kennedy), from hanging. At first Cole is a loyal companion, and saves Glyn's life when the two men ambush a band of marauding Indians. Gradually, though, Cole's crooked instincts get the better of him, and it ends with a confrontation between the two men in the Snake River of the title, with the settlers' vital provisions at stake.

This was the second of the five westerns director Anthony Mann made with James Stewart after *Winchester 73* (1950), which brought out a new, tougher Stewart than the drawling charmer of previous pictures. Here he is bitterly confronted with his past, personified by a corrupt Arthur Kennedy, who he must overcome. Stewart still bears the mark of the hangman's noose around his neck from which he escaped. The narrative spring is as tightly coiled as ever, moving with the inevitability of a Greek tragedy. There is also the conflict between the homesteaders and gold seekers that sets up the two sides of the Old West, the landscape of which is beautifully captured.

High Noon

Will Kane (Cooper) is about to marry a Quaker girl (Kelly) and retire as marshal of the small frontier town of Hadleyville, when he is warned that the Miller gang, whose leader Kane had previously arrested, is arriving on the noon train to get him. Instead of leaving, as he is urged to do, Kane stays to fight them. From 10.45 to 11.45 he attempts to get support from the worthy people of the town. Nobody will stand by him. Even his bride-to-be threatens to leave, until she is appealed to by Kane's Mexican ex-flame (Jurado). Finally, the hero overcomes the gang and leaves the town with his bride.

As Tex Ritter famously sings 'Do Not Forsake Me Oh My Darlin',' on the soundtrack, director Fred Zinnemann builds up the tension in masterly fashion, making this the high-water mark of his career. The pulsating action takes place in the same time scale as the 90-minute running time of the film, respecting the unity of time and place. Despite the intended analogy with McCarthyism, *High Noon* is a classic (much imitated) Western tale of a loner 'doing what a man has to do'. The townsfolk are well characterized, while Katy Jurado, dark and fiery, is contrasted vividly with Grace Kelly, blonde and cool. But it is 51-year-old Gary Cooper, still possessed of a mythic aura which he assumes with such easy masculine (though never aggressively macho) elegance, who gives his most soulful and agonizing performance.

USA, 1952
DIRECTOR:
Fred Zinnemann
CAST INCLUDES:
Gary Cooper, Grace Kelly, Thomas Mitchell, Lloyd Bridges, Katy Jurado
SCREENPLAY:
Carl Foreman from the story *The Tin Star* by John W. Cunningham
CINEMATOGRAPHY:
Floyd Crosby
**PRODUCERS/
PRODUCTION COMPANIES:**
Stanley Kramer/United Artists
**ACADEMY AWARD
NOMINATIONS (1953)**
Best Picture: Stanley Kramer
Best Director: Fred Zinnemann
Best Writing,Screenplay:
Carl Foreman
ACADEMY AWARDS
Best Actor in a Leading Role:
Gary Cooper
Best Music, Scoring of a Dramatic or Comedy Picture:
Dmitri Tiomkin
Best Film Editing: Elmo Williams, Harry Gerstad
Best Music, Original Song:
Dimitri Tiomkin, Ned Washington for the song 'High Noon (Do Not Forsake Me, Oh My Darlin')'

The Naked Spur

USA, 1953
DIRECTOR:
Anthony Mann
CAST INCLUDES:
James Stewart, Janet Leigh,
Robert Ryan, Ralph Meeker,
Millard Mitchell
SCREENPLAY:
Sam Rolfe, Harold Jack Bloom
CINEMATOGRAPHY:
William C. Mellor
**PRODUCERS/
PRODUCTION COMPANIES:**
William H. Wright/MGM
**ACADEMY AWARD
NOMINATIONS (1954)**
Best Writing, Story and Screenplay:
Sam Rolfe and Harold Jack Bloom

Howard Kemp (Stewart), a bounty hunter trying to earn money to buy back land he unfairly lost while away at the Civil War, is on the trail of Ben Vandergroat (Ryan), who has a $5,000 price tag on his head. Kemp teams up with an old prospector, Jesse Torte (Mitchell), and a dishonorably discharged Union soldier, Roy Anderson (Meeker). They help capture Vandergroat who is with his girlfriend Lina Patch (Leigh), and decide to cut themselves in as partners for their share of the reward money. But the journey to the county jail is a hazardous one, especially as tension grows among the group.

Another tough, intelligently-written Anthony Mann-James Stewart Western masterpiece, the only one of the five made for

MGM. Aspiring to Greek tragic dimensions, the film is a study in greed, which is the spur of the title. Stewart, revealing a neurotic side, makes a spiritual journey at the same time as the physically arduous one through a varied landscape. Shot in the inspiring Rocky Mountains of Colorado – there are very few interiors – the characters are sometimes dwarfed by the vast landscape. Nevertheless, this action-packed Western is not pretentious and the characterizations are vivid with good James Stewart and evil Robert Ryan as worthy opponents.

Shane

Shane (Ladd), a lone rider, stops at the farm of homesteader Joe Starrett (Heflin), his wife Marian (Arthur) and young son Joey (De Wilde) just before Ryker (Meyer), a powerful and ruthless cattleman, arrives with his cronies to make the farmer a threatening offer for land that he intends to get by any means necessary. When Shane lets the cattle baron know that his gun will back Starrett if there's any trouble, the grateful homesteader offers the stranger a job on the farm. Shane tries to keep out of the conflict between the opposing groups until Ryker brings in a gunslinger, Wilson (Palance) who threatens Starrett. Joey, who hero worships Shane, sees him ride into town to take on Wilson.

Told through the eyes of a young boy with disarming innocence and warmth, *Shane* has the mythic aura of an Arthurian legend. Alan Ladd in buckskins is at his most iconic: serene face, piercing eyes, tenderness behind the tough persona. We learn little of Shane's background – he comes from nowhere and returns to nowhere. He is first seen coming over the horizon between the antlers of a stag and, in the heart-breaking finale, Joey's voice echoes in the wilderness, 'Shane, come back. Come back, Shane.' One of the most beautifully composed of Westerns, it was filmed in the lush landscapes of Wyoming. If Ladd is stamped forever as Shane, Jack Palance made a lasting impression as the gunman in black, menacingly putting on his gloves. He only spoke twelve lines but was nominated for a Best Supporting Actor Oscar.

It was the lovely Jean Arthur's last movie.

USA, 1953
DIRECTOR:
George Stevens
CAST INCLUDES:
Alan Ladd, Jean Arthur, Van Heflin, Brandon De Wilde, Jack Palance, Emile Meyer
SCREENPLAY:
A. B. Guthrie Jr., Jack Sher from the novel by Jack Schaefer
CINEMATOGRAPHY:
Loyal Griggs
PRODUCERS/ PRODUCTION COMPANIES:
George Stevens/Paramount
ACADEMY AWARD NOMINATIONS (1954)
Best Actor in a Supporting Role: Brandon De Wilde
Best Actor in a Supporting Role: Jack Palance
Best Director: George Stevens
Best Picture: George Stevens
Best Writing, Screenplay: A.B. Guthrie Jr., Jack Sher
ACADEMY AWARDS
Best Cinematography, Color: Loyal Griggs

The Searchers

USA, 1956
DIRECTOR:
John Ford
CAST INCLUDES:
John Wayne, Jeffrey Hunter,
Vera Miles, Ward Bond,
Natalie Wood, John Qualen
SCREENPLAY:
Frank S. Nugent from the novel by
Alan LeMay
CINEMATOGRAPHY:
Winton C. Hoch
PRODUCERS/
PRODUCTION COMPANIES:
Merian C. Cooper/Warner Bros.

Ex-confederate Ethan Edwards (Wayne) returns to his brother's house on the Texas frontier in 1868. After he leaves, the brother, wife and a son are killed by Comanches, who also abduct their two daughters. Joined by Martin Pawley (Hunter), an orphan with Cherokee blood adopted by the dead couple, Ethan finds the older girl dead and pursues the younger, Debbie (Wood), who he believes has married within the tribe. The two wander for five years until they discover that Debbie is a squaw of Chief Scar. The Indian-hating Ethan is determined to kill her, but relents when he catches her and holds her in his arms. 'Let's go home, Debbie,' he says finally.

The Searchers is perhaps John Ford's masterpiece, and the last of the golden era of classical Westerns begun with *Stagecoach* (1939). The Western had matured and become less black-and-white (in both senses) since then, and so had John Wayne's character. Ethan, Ford's only real anti-hero, played by Wayne with complete conviction, is a complex, obsessive man, a mixture of good and bad. In a sense, the five-year quest for Debbie is also a quest for himself, as well as Ford's exploration of his own views on Native Americans. The film reiterates the director's reverence for family life from which Ethan is excluded. In the final unforgettable image, Wayne clutches his arm in a gesture borrowed from Ford's first star Harry Carey, as the door closes on him, the symbol of the rejection of the homeless wanderer. The stunning colour photography, the wonderful vistas of Monument Valley and Max Steiner's moving score are all part of the sensual pleasure of the film.

The Tall T

USA, 1956
DIRECTOR:
Budd Boetticher
CAST INCLUDES:
Randolph Scott, Richard Boone,
Maureen O'Sullivan, Arthur Hunicutt,
Henry Silva
SCREENPLAY:
Burt Kennedy from the story *The
Captives* by Elmore Leonard
CINEMATOGRAPHY:
Charles Lawton Jr.
**PRODUCERS/
PRODUCTION COMPANIES:**
Harry Joe Brown/Columbia

Having lost his horse in a bet, Pat Brennan (Scott) hitches a ride with a stagecoach carrying newlyweds, businessman Willard (Hubbard) and Doretta (O'Sullivan). At the next station the coach and its passengers fall into the hands of a trio of outlaws: Usher (Boone) and his two vicious underlings (Silva and Homeier). When Usher learns that Doretta is the daughter of a rich copper-mine owner, he decides to hold her for ransom. While tension builds over the next 24 hours as Usher awaits a response to his demands and as a romantic attachment grows between Brennan and Doretta, a game of bluff and counter bluff ensues.

The second of seven B-Westerns, directed by Budd Boetticher and starring Randolph Scott, is as taut and laconic as its hero. In its concise way, running 78 minutes, made in a couple of weeks, and shot almost entirely outdoors, it says as much about dignity and courage than many longer, more expensive Westerns. The classic plot is told with an unselfconscious narrative force, and each of the characters is finely etched. The distinctive psychopathy of the villains, particularly Richard Boone's unscrupulous but lonely, intelligent figure, is well contrasted with Scott's inherent decency.

3.10 to Yuma

The title refers to the time of the train on which rancher Dan Evans (Heflin) is to escort outlaw Ben Wade (Ford) to the state prison. Dan is a peace-loving rancher, devastated by drought, who, desperately in need of the reward money, has offered to take on the dangerous mission, knowing that Wade's badmen friends will do anything to free their partner in crime. Tension mounts as the two men wait for the train in a hotel room in a small border town. At the climax, Evans has to face Wade's gang alone.

3.10 to Yuma, like *High Noon*, deals with the psychological tensions of waiting, as well as exposing small-town complacency and cowardice. Relying more on suspense and sharp dialogue rather than physical action, the film brilliantly creates a claustrophobic atmosphere, confined as it is for much of the time to a hotel room. Delmer Daves creates this with an excellent use of close-ups and crane shots. At the heart of the film is the almost Faustian relationship between the wicked but persuasive Glenn Ford and the noble Van Heflin trying to resist temptation. There is also a terrific theme song sung by Frankie Laine.

USA, 1957
DIRECTOR:
Delmer Daves
CAST INCLUDES:
Glenn Ford, Van Heflin, Felicia Farr, Richard Jaeckel
SCREENPLAY:
Halsted Welles from the story by Elmore Leonard
CINEMATOGRAPHY:
Charles Lawton Jr.
**PRODUCERS/
PRODUCTION COMPANIES:**
David Heilweil/Columbia

Forty Guns

USA, 1957
DIRECTOR:
Samuel Fuller
CAST INCLUDES:
Barbara Stanwyck, Barry Sullivan,
Dean Jagger, Gene Barry, Eve Brent
SCREENPLAY:
Samuel Fuller
CINEMATOGRAPHY:
Joseph Biroc
**PRODUCERS/
PRODUCTION COMPANIES**:
Samuel Fuller/20th Century-Fox

Jessica Drummond (Stanwyck) more or less runs Cochise County, Arizona, where she makes her own law with a private posse of forty cowboys. The wimpy sheriff (Jagger) cannot control her and an ex-gunslinger turned US Marshall (Sullivan) is sent for. His job is to bring law and order to the place. There is an immediate clash with Jessica, although the cattle queen finds herself falling for the lawman. But, when her psychotic brother Brockie (Ericson) commits murder, the Marshall is forced to kill Brockie, wounding Jessica in the process.

One of the Westerns that strongly influenced Sergio Leone and later Clint Eastwood's *Unforgiven*, it strips the West of all its glamour, being raw and direct. To counterbalance this and to heighten the slightly off-beam drama, Fuller uses a breathtakingly bravura camera style. *Forty Guns* also stands among a number of Westerns of the 1950s that sought to de-mythologize the cowboy and see the frontier with a modern sensibility, such as the myth of masculine power. Barbara Stanwyck is the 'high ridin' woman with a whip' and 'no man can tame her' of the film's theme song. In addition it has an ambivalent hero that resists using violence until the inevitable end. Fuller's comment on America's fascination with guns also includes some amusingly phallic lines. At one stage, when Stanwyck flirtatiously asks a gunfighter if she can feel his pistol, he warns her that it might go off in her face. Another character remarks that he would 'like to stay around long enough to clean her rifle'.

At the stunning beginning, Stanwyck (clad in black leather) is seen riding at the head of her cavalry of forty guns, snaking through the valleys and canyons; this scene sets the vibrant tone of the film.

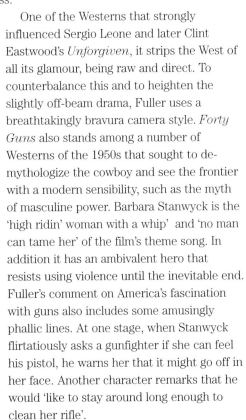

Run of the Arrow

Immediately after the Civil War, a die-hard Irish Virginian infantryman O'Meara (Steiger) who loathes the United States, heads west 'where the savages live'. There he joins a tribe of Sioux after surviving the 'run of the arrow' ritual. He finds a home and nation among them, marrying Yellow Moccasin (Monteil, dubbed by Angie Dickinson), until the US cavalry arrives on Sioux territory, determined to possess the land and build a fort. O'Meara becomes attached as scout to a liberal commanding officer until his old Yankee enemy, Lieutenant Driscoll (Meeker) assumes command, and a fierce battle between the Sioux and the soldiers rages. Though O'Meara sides with his tribe, their brutality forces him to rethink his allegiances.

'The end of this story can only be written by you,' says the final caption of Samuel Fuller's complex off-beat Western, which looks at the virtues and failings of so-called civilization, ethnic allegiance and identity. Rod Steiger, who clashed with Fuller, managing a broad Irish brogue, gives one of his most intense performances. Certainly not an easily liberal film, the script doesn't shirk from showing the ugly side of both Native Americans and later arrivals. However, there is nothing ugly about Joseph Biroc's carefully composed cinematography, shot in Utah.

USA, 1957
DIRECTOR:
Samuel Fuller
CAST INCLUDES:
Rod Steiger, Sara Monteil,
Brian Keith, Ralph Meeker,
Charles Bronson
SCREENPLAY:
Samuel Fuller
CINEMATOGRAPHY:
Joseph Biroc
**PRODUCERS/
PRODUCTION COMPANIES:**
Samuel Fuller/RKO

The Big Country

USA, 1958
DIRECTOR:
William Wyler
CAST INCLUDES:
Gregory Peck, Charlton Heston,
Jean Simmons, Charles Bickford,
Burl Ives, Carrol Baker
SCREENPLAY:
James R. Webb, Sy Bartlett,
Robert Wilder, Jessamyn West
(uncredited) from the novel by
Donald Hamilton
CINEMATOGRAPHY:
Franz Planer
**PRODUCERS/
PRODUCTION COMPANIES:**
Gregory Peck, William Wyler/
United Artists
**ACADEMY AWARD
NOMINATIONS (1959)**
Best Music, Scoring of a Dramatic or
Comedy Picture: Jerome Moross
ACADEMY AWARDS
Best Actor in a Supporting Role:
Burl Ives

Two enemy cattlemen, Major Henry Terrill (Bickford) and Rufus Hannassey (Ives) try to acquire the property of schoolteacher Julie Maragon (Simmons) because it has a well. James McKay (Peck), an Eastern gentleman, comes west to marry the major's spoiled daughter Patricia (Baker) but falls foul of Steve Leech (Heston), the brutish foreman, who eventually wins Patricia while James marries the school ma'm after he's proved himself a real man. The two patriarchs kill each other leaving room for peace.

At the heart of this rousing epic Western is a plea for pacifism, as represented by greenhorn Gregory Peck, something that could make it an anti-Western. But, as in William Wyler's previous film, *Friendly Persuasion*, about a Quaker family, there comes a time when one must act to defend oneself. Thus, *The Big Country* had both sweep and substance, living up to its title on the wide Technirama screen. The film's highlights are the exciting opening sequence involving a carriage chase which recalls *Ben-Hur*, another Wyler picture, accompanied by the celebrated stirring theme music by Jerome Moross; Peck's solitary attempts to master a wild stallion, his moonlight fight with Charlton Heston and the climactic shootout between Burl Ives and Charles Bickford in a giant canyon.

The Left-handed Gun

William Bonney alias Billy the Kid (Newman) gets a job with a cattleman known as 'The Englishman'. But when a crooked sheriff and his men murder his boss, Billy decides to avenge the death by killing the four men responsible, violating the General Amnesty. His outraged friend Pat Garrett (Dehner), who is about to be married, agrees to become sheriff. His sidekick dead, Billy surrenders and faces hanging.

Arthur Penn's debut feature immediately reveals the director's strong sympathy with the outsider and an anti-Establishment stance, a theme that he would develop in later films such as *Bonnie and Clyde*, with the outlaws presented as attractive and vital figures. *The Left-Handed Gun* is considered among the first Freudian Westerns in which a crazy-mixed up Billy the Kid, possibly homosexual, is a young man constantly on the very edge of sanity. Paul Newman (who starred in the original TV version), out-Brandoing Brando, is like a spring always ready to uncoil. Hurd Hatfield (*The Picture of Dorian Gray*) makes an interesting figure as the rather nervous chronicler of the events, inventing much of the mythology of the West, which the film cleverly debunks.

USA, 1958
DIRECTOR:
Arthur Penn
CAST INCLUDES:
Paul Newman, Lita Milan,
John Dehner, Hurd Hatfield,
James Best
SCREENPLAY:
Leslie Stevens from the teleplay *The Death of Billy the Kid* by Gore Vidal
CINEMATOGRAPHY:
J. Peverell Marley
**PRODUCERS/
PRODUCTION COMPANIES:**
Fred Coe/Warner Bros.

Man of the West

USA, 1958
DIRECTOR:
Anthony Mann
CAST INCLUDES:
Gary Cooper, Lee J. Cobb,
Julie London, Jack Lord, Royal Dano,
John Dehner
SCREENPLAY:
Reginald Rose from the novel *The Border Jumpers* by Will C. Brown
CINEMATOGRAPHY:
Ernest Haller
PRODUCERS/
PRODUCTION COMPANIES:
Walter M.Mirisch/United Artists

Link Jones (Cooper), a man of peace who gave up the life of a bank robber twenty years earlier, is faced with the need to use violence once more. The train on which he is travelling is ambushed and he, a card sharp (O'Connell) and a school teacher turned dancehall singer (London) are stranded in the wilderness after being robbed. They come across the hideout of the gang of which Link was once a member. It is now led by a half-crazed outlaw (Cobb) who encourages his depraved crew in their sadism. Gradually, by talk and action, the hero overcomes them all, and rides off with the girl.

Although made in CinemaScope, most of the taut action of this strongly allegorical Western is confined to the small space of the hideout where the characters interact. With a literate script by Reginald Rose (author of *Twelve Angry Men*), the movie is directed with intensity by Western maestro Anthony Mann ('Mann of the West') and Gary Cooper is at his anguished best in his last great role. He represents another one of Mann's deeply troubled heroes with a dark past that catches up with them. Generally dismissed on its first release, the film has since gained in reputation over the years.

Last Train From Gun Hill

US Marshal Matt Morgan (Douglas) is determined to seek revenge on the man who raped and murdered his half-breed wife. The killers leave behind a saddle that he recognizes as the property of his friend Craig Belden (Quinn), a wealthy cattle rancher in the nearby town of Gun Hill. Realizing that Belden's son Rick (Holliman) is one of the killers, Morgan travels to Gun Hill to arrest him. Although sympathetic about the death of Morgan's wife, Belden predictably refuses to turn over his son when the marshal makes known the purpose of his visit, claiming that Morgan owes him for having once saved his life. Not only must Morgan locate and arrest Rick, but he has to do so before the last train leaves Gun Hill at 9 p.m.

This is a superior adult western from director John Sturges, a master of the genre. Rape was not often referred to so explicitly in Hollywood movies of the time, and this depiction is particularly disturbing given its idyllic woodland setting, its racial motivation and the fact that it is witnessed by the victim's young son. Kirk Douglas is at his most intense and uncompromising, never asking for sympathy, while Anthony Quinn matches him in passion. The splendid landscape is the perfect setting for the high-powered action, all the more effective for the gradual eruption.

USA, 1959
DIRECTOR:
John Sturges
CAST INCLUDES:
Kirk Douglas, Anthony Quinn,
Carolyn Jones, Earl Holliman,
Brad Dexter
SCREENPLAY:
James Poe based on the story
Showdown by Les Crutchfield
CINEMATOGRAPHY:
Charles B. Lang Jr
PRODUCERS/
PRODUCTION COMPANIES:
Hal B. Wallis/Paramount

Rio Bravo

USA, 1959
DIRECTOR:
Howard Hawks
CAST INCLUDES:
John Wayne, Dean Martin,
Walter Brennan, Angie Dickinson,
Ricky Nelson, John Russell
SCREENPLAY:
Jules Furthman, Leigh Brackett from
a story by Barbara Hawks
McCampbell
CINEMATOGRAPHY:
Russell Harlan
PRODUCERS/
PRODUCTION COMPANIES:
Howard Hawks/Warner Bros.

Sheriff John T. Chance (Wayne) tries, with his three deputies – Stumpy, a limping old man (Brennan), the drunken Dude (Martin) and Colorado Ryan (Nelson), a trigger-happy youngster– have to hold a murderer in jail for four days until the arrival of the US Marshal, despite the counter-efforts by the prisoner's wealthy brother. Chance also has the support of saloon gal Feathers (Dickinson), on the outside.

Howard Hawks purposely and magnificently abandons the wide open spaces of the traditional Western for the claustrophobic interiors of the prison, town bars and hotel

rooms. It is also Hawks' riposte to *High Noon*, which both the director and Wayne disliked. John Wayne has his motley crew of supporters who may be too old and infirm, too young, too drunk and too female but unlike Gary Cooper, he doesn't reject offers of help, wanting to be surrounded only by willing, loyal people. Dean Martin, giving his most profound performance, is touching as an alcoholic who redeems himself thanks to the cruel-to-be-kind efforts of Wayne. *Rio Bravo* is principally an affectionate, witty and sharply observed study of male camaraderie, with an exciting climax and a great score by Dimitri Tiomkin and a couple of songs warbled by crooner Martin and pop-star Nelson.

The Magnificent Seven

Chris (Brynner) gathers together six other mercenaries to protect a Mexican mountain village from marauding bandits, led by the ruthless Calvera (Wallach). Having fortified the village and won hearts and minds by feeding the kids, they are let down by the peasants' lack of fighting spirit. But the seven overcome the bandits in a climactic battle.

This wonderfully stirring, exciting and humorous Western ingeniously transposes the traditional Japanese jidai-geki genre to the traditional American genre. It was perfectly logical that such a tale could have been adapted from Akira Kurosawa's *The Seven Samurai* given that the great Japanese director himself has acknowledged his debt to the Hollywood Western. A further link with the earlier film was the casting of the oriental-looking Yul Brynner as the leader of the gang of seven. What fascinated director John Sturges was the different lethal skills of the seven, and the development of their self-sacrificial idealism.

The pulsating action, the charisma of the cast and Elmer Bernstein's sweeping music score made it the huge hit it was. The movie boosted the careers of Steve McQueen, James Coburn and Charles Bronson and led Eli Wallach to be cast as the heavy in Spaghetti Westerns a few years later. Three far from magnificent sequels followed.

USA, 1960
DIRECTOR:
John Sturges
CAST INCLUDES:
Yul Brynner, Steve McQueen, Horst Buchholz, Charles Bronson, Robert Vaughn, Brad Dexter, James Coburn, Eli Wallach
SCREENPLAY:
William Roberts, Walter Bernstein, Walter Newman (uncredited)
CINEMATOGRAPHY:
Charles B Lang Jr.
PRODUCERS/
PRODUCTION COMPANIES:
John Sturges/Mirisch-United Artists
ACADEMY AWARD
NOMINATIONS (1961)
Best Music, Scoring of a Dramatic or Comedy Picture: Elmer Bernstein

Two Rode Together

USA, 1961
DIRECTOR:
John Ford
CAST INCLUDES:
James Stewart, Richard Widmark,
Shirley Jones, Linda Cristal,
Andy Devine
SCREENPLAY:
Frank S. Nugent from the novel
Comanche Captives by Will Cook
CINEMATOGRAPHY:
Charles Lawton Jr.
PRODUCERS/
PRODUCTION COMPANIES:
John Ford, Stan Shpetner/Columbia

When Jim Gary (Widmark), an idealistic cavalry officer, asks for help from his old friend, Guthrie McCabe (Stewart), a cynical small-town marshal, in negotiating with the Comanche for the return of some white captives from long-ago raids, McCabe is initially reluctant. But after being guaranteed a bounty for each returned captive, he agrees. On arrival at the Comanche camp, McCabe and Gary find a few of the captives, but they have been completely assimilated into Comanche life and aren't eager to return. The marshal coldly sizes up those he believes he can credibly return for profit and negotiates their release. They can only watch as the alienated children are rejected by the 'civilized' society.

Two Rode Together is in some ways a variation of *The Searchers*, but shows an even darker side. An astute blend of black comedy and tragedy, the film reveals a society dominated by greed and double standards. At its centre, however, are the performances of James Stewart and Richard Widmark playing off each other brilliantly. The friendship between the two contrasting friends is beautifully expressed by John Ford in a leisurely single-take shot as they sit by the river to talk things over. The more garrulous Stewart offers a complex portrayal of avarice and corruption, while Widmark is all stoic integrity. One of Ford's most underestimated late films.

Lonely Are The Brave

Jack Burns (Douglas) is an itinerant cowboy who gets himself sent to prison in order to free a friend who has been sentenced for helping illegal immigrants from Mexico. However, his friend prefers to serve out his sentence, so he escapes alone and goes on the run. He is pursued relentlessly by the sheriff (Matthau) and his posse, which uses helicopters and jeeps, making the power and speed of Jack's horse tragically irrelevant.

USA, 1962
DIRECTOR:
David Miller
CAST INCLUDES:
Kirk Douglas, Gena Rowlands,
Walter Matthau, George Kennedy
SCREENPLAY:
Dalton Trumbo from the novel *Brave Cowboy* by Edward Abbey
CINEMATOGRAPHY:
Philip Lathrop
**PRODUCERS/
PRODUCTION COMPANIES:**
Edward Lewis/Universal

This poignant and pointed Western, set in contemporary times, was Kirk Douglas' favourite film. It was he that convinced Universal to make it. 'It happens to be a point of view I love. This is what attracted me to the story – the difficulty of being an individual today.' Douglas convincingly plays an anachronism. The opening scene immediately sets up the theme when Douglas, dragging on a cigarette, looks up at the sky and watches the long trail of three streaking jet planes. But the film not only shows the way that the Old West, and some of its better values, are obliterated by the pervasive automobile and advancing technology, but makes a statement about the inability of the USA to tolerate misfits. The lengthy mountain chase that is the climax of the film is enhanced with stunning black-and-white location photography.

The Man who Shot Liberty Valance

Senator Ransom Stoddard (Stewart) and his wife Hallie (Miles) return to the small town of Shinbone where Stoddard first settled to practice law. He has come for the funeral of his friend Tom Doniphon (Wayne) and takes the opportunity to talk to a journalist about the story that made him a legend and furthered his career – the fact that he shot and killed violent outlaw Liberty Valance (Marvin). In flashback, we see what really happened. It was the unsung Tom, even though he had lost Hallie to Ransom, who shot Valance from a hidden place, allowing the unsuspecting tenderfoot to think that the fatal bullet had come from his gun.

When the newspaper editor hears the truth, he refuses to print Stoddard's 'confession' by saying, 'When the legend becomes fact, then print the legend'. This effectively sums up the plot of this nostalgic, melancholy and moving late Western by the 67-year-old John Ford. With his wonderful repertory of familiar actors, Ford seems to be summing up his whole career, showing his beloved populist west becoming eaten away by democracy, law and literacy (in the person of James Stewart). John Wayne represents this decline from the cocky hero in *Stagecoach* (1939) to the moment in *The Man Who shot Liberty Valance* when the gunslinger enters the political meeting toward the end, drunken, unshaven and shabby, putting up a brave front. Even though he is defeated in the film, we know that he is a winner, as is the film in all its autumnal glory.

USA, 1962
DIRECTOR:
John Ford
CAST INCLUDES:
James Stewart, John Wayne,
Lee Marvin, Andy Devine, Vera Miles,
Edmond O'Brein
SCREENPLAY:
James Warner Bellah, Willis Goldbeck
from the story by
Dorothy M. Johnson
CINEMATOGRAPHY:
William H. Clothier
**PRODUCERS/
PRODUCTION COMPANIES:**
John Ford/Paramount
**ACADEMY AWARD
NOMINATIONS (1963)**
Best Costume Design, Black-and-
White: Edith Head

Ride the High Country

Ex-sheriff Steve Judd (McCrea) takes a job escorting a shipment of gold bullion down from the high Sierras to a bank, and is joined by former partner Gil Westrum (Scott.) Along for the hazardous ride are Gil's rowdy young assistant Heck Longtree (Starr) and Elsa Knudsen (Hartley), fleeing her zealously religious father to join her fiancé Billy Hammond (Drury) at the mining camp. After a grotesque marriage ceremony in the local brothel, Elsa has to be rescued from the brutal attentions of the five Hammond brothers. On the return journey, pursued by the Hammonds, Judd foils his partner's attempts to steal the money. But they assist each other to defeat the Hammonds and complete their mission.

Elsa asks Judd, 'My father says there's only right and wrong – good and evil with nothing in between. But it's not that simple, is it?' 'No. It should be, but it isn't,' Judd replies, reflecting Sam Peckinpah's own philosophy. *Ride the High Country*, shot beautifully by Lucien Ballard, astoundingly in 26 days, against an appropriate autumnal landscape, is significant in being only Peckinpah's second film, but his first Western. Here immediately is established not only his unpretentious, affectionate nostalgia for the Old West but, by casting two icons of the genre, 59-year-old Randolph Scott in his last role and 57-year-old Joel McCrea in his last important role, Peckinpah also expresses his nostalgia for the Old Western.

USA, 1962
DIRECTOR:
Sam Peckinpah
CAST INCLUDES:
Randolph Scott, Joel McCrea,
Ronald Starr, Mariette Hartley,
James Drury
SCREENPLAY:
N.B. Stone Jr.
CINEMATOGRAPHY:
Lucien Ballard
**PRODUCERS/
PRODUCTION COMPANIES:**
Richard E. Lyons/MGM

Ride in the Whirlwind

USA, 1965
DIRECTOR:
Monte Hellman
CAST INCLUDES:
Jack Nicholson, Cameron Mitchell,
Millie Perkins, Harry Dean Stanton
SCREENPLAY:
Jack Nicholson
CINEMATOGRAPHY:
Gregory Sandor
PRODUCERS/
PRODUCTION COMPANIES:
Monte Hellman, Jack
Nicholson/Proteus Films

Three cowboys, Wesp (Nicholson), Vern (Mitchell) and Otis (Filer), pursued by an unseen character called Cain, come across a gang of outlaws hiding from vigilantes in a mountain shack. The outlaws offer them better hospitality than the 'good citizens' of the Western towns, and the cowboys find themselves on the wrong side of the law.

This stark and original Western was made back to back in three weeks with *The Shooting*, in the Utah desert, at a cost of $75,000, with a minimal crew and two cameras. It was devised by Jack Nicholson after reading some old diaries of the period as well as being influenced by a low-budget Italian film *The Bandits at Orgosolo* (1961) set in Sardinia. The film follows the cowboys across the sun-baked desert, with Vern regretting their banishment, while Wesp (29-year-old Nicholson brilliant in the sort of role he was to make his own – that of the quixotic loner) is at home in exile. Unfortunately, the film was deemed too off-beat and Nicholson too unknown (though he was beginning to have an underground reputation) to gain it a proper distribution in America. Needless to say, both *The Shooting* and *Ride in the Whirlwind* have accrued a cult following.

The Good, The Bad and The Ugly

Il buono, il brutto, il cattivo

Blondie (Eastwood) and Tuco (Wallach) operate a racket whereby Blondie captures Tuco, gets a reward, then rescues him from the rope at the last minute. But they keep doublecrossing each other in the dangerous game. Along comes cold-blooded Setenza (Van Cleef) who thinks nothing of shooting a man's face through a pillow. He's after a box containing $200,000 of stolen money. This leads the three of them to a cemetary where it's buried, and a showdown.

'When you have to shoot, don't talk, shoot,' seemed to be the philosophy behind the film. The concluding part of the *Dollars* trilogy (after *A Fistful of Dollars* and *A Few Dollars More*) is more violent but it also has more depth and dark humour. Despite the title none of the characters is good, all were monosyllabic, bad and ugly, except Clint 'Golden-haired Angel' Eastwood who is monosyllabic, bad and handsome. The film has an amoral mythic grandeur along its bloody way to the gripping climax, the mother of all showdowns. Sergio Leone swings his camera around 180 degrees as the tricky trio face each other with long, lingering looks, while Ennio Morricone's pulsating music adds to the drama.

ITALY, 1966
DIRECTOR:
Sergio Leone
CAST INCLUDES:
Clint Eastwood, Lee Van Cleef,
Eli Wallach, Aldo Giuffre
SCREENPLAY:
Luciano Vincenzoni, Sergio Leone,
Age Scarpelli
CINEMATOGRAPHY:
Tonino Delli Colli
**PRODUCERS/
PRODUCTION COMPANIES:**
Alberto Grimaldi/United Artists

USA, 1966
DIRECTOR:
Richard Brooks
CAST INCLUDES:
Burt Lancaster, Lee Marvin,
Robert Ryan, Jack Palance,
Ralph Bellamy, Claudia Cardinale,
Woody Strode
SCREENPLAY:
Richard Brooks from the novel *A Mule For The Marquesa* by
Frank O'Rourke
CINEMATOGRAPHY:
Conrad Hall
**PRODUCERS/
PRODUCTION COMPANIES:**
Richard Brooks/ Columbia
**ACADEMY AWARD
NOMINATIONS (1967)**
Best Director: Richard Brooks
Best Writing, Screenplay Based on
Material from Another Medium:
Richard Brooks
Best Cinematography, Color:
Conrad Hall

The Professionals

The Mexican-US border 1917. Four mercenaries – an explosives expert (Lancaster), a sharpshooter and tracker (Strode), a horse handler (Ryan) and one skilled in tactics and weaponry (Marvin) – are hired by a wealthy Texan oil baron (Bellamy) to rescue his wife (Cardinale) from a Mexican revolutionary hero (Palance) who has kidnapped her. They make their way across the treacherous landscape to Mexico, carry out the rescue only to discover that she does not want to return.

One of the most financially successful Westerns of the 1960s, (grossing almost $9 million in domestic rentals), it was, despite its 2-hour length, tightly directed and written by Richard Brooks. He also managed to integrate serious themes of loyalty and the need for personal ethics, with a great deal of slam-bang action and humour, while cynicism gives way to romance. The magnificent four – Lancaster, Ryan, Marvin and Strode – present us with four complex and flawed personalities. It all takes place against stunning landscapes. Conrad Hall's cinematography brilliantly evokes the mountains, the ochre-coloured desert and heat that our heroes have to conquer. The atmosphere, plot and setting obviously influenced Sam Peckinpah's *The Wild Bunch*, three years later.

Hombre

John Russell (Newman), a white man brought up by Apaches, while riding a stagecoach, is at first shunned by his seven fellow travellers who think he is an Indian, especially by a banker (March) and his snobbish wife (Rush). He only gets some sympathy from Jessie (Cilento), the rejected mistress of the sheriff. But when the coach is held up by a bandit-chief Grimes (Boone), they turn to Russell for help. The latter proves himself the bravest of the passengers, sacrificing his own life to save them and overcome the bandits. 'People must help each other,' he concludes.

USA, 1967
DIRECTOR:
Martin Ritt
CAST INCLUDES:
Paul Newman, Diane Cilento,
Fredric March, Richard Boone,
Cameron Mitchell, Barbara Rush
SCREENPLAY:
Irving Ravetch, Harriet Frank Jr. from
the novel by Elmore Leonard
CINEMATOGRAPHY:
James Wong Howe
PRODUCERS/
PRODUCTION COMPANIES:
Martin Ritt, Irving Ravetch/Hombre
Productions, 20th Century-Fox

This is an entertaining and unusual variation on *Stagecoach*, with an underlying criticism of the treatment of Native Americans. Not surprising from the idealistic and sensitive director Martin Ritt, who delivers the liberal message without preaching. Beautifully shot in the harsh sun of Death Valley by veteran cinematographer James Wong Howe, there is plenty of action – gunfights and tight corners – and vivid characterizations, especially by cigar-chomping Richard Boone, who makes the murderous bandit almost likeable. Paul Newman, his blue eyes seldom as penetrating, gives another great portrayal of a brooding outsider.

Once Upon a Time in the West

C'era una volta il West

Frank (Fonda), a cold-blooded, psychopathic gunman, suffers no conscience pangs after annihilating an entire family (except the wife who arrived after the slaughter) on the orders of a crazy, crippled railroad tycoon (Ferzetti), who wants the land. But now he must deal with the widow (Cardinale), a mysterious harmonica playing cowboy (Bronson), and a half-breed outlaw (Robards) accused of the killings.

A compendium of almost every Western ever made, this amorality tale of epic grandeur is the apotheosis of the Sergio Leone style of long lingering shots and meaningful close-ups. Skillfully using natural sound – water drops, footsteps, squeaky door hinges and a buzzing fly – the tension is immediately built up in the first fourteen minutes as a trio of villains descend on a train station, awaiting their prey. Much of the effect of this lyrical and bloody film comes from the music of Ennio Morricone, as important as any character, making the movie into a quasi-opera. Henry Fonda is inspiringly cast as a heavy, while Charles Bronson does more with silence than most of the actors with dialogue. The film also addresses the question of race and tackles the sneaky dealings behind how the railroads conquered the West.

ITALY/USA, 1968
DIRECTOR:
Sergio Leone
CAST INCLUDES:
Henry Fonda, Claudia Cardinale,
Jason Robards, Charles Bronson,
Gabriele Ferzetti
SCREENPLAY:
Sergio Leone, Sergio Donati,
Bernardo Bertolucci
CINEMATOGRAPHY:
Tonino Delli Colli
**PRODUCERS/
PRODUCTION COMPANIES:**
Fulvio Morsella/Paramount

Butch Cassidy and the Sundance Kid

USA, 1969
DIRECTOR:
George Roy Hill
CAST INCLUDES:
Paul Newman, Robert Redford,
Katherine Ross, Strother Martin
SCREENPLAY:
William Goldman
CINEMATOGRAPHY:
Conrad Hall
PRODUCERS/
PRODUCTION COMPANIES:
John Foreman/20th Century-Fox
ACADEMY AWARD
NOMINATIONS (1970)
Best Picture: John Foreman
Best Director: George Roy Hill
Best Sound: David Dockendorf,
William E. Edmondson
ACADEMY AWARDS
Best Cinematography: Conrad L. Hall
Best Original Score: Burt F. Bacharach
Best Original Screenplay:
William Goldman
Best Music, Original Song: Hal David,
Burt Bacharach for the song
'Raindrops Keep Fallin' on My Head'

In the early 1900s, Butch Cassidy (Newman) and the Sundance Kid (Redford) are members of the 'Hole-in-the Wall' gang. They rob banks and trains. But Butch's ambition is to go to Bolivia, which has silver, tin and gold mines. The two buddies are endlessly pursued by a remote and relentless posse forcing them into the hills. At one stage, they are trapped and cornered by the posse on a ledge at the edge of a steep rock canyon with nowhere else to go. They are faced with a choice between a hopeless shoot-out and a near-suicidal leap. Although the Kid confesses he can't swim, they jump in tandem, the swift current carries them to safety. After a romantic interlude during which both men vie for a schoolteacher Etta Place (Ross), they get to Bolivia where the army catches up with them.

This romanticized version of a true story (the opening title claims: 'Most of What Follows Is True') is vastly entertaining and likeable. The film opens with the credits next to a silent sepia-toned 'film within a film' portraying the legendary outlaw gang holding up a train. Paul Newman and Robert Redford (in the role that brought him real stardom) make perfect buddy-buddies, Newman an independent, unconventional thinker, disrespectful of both the law and the establishment; Redford (in a part first offered to Jack Lemmon!), is more level-headed, more the traditional Western hero. Instead of the ultra-violence typical of other outlaw films of the day, the film, borrowing from *Jules et Jim* and *Bonnie and Clyde*, uses an ironic mixture of slapstick comedy and conventional Western action to comment on the clichés of the cowboy genre. There is even the famous anachronistic song, 'Raindrops Keep Falling On My Head' which accompanies Newman and Ross doing tricks on a bicycle (which, it is hinted, will soon replace the horse).

True Grit

Rooster Cogburn (Wayne), a hulking, one-eyed, drunken, cantankerous old US marshal, is hired by 14-year-old Mattie Ross (Darby) to find Tom Chaney (Corey), who killed her father. The headstrong Mattie has selected the ageing Cogburn because she believed he had 'true grit'. Also heading into Indian territory in search of Chaney is Texas Ranger La Boeuf (Campbell), who wants to collect the reward placed on the fugitive's head for his earlier crimes. With him are three ruthless villains, Ned Pepper (Duvall), Quincy (Slate) and Moon (Hopper), who put both the lives of Cogburn and Mattie in danger.

'If I'd known, I'd have put the eye-patch on 35 years earlier,' the 62-year-old John Wayne quipped on receiving his first Best Actor Oscar for his 139th film. The award was not only long overdue but fully merited. What Wayne manages to do is create an ageing, uncouth, mean-tempered man, undoubtedly brave who, under the boorish exterior conceals a tender heart without lapsing into mawkishness. The straight-shooting film, directed with supreme expertise by the 71-year-old Henry Hathaway, who had directed Wayne several times previously, had the refreshing presence of newcomer Kim Darby. In 1975, Wayne repeated his *True Grit* characterization opposite Katharine Hepburn in *Rooster Cogburn*, but the film failed to match its predecessor.

USA, 1969
DIRECTOR:
Henry Hathaway
CAST INCLUDES:
John Wayne, Glen Campbell,
Kim Darby, Robert Duvall,
Dennis Hopper
SCREENPLAY:
Marguerite Roberts from the novel
by Charles Portis
CINEMATOGRAPHY:
Lucien Ballard
**PRODUCERS/
PRODUCTION COMPANIES:**
Hal B. Wallis/Paramount
**ACADEMY AWARD
NOMINATIONS (1970)**
Best Music, Original Song: Don Black,
Elmer Bernstein for the song
'True Grit'
ACADEMY AWARDS
Best Actor in a Leading Role:
John Wayne

The Wild Bunch

USA, 1969
DIRECTOR:
Sam Peckinpah
CAST INCLUDES:
William Holden, Ernest Borgnine,
Robert Ryan, Edmund O'Brein,
Warren Oats, Ben Johnson,
Jaime Sanchez
SCREENPLAY:
Walon Green, Sam Peckinpah
CINEMATOGRAPHY:
Lucien Ballard
PRODUCERS/
PRODUCTION COMPANIES:
Phil Feldman/Warner Bros.
ACADEMY AWARD
NOMINATIONS (1970)
Best Music, Original Score for a
Motion Picture (not a Musical):
Jerry Fielding
Best Original Screenplay: Sam
Peckinpah, Walon Green

Pike Bishop (Holden) is the leader of the Wild Bunch, a group of middle-aged, saddle-weary outlaws who find their way of life quickly growing obsolete in 1913. After surviving an ambush by bounty hunters, Pike realizes that the Wild Bunch cannot last forever and wants to plan one last job – 'doing' a railroad office near the Texas border – to make them wealthy before they ride off into the sunset. Deke Thornton (Ryan), the sixth member of the bunch, seeing no future in remaining with Bishop, has gone straight and is working as a bounty hunter determined to destroy his ex-cohorts. But death is not far away for the bunch.

Sam Peckinpah's bloody and meditative tale of the American West is considered by many to be the director's masterpiece. The Western was a dying breed when Peckinpah, along with

Bonnie and Clyde, two years earlier, ushered in a new breed of Hollywood film, depicting a harsh reality where lines between right and wrong became blurred. The film's sympathy is plainly with the outlaws who try to live from another age, although the scenes of carnage reflect the year the film was made. Many critics argued that the way Peckinpah filmed it made violence look good. Every killing was accentuated in slow motion, lending a distinctly lyrical touch as another gringo bit the dust. But it is clearly designed to show that violence doesn't pay. The film also deals with themes of ageing, friendship, loyalty, betrayal, and deception. Peckinpah directed superbly with a sharp sense of characterization and atmosphere, making it into a moving elegy for the end of an era.

The Ballad of Cable Hogue

Cable Hogue (Robards), an itinerant prospector, is left to die in the desert by his two double-crossing partners until he miraculously discovers a water hole. 'I found water where there wasn't,' he claims. It is in just the right spot for a much needed rest stop on the local stagecoach line, and Hogue uses this to his advantage. He builds a house and makes money from the stagecoach passengers. Having made his fortune, and having gained the love of a gold-hearted hooker (Stevens), he is determined on revenge. Hogue has everything going his way until the advent of the automobile ends the era of the stagecoach.

Sam Peckinpah's characteristic use of graphic violence was toned down somewhat in this gem of a Western ballad, but his affectionate view of the Old West is very much in evidence throughout, as is his irony and edgy sense of humour. It could be considered the comic side of *The Wild Bunch*, the film's companion piece. In both films, the main characters' attempts to stem the advance of the new-style west, end in death. Peckinpah described *The Ballad of Cable Hogue* as 'a new version of Sartre's *The Flies* and the *Keystone Kops*'. Jason Robards and Stella Stevens make a likeable couple while David Warner is effective as a god-defying Luciferian preacher.

USA, 1970
DIRECTOR:
Sam Peckinpah
CAST INCLUDES:
Jason Robards, Stella Stevens,
David Warner, Strother Martin
SCREENPLAY:
John Crawford, Edmund Penney
CINEMATOGRAPHY:
Lucien Ballard
**PRODUCERS/
PRODUCTION COMPANIES:**
Sam Peckinpah/Warner Bros.

USA, 1970
DIRECTOR:
Arthur Penn
CAST INCLUDES:
Dustin Hoffman, Faye Dunaway,
Martin Balsam, Chief Dan
George, Richard Mulligan, Jeff Corey,
Thayer David
SCREENPLAY:
Calder Willingham from the novel by
Thomas Berger.
CINEMATOGRAPHY:
Harry Stradling
PRODUCERS/
PRODUCTION COMPANIES:
Stuart Millar/Cinema Center 100
Productions, Stockbridge-Hiller
Productions
ACADEMY AWARD
NOMINATIONS (1971)
Best Actor in a Supporting Role:
Chief Dan George

Little Big Man

Jack Crabb (Hoffman) is a 121-year-old survivor of Custer's Last Stand, who reminisces over his long and eventful life. In 1859, as a 10-year-old abandoned orphan, he is found and adopted by the Cheyenne and is made a brave called Little Big Man by Chief Old Lodge Skins (George). Aged sixteen, he rides into battle against white soldiers but is captured and taken in by a Reverend (David) and his wife (Dunaway). In his mid-20s, he joins Custer (Mulligan). But shifting loyalties, he determines to kill Custer, then offers himself to the General as an Indian scout. At the last battle, Crabb is saved by Younger Bear, who had owed him a life since childhood.

This entertaining revisionist Western views the past from a modern standpoint. For example, a sequence when Custer attacks an Indian village could not help but remind audiences of the time of the My Lai massacre in Vietnam. Director Arthur Penn manages astutely to veer from broad comedy to burlesque in the *Blazing Saddles* manner (there is even a gay Indian and bluesy music), to making serious comments about Indian culture – the Cheyennes are presented as an ideal alternative to the white world – and analogies between their treatment by the whites and the Vietnam War. It was not the first Hollywood movie to attempt to redress the balance in favour of the Native Americans, but it began a new trend in which the Western was appropriated by directors in order to express their liberal views. Dustin Hoffman is brilliantly convincing as a very old man as well as being able to look and behave like a very young man when necessary.

McCabe and Mrs. Miller

In the north western zinc-mining town of Presbyterian Church at the turn of the century, McCabe (Beatty), a bumbling small-time gambler, in the guise of a notorious gunslinger, becomes a business partner in a bordello run by the tougher more sophisticated, opium-smoking Mrs. Miller (Christie). They fall in love and he dreams of building a city out of the muddy frontier settlement but he has to face gunmen sent by a powerful mining company to kill him.

In a way, Robert Altman's first film of this genre (like his only other one to date, *Buffalo Bill and the Indians*) could be considered an anti-Western, exposing the myth of the heroic westerner and replacing it with an almost Marxist view of the westerner as an opportunistic financier, spreading capitalism and corruption. Awash with contemporary allusions, this personal film is very much enhanced by Vilmos Zsigmond's atmospheric photography – especially the memorable closing sequence in the snow – and the convincing creation of a mythical American town. Warren Beatty, glowering handsomely, makes McCabe an unheroic, uneducated figure, who doesn't wear a gun. On the soundtrack, commenting on the action, are Leonard Cohen songs which conjure up the spirit of the 1970s.

USA, 1971
DIRECTOR:
Robert Altman
CAST INCLUDES:
Warren Beatty, Julie Christie, René Auberjonois, John Schuck, Bert Remsen, Keith Carradine
SCREENPLAY:
Robert Altman, Brian McKay from the novel *McCabe* by Edmund Naughton
CINEMATOGRAPHY:
Vilmos Zsigmond
PRODUCERS/ PRODUCTION COMPANIES:
David Foster, Mitchell Bower/ Warner Bros.

Bad Company

USA, 1972
DIRECTOR:
Robert Benton
CAST INCLUDES:
Jeff Bridges, Barry Brown, Jim Davis,
David Huddleston, Jerry Houser,
John Savage
SCREENPLAY:
Robert Benton, David Newman
CINEMATOGRAPHY:
Gordon Willis
**PRODUCERS/
PRODUCTION COMPANIES:**
Stanley R. Jaffe/Paramount
**ACADEMY AWARD
NOMINATIONS (1973)**
Best Drama Written Directly for the
Screen: Robert Benton,
David Newman

Two young deserters from the Union army, conman Jake Rumsey (Bridges) and the god-fearing Drew Dixon (Brown) join up while fleeing the American Civil War. They first meet when Drew is mugged by Jake. With two other draft dodgers Loney (Savage) and Arthur (Houser), they set off towards the Mississippi and the West, becoming outlaws, while dodging a professional criminal (Huddleston), cut-throats, sheriffs and recruiting officers.

This was the first feature directed by Robert Benton who, with David Newman, wrote the sensational *Bonnie and Clyde*. The same team's *Bad Company* shares the same black humour, amorality and loving concern for the feel of the period. As the earlier film demythologized the gangster movie, this one does the same with the Western. Here, survival depends on crime, the only activity that pays. Wonderfully photographed by Gordon Willis (*The Godfather*) in a variety of autumnal browns, this is an unjustly neglected masterpiece of the 1970s. Because of the Vietnam War, this episodic tale of deserters and draft dodgers had a resonance with young audiences.

The Life and Times of Judge Roy Bean

After being run out of the outlaw town of Vinegaroon, the robber and rapist Roy Bean (Newman) is left for dead. But Bean returns to take his revenge. He sets himself up as a judge and has an affair with Maria Elena, a local Mexican girl (Principal), who saved Bean's life. Under his own brand of frontier justice, robbing or killing anyone that tries to make their way through the town, renamed Langtry, in honour of the actress Lily Langtry (Gardner), his feminine ideal, prospers. Gradually the town achieves respectability, and Bean loses his power. So he leaves, only to return twenty years later to seek revenge again, but he finds it full of automobiles and oil derricks.

Shot in Mexico, this episodic somewhat surreal, tale of the famous 'hanging judge' obsessed with actress Lily Langtry, is a bizarre mixture of drama and comedy, romanticism and cynicism. The same story, though far less wide-ranging, was told in William Wyler's *The Westerner* (1940), in which Bean was a villain portrayed by Walter Brennan. As played here by Paul Newman, he is more of a misunderstood anti-hero, whose seen differently by a variety of well-cast characters, including Anthony Perkins as an itinerant preacher, resembling a black crow, who comes to bury Bean's victims. The director John Huston, who also has a cameo role, seems to have enjoyed himself making it, an enjoyment communicated to audiences.

USA, 1972
DIRECTOR:
John Huston
CAST INCLUDES:
Paul Newman, Victoria Principal, Anthony Perkins, Tab Hunter, Ava Gardner
SCREENPLAY:
John Milius
CINEMATOGRAPHY:
Richard Moore
PRODUCERS/ PRODUCTION COMPANIES:
John Foreman/First Artists
ACADEMY AWARD NOMINATIONS (1973)
Best Music, Original Song: Maurice Jarre, Alan and Marilyn Bergman for 'Marmalade, Molasses & Honey'

Ulzana's Raid

USA, 1972
DIRECTOR:
Robert Aldrich
CAST INCLUDES:
Burt Lancaster, Bruce Davison,
Jorge Luke, Richard Jaeckel,
Joaquin Martinez
SCREENPLAY:
Alan Sharp
CINEMATOGRAPHY:
Joseph Biroc
PRODUCERS/
PRODUCTION COMPANIES:
Carter De Haven/Universal

Angered at their mistreatment by whites, a group of renegade Apaches led by Ulzana (Martinez) escape from their reservation and embark on a rampage of murder, rape and destruction. A small detachment of troops under the inexperienced DeBuin (Davison), accompanied by two army scouts, the veteran McIntosh (Lancaster) and an Apache (Luke), are assigned to track down the Indians. As DeBuin, McIntosh, and their party venture into the unfriendly landscape, issues start to surface about the morality of their mission. Soon the white men are fighting amongst themselves, divided over the task at hand. Meanwhile, their efforts to stop Ulzana's Raid seem fruitless.

Robert Aldrich's intelligent, edgy and graphic *Ulzana's Raid* contains many of the features one expects from the director: characters verging on insanity, eruptions into violence, told in a style full of overhead shots, vast close-ups and shock cuts. Given this virile approach, Aldrich is best, as here, in all-male subjects, demonstrating his theme of 'man's efforts to prevail against impossible odds'. The film also attempts to draw parallels with contemporary society. While the cavalry, like the US troops in Vietnam, try to fight conventionally, the Indians use guerrilla tactics like the Vietcong. The veteran soldiers behave almost as savagely as the Indians, much as some soldiers did in the Vietnam conflict. At the film's centre is Burt Lancaster's mature and calming presence. Joseph Biroc's magnificent cinematography evokes the scorching heat of the barren desert.

High Plains Drifter

A stranger (Eastwood), mysteriously materializes out of the desert heat, riding into the small town of Lago. He seems to have returned from the dead to exact revenge on the townsfolk of Lago who once stood by and watched him, their sheriff, whipped to 'death' by a trio of hired gunmen. He requires the inhabitants to literally paint the town red and change its name to Hell. The townspeople are scared of him, and the three gunmen try, unsuccessfully, to kill him again.

Clint Eastwood's second film as star and director, and his first Western, is a stylish revenge drama that pays tribute to Clint's mentors Sergio Leone and Don Siegel. (Among the graves in the cemetery are those of 'Donald Siegel' and 'S. Leone'.)

But it is more allegorical and offbeat than even their pictures, with an added eerie supernatural element, emphasized by Bruce Surtees' almost surreal camerawork. This is counterbalanced by realistic images of a tougher West, cold and gritty, peopled with unshaven men and plain women. Universal wanted the film to be shot on the studio lot but, instead, Clint had a whole town built (and burned to the ground) in the desert near Lake Mono in the California Sierras.

USA, 1973
DIRECTOR:
Clint Eastwood
CAST INCLUDES:
Clint Eastwood, Verna Bloom,
Marianna Hill, Mitchell Ryan,
Jack Ging
SCREENPLAY:
Ernest Tidyman
CINEMATOGRAPHY:
Bruce Surtees
**PRODUCERS/
PRODUCTION COMPANIES:**
Robert Daley/Malpaso-Universal

The Outlaw Josey Wales

USA, 1976
DIRECTOR:
Clint Eastwood
CAST INCLUDES:
Clint Eastwood, Chief Dan George,
Sondra Locke, Bill McKinney,
John Vernon
SCREENPLAY:
Phil Kaufman, Sonia Chernus from
the novel *Gone To Texas* by
Forrest Carter
CINEMATOGRAPHY:
Bruce Surtees
PRODUCERS/
PRODUCTION COMPANIES:
Robert Daley/Warner Bros.
ACADEMY AWARD
NOMINATIONS (1977)
Best Music, Original Score:
Jerry Fielding

Josey Wales (Eastwood) is a peaceful Missouri farmer whose wife and children are brutally murdered by a band of marauding Unionist guerillas. He joins a Confederate gang and exacts bloody revenge on the Unionists. When the war ends, as an outlaw with a price on his head, he makes a journey to Texas, picking up various companions along the way and eventually setting up a commune where, gradually, his thoughts return from killing to farming.

This inspired epic of great scope, structured as a series of brilliant set-pieces, was originally to have been directed by Clint Eastwood's co-scenarist Phil Kaufman, but the former took over after shooting had already begun because of a disagreement as to the nature of the eponymous character. In the event, it turned out to be one of Eastwood's finest achievements both as actor and director. The lyrical landscape photography of Bruce Surtees, Jerry Fielding's fine score and some of the relationships, make this a tender film despite the violence, necessary in this picture of a harsh existence. Chief Dan George as an old Cherokee brave lends the film light relief.

The Shootist

After J. B. Books (Wayne), a retired gunfighter, learns from Dr. Hostetler (Stewart) that he's dying of stomach cancer and has no more than two months to live, he moves into a boarding house in Carson City run by prim widow Bond Rogers (Bacall) and her impressionable son, Gillom (Howard), to die quietly. But when word gets around that the old 'shootist' is in town, there are those who contemplate a showdown with the legend. Annoyed by the attention and realizing that if he waits long enough, he'll die in great pain, Books decides to seek out his enemies and go down with guns blazing. In the finale, he kills three local villains, but he manages to persuade Gillom to foreswear the life of violence he's led.

This graceful valediction to a great star opens with a moving black-and-white montage from John Wayne's earlier Westerns, which is offered as a back story to the J.B. Books character. Wayne, like Books, was dying of cancer as the film was being shot. This makes the parallels between fiction and reality all the more poignant. As much a meditation on the burden of celebrity as an elegy for the Old West, it ends with the gunfighter/star's renunciation of violence. In his consciously chosen swan song, Wayne never seeks sympathy but brings a disarming self-awareness and dignity to the role of a gunslinger, with his emphasis on a code of honour, out of place in the cynical days at the turn of the last century (read also the 1970s).

USA, 1976
DIRECTOR:
Don Siegel
CAST INCLUDES:
John Wayne, Lauren Bacall,
Ron Howard, James Stewart,
John Carradine, Richard Boone,
Hugh O'Brian
SCREENPLAY:
Miles Hood Swarthout, Scott Hale
from the novel by
Glendon Swarthout
CINEMATOGRAPHY:
Bruce Surtees
**PRODUCERS/
PRODUCTION COMPANIES:**
M. J. Frankovich, William
Self/Paramount
**ACADEMY AWARD
NOMINATIONS (1977)**
Best Art Direction-Set Decoration:
Arthur Jeph Parker, Robert F. Boyle

The Long Riders

USA, 1980
DIRECTOR:
Walter Hill
CAST INCLUDES:
James Keach, Stacy Keach,
David Carradine, Keith Carradine,
Robert Carradine, Dennis Quaid,
Randy Quaid, Christopher Guest,
Nicholas Guest
SCREENPLAY:
Bill Bryden, Steven P. Smith,
Stacy and James Keach
CINEMATOGRAPHY:
Ric Waite
**PRODUCERS/
PRODUCTION COMPANIES:**
Tim Zinnemann/United Artists

Cole, Jim and Bob Younger (the Carradine brothers), Frank and Jesse James (the Keach brothers), Ed and Clell Miller (the Quaid brothers) and Charlie and Bob Ford (the Guest brothers), a loosely-knit gang of bank and train robbers, are relentlessly pursued by the Pinkerton Detective Agency. However, they are fiercely protected by their neighbours and relatives while the gang goes robbing. Occasionally they go their own ways, only to come together again, despite the tensions among them. The spectacular but disastrous Northfield Minnesota Raid followed by the murder of Jesse by the treacherous Ford brothers, ends the criminal careers of the legendary outlaws.

'We started robbing banks and we just kept going,' was the main motivation given by the notorious James gang, but there is far more to Walter Hill's visually poetic, but gritty and violent Western. The film firmly places the gang within the rural folk culture of post-Civil War Missouri, stressing the tight family relationships and the social rituals. The same subject was treated in *The Great Northfield Minnesota Raid* (1971), which also tried for accurate period detail and a symbolic treatment of the outlaw's existence. But Hill's use of slow motion, flashbacks, distorted sound, and the extremely unusual but effective casting of four sets of brothers in the main roles injected new life into old material. There is also a superb score by guitar maestro Ry Cooder.

Young Guns

British ranch owner John Tunstall (Stamp) hires six young men to help him tend and guard his ranch. In addition he also teaches them to read and to be civilized. When Tunstall refuses to sell his land to corrupt and ruthless ranch owner Lawrence Murphy (Palance), he is brutally murdered by Murphy's men. The six 'young guns' are then made lawmen named the Regulators, and have sworn to bring the murderers to justice. But, one of their number, William H. Bonney, later Billy the Kid (Estevez), has his own plans for the men who killed their father-figure – gun them down, one by one. Due to Billy's actions, the Regulators are soon branded outlaws, wanted dead or alive.

This oft-repeated tale of Billy the Kid has been adapted in every era to suit the climate and audiences of the time. Since the first full-scale screen version, King Vidor's *Billy The Kid* (1930), there have been dozens of features, the notorious young outlaw being played by, among others, Robert Taylor (30), Paul Newman (32) and Kris Kristofferson (37). Christopher Cain's good-humoured 'modern' take on the story – the dialogue contains expressions like 'kiss my ass' – certainly appealed to young audiences, followers of the Brat Pack, with Emilio Estevez (26) and the others closer to the right age of the outlaws, and provides Jack Palance for those older spectators who prefer the more classical westerns. Tom Cruise has an unbilled cameo as a bad guy who gets shot. A sequel, *Young Guns II* (1990) was inevitable.

USA, 1988
DIRECTOR:
Christopher Cain
CAST INCLUDES:
Emilio Estevez, Kiefer Sutherland,
Lou Diamond Phillips, Charlie Sheen,
Terence Stamp, Jack Palance
SCREENPLAY:
John Fusco
CINEMATOGRAPHY:
Dean Semler
PRODUCERS/
PRODUCTION COMPANIES:
Christopher Cain, John Fusco/20th
Century-Fox

Dances with Wolves

USA, 1990
DIRECTOR:
Kevin Costner
CAST INCLUDES:
Kevin Costner, Mary McDonnell,
Graham Greene, Rodney A Grant,
Floyd 'Red Crow' Westerman
SCREENPLAY:
Michael Blake from his novel
CINEMATOGRAPHY:
Dean Semler
**PRODUCERS/
PRODUCTION COMPANIES:**
Kevin Costner, Jake Eberts,
Jim Wilson/Tig Productions,
Majestic Films International
**ACADEMY AWARD
NOMINATIONS (1991)**
Best Actor in a Leading Role:
Kevin Costner
Best Art Direction-Set Decoration:
Lisa Dean, Jeffrey Beecroft
Best Costume Design: Elsa Zamparelli
Best Actor in a Supporting Role:
Graham Greene
Best Actress in a Supporting Role:
Mary McDonnell
ACADEMY AWARDS
Best Picture: Jim Wilson Kevin Costner
Best Director: Kevin Costner
Best Writing, Screenplay Based on
Material from Another Medium:
Michael Blake
Best Cinematography: Dean Semler
Best Sound: Russell Williams
Best Film Editing: Neil Travis
Best Music, Original Score: John Barry

Lieutenant John J. Dunbar (Costner), a Unionist officer decorated for bravery against Confederate troops, asks to be posted to the western frontier. Living alone at the mysteriously abandoned Fort Sedgewick, 'the furthermost outpost of the realm', he befriends a wolf (Two Socks) and members of the Sioux tribe. By alerting his Sioux neighbours to the presence of a buffalo herd and then going hunting with them, he earns their trust and confirms his place among them. They rename him Dances with Wolves. He then falls in love with Stands With A Fist (McDonnell), a white woman adopted by the Sioux when she was a girl, and marries her according to Sioux rites. Returning to the fort to collect his journals, he is captured by the newly-arrived cavalry and brutally treated as a turncoat.

As a debut director, Kevin Costner displayed extraordinary confidence, handling both the big scenes and the more intimate ones with real feeling for the medium, and he succeeded in getting unstereotypical performances from his Native American actors who even speak their own languages with subtitles. He really proved himself worthy of the Best Director Oscar, especially with his handling of the breathtaking buffalo hunt. In fact, he breathed life into what was considered a dying genre. In the 1990s, it was one of only two films lasting longer than three hours to have grossed more than $100 million domestically (the other being *Titanic*), showing that the public loved it as much as the critics.

Unforgiven

USA, 1992
DIRECTOR:
Clint Eastwood
CAST INCLUDES:
Clint Eastwood, Gene Hackman,
Morgan Freeman, Richard Harris,
Frances Fisher, Saul Rubinek
SCREENPLAY:
David Webb Peoples
CINEMATOGRAPHY:
Jack N. Green
**PRODUCERS/
PRODUCTION COMPANIES:**
Clint Eastwood/Warner Bros.
**ACADEMY AWARD
NOMINATIONS (1993)**
Best Actor in a Leading Role:
Clint Eastwood
Best Art Direction-Set Decoration:
Janice Blackie-Goodine,
Henry Bumstead

When Little Bill Daggett (Hackman), a sadistic, dictatorial sheriff of a small frontier town, denies justice to the prostitutes of the local brothel, one of whom has been viciously slashed by two clients, the women hire Bill Munny (Eastwood), a retired once-ruthless gunfighter, now a gentle widower and hog farmer for $500 to shoot the culprits. He accepts the job to help support his two motherless children, and is joined by his former partner (Freeman) and a cocky greenhorn (Woolvett), However, Munny must contend with his new moral code in the face of revisiting the life he left behind.

Dedicated 'to Sergio and Don', the two directors, Leone and Siegel, who served as his most important mentors, *Unforgiven*, according to Clint Eastwood 'summarized everything I feel about the Western. The moral is the concern with gunplay.' Eastwood's tenth western is also his crowning achievement in the genre in which he made his name. He had acquired the script some ten years earlier, but he had wanted to 'age' into it. At 62, he was ready to play the role to perfection. This 'revisionist' Western, exploring the darker side of the myths of the Old West, gave the kiss of life to the genre. It is striking in its willingness to confront the effects of violence on both those who commit it and those who suffer it, and for the sense of the characters' realization of their own mortality. Gene Hackman at 63, as a brutal sheriff, is a worthy opponent and contrast to Eastwood's compassionate hero.

ACADEMY AWARD NOMINATIONS CONTINUED
Best Writing, Screenplay Written Directly for the Screen:
David Webb Peoples
Best Sound: Vern Poore
Best Cinematography: Jack N. Green
ACADEMY AWARDS
Best Picture: Clint Eastwood
Best Director: Clint Eastwood
Best Actor in a Supporting Role:
Gene Hackman
Best Film Editing: Joel Cox

The Last of The Mohicans

Hawkeye (Day-Lewis) is a European-born adopted son of Chingachgook (American Indian Movement leader Russell Means) a patrician Mohican. Hawkeye, a fur trapper, gets caught between two cultures when he falls for Cora Munro (Stowe), a British army officer's daughter, whom he had rescued, from a Huron war party. Hawkeye serves as a guide for the British at Fort William Henry (reconstructed exactly from historical documents), until it falls to the French (and their Indian allies) with Colonel Munro (Roëves) surrendering to General Montcalm (Chéreau).

The third Hollywood version of the James Fenimore Cooper classic adventure yarn is also the most wildly romantic, the most exciting, the most attractive (it is beautifully lit and photographed) and the most violent – the scalpings are pretty graphic. Daniel Day-Lewis, with flowing mane and heaving pecs, makes a virile but sensitive hero. Director Michael Mann brilliantly captures the essence of the era (the 1750s) – the hand-to-hand battles, the harsh life in the wilderness. The film was shot on location in North Carolina's Smoky Mountains and the old-growth forests stand in spectacularly for the New York State of Cooper's novel.

USA, 1992
DIRECTOR:
Michael Mann
CAST INCLUDES:
Daniel Day-Lewis, Madeleine Stowe, Russell Means, Jodhi May, Eric Schweig, Maurice Roëves, Patrice Chéreau, Wes Studi
SCREENPLAY:
Michael Mann, Christopher Crowe
CINEMATOGRAPHY:
Dante Spinotti
PRODUCERS/ PRODUCTION COMPANIES:
Hunt Lowry/20th Century-Fox
ACADEMY AWARDS (1993)
Best Sound: Chris Jenkins, Doug Hemphill, Mark Smith, Simon Kaye

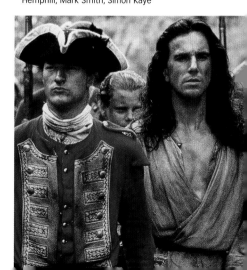

541

All images are courtesy of The Kobal Collection.These images are publicity photos issued by film distribution and production companies to promote their films. We apologise in advance for any omission or neglect and will be pleased to insert the appropriate acknowledgements in any future edition.

page   Film Co.   photographer

page	credit
10	Metro *Nelson Evans*
11	Fox
12	SGF/Gaumont
13	Paramount
14	Mosfilm
15	Warner Bros.
16	MGM/Selznick
17	Warner Bros.
18	Warner Bros.
19	Romulus/Horizon
20	Filmsonor/CICC/Vera-Fono Roma
21	Toho
22	Paramount
23	Paramount
24	United Artists/Bryna
25	MGM
26	MGM
27	Universal/Bryna
28	Columbia/Horizon
29	Diamond
30	MGM
31	United Artists/Woodfall
32	Avco Embassy
33	Mosfilm/DeLaurentiis
33	Werner Herzog
34	20th Century Fox
35	Warner Bros./Concord
36	Corona/Allied Artists/Solar
36	20th Century Fox/Warner Bros.
37	Allied Artists/Columbia/Devon
38/9	Lucasfilm/Paramount
40	Herzog/Verlag der Autoren/ZDF
41	Columbia/Goldcrest
42	Warner Bros./Ladd Co.
43	Warner Bros.
44	EMI/Columbia *Ken Bray*
45	Herald/Ace/Nippon/Greenwich
46	Warner Bros./Goldcrest *David Appleby*
47	Paramount
48/9	Yanco/Tao/Recorded Releasing Co.
50	20th Century Fox *Peter Sorel*
51	20th Century Fox *Richard Foreman*
52	20th Century Fox/Lightstorm *Zade Rosethal*
53	Paramount/20th Century Fox/Ladd/Icon *Andrew Cooper*
54	Columbia/Sony *Chankam Chuen*
55	Universal/Dreamworks *Jaap Buitendijk*
56	New Line/Saul Zaentz/Wing Nut *Pierre Vinet*
57	20th Century Fox/Universal/Miramax *Stephen Vaughan*
58	Walt Disney
59	Warner Bros./Helena *Alex Bailey*
62	Hal Roach/Pathe Exchange *Gene Kornman*
63	United Artists
64	MGM
65	Paramount
66	Paramount
67	Charles Chaplin/UA
68	Selznick/UA (Ted Allan)
69	Hal Roach/MGM
70	Paramount
71	RKO
72	Paramount
73	Columbia
74	Paramount
75	United Artists
76	Paramount
77	Ealing Studios
78	Columbia *Van Pelt*
80	Cady/Discina
81	United Artists *Bernie Abramson*
82	20th Century Fox *James Mitchell*
83	United Artists
84	MGM
85	Embassy Pictures
86	Paramount
87	Paramount
88	Warner Brothers *Bruce McBroom*
89	United Artists
90/1	Warner Brothers

page	credit
93	Universal *Christine Loss*
93	Paramount *John Monte*
94	Columbia *Brian Hamill*
95	Paramount *Josh Weiner*
96	Universal *Fred Sapine*
97	Embassy Pictures *Kristin York*
97	Paramount
98	Paramount
99	MGM/UA *David James*
100	Paramount *Elliott Marks*
101	20th Century Fox *Brian Hamill*
102	20th Century Fox *Don Smetzer*
103	Columbia *Louis Goldman*
104	Hollywood Pictures *Melinda Sue Gordon*
105	New Line *Blake Little*
106	Polygram *Merrick Morton*
108	20th Century Fox *Glenn Watson*
109	Universal/Dreamworks *Phillip Caruso*
110	UGC/Studio Canal +
111	Focus Features *Yoshio Sato*
114	Columbia
115	20th Century Fox
116/7	RKO
118	Pathe
119	Paramount
120	RKO/Goldwyn
121	Rank/Cineguild
122/3	RKO
124	De Sica
125	20th Century Fox
126	Paramount
127	Paramount
128	Columbia
129	Warner Bros.
130	United Artists/Orion-Nova
131	Svensk Filmindustri
132	United Artists/Hecht,Hill,Lancaster
133	Paramount
134	Universal
135	Cineriz
136	Columbia/Open Road
137	Paris/Five Film
138	Embassy
139	Columbia
140	Columbia/Rayburt
141	Columbia
142	20th Century Fox
143	Paramount
144	United Artists/Fantasy Films *Peter Sorel*
145	Warner Bros. *Louis Goldman*
146	United Artists *Elliott Marks*
147	Columbia
148	United Artists/Chartoff-Winkler
149	20th Century Fox/Embassy *Etienne George*
150	Paramount *Andrew Schwartz*
151	Warner Bros./Lorimar/NFH
152	United Artists/Guber-Peters/Mirage *Stephen Vaughan*
153	Universal *David Lee*
154	Era
155	Zupnik/GGR/New Line
156	Spelling Entertainment
157	Paramount *Phillip Caruso*
158/9	Castle Rock *Michael Weinstein*
160	Universal/Imagine *Ron Batzdorf*
161	Universal/Miramax *Laurie Sparham*
162	Paramount *Melinda Sue Gordon*
163	El Deso/Renn/France 2
164	Dreamworks *Sebastian Lorey*
165	Bedford Falls/Initial Ent./USA Films *Bob Marshak*
168	Prana-Film
169	Universal
170	MGM
171	RKO
172	Universal *Roman Freulich*
173	Rank
174	Filmsonor
175	Hammer
176	Universal
178	Anglo Amalgamated
179	MGM
180	Warner Brothers

page	credit
181	Universal
182/3	MGM
184	Paramount
185	Image Ten
186	Warner Brothers
187	Warner Brothers *Josh Weiner*
188	Casey Prod./Eldorado Films
189	British Lion
190	Vortex-Henkel-Hooper/Bryanston
192	Universal *Louis Goldman*
193	20th Century Fox *Bob Penn*
194	United Artists *Dave Friedman*
195	AFI/Libra
196	Falcon International *Kim Gottlieb*
197	United Film *Katherine Kolbert*
198	Warner Brothers
199	Warner Brothers
200	Debra Hill Productions *Kim Gottlieb*
201	Polygram/Universal
202	Universal
203	MGM/SLA Entertainment
204	Warner Brothers *Ralph Nelson Jr.*
205	New Line *Joyce Rudolph*
206	De Laurentiis Group
207	Rosebud/Renaissance *Mike Ditz*
207	Union-Carolco/Tri-star *George Kontaxis*
208	United Artists
209	Castle Rock *Merrick Morton*
210	Universal *Peter Lovino*
211	Orion *Ken Regan*
212	Miramax *David Moir*
214	Hollywood Pictures *Ron Phillips*
215	Artisan Pictures
216	Universal *Keith Hamshere*
217	Omega
218	Miramax/Canal +/Sogecine *Teresa Isasi*
219	DNA/Figment/Fox *Peter Mountain*
222	Warner Bros.
223	Warner Bros.
224	RKO
225	RKO
226	Universal
227	20th Century Fox
228/9	MGM
230	MGM
231	Warner Bros.
232	Columbia *George Hurrell*
233	20th Century Fox
234	MGM
235	MGM
236	Rank/Archers *George Cannon*
237	MGM
238	MGM
239	MGM
240	MGM
241	20th Century Fox
243	Warner Bros.
242	MGM
244	20th Century Fox/Magna *Schuyler Crail*
245	MGM
246	20th Century Fox
247	Paramount
248	Columbia
249	20th Century Fox
250	Mirisch/7 Arts/UA
251	MGM
252	United Artists/Proscenium
253	Walt Disney
254	Warner Bros.
255	Parc/Beta Film
256	20th Century Fox
257	Columbia
258	20th Century Fox/Chenault
259	Warner Bros./Wadleigh
260	ABC/Allied Artists *Lars Looschen*
261	20th Century Fox *John Jay*
263	United Artists *Bruce McBroom*
262	Paramount/Robert Stigwood
264	Paramount
265	20th Century Fox/Columbia *Josh Weiner*
266	Universal
267	MGM *Catherine Bushnell*

543

268 Warner Bros *Murray Close.*
269 Vestron
270 20th Century Fox *Sue Adler*
271 Miramax *David James*
274 Fox
275 Columbia
276 MGM
277 United Artists
278 MGM
279 MGM
280 MGM
281 Paramount
282/3 Warner Bros.
284 Warner Bros.
285 MGM
286 Cineguild/Rank
287 Andre Paulve
288 20th Century Fox
289 MGM
290 Republic
291 Paramount
292 Paramount
293 Universal
294 20th Century Fox
295 20th Century Fox/Jerry Wald
296 Universal *Ray Jones*
298 United Artists/Mirisch
299 Paramount
301 Paramount
302 Paramount
303 Paramount
304 Columbia
305 United Artists/Annie Hall *Brian Hamill*
306 Orion/Warner Bros. *Bruce McBroom*
307 United Artists/Juniper Films
308 Paramount
309 Universal/Mirage *Frank Connor*
310 MGM/UA *Barry Wetcher*
311 Gladden/Mirage/Tobis *Lorey Sebastian*
312 Castle Rock/Nelson/Columbia
313 Touchstone/Warners *Ron Batzdorf*
314 Paramount *Peter Sorel*
315 Touchstone/AFFC/Sedif/UCG *Francois Duhamel*
316 Columbia *Phillip Caruso*
317 Tri-Star *Bruce McBroom*
318 Hollywood Pictures *Michael Weinstein*
319 20th Century Fox *Merrick Morton*
320 Tiger Moth/Miramax/Saul Zaentz *Phil Bray*
321 20th Century Fox/Paramount *Merie W. Wallace*
322 TriStar/Gracie Films
323 Block 2 Pics/Jet Tone
326 Ufa
327 Columbia
328 Ealing/Rank
329 20th Century Fox
330 Paramount
331 MGM
332 Allied Artists/Walter Wanger
333 Universal
334 Columbia
335 Columbia/Hawk
336 Anglo Enterprises/Vineyard
337 20th Century Fox
338/9 MGM/Polaris
340 Warner Bros./Polaris/Hawk
341 Universal
342 Mosfilm
343 United Artists/Rollins-Joffe
344 MGM
345 Jack Harris Ents/USC
346/7 Columbia
348 20th Century Fox/Lucasfilm
349 Warner Bros./DC Comics
350 20th Century Fox
351 Warner Bros./Kennedy-Miller *Carolyn Jones*
352 Film Plan Int./CFDC
353 Handmade Films *Clive Coote*
354 Ladd Co./Warners
355 Universal/Amblin
356 Paramount
357 Walt Disney
358 Columbia
359 Orion
360 Universal/Amblin
361 Universal/Embassy *David Appleby*

362 20th Century Fox *Bob Penn*
363 20th Century Fox
364 Orion *Deana Newcomb*
365 Warner Bros./DC Comics
366 Carolco/TriStar
367 Recorded Picture Co/First Independent
368 Universal/Amblin
369 Polygram/Universal *Phillip Caruso*
370 20th Century Fox *Claudette Barius*
371 Columbia *Melinda Sue Gordon*
372 Warner Bros./Village Roadshow
373 20th Century Fox/Marvel
374 Warner/Amblin/Dreamworks *David James*
375 Warner Bros. *Peter Mountain*
376 20th Century Fox/Dreamworks/Amblin *David James*
377 Columbia/ Marvel
380 Warner Bros./First National
381 Warner Bros.
382 Selznick International
383 Warner Bros.
384 Paramount
385 Warner Bros.
386 20th Century Fox
387 London Films
388 MGM
389 Warner Bros.
390 Columbia
391 Paramount
392 United Artists
393 Indus/Pathe/Prima
394 United Artists/Harris-Kubrick
395 Universal
396 Universal
397 Danjaq/Eon/UA
398 Warner Bros./Tatira-Hiller
399 United Artists/Mirisch
400 MGM
401 Warner Bros./7 Arts/Solar
402 Simkoe/Solar/Mirisch
403 Paramount
404 Warner Bros.
405 20th Century Fox
406/7 Paramount
408 Taplin/Perry/Scorsese
409 Paramount/De Laurentiis
410 Universal
411 Paramount
412 Paramount
413 Warner Bros.
414 Columbia
415 Universal *Sidney Baldwin*
416 Paramount
417 Paramount
418 Warner Bros. *Dirck Halstead*
419 20th Century Fox *Patti Perret*
420 Carolco/Studio Canal+/TriStar
421 Live Entertainment/Dog Eat Dog
422/3 Miramax/A Band Apart/Jersey Films *Linda R. Chen*
425 New Line *Peter Sorel*
426 Polygram/Spelling/Bad Hat/Roscoe *Linda R. Chen*
427 Polygram/Working Title
428 Warner Bros./Monarchy/Regency
429 X-Filme Creative Pool/WDR/arte *Bernd Spauke*
430 I Remember Prods./Summit Entertainment
     Danny Rothenberg
431 Globo Films/02/Hank Levine
434 First National
435 Paramount
436 Universal
437 Realisations D'art Cinematographique
438 Warner Bros. *Mac Julian*
439 Two Cities/British Lion
440 Paramount
441 The Archers
442 Excelsa/Mayer-Burstyn
443 United Artists
444 MGM
445 MGM
446 Republic
447 20th Century Fox
448 20th Century Fox
449 MGM
450 Ealing
451 Columbia
452 Paramount

453 Warner Bros.
454 United Artists
455 Nikkatsu Corp.
456/7 Columbia/Horizon
458 United Artists
459 Mosfilm
460 Columbia
461 20th Century Fox
462 Mirisch/United Artists
463 United Artists
464 Columbia
465 20th Century Fox
466 MGM
467 Selmur
468 MGM *John Jay*
469 Paramount-Filmways
470 20th Century Fox
471 20th Century Fox/Apsen
472 20th Century Fox
473 Anglo-EMI-/Rapid/Terra *Lars Looschen*
474 Columbia-EMI
475 Zoetrope/United Artists
476 Lorimar/United Artists *Laurel Moore*
477 Bavaria/Radiant *Karl-Heinz Vogelmann*
478 Enigma/Goldcrest *David Appleby*
479 Mosfilm
480 Orion/Hemdale *Ricky Francisco*
481 Warner Bros.
482 Touchstone *Bonnie Schiffman*
483 Universal/Amblin *David James*
484/5 Dreamworks *David James*
488 Paramount
489 United Artists/Walter Wanger
490 20th Century Fox
491 Selznick/RKO
492 20th Century Fox
493 RKO
494 United Artists
495 RKO
496 20th Century Fox
497 Universal
498 Universal
499 Stanley Kramer/UA
500 MGM
501 Paramount
502/3 Warner Bros.
504 Columbia/PAC
505 Columbia
506 20th Century Fox
507 Universal/RKO
508 United Artists
509 Warner Bros.
510 United Artists/Mirisch
511 Paramount
512 Warner Bros.
513 United Artists/Mirisch
514 Columbia
515 Universal
516 Paramount
517 MGM
518 Proteus
519 P.E.A./Grimaldi
520 Columbia
521 20th Century Fox
522/3 Paramount/Rafran
524 20th Century Fox
525 Paramount
526 Warner/Seven Arts
527 Warner Bros.
528 Cinema Center/Stockbridge-Hiller
529 Warner Bros.
530 Paramount
531 First Artists
532 Universal
533 Universal
534 Warner Bros.
535 Paramount
536 United Artists
537 20th Century Fox
539 20th Century Fox/Morgan Creek *Frank Connor*
539 Warner Bros.